Dictionary of Literary Biography

1 *The American Renaissance in New England,* edited by Joel Myerson (1978)

2 *American Novelists Since World War II,* edited by Jeffrey Helterman and Richard Layman (1978)

3 *Antebellum Writers in New York and the South,* edited by Joel Myerson (1979)

4 *American Writers in Paris, 1920-1939,* edited by Karen Lane Rood (1980)

5 *American Poets Since World War II,* 2 parts, edited by Donald J. Greiner (1980)

6 *American Novelists Since World War II, Second Series,* edited by James E. Kibler Jr. (1980)

7 *Twentieth-Century American Dramatists,* 2 parts, edited by John MacNicholas (1981)

8 *Twentieth-Century American Science-Fiction Writers,* 2 parts, edited by David Cowart and Thomas L. Wymer (1981)

9 *American Novelists, 1910-1945,* 3 parts, edited by James J. Martine (1981)

10 *Modern British Dramatists, 1900-1945,* 2 parts, edited by Stanley Wein-traub (1982)

11 *American Humorists, 1800-1950,* 2 parts, edited by Stanley Trachtenberg (1982)

12 *American Realists and Naturalists,* edited by Donald Pizer and Earl N. Harbert (1982)

13 *British Dramatists Since World War II,* 2 parts, edited by Stanley Wein-traub (1982)

14 *British Novelists Since 1960,* 2 parts, edited by Jay L. Halio (1983)

15 *British Novelists, 1930-1959,* 2 parts, edited by Bernard Oldsey (1983)

16 *The Beats: Literary Bohemians in Postwar America,* 2 parts, edited by Ann Charters (1983)

17 *Twentieth-Century American Historians,* edited by Clyde N. Wilson (1983)

18 *Victorian Novelists After 1885,* edited by Ira B. Nadel and William E. Fredeman (1983)

19 *British Poets, 1880-1914,* edited by Donald E. Stanford (1983)

20 *British Poets, 1914-1945,* edited by Donald E. Stanford (1983)

21 *Victorian Novelists Before 1885,* edited by Ira B. Nadel and William E. Fredeman (1983)

22 *American Writers for Children, 1900-1960,* edited by John Cech (1983)

23 *American Newspaper Journalists, 1873-1900,* edited by Perry J. Ashley (1983)

24 *American Colonial Writers, 1606-1734,* edited by Emory Elliott (1984)

25 *American Newspaper Journalists, 1901-1925,* edited by Perry J. Ashley (1984)

26 *American Screenwriters,* edited by Robert E. Morsberger, Stephen O. Lesser, and Randall Clark (1984)

27 *Poets of Great Britain and Ireland, 1945-1960,* edited by Vincent B. Sherry Jr. (1984)

28 *Twentieth-Century American-Jewish Fiction Writers,* edited by Daniel Walden (1984)

29 *American Newspaper Journalists, 1926-1950,* edited by Perry J. Ashley (1984)

30 *American Historians, 1607-1865,* edited by Clyde N. Wilson (1984)

31 *American Colonial Writers, 1735-1781,* edited by Emory Elliott (1984)

32 *Victorian Poets Before 1850,* edited by William E. Fredeman and Ira B. Nadel (1984)

33 *Afro-American Fiction Writers After 1955,* edited by Thadious M. Davis and Trudier Harris (1984)

34 *British Novelists, 1890-1929: Traditionalists,* edited by Thomas F. Staley (1985)

35 *Victorian Poets After 1850,* edited by William E. Fredeman and Ira B. Nadel (1985)

36 *British Novelists, 1890-1929: Modernists,* edited by Thomas F. Staley (1985)

37 *American Writers of the Early Republic,* edited by Emory Elliott (1985)

38 *Afro-American Writers After 1955: Dramatists and Prose Writers,* edited by Thadious M. Davis and Trudier Harris (1985)

39 *British Novelists, 1660-1800,* 2 parts, edited by Martin C. Battestin (1985)

40 *Poets of Great Britain and Ireland Since 1960,* 2 parts, edited by Vincent B. Sherry Jr. (1985)

41 *Afro-American Poets Since 1955,* edited by Trudier Harris and Thadious M. Davis (1985)

42 *American Writers for Children Before 1900,* edited by Glenn E. Estes (1985)

43 *American Newspaper Journalists, 1690-1872,* edited by Perry J. Ashley (1986)

44 *American Screenwriters, Second Series,* edited by Randall Clark, Robert E. Morsberger, and Stephen O. Lesser (1986)

45 *American Poets, 1880-1945, First Series,* edited by Peter Quartermain (1986)

46 *American Literary Publishing Houses, 1900-1980: Trade and Paperback,* edited by Peter Dzwonkoski (1986)

47 *American Historians, 1866-1912,* edited by Clyde N. Wilson (1986)

48 *American Poets, 1880-1945, Second Series,* edited by Peter Quartermain (1986)

49 *American Literary Publishing Houses, 1638-1899,* 2 parts, edited by Peter Dzwonkoski (1986)

50 *Afro-American Writers Before the Harlem Renaissance,* edited by Trudier Harris (1986)

51 *Afro-American Writers from the Harlem Renaissance to 1940,* edited by Trudier Harris (1987)

52 *American Writers for Children Since 1960: Fiction,* edited by Glenn E. Estes (1986)

53 *Canadian Writers Since 1960, First Series,* edited by W. H. New (1986)

54 *American Poets, 1880-1945, Third Series,* 2 parts, edited by Peter Quartermain (1987)

55 *Victorian Prose Writers Before 1867,* edited by William B. Thesing (1987)

56 *German Fiction Writers, 1914-1945,* edited by James Hardin (1987)

57 *Victorian Prose Writers After 1867,* edited by William B. Thesing (1987)

58 *Jacobean and Caroline Dramatists,* edited by Fredson Bowers (1987)

59 *American Literary Critics and Scholars, 1800-1850,* edited by John W. Rathbun and Monica M. Grecu (1987)

60 *Canadian Writers Since 1960, Second Series,* edited by W. H. New (1987)

61 *American Writers for Children Since 1960: Poets, Illustrators, and Nonfiction Authors,* edited by Glenn E. Estes (1987)

62 *Elizabethan Dramatists,* edited by Fredson Bowers (1987)

63 *Modern American Critics, 1920-1955,* edited by Gregory S. Jay (1988)

64 *American Literary Critics and Scholars, 1850-1880,* edited by John W. Rathbun and Monica M. Grecu (1988)

65 *French Novelists, 1900-1930,* edited by Catharine Savage Brosman (1988)

66 *German Fiction Writers, 1885-1913,* 2 parts, edited by James Hardin (1988)

67 *Modern American Critics Since 1955,* edited by Gregory S. Jay (1988)

68 *Canadian Writers, 1920-1959, First Series,* edited by W. H. New (1988)

69 *Contemporary German Fiction Writers, First Series,* edited by Wolfgang D. Elfe and James Hardin (1988)

70 *British Mystery Writers, 1860-1919,* edited by Bernard Benstock and Thomas F. Staley (1988)

71 *American Literary Critics and Scholars, 1880-1900,* edited by John W. Rathbun and Monica M. Grecu (1988)

72 *French Novelists, 1930-1960,* edited by Catharine Savage Brosman (1988)

73 *American Magazine Journalists, 1741-1850,* edited by Sam G. Riley (1988)

74 *American Short-Story Writers Before 1880,* edited by Bobby Ellen Kimbel, with the assistance of William E. Grant (1988)

75 *Contemporary German Fiction Writers, Second Series,* edited by Wolfgang D. Elfe and James Hardin (1988)

76 *Afro-American Writers, 1940-1955,* edited by Trudier Harris (1988)

77 *British Mystery Writers, 1920-1939,* edited by Bernard Benstock and Thomas F. Staley (1988)

78 *American Short-Story Writers, 1880-1910,* edited by Bobby Ellen Kimbel, with the assistance of William E. Grant (1988)

79 *American Magazine Journalists, 1850-1900,* edited by Sam G. Riley (1988)

80 *Restoration and Eighteenth-Century Dramatists, First Series,* edited by Paula R. Backscheider (1989)

81 *Austrian Fiction Writers, 1875-1913,* edited by James Hardin and Donald G. Daviau (1989)

82 *Chicano Writers, First Series,* edited by Francisco A. Lomelí and Carl R. Shirley (1989)

83 *French Novelists Since 1960,* edited by Catharine Savage Brosman (1989)

84 *Restoration and Eighteenth-Century Dramatists, Second Series,* edited by Paula R. Backscheider (1989)

85 *Austrian Fiction Writers After 1914,* edited by James Hardin and Donald G. Daviau (1989)

86 *American Short-Story Writers, 1910-1945, First Series,* edited by Bobby Ellen Kimbel (1989)

87 *British Mystery and Thriller Writers Since 1940, First Series,* edited by Bernard Benstock and Thomas F. Staley (1989)

88 *Canadian Writers, 1920-1959, Second Series,* edited by W. H. New (1989)

89 *Restoration and Eighteenth-Century Dramatists, Third Series,* edited by Paula R. Backscheider (1989)

90 *German Writers in the Age of Goethe, 1789-1832,* edited by James Hardin and Christoph E. Schweitzer (1989)

91 *American Magazine Journalists, 1900-1960, First Series,* edited by Sam G. Riley (1990)

92 *Canadian Writers, 1890-1920,* edited by W. H. New (1990)

93 *British Romantic Poets, 1789-1832, First Series,* edited by John R. Greenfield (1990)

94 *German Writers in the Age of Goethe: Sturm und Drang to Classicism,* edited by James Hardin and Christoph E. Schweitzer (1990)

95 *Eighteenth-Century British Poets, First Series,* edited by John Sitter (1990)

96 *British Romantic Poets, 1789-1832, Second Series,* edited by John R. Greenfield (1990)

97 *German Writers from the Enlightenment to Sturm und Drang, 1720-1764,* edited by James Hardin and Christoph E. Schweitzer (1990)

98 *Modern British Essayists, First Series,* edited by Robert Beum (1990)

99 *Canadian Writers Before 1890,* edited by W. H. New (1990)

100 *Modern British Essayists, Second Series,* edited by Robert Beum (1990)

101 *British Prose Writers, 1660-1800, First Series,* edited by Donald T. Siebert (1991)

102 *American Short-Story Writers, 1910-1945, Second Series,* edited by Bobby Ellen Kimbel (1991)

103 *American Literary Biographers, First Series,* edited by Steven Serafin (1991)

104 *British Prose Writers, 1660-1800, Second Series,* edited by Donald T. Siebert (1991)

105 *American Poets Since World War II, Second Series,* edited by R. S. Gwynn (1991)

106 *British Literary Publishing Houses, 1820-1880,* edited by Patricia J. Anderson and Jonathan Rose (1991)

107 *British Romantic Prose Writers, 1789-1832, First Series,* edited by John R. Greenfield (1991)

108 *Twentieth-Century Spanish Poets, First Series,* edited by Michael L. Perna (1991)

109 *Eighteenth-Century British Poets, Second Series,* edited by John Sitter (1991)

110 *British Romantic Prose Writers, 1789-1832, Second Series,* edited by John R. Greenfield (1991)

111 *American Literary Biographers, Second Series,* edited by Steven Serafin (1991)

112 *British Literary Publishing Houses, 1881-1965,* edited by Jonathan Rose and Patricia J. Anderson (1991)

113 *Modern Latin-American Fiction Writers, First Series,* edited by William Luis (1992)

114 *Twentieth-Century Italian Poets, First Series,* edited by Giovanna Wedel De Stasio, Glauco Cambon, and Antonio Illiano (1992)

115 *Medieval Philosophers,* edited by Jeremiah Hackett (1992)

116 *British Romantic Novelists, 1789-1832,* edited by Bradford K. Mudge (1992)

117 *Twentieth-Century Caribbean and Black African Writers, First Series,* edited by Bernth Lindfors and Reinhard Sander (1992)

118 *Twentieth-Century German Dramatists, 1889-1918,* edited by Wolfgang D. Elfe and James Hardin (1992)

119 *Nineteenth-Century French Fiction Writers: Romanticism and Realism, 1800-1860,* edited by Catharine Savage Brosman (1992)

120 *American Poets Since World War II, Third Series,* edited by R. S. Gwynn (1992)

121 *Seventeenth-Century British Nondramatic Poets, First Series,* edited by M. Thomas Hester (1992)

122 *Chicano Writers, Second Series,* edited by Francisco A. Lomelí and Carl R. Shirley (1992)

123 *Nineteenth-Century French Fiction Writers: Naturalism and Beyond, 1860-1900,* edited by Catharine Savage Brosman (1992)

124 *Twentieth-Century German Dramatists, 1919-1992,* edited by Wolfgang D. Elfe and James Hardin (1992)

125 *Twentieth-Century Caribbean and Black African Writers, Second Series,* edited by Bernth Lindfors and Reinhard Sander (1993)

126 *Seventeenth-Century British Nondramatic Poets, Second Series,* edited by M. Thomas Hester (1993)

127 *American Newspaper Publishers, 1950-1990,* edited by Perry J. Ashley (1993)

128 *Twentieth-Century Italian Poets, Second Series,* edited by Giovanna Wedel De Stasio, Glauco Cambon, and Antonio Illiano (1993)

129 *Nineteenth-Century German Writers, 1841-1900,* edited by James Hardin and Siegfried Mews (1993)

130 *American Short-Story Writers Since World War II,* edited by Patrick Meanor (1993)

131 *Seventeenth-Century British Nondramatic Poets, Third Series,* edited by M. Thomas Hester (1993)

132 *Sixteenth-Century British Nondramatic Writers, First Series,* edited by David A. Richardson (1993)

133 *Nineteenth-Century German Writers to 1840,* edited by James Hardin and Siegfried Mews (1993)

134 *Twentieth-Century Spanish Poets, Second Series,* edited by Jerry Phillips Winfield (1994)

135 *British Short-Fiction Writers, 1880-1914: The Realist Tradition,* edited by William B. Thesing (1994)

136 *Sixteenth-Century British Nondramatic Writers, Second Series,* edited by David A. Richardson (1994)

137 *American Magazine Journalists, 1900-1960, Second Series,* edited by Sam G. Riley (1994)

138 *German Writers and Works of the High Middle Ages: 1170-1280,* edited by James Hardin and Will Hasty (1994)

139 *British Short-Fiction Writers, 1945-1980,* edited by Dean Baldwin (1994)

140 *American Book-Collectors and Bibliographers, First Series,* edited by Joseph Rosenblum (1994)

141 *British Children's Writers, 1880-1914,* edited by Laura M. Zaidman (1994)

142 *Eighteenth-Century British Literary Biographers,* edited by Steven Serafin (1994)

143 *American Novelists Since World War II, Third Series,* edited by James R. Giles and Wanda H. Giles (1994)

144 *Nineteenth-Century British Literary Biographers,* edited by Steven Serafin (1994)

145 *Modern Latin-American Fiction Writers, Second Series,* edited by William Luis and Ann González (1994)

146 *Old and Middle English Literature,* edited by Jeffrey Helterman and Jerome Mitchell (1994)

147 *South Slavic Writers Before World War II,* edited by Vasa D. Mihailovich (1994)

148 *German Writers and Works of the Early Middle Ages: 800-1170,* edited by Will Hasty and James Hardin (1994)

149 *Late Nineteenth- and Early Twentieth-Century British Literary Biographers,* edited by Steven Serafin (1995)

150 *Early Modern Russian Writers, Late Seventeenth and Eighteenth Centuries,* edited by Marcus C. Levitt (1995)

151 *British Prose Writers of the Early Seventeenth Century,* edited by Clayton D. Lein (1995)

152 *American Novelists Since World War II, Fourth Series,* edited by James and Wanda Giles (1995)

153 *Late-Victorian and Edwardian British Novelists, First Series,* edited by George M. Johnson (1995)

154 *The British Literary Book Trade, 1700-1820,* edited by James K. Bracken and Joel Silver (1995)

155 *Twentieth-Century British Literary Biographers,* edited by Steven Serafin (1995)

156 *British Short-Fiction Writers, 1880-1914: The Romantic Tradition,* edited by William F. Naufftus (1995)

157 *Twentieth-Century Caribbean and Black African Writers, Third Series,* edited by Bernth Lindfors and Reinhard Sander (1995)

158 *British Reform Writers, 1789-1832,* edited by Gary Kelly and Edd Applegate (1995)

159 *British Short-Fiction Writers, 1800-1880,* edited by John R. Greenfield (1996)

160 *British Children's Writers, 1914-1960,* edited by Donald R. Hettinga and Gary D. Schmidt (1996)

161 *British Children's Writers Since 1960, First Series,* edited by Caroline Hunt (1996)

162 *British Short-Fiction Writers, 1915-1945,* edited by John H. Rogers (1996)

163 *British Children's Writers, 1800-1880,* edited by Meena Khorana (1996)

164 *German Baroque Writers, 1580-1660,* edited by James Hardin (1996)

165 *American Poets Since World War II, Fourth Series,* edited by Joseph Conte (1996)

166 *British Travel Writers, 1837-1875,* edited by Barbara Brothers and Julia Gergits (1996)

167 *Sixteenth-Century British Nondramatic Writers, Third Series,* edited by David A. Richardson (1996)

168 *German Baroque Writers, 1661-1730,* edited by James Hardin (1996)

169 *American Poets Since World War II, Fifth Series,* edited by Joseph Conte (1996)

170 *The British Literary Book Trade, 1475-1700,* edited by James K. Bracken and Joel Silver (1996)

171 *Twentieth-Century American Sportswriters,* edited by Richard Orodenker (1996)

172 *Sixteenth-Century British Nondramatic Writers, Fourth Series,* edited by David A. Richardson (1996)

173 *American Novelists Since World War II, Fifth Series,* edited by James R. Giles and Wanda H. Giles (1996)

174 *British Travel Writers, 1876-1909,* edited by Barbara Brothers and Julia Gergits (1997)

175 *Native American Writers of the United States,* edited by Kenneth M. Roemer (1997)

176 *Ancient Greek Authors,* edited by Ward W. Briggs (1997)

177 *Italian Novelists Since World War II, 1945-1965* edited by Augustus Pallotta (1997)

178 *British Fantasy and Science-Fiction Writers Before World War I,* edited by Darren Harris-Fain (1997)

179 *German Writers of the Renaissance and Reformation, 1280-1580,* edited by James Hardin and Max Reinhart (1997)

180 *Japanese Fiction Writers, 1868-1945,* edited by Van C. Gessel (1997)

181 *South Slavic Writers Since World War II,* edited by Vasa D. Mihailovich (1997)

182 *Japanese Fiction Writers Since World War II,* edited by Van C. Gessel (1997)

183 *American Travel Writers, 1776-1864,* edited by James J. Schramer and Donald Ross (1997)

184 *Nineteenth-Century British Book-Collectors and Bibliographers,* edited by William Baker and Kenneth Womack (1997)

185 *American Literary Journalists, 1945-1995, First Series,* edited by Arthur J. Kaul (1998)

186 *Nineteenth-Century American Western Writers,* edited by Robert L. Gale (1998)

187 *American Book Collectors and Bibliographers, Second Series,* edited by Joseph Rosenblum (1998)

188 *American Book and Magazine Illustrators to 1920,* edited by Steven E. Smith, Catherine A. Hastedt, and Donald H. Dyal (1998)

189 *American Travel Writers, 1850-1915,* edited by Donald Ross and James J. Schramer (1998)

190 *British Reform Writers, 1832-1914,* edited by Gary Kelly and Edd Applegate (1998)

191 *British Novelists Between the Wars,* edited by George M. Johnson (1998)

192 *French Dramatists, 1789-1914,* edited by Barbara T. Cooper (1998)

193 *American Poets Since World War II, Sixth Series,* edited by Joseph Conte (1998)

194 *British Novelists Since 1960, Second Series,* edited by Merritt Moseley (1998).

195 *British Travel Writers, 1910-1939,* edited by Barbara Brothers and Julia M. Gergits (1998).

Documentary Series

1 *Sherwood Anderson, Willa Cather, John Dos Passos, Theodore Dreiser, F. Scott Fitzgerald, Ernest Hemingway, Sinclair Lewis,* edited by Margaret A. Van Antwerp (1982)

2 *James Gould Cozzens, James T. Farrell, William Faulkner, John O'Hara, John Steinbeck, Thomas Wolfe, Richard Wright,* edited by Margaret A. Van Antwerp (1982)

3 *Saul Bellow, Jack Kerouac, Norman Mailer, Vladimir Nabokov, John Updike, Kurt Vonnegut,* edited by Mary Bruccoli (1983)

4 *Tennessee Williams,* edited by Margaret A. Van Antwerp and Sally Johns (1984)

5 *American Transcendentalists,* edited by Joel Myerson (1988)

6 *Hardboiled Mystery Writers: Raymond Chandler, Dashiell Hammett, Ross Macdonald,* edited by Matthew J. Bruccoli and Richard Layman (1989)

7 *Modern American Poets: James Dickey, Robert Frost, Marianne Moore,* edited by Karen L. Rood (1989)

8 *The Black Aesthetic Movement,* edited by Jeffrey Louis Decker (1991)

9 *American Writers of the Vietnam War: W. D. Ehrhart, Larry Heinemann, Tim O'Brien, Walter McDonald, John M. Del Vecchio,* edited by Ronald Baughman (1991)

10 *The Bloomsbury Group,* edited by Edward L. Bishop (1992)

11 *American Proletarian Culture: The Twenties and The Thirties,* edited by Jon Christian Suggs (1993)

12 *Southern Women Writers: Flannery O'Connor, Katherine Anne Porter, Eudora Welty,* edited by Mary Ann Wimsatt and Karen L. Rood (1994)

13 *The House of Scribner, 1846-1904,* edited by John Delaney (1996)

14 *Four Women Writers for Children, 1868-1918,* edited by Caroline C. Hunt (1996)

15 *American Expatriate Writers: Paris in the Twenties,* edited by Matthew J. Bruccoli and Robert W. Trogdon (1997)

16 *The House of Scribner, 1905-1930,* edited by John Delaney (1997)

Yearbooks

1980 edited by Karen L. Rood, Jean W. Ross, and Richard Ziegfeld (1981)

1981 edited by Karen L. Rood, Jean W. Ross, and Richard Ziegfeld (1982)

1982 edited by Richard Ziegfeld; associate editors: Jean W. Ross and Lynne C. Zeigler (1983)

1983 edited by Mary Bruccoli and Jean W. Ross; associate editor: Richard Ziegfeld (1984)

1984 edited by Jean W. Ross (1985)

1985 edited by Jean W. Ross (1986)

1986 edited by J. M. Brook (1987)

1987 edited by J. M. Brook (1988)

1988 edited by J. M. Brook (1989)

1989 edited by J. M. Brook (1990)

1990 edited by James W. Hipp (1991)

1991 edited by James W. Hipp (1992)

1992 edited by James W. Hipp (1993)

1993 edited by James W. Hipp, contributing editor George Garrett (1994)

1994 edited by James W. Hipp, contributing editor George Garrett (1995)

1995 edited by James W. Hipp, contributing editor George Garrett (1996)

1996 edited by Samuel W. Bruce and L. Kay Webster, contributing editor George Garrett (1997)

1997 edited by Matthew J. Bruccoli and George Garrett, with the assistance of L. Kay Webster (1998)

Concise Series

Concise Dictionary of American Literary Biography, 6 volumes (1988-1989): *The New Consciousness, 1941-1968; Colonization to the American Renaissance, 1640-1865; Realism, Naturalism, and Local Color, 1865-1917; The Twenties, 1917-1929; The Age of Maturity, 1929-1941; Broadening Views, 1968-1988.*

Concise Dictionary of British Literary Biography, 8 volumes (1991-1992): *Writers of the Middle Ages and Renaissance Before 1660; Writers of the Restoration and Eighteenth Century, 1660-1789; Writers of the Romantic Period, 1789-1832; Victorian Writers, 1832-1890; Late Victorian and Edwardian Writers, 1890-1914; Modern Writers, 1914-1945; Writers After World War II, 1945-1960; Contemporary Writers, 1960 to Present.*

Dictionary of Literary Biography® • Volume One Hundred Ninety-Five

British Travel Writers, 1910–1939

Dictionary of Literary Biography® • Volume One Hundred Ninety-Five

British Travel Writers, 1910–1939

Edited by
Barbara Brothers
and
Julia M. Gergits
Youngstown State University

A Bruccoli Clark Layman Book
Gale Research
Detroit, Washington, D.C., London

Matthew J. Bruccoli and Richard Layman, Editorial Directors
C. E. Frazer Clark Jr., Managing Editor
Karen Rood, Senior Editor

Printed in the United States of America

Library of Congress Cataloging-in-Publication Data

British travel writers, 1910–1939 / edited by Barbara Brothers and Julia M. Gergits.
p. cm.–(Dictionary of literary biography; v. 195)
"A Bruccoli Clark Layman book."
Includes bibliographical references and index.
ISBN 0-7876-1850-0 (alk. paper)
1. Travelers' writings, English–Bio-bibliography–Dictionaries. 2. English prose literature–20th century–Bio-bibliography–Dictionaries. 3. British–Travel–Foreign countries–History–Dictionaries. 4. Authors, English–20th century–Biography–Dictionaries. 5. Travelers–Great Britain–Biography–Dictionaries. 6. Travel writing–Bio-bibliography–Dictionaries. I. Brothers, Barbara, 1937- . II. Gergits, Julia Marie. III. Series.
PR808.T72B74 1998
820.9'355–dc21 98-21847
[b] CIP

10 9 8 7 6 5 4 3 2 1

To present and future travelers—
Carl Florian and Joseph Marion Gergits Schramer
Mark, Corinne, and Claire Brothers
Jill and Evan Brothers

Contents

Plan of the Series

. . . Almost the most prodigious asset of a country, and perhaps its most precious possession, is its native literary product – when that product is fine and noble and enduring.

Mark Twain*

The advisory board, the editors, and the publisher of the *Dictionary of Literary Biography* are joined in endorsing Mark Twain's declaration. The literature of a nation provides an inexhaustible resource of permanent worth. We intend to make literature and its creators better understood and more accessible to students and the reading public, while satisfying the standards of teachers and scholars.

To meet these requirements, *literary biography* has been construed in terms of the author's achievement. The most important thing about a writer is his writing. Accordingly, the entries in *DLB* are career biographies, tracing the development of the author's canon and the evolution of his reputation.

The purpose of *DLB* is not only to provide reliable information in a convenient format but also to place the figures in the larger perspective of literary history and to offer appraisals of their accomplishments by qualified scholars.

The publication plan for *DLB* resulted from two years of preparation. The project was proposed to Bruccoli Clark by Frederick C. Ruffner, president of the Gale Research Company, in November 1975. After specimen entries were prepared and typeset, an advisory board was formed to refine the entry format and develop the series rationale. In meetings held during 1976, the publisher, series editors, and advisory board approved the scheme for a comprehensive biographical dictionary of persons who contributed to North American literature. Editorial work on the first volume began in January 1977, and it was published in 1978. In order to make *DLB* more than a reference tool and to compile volumes that individually have claim to status as literary history, it was decided to organize volumes by topic, period, or genre. Each of these freestanding volumes provides a biographical-bibliographical guide and overview for a particular area of literature. We are convinced that this organization–as opposed to a single alphabet method–constitutes a valuable innovation in the presentation of reference material. The volume plan necessarily requires many decisions for the placement and treatment of authors who might properly be included in two or three volumes. In some instances a major figure will be included in separate volumes, but with different entries emphasizing the aspect of his career appropriate to each volume. Ernest Hemingway, for example, is represented in *American Writers in Paris, 1920–1939* by an entry focusing on his expatriate apprenticeship; he is also in *American Novelists, 1910–1945* with an entry surveying his entire career, as well as in *American Short-Story Writers, 1910–1945, Second Series* with an entry concentrating on his short stories. Each volume includes a cumulative index of the subject authors and articles. Comprehensive indexes to the entire series are planned.

Since 1981 the series has been further augmented by the *DLB Yearbooks,* which update published entries and add new entries to keep the *DLB* current with contemporary activity. There have also been *DLB Documentary Series* volumes which provide biographical and critical source materials for figures whose work is judged to have particular interest for students. One of these companion volumes is entirely devoted to Tennessee Williams.

We define literature as the *intellectual commerce of a nation:* not merely as belles lettres but as that ample and complex process by which ideas are generated, shaped, and transmitted. *DLB* entries are not limited to "creative writers" but extend to other figures who in their time and in their way influenced the mind of a people. Thus the series encompasses historians, journalists, publishers, book collectors, and screenwriters. By this means readers of *DLB* may be aided to perceive literature not as cult scripture in the keeping of intellectual high priests but firmly positioned at the center of a nation's life.

**From an unpublished section of Mark Twain's autobiography, copyright by the Mark Twain Company*

DLB includes the major writers appropriate to each volume and those standing in the ranks behind them. Scholarly and critical counsel has been sought in deciding which minor figures to include and how full their entries should be. Wherever possible, useful references are made to figures who do not warrant separate entries.

Each *DLB* volume has an expert volume editor responsible for planning the volume, selecting the figures for inclusion, and assigning the entries. Volume editors are also responsible for preparing, where appropriate, appendices surveying the major periodicals and literary and intellectual movements for their volumes, as well as lists of further readings. Work on the series as a whole is coordinated at the Bruccoli Clark Layman editorial center in Columbia, South Carolina, where the editorial staff is responsible for accuracy and utility of the published volumes.

One feature that distinguishes *DLB* is the illustration policy–its concern with the iconography of literature. Just as an author is influenced by his surroundings, so is the reader's understanding of the author enhanced by a knowledge of his environment. Therefore *DLB* volumes include not only drawings, paintings, and photographs of authors, often depicting them at various stages in their careers, but also illustrations of their families and places where they lived. Title pages are regularly reproduced in facsimile along with dust jackets for modern authors. The dust jackets are a special feature of *DLB* because they often document better than anything else the way in which an author's work was perceived in its own time. Specimens of the writers' manuscripts and letters are included when feasible.

Samuel Johnson rightly decreed that "The chief glory of every people arises from its authors." The purpose of the *Dictionary of Literary Biography* is to compile literary history in the surest way available to us–by accurate and comprehensive treatment of the lives and work of those who contributed to it.

The *DLB* Advisory Board

Introduction

By all accounts the years from 1910 to 1939 were a golden period for travelers. In *The Golden Age of Travel, 1880–1939* (1990) Alexis Gregory places the climax of this period before World War I, in the first decade of the twentieth century. Paul Fussell, however, argues in *Abroad: British Literary Traveling Between the Wars* (1980) that 1920–1940 was the period of British obsession with travel. The British urge to travel seems always to have been strong, but the means, motives, destinations, and kinds of individuals who traveled changed as education, technology, and politics transfigured the world. Just how travel and travel writing were transformed in the years leading up to World War I and in the period between two world wars is the subject of this introduction.

Tracing the development of popular travel in his *Cook's Tours: The History of Popular Travel* (1982), Edmund Swinglehurst identifies 1882 as the year when the pleasure-leisure motive began to dominate the travel industry. Gregory argues that the introduction of luxury steamers and railway cars in the 1880s began a Golden Age that reached its climax in the Edwardian era with its grand hotels and stylish restaurants, many of which had their reputations made by the patronage of Edward, Prince of Wales, who lent his name to the first decade of the twentieth century. Greater ease of travel and a reduction in travel costs combined with the rise of the middle class and increased leisure time resulting from a shortened work week to motivate people to leave home, if only for the weekend, to become travelers or, to be more accurate, tourists. Robert Graves's *The Long Week End* (1940), which relates the social history of Great Britain from 1918 to 1939, describes the factors that contributed to increased leisure and money to enjoy that leisure.

Seeking blue water and white sand, the twentieth-century spiritual restorative, people flocked to the Riviera. Queen Victoria and her son Edward VII traveled there in the 1890s. Russian and European royalty and American millionaires flocked there, and it continued to attract the upper-middle and wealthy classes until World War I and the Russian Revolution. According to Maxine Feifer in *Tourism in History: From Imperial Rome to the Present* (1986), fifty thousand tourists spent fifty million gold francs on the Riviera during the winter of 1913–1914. Following World War I the popularity of the Riviera grew as the strength of the dollar and the pound increased and swift and opulent ocean liners and new luxury trains—such as the *Blue Train,* introduced in 1922—made it even more accessible. People crossed the Atlantic for pleasure, bound for the northern shores of the Mediterranean rather than the coasts of the North Atlantic. At the beginning of the nineteenth century the man of wealth traveled to Italy and the Mediterranean for the completion of his education, but by the beginning of the twentieth he went to the South of France to gamble and eat. As the Victorian middle class had followed in the footsteps of their "betters" to view the artworks in Venice, Florence, and Rome, in the 1920s and 1930s they walked along the beach at Cannes, making the suntan the badge of leisure rather than of work.

In the twentieth century the development of air transportation had a major impact on travel. As early as 1920 there were three-hour flights from London to Paris, but the lower-middle class had to wait until the introduction of tourist-class fares in the 1950s to take to the air. United Airlines introduced stewardesses to assist passengers by 1930, and in 1935 Imperial Airways offered round-the-world service. Air France, Pan Am, TWA, and the Dutch airline KLM were all in existence before World War II.

The advent of color film and motion-picture cameras also revolutionized travel and records of it. Late-nineteenth-century travel writers had included photographs in their narratives, comfortably assuming the technology into the genre. Natural color photography became possible in 1931, and glossy travel magazines became the ideal of a travel narrative for many readers. Furthermore, travel books took on a different role once film could record areas, people, and events for armchair travelers back home. As social historians have discussed, the fabric of what makes "truth" came under discussion when photographs become part of historical records. Documentary movies made travel books obsolete as historical record and forced changes in the genre that took decades to mature.

The primary literary result of the twentieth-century travel boom was not entertaining and informative books for the armchair traveler and the peripatetic voyager but an increase in the market for guidebooks. Eighteenth- and early nineteenth-century travelers had guidebooks, but they did not develop into their present mass-produced form until the second half of the nineteenth century. Most travelers use guidebooks and depend on their advice about where to eat and stay.

Yet twentieth-century travelers and travel writers continued the rich tradition of exploration, adventure, and research established by the Victorians, motivated by many of the same urges as earlier Royal Geographical Society explorers such as Richard Burton, John Hanning Speke, or Isabella Bird. In the period of 1910–1939, however, travel was not only faster but also more politically motivated. Some writer-travelers worked as journalists, observing the formation of fledgling socialist nations and witnessing warfare on a global scale. Other times their reporting assignments, which they frequently turned into books, were far more mundane. The age of the amateur scientist-traveler was essentially over, and the age of professional travel writers had begun.

Religion, which propelled earlier travelers to take part in crusades and pilgrimages and nineteenth-century travelers to journey to Africa and the Middle East, continued to motivate twentieth-century travelers though they were fewer in number. In 1901 missionary work took Mildred Cable to China, where she met Francesca and Evangeline French. These three women wrote more than twenty books, many of them travel books on China. One of them, *The Gobi Desert* (1942), won an award from the Royal Central Asian Society. Cable and the French sisters were not the only traveling missionaries who wrote about their journeys, as the titles of some books published during this period testify. They include *By the Equator's Snowy Peak: A Record of Medical Missionary Work and Travel in British East Africa* (1913), by E. May Crawford, and *Across the Prairie in a Motor Caravan: A 3,000-Mile Tour by Two Englishwomen on Behalf of Religious Education* (1922), by F. H. Eva Hasell and Winifred Ticehurst and many others published by the Society for Promoting Christian Knowledge.

Some travelers believed that exploration of the settings for the Old and New Testaments would renew their faith while authenticating the Scriptures for others. In the 1930s and 1940s Louis Golding pursued his Jewish roots in the Mediterranean and Middle East while H. V. Morton produced travel books based on his journeys to the Holy Land in search of his Christian roots. Thomas Cook and other travel companies served the needs of less-adventuresome tourists who wanted to make pilgrimages to biblical sites in Palestine and Egypt with the aid of guide and guidebook. For armchair travelers there were also books such as Edith Louisa Floyer's *Egypt as We Knew It* (1911), Ada M. Goodrich-Freer's *Things Seen in Palestine* (1913), and Lady Evelyn Cobbold's *Pilgrimage to Mecca* (1934). A few other travelers had religious motivations that were not connected with organized religion. D. H. Lawrence's journeys to Italy and later to Mexico were quests for spiritual education and fulfillment through place, as were the travels of Norman Douglas and E. M. Forster.

Following in the grand Victorian tradition, many twentieth-century travelers and travel writers were fulfilling a desire to improve their minds by extending their knowledge of the history and arts of earlier civilizations. The eighteenth- and nineteenth-century British tradition of going abroad to complete one's education continued, but it was no longer confined to rich males. Increased prosperity and shifting manners and mores allowed women and middle-class men to avail themselves of once-exclusive cultural opportunities. Robert Byron became an authority on Byzantine art, architecture, and history through his travels to Greece, India, Tibet, Afghanistan, Persia, and Russia. His travel books educated the generation between the wars about the achievements of the Byzantine Islamic and Christian cultures. While some writers, such as Byron, traveled beyond Greece and that most popular of destination, Italy, the Mediterranean countries were still the ones most frequently visited by students of earlier civilizations. The popularity of travel to the Mediterranean is apparent in the number of travel books written about the region, books such as Sophie Atkinson's *An Artist in Corfu* (1911), Mrs. Colquhoun Grant's *Through Dante's Land: Impressions in Tuscany* (1912), and Edward Hutton's *The Cities of Romagna and the Marches* (1913) or, toward the end of the period, John Gibbons's *Afoot in Italy* (1930), Cecily Hamilton's *Modern Italy, As Seen by an Englishwoman* (1932), and Kate O'Brien's *Farewell Spain* (1937).

Research for books of art criticism drew Beatrice Erskine to Italy and Spain; research for biographies of Baudelaire and George Gordon, Lord Byron, drew Peter Quennell to Paris. Then the love of traveling and writing about their journeys led them farther afield. Erskine traveled to Arabia and Palestine and earned membership in the Geographical, Empire, and Asiatic Societies. Quennell went to Africa, Asia, and North America. After graduation from Cambridge E. M. Forster traveled to Italy and Greece, and later he went to Egypt and India. Italy and India became settings for some of his novels and the subjects of his travel writings. In his fiction Forster came to understand and depict travel as a metaphor for self-understanding. Yet for him, as for D. H. Lawrence, travel writing was a sideline. It was also of secondary importance for Walter Starkie and T. E. Lawrence. Walter Starkie, a professor of Spanish and Italian literature at Trinity College in Dublin, produced travel books from his journeys abroad to study gypsy life; T. E. Lawrence's research on medieval architecture took him to Syria and Mesopotamia. His exploits as military adviser to the Arab leader Faisal during World War I, popularized first by American journalist Lowell Thomas and later by Lawrence's account of his wartime travels, *The Seven Pillars of Wisdom* (1926), transformed him in the public eye into the larger-than-life Lawrence of Arabia.

The desire to map remote areas of Africa took explorers to the Arctic and Antarctic, China and Tibet, Turkistan, northern India, and the remote recesses of Arabia, the Amazon, New Guinea, and Borneo. Titles of the travel books about Africa began to sound like those about travel excursions or stays in familiar parts of the world. These books include Charlotte Cameron's *A Woman's Winter in Africa* (1913), Lady Dorothy Rachel Mills's *The Golden Land, A Record of Travel in West Africa* (1929), William John W. Roome's *Tramping through Africa: A Dozen Crossings of the Continent* (1930), and Evelyn Brodhurst-Hill's *The Youngest Lion: Early Farming Days in Kenya* (1934). More and more the audacious were challenged by the jungles of South America and Southeast Asia or the mountaintops and frigid regions of the world, rather than by the heart of Africa and its mysteries, even though Egypt and other destinations of nineteenth-century explorers had secrets left to yield. In 1915 the excavation of the Cretan palace at Mallia began, and in 1922 the Tomb of Tutankhamen was discovered in Egypt.

The Royal Geographical Society continued to sponsor and reward travel in little-known areas such as Arabia and Persia. Among the winners of the Royal Geographic Society medals for the period 1910 to 1940 were writer-travelers Douglas Carruthers (1912), Charles Doughty (1912), Gertrude Bell (1918), H. St. John B. Philby (1920), Bertram Thomas (1931), and Maj. R. E. Cheesman (1936)–all of whom focused their attentions on the region. Also lifting the veil from the remote recesses of Arabia and Persia during this period were Mr. and Mrs. Harold Ingrams, who won a Gold Medal in 1940 for "exploration and studies" in the Hadhramawt, and Freya Stark, one of most inveterate travelers and most prolific travel writers of the twentieth century, who received a Gold Medal in 1942 for her travels and writing on Arabia during the 1930s and 1940s.

Tibet, a land veiled by mystery, was penetrated by Europeans during the first half of the twentieth century. Sir Francis Younghusband's famous British expedition of 1903–1904, in which F. M. Bailey took part, marked the beginning of many journeys of discovery to the region that ended when the Chinese closed the borders of Tibet in 1950. Explorer-writers Bailey and Francis Kingdon Ward earned Royal Geographic Society medals in 1916 and 1930 respectively for their travels in Tibet. Bailey did not publish his accounts of his journeys until after World War II–*China-Tibet-Assam* (1945), *Mission to Tashkent* (1946), and *No Passport to Tibet* (1957). While Bailey was an adventurer, Kingdon Ward was a scientist, primarily a biologist. Ward described the flora of Tibet in *The Land of the Blue Poppy* (1913) and its rivers in *The Mystery Rivers of Tibet* (1923). Ward and Bailey were both part of the 1924 expedition that identified the source of the Brahmaputra-Tsangpo River. Many novelists and travel writers have addressed the closing of the Tibetan borders, testifying to a continuing fascination with Tibet and its people. A wonderful spy novel set during the end of Tibet exploration is Lionel Davidson's *The Rose of Tibet* (1962), which depicts the rigors of traveling in its mountainous regions. Peter Fleming's novel *Bayonets to Lhasa* (1961) was published after he had traveled to Brazil, central Asia, and other parts of the world.

In much that has been written about Tibet following the 1903–1904 expedition writers repeated legends about the Tibetan people and their culture, drawing more on the imagination than on unbiased observation. (See the bibliography of travel writing in the appendix to this volume.) Mark Cocker provides several examples of this phenomenon in *Loneliness and Time: The Story of British Travel Writing* (1992), but he does find a significant change in attitude from nineteenth-century writers. While nineteenth-century writers tended to view Tibetans as "filthy, barbarous and savage," twentieth-century writers often saw them as the "final guardians of a portion of the human spirit that had been extinguished everywhere else." Worship of the primitive appears in the writings of twentieth-century travelers to other parts of the world as well, reflecting attitudes discussed by Sigmund Freud in *Civilization and Its Discontents* (1930).

Adventure is part of the lure of exploration. Expeditions to the Arctic and Antarctic, which also attracted many twentieth-century explorers, provided opportunities for individuals to prove their courage as well as to discover important scientific information. Sometimes their journeys proved so hazardous that they did not return. In 1913 the

Royal Geographic Society presented to the widow of Comdr. Robert Scott a casket containing the Patron's Medal and a special Antarctic Medal posthumously awarded to her husband. His 1910–1913 expedition is the subject of Apsley Cherry-Garrard's extremely popular *The Worst Journey in the World* (1922). Previously, Commander Scott (1904), Capt. Roald Amundsen (1907), and Dr. William Speirs Bruce (1910) had earned Royal Geographic Society medals for travels in the Arctic and Antarctic. In 1911 Bruce published *Polar Exploration,* an account of his travels. A medal for exploration of the Antarctic was presented to another explorer in 1913, and at least one of the two Royal Geographic Society medals awarded in 1915, 1921, 1923, 1926, 1930, 1931, 1932, 1933, 1934, 1937, and 1939 was for exploration of a polar region, nearly one-fourth of all the medals presented. Many of the explorers were not British and wrote nothing about their journeys; yet accounts of polar travel continue to appeal to a large audience.

Well supported by the Royal Geographic Society, mountain-climbing exploits continued to capture the imagination of the British reading public. Perhaps that popularity stems from the combination of sport and adventure that characterizes the activity. In 1922 alone readers were offered Douglas Freshfield's *Below the Snow Line,* Helen Hamilton's *Mountain Madness,* and Lt. Col. Charles Howard-Bury's *Everest: The Reconnaissance, 1921.* Some mountain climbers were also explorers, and the Royal Geographic Society presented medals and awards to several individuals for exploration of the Himalayas and the Caucasus mountains. The Royal Geographic Society helped to sponsor the Mount Everest expedition of 1922 and presented an award to its leader, Col. C. K. Howard-Bury. Other awards for Himalayan exploration were presented to Englishmen in 1915, 1928, 1932, and 1934 while one in 1935 was presented to a German for his exploration of the Caucasus mountains.

In 1938 the Royal Geographic Society gave an award to mountain climber Eric Shipton, who wrote about his exploits in *Nanda Devi* (1936) and *Blank on the Map* (1938), as well as in several more books after World War II. Another account of climbing the Himalayan peak Nanda Devi was published by Howard Tilman in 1937, and accounts of ascents of Mount Everest were published by Sir Francis Younghusband in 1936 and by Hugh Ruttledge in 1937. Books about mountain-climbing exploits were published by men and women throughout this period. Francis Smythe, who along with Shipton was a part of a Royal Geographic Society–sponsored expedition to reach the summit of Mount Everest, wrote about and photographed his climbs in the Alps, the Himalayas, and the Canadian Rockies. He also wrote about Edward Whymper. The subtitle of Frederick Spencer Chapman's *Lhasa, the Holy City: Memoirs of a Mountaineer* (1938) reminds the reader that the exploration of Tibet necessitated mountain-climbing skills. Published travel accounts of journeys to northern Greenland, Iceland, and Lapland–for example, Olive Murray Chapman's *Across Iceland, The Land of Frost and Fire* (1930) and *Across Lapland with Sledge and Reindeer* (1932)–reveal how much of the search for adventure and knowledge of the unknown in the first half of the twentieth century led to remote lands of ice and snow.

While readers enjoyed books about the exploits of mountain climbers and polar expeditions, they had little exposure to information about the scientific and archaeological discoveries occurring rapidly throughout the world. Nineteenth-century travelers such as Sir Samuel White Baker, Sir Richard Francis Burton, Charles Darwin, Sir Francis Galton, Sir Austen Henry Layard, Harriet Martineau, Marianne North, and Amelia Edwards wrote travel books for lay audiences, providing scientific information about the countries and regions they visited and relaying their discoveries in digging up the past and observing the present. They not only wrote about the flora, fauna, geography, peoples, architecture, and archaeological treasures but also frequently collected and brought back specimens and objects to British museums. By contrast Leonard Woolley, a member of the same archaeological expedition to the Middle East that gave T. E. Lawrence his introduction to Arabia, did not write a widely available book about his travels until he published his autobiography, *Digging Up the Past* (1949). That he did not has much to do with the professionalization of the sciences and social sciences, including history. Many of the works of modern sociologists, archaeologists, botanists, and Egyptologists were written only for other specialists. There were, however, a few exceptions, notably Evelyn Cheesman, an entomologist who first worked as an insect keeper at Regent's Park Zoo and then got her chance to advance her career when she became part of a zoological expedition to the Marquesas and Galapagos Islands in 1924. Her five books on her travels in the islands of the southwestern Pacific and her two autobiographies carry on the nineteenth-century tradition exemplified in the work of Marianne North.

While some travel writers included in this volume–such as Helen Cameron Gordon, Lady Russell, and Olive Chapman–could still be classified as amateur cultural anthropologists, others might be called social explorers, a term Joanne Shattock uses in "Travel Writing Victorian and Modern," included in *The Art of Travel* (1982), and by Peter Keating in his *Into Unknown England 1866–1913* (1976). George Orwell's books, such as *The Road to Wigan Pier* (1937) and some of W. H. Hudson's work fit the narrow application she has in mind. Yet, applied more broadly, the phrase aptly describes not just the impulse that made British people from one class become the observers of those from another but also the motivation that sent many to Russia, the Balkans, and other parts of the globe to investigate the politics and ideologies of other cultures. Rather than as social scientists–economists, anthropologists, or historians–these individuals went as professional writers, as journalists, investigating the lives, beliefs, and actions of people who were of interest to their English readers.

For example, Russia is one of the most written-about places of the twentieth century. Early-twentieth-century visitors include Stephen Graham, who began his love affair with Russia by tramping through the Caucasus and Ural Mountains before the Revolution of 1917 and wrote several books about Mother Russia. Most visitors to Russia, however, went to observe the effects of post-Revolutionary economics and politics. There were a few others like Graham, of course: Ella Christie was fascinated by Turkistan, its people and places, and wrote about it in her only travel book, *Through Khiva to Golden Samarkand* (1925). Some, such as Ella Maillart, went ostensibly to study film though she was drawn as much by a desire to study communism and wrote *Turkestan Solo* (1934) about her journey from Moscow to Soviet Turkistan. Later visitors of the 1930s frequently extolled the benefits of communism and wrote tracts rather than travel books. Ethel Mannin, who made several journeys to Moscow and was a strong supporter and believer in Russian socialism, eventually became disenchanted with the Soviet system and chronicled her change of heart in *South to Samarkand* (1936). E. M. Delafield went to Russia at the behest of her publisher, who wanted her to write a book with "a humorous slant on Russia." Calling herself the new Mrs. Trollope, she did just that, producing *Straw Without Bricks* (1937; published in the United States as *I Visit the Soviets*), a funny book about the people of Russia and those who travel there. She made no pretense of examining Russian history or its institutions. The popularity of the Soviet Union as a travel destination can be assessed by perusing the selected list of travel books provided for this period. Writers included in this volume who visited and wrote about the Soviet Union include Eileen Bigland, Rosita Forbes, Byron, and Fleming.

The Arabian peninsula was also a frequent destination for travelers, largely because of its political importance to the world. Gertrude Bell, for example, was famous not only for her travel writing about the Middle East but also for the use the British government made of her knowledge. Not all travelers to the region agreed with British government policies. T. E. Lawrence is the best known of those who sided against British policies toward the Arabs, but Beatrice Erskine also earned the government's ire.

Other places that gained attention through political upheaval and conflict include the Balkans, which journalist-traveler Mary Edith Durham wrote about in *High Albania* (1909). W. H. Auden and Louis MacNeice's *Letters from Iceland* (1937) is less the travel book they were commissioned to write than a comment on the developing political crises in Europe. The 1930s were difficult times. In *On the Frontier* (1937) Auden reflected in poetry on his visit to Spain, and *Journey to a War* (1938) comprises Auden's poems and Christopher Isherwood's prose account about their journey to China during the Sino-Japanese War. Journalists such as Peter Fleming and Ella Maillart were sent on assignment to cover that war and recounted their journeys in travel books. Accounts of other battlefronts were also published, including George Orwell's *Homage to Catalonia* (1938), about the Spanish Civil War, and Somerset Maugham's *France at War* (1940), about French preparations about the German invasion.

Diplomats or diplomats' spouses still wrote books about their experiences, albeit fewer than in the nineteenth century. Maurice Collis, a colonial administrator for Burma (now Myanmar) in 1912–1936, wrote several travel books on China and the Asian colonies. Vita Sackville-West, who visited her diplomat husband in Persia (now Iran) in 1926 and 1927, wrote two books about her travels. Helen Cameron Gordon, Lady Russell, first lived for a time in India as a young girl and then in Cyprus as the wife of the attorney general. While she considered herself a linguist and folklorist as much as a travel writer, she was made a fellow of the Royal Geographic Society on the basis of her extensive travels and her books about them.

Some travelers seem always to have traveled merely for the sake of traveling. In some cases it may have been to escape constraints of home, but in other cases the individual seems to have been born with the spirit of wanderlust. The twentieth century has produced many such globe-trotters and expatriates who have written significant bodies of travel literature about experiences. At twenty-five Somerset Maugham returned to Paris, where he had spent his early childhood, and made it his base for his travels throughout the world. Southern climes and sunshine seduced many British into taking up residence abroad. Southern Italy, particularly the Isle of Capri, was Norman Douglas's choice of home though he wrote about North Africa as well. Italy served as the place of refuge for Osbert Sitwell, but like Maugham he traveled extensively throughout the world. The title of his final travel book reflects his peripateticism: *The Four Continents: Being More Discursions on Travel, Art and Life* (1954).

Following in the illustrious footsteps of female travelers such as Isabella Bird and Mary Kingsley, twentieth-century women traveled widely and wrote extensively. Among the most famous of the women globe-trotters was Forbes, an adventurer turned writer, whose career began after she crossed the Libyan Desert when she was only in her twenties. There are few spots in the world that she did not visit and few famous and infamous political leaders that she did not interview. Her exploits earned her gold medals from the Royal Antwerp Geographical Society, the French Geographical Society, and the Royal Society of Arts. She was also a Fellow of the Royal Geographical Society. Charlotte Cameron was a journalist and foreign newspaper correspondent whose work took her from Alaska to Mexico and from the southern seas to Africa. The title of one of her travel books refers to her as *Cheechako* (tenderfoot), or "woman alone wandering." Other female writer globe-trotters of the first half of the twentieth century include Ethel Mannin and Lady Dorothy Mills.

In an age in which frontiers ceased to exist, even in the polar regions, those addicted to travel sought adventure or individuality through unusual methods of travel. For many travelers the means of conveyance became an integral part of their experience. Walking tours were still popular at home and abroad; John Gibbons's *Afoot in Italy* and *Tramping through Ireland* were both published in 1930. Sailing fascinated many others, and Lady Annie Brassey's nineteenth-century tales were followed in the twentieth century by Ella Maillart's autobiographical writings, Dorothy Ratcliffe's stories of traveling on the family yawl, the *Sea Swallow,* and Maude Speed's *A Yachtswoman's Cruises and Steamer Voyages* (1911), an account of her adventures aboard her husband's sailboat. Neil Gunn's *Off a Boat* appeared in 1938. H. M. Tomlinson's fascination with shipping led him to travel by steamer and ocean liner and then to a career in writing, including travel books. Robert Gibbings traveled by boat to explore cultures at home and abroad.

In other instances new means of travel, such as the automobile, not only replaced older means of travel but also began to appear in book titles such as Jan and Cora Gordon's *On Wandering Wheels: Through Roadside Camps from Maine to Georgia in an Old Sedan Car* (1928) and Stella Court Treatt's *Cape to Cairo: The Record of a Historic Motor Trip* (1927). The British seemed to have developed a love affair with train travel, which was reflected in detective novels and thrillers such as Graham Greene's *Stamboul Train* (1932) and Agatha Christie's *Murder on the Orient Express* (1934). They also developed a fascination with air travel as a means of exploring the globe, and travel books such as Mildred Bruce's *The Bluebird's Flight* (1931) took it as their subject.

In fact travel became so easy and popular that Aldous Huxley, who wrote *Jesting Pilate* (1926) about his travels around the world, also wrote "Why Not Stay at Home" (1925), and Evelyn Waugh seemed at times to have traveling itself rather than place as the subject of his travel books. The jaded spirit of modernism was evident in the writings of Norman Douglas, D. H. Lawrence, Helen Cameron Gordon, and others who charged the West with contaminating the earth rather than civilizing it. In other cases writers such as Peter Fleming created antiheroic narrators to "demythologize the romance of travel and imperial adventure" or, like H. M. Tomlinson, they posed as reluctant travelers.

The means for travel may have changed during the years 1910–1939, but the motives at most metamorphized rather than becoming completely new or different. As always travelers journeyed to learn, to explore, to escape, to re-create life as adventure or romance, and to seek health, freedom from restraint, vice, or spiritual rejuvenation. In this era marred by World War I, a worldwide depression, and the approach of World War II, travelers continued to dream, explore, and share their adventures.

–Barbara Brothers and Julia M. Gergits

Acknowledgments

This book was produced by Bruccoli Clark Layman, Inc. Karen L. Rood, senior editor for the *Dictionary of Literary Biography* series, was the in-house editor.

Administrative support was provided by Ann M. Cheschi, Carol Cheschi, and Tenesha S. Lee.

Bookkeeper is Joyce Fowler. Assistant bookkeeper is Beverly Dill.

Copyediting supervisor is Samuel W. Bruce. The copyediting staff includes Phyllis A. Avant, Charles Brower, Patricia Coate, Christine Copeland, Margo Dowling, Thom Harman, Jannette L. Giles, Nicole M. Nichols, and Raegan E. Quinn. Freelance copyeditors are Rebecca Mayo and Jennie Williamson.

Editorial associate is Jeff Miller.

Layout and graphics staff includes Janet E. Hill, Mark J. McEwan, and Alison Smith.

Office manager is Kathy Lawler Merlette.

Photography editors are Melissa D. Hinton, Margaret Meriwether, and Paul Talbot. Photographic copy work was performed by Joseph M. Bruccoli.

Production manager is Philip B. Dematteis.

SGML supervisor is Cory McNair. The SGML staff includes Linda Drake, Frank Graham, Jennifer Harwell, and Alex Snead.

Systems manager is Marie L. Parker.

Database manager is Javed Nurani. Kim Kelly performed data entry.

Typesetting supervisor is Kathleen M. Flanagan. The typesetting staff includes Pamela D. Norton, Karla Corley Price, and Patricia Flanagan Salisbury. Freelance typesetters include Deidre Murphy and Delores Plastow.

Walter W. Ross and Steven Gross did library research. They were assisted by the following librarians at the Thomas Cooper Library of the University of South Carolina: Linda Holderfield and the interlibrary-loan staff; reference-department head Virginia Weathers; reference librarians Marilee Birchfield, Stefanie Buck, Stefanie DuBose, Rebecca Feind, Karen Joseph, Donna Lehman, Charlene Loope, Anthony McKissick, Jean Rhyne, and Kwamine Simpson; circulation-department head Caroline Taylor; and acquisitions-searching supervisor David Haggard.

Dictionary of Literary Biography® • Volume One Hundred Ninety-Five

British Travel Writers, 1910–1939

Dictionary of Literary Biography

Eileen Bigland

(1898 - 1970)

Holly Dworken Cooley

BOOKS: *Doctor's Child: A Novel* (London: Barker, 1934);

Gingerbread House: A Novel (London: Barker, 1934; New York & London: Appleton-Century, 1934);

Alms for Oblivion (London: Hodder & Stoughton, 1937);

Laughing Odyssey (London: Hodder & Stoughton, 1937; New York: Macmillan, 1938);

Conflict with a God (London: Hodder & Stoughton, 1938);

This Narrow World (London: Hodder & Stoughton, 1938);

The Lake of the Royal Crocodiles (London: Hodder & Stoughton, 1939; New York: Macmillan, 1939);

Into China (London: Collins, 1940; New York: Macmillan, 1940);

Pattern in Black and White (London: Drummond, 1940);

The Riddle of the Kremlin (London: Collins, 1940);

Tiger in the Heart (London: Hodder & Stoughton, 1940);

You Can Never Look Back (London: Hodder & Stoughton, 1940);

The Key to the Russian Door (London: Putnam, 1942);

Awakening to Danger (London: Nicholson & Watson, 1946);

The Story of the W.R.N.S. (London: Nicholson & Watson, 1946);

Britain's Other Army; the Story of the A.T.S. (London: Nicholson & Watson, 1946);

Miranda (London: Jarrolds, 1947);

Understanding the Russians (London: People's Universities Press, 1948);

Journey to Egypt (London & New York: Jarrolds, 1948);

Clown Without Background (London & New York: Jarrolds, 1950);

Ouida: The Passionate Victorian (London & New York: Jarrolds, 1950; New York: Duell, Sloan & Pearce, 1951);

In the Steps of George Borrow (London & New York: Rich & Cowan, 1951);

Flower without Root (London: Jarrolds, 1952);

The Indomitable Mrs. Trollope (London: Barrie, 1953; Philadelphia: Lippincott, 1954);

Marie Corelli, The Woman and the Legend (London & New York: Jarrolds, 1953);

Madame Curie (London: Muller, 1955; New York: Criterion, 1957);

The True Book About Sister Kenny (London: Muller, 1956);

Lord Byron (London: Cassell, 1956); republished as *Passion for Excitement: The Life and Personality of the Incredible Lord Byron* (New York: Coward-McCann, 1956);

The True Book About Madame Curie (London: Muller, 1956);

The True Book About Helen Keller (London: Muller, 1957);

The True Book about Heroines of the Sea (London: Muller, 1958);

Mary Shelley (London: Cassell, 1959; New York: Appleton-Century-Crofts, 1959);

Russia Has Two Faces (London: Odhams, 1960);

Queen Elizabeth I (New York: Criterion, 1965).

A prolific writer of fiction and nonfiction, Eileen Bigland is most notable for her books about her travels to places that were undergoing political

LAUGHING ODYSSEY

BY

EILEEN BIGLAND

LONDON

HODDER AND STOUGHTON LIMITED

1937

Frontispiece and title page for Bigland's first travel book, an account of her 1936 journey to the Soviet Union

and social upheaval. Always adventurous, she was, for instance, the first white or Western woman to travel the Burma Road in China, and her choices of destinations corresponded to her political leanings. During the 1930s and later she enthusiastically explored how Communism was reshaping the East, and she also wrote about traveling in central Africa.

Except for the information in Bigland's autobiography, *Awakening to Danger* (1946), which focuses largely on her travels, little is known about Bigland's personal life. Born in 1898 in Edinburgh, Scotland, to a family that was half Calvinist Scot and half Russian, Eileen Bigland was fascinated early on by her grandmother's Slavic heritage. From her grandmother she learned enough Russian to facilitate her later travels. She had two older sisters, Francesca and Mary, as well as two other siblings who had died before she was born, and a father who died young. Eileen Bigland began serious training for the ballet, but after she went to France to study dance, she met Isadora Duncan, who befriended her and dissuaded her from a career as a dancer. Bigland married and eventually had three children. Her marriage ended in the late 1930s. During that decade she wrote fiction and worked as a reader for a publisher, where she "discovered" mystery writer Eric Ambler. Later, after she began writing about her travels, she lectured and broadcast travel talks for the BBC.

By her own account none of Bigland's novels is particularly memorable. During World War II she wrote *The Story of the W.R.N.S.* (1946), about the Women's Royal Navy Service, and *Britain's Other Army; the Story of the A.T.S.* (1946), about the Auxiliary Territorial Service. She is also the author of popular biographies for adults and young people, including *Ouida: The Passionate Victorian* (1950), *In the Steps of George Borrow* (1951), *Marie Corelli, The Woman and the Legend* (1953), *The Indomitable Mrs. Trollope* (1953), *Lord Byron* (1956), *The True Book*

Dust jacket for the U.S. edition of Bigland's book about her 1938 travels in East Africa

About Sister Kenny (1956), *The True Book About Madame Curie* (1956), *The True Book About Helen Keller* (1957), *The True Book About Heroines of the Sea* (1958), *Mary Shelley* (1959), and *Queen Elizabeth I* (1965).

All of Bigland's writings reveal a true humanist's fascination with people. In a *Chicago Sunday Tribune* review of *Mary Shelley* Edward Wagenknecht commented that "her book reads as vividly as a novel" (4 October 1959). This appraisal could be applied to all Bigland's writing. Perfect for the armchair traveler, Bigland's style is eminently readable and seemingly effortless. Remembered conversations, presented in the form of dialogue, let people she has met speak in their own words. By indicating how she phrased her questions she also reveals how she may have influenced the answers. This technique lends immediacy and apparent authenticity to her reports. The reader is less aware of Bigland than of the country and its people, who often speak in their own words and express their own attitudes. The major theme of Bigland's travel writing seems to be that people should try to understand each other.

Bigland's first travel book, *Laughing Odyssey* (1937), opens with the enigmatic line "I went to Soviet Russia in search of happiness." With the world on the verge of war in 1936, her grandmother's stories of old Russia gave Bigland hopeful expectations about journeying to a land of cherished memories that was being transformed by Communism. Looking at people rather than systems, Bigland humanized what others might have seen in theoretical terms. She looked for the individual in the collectivization of a continent. The title appears to be more

THE RED ARMY STANDS GUARD AT
RUSSIA'S DOOR
frontispiece

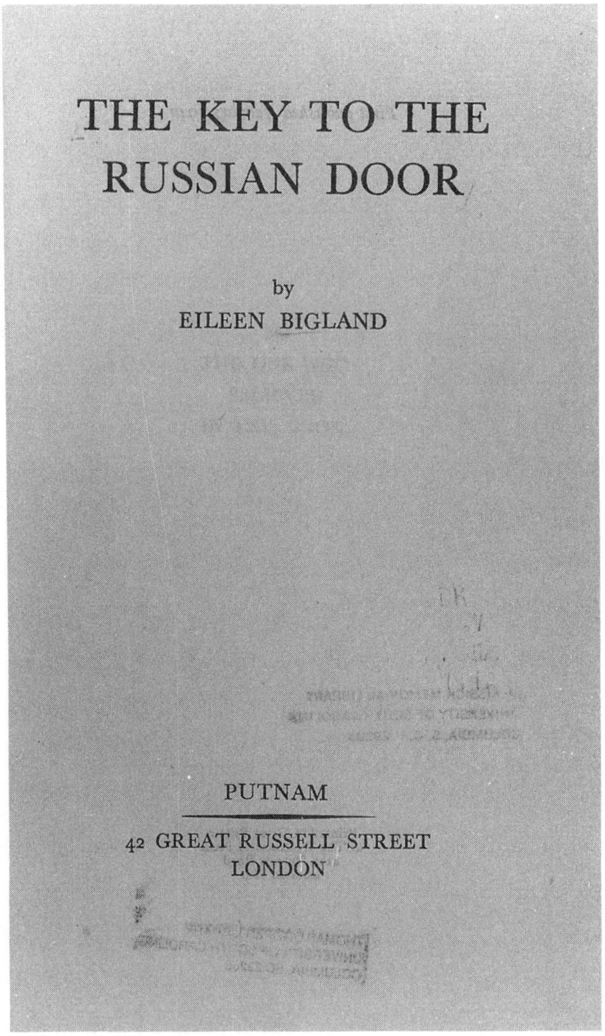
THE KEY TO THE
RUSSIAN DOOR

by
EILEEN BIGLAND

PUTNAM
42 GREAT RUSSELL STREET
LONDON

Frontispiece and title page for Bigland's 1942 book, an attempt to allay British and American fears of Soviet Communism with "a portrait of the Soviet Russian as he really is"

flippant than it actually is: laughter is the writer-traveler's answer to situations that might provoke disturbing responses. Indeed Bigland looked back on her summer in Russia as one of the happiest times in her life. A reviewer for *The New York Times Book Review* (27 February 1938) evidently felt that the book conveyed her joy, calling her account "delightful."

Notable in Bigland's account of her travels through Soviet Russia is her presentation of subjects such as hospital treatment, the abolition of legalized abortion, and the manner in which the marriage bureau dealt with bigamy. After presenting a Soviet method she sometimes commented that it was not the usual Western way or even that it was unfathomable to her, but she was careful never to present Soviet customs in terms of Western ones or to pass judgment on them. Achieving the enormous task of traveling in a country that suffered under repressive czarist regimes in the past and Stalinist purges in the present, Bigland remained objective and hopeful, refusing to be misled by political posturing and asserting, "for myself, who am neither Tsarist or Communist, I prefer Russia as she is at present, a vast country struggling to make life happy for her people."

Bigland wrote more books on Russia than on any other country. It became something of a mission for her to convince the West that Communism had improved the Russians' lot and that Soviet politics should not be a barrier to their association with democratic nations. *The Riddle of the Kremlin,* which appeared in 1940, was followed in 1942 by *The Key to the Russian Door,* which was aimed at replacing British and American fears with "a portrait of the Soviet Russian as he really is." *Understanding the Russians*

(1948) is an attempt to explain the Russian historical background and character in light of present actions. In 1958 Bigland returned to Russia. Her account of this second journey, *Russia Has Two Faces* (1960), is even more enthusiastic about what the country had accomplished in its race for modernization. Again her dramatic narratives help readers to relive her journeys.

Bigland's 1938 visit to Shiwa Ngandu in what was then known as northern Rhodesia (present-day Zambia and northeastern Zimbabwe) led to *The Lake of the Royal Crocodiles* (1939), in which she describes relationships between the European friends she visits and members of the Bemba tribe. She also visited Kenya and Tanganyika (now part of Tanzania) and encountered missionaries, government workers, and members of various other African tribes. In the Belgian Congo (now the Republic of the Congo) she became the first woman to descend into one of the copper mines. Nonpolitical in her treatment of Africa, Bigland presented an enlightened picture of African self-government that seems at odds with most opinions of the time. Reviews of this book seemed more positive than those for her books on Russia. A writer for *The New York Times Book Review* (2 April 1939) called *The Lake of the Royal Crocodiles* "decidedly superior" to the usual "my-trip-to-Africa" narrative, finding Bigland's book "more original, more objective, more searching and much wittier." Bigland's talents for close observation, objectivity, and humor even in discomfort are characteristic of her thinking and writing, no matter where she visited.

Issues that Bigland touched on in *The Lake of the Royal Crocodiles* are explored in *Pattern in Black and White* (1940), in which she analyzed what white settlers have done to the black man's Africa, viewing the colonization process as a betrayal of black by white and warning that ignoring African problems might lead to more difficulties between blacks and whites on that continent. *Pattern in Black and White* seems the most political of Bigland's works.

Into China (1940), Bigland's account of her journey to the other great Eastern power, alludes to "The Puzzle of China," what she described as its people's serenity despite war-induced hardships. She might also have called the book "The Burma Road." For three weeks she traveled with only Chinese companions in the first passenger bus of an ammunition convoy from Lashio in Burma to Kumming, China. The first white woman to have the dubious pleasure, Bigland approached the experience with her characteristic sense of humor. Her enthusiasm for the Chinese and their kindliness is topped only by her regard for the Russians. Her reviewers seem to agree with P. J. Searles, who wrote that Bigland "holds the reader's absorbed interest on every page" (*Boston Transcript,* 25 January 1941).

All Bigland's books are out of print, including her last travel book, *Journey to Egypt* (1948). Their lack of availability is a great loss, for Bigland saw in person most of the notable players in the great upheavals between the two world wars–including Benito Mussolini, Joseph Stalin, and Adolf Hitler–and in every country she visited, she lived with the people who were affected by the actions of these leaders. Because she involved herself in the events taking place around her, from changing bandages, to saying the wrong thing and being thrown in jail, to sleeping in a bathtub because there was no bed for her in a crowded hospital, she was a participant as well as a correspondent. Her keen apprehension of the necessity of valuing all human life and her fears of isolationist societies are as useful and poignant in the late twentieth century as they were when she wrote them.

Bigland's writings always focus on humanity, regardless of color, race, or ethnicity. When she became irritated with a people, she was not motivated by racist feelings but by her humanitarian impulses. An inveterate traveler, who called herself a sponge, she was an effective travel writer because she did not consciously impose herself or her views on her surroundings. She put herself in the way of adventures and people and watched what happened, seemingly immune to hardship–or at least not complaining about it. She was hardly motivated by a desire for fame and seemed to see her writing not as an art but as a means of making money to support herself and her family.

Although at times Bigland's prose may become melodramatic, her books are suspenseful, readable, and memorable, especially for their anecdotes and conversations. Bigland's real subject is people. Scenery and machines are important only insofar as they relate to people. Her use of the words *riddle, key,* and *pattern* in three of her book titles implies that there is something to be understood in human behavior, whether or not her books solve the riddles, locate the keys, or detect the patterns. All Bigland's travel writings demand that her readers attempt to understand their fellow human beings.

Reference:

Jane Robinson, *Wayward Women: A Guide to Women Travellers* (New York: Oxford University Press, 1990).

Robert Byron

(26 February 1905 - 24 February 1941)

Michael Coyle
Colgate University

BOOKS: *Europe in the Looking-Glass: Reflections of a Motor Drive from Grimsby to Athens* (London: Routledge, 1926);

The Appreciation of Architecture (London: Wishart, 1927);

The Station: Athos, Treasures and Men (London: Duckworth, 1928; New York: Knopf, 1928);

The Byzantine Achievement: An Historical Perspective, A.D. 330–1453 (London: Routledge, 1929; New York: Knopf, 1929);

The Birth of Western Painting, by Byron and David Talbot Rice (London: Routledge, 1930; New York: Knopf, 1931);

An Essay on India (London: Routledge, 1931);

First Russia, Then Tibet (London: Macmillan, 1933);

Innocence and Design, by Byron and Christopher Sykes, as Richard Waughburton (London: Macmillan, 1935);

Shell Guide to Wiltshire (London: Architectural Press, 1935);

The Road to Oxiana (London: Macmillan, 1937);

Imperial Pilgrimage, London in Your Pocket Series (Westminster: London Transport, 1937).

OTHER: "Timurid Architecture," in *Survey of Persian Art: From Prehistoric Times to the Present,* 6 volumes, edited by Arthur Upham Pope (London & New York: Oxford University Press, 1938–1939), III: 1119–1143;

Byron's diary of his 1938 visit to the Parteitag in Nuremberg, in *Articles of War: The Spectator Book of World War II,* edited by Fiona Glass and Philip Marsden-Smedley (London: Grafton, 1989), pp. 3–20.

SELECTED PERIODICAL PUBLICATIONS–UNCOLLECTED: "Fascism in the Dodecanese," *Nation,* 149 (14 April 1926): 554-556;

"Liberal Education," *New Statesman,* 34 (7 December 1929): 290–292;

"Freedom of the Skies," *New Statesman,* 35 (14 June 1930): 298–300;

Robert Byron, circa 1936–1937, working on The Road to Oxiana *(photograph by Lucy Butler)*

"Black Pagoda of Kanarak," *Architectural Review,* 68 (November 1930): 194–200, 223–224;

"New Delhi," *Architectural Review,* 69 (January 1931): 1–30;

"Tibetan Applique-work," *Burlington Magazine,* 58 (June 1931): 267–269;

"Byzantine Exhibition in Paris," *Burlington Magazine,* 59 (July 1931): 27–33;

"Landscape and the Artist," *New Statesman and Nation,* 2 (15 August 1931): 198;

"Russian Scene: Foundations," *Architectural Review,* 71 (May 1932): 174–200;

"Broadcasting House," *Architectural Review,* 72 (August 1932): 47–49;

"New Mosaic in the Kahrieh," *Burlington Magazine,* 62 (January 1933): 40–41;

"Formation of Byzantine Art," *Architectural Review,* 73 (February 1933): 78–79;

"Anatomy of Broadcasting," *New Statesman and Nation,* 5 (6 May 1933): 564–565;
"Can We Save Central London?," *Architectural Review,* 73 (June 1933): 227–228;
"Shrine of Khwajn Abu Nasr Parsa at Balkh," *American Institute for Persian Art and Archaeology Bulletin,* 7 (December 1934): 1;
"Note on the Qal'a-i Duhktar at Firuzabad," *American Institute for Persian Art and Archaeology Bulletin,* 7 (December 1934): 3–6;
"Photographic Essay of Persian Islamic Architecture," *American Institute for Persian Art and Archaeology Bulletin,* 7 (December 1934): 36–38;
"In Pursuit of Persian Islamic Architecture," *Asia,* 35 (May 1935): 284–289;
"Early Rock Carving at Nagsh-i-Rustam," *American Institute for Persian Art and Archaeology Bulletin,* 4 (June 1935): 39;
"Russian Art," *New Statesman and Nation,* 9 (8 June 1935): 862;
"New Russia," *Times* (London), 16 March 1936, pp. 13–14; 17 March 1936, pp. 17–18; 18 March 1936, pp. 15–16, 18;
"Cost of Communism," *American Mercury,* 41 (May 1937): 68–74;
"How We Celebrate the Coronation: A Word to London's Visitors," *Architectural Review,* 81 (May 1937): 217–224;
"Persian Triumph," *Architectural Review,* 81 (June 1937): 297;
"Destruction of Georgian London," *New Statesman and Nation,* 14 (11 December 1937): 1009;
"Firmness, Commodity, Delight," *New Statesman and Nation,* 15 (22 January 1938): 120–121;
"Clerk's Apology," *New Statesman and Nation,* 15 (26 March 1938): 517–518;
"Secrets of Abingdon Street," *New Statesman and Nation,* 15 (4 June 1938): 949–950;
Review of *Modern Architecture* by J. M. Richards, *New Statesman and Nation,* 19 (30 March 1940): 428–430.

On 24 February 1941 the destroyer transporting Robert Byron to Meshed, Iran, was torpedoed off the north coast of Scotland above Stornoway. There were no survivors. At the time the newspapers reported that he had been on his way to Cairo to serve as a journalist. After the war Byron's friend Christopher Sykes suggested that Byron's last journey had a further purpose, that "secret as such matters always were in the war," his destination "was so blatantly obvious": "his name was Byron and the battle of Greece was drawing near." Although Paul Fussell has since determined that Byron's actual destination had been to report to British Intelligence on Soviet activity in the Middle East, previous speculations such as Sykes's illustrate how thoroughly Byron's readers associated him with daring and even romance. Byron's hatred of the Nazis in the years immediately preceding World War II had been so ferocious and had so often led him to embarrass influential people that when fighting actually began he was passed over for positions he wanted. The fateful mission to Iran came late, only after the retreat of Allied forces from Dunkirk (26 May – 4 June 1940). Byron found death much as he had found life: in the passionate fight for an embattled cause.

Byron was, as Sykes proposes, "a man born to controversy." Yet in every case–whether in his defenses of Byzantine or Islamic art and culture, in his work on India or on Soviet Russia, or even in his writings on England itself–Byron's cultural engagements developed fundamentally as travel writings. Even the novel that he wrote with Sykes, *Innocence and Design* (1935), resulted from travels in Persia. Fussell has explained that "Richard Waughburton," the pseudonym under which they published the novel, is an amalgam of the names Richard Halliburton–an American travel writer whose *Royal Road to Romance* was one of the best-sellers of 1925–and Alec and Evelyn Waugh–who were both already celebrated travel writers. The name metaphorically suggests the scope and importance of Byron's career: that combination of adventure and learning that marks the work of the Victorian traveler Richard Burton, joined to the aesthetic sensibilities–and self-conscious Englishness–of Byron's sometime friend and bitter enemy Evelyn Waugh. In a career of scarcely fifteen years Byron nearly reinvented the travel narrative, investing it with new credibility as a form suitable for serious cultural commentary.

Byron was born on 26 February 1905 in Wembley, Middlesex. The only son of three children born to Eric Byron, civil engineer, and his wife Margaret, Byron was in fact only distantly related to the great poet whose name he shared. He was educated at Eton and at Merton College, Oxford, where he obtained a third class in modern history in 1925. Byron's lackluster academic performance suggests how distracted he was by the excitement of travel. He made his first trip abroad in 1923, spending five weeks in Italy. "But for that first sight of a larger world," he later maintained, "I might have been a dentist or a public man." The next year he visited Hungary, and then, in the fall of 1925, Byron and two Oxford friends, David Henniker and Simon O'Neill, motored through Germany, Italy, and Greece. The conditions of European roads and cross-channel transport required the traveler to ex-

Byron's traveling eompanions David Talbot Rice and Mark Ogilvie-Grant with the guest master at the Monastery of Docheiariou, which they visited on their journey to Athos (photograph by Byron; from The Station: Athos, Treasures and Men, *1928)*

hibit considerable pluck and good humor, and these motor trips became the subject of Byron's first book, *Europe in the Looking-Glass: Reflections of a Motor Drive from Grimsby to Athens* (1926).

Byron later came to consider this high-spirited book jejune; yet it set the stage for his finest work. Byron fell in love with Greece, and in the course of this journey he reviewed a performance of Gioacchino Rossini's *Moses* at the celebrated Roman Arena in Verona. The review, published a fortnight later in the *Times* of London (29 August 1925), suggested to Byron that the travel that inspired his pen could also be financed by it. All of Byron's subsequent travel books were partially financed by short pieces and series of pieces that he wrote along the way. Finally, *Europe in the Looking-Glass* challenges English readers to recognize their vital connection with the rest of Europe. In the conceit of the book's title, by leaving Britain for the Continent he had taken the measure of his own identity as a European. At the end of chapter 1 Byron declares that his aim in representing "the continent of which England forms a part" is to "further a new sense of European Consciousness": "Europe, taken as a whole, is such an unknown quantity to most of her inhabitants, nurtured in the disastrous tradition of the armed and insular state, that they are unable to gauge the contrast between their own corporate civilization, the laborious construction of two thousand years, and the retrograde industrialism sprung up in a night on the other side of the Atlantic."

In other words, even as a first-time author, Byron imagined his role in larger cultural struggles, some of them immediately political. While in Athens, Byron was contacted (because of his name) by

Skevos Zervos, the leader of the Dodecanese islands in their struggle to gain freedom from Italy (which had captured them from the Turks in 1912) and reunite with Greece. Byron was moved by Zervos's entreaty and wrote "Fascism in the Dodecanese" (*Nation,* 14 April 1926) on behalf of his cause. Promises forgotten or destroyed in the debacle of World War I are not treated overtly in Byron's first book, but he generally refused to accept that the war and its consequences had shattered the ideals of earlier ages. This choice, made earnestly and self-consciously, portended an almost definitive gesture. Harold Acton, Byron's friend at Eton and Oxford, recalled as much in his autobiographical *Memoirs of an Aesthete* (1948). Among his fellows Byron was given to a flamboyant dislike of the Bloomsbury group and its vision of a modernity cut off or set free from Victorian tradition, and Acton remembers Byron's insistence that "it was necessary to discard the intellectual conventions of a mentality that will never finish recovering from the war." Evidently Byron was little disposed to see himself as the victim of anything or as needing an absolute escape (as opposed to trips away) from England. The author of *Europe in the Looking-Glass* remembers even in his exuberant departure that his ultimate destination is home.

Only two years later Byron discovered his true mettle and in the process essentially created a new genre. Written when he was twenty-two years old, *The Station: Athos, Treasures and Men* (1928) recounts a journey he made with David Talbot Rice, Mark Ogilvie-Grant, and Gerald Reitlinger to the "holy mountain" of Athos, the southern point of the Aktian peninsula, on the northern Aegean shore of Greece. The holy mountain has been the site of a monastic community since 881 A.D., remaining politically autonomous with its way of life essentially unchanged over the centuries. Byron regarded Athos as the one surviving site of Byzantine civilization; indeed he hailed it in Ruskinian terms, finding in this one surviving part the life of all that was Byzantium, "one fragment, one living, articulate community of my chosen past, has been preserved. . . . Of the Byzantine Empire, whose life has left its impress on the Levant and whose coins were once current from London to Peking, alone, impregnable, the Holy Mountain conserves both the form and the spirit." This polemical claim simultaneously marks Byron's blindness and his insight. He noisily dismissed the received tendency of Western Europe to idolize the Greece of antiquity and to dismiss Byzantine or Christian Greece, in William Lecky's Gibbonesque words (1869), as "absolutely destitute of all the forms and elements of greatness," a charge Byron quoted in the epigraph to *The Byzantine Achievement* (1929). Byron wrote to his mother that *The Station* "is of the same inconsequence as *Europe in the Looking-Glass*–but much better." Yet *The Station* is also an advance on his first book because this second attempt journeys across time as well as space.

This proposition informs the distinguishing generic features of Byron's writing. Mixing personal narration with art criticism and cultural and political history, *The Station* anticipates the richness of such late-twentieth-century travel narratives as Leila Philip's *The Road Through Miyama* (1989). For Byron this generic heterogeneity was suggested by the work of Victorian aesthetician and cultural theorist John Ruskin. Ruskin's example is easy to mistake given Byron's dismissive remarks in the Verona chapter of *Europe in the Looking-Glass,* where he laments Ruskin's "repellent" popularization of Venetian Gothic. Nevertheless, Ruskin's work informs much of Byron's, and along with Byron's unfashionable love of Victorian culture this Ruskinianism is largely what distinguishes him from so many of his modernist contemporaries, whether from Bloomsbury circles (Virginia Woolf or Lytton Strachey) or Oxford (W. H. Auden or Evelyn Waugh). Acton recalled that even while at Eton, Byron "was saturated in Ruskin" and "supported whatever was retrograde." Acton also commented that Byron found in Ruskin's vision of a "large-limbed, high-coloured Victorian England, seated in honor and plenty," a resplendent antidote to the thin urbanity of postwar sophistication–that "mentality that will never finish recovering from the war." That vision regularly found comic and self-mocking expression; Acton recalled that Byron once arrived at a costume party dressed as Queen Victoria. Other friends remembered that Byron imagined he actually resembled the late queen and that he liked to imitate her. It seems no accident that G. M. Young, who later became the first modern authority on Victorian life, should have figured among Byron's closest friends.

More than mere fancy and by no means merely retrograde, Byron's interest in Victorian culture provided the basis for his sometimes radical critique of twentieth-century culture. In *First Russia, Then Tibet* (1933), for instance, Byron insisted that "real knowledge must come from a study not of this or that particular cell, but of the relationship between them all." In referring to that relation as an "organic harmony," he presented his Ruskinian credentials in quite explicit terms. Rather in the same Ruskinian fashion *First Russia, Then Tibet* opens by disavowing any intention ei-

Byron (right) with Father Bartholomew at the Monastery of Lavra (photograph by David Talbot Rice; from The Station: Athos, Treasures and Men, *1928)*

ther to "instruct or improve" its readers, claiming to "entertain by its art alone." For Byron art represented the harmonious arrangement of particular perceptions, and he considered that no other genre so lent itself to the art of writing and so affirmed the value of "personal knowledge" as the travel narrative. Unlike the specialist the traveler seeks to move from the intense–because unfamiliar–perception of particulars to a vision of a culture as a whole. Such idealism tempered Byron's resistance to what he saw as the unchecked materialism of both Russia and America so that what otherwise might have developed as British snobbery emerged instead as moral conviction. Yet as his travels broadened his knowledge of Byzantine and Russian, Persian and Islamic, or Indian, Chinese and Tibetan cultures, they simultaneously gave edge to his valorization of that British heritage so often and–he thought–so shamefully neglected by modern Britons.

The Station exemplifies his sometimes lyrical pursuit of cultural wholeness. Distinguishing generally between Athos and the sacred monuments of medieval Catholicism, he proposed that Gothic architecture reaches to the firmament while Byzantine architecture re-creates it. The formulation represents Byron at his best: it acknowledges the accomplishments of Western Christianity even while offering a new, doubtless iconoclastic, perspective that inspires a sense of wonder and admiration for its long-maligned Eastern counterpart. Undermining received academic opinion by showing its limits, Byron's comparison does not simply describe an architectural style; it imagines, in good Ruskinian tradition, a vision of the cosmos and humanity's place in it. It reads architectural style as a symptom of a larger cultural unity.

Ultimately, however, Byron does not even allow that the Western middle ages ever accomplished such a whole; in contradistinction to Thomas Carlyle, Augustus Welby Pugin, and the Victorian medievalists, Byron charges that in the West "the ways of men were divided," but in the East "the world and the Church were one." Such a charge, especially when considered in view of Byron's Ruskinian bearings, amounts to the denial that the West ever gave life to a genuine culture. This kind of extremity vitiates some of the best work in *The Station,* but a half century later the reader should see that this proximity of excellence and excess is not accidental. That Byron experienced intellectual life passionately, and was little attracted to Arnoldian notions of "disinterestedness," is largely why, after more than a half-century, his work still claims our attention.

The Station led directly to the two revisionist histories that followed. *The Byzantine Achievement* (1929) is a popularizing account of a subject that otherwise had attracted little such attention and that Byron felt had been dismissed by tired academic prejudice. Sykes proposed that the book "is the only example of Robert's work as an historian pure and simple"; yet, despite what its popularizing ambitions might suggest, it is not history "pure and simple." Rather, Byron overtly offers the achievement of Byzantine civilization as a measure for the scientific and "encyclopaedic civilisation now being launched," one whose vitality derives "from the scope and unity of its embrace." Although not travel writing, *The Byzantine Achievement* expansively links Byron's early writing with the ambitious sweep of later books such as *First Russia, Then Tibet* and *The Road to Oxiana* (1937).

The Birth of Western Painting (1930) forms an important sequel to *The Byzantine Achievement.* It is no more a conventional art history than its predecessor is a simple history, for *The Birth of Western Painting* strives to revise the reader's common sense of the origins of Western culture by emphasizing the seminal importance of later, rather than classical, Greek civilization–particularly El Greco, whom Byron celebrates as the triumph of Byzantine painterly tradition. Nevertheless, the book does not simply argue that the modern West owes everything to the Byzantines; instead it accepts the great tradition of Renaissance painting, but it submits that the Renaissance notion of "interpretational art" is but one school in a more broadly conceived sense of "tradition" and that even such humanist "interpretational art" derives from Byzantine examples.

The Birth of Western Painting, An Essay on India (1931) exemplifies the consequences of carrying Byron's inclusive sense of tradition beyond the record of travel and into cultural-political critique. Byron's arrival in India is, in itself, quite a story. "A chance invitation to Sikkim," as his sister put it, inspired Byron to offer William Aitken, Lord Beaverbrook, a series of articles for *The Daily Express* on the new airmail service to India. Byron proposed to report on the service by traveling from Cairo to Karachi on the mail plane and dispatching his articles from various stops along the way. (*The Daily Express* published his articles on 11, 12, 13, and 17 September 1929, and Byron redacted his account in part 2 of *First Russia, Then Tibet.*) The articles display Byron's characteristic wit and humor, but *An Essay on India*–which he had half-finished by early December–is programmatically serious. In a 10 December 1929 letter to his mother he expressed his intention to call the book "The British Evening in the Morning-Lands," jocularly pleading with her not to object to the title. Whatever her response, the published title is less aggressive, but Byron's thesis remained unchanged. He was not on principle opposed to imperialism, but he had no patience for inept or stupid administration. Although he compared the British Raj favorably with the Russian dominion of central Asia, Byron foretold its end.

Remarkably, the book is based on a visit of only eight months, between August 1929 and April 1930. During that visit Byron traversed the Indian subcontinent from Karachi to Calcutta, from Sikkim to Sri Lanka, making a study of four architectures: Hindu, Muslim, Buddhist, and–with the work of Sir Edwin Lutyens in New Delhi–Christian. Byron found Lutyens's design for the new capital particularly exciting; before this visit he "had never felt, nor wished to feel, any interest in India." Perhaps that prior lack of interest is why Byron's admiration for Lutyens did not translate to the British imperial presence as a whole. Byron came to feel that British rule was providing Western culture with "the supreme and ultimate test of its practical value." In other words India fascinated him less for its own marvels than for the challenge he saw it presenting to its imperial lords. Nothing he had read before his arrival prepared him for this strain, and he determined to provide a more completely contextualized account. On this score he was particularly pointed, objecting that no account of classical Greece or renaissance Italy would ever find general approval if it omitted mention of the arts; yet no British account of India had brought the arts to bear on political considerations. The British had no real notion of Indian culture. Byron's *Essay on India* was meant to rectify that want and to do so on an overtly personal basis–the experience of one educated and cultured traveler.

The results were surprisingly critical, especially on the question of British racial superiority, which prejudice Byron historicized and showed to have been institutionalized only after the Sepoy Mutiny of 1857–1858. Ultimately Byron charged that the defeat of British dreams of unification owes much more to institutionalized empiricism and racial prejudice than to Mohandas Gandhi and the Congress Party. These conclusions were hardly likely to win applause from so huge and so formal a thing as the empire, and critical reaction was curt. Nonetheless, Sykes recalled the opinion of the viceroy, Freeman Freeman-Thomas, Lord Willingdon, who called the book "the best brief statement of the modern problem of India." Sykes himself went further, declaring it among "the best books written on any Asiatic subject by an Englishman" and suggesting that its attacks on Winston Churchill and Sidney Harmsworth, Lord Rothermere, distracted readers from its masterful analysis. Lucy Butler thinks that incidental factors cost the book its proper audience, speculating that the deepening eco-

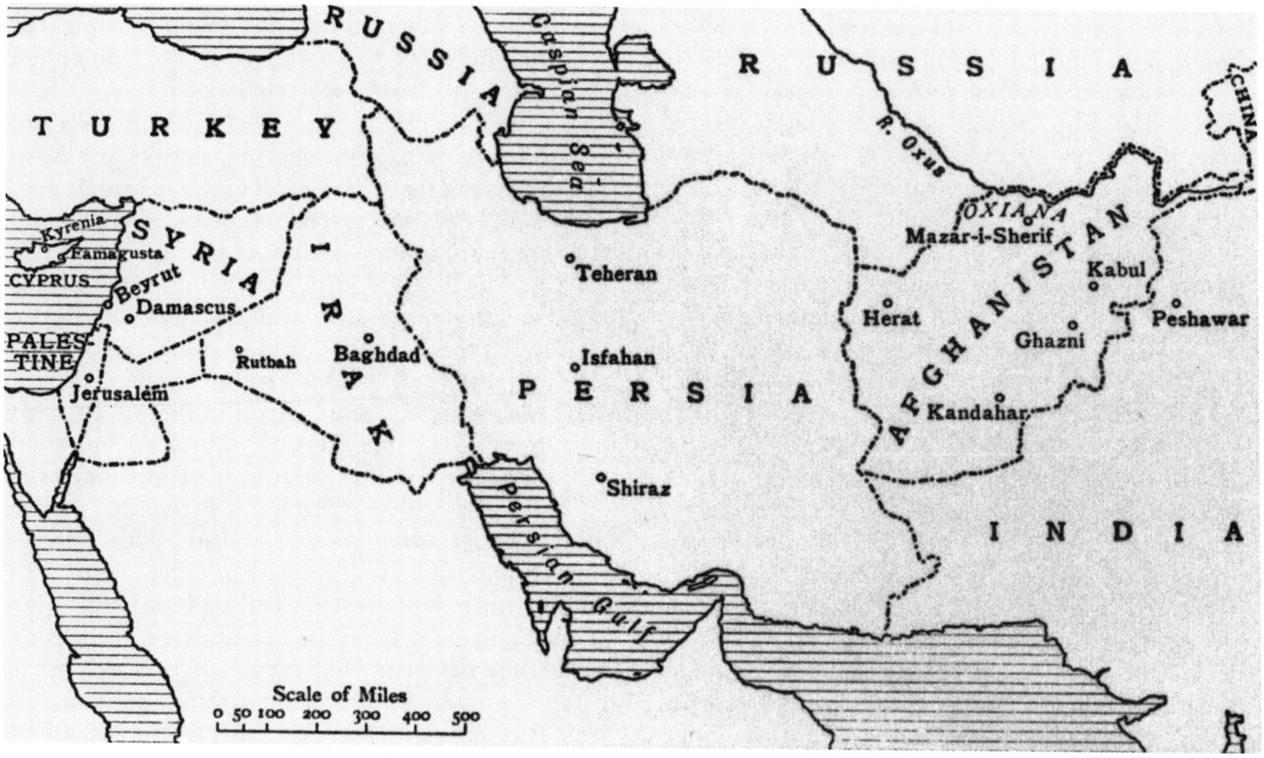

Map published in The Road to Oxiana *(1937)*

nomic depression of 1931 caused *An Essay on India* to attract relatively small notice. No doubt Byron made a habit of choosing powerful enemies, and declining economic fortunes doubtless stiffened the resolve of the many who depended on the empire for their livelihood. Even had Byron recognized the conditions that must shape the reception of his book, it is unlikely that he would have written it differently. He loved England but served it by fidelity to his vision. *An Essay on India* remains Byron's most sustained serious address of immediate political issues.

First Russia, Then Tibet (1933), even while venturing to the source of so much contemporaneous political anxiety, subordinated Byron's enduring political and social concerns to the more familiar features of travel writing. Based on six weeks of travel with Sykes, it opens with a "Traveller's Confession" submitting that "a book that entertains by its art alone will always be more welcome than one which forces attention upon its learning or righteousness." Nevertheless Byron acknowledged that the motives prompting his journeys to Russia and Tibet were not in any simple way "innocent." He sought, "as a member of a community, and heir to a culture, whose joint worth is now in dispute," to "discover what ideas, if those of the West be inadequate, can with greater advantage be found to guide the world." This inquiry, enlarging on the project of *Europe in the Looking-Glass,* no doubt speaks even more eloquently to Western sensibilities at the end of the millennium than it did in Byron's own day and testifies to Byron's extraordinary combination of national pride and self-critique. His "Traveller's Confession" develops into a considered justification of traveling: "when the impulse [to travel] is so imperious that it amounts to a spiritual necessity, then travel must rank with the more serious forms of endeavor." The conditional "when" acknowledges the difference between his own activity and the more casual motives of most travelers, and it responds to the pressure on travel accounts from the increasingly specialized and academicized disciplines that require their own kinds of travel.

Byron frames his account paradigmatically: "the ideas of Russia are preached, and act, as a challenge to those of the West" while "the ideas of Tibet offer no challenge; they maintain, simply, a passive resistance towards those of the West." In other words, while Byron's journeys to Russia and Tibet may bear only accidental relations to one another, their juxtaposition in his book is designed to establish "an absolute standard of worth capable of unlimited extension." One reason for making his design so explicit was, of course, that any Englishman's account of Soviet Russia would ordinarily be regarded as political polemic. In fact, for all of his dislike of the Soviet state, Byron regularly checked himself. Acknowledging that he shared the inclination of other visitors to laugh at "the Russian cult of the machine," he suggested that English readers remember "Macaulay's panegyric on his country's factories and railroads, couched in the language of an artist before the Parthenon; and having read, let them envy rather than despise a country that can still enjoy, in the twentieth century, that blend of assurance, novelty, and excitement which produced our own greatness in the nineteenth."

Modern Russia is but "in its embryonic stage." This warning recalls that sense of decline signified in his proposal to call *An Essay on India* "The British Evening in the Morning-Lands"–and that book too invokes Thomas Babington Macaulay in its opening epigraph. Clearly Byron had matured a great deal as a writer since the unqualified and positive assertions of his earliest works. Although *First Russia, Then Tibet* abounds with political judgments, politics were not for him the important issue; he was less interested in "information about Russia of a detached, scientific kind"–the likely fate of the five-year plan–than he was in considering the mediating role of Russia between Byzantium and the modern West.

Here as elsewhere Byron's best observations were summoned by architecture. His chapter "The Russian Aesthetic" offers a lyrical description of how the earliest expressions were–literally–an enlargement of Byzantine models, around which subsequently "grew walls and towers of Tartar pattern, to form the local Kremlins and fortified monasteries." In this and other accounts Byron continued to reproduce the language of Ruskin, while finding in organic relations the expressions of historical struggle rather than of religious faith. Indeed the chapter ends with a consideration of a projected new Soviet style for official Moscow, one that would distinguish itself stylistically from the antique splendor of the Kremlin. "There are those Russians," Byron commented, who "regard such discord as the very purpose of their artistic efforts. These victims of Materialist novelty fail to distinguish between 'discord' and 'difference.' The first is mean. The second may be mean. But it can also imply a contrast between equals in artistic merit which provides the highest form of intellectual stimulus and contains in itself a ground of harmony between the opposing monuments." This harmony–again, that aesthetic standard–entails an affirmation of modernity that draws strength from the legacy of the past: history at once the basis of inevitable departure from the past, and the process wherein one develops the promise of that past.

What Byron had to say about Soviet architectural policy in *First Russia, Then Tibet* shows up again five years later in his efforts to preserve the architecture of Georgian London. This episode marks an extremely interesting moment in Byron's career–in effect the return home anticipated in *Europe in the Looking-Glass* and the domestication of his traveler's sensibility. Essays such as "Can We Save Central London?" (*Architectural Review,* June 1933), "How We Celebrate the Coronation" (*Architectural Review,* May 1937), "Destruction of Georgian London" (*New Statesman and Nation,* 11 December 1937), and "Secrets of Abingdon Street" (*New Statesman and Nation,* 4 June 1938) essentially directed the eyes of his countrymen to treasures they passed daily without notice. As always, Byron was particularly interested in architecture, which he regarded as a public expression of national genius and the spirit of the people–an important link between past and future.

Acting on these convictions, Byron became one of the founding members of the Georgian Group, founded in 1937 to bring up to date the work of the Society for the Protection of Ancient Buildings (SPAB)–a group William Morris had founded sixty years before to protect medieval and renaissance architecture from the mid-Victorian mania for "restoration." Although nominally an offshoot of the SPAB, the Georgian Group was quite different in tone; young and aggressive, it inspired some of Byron's most furious invective. This intemperance is less important to remember than the rich accounting of a national heritage that came with it. In a BBC broadcast Byron argued that Georgian architecture should be preserved not just because it "really *suits* London" nor even because it commemorates that historical moment when English taste and political ideas "had suddenly become the admiration of Europe." Rather it was to be valued because "it corresponds, almost to the point of dinginess, with our national character. Its reserve and dislike of outward show, its reliance on the virtue and dignity of proportions only, and its rare bursts of exquisite details all express as no other style has ever done that indifference to self-advertisement, that quiet assumption of our own worth, and that sudden vein of lyric affection, which have given us our part in civilisation."

In demonstrating the imaginative impact of his travels on his sense of home, Byron attended to features few before him had found reason to notice. The *Shell Guide to Wiltshire* (1935), which he edited and for the most part wrote, is the most conventional travel guide Byron ever wrote. It is organized into different departments–such as "The Face of

The Tower of Kabus, built in 1007, and Byron in "lower middle-class Persian" dress, photographs from The Road to Oxiana

Wiltshire," "Antiquities," "Industries," and "Sport"–and though rich in local anecdotes it is written in an "objective" voice. Indeed it is a sign of the strength of Byron's literary "voice" that even in this book his intelligence is everywhere evident, often, irresistibly no doubt, surfacing in rapier-like quips and strongly asserted unorthodoxies.

Largely undertaken for the money, the *Shell Guide to Wiltshire* left Byron increasingly restless. For one thing, responding to increasing economic pressures of the Depression, Shell cut salaries of those employees it was able to retain by 25 percent. Byron found himself even shorter of patience than he was of money; to his mother he wrote, "I am afraid I shall be permanently discontented until I am again embarked on some *work*–not mere money making, but something calling for a real mental effort." According to Sykes, while at work on *The Byzantine Achievement* Byron had expected to write a sequel giving the "history of the contemporary Eastern Mediterranean." After writing the *Shell Guide to Wiltshire* he put aside that idea in favor of a different way of addressing the cultural condition of the modern world. In 1935 he applied to Macmillan, publisher of *First Russia, Then Tibet* and *Innocence and Design,* for a retainer to write a history of World War I. After lengthy deliberation, as Butler explains, Macmillan finally declined his proposal but did offer to advance him £100 for a travel book. This money became the seed for the most important of all Byron's books–*The Road to Oxiana.*

The direction and object of Byron's travel were not immediately clear. Before receiving the money from Macmillan, Byron had considered exploring Chinese Turkestan, but he was denied permission by the Foreign Office. He next thought to go to the Lake Van region of eastern Anatolia to study early Armenian churches, but this time the Turkish general staff refused him permission. After this second refusal came the Macmillan advance, and Byron's curiosity returned to a problem he had first encountered in India. His studies of Mogul architecture had left him unable to explain the origins of the elaborate facades of Islamic architecture. Having met Arthur Upham Pope, an expert on Persian art for whom Byron later wrote an account of Timurid architecture, Byron saw photographs of Seljuk towers that persuaded him the answer was to be found in Oxiana.

That destination could not have seemed immediately propitious; Byron had already been denied access to the frontier regions of Turkestan and Armenia, and again he named another frontier as his destination. These choices suggest much about his imagination: Byron was drawn to frontiers, places where the order of things is polyglot and heterogeneous, places where cultures interact, clashing or bleeding together. Oxiana–the area watered by the Oxus (Amu Darya) River but culturally the region between Persia and central Asia–has always been such a place. The empires of Cyrus and Alexander reached so far but no farther; Oxiana similarly marked the furthest reach of the post-Hellenistic empires of the Parthians or Sassanids, the Abbasid caliphate, and the Mongols, who destroyed it in 1258, successfully extending their power from Baghdad across Oxiana. After the death of Timur (Tamerlane) in 1405 Oxiana reassumed its outlandish mystery for the capitals of Europe and Western Asia. By the nineteenth and twentieth centuries Oxiana marked the uneasy frontier between British and Russian Asia, remaining as always accessible only to the intrepid. Byron called his book *The Road to Oxiana* because he never got there: he came close, actually glimpsing the Oxus shimmering in the distance below, but he was turned away at last by Afghan authorities.

In reading *The Road to Oxiana* (1937), or the letters that he wrote to his mother while making that journey, it can seem a wonder he got as far as he did. As Butler explains, Byron's friend Bosworth Goldman had originally proposed they travel in "cars running not on petrol, difficult to obtain in those remote regions, but on charcoal." This scheme helped Byron raise funds for the trip, but the charcoal burners proved utterly unreliable. Goldman and the motor party returned home in secret, so as not utterly to compromise the expedition, while Byron and Sykes, after rendezvousing in Cyprus, pressed on to Baghdad. There they got a car and drove into Persia, and the various comedies, maladies, and misadventures are retold in the book. The glimpse of the Oxus that Byron and Sykes finally managed is, however, more a denouement than a climax. The intense excitement came earlier, with a visit to the thirteenth-century burial Towers of Kabus (or Qabus) and Byron's return trip to the fifteenth-century mausoleum and College of Gohar Shad, daughter-in-law of Timur. Byron became so swept up by Gohar Shad that he wrote a long inset narrative of her career–the seven-page entry for 13 May. Such passages give weight to Sykes's conviction that the theme of the book is Byron's "quest for the origins of Islamic Art." Other factors suggest a different description; the quest for "the origins of Islamic Art" was the object of Byron's journey, but the book itself embodies something more. One might say that it is more about "the road," about journeying itself, than it is about Oxiana.

It is nowhere more important to recognize the literary character of a travel book, to consider the difference between the book and the journey that it purports to record, than with *The Road to Oxiana*. Publishing his *Four Studies in Loyalty* in 1947, Sykes thought otherwise, that the book was in "the same style in which the original notes were made"; his position conveniently marks the impact of a half-century of modernist formal experiments. Sykes's concern that Byron's formal experiments would be misread thus seems less urgent today. It is evident now that Byron's use of journal-like form does not remove the literary mediation of experience but rather mediates and represents that experience differently. Byron subordinates retrospective and narrative order to the uncertainty and intensity of discovery.

Certainly the form of the book, unfolding in daily journal entries, departs from the narrative style of Byron's or nearly anyone else's histories of art. Byron's form and style are virtually antinarrative, emphasizing not so much the connections among successive experiences as the singularity of each. This emphasis marks the distinctively "aesthetic" nature of Byron's account–his recurrent absorption in the quality of particular perceptions above the recitation of guidebook-like facts. For instance, his entry for 2 March reflects on the difference between modern, motor-driven travel and the older mode of travel by beast. The old mode, Byron thought, left one "alone with the ancient world. You saw Asia as the Greeks saw it, and you felt their magic breath stretching out towards China itself. Such emotions left no room for the aesthetic question, or for any question." By contrast, he continued, modern travel introduces new factors–cars and lorries, hostels, mean academic claims to privileged access–that "clarify the intelligence." These factors occasion a new experience of distance that simultaneously opens space for the "mood of romance" and also for detached criticism; such, Byron judged, "is the penalty of greater knowledge." It is moreover the measure of modernity, the uneasy alternation between romance and clinical evaluation symptomatic of the modern alienation from experience. One knows more but enjoys less.

Again, this tendency to regard cultural particulars symptomatically recalls the distinctive mode of Ruskinian analysis; in this case Byron finds in his own deepest responses to Persepolis the signs of his and his culture's condition. His entry for 26 August, while taking ship from Venice to Cyprus at dawn, records his annoyance with a "moustachio'd and portly gondolier." Byron's response was to regret the translation of Europe into the picturesque: "give me Venice as Ruskin first saw it–without a railway" and without "the human museum." In the entry for 22 May, Byron offhandedly suggested a nearly ideal figure for this obsession with his own aesthetic propensities: "I have been reading Proust for the last three days (and begin to observe the infection of uncontrolled detail creeping into this diary)." This comparison is at once the most unlikely and the most appropriate of choices, not least because Marcel Proust translated and wrote an introduction to Ruskin's *Sesame and Lilies* (1865). It is unlikely (as Byron guessed) that someone facing daily physical peril should be reading so refined and withdrawn a book as a novel by Proust, and it is appropriate because Proust too seldom distinguished between self-scrutiny and cultural critique.

The Road to Oxiana abounds with such surprises. It is a book whose art strives to conceal itself, displaying a most acutely active sensibility while presenting itself as a nearly spontaneous record of rough travel. The irony here is worthy of Byron's celebrated relation, especially given Sykes's recollection that Byron "had the greatest contempt for showy travellers who 'rough it' for the sake of 'roughing it.'" (At the same time the reader should remember Acton's comment that Byron "would always sacrifice comfort to aesthetic pleasure.") Sykes was, however, dead-on in considering *The Road to Oxiana* to be "an astonishing document of . . . the first modernity-mad age as it was terribly reflected in Asia from Europe, and also as an absolutely reliable guide to the puzzling question of Islamic art and its origins." Sykes worried that reviewers, save for G. M. Young, did not recognize the kind of book it really was. In November 1937, however, *The Road to Oxiana* won the *Sunday Times* Gold Medal for the most outstanding travel book of the year.

In his admiration for its accomplishment Paul Fussell seeks to dissociate *The Road to Oxiana* from more typical accounts of travel; it is, he affirms, a work of fiction, "an artfully constructed quest myth in the form of an apparently [but only apparently] spontaneous travel diary." Acknowledging that the artful deception extends even to calling the table of contents "Entries," Fussell rightly observes that "the book is fully written": Byron worked on it for nearly three years, at certain points for ten hours a day. The travel-diary conceit "enabled him to overcome what had been his defect as an artist: stylistic affectation and a leaning toward 'fine writing' and arch pedantry." With this book, Fussell concludes, Byron "mastered the secret of the travel book. He had now learned to make essayistic points seem to emerge empirically from material data intimately experienced." This conclusion, valuable in itself, suggests a further one that more particularly situates Byron within the genre of travel writing: he was as much interested in the *writing* as he was in the travel, and he took up travel writing because he believed it emphasized a distinct kind of writing. Three months into his Persian travels he wrote to his mother: "I have read *Anna Karenina* with great pleasure. But it isn't what I call *writing*. No Russian book is–no novel either for that matter." Byron did not live to write the essays that might have developed this point, but the letter says enough to make clear how serious he was in his choice of literary form.

Unfortunately *The Road to Oxiana* was Byron's last major book. After returning to England in June 1934 he traveled extensively: to America to lecture in January and February 1935; across Russia and Siberia by rail that same September and November; from there to Beijing, where he stayed through the end of May 1936; to Japan in June; by ship (his least favorite form of travel) to San Francisco and by plane to Washington, D.C.; and to Eastern Europe for the British Council in February and March. In the months after that trip he wrote "How We Celebrate the Coronation" and did other work for the Georgian Group. His essay "Timurid Architecture," exhaustively researched and written earlier but cut and revised drastically under pressure from Upham Pope, was published in 1938 in *Survey of Persian Art*.

By this time Byron's attention had turned to his last passion: his fierce hatred of the Nazis. On 26 March 1938 *The New Statesman and Nation* published Byron's "Clerk's Apology," an indictment of the intellectual lassitude of Britain toward its inevitable foe. Byron also began doing volunteer propaganda work for the BBC, ultimately setting aside all else to awaken his countrymen and Europe to what he knew was imminent peril. In November 1938 he managed to get an invitation from Unity Mitford, an Englishwoman living in Germany and a friend of Adolf Hitler, to attend the Parteitag–the Nazis' last Party Day rally in Nuremberg. Byron's diary from this trip, published in 1989, shows his perceptions were keener than ever: for all his hatred of the Nazis he was able to distinguish between what they stood for and German culture. All the same, after two weeks in Germany, Byron's last entry concludes, "I want to be home. Or shall we wake up one day?" The next month he made his last trip, again to the United States, on behalf of the Petroleum Information Bureau. He devoted his last two years to the war effort, contemplating no sustained project (according to Sykes) other than the history of World

War I that he had given up to write *The Road to Oxiana*. The gathering clouds of a second world war seemed to give a new importance to confronting the lessons of the first.

In 1946 Sykes submitted that Byron "never became a well-known writer, but time has shown him to be an influential writer." Since then, other travelers have testified to the power of Byron's example. Bruce Chatwin has described sitting cross-legged on the floor of the Sheikh Lutf'ullah Mosque in Isfahan reading *The Road to Oxiana,* "marvelling both at the tile work and Byron's description of it." Judging that book to put Byron "at least in the rank of Ruskin," Chatwin carried his own "spineless and flood-stained" copy throughout four journeys to central Asia. Introducing the Lehmann edition of *The Road to Oxiana* (1950) Rice describes Byron's pioneering of "a new genre, travel books not concerned with game or sport, like those of the nineteenth century, nor even with peoples and customs, like many of those of the early twentieth, but rather with buildings, paintings and works of art; 'art-travel' books one might perhaps call them." For all their gaiety of telling Byron's books are as ambitious as they are serious. In focusing on the art of remote places and ages Byron takes them up at their best and then finds in them a challenge to the vitality of his own culture. His work avoids the shallowness of much late-twentieth-century ethnotourism because he never fantasizes about changing his skin or facilely finds fault with his own culture. For Byron knew that the continued vitality of the West faces a road more perilous and difficult than any he was likely to travel abroad.

Letters:

Letters Home, edited by Lucy Butler (London: Murray, 1991).

References:

Harold Acton, *Memoirs of an Aesthete* (London: Methuen, 1948);

Neil Brennan, "The Eton Society of the Arts," in his *Anthony Powell* (New York: Twayne, 1974), pp. 34–41;

Bruce Chatwin, Introduction to *The Road to Oxiana* (London: Picador, 1981);

Virginia Cowles, "The German Merry-Go-Round," in her *Looking for Trouble* (New York & London: Harper, 1941);

Paul Fussell, Introduction to *The Road to Oxiana* (New York: Oxford University Press, 1982);

Fussell, "Sancte Roberte, Ora Pro Nobis," in his *Abroad: British Literary Traveling Between the Wars* (New York: Oxford University Press, 1980), pp. 79–112;

Fussell, "Stubborn, Self-taught Byzantinist," *Times Literary Supplement,* 12 April 1991, p. 20;

William Gaunt, Review of *The Birth of Western Painting, Atelier,* 1 (April 1931): 377;

Robert Irwin, "Open to the Infidel," review of the Courtauld Institute Galleries exhibition *Along the Golden Road to Samarkand: Photographs of Monuments in the Middle-East by A. W. Lawrence, T. E. Lawrence, and Robert Byron, Times Literary Supplement,* 21 February 1922, p. 19;

David Talbot Rice, Introduction to *The Road to Oxiana* (London: John Lehmann, 1950), pp. v–xii;

Sacheverell Sitwell, Review of "The Road to Oxiana," *Architectural Review,* 52 (January 1937): 33–34;

Gavin Stamp, "Origins of the Group," *Architect's Journal,* 175 (31 March 1982): 35–38;

Christopher Sykes, *Evelyn Waugh: A Biography* (Boston: Little, Brown, 1975), pp. 41–71, 140–177, 342–343;

Sykes, Introduction to *The Station: Athos, Treasures and Men* (New York: Knopf, 1949), pp. 7–13;

Sykes, "Robert Byron," in his *Four Studies in Loyalty* (London: Collins, 1947), pp. 87–185;

Evelyn Waugh, *Essays, Articles and Reviews,* edited by Donat Gallagher (Boston: Little, Brown, 1984), pp. 45–47, 197–199, 319–320, 532–536, 592–599;

G. M. Young, "Cities and Harvests," in his *Daylight and Champaign: Essays* (London: Rupert Hart-Davis, 1937), pp. 28–34;

Young, "Robert Byron," in his *Today and Yesterday: Collected Essays and Addresses* (London: Rupert Hart-Davis, 1948), pp. 9–15.

Papers:

Byron's papers are in the possession of his family, and his sister, Lucy Butler, has been his literary executor since the time of his death. Byron's most prolific correspondent was Michael Rosse, and his weekly letters to Rosse are held by the earl of Rosse, Birr Castle, County Offaly, Ireland. New York University holds Byron's correspondence with Harold Acton and Arthur Upham Pope. The Fogg Museum in Boston holds Byron's letters to Eric Schroeder, with whom Byron was planning a study of Persian architecture until the intervention of war made the project impossible. The Lambeth Palace Library in London holds Byron's correspondence with John Douglas, and the British Library holds Byron's correspondence with Macmillan.

Mildred Cable
(21 February 1878 – 30 April 1952)

Francesca French
(12 December 1871 – 2 August 1960)

Evangeline French
(27 May 1869 – 8 July 1960)

Laura Brady
West Virginia University

BOOKS: *The Fulfilment of a Dream of Pastor Hsi's: The Story of the Work in Hwochow,* by Cable (London: Morgan & Scott, 1917);

Despatches from North West Kansu, by Cable and Francesca French (London & Philadelphia: China Inland Mission, 1925);

Through Jade Gate and Central Asia, by Cable and Francesca French (London: Constable, 1927; Boston: Houghton Mifflin, 1927);

The Challenge of Central Asia: A Brief Survey of Tibet and Its Borderlands, by Cable, F. Houghton, R. Kilgour, A. McLeish, R. W. Sturt, and Olive Wyon (London & New York: World Dominion Press, 1929);

Something Happened, by Cable and Francesca French (London: Hodder & Stoughton, 1933; New York: Stokes, 1934);

A Woman Who Laughed, by Cable and Francesca French (London & Philadelphia: China Inland Mission, 1934);

A Desert Journal: Letters from Central Asia, by Cable, Evangeline French, and Francesca French (London: Constable, 1934);

The Making of a Pioneer: Percy Mather of Central Asia, by Cable and Francesca French (London: Hodder & Stoughton, 1935; New York: Stokes, 1936);

Ambassadors for Christ, by Cable and Francesca French (London: Hodder & Stoughton, 1935);

The Story of Topsy: Little Lonely of Central Asia, by Cable and Francesca French (London: Lutterworth Press, 1937);

Grace: Child of the Gobi, by Cable and Francesca French (London: China Inland Mission, 1938);

Towards Spiritual Maturity, by Cable and Francesca French (London: Hodder & Stoughton, 1939);

The Gobi Desert, by Cable and Francesca French (London: Hodder & Stoughton, 1942);

China: Her Life and Her People, by Cable and Francesca French (London: University of London Press, 1946);

The Book Which Demands a Verdict, by Cable and Francesca French (London: S. C. M. Press, 1946); republished as *The Bible in Mission Lands* (New York & London: Revell, 1947);

The Spark and the Flame, by Cable and Francesca French (London: British and Foreign Bible Society, 1948);

George Hunter, Apostle of Turkestan, by Cable and Francesca French (London: China Inland Mission, 1948);

Journey with a Purpose, by Cable and Francesca French (London: Hodder & Stoughton, 1950);

Why Not for the World: The Story of God through the Bible Society, by Cable and Francesca French (London: British and Foreign Bible Society, 1952);

Luckchild: The Boy and the Man, by Francesca French (London: Marshall, Morgan & Scott, 1954);

Miss Brown's Hospital: The Story of the Ludhiana Medical College and Dame Edith Brown. O.B.E., Its Founder, by Francesca French (London: Hodder & Stoughton, 1954);

Thomas Cochrane, Pioneer and Missionary Statesman, by Francesca French (London: Hodder & Stoughton, 1956).

Mildred Cable, Evangeline French, and Francesca French traveled across China for the China Inland Mission—a Bible society established in 1865 to convert the people of China to Christianity. From the time of Evangeline French's arrival in China in 1893 until the three women (often referred to as the

The "Trio": Evangeline French, Mildred Cable, and Francesca French

"Trio") permanently retired to England on the eve of World War II, their books, credited mainly to Cable and Francesca French, chronicled their work and travels in China. These works might best be grouped into three broad categories: handbooks and missionary biographies written to fellow evangelists, children's books, and travel memoirs. The first two groups are a natural extension of their missionary work; their purpose is to guide and instruct others. Unlike these works, the travel memoirs, which describe the Trio's active participation in Chinese culture, are refreshingly free of didacticism and appeal to a broader audience. It is not surprising that the travel books, such as *The Gobi Desert* (1942), have been and continue to be the best known and most popular of the Trio's writings.

The daughters of Elizabeth and John French, Evangeline "Eva" French, born in Algeria, and Francesca French, born in Belgium, were educated in Geneva, Switzerland. Born in Dorset, England, and reared in Guilford, Surrey, Alice Mildred Cable was the daughter of John C. Cable, a master draper, and Eliza Kindred Cable. She decided to become a missionary to China when she was only fifteen, after hearing a preacher talk about the Chinese. Her parents readily supported her decision despite their worries over the political unrest in China at the turn of the century.

Having decided to become a missionary in 1890, Evangeline French went to China in 1893, joining the China Inland Mission, which had been founded fewer than twenty years earlier. She was there in 1900, the time of the Boxer Rebellion, an attempt to drive out foreign and proselytizing influences, during which many Chinese Christians and Western missionaries were killed. Her own life was threatened, and she was, in fact, reported dead at one point.

In 1901 Mildred Cable set out for China, where she and Eva French were given the daunting assignment to survey the effects of the Boxer Rebellion on various mission sites. The missionary who had recruited them was one of the missionaries

Evangeline French (second row, far right) and other missionaries who escaped from Shanxi province during the Boxer Rebellion

killed by the Boxers, who had also killed two female missionaries who served in Huoxian, Shanxi province, before Cable and Eva French arrived there. Mildred and Eva's friendship began during the months they spent reconstructing the Huoxian mission house and the mission projects. They helped to establish a teaching center, where they taught literacy skills and performed evangelical work. Although correspondence between the French sisters shows that Francesca also had an early interest in China, she was caring for her mother and did not join Eva and Mildred until 1909, when her mother's death left her free to pursue missionary work.

In China the three women adopted Chinese dress: loose tunics and jackets and soft shoes–clothing that Marina Warner describes as giving them "the soft, rounded, loose look of the Oriental, in exact reversal of the corseted, hard, tormentingly encased bodies of their sisters in Europe." They made efforts to assimilate themselves to China despite their mission to "convert" the Chinese.

The three shared beliefs and training and were, no doubt, influenced by the narratives of other missionaries. Their shared goals and influences helped to shape and unify the tone and style of their narratives. The first book about their travels, *Despatches from North West Kansu* (1925), could be viewed as a draft for the more complete account in *Through Jade Gate and Central Asia* (1927), while this second book and *A Desert Journal* (1934) might be considered early versions of *The Gobi Desert* (1942). *Through Jade Gate and Central Asia* provides an account of the Trio's six-thousand-mile journey in 1926 from Shanxi Province in China to England by way of the Gobi Desert, Turkestan, southern Siberia, and Moscow. This journey came at the end of three years' work as itinerant evangelists for the China Inland Mission, undertaken after about two decades at the school they had helped to establish in Shanxi Province. At a point when their colleagues might have retired from foreign mission work, the three women, all over forty, took on the most challenging assignment of their careers.

Through Jade Gate and Central Asia is divided into four parts: "From Hwochow [Huoxian] to Kanchow [Zhangye]," "In the Far North-West," "Across the Gobi Desert," and "In the Land of the Reds." The first two sections describe the Trio's missionary work in Huoxian and the Central Asian province of Gansu (then spelled Kansu), where the Trio had begun work in 1923. The most interesting part of the book, however, is the third section, which describes how the Trio became the first Western women to cross the Gobi Desert. Returning home to England for leave in 1926, during a period of political unrest in China, they traversed most of the Gobi by mule cart, recording without much comment their exhaustion at the end of each difficult day's journey and horrifying sights such as bleached bones of abandoned caravan animals, which provided a grim incentive to keep moving. When they found an unconscious man by the side of the road, their driver urged the women to leave him because their caravan could not risk the extra strain that another person would put on their mules and their supplies of food and water. Despite warnings, the women took the man into their cart and took turns walking to spare the mules. Never dwelling on personal discomfort or anxiety, *Through Jade Gate and Central Asia* focuses instead on descriptions of climate, topography, language, customs, and political events. Published while the Trio was on leave in England, *Through Jade Gate and Central Asia* presents a picture of three strong, tolerant, and committed women, but the book includes few personal details.

The Trio returned to Gansu in 1928, but in 1932 political conditions again made it necessary for them to return to England, where they remained until 1935. During this time they prepared two books for publication, the autobiographical *Something Happened* (1933) and *A Desert Journal* (1934), which covers their travels in China from June 1928 until June 1932.

Something Happened (1933) fills in some biographical details missing from the travel books and provides background for the travel writing. This book recounts moments of epiphany–when each woman recognized her vocation or discovered the next stage of their mission work in China. The words *something happened* function as both the title of the book and as a refrain to mark the various changes in their lives. These transformations are often religious in nature (a calling, a conversion, a vision), but something also happened to the three women's social positions as they left England, its conventions, and the domestic sphere of their families, locating themselves in China, in history and politics. Outside both British and Chinese cultures, they found a space for their lives, their writing, and their work.

Although it is an autobiography, *Something Happened* is cast almost entirely in the third person, creating a curiously distanced tone that positions the narrative persona as an outside observer. The women's active participation in Chinese culture is described in the first person, the point of view used in most of their travel writing. *Something Happened* also draws analogies between the women's desert travels and their "mission," as in this passage that uses the image of a mule team to illustrate their collaboration as preachers, travelers, and writers:

> They have often seen themselves depicted in the similitude of the mule team, which has drawn them over so many mountains, through such dangerous rivers and across burning desert plains. The alert beast in the traces gets the first flick of the whip when there is difficulty ahead. She responds with a bound, but before the impetus of her pull has slackened, the driver has touched the steady reliable mule in the shafts, which can be counted on to brace itself to bear the strain. Then the two pull together to one purpose and one end, but without the third mule, hitched so as to get an equal share of the weight, the mountain pass would never be crossed, nor the exhaustion of the wearisome plain endured. The beasts of the team do not select each other, that is the driver's business, as it is his to give the signals.

The mule-team metaphor never makes explicit which of the three women is the lead mule, which is the "steady reliable mule in the shafts," and which is the weight-bearing center mule, but it is fairly clear that the mule-team driver is Christ, who selects the team and gives the signals.

In addition to describing themselves as beasts of evangelical burden, the three women called themselves soldiers who would "capture" trade routes for the gospel and laborers who would build a "highway for the Lord . . . a pathway for God":

> To capture these trade routes for Him, to throw up a highway for the Lord, to make ready in the desert a pathway for God, became their ambition. With such a glorious task ahead what mattered physical discomforts, dirty inns, blue-bottles, mosquitoes, bitter desert water, heat and cold, occasional shortness of food and a hard life?

While the metaphors–soldiers and laborers for Christ–are conventional, the direct parallels to their travels are not: the images allude to the way the three women traveled by mule caravan on the ancient trade routes crossing the Gobi Desert.

Situated on the border between Chinese and British conventions, the three women were allowed freedoms that would not have been available in either British or Chinese culture. Their unease about returning to "domestic" life in Britain appears in a passage near the end of *Something Happened,* where they describe their return to England in 1932:

Topsy, the deaf-mute child the Trio adopted in 1928

> The last lap of the long journey, Berlin to Victoria–and during its hours time to think of what awaited them over the threshold of London life. Among the peoples of the East they had lived and dressed as Chinese and were used to slow, decorous methods of life. . . .
>
> During the long years of their exile they were conscious of having lost most of the things that the world prizes, together with the easy sense that no situation could arise which might take them at a disadvantage. One thing they had gained and that they esteemed so highly, that everything else might go, provided they retain it. Moving slowly through desert solitudes they had learnt to measure life, not by the fretful ticking of the clock, but by the majestic course of the stars, and among those silences the relative value of things temporal and eternal had been settled for ever. In the wild rush of accelerated life, could the poise of spirit essential to that true discrimination be retained?

There are two striking images in this passage: the threshold and the exile. The women are conscious of the transition between their life in China and that which awaits them in England, and they cast that transition in terms of a domestic space–a doorway or "threshold." Though they wrote of returning from exile, they were in fact exiles from both England and China. Their previous "losses" (that is, those things they lost in their exile from domestic England) are clearly aligned with the temporal.

The theme of "the poise of spirit essential to that true discrimination" between the temporal and the eternal recurs in several of their biographies of fellow missionaries. *A Woman Who Laughed* (1934) is a biography of Henrietta Soltau, who worked in England for the China Inland Mission from 1877 until her retirement in 1919. *The Making of a Pioneer: Percy Mather of Central Asia* (1935) and *George Hunter, Apostle of Turkestan* (1948) are about two other missionaries whose work the Trio knew firsthand. The biography of Mather is based on letters that he wrote to his parents and sisters between 1910 and his death in China in 1933. The Trio spent time with Mather on at least one of their travels across the Gobi, and they carried his translations with them on their evangelical missions. The biography of Hunter was likewise inspired by the Trio's friendship with this "pioneer" evangelist for the China Inland Mission.

The Trio returned to Gansu province in 1935, but by August 1936 the political situation again necessitated their return to England. Their first literary effort was a children's book, *The Story of Topsy* (1937), about a small, deaf-mute Chinese girl whom the Trio adopted in 1928 and nicknamed "Topsy." (The parallels to the character of Topsy in Harriet Beecher Stowe's 1852 best-selling novel, *Uncle Tom's Cabin,* are presumably deliberate.) The book also describes the people and customs of China and a grueling trek across the Gobi Desert. One of the central villains in the story is Gen. Ma Chung Ying, leader of a successful 1927 uprising in Gansu province. (In 1930 General Ma held the women as prisoners for several days because he needed their medical assistance.) *The Story of Topsy* purports to teach a lesson of what happens when law and order break down, and most contemporary readers would find it painfully didactic. Implying that Christianity is the "true" source of material and spiritual salvation, the Trio's children's fiction in general has little enduring literary merit. The same message and didactic tone characterize *Grace: Child of the Gobi* (1938), the story of a crippled slave girl whom the Trio adopted.

In welcome contrast *The Gobi Desert* (1942) is a distinctly nonevangelical text. The book begins in

June 1923, when Mildred Cable (age forty-five), Eva French (age fifty-four), and Francesca French (age fifty-two) receive orders to travel and preach in the "Great North-West," and it covers their experiences in that part of China until their retirement in 1936. During those years the three women made five crossings of the Gobi Desert, which measures roughly fifteen hundred miles from north to south and two thousand miles from east to west. It is still a remote and grueling desert to cross. During their travels the Trio typically carried books in seven languages–many of them religious tracts and translations of the Bible–and dispensed medical aid along with their evangelical messages.

For all the writers' evangelical zeal, the book is surprisingly undogmatic. The descriptions of desert life, landscape, and customs include amazing desert sights: the Caves of the Thousand Buddhas, the sapphire Crescent Moon Lake, the Singing Sands, temples, towns, and markets. They write of the desert itself: its sandspouts and mirages; its grasses, which serve as building materials; its oases and ancient buildings; its rare birds and animals; and its starry night skies and silences. They describe individuals they met: a professional storyteller, a guild of beggars, a theatrical troupe, camel men, carters and innkeepers, the "tiger Prince," the Living Buddha, and General Ma. They also contrast "repressed" Muslim women and "free" Mongol women, who ride and herd cattle, implying that the Trio offers a new perspective on women (or at least Western women) to Muslim and Moguls alike, although the Mongol women accept the missionaries more readily.

The Gobi Desert begins with the same image that ends *Something Happened:* the threshold. The first chapter, "On the Threshold of the Desert," opens at the fortress from which the three women began their first desert trek. A great stone table marks the threshold to the desert and bears the inscription "Earth's Greatest Barrier." As they left the relative safety and community of the fortress behind them, "The gate swung to, and we heard them shoot the heavy bar. We were irrevocably launched on the long trek." As in *Something Happened,* the crossing of the threshold is linked to a sense of exile or exclusion. They are outside the gates, barred from the safety of the fortress. When the narrative voice goes on to say "Anything might happen," however, it speaks with a sense of anticipation rather than dread. The three women and their small band of carters are drawn by "The Lure of the Gobi," the title of chapter two.

Except for the prologue, the narrative of *The Gobi Desert* is written in the first-person singular. As the prologue explains, "These experiences were shared by three people, but for obvious reasons the record is written in the first person singular." The reasons for using the first-person singular are by no means "obvious," but the use of the first person for a book describing the collective experiences of three people is distinctive.

In direct reversal of their missionary purpose, the prologue promises a story of what they learned, rather than what they taught: "Once the spirit of the desert caught us, it lured us on and we became learners in its severe school." In the sense that the narrative has a teaching function, they emphasize place over people or culture. In this book the women resist their roles as missionaries or teachers.

In a review of the 1987 edition of *The Gobi Desert,* geographer Robert McColl recognized the importance of the geographic descriptions and analyses in the book, praising Cable and the French sisters for their insights on "human/land relationships." McColl also notes the value of *The Gobi Desert* for "anthropologists [and] botanists (for the types and uses of various plants), [and] for an introduction to the agricultural practices of the 1930s and how human beings overcame the marginal capacity of the desert to produce." The practical observations are based on both academic training and decades of life experience in China. All three women spoke Chinese and Turkish; Francesca French had medical training, and Mildred Cable had studied both medicine and botany.

The Gobi Desert is filled with passages such as this account of the sand dunes between Tunhwang (Dunhuang) and Shachow (Shazaoyuan) that hide the "Caves of the Thousand Buddhas": "The volcanic range which has formed the foothills of the South Mountains meets the first sand-hills of a line which stretches westward through the Desert of Lob. . . . Each clean-cut edge of sand-hill presents a striking contrast of light and shade, for one side of the projecting angle reflects the brilliant sun in warm tones, while the surface which lies in the shade has a lustreless cold hue." Such geographic descriptions are often accompanied by historic or anthropological information. The reader is told that Tunhwang, for instance, has a history as "a military outpost and as an important business center on the old Silk Road which connected Cambaluc (Peking) in China with Rome in the Western world, even before the days of the Han dynasty." In addition to "objective" observations about landscape and history, *The Gobi Desert* also conveys a subjective sense of nostalgia for China. The same passage that describes geographic, anthropological, and historic aspects of the Lake of the Crescent Moon and the

Topsy, Mildred Cable, and Francesca French seated in front of their tent in the Gobi Desert

Caves of the Thousand Buddhas ends with an expression of longing for those vistas:

> Between the pages of a book I have pressed a small branch of sand-jujube flowers, and whenever I catch its subtle but fading fragrance, I . . . long for a place that seems so near and yet is so far away. Sick with longing I walk among the crowds while my spirit flees to the quiet which is found by the hidden lake among the dunes.

When *The Gobi Desert* was published, the Trio retired and settled permanently in England. This passage offers an intriguing glimpse into the way that Mildred Cable and Eva and Francesca French viewed themselves and China as they reflected on their experiences. They position themselves as exiles, but the origin of their exile has shifted. They close the book with a longing for "the inviolate spirit of the desert" in the midst of the "new era of Gobi life" that followed the Japanese invasion of China in 1937. They are exiles of both time and place:

> the machine-minded men are now in control, who discuss the Gobi in terms of profit and loss, and propose to lay iron rails across it and commercialise its ancient sites.
>
> They may conquer the desert spaces and shatter its silences, but they can never capture its magic charm, and those who have been disciplined and instructed by its austerity still find that the elusive spirit of the desert can call them at will, to roam again in the Gobi that once was.

The "Gobi that once was" is now a "magic" place that no longer exists.

The Trio's books about their travels earned them recognition. Shortly after the publication of *The Gobi Desert* Mildred Cable was awarded the Lawrence Memorial Medal of the Royal Central Asian Society, and a year later, in 1943, all three women were recognized with the Livingstone Medal of the Royal Scottish Geographical Society. The women also found a ready audience for their evangelical writing. The Bible Society used several of their books as handbooks or primers for future missionaries. Mildred Cable and Francesca French had already published missionary handbooks such as *Ambassadors for Christ* (1935) and *Towards Spiritual Maturity* (1939), and they went on to write three others: *China: Her Life and Her People* (1946), *The Book Which Demands a Verdict* (1946), and *The Spark and the Flame* (1948).

China: Her Life and Her People announces, "In the course of a lifetime spent in China [the writers] have watched her emergence and wish to share their knowledge of the Chinese people with all who desire to understand them better, and specially with any expecting to go to the Far East." The table of contents suggests the wide range of subjects the book covers: "The Riches of the Land" (geography), "Life in North China Villages," "Life in South China Villages," "Life on the Waterways," Life in Towns" (geography and anthropology), "Chinese Art and Poetry," "The Religions of China," "A Chinese Who's Who," and "China at War" (politics). The preface concludes with an analogy to the prophet Ezekiel, who made a point of studying the people to whom he spoke, implying an admonition to future missionaries to study and observe before preaching. As a result *China: Her Life and Her People* spends more time on the history of the people and their culture than on the role of the missionary. Only the final three chapters focus on "How Christianity Came to China," and the last section of the book consists of "Questions for Study Circles," geared toward an audience of future missionaries.

The Book Which Demands a Verdict (1946), republished in the United States as *The Bible in Mission Lands* (1947), traces the influence of the Bible in England, China, Japan, India, and Africa. It also treats issues such as the need for literacy and accessible translations of the Bible. In discussing the world-literacy campaign the Trio transferred their missionary zeal from teaching the word of God to teaching the written word.

The Spark and the Flame, published as the "Annual Popular Report" of the British and Foreign Bible Society, draws an extended analogy between the necessity of fire for desert survival and the necessity of religious fire for spiritual survival. The dual emphasis on preaching and teaching found in many of the Trio's books is not surprising. The three women were, after all, missionaries for their entire lives. Even after their retirement to England, they continued to work, write, and travel on behalf of the Bible Society. *Journey with a Purpose* (1950) recounts the Trio's travels in Australia, India, and New Zealand on behalf of the Bible Society after World War II. *Why Not for the World: The Story of God through the Bible Society* (1952) discusses the ongoing missionary work of the British and Foreign Bible Society and the Overseas Missionary Fellowship (formerly the China Inland Mission).

Yet China–and specifically the Gobi Desert–seems to have been the Trio's favored subject. Their representations of China and its culture–ranging from primarily descriptive accounts of the topography such as *The Gobi Desert* to evangelical tracts such as *The Story of Topsy* and *China: Her Life and Her People*–raise important questions about how "representative" any travel narrative can be. How large or small a part of the "native" culture do their works represent? How did their faith and their mission color their perceptions? Writing as evangelical missionaries, they provided a chronicle of religious colonization in China. Their travel writing is more complicated. Neither as dogmatic nor as reductive as their evangelical works, books such as *The Gobi Desert* appear to be unified by nature, not religion. The tension between spiritual and material survival creates a much more problematic–and interesting–text.

Biographies:

W. J. Platt, *Three Women: Mildred Cable, Francesca French, Evangeline French* (London: Hodder & Stoughton, 1964);

Alexandra Allen, "Mildred Cable and Evangeline and Francesca French," in *Travelling Ladies–Victorian Adventuresses* (London: Jupiter Press, 1980), pp. 190–224.

References:

Robert McColl, Review of *The Gobi Desert, Focus,* 38 (Fall 1988): 34.

Marina Warner, Introduction to *The Gobi Desert* (Boston: Beacon/Virago, 1987), pp. xi–xxi.

Olive Murray Chapman

(1892 - 11 June 1977)

Robert H. Sirabian
Mississippi Valley State University

BOOKS: *Across Iceland, The Land of Frost and Fire* (London: John Lane / New York: Dodd, Mead, 1930);

Across Lapland with Sledge and Reindeer (London: John Lane, 1932; New York: Dodd, Mead, 1932);

Across Cyprus (London: John Lane, 1937);

Across Madagascar (London: E. J. Burrow, 1943).

Olive Murray Chapman in Lapp dress (photograph by Pearl Freeman)

Social restraints and lack of opportunities prevented most women from participating in the notable historical periods of global exploration and travel, but during the nineteenth and early-twentieth centuries a growing number of female explorers and travelers documented their journeys. The contributions of these women were often ignored or subordinated to the accomplishments of male travelers, especially when husbands and wives traveled as teams. Writing between World Wars I and II, Olive Murray Chapman is the author of travel narratives that balance the romantic longing for and freedom of travel with the scientific quest to reach unknown places and achieve personal contact with indigenous peoples. Her accounts of her journeys to Iceland, Lapland, Cyprus, and Madagascar established her reputation as an independent, resourceful traveler who was not afraid to take risks or to explore the least-traveled paths. Not mentioned in many studies about travel writing, Chapman is an intriguing figure because her writings helped to expand the definition of traveler to include the capable, independent woman, and at the same time they reveal nineteenth-century preoccupations about adventure and colonial exploration.

Little information is available about Olive Chapman's personal life, which her obituary in the London *Times* (14 June 1977) suggests was a private one: "Cremation private. . . . No mourning, No flowers." Born in 1892, Chapman was the daughter of G. A. Garry Simpson, a member of the Royal College of Surgeons, and Ethel Maud Gibbon Simpson. Chapman's husband was C. H. Murray Chapman, a flight lieutenant in the Royal Navy who was killed in active service in 1916. Chapman was educated at Queen's College and Heatherley's Art School in London. As a fellow of the Royal Geographical Society, she lectured to that organization about her travels, as well as to the Royal Scottish Geographical Society and the Royal Asiatic Society. She also lectured in the United States. Chapman held three one-woman shows of her watercolor paintings in Bond Street, London, and she produced *Winter with the Laps* (1933), a short sound travel

"A Lapp Wedding Procession at Karasjok," illustration by Chapman for Across Lapland with Sledge and Reindeer *(1932)*

documentary made during her visit to Lapland, which was shown at the Academy Cinema in London. She died at age eighty-five in Suffolk, England, on 11 June 1977.

At the time of Chapman's travels, a growing interest in commercialized tourism helped to create a distinction between the terms *tourist* and *traveler*. In *Across Lapland with Sledge and Reindeer* (1932) Chapman explained that when she first talked with an official at the Swedish travel bureau in Stockholm about traveling to Lapland, he vehemently exclaimed, "No, no! What you propose to do is an adventure, not an ordinary tourist's journey. We cannot help you here at all nor be responsible." Chapman remarked, "I made a mental note that he had probably exaggerated the difficulties, and determined not to be put off by his remarks." She did not perceive of herself as a tourist interested in the safe and leisurely pursuit of novelty. She viewed herself as an independent, goal-oriented traveler, seeking freedom and adventure while investigating the geography and cultures of lesser-known places. The Swedish official's reaction to her proposed journey reveals the skepticism Chapman encountered throughout her travels.

The emphasis of Chapman's first book, *Across Iceland, The Land of Frost and Fire* (1930), is on the geography and natural wonders of the island, then a Danish colony, whose climate and landscape are characterized by extreme variations. Written in a well-established tradition of English travel narratives about Iceland by authors such as Joseph Banks, W. G. Collingwood, and Frederick Blackwood, Lord Dufferin, Chapman's book begins with a history of the country, describing the great debate about Christianity by the early Icelandic parliament, the Althing, and discussing the noted poets and historians of Iceland while largely ignoring modern colonial history. Hoping to correct misconceptions that Iceland is an uninteresting and insignificant country, Chapman next reveals the conception of the trip and her reasons for undertaking it: to gain an understanding of the geography, history, language, and art of Iceland, as well as an appreciation of the lives of its women, especially those living in remote regions.

After an initial overview of the culture the book focuses on Chapman's journey through Iceland. Starting in the north, she traveled mainly by ponies across rugged and changing terrain. Once she was almost thrown from a pony that became frightened at the rare appearance of a motorized lorry. Even when she traveled by car, the crude roads and outdated automobiles made her journey anything but comfortable. Before her journey ended she observed imposing volcanoes, spectacular waterfalls, and vast lava deserts, in addition to the processes of haymaking, salting fish, and preparing wool. Chapman's book also comments on social issues such as education and crime and on the rural life of farmers, whom she notes were always hospitable. Improvements in Iceland brought about by outside technology, such as the wireless and construction of new roads, are viewed as a positive effect of civilization. Chapman also had a special understanding for the difficult lives of rural women.

Chapman created and verified her position of authority as a traveler by setting her own goals and undertaking her journey according to her own agenda. Unlike earlier female travelers whose journeys were verified or described by others, she recorded events as she directly experienced them. Occupying the subject position of her narrative rather than the object position of someone else's account, she is active and independent, not constrained or stationary–behavior patterns that reinforce notions of domesticity and dependence–and she maintained the authenticity of her narrative by refusing to place limits on her participation or to abandon travel plans that were prescribed as too dangerous and strenuous for women. The skepticism of officials and surprise of other travelers (or tourists) strengthened her resolve to achieve her goals. Her photographs and paintings, which accompany her narrative, document her achievements. Although she relied on guides, without whom managing language barriers and traveling through unmarked country would have been impossible, Chapman carried out every phase of the journey herself. In one instance, intent on viewing a bubbling crater emitting noxious fumes in the sulfurous mountains at Námaskard, Chapman had to be wary of the thin ground surrounding the crater, which might have collapsed under her. Another time, while riding a pony, she crossed a river with swift, dangerous currents. She also visited the farms of the rural south, staying in rustic farmhouses and sampling hardy, simple food. For women, life in these rural settings afforded few luxuries or conveniences.

Across Lapland with Sledge and Reindeer follows the overall narrative structure of *Across Iceland,* a structure that is repeated in Chapman's other two travel books as well. Each book includes a detailed map of the author's travel routes, and some have appendices offering practical advice to future travelers. In *Across Lapland* Chapman again showed herself to be resourceful and intelligent, noting information pertaining to geography, history, and culture. As was the case with her Iceland journey, she sought adventure and knowledge about a little-known place and its people, with a special interest in the lives of women. In *Across Lapland,* however, the matter-of-fact style is balanced with more colorful descriptions of landscapes and natural settings. Crossing the Arctic Circle on her way to Lapland, Chapman noted: "Later, the sun rose behind the frosted peaks of the grand coast-line past which we were steaming, and cast a rosy glow over the mountain-tops, while the snow-covered slopes below were steeped in purple and blue shadow down to the water's edge." Watercolor sketches and photographs are an integral part of *Across Lapland* as well as of Chapman's other books. Her main subjects are landscapes, historical points of interest, and indigenous peoples; and although her paintings and photographs sometimes have romanticized elements, they are usually unstylized, realistic renditions of natural wonders. Although drawing and photography were sometimes idle pursuits used by travel writers to combat boredom, Chapman used photography and drawing to establish accuracy and to capture the beautiful sites of her journeys.

Beginning with an overview of her purpose and destination, *Across Lapland* introduces readers to the people and culture of Lapland at the festive market at Bossekop, discussing the effects of religion and alcoholism and the differences in dress between men and women. The book also notes the importance of reindeer in Lap (or Saami as they call themselves) culture and discusses their characteristics and habits. After reciting the interesting history of ancient beliefs and folktales, Chapman takes the reader along her journey south from Bossekop through parts of Finland and Sweden and then west across the Norwegian border to Narvik, traveling mainly by reindeer-pulled sledge, a primary means of transportation in the frozen winter landscape of Lapland. On her journey she persevered through blizzards, a dog attack, a case of mild frostbite, and a marriage proposal by an elder Saami man. *Fjellstues*–mountain or rest huts maintained for travelers–provided shelter for Chapman and her guides, who were indispensable in helping her navigate the frozen landscape and language barriers. Describing natural features such as the aurora borealis, great reindeer herds, and wooded, snow-covered landscapes, she also commented on religion during an Easter service she attended and about the Saami educational system.

Chapman's discussion about her determination to learn to drive a reindeer-pulled sledge shows her independence and fortitude as well as her sense of humor. Dressed in a heavy pesk (a Saami winter coat made of reindeer hides), she put her ego aside and laughed at her initial failures when riding in a canoe-shaped sledge and managing a reindeer, an animal that can be stubborn, willful, and sometimes dangerous. Describing one incident, when her reindeer became frightened and dashed off while she was still inside the sledge, Chapman wrote: "I clung

Chapman with a Lapp woman from Kautokeino and a Karasjok Lapp bride and groom (photographs by Chapman; from Across Lapland with Sledge and Reindeer*)*

to the side of the sledge weak with laughter, till at last the reindeer became wound up in his rope and we came to a standstill." Her ability to drive a sledge with success was a source of pride for her, not in any outwardly boastful manner but as a sense of personal accomplishment. She authenticated her travel accounts by accomplishing goals rather than through rhetorical heroic posturing.

Chapman's empathy for the life of Saami women reveals compassion and an understanding of a routine lifestyle offering few personal opportunities. Marriages were arranged in Saami culture and predicated on wealth (measured by sizes of reindeer herds), and bigamy was practiced in Lapland at the time of her journey. Domestic life for women was onerous and dangerous, as they were expected to collect snow, feed dogs, and milk reindeer, whose kicks may result in serious injury or even death. Childbirth was also dangerous because of rural conditions, and there was a high death rate for babies and their mothers. Revealing her conditioning as a proper English lady, Chapman clearly preferred the comforts of civilization when it comes to matters of sleeping, hygiene, and food, but she embraced her rough and sometimes dirty conditions in the spirit of experiencing other cultures.

Chapman adopted the discourse of colonialism when she discussed the Saami people and their cultural practices. In describing fairy tales and magic as part of the Saami's ancient beliefs, Chapman placed Christianity above "superstition." Although her judgment is not as harsh as a Swedish historian whom she quotes as condemning superstition, she dismisses ancient Saami beliefs as curiosities of "primitive folk." For Chapman and others, the Saami of remote districts who subscribed to ancient beliefs were isolating themselves from the enlightenment of Christianity. On the other hand, Chapman was critical of evangelical sects in Lapland and what she viewed as their extreme, austere forms of religious practice. She also entertained romanticized notions of the Saami, viewing them sometimes as children, a common response of nineteenth-century European travelers when encounter-

Chapman learning to drive a Lapp pulka, *or sled*

ing indigenous peoples. Chapman offered Saami children and women gifts of balls and Woolworth bead necklaces, which recalls more organized attempts by outsiders to interest Saami women and children in arts and crafts as a means of "Westernizing" them. Even though it is framed within cultural norms that shape Chapman's own experiences and beliefs, *Across Lapland* leaves readers with the picture of a self-reliant, astute traveler who is interested in understanding and appreciating the culture of the Saami.

Writing about Saint Hilarion in *Across Cyprus* (1937), Chapman explained what seeing the castle meant to her: "It is the picture that still comes first to my mind when I think of Cyprus; the vision of a Fairy castle, dream-like and unreal, poised between heaven and earth, mounting guard over the enchanted isle to which it belongs." *Across Cyprus* reveals Chapman's interests in the history and culture of the island while more openly praising the benefits provided by a governing power than she had done in her previous two travel books. Her account of Cyprus is much more than an effete observer's romantic rendering of landscapes and history. In order to visit ancient monasteries and castles perched atop mountains, Chapman traversed rugged and in many cases unmarked terrain. In her climb to the castle of Buffavento, for example, following only an account of a similar ascent by Dutch traveler Cornelius de Bruyn (whom she calls Van Bruyn), in 1683, Chapman had to invent her own route: "Up and up I climbed, and soon, like Van Bruyn, found myself gripping on to rock ledges while I had to take the greatest care not to slip upon rolling stones and in places was occasionally reduced, like him, to crawling upon hands and feet." Her description shows her bravado in originally doubting the necessity of crawling but acknowledges her humbling before the mountain. Chapman's narrative is rooted in adventure and danger, characteristic of nineteenth-century travel accounts; yet her experience is direct–she makes the climb to Buffavento alone without a guide–and her account reveals varied perspectives of her experiences, both realistic and romantic, perspectives that work interdependently in providing a notion of the experience of travel and that depart from the uniform perspective of the tourist or recreational traveler. Chapman's narrative reveals her disappointment with uniform accounts of traveling, which stress convenience and luxury, given to her by "tourists" about the most popular time to visit Cyprus and the advantages of hotels and English clubs: "This account, typical of the average Briton's requirements abroad, depressed me, being far removed from what I was hoping to enjoy in Cyprus."

A notable example of Chapman's descriptions of the people and culture of Cyprus is her account of the spring fair at Famagusta, where masses of people from all over the island buy and sell food, goods, and animals. After landing at Famagusta and exploring the surrounding areas, Chapman worked her way south and then north and east. Pointed in her remarks about the advantages of Cyprus having be-

The Old Town, Nicosia, Cyprus (photograph by Chapman; from Across Cyprus, *1945)*

come a British colony in 1925, she sketches the turbulent history of the island and its changes of rulers, including the failed reign of Richard I (Richard the Lion Hearted) of England, who captured the island in 1191 during the Third Crusade but sold it to the Lusignan dynasty the following year. Chapman's historical overview concludes with a description of Cyprus as "a little colony of whom Britain may be proud, teeming with archaeological interest, and whose fame and importance from a strategic point of view is only now beginning to be recognized." Chapman agreed that developing modern roads for greater access to some of the ancient ruins threatens to destroy their mystery and integrity, and she also noted the negative effects of the encroachment of modernization on the ancient architecture. Still, she clearly sanctioned "improvements" to the economic and social structure that were made possible under British rule. As in her other travel accounts, she included observations about religion, education, and the domestic requirements and codes placed on women, but *Across Cyprus* is largely Chapman's celebration of the history and ancient ruins that she felt were overlooked and underappreciated.

Across Madagascar (1943), Chapman's final travel book, has as its dramatic background the approaching outbreak of World War II and the author's worries about becoming trapped on the other side of the globe. Like *Across Cyprus, Across Madagascar* expresses Chapman's approval of colonial rule, in this case by the French. After documenting a turbulent and violent history, including a struggle by many Malagasies (who were encouraged by Western missionaries) to adopt Christianity over "superstition," Chapman's book states her opinion that the people of Madagascar have to "earn" the right of French citizenship. She viewed the adoption of Christianity, a practice linked to colonialism, as bringing an end to superstition and primitive practices, and just as with the Saami of Lapland, the Malagasies were better served, according to Chapman, by abandoning ancient (primitive) beliefs.

Because of the terrain of the Madagascar rain forests, Chapman's source of travel in the north, after landing in Tamatave (Toamasina), is a *filanzana* (riding chair) carried by Malagasy porters. Chapman had difficulty adjusting to riding in a filanzana–which is not overly comfortable or stable, especially when traversing rough terrain–but she accepted these conditions in the spirit of her journey. At one point, when Chapman's footrest broke during the descent of a steep hill, she and her bearers almost fell: "The porters staggered and all but fell with me down the precipitous hillside, below which was a rushing torrent, but with incredible skill they recovered themselves just in time to lower me safely to the ground. . . ." Chapman admired the skill and stamina of her bearers though she never questioned their subordinate position to herself or that they were being exploited by a colonial system. Her narrative is sometimes susceptible to conventionalized descriptions of the Malagasies, and the foreword of the book notes her desire for adventure and encounters with "primitive" tribes.

Attitudes that privilege European culture surface throughout the narrative. Chapman received preferential treatment by French officials, who helped her with guides, and she avoided direct contact with indigenous people when riding on crowded buses. One French official, in talking about the possibilities of mining mica in Madagascar, told Chapman that the heat, insects, and rough terrain made the island unfit for white men and that the "natives" were too lazy to be useful. Chapman also asked an official about comments she had heard in England that Madagascar would be an appropriate place for the settlement of "impecunious Jews." Although she was never disrespectful to the people of Madagascar and learned terms in their language, she never questioned the colonial system or took the view that the Malagasy culture might coexist with European culture rather than be subordinated to it.

During her trip to Fort-Dauphin (Tôlanaro) in the south, Chapman encountered many natural wonders and traveled through untouched rain forests that are host to mosquitoes, other biting insects, and plant species that cause skin disease and eye irritation, as well as to crocodiles and other exotic animals. Along with excessive heat and humidity, she had to contend with a painful case of jiggers in one foot and a mild fever, none of which she allowed to interfere with her schedule. She had direct contact with the Tanala people, in whose village she witnessed a dance, and visited an ancient Tanala burial place. She received her share of excitement on a crowded mail bus when the driver, who backed up to avoid an oncoming lorry, misjudged the narrow width of the road and the off-side wheels of the bus rolled over the steep banks. With the bus partially suspended, Chapman and the other passengers managed to jump out without causing the bus to roll down the embankment. She reacted to this nearly fatal accident with her characteristic fortitude and optimism, glad that she had not been killed in such a pedestrian manner. Before her trip ended she found time to visit various churches, mosques, and several Malagasy villages, which helped make her trip a memorable experience.

Chapman's concern for the plight of women is seen toward the end of the book in observations about the treatment of the wife of the deputy governor of Madagascar. Because she is Malagasy, she is ostracized by French officials and their wives, but after meeting and talking with her, Chapman concluded that this prejudice was unfair. The end of Chapman's narrative is dominated by her concern about the approaching war, causing her to affirm the French colonial empire as a symbol of democracy. (*Across Madagascar* is dedicated to "General De Gaulle and the fighting French.") Even with the real fear of becoming trapped far from home, Chapman, marveling at the people and beautiful natural scenes, ended the book with an overview of all of her journeys and expressed the joy and personal satisfaction she had experienced by setting goals and seeing new places.

While sometimes critical of her style and her penchant for romanticized observations, British and American reviews of Chapman's first two travel books praised her interesting and informative accounts. The several reprintings and positive reviews of her first two books indicate the appeal of Chapman's travel accounts. With fewer reprintings and reviews of her last two books, Chapman's popularity may have waned, possibly, in part, because she was writing these books against the cataclysmic backdrop of World War II. Though she never attained recognition equal to that of well-known women travel writers such as Mary Kingsley or Lady Anne Blunt, Chapman was invited to talk before several royal geographical societies.

Olive Chapman enjoyed the adventure and excitement of travel as well as the contemplation of natural wonders. She sought to understand unknown cultures and to promote an interest in travel beyond the beaten track. A review of her first travel book in *The New York Times* (21 August 1932) gives an overview of her approach to traveling: "Everybody told her she couldn't do it, that nobody ever had done it, and so she set forth and did it, to the accompaniment of interesting and fascinating contacts and experiences from beginning to end of the journey."

References:

Ali Behdad, *Belated Travelers: Orientalism in the Age of Colonial Dissolution* (Durham, N.C.: Duke University Press, 1994);

James Buzzard, *The Beaten Track: European Tourism, Literature, and the Ways to Culture, 1800–1918* (Oxford: Clarendon Press, 1993);

Paul Fussell, *Abroad: British Literary Traveling Between the Wars* (New York: Oxford University Press, 1980);

Sara Mills, *Discourses of Difference: An Analysis of Women's Travel Writing and Colonialism* (London: Routledge, 1991).

Evelyn Cheesman

(unknown 1881 - 15 April 1969)

Marcia B. Dinneen
Bridgewater State College

BOOKS: *Everyday Doings of Insects* (London: Harrap, 1924; New York: McBride, 1925);
The Great Little Insect (London: Hodder & Stoughton, 1924);
Islands Near the Sun: Off the Beaten Track in the Far, Fair Society Islands (London: Witherby, 1927);
Marooned in Du-Bu Cove (London: Bell, 1930);
A First Book of Nature Study (London: Allan, 1931); republished as *The Growth of Living Things: A First Book of Nature Study* (New York: McBride, 1932);
Hunting Insects in the South Seas (London: Allan, 1932; New York: Ballou, 1933);
Insect Behaviour (London: Allan, 1932; New York: Ballou, 1933);
Backwaters of the Savage South Seas (London: Jarrolds, 1933);
The Two Roads of Papua (London: Jarrolds, 1935);
The Land of the Red Bird (London: Joseph, 1938);
Camping Adventures in New Guinea (London: Harrap, 1948);
Six-Legged Snakes in New Guinea: A Collecting Expedition to Two Unexplored Islands (London: Harrap, 1949);
Camping Adventures on Cannibal Islands (London: Harrap, 1949; New York: McBride, 1950);
Landfall the Unknown: Lord Howe Island (Harmondsworth, U.K.: Penguin, 1950);
Insects Indomitable (London: Bell, 1952); republished as *Insects: Their Secret World* (New York: Sloane, 1953);
Sealskins for Silk: Captain Fanning's Voyage Round the World in a Brig in 1797–99 (London: Methuen, 1952; New York: Abelard-Schuman, 1956);
Charles Darwin and His Problems (London: Bell, 1953; New York: Abelard-Schuman, 1955);
Things Worth While (London: Hutchinson, 1957);
Look at Insects (London: Hamilton, 1960);
Time Well Spent (London: Hutchinson, 1960);
Who Stand Alone (London: Bles, 1965).

SELECTED PERIODICAL PUBLICATIONS–UNCOLLECTED: "The Island of Malekula, New Hebrides," *Geographical Journal,* 81 (March 1933): 133–210;
"Two Unexplored Islands Off Dutch New Guinea: Waigeu and Japen," *Geographical Journal,* 95 (March 1940): 208–217;
"Japanese Operations in New Guinea," *Geographical Journal,* 101 (March 1943): 97–110.

Evelyn Cheesman was principally an entomologist and incidentally an explorer. In her search for insects and her attempt to prove a theory concerning a land bridge between Asia and Australia, she traveled throughout the South Pacific, camping in areas where no white man, let alone a white woman, had ever been. Although she did not intentionally write travel books, her descriptions of her insect-hunting expeditions provide insights into the places where she lived and the people she encountered. Jane Robinson describes Cheesman as a woman who "travelled professionally," but this description is misleading. Travel was never Cheesman's main focus; it was the means for finding new species of insects or proving her theory. Her books, which sold well, were written to fund her expeditions.

Born in Westwell, Kent, Lucy Evelyn Cheesman (who neither liked nor used her first name) was the daughter of Robert Cheesman, a farmer, and his wife, Florence Maud Tassell Cheesman. Brought up in the comfort of Court Lodge with three brothers and one sister, Cheesman developed a lifelong love of nature. In *Things Worth While* (1957) she describes her youth as "care-free happy days soaking in wild life." Her brothers were sent to good boarding schools, but Cheesman and her sister, as was usual then, went to local schools. An aunt paid their tuition. Cheesman attended school in Ashford and spent a year at the Misses Collingwood School in Brighton; then she had to earn her own living. She worked at the only career open to women of her social class, that of governess, for three years.

While working for a family at Gumley, in the Midlands, Cheesman spent a year in Germany, learning German and teaching English. When the twenty-nine-year-old Cheesman realized that the

Evelyn Cheesman

family that had hired her no longer required her services, she attempted unsuccessfully to fulfill her ambition to become a veterinarian, a profession that was not open to women at that time. Unhappy as a governess, she realized that she "might not be a misfit in another environment" and became a canine nurse, studying anatomy on her own, in the hope that the practical experience would be useful when the Royal Veterinary College finally opened its doors to women.

Circumstances determined that canine nurse would not be her ultimate career. During World War I she worked as a temporary civil servant, and after the war a friend got her a job as curator of the insect house at the Regent's Park Zoo. For someone who had grown up collecting insects, the position was a natural. (As a child, she once collected thirty-two glowworms in one evening, a family record.) The insect house had been neglected during the war, and Cheesman built it back up, providing interesting exhibits and giving talks to children. She also attended a two-year course in entomology offered by Professor Maxwell Lefroy at the Royal College of Science.

Because of her success at the zoo, she was offered a position as official entomologist on an expedition to the Pacific Islands, allowing her to fulfill a lifelong dream of visiting that part of the world. Her passage would be free. Encouraged by Professor Lefroy, she took a leave of absence from the zoo and joined the St. George Expedition of 1924, embarking with ten pounds in her pocket and beginning a lifetime of travel to study insect life.

As a member of the St. George Expedition, she was continually frustrated by having to stick to a schedule determined by others. When the group arrived at Tahiti, she found a check for £100 from her brother Percy, which made it possible for her to set out alone in 1925 to journey through Tahiti, Raiatea, and Bora Bora.

This expedition was the first of Cheesman's eight solo expeditions to the South Pacific, which provided the raw material for her travel books. Cheesman wrote sixteen adult books, some centering on a specific location, others ranging over several expeditions. She also wrote children's books, as well as scholarly articles.

Understandably dedicated to her brother Percy, *Islands Near the Sun: Off the Beaten Track in the Far, Fair Society Islands* (1927) describes Cheesman's first solo expedition in 1925. She traveled inland into the mountains on her collecting trips, away from the tourist areas along the beaches. Stating that one "can't describe Tahiti from sea level," she wrote that the spirit of Tahiti and its people has "been driven into the mountains, and can only be traced here and there among the Tahitians of to-day as a faint echo of the past."

Each of Cheesman's travel books has a focus, either on a particular location or on her theory of the origin of a place. *Islands Near the Sun* describes the islands she visited in detail and includes references to previous visitors, such as Pierre Loti, Herman Melville, and Louis Agassiz. Her compatibility with the natives and her regret at the decline of the native Polynesians are apparent. She also includes fascinating information on topics such as the cultivation of vanilla. As in all her travel books, Cheesman's own personality comes through. She describes her pleasure in her simple hut outside Papeete and her sickness from eating an inedible fish, resulting in abscesses and boils on her feet and legs. Rather than giving up her collecting projects during this illness, she kept close to her home base, "and for a fortnight only covered those distances which could be accomplished by limping on one foot–a tedious performance."

As the title states, *Hunting Insects in the South Seas* (1932) is mainly about Cheesman's quests for insects, but her descriptions of the places she visited in the process demonstrate her sensitivity to her surroundings and ability to appreciate beauty, even while searching for food for the finicky caterpillars she was raising. This book includes materials from her 1924–1925 expedition to the Society Islands as well as a 1929–1930 expedition to the New Hebrides (Vanuatu).

Although Cheesman took her work as an entomologist seriously, she described it as the "game of collecting," and throughout each of her books this "thrill of the hunt" in locating different insects is apparent. *Hunting Insects* also describes her excitement in finding violets on Tahiti and in coming upon a valley on the Marquesas Islands made famous by Melville in *Typee* (1846). Though she concluded that Melville did not exaggerate its beauty, Cheesman did note that he had neglected to mention the torture inflicted by the sand flies that make the valley "practically uninhabitable." She was bitten so badly that "for a whole day afterwards I could not walk but had to spend hours in bathing swollen limbs." The book also includes an in-depth description of the "bush" of Vanuatu, the dense forest, the flowers, and, particularly, the banyan trees.

Backwaters of the Savage South Seas (1933) is about Cheesman's 1929–1930 expedition to the large island of Malekula in Vanuatu, contrasting this island with the Society Islands, particularly with reference to the people. On Malekula Cheesman encountered cannibals, writing that "the only real dangers apart from accidents that attend a white woman, who wanders about in the bush thinking only of suitable spots for collecting insects, are, the breaking of a tambu [taboo] unwittingly, getting the reputation for sorcery, or rousing the ire or the jealousy of the sorcerer of the tribe."

Fortunately, she had a taboo set on her to signify that "my person was sacred and I must not be interfered with, and that anyone accompanying me was tambu also." Protected by this taboo and by her caring attitude toward her native assistants, Cheesman had no problems with the cannibals and was invited by King Ringapat of the Big Nambas to stay in his village. Her description of the customs, the ceremonies, and the position of women in this society is instructive and entertaining. For example, pigs were used as currency when purchasing a wife.

Backwaters of the Savage South Seas explains cannibalism as a social rite in which the entire tribe partakes in eating an enemy so that his spirit is "annihilated and his debbil-debbil cannot appear" to take revenge. King Ringapat had renounced cannibalism and substituted a pig as a sacrifice in tribal celebrations. His father, however, was a notorious cannibal, who had taken "latterly to eating children" because he enjoyed the taste.

The Two Roads of Papua (1935) covers Cheesman's expedition to British New Guinea (now part of Papua New Guinea) in 1933–1934, during which she studied insects and geological evidence in search of proof for a theory that a land bridge once connected Asia with Australia. The description of her arrival at Port Moresby reads like a true travel book as she details the difficulty of finding suitable accommodations. Expeditions to a variety of camps are described, including some of the minutiae of daily life. At Kokoda, for example, the hut she rented was overrun by rats "who were dreadfully bold." She found them everywhere, even in a basket of scrap paper.

Cheesman also has one of her recurring attacks of malaria, to which she alludes in her typically understated style: "There is nothing worth even a passing interest when you have had fits of vomiting for twenty-four hours on end and are feeling like a well-sucked orange skin." After describing a variety of "discomforts," she wrote: "Few people can realize the pleasure to be derived from peeling off a wet suit, soaking yourself in a tin bath, with a little ammonia in it, and watching the leeches squirm and curl up which had secreted themselves in your clothing."

One reason Cheesman's travel books sold so well was her power of description, as in this passage about the mosquitoes of Boroka: "With the sun just sinking there would be a noise like a fife-and-drum band, as thousands of mosquitoes poured out of the marshes in solid streams, attacking so fiercely that nobody could sit still." People would gather around a smouldering log, coughing on the smoke, which "was preferable to being pierced by hundreds of stilettos at once." Each night the mosquitoes sang their "Hymn of Hate outside the mosquito nets until dawn."

The Land of the Red Bird (1938) describes another expedition to the island of New Guinea, specifically the Cyclops and Torricelli mountain ranges. During this expedition she confirmed the land-bridge theory. The book also provides a great deal of information about the history, geology, and weather of the mountains. Cheesman traveled with tourists to the coast of New Guinea but later went "quite off the rubber-neck track" into Humboldt (Kayo) Bay, on the northwest coast of the part of the island that is now Irian Barat, Indonesia. Though the bay has "some of the most beautiful islands imaginable," the area has "nothing to tempt tourists."

A particularly interesting aspect of the book is the information on the plumage trade. The "Red Bird" in the title of the book is the Red Bird of Paradise, once common all over New Guinea. The birds were almost wiped out before Cheesman went to New Guinea, and although it had become illegal to import the plumage into Great Britain, smuggling the feathers into Europe was big business.

Despite being an entomologist Cheesman had no love of leeches, especially on this trip, where the leeches had "something more poisonous than usual in their bites." Traveling through leech-infested areas, she had to scrape them off herself every few yards. She had intended to spend a month in a rain forest, but broke camp "rather suddenly owning to an untoward incident, for I found a leech in the teapot. . . . It suddenly occurred to me that nobody but an idiot would remain in any place where there were leeches in the teapots."

Despite such adversity Cheesman remained in New Guinea until the outbreak of World War II. She was on the last boat out of New Guinea before the Japanese invasion of 1942. During the war she worked first in the censorship office, then as a plane spotter, and finally as a lecturer to the British military, giving 1,020 speeches on the Pacific war zone. She also wrote several articles for professional journals and organized her diaries and notes into a book. *Six-Legged Snakes in New Guinea: A Collecting Expedition to Two Unexplored Islands* (1949) details her collecting expedition to the islands of Waigeu (Waigeo) and Japen (Yapen), off the coast of Dutch New Guinea (Irian Jaya), where she lived from February 1938 to June 1939, researching the migration of various insect species from Asia to New Guinea.

Near the end of the war, Cheesman was injured in a train accident. The resulting headaches and back pain were not treated properly. Three doctors said the pain was caused by rheumatism, and nothing could be done. Walking was impossible, and she was "steadily becoming more crippled" until she consulted an osteopath who was able to put some displaced vertebrae back in place. Able to walk again, Cheesman began to plan another expedition. To help finance the forthcoming trip, she wrote *Camping Adventures in New Guinea* (1948), based on a previous expedition. *Camping Adventures on Cannibal Islands* (1949), about Vanuatu, is also based on an earlier trip.

Cheesman traveled to New Caledonia and the Loyalty Islands in 1949. During this time she continued to be plagued by pain and resolved to give up travel and stay at home in London. In 1953, however, she had a successful operation that allowed her to walk and travel once again. In 1954 Cheesman returned to Aneityum in Vanuatu on her last solo expedition. She was more than seventy years old.

The foreword to *Things Worth While* (1957) states that the book is "not intended to be an autobiography," but the "reactions of one person. The person herself is not interesting." The book reveals a great deal of information about Cheesman's early life, showing how she became the courageous woman she was, and it provides additional details on her eight solo expeditions. The reader learns about the importance of her trek to Buna in Papua New Guinea, which gave her personal knowledge of the terrain that was valuable to Allied forces during World War II. One of her contour maps was used by five governments in locating enemy strongholds.

Time Well Spent (1960) was written in response to the many letters she received from readers who wanted to know the "nitty-gritty" of her life in the bush: what she ate, wore, and read. The book details Cheesman's daily regimen, stressing the importance of living a frugal life "when outside the bounds of civilization." Unlike many travelers she insisted that drinking during the day contributes to thirst. She would only suck the juice of a lime because "it is a waste of time to pour liquid into your body only so that it could ooze out again." Cheesman was also against sleeping during the daytime, insisting that it was "expedient" to sleep fewer hours in the tropics.

Cheesman traveled light. Her collecting gear was her primary concern; physical comforts were secondary. She slept in a hammock and once lived on sweet potatoes for five weeks because she believed in living off the land whenever possible. After initially refusing to try them, she found that fruit bats were delicious once the heads were removed.

To begin each day Cheesman read a chapter from Marcus Aurelius's *Meditations.* She was always concerned for the health and well-being of the natives she employed and met. At times she administered medicine to them as well as treating her own ailments. To the natives of Papua she was "the woman who walks." In Hollandia (Jayapura), Dutch New Guinea (Irian Jaya), she was known as "nona di gunung," Malay for "lady of the mountains." Being called "nona"–lady–and not "perempuam"–woman–pleased her: "I was snobbishly proud of that distinction."

Another name for Cheesman came from her clothing. Being a sensible woman, Cheesman made herself a "bush suit," which was sturdy and practical but caused a commotion among the sisters at a Catholic mission in New Guinea. The natives called her "the sinnabudda belong good feller calico" (the mistress with sensible clothes), but the nuns thought her tunic, bloomers, and stockings were "scandalous."

Throughout her travels male settlers were appalled at Cheesman's activities. The assistant resident at Buna, for example, was "perturbed by the manner in which I travelled. It was customary, if a white woman happened to make a bush trip, to have her carried in a cane-chair slung on poles." Cheesman walked. He was also astounded to discover that she slept in a hammock. A plantation owner saw her as "a freak," and to his wife "I must have appeared as a monstrous female from another planet." Usually covered with mud and wielding an insect net, she was, indeed, a rare sight.

When people remarked on Cheesman's courage at traveling alone in wild places such as New Guinea, she stated that it was "not so much courage that is called for but endurance. I should place independence first and then endurance, neither of which

Cheesman in New Guinea

are virtues but acquired habits." Aware of highly critical male and female attitudes toward her and her work, she commented that independence is regarded "as an unsociable habit, especially in a woman."

Cheesman's final collecting expedition was in 1958, when she and another woman, a botanist, mounted an expedition to Tarifa in Spain. The description of this trip in *Time Well Spent* reads more like a travel book than Cheesman's other accounts of expeditions, as she describes hotels, people they meet, and schedules. Except for her expedition to Tarifa, Cheesman traveled alone. Natives carried her equipment, and occasionally a "European" male would accompany her on short treks, but she was mostly on her own. Yet for Cheesman, "Isolation from human intercourse holds no penalty except for those with a weak mental directive. . . . Real isolation is freedom of the mind." Busy with her collecting projects, Cheesman found the solitude of camp life something to "savour."

The effects of isolation are the basis for Cheesman's last book, *Who Stand Alone* (1965), which shows how white people living far from home in New Guinea and Vanuatu are affected by their environment. The book begins with a quotation from

Henrik Ibsen: "The Strongest Man of Earth is He Who Stands Most Alone." This statement could be a description of Cheesman. Although she was a slight woman and only 5' 2" tall, Cheesman did not fear physical harm or feel dismay at the lack of "civilized" society while living in the bush. Her only anxiety was that she had overlooked something or missed an opportunity to investigate a new place.

According to *Who Stand Alone,* white female settlers were the chief sufferers from isolation because the men had their work. Many of these women "were haunted by their isolation: they resented it fiercely, daily and hourly." Such resentment took its toll; some of them "ended in mental homes in Australia." Cheesman decided that there were two types of settlers: those who refused to adapt to what is strange and those who are "keen to master difficulties, . . . assimilating the new environment and imprinting it with their own personality."

Frugal by necessity, Cheesman lived simply. After the St. George Expedition, she resigned from her work at the insect house in Regent's Park and worked, unpaid, for the rest of her career at the Natural History Museum in London. Although she did receive some grants, she financed her travel mainly through her writing. In 1953 she received a Civil List Pension, which helped to ease her financial concerns. That same year she was awarded an Order of the British Empire to acknowledge her contributions to science. A fellow of the Royal Entomological Society, an honorary associate of the Entomological Department of the British Museum, and a fellow of the Zoological Society, Cheesman died on 15 April 1969.

Although she did not initially set out to become a travel writer, Cheesman's insect-collecting expeditions took her to exotic places, some of which had never been described in writing. In the best sense of what a travel writer should do, Cheesman made the islands in the South Pacific, and the other places she wrote about, real to readers unable to make the journeys. Her books provide a wealth of information about the places she visited and the people she met. Her descriptions are vivid, and her sense of humor is understated. For example, in describing some New Guinea natives who had been given some colored muslin fabric in exchange for food, she wrote: "Thereafter the men of the village strutted about with red or blue rags draped round their necks or tied round their heads; the rest of their clothing consisted of half a gourd and a black beard–the effect was devastating."

Cheesman possessed a lifelong enthusiasm for collecting insects, discovering new places, meeting new people, adapting to difficult conditions, and describing the beauty she could always find around her. At a meeting of the Royal Geographical Society, after Cheesman had given a paper on the island of Malekula, a Dr. Ivens of the Melanesian Mission stated: "For a man to have done what Miss Cheesman has done would have been remarkable. It is amazing that a woman should have gone to these wild places to do what she has done and then think nothing of it."

References:

Daniel B. Baker, ed., *Explorers and Discoverers of the World* (Detroit: Gale Research, 1993), p. 138;

"Miss Evelyn Cheesman: Entomologist and Explorer," *Times* (London), 17 April 1969, p. 11;

Jane Robinson, *Wayward Women: A Guide to Women Travellers* (New York: Oxford University Press, 1990), pp. 130–131;

Marion Tinling, "Lucy Evelyn Cheesman," in her *Women into the Unknown: A Sourcebook on Women Explorers* (Westport, Conn.: Greenwood Press, 1989), pp. 85–90.

Papers:

Cheesman's expedition notebooks and diaries, photographs, sketches, maps, and correspondence are at the Natural History Museum, also known as the British Museum (Natural History), in London. The Cheesman Collection also includes personal copies of her books, with her annotations and drawings.

Maurice Collis

(10 January 1889 - 12 January 1973)

Maria Noëlle Ng
University of British Columbia

BOOKS: *Danse Macabre* (London: Selwyn & Blount, 1922);

Siamese White (London: Faber & Faber, 1936);

She Was a Queen (London: Faber & Faber, 1937; New York: Criterion, 1962);

Trials in Burma (London: Faber & Faber, 1938);

Lords of the Sunset, A Tour in the Shan States (London: Faber & Faber, 1938);

Sanda Mala (London: Faber & Faber, 1939; New York: Carrick & Evans, 1940);

Courts of the Shan Princes (London: China Society, 1939);

The Dark Door (London: Faber & Faber, 1940);

The Great Within (London: Faber & Faber, 1941);

British Merchant Adventurers (London: Collins, 1942);

The Motherly and Auspicious, Being the Life of the Empress Dowager Tz'u Hsi in the Form of a Drama (London: Faber & Faber, 1943; New York: Putnam, 1944);

The Land of the Great Image, Being Experiences of Friar Manrique in Arakan (London: Faber & Faber, 1943; New York: Knopf, 1943);

The Burmese Scene: Political, Historical, Pictorial (London: Crowther, 1943);

New Sources for the Life of the Empress Dowager Tz'u Hsi (London: China Society, 1944);

White of Mergen (London: Faber & Faber, 1945);

Quest for Sita (London: Faber & Faber, 1946; New York: Day, 1947);

Foreign Mud (London: Faber & Faber, 1946; New York: Knopf, 1947);

Lord of the Three Worlds (London: Faber & Faber, 1947);

The First Holy One (London: Faber & Faber, 1948; New York: Knopf, 1948);

The Descent of the God (London: Faber & Faber, 1948);

The Grand Peregrination, Being the Life and Adventures of Fernão Mendez Pinto (London: Faber & Faber, 1949);

Marco Polo (London: Faber & Faber, 1950; New York: New Directions, 1961);

Maurice Collis, 1939

The Mystery of Dead Lovers (London: Faber & Faber, 1951);

The Discovery of L. S. Lowry: A Critical and Biographical Essay (London: Reid & Lefevre, 1951);

The Journey Outward: An Autobiography (London: Faber & Faber, 1952);

Into Hidden Burma: An Autobiography (London: Faber & Faber, 1953);

Cortés and Montezuma (London: Faber & Faber, 1954; New York: Harcourt, Brace, 1955);

Last and First in Burma (London: Faber & Faber, 1956; New York: Macmillan, 1956);

The Hurling Time (London: Faber & Faber, 1958);

Nancy Astor: An Informal Autobiography (London: Faber & Faber, 1960; New York: Dutton, 1960);
Stanley Spencer: A Biography (London: Harville, 1962);
Wayfoong: The Hongkong and Shanghai Bank Corporation (London: Faber & Faber, 1965);
Raffles (London: Faber & Faber, 1966);
Somerville and Ross: A Biography (London: Faber & Faber, 1968);
The Journey Up: Reminiscences, 1934–1968 (London: Faber & Faber, 1970).

Maurice Collis belongs to a group of British writers who took former Asian colonies of Great Britain as themes for their writings, in his case writing mainly about Burma (now called Myanmar). His many travel narratives and historical works on Burma not only contribute to the historical record of that country but also illustrate the sorts of predicaments colonial administrators encountered there, illuminating the cultural complexities of a colonial society.

Maurice Stewart Collis was born in Dublin on 10 January 1889. His parents, William Stewart Collis, a lawyer, and Edith Barton Collis, came from the Protestant gentry class. Collis was educated at Rugby School and Corpus Christi, Oxford, where he studied modern history. One of his friends from the Oxford days was Geoffrey Faber, who later founded Faber and Faber, which became Collis's chief publisher.

Collis's fascination with Asia began in his early years. In his autobiography *The Journey Outward* (1952) Collis recalled writing to his aunt in India when he was ten years old, asking her to send him a lion's or tiger's tooth: "Are there any tigers near where you lieve [*sic*], does Uncle George ever go hunting tigers and shute [*sic*] some and bring home some skins?" Collis's academic performance was acceptable if not brilliant, and he excelled in games. In 1910, after taking a first in history honors (T. E. Lawrence was another first), Collis prepared for the required examinations to enter the Indian Civil Service. Over a period of twenty-five days a candidate for the service was asked to write papers on subjects such as English literature, the French language and literature, Roman history, Roman law, and English law. Although Collis did not make the first list, he received an appointment after a candidate failed the second round of examinations. Thus Collis set out for Burma in October 1912 and served as a colonial administrator there until 1936, when he retired and became a writer. In 1912 he married Dorothy Tuney-Bassett, by whom he had two sons. The marriage was dissolved in 1917, and in 1922 he married Eleanor Bourke. They had two sons and one daughter. Eleanor Collis died in 1967.

Strictly speaking, Collis wrote only one travel book, *Lords of the Sunset,* (1938), but his four autobiographies–*Trials in Burma* (1938), *The Journey Outward* (1952), *Into Hidden Burma* (1953), and *The Journey Up* (1970)–as well as some of his historical narratives also deal with the history of Burma. Collis's first book published by Faber and Faber, significantly, was *Siamese White* (1936), an account of the adventures of Samuel White, a seventeenth-century English merchant pirate who operated from the southern tip of Burma, which was then part of the Siamese kingdom and in Collis's time was known as Tenasserim. *Siamese White* established Collis's reputation as a writer who knew the East. The title page of *The Burmese Scene* (1943) calls him "The authority on the Far East." *Siamese White* captivated readers in the last years of the colonial empire with its account of English adventures in the East, but readers in the late twentieth century tend to be more interested in Collis's uneasy attempt to balance imperial pride with a growing awareness of the Eurocentric assumptions of colonialism. This internal tension, already detectable in *Siamese White,* became more apparent in his later publications and provides useful insight into the dilemmas encountered by colonialists.

Trials in Burma begins with an elegiac description of Collis's impression of Burma as he returned from a leave of absence in England: "There, bathed in sunshine, secret and still, was Buddhist Burma. Coming upon it suddenly, after long leave in London, it seemed like a picture in an old book of travels." According to Collis, society in the capital city of Rangoon (Yangon) "was wholly English and it was composed of the members of three great clubs. . . . Wealth or attainments or character was irrelevant; only race counted." It is obvious from such defensive remarks that he was not as severe a racist as some of his compatriots, but he nonetheless accepted the racial segregation practiced by Anglo-Burmese society, commenting that "all foreigners are rather exhausting." *Trials in Burma* also includes an account of an infamous 1930 traffic accident involving a young lieutenant of the Cameron Highlanders and three non-Europeans. As presiding judge at the trial, Collis was under considerable pressure from the colonial community to find the Englishman not guilty against all evidence; yet he sentenced the lieutenant to "three months' imprisonment and a fine of thirty pounds." This uncompromising sense of fair play cost Collis his future in the civil service and led to his eventual retirement in 1936.

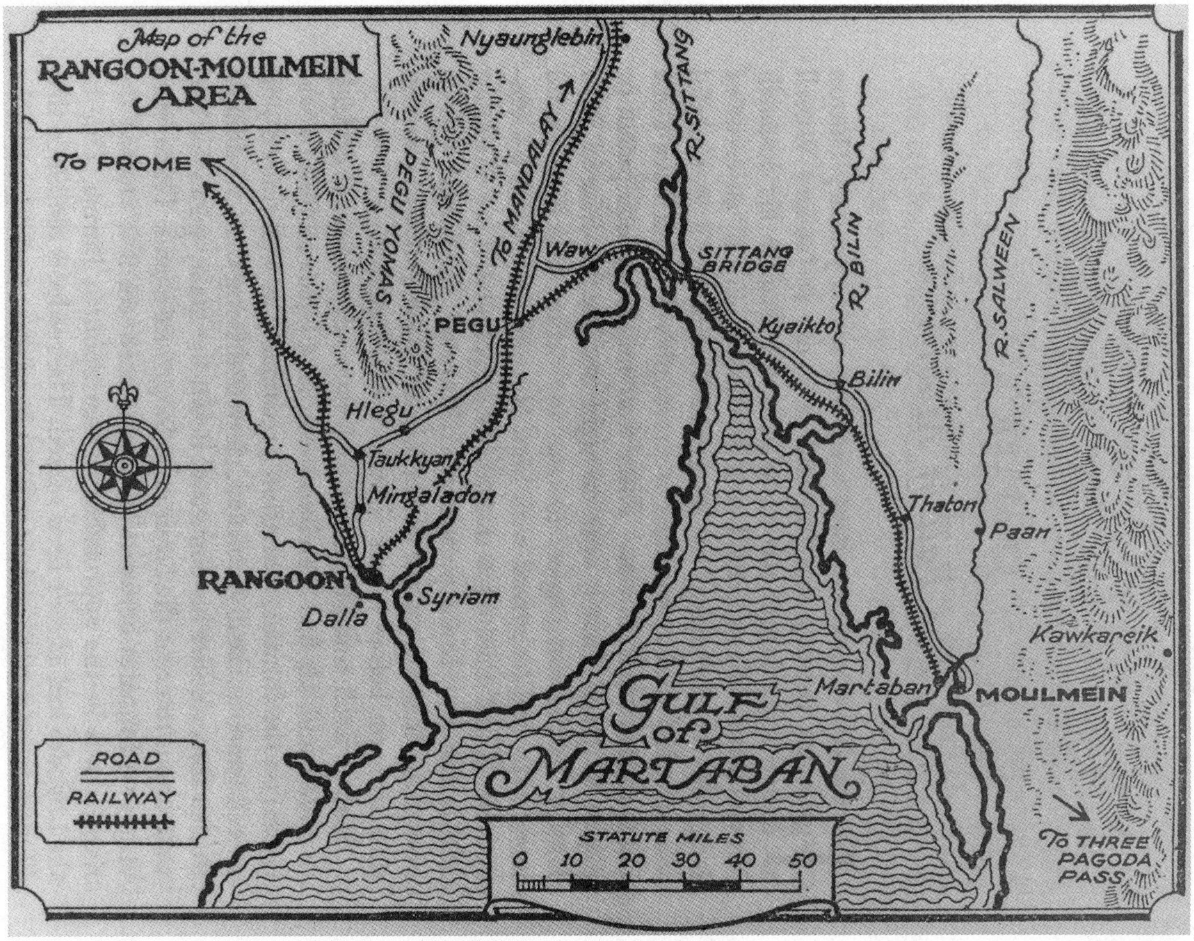

Map from Last and First in Burma *(1956)*

Collis's last posting in Burma was in Mergui, where the India Office sent him as a kind of punishment for the sentence he handed down in the traffic-accident case. It was also the place where Samuel White had erected a lawless outpost in the seventeenth century, thus planting the seed for Collis's career as a writer.

After Collis retired, the commissioner of the Shan States in northern Burma invited him to pay a visit to that district. This trip was financed by Faber and Faber, which published the resulting travel book, *Lords of the Sunset* (1938). A guest of the commissioner, Collis carried letters of introduction to other British notables, including a man called Livesey, whom Collis believed to merit a visit because "The English public is always interested in Eton boys, particularly if they take to living on a lake in the middle of Asia." Yet Collis spent much of his time visiting the Shan princes and their families. He respected the Burmese nobility and wrote affectionately of those he met. In describing the modest dwelling of the former ruler of Keng Kam (Keng Hkam), Collis wrote: "I glanced round the little room, trying to arrange my legs. Had there been chairs, there would have been no space for anything else. . . . [The prince] had no chairs; that was the end of it. To send out for chairs would not be good manners. These were subtleties which gentlemen understood." Collis was at his best when describing a simple country scene, and his prose comes alive in spite of his caveat:

> Thence the road entered that kind of country which I find so wearisome. The plain was left and we were enclosed among wooded hills for a long while. There were many people on the road, Kachins in their red clothes, Chinese caravans, their ponies or bullocks laden with silk, a few Shans, and once a Lama from Thibet [*sic*] in his dark yellow robe and curving hat.

During this trip Collis also visited silver mines and tung plantations, which were commercial enterprises of economic importance to the British government. In a poignant scene Collis and some Shan nobles gathered to listen to the radio and heard the

Collis in his study with some of his Asian artifacts, 1959 (photograph by Gerti Deutsch)

news of a Europe menaced by Francisco Franco, Adolf Hitler, and Benito Mussolini. Seeming little aware of the dawning catastrophe of World War II, Collis wrote: "It had been a very pleasant evening. The company was unusual, but I have rarely been where I felt more at my ease."

During World War II, Collis continued to write books on Asia. Following the advice of Geoffrey Faber, Collis turned his attention to Asian countries other than Burma. In 1941 Collis wrote *The Great Within,* a book about China, which he described in *The Journey Up* as "a sketch of European relations with that country from A.D. 1600 to 1912." The book was reviewed favorably by Harold Acton in *The Listener* (December 1941). Though Collis had never studied Chinese history nor its language, he was encouraged by the reviews and the sales of this book to write several more books on China, a decision that supports Edward Said's claim in *Orientalism* (1978) that people who study the so-called Orient do not always have intimate knowledge of Asian cultures.

During the war Burma came to international attention as the Japanese and the Allies battled to control it. In response to this situation Collis produced *The Burmese Scene,* a superficial sixty-page gallop through the history of Burma. Written in a jingoistic tone, the book ends with a last hurrah for the British in Burma: "I believe that when Wingate came out of Burma in his battered pith helmet, with his shirt in ribbons, he had scored the first victory for Britain against the Japs." To take advantage of the general interest in Burma, Collis also published *The Land of the Great Image* (1943), a historical account of Friar Manrique, a Portuguese Augustinian, and his travels in the Arakan (Rakhine) state of Burma. The book provides some colorful background information on Portuguese exploits in India and their settlements in Goa. As with Collis's first book, *Siamese White*, the style is adequate but uninspiring.

In 1952 and 1953 Collis produced *The Journey Outward* and *Into Hidden Burma,* autobiographies that cover his childhood in Dublin, his student years at Rugby and Oxford, and his civil-service years. Also the author of biographies, Collis was most successful in writing his own life. The Burma he portrayed is a land of enchantment and ancient history. These books are imbued with a sense of nostalgia and irrevocable loss that one does not detect as much in *Lords of the Sunset.* Here is a typical description from *Into Hidden Burma:*

> Kyaukpyu struck me at once as a beautiful place. First you saw a long beach of firm sand and shells with the open sea breaking on it in fresh little waves. Standing

> close to the water's edge was the deputy commissioner's house, a large two-story building, with a row of tall casuarinas beside it, the red wood trees which look like pines but are unrelated to that family. They are found on these coasts everywhere, and the sea breeze makes a perpetual music in their needles.

Collis was genuinely enchanted by the simplicity of the Burmese countryside and the people, writing, "They had never seen an aeroplane, there was not one motor-car in the place, no one had even a bicycle or a gramophone." Collis was aware of the paradox of the colonial culture: gradually introduced to the modern world through the British administration, these people began to desire the "novelties of the modern world."

During his last posting at Mergui, Collis consoled himself by collecting artifacts and antique porcelain pieces dug up in the area. This interest in collecting was the beginning of Collis's secondary career as an expert on Asian ceramic art, a subject on which he lectured in the 1930s. Though the place was isolated from the European communities, Collis appreciated its beauty, describing it with affection in *Into Hidden Burma:*

> I sat in the upper veranda of the residence and looked westwards into the great bay. The house stood on a ridge over the port, a bluff of one hundred and fifty feet that rose abruptly from the stretch of flat between the ridge's foot and the sea. On the flat immediately below the house . . . were the port buildings, opening inwards on a little square where stood an ancient banyan tree, covered with ferns and other growths.

Collis continued writing into his eighty-first year, when he published his last memoir, *The Journey Up* (1970). In this book Collis's position regarding British colonial history in Asia, and especially in Burma, remains unresolved. He was understandably proud of the tradition of the India Civil Service, which recruited "men of first-class education," usually graduates of Oxford or Cambridge. Yet he seemed unaware that this "first-class education" was not always sufficient to help these civil servants understand Asian cultures. He was ambiguous toward the civil-service career. On the one hand a civil servant was "cut off from the world of ideas" and became dull. On the other hand he became committed to his "mission in life to take care of and instruct a backward oriental people." Collis's comments on a civil servant's restricted mentality is supported by other colonial accounts, such as Leonard Woolf's *Growing* (1962). The idea that the "backward oriental people" are the white man's burden and charge has little acceptance in a postcolonial and postimperial age.

The first half of the twentieth century produced a plethora of British travel (and colonial) literature. Collis's works belong to this general category, but they differ from the Southeast Asian writings of W. Somerset Maugham and Joseph Conrad, for example, in one specific instance. Collis, though not fluent in everyday Burmese, could understand the language superficially. He had worked with various Burmese ethnic groups and lived in the country for almost twenty years. His records are more complex and, as much as his official position allowed, more accurate observations of Burmese scenes than Maugham's travel writing or Conrad's fiction. Collis's criticisms of narrow-mindedness and racial injustice in British colonial culture are valuable commentaries on the last decades of the colonial era in Asia. Of course, accuracy does not always make for exciting literature. Collis's books on Burma are not literary gems, but they provide a distinctive view of the colonial history of an Asian country not much discussed in postcolonial studies. Maurice Collis deserves more than a footnote in the history of travel and colonial literature.

Norman Douglas

(8 December 1868 – 7 February 1952)

Jeffrey Gray
Seton Hall University

See also the Douglas entry in *DLB 34: British Novelists, 1890–1939: Traditionalists.*

Norman Douglas, 1892

BOOKS: *On the Herpetology of the Grand Duchy of Baden* (London: Printed by Adams Brothers, 1894);

Report on the Pumice Stone Industry of the Lipari Islands, British Foreign Office, Miscellaneous Series, no. 378, Reports on Subjects of General and Commercial Interest (London: Printed for Her Majesty's Stationery Office by Harrison & Sons, 1895);

Unprofessional Tales, by Douglas and Elsa FitzGibbon, as Normyx (London: Unwin, 1901);

The Blue Grotto and Its Literature, part 1 of *Materials for a Description of Capri* (London: Printed by Adams Brothers, 1904);

The Forestal Conditions of Capri, part 2 of *Materials for a Description of Capri* (London: Printed by Adams Brothers, 1904);

Fabio Giordano's Relation of Capri, part 3 of *Materials for a Description of Capri* (Naples: Printed by Luigi Pierro, 1906);

Three Monographs ["The Lost Literature of Capri," "Tiberius" and "Saracens and Corsairs in Capri"], parts 4, 5, and 6 of *Materials for a Description of Capri* (Naples: Printed by Luigi Pierro, 1906);

The Life of the Venerable Suor Serafina di Dio, part 7 of *Materials for a Description of Capri* (London: Printed by Dunn & Duncan, 1907);

Some Antiquarian Notes, part 8 of *Materials for a Description of Capri* (Naples: R. Tipographia Francesco Giannini & Figli, 1907);

Siren Land (London: Dent / New York: Dutton, 1911; revised edition, London: Secker, 1923);

Fountains in the Sand: Rambles Among the Oases of Tunisia (London: Secker, 1912; New York: Pott, 1912);

Disjecta Membra, part 9 of *Materials for a Description of Capri* (London: Printed by Dunn & Duncan, 1915);

Old Calabria (London: Secker, 1915; Boston & New York: Houghton Mifflin, 1915);

Index, part 10 of *Materials for a Description of Capri* (London: Printed by Dunn & Duncan, 1915);

London Street Games (London: St. Catherine Press, 1916; revised and enlarged edition, London: Chatto & Windus, 1931);

South Wind (London: Secker, 1917; New York: Dodd, Mead, 1918);

They Went (London: Chapman & Hall, 1920; New York: Dodd, Mead, 1921);

Alone (London: Chapman & Hall, 1921; New York: McBride, 1922);

Together (London: Chapman & Hall, 1923; New York: McBride, 1923);

D. H. Lawrence and Maurice Magnus: A Plea for Better Manners (Florence: Privately printed, 1925);

Experiments (Florence: Privately printed, 1925; New York: McBride, 1925; London: Chapman & Hall, 1925);

Birds and Beasts of the Greek Anthology (Florence: Privately printed, 1927; London: Chapman & Hall, 1928; New York: Cape & Smith, 1929);

In the Beginning (Florence: Privately printed, 1927; New York: Day, 1928; London: Chatto & Windus, 1928);

Some Limericks Collected for the Use of Students, & Ensplendour'd with Introduction, Geographical Index, and with Notes Explanatory and Critical (Florence: Privately printed, 1928; New York: Privately printed, 1928);

Nerinda (Florence: Orioli, 1929; New York: Day, 1929);

One Day (Chapelle-Réanville, France: Hours Press, 1929);

How About Europe? Some Footnotes on East and West (Florence: Privately printed, 1929); republished as *Good-bye to Western Culture: Some Footnotes on East and West* (New York & London: Harper, 1930); published again as *How About Europe? Some Footnotes on East and West* (London: Chatto & Windus, 1930);

Paneros (Florence: Privately printed, 1930); republished as *Paneros: Some Words on Aphrodisiacs and the Like* (London: Chatto & Windus, 1931; New York: McBride, 1932);

Summer Islands: Ischia and Ponza (London: Harmsworth, 1931; New York: Colophon, 1931);

Looking Back: An Autobiographical Excursion (2 volumes, London: Chatto & Windus, 1933; 1 volume, New York: Harcourt, Brace, 1933);

An Almanac (Lisbon: Privately printed, 1941; London: Chatto & Windus / Secker & Warburg, 1945);

Late Harvest (London: Drummond, 1946);

Footnote on Capri (London: Sidgwick & Jackson, 1952);

Venus in the Kitchen or Love's Cookery Book, as Pilaff Bey (London: Heinemann, 1952; New York: Viking, 1953).

Collections: *Three of Them* (London: Chatto & Windus, 1930)–comprises *One Day, Nerinda,* and *On the Herpetology of the Grand Duchy of Baden*;

Capri: Materials for a Description of the Island, parts 1–10 of *Materials for a Description of Capri* (Florence: Orioli, 1930);

Norman Douglas: A Selection from His Works, edited by D. M. Low (London: Chatto & Windus, 1955).

OTHER: A. J. Olsen, *The Beaver in Norway,* translated by Douglas (London: West, Newman, 1895);

John Gaston de Medici, *The Last of the Medici,* translated by Harold Acton, with an introduction by Douglas (Florence: Privately printed, 1930).

SELECTED PERIODICAL PUBLICATIONS–UNCOLLECTED: "Zur Fauna Santorius," *Zoologischen Anzeiger* (12 December 1892): 453–455;

"Contributions to an Avifauna of Baden," *Zoologist* (May 1894): 166–177;

"On the Darwinian Hypothesis of Sexual Selection," *Natural Science,* 7 (November 1895): 326–332; (December 1895): 398–406.

Norman Douglas wrote scientific monographs, memoirs, polemics, novels, a collection of obscene limericks, and even an aphrodisiac cookbook, but he is best known as a travel writer. He spent more than half his life in Italy, and it was chiefly as an interpreter of southern Italy that he achieved renown in England, where his work ranks with that of Charles Doughty, T. E. Lawrence, and D. H. Lawrence. Douglas virtually invented the modern travel book, as a portmanteau genre whose themes of leisure and unconstrained pleasure are reflected in a loose, digressive construction. In America his reputation rests on his novel *South Wind* (1917), which made expatriate life in Europe irresistible to a large audience of young readers impatient with life at home. In this regard Douglas may be credited with having helped give birth to the "lost generation."

George Norman Douglass was born on 8 December 1868 at Falkenhorst, the family home at Thüringen, in the Vorarlberg state of Austria. (He later dropped his first name and the final *s*.) He was the third son of a Scottish father, John Sholto Douglass, fifteenth Laird of Tilquhillie, who owned cotton mills in the Vorarlberg. Douglas's mother, Vanda von Poellnitz, was half Scot, half German; her father was a baron, and her mother was the daughter of James Ochoncar Forbes, seventeenth Lord Forbes, premier baron of Scotland. The Douglass family seat in Scotland was Tilquhillie Castle, near Banchory, Aberdeen, which Douglas first saw at the age of six, after the death of his father in a September 1874 hunting accident. Because he intensely disliked his English school at Uppingham, Douglas was sent to the gymnasium at Karlsruhe, Germany, in 1883, where he received a scientific education and became an excellent linguist. He was bilingual

Villa Maya, the house overlooking the Bay of Naples that Douglas bought in 1896

in English and German and became fluent in Russian, French, and Italian.

Douglas joined the British Foreign Office in 1893, and the following year he was posted to the British Embassy in Saint Petersburg, where he served first as attaché and then as third secretary. In 1896, on receiving an inheritance, he resigned from the Foreign Office, bought the Villa Maya on Posilipo, above the Bay of Naples, and traveled around Europe and to India. On 25 June 1898 he married his first cousin, Elsa FitzGibbon. The couple had two sons, Louis Archibald (born in 1899) and Robert Sholto (born in 1902). They were divorced in 1903, at about the time Douglas moved to Capri, where his love of the Mediterranean began. He lived and traveled extravagantly, running through his money. As a result, from 1907 onward, he earned his living by writing.

Douglas wrote not merely about travel but about the philosophy of travel. His books recommended a way of life, an attitude toward the physical world, and a kind of ideal traveler's subjectivity. The traveler-writer for Douglas is first of all an aristocrat, a man (always a man) above politics and prejudices, a law unto himself; he is both aesthete and gourmand, an unabashed critic of home and abroad, a sensualist with little use for idealism or otherworldliness, whether in the form of Christianity, socialism, or democracy. Indeed he is one who sees all creeds as deplorable declensions from a serene and sunlit antiquity.

In his book *Experiments* (1925), while praising Charles Doughty's *Travels in Arabia Deserta* (1888), Douglas set out the desiderata of a "good" travel book:

> It seems to me that the reader of a good travel-book is entitled not only to an exterior voyage, to descriptions of scenery and so forth, but to an interior, a sentimental or temperamental voyage, which takes place side by side with that outer one; and that the ideal book of this kind offers us, indeed, a triple opportunity of exploration–abroad, into the author's brain, and into our own.

Books of this kind were no longer likely to be written, thought Douglas, because travelers whose brains were worth exploring had, apart from himself, disappeared. Voyages were once costly undertakings; travelers were gentlemen-scholars and individualists. With D. H. Lawrence, Douglas believed that standardization, world communication, modern education, and democracy had alienated man from the land and blunted his individual edges. Precisely what made travel easier made it, for Douglas, less worthwhile. He thought that travel should be the preserve of an educated and eccentric elite, a group of which he clearly considered himself a member.

In Douglas's work one may see elitism and transgressiveness indissolubly linked. While Victorian and Edwardian society resisted eccentricity, it deplored sexual transgression even more, particularly after Oscar Wilde's imprisonment for homosexual activity in 1895. As homoerotic traveler Douglas was part of a group including Sir Richard Burton, Robert Byron, T. E. Lawrence, Lawrence Durrell, Gavin Maxwell, and many others. With T. E. Lawrence, Douglas may also be seen as fleeing northern softness for a tougher, more elemental life in the Mediterranean. Paradoxically, one finds in Douglas the celebration of both sybaritic sensuality and elemental toughness, neither of which he could find in England.

Douglas became a professional writer relatively late in life. He had already published some pamphlets about Capri at his own expense, but he was forty when his articles appeared on the English literary scene, having first circulated and won support among the London literati, including Joseph Conrad, whom Douglas had met in Capri in 1905, and Ford Madox Ford, then editor of *The English Review*. In February 1909 "The Island of Typhoëus" was published in *The English Review*. This essay about Ischia and another piece on the islands of Ponza (first published in *The English Review,* April 1913) were much later published as *Summer Islands: Ischia and Ponza* (1931). In 1909 Douglas also published "The Brigand's Forest," which became part of *Old Calabria* (1915), in the February issue of *The Cornhill Magazine,* and "Sirens" and "Tiberius" in *The English Review* (May and August).

Douglas's first travel book, *Siren Land* (1911), based on years of research on the Sorrentine Peninsula and Capri, established his characteristic style: carefully detailed descriptions, Dionysiac energy, pedantic digressions, repetitions and ellipses, and a combination of rhetorical flourish and classical restraint. Like all his books–with the arguable exception of his three novels, *South Wind* (1917), *They Went* (1920), and *In the Beginning* (1927)–*Siren Land* is discursive and haphazard, consisting of narrative and descriptive sections interlarded with essays on local winds, the character of Tiberius, caves and their legends, local wines, and other subjects. Underlying the miscellany runs Douglas's principal theme: the damage done by the Cartesian opposition between body and spirit, "the most pernicious piece of crooked thinking that ever oozed out of our poor deluded brain." Yet the criticism of Western thinking in *Siren Land* has neither the intensity nor the pervasiveness it has in Douglas's later books. In *Siren Land* the mood is serene, like the landscape it depicts, where "an azure calm, a calm of life, streams down from on high, permeating every sense with tremulous scintillations of vitality."

The first chapter of *Siren Land,* and much of the rest of the book, consists of responses to a single question: who were the Sirens? Douglas also took up this subject in his last book on Italy, *Footnote on Capri* (1952). In *Siren Land* Douglas argues that the Sirens were "vampires, demons of heat, of putrefaction, of voluptuousness, of lust" until the Greeks turned them into virginal, angelic creatures, "deodorised" and full of charm. Homer began this transformation though Homer too suggested the sirens' demonic and cannibalistic ferocity.

Douglas's scope widens to include siren lore in China, Brazil, and Chile, but the unity of the book lies in its focus on a region. Toward the end of the first chapter the reader is led to the summit of Mount San Costanzo, overlooking the Bay of Naples and the Gulf of Salerno. To the south lie the islets of the Sirens, now known as the Galli; to the west lies Capri; and Sorrento lies on the northern slope. Altogether it is "a tongue of limestone about three miles across and six long, jutting into the sea," a microscopic territory overgrown with ancient tradition, of which the Sirens are only one example.

Description in Douglas, while often offered for its own sake, is just as often tied to the theme of north-south distinctions that lies at the heart of his work. In "The Philosophy of the Blue Grotto," for example, Douglas describes the greatest tourist attraction on Capri, discovered during the wave of cavern and ruin worship that swept northern Europe during the nineteenth century. The locals, uncorrupted by the pathetic fallacy, find the grotto inconsequential. In other chapters too, Douglas praises the unsentimentality of the South, particularly the South of ancient times. For the Greeks Man was the restrainer of savagery, and Nature was the common enemy. For this reason infants were seldom portrayed in Greek art: with their convulsive movements, flat noses, and crooked legs, they represented something abortive, incomplete, and offensive. Christian art, on the other hand, idealized chil-

Douglas and his half sister, Mrs. Olaf Gulbrannson, on the island of Ischia, 1908 (photograph by Olaf Gulbrannson)

dren, expunging the simian traits and endowing them with piety or wisdom.

As with children, so with all emblems of the wild, the picturesque, the exotic: for the Greeks these popular subjects of Western art are abuses of man's higher faculties. Douglas sees this contrast of the then and now as a contrast of the best and worst, the aristocrat's perception versus the tastes of the herd. "They *will* wallow, these good folk, having, as Schopenhauer observed, 'no height from which to fall. . . .'"

The last pages of *Siren Land* celebrate the Mediterranean as the ne plus ultra of beauty in landscape, better than the North because brighter, better than the tropics because cooler. Only in the Mediterranean do the works of man stand in just relation to those of nature, each supplementing the other.

A sense of easeful drifting permeates *Siren Land* as it does many passages in Douglas–redolent of a way of life at the same time that it is suggestive of an aesthetic of the travel book as a genre in which to loiter. A cultivated idleness, for Douglas, was the best recipe for writing and living.

Douglas made his first visit to Tunisia in 1899 with his wife, Elsa, and his second alone in 1910. He had contemplated a book on Tunisia, but, as in other cases, his motive for travel was complex. He had met a Miss Iseman, had had an affair, felt he was not in the marrying mood, and thought it best to get out of Italy. The "slice of sea" that Douglas thought it best to put between himself and the young woman was that between Naples and Tunisia.

Fountains in the Sand: Rambles Among the Oases of Tunisia (1912) has not been regarded as highly as *Siren Land* or *Old Calabria* (1915); indeed, it is a different sort of book. In the books about Italy, Douglas wrote as an informed insider, knowledgeable and sympathetic. In Tunisia he saw only the ruins of Roman civilization and a once fertile country buried in sand. Instead of scholarship Douglas offered a sharp eye and a mordant wit. Instead of discoursing on antiquity he criticized the natives.

Like other travel narratives that purport to lead the reader back in time, *Fountains in the Sand* depends on a view of the native not just as underdeveloped but as incapable of development. Seeing a family crouched near a hollow rock, Douglas notices a heap of bones and imagines cannibalism. Of these "primitives of Gafsa" he singles out a woman for description:

> The wild-eyed young wench, with her dishevelled hair, ferocious bangle-ornaments, tattooings, and nondescript blue rags open at the side and revealing charms well fitted to disquiet some robust savage–what has such a creature in common with the rest of us? Not even certain raptures, misdeemed primeval; hardly more than what falls to man and beast alike.

At times the descriptions betray sympathy for people whose lives are impoverished and whose prospects are dim, but when it comes to generalizations, Douglas is unsparing. Describing the inadequacy of the Arab burnoose (or burnous), for example, Douglas draws a conclusion about the entire people: "The character of the race is summed up in that hopeless garment, which unfits the wearer for every pleasure and every duty of modern life."

In Douglas's view the Arabs lack a sense of proportion and tend to err in extremes–drunkards or teetotalers. Because all is ordained by Allah, they bear extremes of hunger or "gorge like Eskimos, like boa-constrictors. *Mektoub* [meaning "It is written"] is the intellectual burnous of the Arabs. . . ." Yet Douglas commended this fatalism a few pages earlier, contrasting it with northern neurosis and calling it "an underlying primitive sanity which we would do well to foster within us."

Douglas's response to the "backward" peoples among whom he traveled is thus deeply ambivalent. His travel writings criticize and aestheticize, loathe and envy. But he can generally be counted on to rel-

Photograph of Capri taken by Douglas from the Sorrentine Peninsula

ish natives insofar as they confirm his rejection of home. He notes with admiration that the "chief mental exercise of the Arab . . . consists in thinking how to reduce his work to a minimum" and comments that this is precisely his own ideal of life. When Douglas turns to Arab women, "the repository of all the accumulated nonsense of the race," his misogyny and slave-master mentality are obvious, but so is the mischievous desire to shock. He offers advice on the purchase of child-brides:

> As brides for a lifetime (slaves) they cost from a hundred to six hundred francs apiece; and you will do well to *abonner* yourself with the family before hand, in order to be sure of obtaining a sound article. . . . They are less nimble and amiable than the boys, and often require more beating than a European has time to give them. You can always sell them again, of course; and sometimes (into the towns) at a good profit.

Douglas relished the outrage he knew such comments would elicit. The voice–that of the bemused and unshockable outsider–anticipates Evelyn Waugh in Ethiopia twenty years later.

Douglas meditates on the foreigners in Tunisia: Jews ("their dirt does not detract from their astuteness"), Sicilians ("the cancer of Tunisia"), Maltese ("Not merely cantankerous and bigoted Arabs, but also sober, industrious, and economical"), and Corsicans ("Cave-hunting savages at heart, and enemy to every man save their own blood relations"). Yet, apparently without irony, he presents himself as a fair-minded tourist among bigoted French colonials. In *Fountains in the Sand* it is frequently not the narrator but a Frenchman who says of the Arabs, "What fools they are!" or "They're only children," sentiments of which the reader is tacitly invited to disapprove.

In spite of his aspersions on foreigners, Douglas prefers the mixture of races and cultures to the "pure-race" groups living outside of Gafsa, who seem to possess "almost undiluted, the features of the savage Neanderthal brood." As for the poverty-stricken, "They die like flies. Naturally enough; for it is not too much to say, of the poorer classes, that they eat dirt, and that only once a day."

Fountains in the Sand offers many examples of Douglas's elaborate descriptions of nature, at once sensitive, scientific, and allegorical, *paysages moralisés*:

> Contrast with the wanton blaze of green, the contorted trunks and labyrinthine shadow-meanderings of our woodlands, these palm groves, despite their frenzied exuberance, figure forth the idea of reserve and chastity; an impression which is heightened by the ethereal striving of those branchless columns, by their joyous and effective rupture of the horizontal, so different from the careworn tread of our oaks and beeches.

The conclusion of *Fountains in the Sand* examines the truism that the desert is responsible for the

Douglas at Villa Daphne, Capri, in 1912, just before he left for London to become assistant editor of The English Review

Arab mentality, that the desert (like the jungle in Conrad) "decomposes the intellectual fabric of mankind . . . into its primordial elements of ecstasy and emotionalism." Douglas argues that this belief is untrue, that Arabia and Africa were different before "these ardent shepherds appeared on the scene, with their crude and chaotic monotheism." The physical abandonment and social decay of North Africa are the work not of the desert but of "the man of Mecca. Mahomet is the desert-maker."

From 1912 to 1916 Douglas lived principally in London, working as assistant editor of *The English Review,* first under Ford Madox Ford and later under Austin Harrison. During this period, probably by the end of 1913, he finished *Old Calabria* (1915) and began work on other projects, including *South Wind.*

Old Calabria was the result of several tours through "the Sahara of Italy" by train, car, and on foot in 1907 and 1911. It is Douglas's most highly praised travel book, equal if not superior to the best of Charles Doughty and D. H. Lawrence. Its reception today would no doubt be different, given its unabashed colonialism, uncompromising Latinity, and leisurely but often weighty divagations. The casual and aimless discursiveness alone might disqualify *Old Calabria* from a late-twentieth-century appreciation.

It is helpful to see *Old Calabria* in the context of a gradual subjectivization in Douglas's work. *Siren Land,* more unified in time and place, offers landscape and history rather than self-revelation. In *Fountains in the Sand* the presence of the author is more pronounced as the reader follows the trail of his sensations, whether smoking kef or collecting flints. *Old Calabria* extends the autobiographical and subjective material. By the time of *Alone* (1921) Douglas's manner became much more relaxed and conversational, with far fewer learned digressions and with the author slipping freely in and out of autobiographical mode. Finally, in *Together* (1923) Douglas reached the opposite extreme from *Siren Land:* autobiography replaced landscape and history as the chief feature of the book though all the elements continue to be integrated. *Old Calabria* marks the midway point in this process.

Old Calabria would seem to be a collection of notes and articles Douglas had to hand at the time of writing; little effort was made to provide transition or continuity. As with virtually all his books, *Old Calabria* includes both material derived from observation and that derived from research, often alternating whole chapters of one with the other but more frequently combining the two in shorter sections within each chapter.

Douglas begins in Saracen Lucera, near the east coast, then travels to Manfredonia, moving southward through Venosa, Taranto, and Cosenza. As in *Fountains in the Sand,* there is no introduction to explain the purpose of the book. The absence is more conspicuous in *Old Calabria* since the book is much more a potpourri, with little logic or continuity of mood. A typical transition in *Old Calabria* reads, "Then my thoughts wandered to the Hohenstaufen. . . . " Apropos of nothing, Douglas begins to discuss Frederick II, Manfred, and other princes, popes, and pretenders of the thirteenth century. One rhetorical question, randomly chosen from a paragraph made entirely of them, suggests the style: "Why did Roger de Lauria not profit by his victory to insist upon the restitution of the young brothers of Beatrix, of those unhappy princes who had been confined as infants in 1266, and whose very existence seems to have faded from the memory of historians?" Such erudition is showy and pointless. It is not only from the memory of historians that these and other figures have faded.

Calabrian life, as Douglas painted it, is fierce, corrupt, and difficult. The peasants lack all sense of color, having not even a vocabulary for it. Their music is "utterly unpalatable to a civilized northerner . . . a soulless cult of rhythm." Moreover, they are humorless. A hard, penurious life accounts for these deficiencies. Unromantically and inconsistently, Douglas favors the city over the country. City dwellers, he reflects, may have "flashes of enthusiasm and self-abnegation never experienced by this shifty, retrogressive and ungenerous brood, which lives like the beasts of the field and has learnt all too much of their logic." The peasants' acceptance of fate, however, is not indifference, Douglas says; it is true philosophy. In a familiar reversal Douglas praises the virtue of the *Mektoub,* which, virtually in the same breath, he both condemned and praised in the Arabs of *Fountains in the Sand.*

Douglas's judgments are not confined to human beings; they include sunsets, mountains, whole landscapes. Occasionally the effect is wildly disproportionate. At one point, disgusted by the eucalypti, he writes of their "demoralizing aspect of precocious senility and vice, their peeling bark suggestive of unmentionable skin diseases, and that system of radication which is nothing short of a scandal on this side of the globe. . . . "

If there is a controlling idea in *Old Calabria,* it is the question of what is finally the difference between the Italians and "ourselves." In mundane matters the Italian's judgment, Douglas finds, "is apt to be turbid and perverse," but it becomes "serenely impartial" in questions of pure intelligence. The Englishman, on the other hand, is clear-sighted in practical matters but finds it hard to reason dispassionately on nonpractical subjects.

Having reduced cultural difference to such simple terms, Douglas nevertheless warns that we must rid ourselves of that "incubus of 'immutable race characters,' " noting the difference between the Englishman of George Gordon, Lord Byron's time and today and explaining, "Such differences as exist between races of men, exist only at a given moment." Thus Douglas's drive to simplify is always arrested by the irreducibility of his subject matter. That conflict between the mind and its unassimilable objects is at the heart of Douglas's writing, perhaps accounting for his purported inability to construct a plot, his limitless digression, as well as for the richness of his texts–the hundreds of scenes, histories, etymologies, and explanations–as though circumlocution and allusion might better convey the unevenness of human experience than narrative linearity.

From time to time, notably in his conclusions, Douglas offers the kind of transcendent moment for which the traveler lives. The closing paragraphs of *Old Calabria* exhibit the heightened consciousness he cherished and recommended as a way of life:

Douglas in Settignano, Italy, 1921, photographed by "René," or "Mr. R," Douglas's traveling companion in Alone *(1921) and* Together *(1923)*

> Meanwhile it is good to rest here, immovable but alert, in the breathless hush of noon. Showers of benevolent heat stream down upon this desolation, not the faintest wisp of vapour floats upon the horizon; not a sail, not a ripple, disquiets the waters. The silence can be felt. Slumber is brooding over the things of earth. . . .
>
> Such a torrid splendour, drenching a land of austerest simplicity, decomposes the mind into corresponding states of primal contentment and resilience. There arises before our phantasy a new perspective of human affairs; a suggestion of well-being, wherein the futile complexities and disharmonies of our age shall have no place. To discard these wrappings, to claim kinship with some elemental and robust archetype, lover of earth and sun–
>
> How fair they are, these moments of golden equipoise!
>
> Yes, it is good to be merged awhile into these harshly-vibrant surroundings, into the meridian glow of all things.

Such a moment, such a landscape

> brings us to the ground, where we belong; it medicines to the disease of introspection and stimulates a capacity

> which we are in danger of unlearning amid our morbid hyperborean gloom–the capacity for honest contempt: contempt of that scarecrow of a theory which would have us neglect what is earthly, tangible. What is life well lived but a blithe discarding of primordial husks, of those comfortable intangibilities that lurk about us, waiting for our weak moments?

These passages supply the unity missing in Douglas's drift of observation, musing, description, and invective. In addition this final passage confirms the impression garnered throughout *Old Calabria* that the speaker has lived deeply in this place, that its genius has permeated his vision. One sees, moreover, something of the psychology of the traveler here; "immovable," "silence," "slumber"–all suggest the calm one comes so far to find, a calm due as much to absences as to presences. The absences are "our" absences: absences of "complexities and disharmonies" associated with home, that "hyperborean" clime. One has had to get away, "to discard" that place and its sicknesses, particularly its Christian and Cartesian mind-body split ("that scarecrow of a theory"), in order to unlearn, to be cured, and to claim kinship with the Other Place, which is "elemental," "robust," "benevolent," and of "austerest simplicity."

To travel in this way is to *un*do oneself. The austerity of the land "decomposes" the mind into a state of primal simplicity. To undo oneself is to extricate oneself and then, in the other place, to surrender. The alternative metaphor is that of the shedding of husks. The passage subsumes the many descriptions and disquisitions of the book, but it also transcends them. One hears little of Douglas the aristocratic, egoistic, scholarly epicure whose foremost demand is the satisfaction of appetites.

Most of Douglas's commentators have considered *Old Calabria* to be his masterpiece; the popular preference, however, has always been *South Wind,* the first and by far the best of his three novels. Its setting and theme were suggested to Douglas by Joseph Conrad. Often called a minor classic, *South Wind* is a travel book disguised as a conversational novel in the manner of Thomas Love Peacock. It has the same loose structure as Douglas's nonfiction travel books, the same satyr's paean to pleasure, the same indictment of progress and the cold climates, and the same vivid Italian scenes. The book appealed to American "Jazz Age" readers, who saw it as an invitation to live the eccentric expatriate life, to identify with the cosmopolitan members of a "lost generation" settled on an ancient Mediterranean island.

As *South Wind* was taking shape, Douglas experienced one of the most trying moments of his life. In October 1916 he was arrested and jailed in London on charges of child molestation. The initial charge concerned a boy he had picked up at the Natural History Museum and taken to his apartment; the boy afterward went to his schoolmaster, who signed the charges. Parents of two other boys brought similar charges, but these were dismissed on the grounds that Douglas had been in Capri at the time, as his passport showed. Two friends stood bail, but most of Douglas's circle, including Joseph Conrad, abandoned him. Discharged, without money, and awaiting trial on the one serious count, Douglas obtained visas to France and Italy and set off from England in January 1917. He was forty-eight years old and virtually penniless. Once in Capri, he corresponded with his publisher and saw *South Wind* through to publication in June 1917. The book was an immediate success.

Set on the island of Nepenthe–an idealized version of Capri–the plot of *South Wind* accommodates the digressions–essays on topography, mineralogy, customs, flora, and fauna–characteristic of all of Douglas's writing, and it bears the weight of Douglas's favorite theme: the freedom of the "other" country, the character of the place that allows one, or induces one, to behave intuitively. Like the Marabar Caves in E. M. Forster's *A Passage to India* (1924), the sirocco wind that haunts Nepenthe liberates or even unhinges the tourists who visit, particularly the protagonist, an Anglican bishop whose "moral pores" are opened by the sunny and hedonistic atmosphere. After only twelve days on the island the bishop watches his cousin throw her husband over a cliff and is able to pardon, even approve of, the crime.

Douglas's mouthpiece in the novel is the expatriate Mr. Keith, who not only expounds Douglas's pagan philosophy but also helps him settle his real-life score with the British police. Mr. Keith asks the bishop, "How would you like to be haled before a Court of Law for some ridiculous trifle, which became a crime only because it used to be a sin, and became a sin only because some dyspeptic or impotent old antediluvian was envious of his neighbour's pleasure?"

As a result of *South Wind,* Douglas became a living symbol of the pagan expatriate in revolt against Victorian moral standards. He also became a model for characters in other novels–James Argyle in D. H. Lawrence's *Aaron's Rod* (1922) and Scrogan in Aldous Huxley's *Crome Yellow* (1921) among them. Graham Greene once remarked, "My generation was brought up on *South Wind.*"

Douglas's other two novels, having little to do with the travel genre, warrant only brief men-

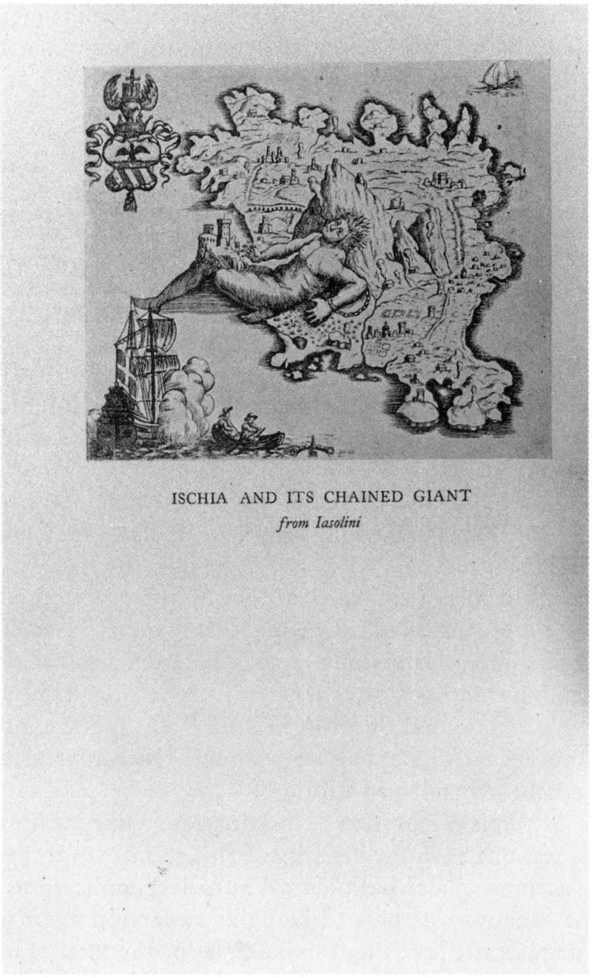

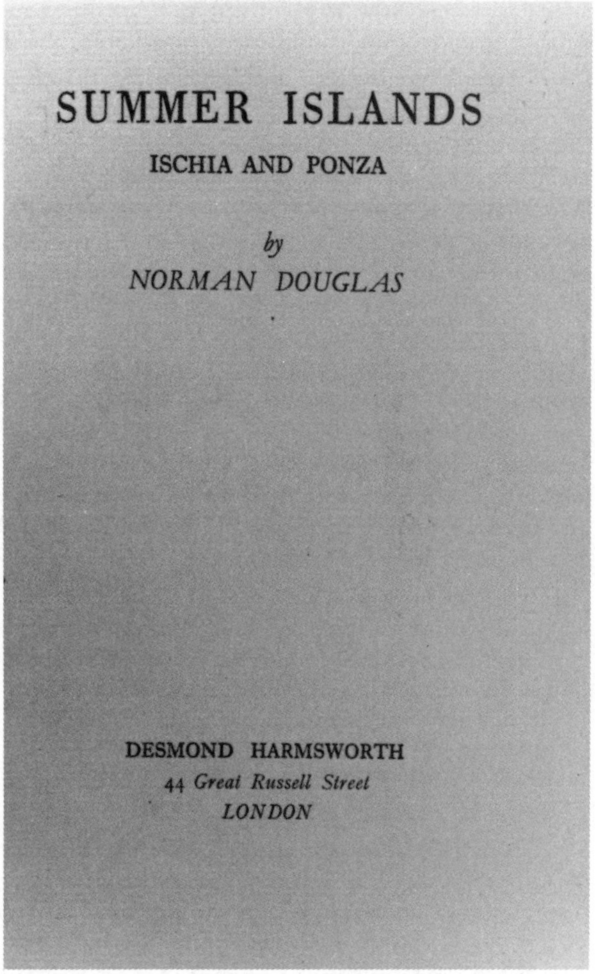
SUMMER ISLANDS

ISCHIA AND PONZA

by

NORMAN DOUGLAS

DESMOND HARMSWORTH

44 *Great Russell Street*

LONDON

Frontispiece and title page for the 1931 book in which Douglas collected two of the travel essays he published in The English Review *during 1909–1913*

tion. *They Went* (1920) is, in spite of its title, not a travel book but a fable set in a mythical kingdom of princesses, magic spells, dwarfs, and magicians. Neither *They Went* nor *In the Beginning* (1927) has the realism, the philosophy, or the energy of *South Wind,* nor were they widely read or well received.

In 1919 Douglas settled in Florence, which became his home for the next twenty years. In the early 1920s he met Giuseppi "Pino" Orioli, a well-liked publisher with whom he became close. The two lived in adjoining apartments in Florence and dined and toured together. As a joint publishing venture they began the Lugarno series, publishing the work of Somerset Maugham, Richard Aldington, D. H. Lawrence, and other authors thought too risky for conventional publishers.

Alone (1921) was Douglas's favorite among his travel books. Written in 1917 and titled "Sunshine" in manuscript, the book recounts "the months when, at the age of fifty, I exhaled the last breaths of an inconstant youth by the wayside of a beaten track in Italy," as Douglas wrote in *Late Harvest* (1946).

The only reference in *Alone* to its title lies in a footnote on the last page. The narrator's description of an afternoon spent with friends in a hazel grove–drinking, eating, slumbering, and joking–is followed by this note: "The title *Alone* strikes me, on reflection, as rather an inapt one for this volume. Let it stand!" On the penultimate page Douglas mentioned for the first time "my companion," his young friend Eric, without naming or describing him.

Alone sets travel in the context of duty and obligation. Douglas recounts several attempts to serve his country in World War I, waiting in line at the Board of Trade Labour Emergency Bureau, the War Office, and the Foreign Office. After months of interviews, forms, and misdirections, the incident with the young boy in 1916, "the God-sent little accident, the result of sheer boredom," sent him to the

Mediterranean, where, according to *Alone,* he abandoned further thoughts of service to country.

Alone is a collection of observations of Italian customs, cuisine, and geography interspersed with clever conversations that show Douglas lording over his inferiors. There is virtually no narrative. The chapters "Siena," "Pisa," "and Viareggio" concern his neighbor "O," "who was carried out of the train at this very [Pisa] station, dead, because he refused to follow my advice." "O" was a decadent aristocrat with a shooting lodge in the Alps, who indulged perverse desires, heaped abuse on his servants, and died of excess. Among many grotesque anecdotes, one stands out. On receiving a telegram bearing a single word, "Rats," Douglas would ride down to O's place for a grand day of rat hunting in the fields. One day they gave a huge rat to an old sow to eat:

> She ate it as you would eat a pear. She engulfed the corpse methodically, beginning at the head, working her way through breast and entrails while her chops dripped with gore, and ending with the tail, which gave some little trouble to masticate, on account of its length and tenuity. Altogether, decidedly good sport. . . .

It is the last line, of course, that identifies the writing as Douglas's. Whether his taste for the gory and macabre was feigned or genuine is difficult to know, but certainly there are many instances of it. Much later, when Douglas learned that D. H. Lawrence's remains were to be exhumed in the south of France to be shipped to Taos, New Mexico, Douglas wrote to his "Auntie" (Martha Harriet Gordon Crotch): "Now do tell me more–about bones and skull, etc. I love macabre details. . . . Do send those photos of the exhumation, and I shall be delighted to pay for them."

"Rome" describes an encounter with an English tourist in a restaurant, who comments, "I don't care what I eat." Douglas uses this remark to expand on a favorite set of topics: food, taste, cultivation. Douglas warns, "Beware of gross feeders. They are a menace to their fellow creatures. Will they not act, on occasion, even as they feed? Assuredly they will." (One might note the application of these sentences to Douglas himself: his documented selfishness at the table, his secretiveness regarding good places to eat, his finicky tastes and impatience with waiters and cooks, and his stinginess when it came to paying the bill.)

Douglas's chapters on Rome bring him to a central question of travel. One travels to Italy, he suggests, to be in contact with beauty and antiquity, with physical well-being, sunshine, and a freer mode of self-expression. But, more important, one comes to Italy to be able to remember and reconstruct at a distance. This aim seems to Douglas the chief purpose of travel:

> For a haze of oblivion is formed by a lapse of time and space; a kindly haze which obliterates the thousand fretting annoyances wherewith the traveller's path in every country is bestrewn. He forgets them; forgets that weltering ocean of unpleasantness and remembers only its sporadic islets–those moments of calm delight or fiercer joy which he would fain hold fast for ever.

For a moment Douglas imagines seeing England the same way, as a tourist. How attractive it would seem, provided one knew for certain that one would never have to live there. In such a case, "What lovely things one could say about England, in Timbuktu!"

In *Alone* Douglas describes his writing method as a dredging up of fragments from memory–a voice or glimpse of landscape–and letting each detail elicit another until a sort of skeleton is constructed, after which imagination provides the flesh, blood, and movement. "Imagination–why not? One suppresses much; why not add a little?"

This celebration of imagination, while it raises questions as to the veracity of Douglas's own travel "accounts," also has political-historical implications. It functions as part of Douglas's reaction against democratic leveling, as nostalgia for the virtues of aristocracy, erudition, taste, and individualism. For Douglas "imagination" is the faculty of the "gentleman."

Alone ends with an image of Douglas's remembered countrymen, "taking themselves seriously and rushing about, haggard and careworn, like those sagacious ants that scurry hither and thither, and stare into each others' faces with a kind of desperate imbecility. . . . " Douglas does not complete the analogy by presenting himself as the irresponsible grasshopper, but his refusal to acknowledge or accept obligation renders the comparison implicit: "As for ourselves, we took our ease. We ate and drank, we slumbered awhile, then joked and frolicked for five hours on end, or possibly six. I kept no count of what we said nor how the time flew by." Keeping no count is as much an assertion of independence as it is a praise of idleness and a rejection of an age in which the quantitative is prized.

Douglas's friends often said that each of his books was inspired by a particular love affair. *South Wind* owed a debt to several companions, *Siren Land* to a boy named Amitrano, *Old Calabria* to Eric, and both *Alone* and *Together* (1923) to René. René, called "Mr. R.," figures more prominently in *Together* than

Ian Greenlees, Pino Orioli, Douglas, and Osbert Sitwell in Florence, 1933

in *Alone,* where he goes virtually unmentioned. "To René also, and above all, is due the leisurely and attractive ease, the wistfulness and joy, the concentrated homogeneous atmosphere of reminiscence in *Together,*" wrote Douglas.

Together, the result of two visits to the Vorarlberg with René in 1921 and 1922, occupies a category of its own among Douglas's travel books. While it explores a region and its history, geology, botany, zoology, and sociology in Douglas's usual manner, the book is also an exploration of the author's childhood. It expresses three kinds of love–for his companion, for the sights and sounds of the journey, and for the personal past and its associations. The mixture of observation with autobiographical recollection is not a complete blend, as it was in *Alone,* but rather a folding-in. As René and Douglas hike through the province, the memories are selective: there is nothing about Douglas's mother or her second husband but much about his father and grandfathers, his sister and governess, and various local people.

The book begins with Douglas in the Alpine village of his childhood, savoring a respite from the heat of the South. Even at "home," travel functions as escape: *from* one's native land or *to* that native land from one's adopted home. Like Marcel Proust's madeleine, the view of the landscape from the window of Douglas's childhood room prompts a flood of memories–the aurora borealis, the sound of the church bells, the thrill of sliding down the hills on a fir branch, the tastes of his favorite dishes. Douglas is, he says, "ghost-hunting": wherever he goes, the memories,

Douglas and two Arab boys at Kaabi Spring in Tunisia, 1938

whether of legend or of childhood, rise up like steam.

"Gamsboden" describes their visit to the spot where Douglas's father fell to his death while chamois hunting. Douglas explains to René the varieties of shale by the cliff and the ability of the chamois to leap onto this shale without plunging to their deaths. His father fell at least a thousand feet from this cliff; "there was nothing about him that was not shattered: his gun, his watch, even his alpenstock."

"Blumenegg" is a chapter of praise for a twelfth-century castle in the forest. Lying with René on the sun-warmed moss of the castle floor, Douglas muses on other castle ruins of Europe, now polluted by tourists. Southern ruins are impressive, he says, but bleak; their ravages are naked and revealed. Here the ravages are healed; trees and moss adorn the ruins so that a refined tonality pervades the site. Of course, these remarks contradict Douglas's avowed preference, in *Siren Land* and elsewhere, for the Mediterranean, where man's ruins are in harmony with nature, neither crushed under its cold and rain as in the North nor scorched by it as in the tropics.

Yet in such passages the reader sees Douglas at his most representative, showing the love of nature over civilization *and* the love of ancient remnants and relics, showing, in other words, the place of tradition in nature and vice versa. Moreover, the real beauty of Blumenegg is its remoteness. It exists in a sort of enchanted shadow, to be appreciated only by the initiated.

In "Rosenegg," passing another twelfth-century castle ruin, Douglas begins to discuss the stones to be found in the area, and an odd memory emerges: passing once below this tower and hearing an unusual sound, he discovered its source to be a putrid stag, "so alive with worms as to make itself heard."

The image, at once naturalistic and surrealistic, shocks the reader. The aesthete of decay, fascinated by what Charles Baudelaire called "the phosphorescence of putrescence," is combined in Douglas with a robust vigor of health and appetite unknown among the Symbolists, whose self-definition was frailty and exquisite sensibility.

At several points in *Together* Douglas expresses fascination for *dorftrottels,* or idiots, "of the genuine Alpine breed." Many come from Raffel, "fertile mother of idiots, because everybody marries into his own family there." Yet the modern idiots–like most things modern– prove to be a disappointment. They can sew and knit, chop wood, even talk: a mediocre idiocy when compared to the truly mad of childhood memory, whom he describes in loving detail.

Toward the end of *Together* Douglas and René come on a marshy tract full of gentians. Douglas isolates this memory out of a flood of impressions from the trip. He has allowed himself and René to become lost because "in so doing, you never fail to see something, however insignificant, which you never saw before."

> They shot up from the wet moss–a blaze of the most perfect blue on earth. Theirs was not a steady light, but shimmering and playful, and of a luster so intense that no African sky, no sapphire could have rivaled it. I plucked one of these portentous flowers. It measured nearly the length of my walking-stick and was alive with

> color from end to end. Conceive a hundred thousand of them, all huddled together among those somber trees. We seemed to be looking down into a lake of blue fire.
>
> Here, I think, is a memory to cherish; a vision to carry away into other lands.

The tone of this passage is typical of *Together,* a book that looks wistfully at things left undone, hills unclimbed, ruins unvisited, delicacies untasted, but concludes, "No matter. We have had a breath of fresh air together."

Experiments (1925) is a collection of book reviews, short stories in the manner of Edgar Allan Poe, and occasional pieces. Its first chapter, "Arabia Deserta," merits attention in a study of Douglas's travel writing. In this chapter he reviews two travel books, one English and one French: Charles Doughty's *Travels in Arabia Deserta,* republished in 1921 with an introduction by T. E. Lawrence, and *Marrakech* (1920) by the brothers Jérôme and Jean Tharaud. Reviewing *Marrakech* allows Douglas to expatiate on the mediocrity of the French travel book in general and, by extension, the inferiority of the French language and finally the limitations of the French themselves: "Your Gaul is a centripetal fellow, a bad nomad. His affinities with foreign folk are only skin-deep–aesthetic rather than constitutional."

To these effete and impersonal French writers, Douglas contrasts the English traveler Charles Doughty, in whom he finds an intimacy distinctively Anglo-Saxon. Doughty's tough, unpolished, even harsh style suits the "crudeness of Arabian character and landscape." Although Douglas, like many other readers, finds *Travels in Arabia Deserta* to be oppressively long and weighty, "nothing short of eleven hundred pages could do justice to this toilsome, nightmarish epic." It is Doughty's character that unifies the descriptions, folklore, statistics, and history. Character allows the reader to share in the interior voyage, which, in a worthwhile travel narrative, must parallel the exterior one. Doughty is rich in character; Palgrave, who traveled the same regions, is not; and Sir Richard Burton is "A driving force void of savour or distinction; drabness *in excelsis;* a glorified Blue Book."

Douglas's disapproval of French travel writing suggests his other criterion for the travel book: its *Englishness.* Comfortable, verdant England, with its "sense of immemorial tranquillity," is the ideal place in which to "conjure up visions of the traveller's marches under the flaming sky and of all his other hazards in a land of hunger and blood and desolation!" Yet Douglas, though English, is not the same kind of traveler as Doughty, he notes: "Never could I have attained to his infinite capacity of suffering fools gladly. . . . Can there be a greater torture of mind than to travel month after month among peevishly ferocious bigots, repressing an altogether praiseworthy inclination to laugh at them or hit them on the head?"

From his home in Florence, Douglas made many journeys during the 1920s and 1930s–to Austria, France and Monte Carlo, Tunisia, India, Lebanon, Tanganyika, other parts of Italy, and Greece. *One Day* (1929) is the result of a gift of three hundred pounds from the Greek government for a book about Greece. The government hoped for a book written in the manner of the much-admired *Old Calabria,* but when Douglas arrived in Athens, he realized the task would take him years. Moreover, his Greek was rusty from disuse. The project was abandoned in favor of a brief account of a day's visit to some local sites, chiefly around Athens. If not an *"Old Hellas,"* at least, Douglas felt, *One Day* was full of love of Greece, reverence for its traditions, and "shrewd and suggestive observations."

In 1929 Douglas published *How About Europe? Some Footnotes on East and West,* a work best described as a metatravel book. The book was written as a response to Katherine Mayo's *Mother India* (1927), which Douglas found unfairly critical of India. If one is going to scrutinize India's faults, he asked, how about Europe? The book consists of comments scrawled in the margins of *Mother India,* answering Mayo's charges regarding Indian illiteracy, polygamy, and the abuse of women. In each case Douglas shows Europe at least as corrupt as India, if not more so.

Douglas's critique of the West as the source of sin, corruption, and disease indicates his disillusionment as well as his romanticism. Over the East, Douglas writes, "The White Man creeps . . . like some foul skin disease, eating away the bloom of their features." Why are Westerners so evil, so sad, and so ferocious? Douglas finds the answer in Roman vulgarity and imperialism and the welcome Romans gave to "imported pinchbeck like Christianity." Douglas notes, as the one example of reverse pollution, that this Christianity came from the East. The legacies of the West include state idolatry, public education, monotony, and an architecture that "settled upon the whole world like a frost, that chilled all indigenous and divergent blossoming. Everything stereotyped and conventionalized!"

The book offers no solutions to the problems of either East or West. In Douglas's view nothing is going to change. The world grows stupider, he asserted, and, anyway, he was no reformer.

Douglas on Capri, 1947

Rather, he says, apparently echoing Walt Whitman, "I observe, and pass on."

By the 1930s Douglas was in his sixties and no longer willing to involve himself in long writing projects. In 1937 it seemed wise to leave Italy, where fascist suspicion of foreigners, particularly the English, had become heightened. As with the scandal that had forced him to leave England in 1917, there was another reason for flight. He had been sheltering a ten-and-one-half-year-old girl named Renata in his flat in Florence ("I am . . . taking to girls again," he confided to his friend Bryher). Given his high profile and the puritanism of the fascist regime, Douglas's arrangement was imprudent. Neighbors complained, and the authorities intervened. Douglas at the age of sixty-eight was again obliged to "hop it," with only his rucksack. The girl was found to be a virgin, and Douglas lost no friends this time; indeed, friends seemed relieved to find the incident had involved a member of the opposite sex.

Douglas moved to the south of France, living in Vence and Antibes and taking occasional trips, including one to North Africa with his friend Nancy Cunard. In May and June 1940 France fell to the Germans. No one living in France could receive money from England; with shortages of food and other necessities life became difficult. By the end of the year he had obtained visas to Spain and Portugal. In February 1941 he moved to Portugal, where he stayed with friends, first in the countryside, then in Lisbon. Finally, at a loss how to survive, he returned to London in January 1942.

Douglas returned to an England of blackouts, shortages, and bombing, a different kind of "siren land." Many of his friends were gone, and though Nancy Cunard provided camaraderie, much of his time was spent alone. He had lost weight and suffered from rheumatism. In his mid seventies, he could not easily find work. He scraped together a living giving language lessons, but he realized he had to get back to Italy. He proposed to go to Paris, then Antibes to pick up books and papers, then to Naples, where friends would put him up "while I look in the neighbourhood for some convenient hole in which to die when the time comes." The story goes that when the interviewer at the Italian embassy asked Douglas whether he wanted to go back to live in Italy, Douglas responded, "No–I want to go back to die there." The embassy official was so moved that he readily granted permission to travel.

In 1946 Douglas returned to Capri, where he stayed until the end of his life. He was made an honorary citizen of that island, the only Englishman ever to have received the distinction. Douglas worried only about money and health. His tiny fixed income could not match postwar inflation in Capri. *Late Harvest* (1946) had just come out, and Douglas was disappointed with its small print and inferior paper. While it made little impact, the book is interesting for its insights into the background of Douglas's principal earlier books.

Late Harvest looks over a topography not of personages or even experiences but of books, Douglas's own. It is also consistent with those books in its humanistic and elegiac tone. Its first chapter offers the only extensive discussion of homosexuality in Douglas's writings. Referring to the "Hellenism" popular among nineteenth-century literary and artistic circles in Germany, Douglas praises the candor of these men who gloried in being "Greeks." By contrast he points to recent articles in London newspapers proposing to cure the "disease" of homosexuality. Douglas argues that homosexuals have always existed, contributing much of beauty and use to mankind. He places the blame for their oppression on Christianity: "What calls for treatment is not so

Douglas and Nancy Cunard, October 1949

much homosexuality as the diseased attitude adopted towards it in non-Latin countries. This attitude is the outcome of Judaeo-Christian teaching, as interpreted by Puritanism."

Douglas's references to women also deserve comment. There are many remarks throughout Douglas's books such as that in *Late Harvest,* where he refers to "our wives and mistresses," implying that only men are reading his book. Perhaps he is guilty merely of being a man of his time, in thinking of writing and reading as principally male domains. *Some Limericks* (1928), as he says in the introduction to that book, was written for the "Dirty-Minded *Elect,*" by which he meant "gentlemen," who could be relied on to confine their smutty tastes to the smoking room or club. Women were not invited, were indeed meant to be protected from such ideas.

Douglas's final travel book, *Footnote on Capri* (1952), appeared posthumously in the year of his death. It comprises forty pages of prose interspersed with photographs of Capri and Anacapri, the two principal towns on the island. The "footnote" of the title is a reminder of Douglas's penchant for the partial and the unfinished. Yet even in this small book Douglas tells his familiar story of the defacement, if not the erasure, of the old and the beautiful. One is reminded of Claude Lévi-Strauss's complaint in *Tristes Tropiques* (1925): "The first thing we see as we travel round the world is our own filth, thrown into the face of mankind." One photograph bears the caption "Imperial masonry is defaced by modern ironwork on the ruins of Tiberius' villa"; another says, "Fragments of mosaic and reticulated masonry suggest the former richness of this corridor." Yet most of the photographs are breathtaking views of the cliffs and sea around Capri, the monasteries, lighthouses, medieval forts, megalithic walls, and some local inhabitants.

The actual text, the forty-page "footnote," which Douglas introduces as "just a glimpse, a rapid *coup d'oeil,*" is chiefly a history of the island, where Douglas first landed on 26 March 1888. Since Capri–disguised as "Nepenthe"–is a backdrop for foreigners' dramas in *South Wind,* it is significant that Douglas himself first saw it that way, as a place "full of lovable freaks of various nationalities who lived contentedly on next to nothing, and took no heed of the annual invasion of Teutonics. . . . " Of the recent tourists' invasions the succession has been Russian, American, and Italian. Capri has at last been discovered by Neapolitans, "much as the Lake District was discovered by Liverpudlians, and with much the same results. . . . " Douglas sees the island as "defaced," and perhaps so from antiquity since the island was the site of many invasions–by the Phoenicians, Greeks, and Romans, among others.

The Emperor Augustus (63 B.C.–14 A.D.) "discovered" Capri, visiting it off and on for forty-two years and making it his special retiring place. Since then "wanton excavators" exported boatloads of columns and statuary to Naples to be burnt into lime. After Augustus came his son Tiberius (42 B.C.–37 A.D.), who lived on Capri for eleven years, a period when the island became the center of the world, rivaling Rome as the seat of the empire. If one believes Tacitus and Suetonius–Douglas suggests one should not–Tiberius staged elaborate orgies and hurled girl victims over the cliffs. These accounts, if spurious, have done much to build the tourist trade on Capri.

Douglas ends *Footnote on Capri* where he began: with tourism. While the islanders have grown rich from the Blue Grotto and other attractions, the old industries–silk, cheeses, coral fisheries, the export of charcoal and lime–have decayed. The decline of the locals parallels the decline of the tourists: gone are the foreign eccentrics, such as the English peer who on a wager walked naked from Capri to Anacapri. The present tourists are employees from the mainland who intermarry with the natives, debasing the Greek profiles that sentimental travelers have claimed to find on Capri.

The question of corruption, usually by "us," is one of two guilts one may trace in Douglas's travel writing. In addition to the guilt of contamination of the other, so familiar from twentieth-century ethnography as well as from eco-travel writing, there is another guilt apparent, though strenuously denied, in all of Douglas's travel books: the guilt of leaving home, of irresponsibility, of abandonment of duty. This second guilt is problematic in Douglas if only because all his writing is a celebration of that irresponsibility.

Though critics of travel writing have continued to rank Douglas highly, his reputation declined after the 1930s, particularly when it became clear he was not going to repeat the apogee reached by *South Wind.* The tone of some of his later books is cynical, and the candid pederastic sentiments he expressed were repugnant to some readers. Moreover, the later work tended increasingly to be fragmentary, often compilations of or glosses on earlier writing.

The humane sympathy one finds in Douglas is often overwhelmed by aristocratic scorn, and the sense of wonder by a sense of loss and defeat. In most of his books there are generous measures of satiric cruelty and egoism. He claimed to reject Christianity and socialism and indeed any form of idealism; yet his own brand of idealism shows in the admiration he reserved for things remote or vanished. Douglas lived the contradiction between home and abroad: taking the side of the other, insofar as that other stood in apparent opposition to the "West," was a way to shock the home reader while abroad he made no attempt to conceal his distaste and contempt for native ways.

Yet none of these reasons accounts for the decline in popularity of Douglas's work. Indeed, some of them should recommend him to readers in the late twentieth century. H. M. Tomlinson thought that Douglas's work suffered neglect because he could not or would not rest in one category but instead wrote so diversely: monographs on Capri, aphrodisiacs, folklore, animal pigmentation, and the zoology of the Greek anthology; a collection of limericks; a catalogue of games played in London streets; short stories; and novels.

The diversity of Douglas's tastes may account in part for his neglect but not precisely for the reasons Tomlinson suggests. The problem is not that Douglas cannot be easily classified as a writer. Certainly, other authors have had success in several genres. Rather, the problem lies in the diversity of each book. Few readers have patience with an authorial mind that drifts as freely or as self-indulgently across as broad a range of interests as Douglas's did. Moreover, both the learned, supercilious style and the content of the digressions may have lost their audience. The modern reader is unlikely to appreciate the range of subjects that Douglas's readers found interesting: etymologies, treatises on geology, mythology, horticulture, passages of untranslated Latin. As often as not, these digressions do not even concern the place purportedly under discussion.

There are, on the other hand, elements in Douglas which might seem to recommend him powerfully to those present-day readers with a taste for the transgressive and subversive, but these elements–vagabondism, pederasty, hedonism, irresponsibility, rootlessness, atheism, antipatriotism–are inseparable from what would preclude those same readers from accepting him: elitism, aestheticization, apoliticism, pedantry, bigotry, and (though Douglas often denied this last element) Anglo- or at least Eurocentrism.

Given these reservations, Douglas at his most characteristic remains compelling, the more so if his strengths come out of a frivolous, perhaps maimed ego: the unfettered energy and laughter, the restless irritation with humbug, the love of the sunlit and tranquil, the absorbed evocation of landscape and the ancient world, and, through all of this, the sense of endless leisure, of life as an infinitely pleasurable drifting.

Douglas had returned to Capri in 1946, depressed and impoverished by his stay in England. He had been suffering for years from arteriosclerosis and rheumatism and for months from erysipelas, an infectious disease of the skin. In *An Almanac* (1941) he had written, "Why prolong life save to prolong pleasure?" At eighty-three, bedridden and emaciated but too hardy to die easily, he gave himself an overdose of luminal. He remained in a coma for two days, attended by his doctor, and died the night of 7 February 1952. An official date of 8 February was recorded so as to gain a day for funeral preparations. He is buried among cypresses on a Capri hillside overlooking Vesuvius, Ischia, and Sorrento–the summer islands and siren lands he loved.

Bibliographies:

Edward D. McDonald, *A Bibliography of Norman Douglas* (Philadelphia: Centaur Book Shop, 1927);

Cecil Woolf and A. Anderson, *Memorial Exhibition of Works by Norman Douglas* (Edinburgh: Edinburgh Central Library, 1952);

Woolf, *A Bibliography of Norman Douglas* (London: Hart-Davis, 1954);

Woolf, *Notes on the Bibliography of Norman Douglas* (Edinburgh: Tragara Press, 1955).

Biographies:

H. M. Tomlinson, *Norman Douglas* (New York & London: Harper, 1931; revised, 1952);

Nancy Cunard, *Grand Man: Memories of Norman Douglas* (London: Secker & Warburg, 1954);

Richard Aldington, *Pinorman: Personal Recollections of Norman Douglas, Pino Orioli, and Charles Prentice* (London: Heinemann, 1954);

Mark Holloway, *Norman Douglas: A Biography* (London: Secker & Warburg, 1976).

References:

John Davenport, Introduction to *Old Calabria* (New York: Harcourt, Brace, 1956);

Constantine FitzGibbon, *Norman Douglas: A Pictorial Record* (London: Richards, 1953);

R. M. Flint, "Norman Douglas," *Kenyon Review,* 14 (Autumn 1952): 660;

Paul Fussell, *Abroad: British Literary Travelers between the Wars* (New York & Oxford: Oxford University Press, 1980);

Ian Greenlees, *Norman Douglas* (London: Longmans, Green, 1957);

Lewis Leary, *Norman Douglas* (New York & London: Columbia University Press, 1968);

Ralph Lindeman, *Norman Douglas: A Critical Study* (New York: Twayne, 1965);

D. M. Low, Introduction to *Norman Douglas: A Selection from His Works,* edited by Low (London: Chatto & Windus/Secker & Warburg, 1955);

R. MacGillivray (R. M. Dawkins), *Norman Douglas* (Florence: Orioli, 1933); republished under author's real name, (London: Hart-Davis, 1952);

Kenneth MacPherson, *Omnes Eodem Cogimur: Some Notes Written Following the Death of Norman Douglas, 9 February 1952* (Naples: Privately printed, 1953);

H. T. Webster, "Norman Douglas: A Reconsideration," *South Atlantic Quarterly,* 49 (April 1950): 226;

Elizabeth D. Wheatley, "Norman Douglas," *Sewanee Review,* 40 (January 1932): 55.

Papers:

Douglas's letters and manuscripts are scattered among many libraries in Germany, Italy, England, and the United States. One of the major collections of correspondence is in the Rare Books and Special Collections Department, University of California, Berkeley. Other important collections include the Beinecke Rare Book and Manuscript Library, Yale University, and the Houghton Library, Harvard University. The Berg Collection, New York Public Library, holds the copy of *Looking Back* annotated by Douglas and William King, who was briefly Douglas's literary executor.

Mrs. Steuart Erskine

(? - 10 September 1948)

Cecile M. Jagodzinski
Illinois State University

BOOKS: *Lady Diana Beauclerk: Her Life and Work* (London: Unwin, 1903);

London as an Art City, The Langham Series of Art Monographs, volume 6 (London: A. Siegle, 1904; New York: Scribners, 1904);

The Spade Heresy: A Comedy in One Act (London: Johnson, 1904);

Beautiful Women in History & Art (London: Bell, 1905);

The Magic Plumes (London: Methuen, 1907);

A Royal Cavalier: The Romance of Rupert, Prince Palatine (London: Nash, 1910; New York: Appleton, 1910);

The Ring of Necessity (London: Rivers, 1913);

Madrid, Past and Present (London: John Lane, 1922; New York: Dutton, 1923);

Trans-Jordan: Some Impressions by Mrs. Steuart Erskine (London: Benn, 1924);

The Vanished Cities of Arabia, text by Erskine and illustrations by Benton Fletcher (London: Hutchinson, 1924; New York: Dutton, 1925);

The Bay of Naples, text by Erskine and illustrations by Fletcher (London: Black, 1926);

Vanished Cities of Northern Africa, text by Erskine and illustrations by Fletcher (London: Hutchinson, 1927; Boston & New York: Houghton Mifflin, 1927);

In Search of Herself (London: Jenkins, 1927);

Twenty-nine Years: The Reign of King Alfonso XIII of Spain: An Intimate and Authorised Life Story (London: Hutchinson, 1931);

King Faisal of Iraq: An Authorised and Authentic Study (London: Hutchinson, 1933);

Palestine of the Arabs (London: Harrap, 1935).

OTHER: Aureliano de Beruete y Moret, *The School of Madrid,* translated by Erskine (London: Duckworth / New York: Scribners, 1909);

Narcisco Sentenach y Cabañas, *The Painters of the School of Seville,* translated by Erskine (London: Duckworth / New York: Scribners, 1911);

Anna Jameson, *Anna Jameson: Letters and Friendships (1812–1860),* edited by Erskine (London: Unwin, 1915);

Eleanor Julian Stanley Long, *Twenty Years at Court: From the Correspondence of the Hon. Eleanor Stanley, Maid of Honour to her Late Majesty Queen Victoria, 1842–1862,* edited by Erskine (London: Nisbet, 1916);

Edward George Henry Montagu, Earl of Sandwich, *Memoirs of Edward Earl of Sandwich, 1839–1916,* edited by Erskine (London: Murray, 1919);

The Memoirs of Sir David Erskine of Cardross, K.C.V.O., edited by Erskine (London: Unwin, 1926);

Alvaro Alcalá-Galliano, *The Fall of a Throne,* translated by Erskine (London: Butterworth, 1933).

SELECTED PERIODICAL PUBLICATIONS–UNCOLLECTED: "Madrid of Today," *Times* (London), 12 May 1921, p. 7;

"A Dispensary and a Dispensation," *Contemporary Review,* 120 (December 1921): 777–784;

"Winter Sunshine," *Spectator,* 139 (5 November 1927): 762–763;

"Marginal Notes," *Spectator,* 140 (21 January 1928): 72;

"Over the Sea," *Spectator,* 140 (28 January 1928): 108;

"Literary Letter from Madrid," *Spectator,* 140 (14 April 1928): 564;

"The Exhibition at Buenos Aires–And Afterwards," *Spectator,* 146 (31 January 1931): 141–142;

"On Holiday," *Saturday Review,* 154 (3 September 1932): 245;

"Fame," *Saturday Review,* 155 (4 March 1933): 214–215;

"Palestine and the Land," *Times* (London), 18 August 1937, p. 6;

"The Arab Charter for Palestine," *Great Britain and the East,* 51 (18 August 1938): 184;

"The Palestine Problem," *Great Britain and the East,* 51 (6 October 1938): 384;

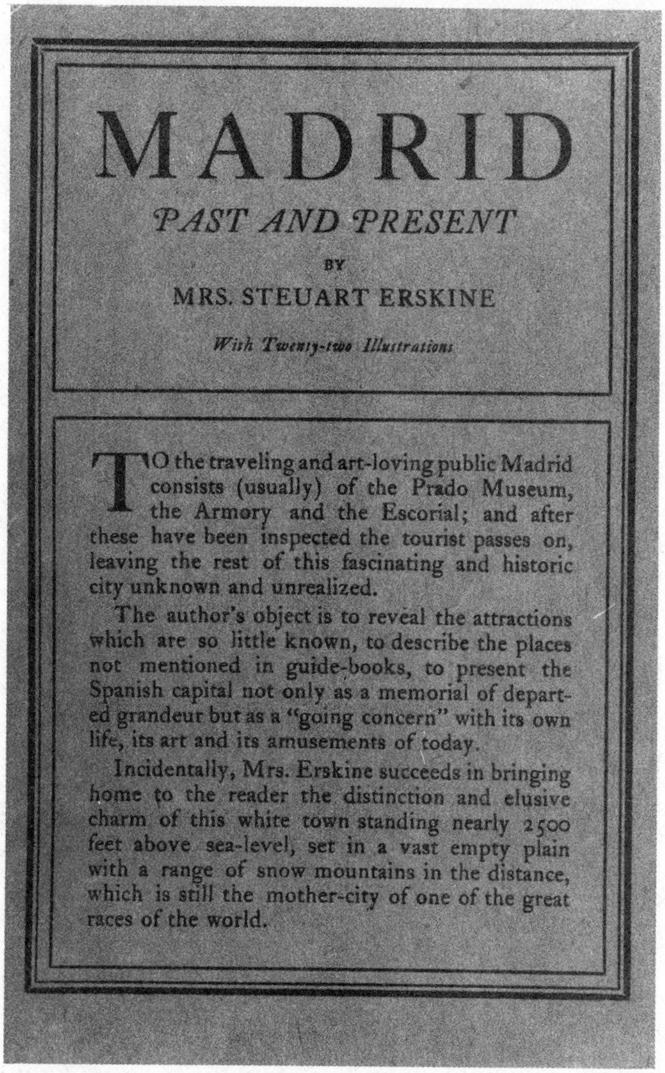

MADRID
PAST AND PRESENT
BY
MRS. STEUART ERSKINE
With Twenty-two Illustrations

TO the traveling and art-loving public Madrid consists (usually) of the Prado Museum, the Armory and the Escorial; and after these have been inspected the tourist passes on, leaving the rest of this fascinating and historic city unknown and unrealized.

The author's object is to reveal the attractions which are so little known, to describe the places not mentioned in guide-books, to present the Spanish capital not only as a memorial of departed grandeur but as a "going concern" with its own life, its art and its amusements of today.

Incidentally, Mrs. Erskine succeeds in bringing home to the reader the distinction and elusive charm of this white town standing nearly 2500 feet above sea-level, set in a vast empty plain with a range of snow mountains in the distance, which is still the mother-city of one of the great races of the world.

Dust jacket for the American edition of Mrs. Steuart Erskine's first travel book

"Our Oldest Colony," *Times* (London), 30 June 1939, p. 12.

Beatrice Caroline Erskine, who published many of her writings under the name Mrs. Steuart Erskine, belongs to that class of early-twentieth-century authors who combine British upper-class sensibilities with the stylistic technique and workaday prose of the journeyman. Aside from what can be gleaned from her writings, little is known of her personal life. Born in London, daughter of H. Linwood Strong, she married R. Steuart Erskine and had memberships in the Royal Geographical Society, the Royal Empire Society, the Royal Central Asia Society, and the Women Geographers, America.

Erskine's writing spanned several decades and a wide variety of forms and genres. Her earliest literary efforts were in belles lettres and the fine arts–plays, poetry, novels, and art criticism. She was also commissioned by various publishers or family members to edit the letters or memoirs of Anna Jameson (1915); Edward Montagu, Earl of Sandwich (1919); Sir David Erskine (1926); and Eleanor Stanley Long, lady-in-waiting to Queen Victoria (1916). A biography of Lady Diana Beauclerk (1903), a minor artist, and *Beautiful Women in History & Art* (1905) are folio-sized examples of what would now be called the coffee-table book, replete with many engraved portraits and art reproductions. These obviously commercial, rather sentimental, volumes contrast sharply with much of Erskine's later work.

Erkine's social consciousness (which never totally erased her consciousness of class) emerged in her support of the fledgling system of British tuberculin dispensaries, set up in 1910 by a lay committee "for the simple reason that the medical authorities had refused to do it themselves." In a December 1921 article for the *Contemporary Review* she indicted the medical establishment and called for universal access of the poor to the tuberculin vaccine:

> Rich patients, and a strictly limited number of poor sufferers, were sent to sanatoria; for the most part the poor were advised to live in the fresh air, to take cod-liver oil, and to be careful not to spit. Very excellent advice, but fresh air is not obtainable for one who may have to live in the basement of a London lodging-house; cod-liver oil, however valuable as food, is not a cure; and to abstain from spitting, although necessary for the protection of others, does not affect the principal sufferer.

Though this article may signal only Erskine's sense of noblesse oblige, it is a radical departure from her earlier writing. Her social awareness became more and more evident in her travel writings of the next two decades.

With her husband, who was also a fellow of the Royal Geographical Society, Beatrice Erskine traveled widely during the fourteen years of their married life. There is little information about the couple's motives for travel or on the immediate reasons for Mrs. Erskine's career as an author. Unlike other, better-known, female travelers she did not fit the mold of lady adventurer. According to Jane Robinson, Erskine traveled "in order to write her books, not (as is so common) the other way round."

The first of Erskine's travel books, *Madrid, Past and Present* (1922), is an outgrowth of her earlier appreciations of art. It was her intent to describe "places of interest that are not mentioned in guidebooks . . . from an absolutely impersonal point of view." Nevertheless, aside from her periodical writings, this book probably reveals much about Erskine's self-image and her concern for her place in "society." Fluent in Spanish and the translator of several books from the Spanish, Erskine was clearly at home in Spain, and in 1921 she gave a lecture on "Madrid of Today," which was published in the London *Times* (12 May 1921). The recommendation in her book that the visitor travel on foot indicates her comfort with that area and its culture. (In later years, however, she preferred to travel by car.) Her apparent hardiness is countered by her concentration on social events, her visits and conversations with the Spanish literary and social elite, and her constant name-dropping. This report of her conversation with a Spanish acquaintance is revelatory:

> Once I ventured to ask a literary man why no great Society novel was written, and I shall never forget the expression of pained surprise with which he regarded me. "Write about our aristocracy?" he said. "But what could be said about them?" It was in vain that I suggested that they have hearts and lives, tragedies and temptations like other people, that, psychologically, the effect of catastrophe or good fortune on educated individuals was more subtle and amusing than it was on the uneducated. In vain. He shook his head, and we changed the conversation.

Erskine's view of Madrid is that of the enlightened British imperialist: Spain might have been, as a Spanish painter told her, "three or four centuries behind the times," but she was charmed by this "image of a man standing, like a sentinel . . . to keep out any innovations that might endanger the customs and the traditions of his beloved land."

Madrid, Past and Present also exhibits Erskine's efforts to combine scholarly research with popular appeal. Her descriptions of the well-known palaces, libraries, and museums of Madrid are accompanied by timeworn guidebook information despite her intention of writing a different sort of travel book. *Madrid, Past and Present* immerses the reader in historical detail and anecdote, and it often fails to document her sources (a failure many contemporary reviewers pointed out). The whole lacks the ring of original scholarship. Clearly not a scholar herself, Erskine remarked, for example, that Konrad Haebler, a great incunabulist, did not make "any attempt to present his subject in an attractive manner," while acknowledging that he "gives a great deal of practical information." This inclination toward the superficial, toward a style more suited to the female society reporter, is one of Erskine's weaknesses as a writer. Yet she has an ability to invoke place and time with extraordinary sensitivity to color, light, and scene, as in this description of the Sahara in *Vanished Cities of Northern Africa* (1927):

> But, in whatever manner you begin, you are bound to get into the heart of the Sahara before long. And the wonder of it steals on you, makes you long to be alone, to live long days and nights in the perfect peace of a place cut off from the tiresome problems of existence.
>
> One of the interesting points about the desert is the change of colour that takes place as the day advances. In the middle of the day all colour seems to vanish: the sand is then dazzlingly white, the shadows curiously black. As the day wanes, the sand gets back its golden hue, the shadows become blue, and the sunset may throw a flaming mantle over some distant sandhill, making it appear like the reflection of a great fire. And then the night!–all white and still, with stars shining out of a summer night sky. . . .

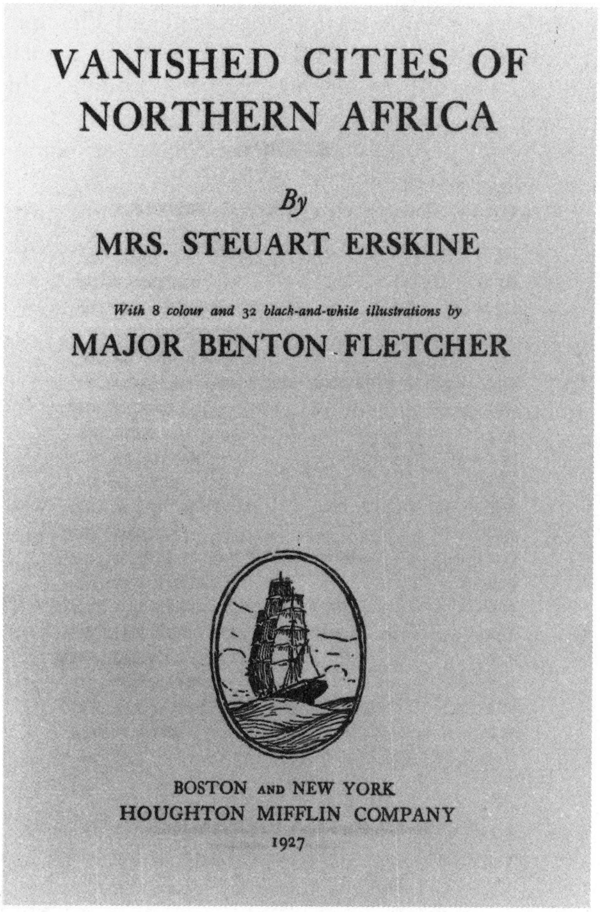

VANISHED CITIES OF NORTHERN AFRICA

By

MRS. STEUART ERSKINE

With 8 colour and 32 black-and-white illustrations by

MAJOR BENTON FLETCHER

BOSTON AND NEW YORK
HOUGHTON MIFFLIN COMPANY
1927

Frontispiece and title page for the American edition of Mrs. Erskine's description of her travels to the sites of Carthage, Timgad, and other ancient cities

Erskine's journeys in Spain, northern Africa, and the Middle East during the 1920s and 1930s coincided with some of the first scientifically conducted archaeological investigations in these regions. The immense public interest in the antiquities of Egypt and the eastern Mediterranean encouraged her romantic views of these areas and their ancient civilizations. At the same time travel seems to have fostered a new breadth of vision, and her writing reflects the battle between the assumptions of her society and her actual experience. *Trans-Jordan* (1924) was written soon after the nation now known as Jordan was established by a mandate that placed it under British protection. The book reports Erskine's impressions of the people and history of the region and displays a characteristic pride in the superiority of British civilization:

> It was certain that the country is in a safer and better state under the Mandate that it was before, a fact of which we may justly be proud. . . . The English flag is still a symbol of freedom; the English are looked on as the natural protectors of small nations.

Despite such imperialism Erskine's travel writings display a surprising sympathy for cultural differences and for the rigors and pleasures of travel. She laughed at the American woman who raced around Jerusalem trying to see the landmarks in one day, and she was careful to ask permission before she photographed inhabitants. She even began to learn Arabic though she never became an expert conversationalist. (When she interviewed King Hussein for an authorized biography nearly ten years later, she spoke to him in French and required an interpreter.) As a woman traveler, she advised other women to try riding astride.

The Vanished Cities of Arabia (1924) was Erskine's first collaboration with illustrator Maj. Benton Fletcher. Fletcher, a veteran of the Boer wars, had joined pioneering archaeologist Sir Flinders Petrie in excavating the temple of Seti I Abydos in Egypt, and, like his mentor, Fletcher was thereafter extremely concerned for the preservation of antiquities and historical monuments. Petrie had deplored the carelessness of the tourists and governments who failed to protect ancient sites, and Fletcher bombarded *The Times* with letters urging the historical preservation of London. He also bought Old Devonshire House, built circa 1667, and established a center for the study of Tudor and Restoration musical instruments.

Erskine shared Fletcher's concern for the past, as her two *Vanished Cities* books demonstrate. Both books trace her journeys through the ruins of ancient cities encircling the Mediterranean. Erskine interjected her thoughts and imagined conversations into a narrative filled with anecdote and legend, sentimental musings on religion and romance. The popular press praised Erskine's romantic depiction of these arid lands (and *romantic* is the operative word), but scholars have deplored the absence of maps, indexes, and consistent archaeological detail. Leonard Woolf, like many other commentators, remarked in *Nation and The Athenaeum* (7 February 1925) that in *The Vanished Cities of Arabia* Erskine "finds her romance in history," and he wished that "she had spared us at least one of Major Fletcher's too romantic colour pieces in order to include a map." A review in *The Times* (9 January 1925) probably represents a more bourgeois point of view, that of the Britisher enamored of the *Arabian Nights* and the adventures of T. E. Lawrence: "It is so easy to be tedious in dealing with a subject which tries hard to run away into architectural or archaeological byways familiar only to the erudite, but Mrs. Erskine rides her steed from vanished Arabia with skill and keeps in the broad path which leads among all manner of interests and subjects." This reviewer and many others complimented Fletcher's illustrations; the reviewer for the *Geographical Journal* (July 1925) went so far as to say that the illustrations "are of exceptional merit and double the value of the book."

Erskine's romanticism, her impressionistic and emotional rather than intellectual response to her experiences, and her cultural snobbishness are probably what attracted the common reader to Erskine's books. Yet they can be irritatingly superficial, as when she invokes an Arab historian's description of the dress of a twelfth-century bride in Tyre, assigns a set of national characteristics to the native populations, and writes "as a wanderer intent rather on the impression of the moment. . . ." In a digression on the ancient theater Erskine deplores the "lowering of the tone of the audiences in Alexandria" and smugly praises the local police and the Arab Legion, grateful that "the advance of civilization has done something to secure for us the peaceful enjoyment of the monuments of the past."

The Bay of Naples (1926) is less a travel book than an anecdotal history and a picture book in which Erskine's text is secondary to Fletcher's illustrations. In the final paragraph Erskine admitted: "The story is told, rather too discursively it is true, but with the sole intention of providing an obbligato or accompaniment to Major Benton Fletcher's fine series of drawings." Erskine's publisher did supply a map, but there are few comments on the actual experience of travel. Instead, biography and history from unnamed sources, descriptions of clothing, and the fictionalized ramblings of historical personages characterize the work. This approach works in a chapter on the lost city of Pompeii, and there is the occasional felicitous simile, revealing just as much about Erskine as about the view: "There is Capri, delicately blue and dreamy on a placid blue sea, and there, all along the coast, are those white houses that suggest a badly threaded pearl necklace."

Eschewing physical exertion, Erskine preferred to ascend Vesuvius via the railway constructed by Thomas Cook and Son and lamented having to share an omnibus with German tourists: "So I cannot help thinking that it is really necessary to order a car beforehand, for no cars are to be had without previous notice, as I found to my cost."

Erskine opened her next book, *Vanished Cities of Northern Africa* (1927), with another tribute to Fletcher and acknowledged her debt to the Compagnie Transatlantique: "Thanks to the initiative of this company, places hitherto almost inaccessible can be visited by motor-car in comfort and security." She justified this mode of travel over that of the traditional caravan on two counts: the caravan required more leisure and more money. It is still the ideal, however; in a caravan "the most restless spirit can become one with the surroundings, wrapped round by the curious fatality, by the intimate strange charm of the waste places of the earth." This book again exhibits Erskine's fascination with the exotic and the fanciful. It is difficult to separate fact from legend in her account of her travels through Tunis and the sites of Carthage, Timgad, and other ancient cities. Yet a transformation of sorts appears to take place as she roams through the deserts: "There is no doubt about it: desert travelling calls for camp-life, with all its freedom." The desert demands the abandonment of a sensible British "middle course": "You must forget your ordinarily reserved and even condescending manner of speaking of other parts of the earth, the half-hearted approval that has always a reserve behind it, for there is no hedging about the desert."

Erskine's next travel book, *Palestine of the Arabs,* was not published until 1935. During the intervening years she made frequent contributions to *The Spectator,* wrote an autobiographical novel, *In Search of Herself* (1927), and translated *The Fall of a Throne* (1933) by Spanish writer Alvaro Alcalá-Galliano. She also wrote sympathetic biographies of Alfonso XIII of Spain (1931) and King Faisal of Iraq (1933). The biography of Faisal generated enough interest in the Middle East to merit translation into Arabic. She continued to travel, mostly in connection with her work. A vacation in Mexico City resulted in an article for *The Saturday Review* (3 September 1932).

Palestine of the Arabs is different from Erskine's travel books of the 1920s. Written in support of the Arab Nationalist Movement, the work is critical of official British policy in Palestine. The book is chiefly a social and political document, though Erskine included token descriptions of the Holy Land and wrote about the lives of the Bedouin population and Arab women. The book is illustrated with her photographs of local sites. Erskine's disapproval of the policy permitting unlimited Jewish immigration to Palestine was shared by many in England during the 1930s, as perhaps were her judgments of the ethnic groups involved: "The oppressed peasants from Russia, Poland, and Germany were mostly rough, uneducated specimens," not "carefully chosen" candidates for immigration, Erskine asserted. Erskine's sympathy for the Arabs and the retention of their lands nearly crosses the line into anti-Semitism. Speaking of the large number of German-Jewish immigrants, she remarks: "Indeed, it sometimes seems as if we had won the War in order to make German the second language, after Hebrew, of the Holy Land." Reviewers acknowledged that it represented an antidote to the many pro-Zionist publications of the period, but they regarded her viewpoint as far from impartial. The reviewer for the journal *International Affairs* (1936) charged that Erskine failed to appreciate "the disastrous influence on the Arab cause of the disunity and rivalries of the Arabs themselves" while the *Geographical Journal* (1936) pointed out Erskine's old penchant for erring "on the side of excessive 'shepherd and peasant' romanticism."

Palestine of the Arabs speaks with the author's new voice. It is better researched and documented than her earlier books, and though Erskine was still class conscious, the reader finds here a different woman from the young one who wrote a one-act play with a game of bridge as its central metaphor (*The Spade Heresy,* 1904). By 1935 work and travel had enlarged her perception of the world in an extraordinary way.

Erskine spent the late 1930s serving as a secretary to the Arab Centre and the Palestine Information Centre (a group whose purpose was to "uphold the rights of the Arab population"). She spent part of World War II in London and agreed to remove herself to Scotland only after eleven bombs fell on her home. Beatrice Erskine died on 10 September 1948. She has disappeared from literary history. Even anthologies of travel writing and research studies on women travelers bypass Erskine. Yet as an individual woman whose life reflected the values of her times and occasionally also challenged them, Mrs. Steuart Erskine deserves renewed attention.

Reference:

Jane Robinson, *Wayward Women: A Guide to Women Travellers* (New York: Oxford University Press, 1990).

Peter Fleming

(31 May 1907 - 18 August 1971)

Chris Hopkins
Sheffield Hallam University

BOOKS: *Brazilian Adventure* (London & Toronto: Cape, 1933; New York: Scribners, 1934);
Variety: Essays, Sketches and Stories (London & Toronto: Cape, 1934);
One's Company: A Journey to China (London & Toronto: Cape, 1934; New York: Scribners, 1934);
News From Tartary: A Journey from Peking to Kashmir (London: Cape, 1936; New York: Scribners, 1936);
The Flying Visit (London: Cape, 1940; New York: Scribners, 1940);
A Story To Tell, and Other Tales (London: Cape, 1942; New York: Scribners, 1942);
The Sixth Column–A Singular Tale of Our Times (London: Hart-Davis, 1951; New York: Scribners, 1951);
A Forgotten Journey (London: Hart-Davis, 1952);
My Aunt's Rhinoceros, and Other Reflections (London: Hart-Davis, 1956; New York: Simon & Schuster, 1958);
Invasion 1940: An Account of the German Preparations and the British Counter-Measures (London: Hart-Davis, 1957); republished as *Operation Sea Lion: The Projected Invasion of England in 1940, An Account of the German Preparations and the British Countermeasures* (New York: Simon & Schuster, 1958);
The Gower Street Poltergeist (London: Hart-Davis, 1958);
With the Guards to Mexico! And Other Excursions (London: Hart-Davis, 1959);
The Siege at Peking (London: Hart-Davis, 1959; New York: Harper, 1959);
Bayonets to Lhasa: The First Full Account of the British Invasion of Tibet in 1904 (London: Hart-Davis, 1961; New York: Harper, 1961);
Goodbye to the Bombay Bowler (London: Hart-Davis, 1961);
The Fate of Admiral Kolchak (London: Hart-Davis, 1963; New York: Harcourt, Brace & World, 1963).

Peter Fleming in the Caucasus, 1934

SELECTED PERIODICAL PUBLICATIONS–UNCOLLECTED: "Colonel Fawcett's Fate," *Times* (London), 10 January 1933, p. 13;
"Journey through Central Asia," *Times* (London), 29 July 1935, p. 12;
"Mr Fleming and His Weapons," *Times* (London), 23 November 1935, p. 15.

Peter Fleming was widely regarded by contemporaries in the 1930s as the archetypal adventurer and travel writer, a reputation based on three travel books published during that decade: *Brazilian Adven-*

Eve Fleming with her four sons: Peter, Richard, Michael, and Ian, 1918

ture (1933), *One's Company* (1934), and *News From Tartary* (1936). Though he was well known for intrepidity, his travel writing is characterized by an antiheroic debunking. Though his witty and modest strategies did not diminish his renown as an adventurer, his main contribution to the travel-writing tradition is the invention of a modest response to strangeness, acknowledging that he and his readers inhabit a world they assume to be normal but may not be. His narrative persona is surprised by nothing and invokes norms that are sometimes comic, sometimes quietly heroic, and sometimes quirky. Paul Fussell in *Abroad–British Literary Traveling Between the Wars* (1980) characterizes Fleming's antiheroism as representing a significant tendency in travel writing after World War I.

In their *Journey to a War* (1939) W. H. Auden and Christopher Isherwood drew attention to Fleming's acting as both joker and hero-explorer. Although Fleming often assumed an older style of heroic masculinity, he remained part of the younger postwar generation. Fleming was not earnest about imperial virtues, but they retain an aura of power in his writing. To illustrate this point Isherwood described Fleming's reaction to a story about a peasant who threw a Japanese officer into a stream and "bashed his head in with a stone" rather than carry the officer on his back across the stream, as ordered. According to Isherwood: "'Oh, jolly good!' exclaimed Fleming, politely assuming the tone of one who applauds a record high jump or a pretty drive to leg." The invocation of the public-school-games ethos is not coincidental. It is a central part of Fleming's persona and appeal. The tradition of the stiff upper lip is only partly parodied. Fleming knew that he was playing a comic role and played it so well that it is convincing.

Fleming's approach to travel writing partly demythologizes the romance of travel and imperial adventure in a way that makes his writing modern. At the same time it suggests that there is a realistic realm of adventure within these powerful imperial fantasies. He is a sophisticated, self-aware narrator of travel, whose sophistication may make the adventure all the more accessible for readers who find earnest and naive heroism difficult to credit.

Born on 31 May 1907, Robert Peter Fleming was the eldest child of Eve Ste Croix Rose Fleming and Valentine Fleming. Peter Fleming's brothers were Ian (creator of James Bond), Richard, and Michael. Both parents were from fairly wealthy and well-connected families. Eve Ste Croix Rose's father and paternal grandfather were both solicitors, and her maternal grandfather was a well-known London surgeon. Valentine Fleming, elected to Parliament in 1910, had inherited £250,000 on reaching the age of twenty-one.

Peter Fleming was ill for a long period as a young child, suffering from the ages of one to six from stomach pains and severe and continuous nausea. His biographer, Duff Hart-Davis, refers to the opinion of many of Fleming's friends that his childhood illness might be the reason for his later "phenomenal appetite for exercise: in persistently driving himself to the limit, they believed, he was subconsciously compensating for the weakness of his boyhood." Both Fleming and his biographer argue that this illness and its treatment had a profound effect on his character. Fleming commented in his unpublished autobiographical fragment "In Those Days" that "I suspect that my childhood ailments, and the semi-convalescence that followed them, helped to make me rather a solitary person and to immunize me–partially, at any rate–against the devastating pangs of loneliness." Hart-Davis also suggests that Fleming's perseverance and enjoyment of travel, as well as his disavowal of heroism and romance, had their roots in this childhood illness, as did his development of a sense of humor, both stemming from an unwillingness to claim attention or express strong emotion.

Fleming's childhood was comfortable in terms of material, but not mental, well-being until the outbreak of World War I in 1914. Valentine Fleming, who held the rank of captain in the Queen's Own Oxfordshire Hussars, went to France almost as soon as war was declared in August, and Peter, then seven, saw his father thenceforth only during his brief leaves. Until this point Peter had been educated at home because of his health, but in this year he was sent to boarding school, the normal course for a boy of his class. Fleming enjoyed the school, Durnford, though it had its eccentricities.

Near the end of his school holidays at Easter 1917, Fleming had his tonsils removed and was unable to return immediately to school. He enjoyed the exclusive and extended attention of his mother, but this pleasure was disrupted by news of his father's death. Fleming recalled it vividly in his autobiographical writing:

> I do remember very clearly walking with my mother through the hall . . . and my aunt Kathleen . . . coming suddenly . . . out of the dining-room door on our right. She had a paper in her hand.
>
> "Eve," she said. "A telegram has come about Val."
>
> Somebody grabbed me and bustled me away upstairs. Behind me in the hall were the terrible sounds of grief. I knew that my father had been killed.
>
> Then a feeling of guilt overcame me. . . . Life had become a nightmare. . . . I remember very clearly what was said to me outside my mother's bedroom door. "You must be very good and brave . . . because now you must take your father's place."

If Fleming's illness might be said to have contributed to his adult character and writing, his father's death reinforced his need to be self-contained and self-reliant. It also established an incontrovertibly heroic figure to live up to (Eve always "invoked him [Valentine] as an example, an ideal").

Fleming went to Eton (1920–1926) and then to Christ Church, Oxford (1926–1929), gaining a degree in English. At both school and university he was well liked and showed himself to be intellectually able. After his graduation his mother and grandfather (much against Fleming's own inclination) decided that he should be apprenticed to a firm of stockbrokers in New York. He was depressed by the job, as witty letters make clear ("Long Island represents the Americans' idea of what God would have done with Nature if he had had the money"). He did, however, travel in Central America on a hunting trip with friends, and he enjoyed this first experience of travel immensely. Fleming soon returned to Europe and became an assistant literary editor for *The Spectator* in the spring of 1931, developing his style in a variety of forms, including reviews of books, plays, and motion pictures, as well as topical commentaries.

His travels in Central America had created a wish to travel further, and in 1931 he arranged to visit China, ostensibly to attend a conference in Shanghai. He obtained a four-month leave from *The Spectator,* took a train to Moscow, and there caught the Trans-Siberian Express to Shanghai. He visited Beijing and returned home by boat and train via Singapore, Yangon, Delhi, Baghdad, and Istanbul.

Though he used part of this experience in his second travel book, for the moment he simply resumed work at *The Spectator*. Soon after his return to England, he met and fell in love with actress Celia Johnson. This interlude at home did not last long, for in April 1932 his attention was caught by a curious advertisement in *The Times:* "Exploring and sporting expedition, under experienced guidance, leaving England June to explore rivers Central Brazil, if possible ascertain fate Colonel Fawcett; abundant game, big and small, exceptional fishing; ROOM TWO MORE GUNS; highest references expected and given–Write Box X, *The Times,* E.C 4." He did not reply at once, but when the 26 April issue of *The Times* included an article about Col. Percy Harrison Fawcett, an explorer who had disappeared in central Brazil in 1925, he could not resist.

Fleming found that he could afford the trip and recruited an Etonian and Oxford acquaintance, Roger Pettiward, to fill the other vacant place on the expedition.

When *The Times* asked if a member of the expedition would cover the trip as its unpaid correspondent, Fleming received his first journalistic commission involving travel. He was also approached by the publisher Jonathan Cape, who asked him to write a book based on the expedition. Despite the claims of the advertisement that the expedition would be under "experienced guidance," it was far from well planned. The two organizers had really intended it as a safari, from which they would make a profit. One of them, Richard Churchward, had added the reference to Fawcett in the advertisement to attract more customers. There had never been any serious intention to pursue Fawcett's trail, and the expedition was in many respects disastrous. It did give Fleming the impetus to write his first travel book, which became a best-seller.

Brazilian Adventure is an account of the expedition's travels along remote Amazonian rivers and of the quarrels between the organizers and some members of the group. They finally split up when Fleming attempted to lead some of them as far as he could go in search of Colonel Fawcett.

The foreword to *Brazilian Adventure* introduces many of the poses that Fleming assumed throughout his travel writing. Suggesting that travel is not really that adventurous after all, he dismisses any scientific, rational motivation behind *Brazilian Adventure:* "Most expeditions have serious, scientific, non-committal books written about them. But ours was not that kind of expedition, and mine is not that sort of book. Only an alienist could have chronicled our activities either seriously or scientifically. I have, however, been as non-committal as I could." He claims to be an amateur, traveling not for some publicly validated reason but for some less serious, less solid reason. The meaning of "non-committal" shifts notably from the first to the second use. In the first it means objective and impersonal; in the second the shift from a scientific to a personal context reinforces the sense that this book is about personal matters and that clear attitudes toward the adventure may not be easily discerned.

The next paragraph develops Fleming's claim of amateur status in a new way. Not only is the expedition not scientifically justifiable, but also the account of it is not going to be a "professional" traveler's tale. He intends instead to tell the exact and unheroic truth:

> Differing as it does from most books about expeditions, this book differs also from most books about the interior of Brazil. It differs in being throughout strictly truthful. I had meant when I started to pile on the agony a great deal; I felt it would be expected of me. In treating of the Great Unknown one has a free hand, and my few predecessors in this particular field had made great play with the Terrors of the Jungle. The alligators, the snakes, the man-eating fish, the lurking savages, those dreadful insects–all the paraphernalia of tropical mumbo-jumbo lay ready to my hand. But when the time came I found that I had not the face to make the most of them. So the reader must forgive me if my picture of Matto Grosso does not tally with his lurid preconceptions.
>
> The hardships and privations which we were called upon to endure were of a very minor order, the dangers which we ran were considerably less than those to be encountered on any arterial road during a heat wave; and if, in any part of this book, I have given a contrary impression, I have done so unwittingly.

Fleming in the Amazon region during the expedition he described in Brazilian Adventure *(1933)*

These lines are the first (and probably the fullest) statement of Fleming's demythologizing aesthetic. He debunks travel writing as romance (full of exotic dangers and properties) but does not reject the romantic possibilities of the travel-book genre. The mention of marvels that are not going to be found does not quite dismiss them from the reader's expectations. Nor does the statement that any dangers faced were less than those "on any arterial road" lead readers to think that the Matto Grosso is as unexciting as a busy road at home. Instead it promises a narrator who is honest and will share his experiences while even underemphasizing their differences from the familiar.

The ambiguity of the narrator's values and of his experience continues throughout *Brazilian Adventure.* The first chapter of part 1, "Through the Looking Glass," asks if adventure is really possible any more, and then it suggests that truly adventurous qualities are found more in ordinary life than on expeditions to out-of-the-way places. The chapter discusses the motivations of modern travelers when "geographical discovery" and "territorial annexation" no longer send young men abroad. Though "there is still plenty of adventure of a sort to be had," many prefer stunts such as driving "a well-known make of car along the Great Wall of China": "These spurious and calculated feats bear about as much relation to adventure as a giant gooseberry does to agriculture." For the most part explorations into the unknown have been replaced by publicity stunts that yield commercial rewards.

Arguing that it "requires far less courage to be an explorer than to be a chartered accountant," he observes that the "courage which enables you to face the prospect of sitting on a high stool in a smoky town and adding up figures over a period of years is definitely a higher as well as a more useful sort of courage than any which the explorer may be called upon to display. For the explorer is living under natural conditions. . . ." Though the speaker asserts the values of staying at home, he is clearly not going to do so. By this means adventure becomes the province, not of the responsible Victorian male, but of whimsical, irresponsible young men who cannot take the pace of office life.

Such commentary about the "younger generation" had a vogue in the late 1920s and early 1930s. It has a distinct resemblance to Evelyn Waugh's journalism and early novels–particularly *Vile Bodies* (1930)–which also deploy a playful mock-seriousness on the generation question. For Fleming and Waugh's contemporaries this ambivalence provided a variety of pleasures, suggesting the sophisticated play of the youthful mind and secretly recovering–without admitting it–the prewar pleasures of sounding certain about things.

Ambivalence about the value of travel continues throughout *Brazilian Adventure.* Indeed, though it is a travel book, the inherently progressive plot shape of a *journey* is undercut repeatedly. Almost every chapter has an episode of delay or nonprogression. For example, the title of chapter 10, "False Start," suggests the failure of adventure to start with any certitude. In chapter 7, "Rio," the narrator observes:

> We ate. We slept. We were bored.
>
> But there is an end to all things, even to delays in Brazil (though that will not prevent me from always referring to them as interminable). On July 8th we caught the night train for Sao Paulo. "We really have started at last," we told each other.
>
> We were wrong.

The first part of the book describes how the expedition progressed only toward further delays. At one point he recorded his impression of Santo Amaro because its status as a nonexperience makes it a symbol of meaninglessness: "it was a magnificently unreal place." The strange nothingness is like the general air of unreality of the expedition. No one knew "where we were going or why we were going there, or whether it wouldn't perhaps be better to go somewhere else instead," and Fleming found that they "gauge the navigability of non-existent rivers, and wrangle over the heights of ranges with which cartographers (those visionaries, those humorists) had arbitrarily embossed the plateau." The unsatisfactory shape of the journey is, of course, part of the truth telling that the reader was promised in the foreword.

The book does progress toward a more serious and conventional travel narrative. As the journey gets under way, the tone shifts, and the debunking of exploration gives way gradually to a sense that the expedition (or Fleming) did genuinely encounter dangers and other ways of life. The initially playful sense that travel writing is often a sham is overtaken by a defense of the genre as something that can, properly used, deliver some sense of the truth. Having revealed the falsity of much adventure writing, Fleming could provide something real.

From the beginning of part 2 there is an increase in descriptions of places and of geographical information: "We had reached the mouth of the Tapirape in the third week in August and camped opposite it, at the foot of a little conical hill on the shores of the island of Bananal, the largest effluvial island in the world." The book discusses the people who live on these rivers, particularly those known as the Carajas, but Fleming still does not feel certain about anything on this trip. He is "appalled when I think how little I know about the Carajas" and says that he "cannot write objectively, for my data are inadequate and unreliable; and I cannot write of them subjectively, for I cannot say for certain that I understand them." Yet he does relate whatever information he has. Thus, he notes that "the use of the

Members of the Brazil expedition: Queiroz, Camaira, Neville Priestley, Fleming, Camariaõ, and Roger Pettiward

tribal mark–the circle cut with a stone on either cheek bone–is said to be dying out."

Fleming provides a detailed description of *carne seca,* the dried meat that forms an important part of their rations. Unlike the apocryphal *tumbo* he mentioned earlier it cannot be said to be an appetizing dish, partly because of the grubs that sometimes infest it. Often in Fleming's travel narratives food becomes a major preoccupation. *Brazilian Adventure* records how the expedition ran short of food and devoted much effort to acquiring it. This aspect of the book is part of Fleming's notion of being in touch with a reality of which civilization has lost sight. Hunger is undesirable, but searching for food and feeling pleasure at its acquisition are fundamentally satisfying.

In the epilogue the discussions of "truth," of distinctions between true and false experience and ways of labeling it, are aspects of Fleming's profound understanding of travel writing. The epilogue stresses comedy, adding to the modernity of *Brazilian Adventure.* Yet within that frivolous–though seriously motivated–frame, there is also a great pleasure in adventure taken seriously as Fleming remembers "the taste of raw farinha: the smell of Carajas: the familiar play of muscles in the paddlers' backs."

Brazilian Adventure was a great success, going through eight impressions in the year of publication and seven more in the following two years. By 1946 it had appeared in twenty-seven printings, and by 1973 it had sold 123,000 hardback copies alone. Its reception by reviewers was excellent. Hart-Davis comments that it represented a new kind of travel writing: "Until he came on the scene, travel and travel books had been treated with excessive reverence and solemnity; but then, with a single, sustained burst of self-mockery, *Brazilian Adventure* blew the whole genre sky-high. Readers–and reviewers–could scarcely believe that a travel book could be so funny."

At the same time some reviewers picked up the real commitment to adventure that hides inside the mockery. Reviewing the book in *The Spectator,* Evelyn Waugh liked it but had some regrets: "For the truth is that Mr Fleming has a really exciting story to tell, but he almost spoils it by going to the extreme limits of depreciation in his anxiety to avoid the pretentious. . . . he is afraid to let himself go: there is a tentative, luminous phrase followed by immediate recession." Critical opinion then and since has shown considerable consensus on *Brazilian Adventure:* it brought a new self-consciousness and hu-

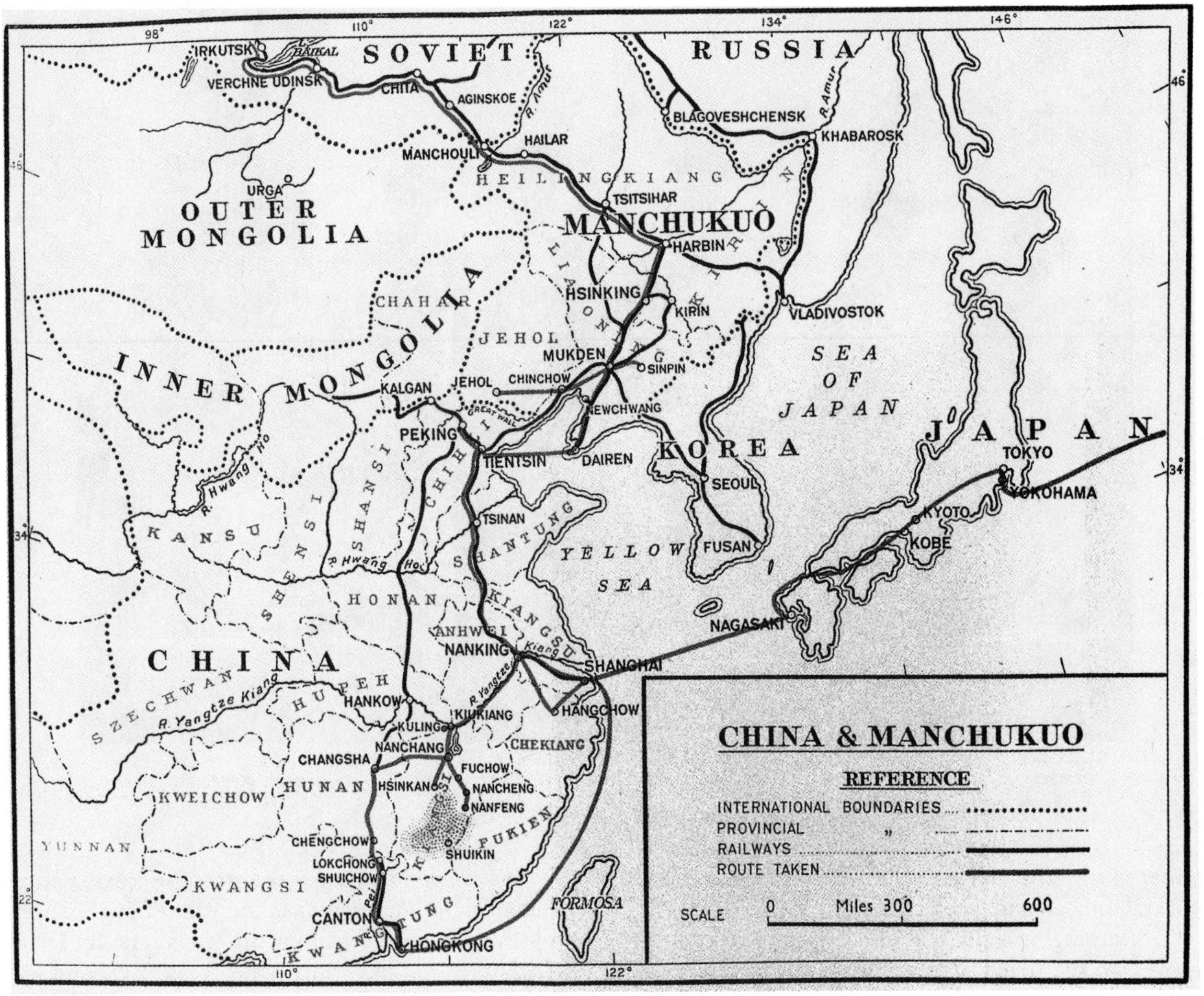

Map of Fleming's route during his 1933 visit to China and Manchuria (from One's Company, *1934)*

mor to travel writing, without sacrificing some of its traditional pleasures.

On his return from Brazil, Fleming wasted little time. He wrote *Brazilian Adventure* in fewer than three months, and before it was published in August 1933 he had set off on another journey. Arguing that he was qualified because of his visit to China in 1931, Fleming persuaded *The Times* that it ought to have a special correspondent to cover Chinese resistance to the Japanese occupation of Manchuria. *The Times* agreed to pay for any articles he wrote, and he negotiated advances for future articles from *The Spectator* and for *Brazilian Adventure* from Cape. Cape also agreed to publish a book about this next journey. Leaving England in June 1933, Fleming traveled by train to Moscow, caught the Trans-Siberian Express to Harbin, in northeast China, and then went to Hsinking, the recently created capital of the puppet Japanese state of Manchukuo. Fleming had little interest in politics. Travel and adventure were his real motives, and he spent five months traveling before returning home. As before, he wrote the book about the journey with considerable speed.

The book based on this trip, *One's Company,* was published in August 1934, a year after his first book. It was also an immediate success, selling some ninety thousand copies by 1946. The book is divided into two parts, "Manchukuo" and "Red China," covering Fleming's visits to the Japanese-occupied areas of Manchuria and the Communist areas of South China. In many respects this book is different from *Brazilian Adventure.* Where that was a book about exploring, *One's Company* is a book about traveling. Rather than a narrative of discovery in the Eurocentric manner of the first book, this second book is the narrative of an outsider traveling in an alien culture. The Fleming approach to travel is still recognizable, however, in his remarks that this book "is a superficial account of an unsensational journey." "One cannot," he observes, "travel through a country without finding out something about it and the reader, following vicariously in my footsteps, may perhaps learn a little. But not much." The modesty, the sense of provisionality and uncertainty, and the build-up to a punch line are familiar. The "Warning to the Reader" contrasts the vastness of China and the extent of its history with the author's youth and ignorance. As in *Brazilian Adventure,* the narrator simultaneously appeals to the romance of adventure and discounts its possibility.

The opening chapters cover the journey through the Soviet Union with Fleming commenting on Russia and long train journeys. For the most part these comments are lighthearted, even on the subject of a train crash: "it would be difficult to imagine a nicer sort of railway accident. The weather was ideal. No one was badly hurt." Relatively serious comment is reserved for the peculiar sensation of such a lengthy train journey, during which "you cannot take your eyes away from the window."

This train journey, however, is only a prelude to the real journey into China, which is described in more detail than the journey in *Brazilian Adventure.* Though Fleming maintains his mocking tone, the descriptions give a distinctive sense of atmosphere and place, as in this description of temples as

> a chain of huge, brightly coloured forts, set dispersedly in a waste of jagged and spectacular hills. They are deserted save by a shy handful of monks, who can less justly be called caretakers than the impotent spectators of decay. In their dark halls the gods gesticulate in silence; a thin filament of smoke . . . is their only certificate against oblivion. Their gold faces scowl importantly among the heavy shadows; their swords are furiously brandished. There are hundreds of them standing there in the half-darkness. . . .
>
> The sense of a splendid spectacle without an audience is striking. The gods perform their gesticulations, but the only spectators are watching over decay, and whatever their scowls and brandishings the gods receive only the recognition of a few joss-sticks.

One's Company lacks a clear structure. Where *Brazilian Adventure* worked both with and against narrative progression, *One's Company* does not arouse expectations of any particular shape in the narrative. This difference is partly a generic distinction between the two books. One has a narrative based on a journey (supposedly) to somewhere specific; the other is about several trips in a region over a period of time. The second book is partially motivated by a series of journalistic quests for information, while the first had (or was meant to have) a single central quest. The multiple foci of the narrative in *One's Company* disperse plot development, but they emphasize incidental meetings with interesting characters and situations. Given Fleming's liking for digression and anecdotes, this structure leaves many of his pleasures room to develop.

Since the book has an unsystematic structure, it is not surprising that it focuses on incongruities and the anomalous assertion of norms (Fleming's and other people's) against all the odds. In Mongolia, Fleming has a memorable exchange with a theater director named Assorgim, who has been appointed to direct plays in Soviet Outer Mongolia. Several of these plays have some English characters, presumably for ideological reasons. Assorgim knows only one English song, which he learned in Moscow, "Tipperary," popular during World War I. The director was worried about using this for several reasons: "Frankly, he was tired of it. Besides, was it modern? Was it representative? Was it *correct?*" Fleming tried to teach him the Eton boating song, "which is the only song I have ever sung more than once."

> After a painful half-hour he had mastered some sort of travesty of this immortal ditty.
>
> He was so eager, so anxious. . . . After all it was better than "Tipperary." . . . I often think of him, a distant gesticulating figure, teaching the Eton Boating Song to the inhabitants of Outer Mongolia.

While there undoubtedly is an element of laughing at another culture's misunderstanding of English cultural icons, Fleming preserves the most important values–Assorgim's self-respect and happiness. The incongruity of an Eton song in modern Soviet dramas in Mongolia may be funny, but it better preserves the community of the two travelers to allow the mistake to be perpetuated than to expose it. Fleming and English culture are as much the comic objects as Assorgim and Soviet-Mongolian culture.

Another complex meeting between norms and incongruities is Fleming's interview with Pu Yi (P'u-i), last emperor of China and puppet ruler of Manchukuo. To every question, P'u-i answers, "Wangtao," which, the interpreter says, means "the Principle of Benevolent Rule": "the more specific the questions you asked, the more certain you were to get Wangtao for an answer." At first Fleming tried political questions. Then he asked an informal question about which part of P'u-i's life had been happiest. The answer was "Wangtao" again. This blatant evasion is in one way alien, yet in another way exactly what a journalist might expect from a political leader. The personal question pretending to move away from politics was quite correctly evaded as also a political question. Indeed the final

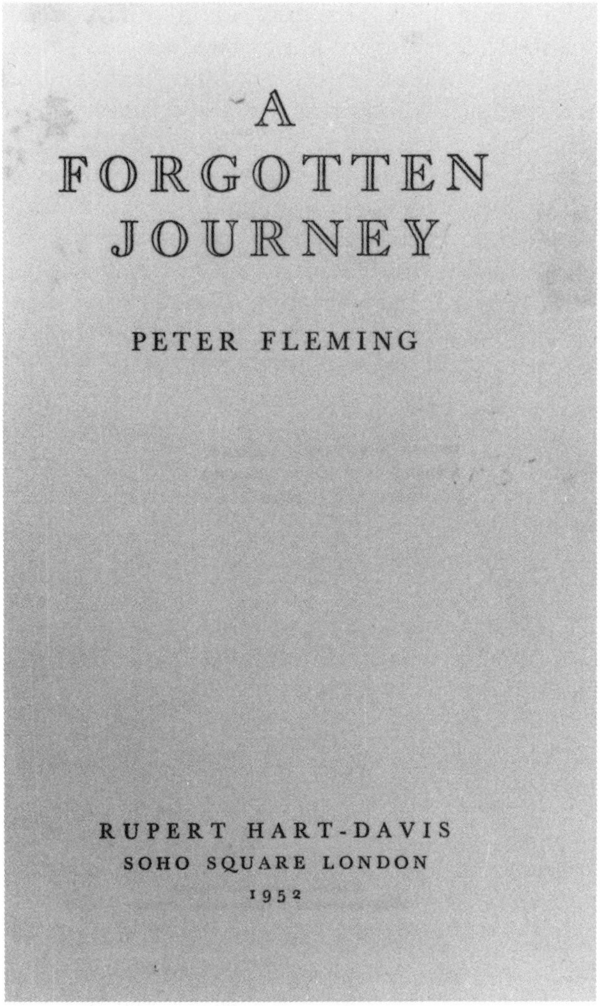
A
FORGOTTEN
JOURNEY

PETER FLEMING

RUPERT HART-DAVIS
SOHO SQUARE LONDON
1952

Frontispiece and title page for the diary Fleming kept during his 1934 visit to the Caucasus region

paragraph on P'u-i acknowledges that Fleming knew P'u-i could not say anything more than "Wangtao" and why: "Officially he is the master. But actually he is at best no more than a privileged spectator. He cannot be unconscious of the fact." That P'u-i's interview is ludicrous does not prevent the book from taking a more serious interest in him immediately afterward. Fleming's humor is characteristically sympathetic rather than destructive.

One's Company undoubtedly has many pleasures, and it offers more real engagement with alien places than does *Brazilian Adventure;* however, the lack of the structure and the lack of the thematic unity in Fleming's second book does tell. The book was well received by reviewers, but comments were a little less enthusiastic than about its predecessor. Vita Sackville-West wrote in *The Spectator* that *One's Company* was an exceptional travel book though a little less so than *Brazilian Adventure.* Harold Nicolson's review in the *Daily Telegraph* complained about a tendency in English writing of the time. In many ways the review does not address specific features of *One's Company,* but it suggests that for some readers not much of substance survived Fleming's wit: "Mr Fleming stands at the end of that long line of iconoclasts who have rendered English literature so intelligent and so uncreative." Most reviewers, though, saw *One's Company* in much the same light as Fleming's first book. A review by Sylvia Lynd quoted in a later printing of *Brazilian Adventure* seems representative: "This is a completely fascinating book with information and fun upon every page. Mr. Fleming went to look for trouble and found instead a ceaseless pageant of strange and decorative and comic scenes which his honest and amiable pen has enabled us to enjoy with him." Lynd's sense of the diversity of *One's Company* seems accurate.

By the time *One's Company* had been published in August 1934, Fleming had begun (though loosely) to plan his next journey. Indeed, three weeks after the book appeared, he left England for the Caucasus region. There he did some shooting, keeping a diary that was later published as *A Forgotten Journey* (1952) before traveling on to Manchuria. In Harbin he met Ella Maillart (known to her friends as Kini). They had traveled together a little on the trip he described in *One's Company.* The two travel writers had independently conceived plans to walk from China to India, originally favoring different routes. It is not clear at what point they decided to travel together, but the precise reason seems to have been that both needed the help of some Russian exiles, the Smigunovs, if they were to have any hope of success. Unlike Fleming, Maillart spoke several useful languages.

Fleming had again negotiated an agreement with *The Times* to act as a special correspondent. On this trip, however, he did not have a book contract set up before departure. In a letter to Geoffrey Dawson, the editor of *The Times,* Fleming specifically says: "I want to get out of that rut and/or racket and–though I may do another travel book if the material inspires me–I shall not start with a publisher's contract in my pocket." This comment may sound dismissive of his travel writing, but it probably stems from a sensitivity about asking the newspaper to finance his writing career. It seems likely that he had every intention of writing a third travel book.

Maillart and Fleming began their journey in Beijing and traveled thirty-five hundred miles through the Chinese provinces of Sichuan, Qaidam, and Xinjiang until they came to the Indian city of Srinagar. They closely followed the ancient Silk Road and entered Xinjiang (Chinese Turkestan, or loosely, Tartary) at a time when it was virtually closed to outsiders. "In 1935," said Fleming, "Sinkiang [Xinjiang], if you substitute political for physical difficulties, shared with the peak of Everest the blue riband of inaccessibility."

The journey was completed by August 1935, and as before Fleming quickly wrote a book about it. *News From Tartary* was published in August 1936. Many of Fleming's contemporaries found it an even more impressive achievement than his previous books, and indeed it still represents the peak of Fleming's contribution to travel writing. Pervaded by Fleming's sense of humor and ability to see situations from different perspectives, *News From Tartary* shows considerable development over *One's Company* and *Brazilian Adventure.* Like Fleming's first book, it has the single focus on a significant journey (though without many of its confusions), and like his second, it shows a serious interest in people and places.

As in his two previous books, Fleming is fascinated with the distinction between true and false adventure and the problem of truthfully representing such journeys. The foreword begins with the now-familiar assertion of amateur status: "The world's stock of knowledge gained nothing from our journey." He also makes a familiar point about how real discovery is no longer possible: "all along the line we have been forestalled, and forestalled by better men. Only the born tourist . . . can follow in their tracks with the conviction that he is not wasting his time." There is, however, a new and plainer statement of his aesthetics of travel writing:

> I have never admired, and very seldom liked, anything that I have written. . . . But it is at least honest in intention. I really have done my best–and it was difficult, because we led such a queer, remote, specialised kind of life–to describe the journey without even involuntary falsification, to tell what it felt like at the time, to give a true picture of a monotonous, unheroic, but strange existence. On paper it was a spectacular journey, but I have tried to reduce it to its true dimensions.

Fleming no longer depends on contrast with stories of adventure and romance. Instead of mocking adventure, this book suggests that for travelers, experience cannot be neatly slotted into the ready-made categories of "ordinary" and "exotic."

The narrator is no longer one of the younger generation, who cannot be too serious. Instead he provides a subtle range of modulations in tone across a wide scope. Events, situations, and people seem to have inherent oddities, so there is less need for a playful narrator although he is still open to comedy. In *Brazilian Adventure* false starts were a source of comedy (and frustration); in *News From Tartary* the narrator is aware that journeys do not have simple shapes: "most journeys begin less abruptly than they end, and to fix the true beginning of this one . . . is a task which I do not care to undertake." This passage is a suitable start to a narrative in which a desire to progress is frequently checked by uncertainty and obstruction. Also characteristic is the sense that for those involved, what they are attempting is not quite straightforward:

> It was time to take stock of the situation, and this, with a kind of luxurious incredulity, I did. It was a sufficiently improbable situation. I found myself the leader of a party . . . who had left Peking [Beijing] the night before with the undisclosed intention of proceeding overland to India . . . by way of North Tibet and Sinkiang. For the latter province, which had until recently been rent by civil war and which was virtually closed to foreign travellers, we had no passports. . . . I felt extremely cheerful nevertheless.

The chief pleasures of this narrative are the presentation of an enormous undertaking as if it were quite normal and the sheer oddness of the unexpected juxtapositions that occur during the journey. Their stay at the chief settlement of the inordinately romantic Prince of Dzun produces many such strange meetings. The people of Dzungaria (Junggar), as well as its prince, find it hard to classify Maillart and Fleming:

> To the end we remained, I think, a mystery to him and to all the people of the caravan. Very few of them had seen a foreigner before. They addressed me always by a respectful Chinese term which means "Pastor" and is applied to missionaries; Kini, whose native country was not on their map, they spoke of as "that French person." In general they treated us as an obscure kind of joke, of which they could not be certain that they really saw the point; this suited our purposes well enough.

It is characteristic that Fleming sees himself as a source of humor and as of uncertain status.

Another odd adaptation of cultures took place as the Mongolians made their own use of Fleming and Maillart's large number of detective novels by Maurice Leblanc and Georges Simeon:

> We fought each other for these books and dreaded the day when they would be finished. As each was jettisoned the influence of French detective fiction spread gradually throughout the caravan, and it was no uncommon thing to see a Mongol stalking along with the lively cover of *La Demoiselle Aux Yeux Verts* stuck in between his forehead and his fur hat to form an eye-shade. . . . The only other form of literature the Mongols can ever have seen was prayer-books in their own lamaseries; if they thought that our books were prayer-books too we must have struck them as very sacrilegious people.

Many entertainments are offered here. It is striking that the journey–or parts of the journey–produces such a hunger for exciting narrative normally used to enliven the dullness of ordinary life. Boredom and compensating diversions are clearly part of this journey. There is also the joke about the influence of French detective fiction, implying at first a Mongolian caravan gripped by the adventures of Arsene Lupin and Inspector Maigret, before the description of another use for these works.

At the same time that this narrative is about oddities, however, it is also about a return to a normality that modern life has lost. As in *Brazilian Adventure* Fleming draws attention to the ever-present concern with basic needs, particularly food. It was the "one thing that we could always talk about with feeling and animation." At other times a sense of a return to fundamentals goes beyond the shared and intense interest in food. The scenery and isolation brought "contentment at our lot." The sun and mountains were reminders of "the virtues of desolation," and they "felt keenly the compensations of the nomad's life." Their senses were heightened, and they "appreciated the tiny changes in the flavour of our food."

A new thing in *News From Tartary* is the relationship between Fleming and a traveling companion. Fleming comments that "By all the conventions of desert island fiction we should have fallen madly in love with each other; by all the laws of human nature we should have driven each other crazy with irritation." The two travelers' relationship is not constantly in the foreground of the narrative because it is not problematic, but their differences and similarities are part of the experience of a journey that is itself about an equivocal sense of difference and familiarity: "we had come to take each other as much for granted as we took our horses. It was only at times that we would remember, fleetingly, how valuable the other's presence was, how trying the journey would have been alone."

Like Fleming's previous two books, *News From Tartary* was a great success with seven printings in the first year of publication. Most reviewers, indeed, thought it the best of them all. They commented on the usual Fleming characteristics, but they viewed his comedy and "distaste for heroics" (*The Sunday Times)* as less important than his serious approach to travel writing and, indeed, to adventure. Harold Nicolson, who sometimes saw cause for anxiety in Fleming's writing, wrote an almost wholly positive review in the *Daily Telegraph,* calling the book "the best that [Fleming] has yet written." It is, Nicolson felt, both entertaining and informative and more stylistically sophisticated than Fleming's earlier travel narratives. He also praised the "ambiguity of narration" and the way in which this book turns monotony into an "epic of adventure."

Though Nicolson's review looked forward to further development in Fleming's writing, *News From Tartary* was, in fact, Fleming's last full-scale travel book. On his return to England in 1935, he married Celia Johnson on 10 December and became a full-time journalist for *The Times.* He continued to travel, but these journeys did not lead to another travel book. On the whole his marriage marked an acceptance of a more settled life and the necessity for regular employment. In 1936 *The Times* sent the Flemings to tour the capitals of Europe. By this time Peter Fleming was expressing marked disagreements with the policy of the British government under Neville Chamberlain toward Adolf Hitler and

Fleming playing patience and his traveling companion, Ella Maillart, working during their 1935 expedition to Chinese Turkestan, the subject of Fleming's News From Tartary *(1935) and Maillart's* Forbidden Journey *(1937)*

Benito Mussolini. The editorial policy of *The Times* largely supported Chamberlain's strategies of appeasement, and there were incidents in which Fleming came into serious disagreement with other correspondents and with his longtime supporter, editor Geoffrey Dawson.

In February 1938 Peter and Celia Fleming set off for another journey to China, to cover the Japanese war against China. Traveling as a fully accredited war correspondent, Peter Fleming was only too pleased to be sent since he had little enjoyment of the routine aspects of being a journalist in London. He did much useful and conscientious journalistic work, interviewing Chiang Kai-shek, commander in chief of the armies of the Chinese Republic, and forming an increasingly anti-Japanese attitude. Fleming predicted the war would continue without definite result because he thought that while Japan would repeatedly defeat the Chinese armies, Japanese forces would have great difficulty in permanently assimilating Chinese territory. In July 1938 his assignment ended, and the Flemings returned to London.

The first thing they did was to build a house on the family estate at Nettlebed in Oxfordshire, where the Flemings lived thereafter. In January 1939 Celia and Peter Fleming had their first child, Nicholas. While employed by *The Times,* Fleming started work on a novel and a play. Neither progressed well, and his diary entries suggest anxieties about these projects and about the international situation. By the end of January he had already begun to make contact with the War Office to see what war duties might be found for him. As a result he was interviewed by a branch of Military Intelligence, and in May he rejoined the Grenadier Guards officer reserve, having belonged to them from 1930 until 1936. In June, July, and August 1939 he worked for Military Intelligence in the department known as M.I. 2, assuming duties in the Grenadier Guards in September 1939.

During World War II Fleming served with distinction in several theaters. Though he wished to be a front-line officer, his reputation as a traveler ensured that he spent the war involved mainly in intelligence work, particularly in special operations and

Fleming (on horseback) following his guide, Li (riding a yak), during his 1935 visit to Chinese Turkestan

deception. He first went to Norway as part of the British Expeditionary Force, where a newspaper correspondent mistakenly reported that Fleming had been killed, causing *The Times* to publish a premature obituary. He was then ordered to set up an underground force to form the core of resistance to occupying German armies in southern England. In 1941 he went to Greece as part of a commando force ordered to destroy bridges and other strategic targets. By the time the force landed, however, the defeat of the British in Greece was imminent, and soon Fleming was ordered to help evacuate British embassy staff on a commandeered yacht. The yacht was bombed while sailing to Crete, and Fleming was wounded. Nevertheless, he and other survivors escaped capture. Fleming had many other postings, spending the majority of the war in command of deception plans aimed at impeding Japanese operations against India. He survived a glider crash in the Burmese jungle and led the other survivors back to India. He held the rank of lieutenant colonel at the end of the war.

After the war Fleming returned to his house at Nettlebed and devoted himself to caring for the estate. He had not given up writing, having written one short book during the war and published a collection of short stories. From 1952 onward he began to publish books in a variety of forms, and he continued to write until his last book was published in 1963. Fleming also published one last book based on earlier travel experiences. Written in the 1930s, though not published until 1952, the book forms an addendum to Fleming's travel writing. Called *A Forgotten Journey,* the book is a diary of Fleming's trip to Russia and the Caucasus region in 1934, while on his way to Manchuria. Fleming had originally intended to write a book about that journey, but once he had been to Manchuria, he had been too engaged with *One's Company* to return to the earlier part of the trip. In 1952 he decided to publish the diary, partly because his reputation, income, and sense of his writing potential were all at a low ebb. He did not rewrite the diary into a finished travel narrative because he felt that he remembered the events too imperfectly "to recast the material into a more polished and coherent form without some sacrifice of honesty and some risk to truth." The diary is somewhat like *One's Company* in style, with a good deal of comic commentary. Though not in a fully polished form, the book offers the pleasures usually found in Fleming's work, including an account of a comic and bizarre meal of sausages and vodka in Samarkand. The meal was disrupted by a Red Air Force pilot who became drunk, fired a loaded pistol into the air, and was finally disarmed by Fleming. At one time the book Fleming planned to base on this diary

Fleming and a tribesman smoking their pipes during Fleming and Maillart's 1935 travels in Chinese Turkestan

was to be called "Sausages in Samarkand." Sales of *A Forgotten Journey* were only moderate, and Fleming did not publish any further travel books.

Several of Fleming's other wartime and postwar publications have connections to his prewar travel writing and travels. Some of the stories in *A Story To Tell, and Other Tales* (1942) refer to Fleming's travel experiences before the war. The title story concerns the attitude of a character called Hopkinson toward his abduction by Chinese bandits, and the final story, "A Tent in Tibet," dramatizes the travel writer's plight. In the first, while he is held for ransom, Hopkinson's mind is filled by the opportunities he will have of telling his exciting story upon his release. He imagines a future of fascinated audiences in every club in the British Empire though he has in the past been widely known as a bore. As he is being released, however, he cannot resist telling his captors that he will tell the authorities everything he knows about them, including the locations of their hideout. Their leader releases him but cuts out his tongue. Hopkinson will never *tell* his story.

In "A Tent in Tibet" an explorer named Richardson has won fame for traveling and the books he has written about them. He knows, however, that the books are superficial accounts of his experiences: they never tell what he really felt or thought. The story is narrated as he lies in his sleeping bag in a tent in Tibet. The last surviving member of the expedition, with no food or fuel left, he knows that he will die of cold soon. Looking back over his career, he is comforted by the knowledge that the true stories of his travels will be found with his body, because in the tent are the diaries in which he has recorded a truer, more profound version. As the cold gets worse, however, he cannot resist experiencing just a few more minutes of the warmth and uses his diaries as fuel. Again, there is the theme of a narrator's guilt about telling his own story and in the end his guilt about repressing that story. Clearly, Richardson is a Fleming-type character, and the character's guilt reflects on the psychic forces that helped to make Fleming the kind of travel writer he was.

Among Fleming's later books three seem particularly significant in terms of his travel writing. *The Siege at Peking* (1959), *Bayonets to Lhasa* (1961), and *The Fate of Admiral Kolchak* (1963) are exciting historical narratives of events that happened in places Fleming visited in the 1930s. Fleming points out this connection in *Bayonets to Lhasa* with a characteristic blend of understatement and lyricism: "With the Central Asian setting of my narrative–the plateaux and the mountains, the lamaseries and the salt lakes, the bitter winds, the shaggy ponies, the rough people, the rumours round the yak-dung fire–I can claim a peripheral acquaintance."

The Siege at Peking and *Bayonets to Lhasa* are concerned with forgotten but important moments in imperial history and with not only adventure but also the complex relations between different cultures. Both books provide heroic figures with whom Fleming could identify: J. R. L. Macdonald, de facto commander of the Foreign Legations defense forces, and Sir Francis Younghusband, leader of the 1903–1904 British expedition that opened the borders of Tibet, were men after his own heart. (The same is not true of Admiral Alecsandr Kolchak, and it is notable that this book seems less engaged.) *The Siege at Peking* and *Bayonets to Lhasa* provide some of the pleasures of Fleming's earlier travel writing. His discovery of historical writing was liberating, allowing a return to his personal past and to an imperial past, which, though he mocked it in the 1930s, had a strong hold on his loyalties. Such a return was particularly welcome at this period of his life when he felt that the world was changing for the worse. The books received excellent reviews.

After 1963 Fleming produced no more books. He made starts on an autobiography but never came near to completing it. He continued to write regular pieces of whimsical humor and comment for *The Spectator*. He died in 1971, at age sixty-four, while shooting in Scotland, an activity he had pursued with enthusiasm throughout his life.

Fleming's reputation as a travel writer has neither much changed nor diminished since the spectacular success of his first book in 1933. His travel books have remained in print for much of the period since that time. His contemporaries viewed his books as a new and modern kind of travel writing, and his modern critics pick out the same features for comment as contemporary reviewers did, though in a different critical context. Fleming's work did develop, and *News From Tartary* is significantly different from the more playful earlier works. Each of his 1930s travel books, however, shares his distinctive sense of the romance of adventure coupled with a desire to deflate false romanticism. His ability to produce writing from these opposed tendencies sprang partly from his upbringing and childhood experiences in a particular British ethos and partly from his generation's need after World War I to disassociate itself from the past and retain traditional modes of feeling. Indeed Fleming's need to express himself and at the same time not to show off could be seen as part of a wider need for aspects of British culture to both move away from and yet rely on traditional imperial values in the 1930s.

Biography:

Duff Hart-Davis, *Peter Fleming–A Biography* (London: Cape, 1974).

References:

Valentine Cunningham, *British Writers of the Thirties* (Oxford: Oxford University Press, 1988);

Paul Fussell, *Abroad–British Literary Traveling Between the Wars* (New York & Oxford: Oxford University Press, 1980).

Rosita Forbes

(16 January 1893? - 30 June 1967)

Samuel J. Rogal
Illinois Valley Community College

BOOKS: *Unconducted Wanderers* (London & New York: John Lane, 1919);
The Secret of the Sahara: Kufara (London: Cassell, 1921; New York: Doran, 1921);
The Jewel in the Lotus: A Novel (London: Cassell, 1922);
Quest: The Story of Anne, Three Men and Some Arabs (London: Cassell, 1922; New York: Holt, 1923);
A Fool's Hell (London: Butterworth, 1923; New York: Holt, 1924);
El Raisuli, The Sultan of the Mountains: His Life Story (London: Butterworth, 1924); republished as *The Sultan of the Mountains: The Life Story of Raisuli* (New York: Holt, 1924);
From Red Sea to Blue Nile: Abyssinian Adventures (London: Cassell, 1925; New York: Macaulay, 1925); revised as *From Red Sea to Blue Nile: A Thousand Miles to Ethiopia* (New York: Furman, 1935; London: Cassell, 1936);
If the Gods Laugh (London: Butterworth, 1925; New York: Macaulay, 1926);
Sirocco (London: Butterworth, 1927); republished as *Pursuit* (New York: Macaulay, 1928);
Account Rendered, and King's Mate (London: Cassell, 1928); republished as *Account Rendered* (New York: Macaulay, 1929);
Adventure, Being a Gipsy Salad–Some Incidents, Excitements and Impressions of Twelve Highly-Seasoned Years (London: Cassell, 1928; Boston: Houghton Mifflin, 1928);
The Cavaliers of Death (London: Butterworth, 1930; New York: Macaulay, 1930);
One Flesh (London: Cassell, 1930; New York: Putnam, 1930);
Conflict: Angora to Afghanistan (London: Cassell, 1931; New York: Stokes, 1931);
Ordinary People (London: Cassell, 1931); republished as *Promise You Won't Marry Me* (New York: Stokes, 1932);
Eight Republics in Search of a Future: Evolution and Revolution in South America (London: Cassell, 1933; New York: Stokes, 1933);

Rosita Forbes, circa 1920

The Extraordinary House (London: Cassell, 1934; New York: Stokes, 1934);
Women Called Wild (London: Grayson & Grayson, 1935; New York: Dutton, 1937);
The Golden Vagabond (London: Cassell, 1936);
Forbidden Road–Kabul to Samarkand (London: Cassell, 1937; New York: Dutton, 1937); republished as *Russian Road to India: By Kabul and Samarkand* (London: Cassell, 1940);
These Are Real People (London: Jenkins, 1937; New York: Dutton, 1939);
India of the Princes (London: Gifford, 1939; New York: Dutton, 1941);
A Unicorn in the Bahamas (London: Jenkins, 1939; New York: Dutton, 1940);

The Prodigious Caribbean: Columbus to Roosevelt (London: Cassell, 1940);

These Men I Knew (London: Hutchinson, 1940; New York: Ryerson, 1940);

Gypsy in the Sun (London: Cassell, 1944; New York: Dutton, 1944); abridged, with *Appointment with Destiny,* as *Appointment in the Sun* (London: Cassell, 1949);

Appointment with Destiny (London: Cassell, 1946; New York: Dutton, 1946); abridged, with *Gypsy in the Sun,* as *Appointment in the Sun*;

Henry Morgan, Pirate (New York: Reynall & Hitchcock, 1946); republished as *Sir Henry Morgan, Pirate & Pioneer* (London: Cassell, 1948);

Islands in the Sun (London: Evans, 1949).

SELECTED PERIODICAL PUBLICATIONS–UNCOLLECTED: "Adventuring into Stevenson's Country," *Travel,* 34 (December 1919): 29–33;

"Palestine," *Fortune,* 114 (November 1920): 835–845; 116 (July 1921): 131–139;

"Across Morocco," *Mentor,* 14 (February 1926): 1–14;

"You Americans and We English," *Saturday Evening Post,* 198 (10 April 1926): 23;

"When I Was Most Afraid," *Collier's,* 77 (29 May 1926): 7;

"Queen of Sheba," *Mentor,* 14 (June 1926): 1–10;

"Women Who Never Lie," *Collier's,* 78 (21 August 1926): 10;

"Nothing's Improper Somewhere," *Collier's,* 78 (18 September 1926): 22;

"God of the Desert," *Asia,* 27 (August 1927): 642–643;

"Black and White Magic," *Fortnightly Review,* 129 (January 1928): 43–57;

"In the Cordilleras," *Fortnightly Review,* 139 (January 1933): 90–95;

"Impressions of Peru," *Nineteenth Century and After,* 113 (March 1933): 340–351;

"Poetess of the Impossible," *Country Life,* 68 (September 1935): 51–52;

"Behind the Lines in Ethiopia," *Independent Woman,* 14 (November 1935): 364–366;

"Slaves for the Harems of Araby," *Travel,* 67 (May 1936): 51–52;

"Women of the Flame," *Country Life,* 70 (September 1936): 57–60;

"Indian Kaleidoscope," *Country Life,* 71 (April 1937): 66–72;

"Afghan Dictator," *Literary Digest,* 124 (16 October 1937): 29;

"Forbidden Road to Samarkand," *Country Life,* 76 (May 1939): 55;

"And So They Married," *Readers' Digest,* 37 (October 1940): 126;

"Importance of Panama," *Fortnightly,* 154, new series 148 (November 1940): 429–435;

"Mediterranean Highway," *Fortnightly,* 154, new series 148 (December 1940): 584–600;

"Canada," *Fortnightly,* 157, new series 152 (May 1942): 344–352;

"Bridge of Asia," *Fortnightly,* 158, new series 152 (December 1942): 373–381;

"Earth Re-Mapped for British Supplies," *Fortnightly,* 159, new series 153 (June 1943): 378–386.

Rosita Forbes was a significant figure among travel writers between World Wars I and II–and slightly beyond. Publishing many books and articles in popular periodicals, she also lectured widely in England and the United States, achieving a reputation as a traveler, explorer, and adventurer. Indeed, Tibet and New Zealand are the only two countries that she never visited, and she experienced everything she described in her writings.

The year of Forbes's birth varies according to source: the 1961–1970 supplement to *The Dictionary of National Biography* (1970) says she was born in 1890; *The Cambridge Bibliography of English Literature* (1972), *Twentieth-Century Authors* (1942), and the *Longman Companion to Twentieth-Century Literature* (1970) say 1893; and *Contemporary Authors* suggests 1895. Forbes was born Joan Rosita Torr at Riseholme Hall, Swinderley, Lincolnshire, the eldest of the six children of Herbert James Torr, a less-than-wealthy landowner who was a member of Parliament, and Rosita Graham Torr. Forbes's early education–first at home under a governess, then at a school in London–produced at least three significant interests: reading, maps, and horses. She also acquired the ability to learn foreign languages quickly. In 1911 she married Col. Ronald Forbes of Rothiemay Castle, Banffshire, and went to live in India. Garrison life offered little romance, and in 1917 they divorced. In 1921 Forbes married another soldier, Col. Arthur T. McGrath, D.S.O., a member of the general staff of the War Office, whose work took the couple to China, India, and Australia. That union endured until McGrath's death in 1962. Forbes, who had already published her first book by the time of their marriage, continued to use her first husband's surname for professional purposes.

Forbes's first book, *Unconducted Wanderers* (1919), chronicles a journey around the world with a friend who had just been released from the hospital. Bored by government work during World War I, the two young women embarked in England on an Atlantic liner, unmindful of the threat from a German U-boat hovering nearby. After landing in New York they crossed the United States to California and then proceeded to Hawaii, Samoa, Tonga, Fiji, Nausonga, New Guinea, Java, Sumatra, Malaysia, Thailand, Cambodia, various parts of China, and Korea. They traveled together as far as North Africa, where Forbes was introduced to the Arab world, then in a state of disorder brought on by the recent defeat of Turkey during World War I. Visits to Cairo, Damascus, and Beirut aroused an interest in that part of the world that would last for a lifetime and provide the motivation for Forbes's 1920–1921 expedition to the Al-Kufrah oasis in Libya.

The style of *Unconducted Wanderers* helped to establish Forbes's popularity as a writer. She set out not only to inform her readers but also to entertain them with her wit and her emphasis on the dramatic aspects of world travel. Attentive to specifics, she offered a daily account of what she and her companion saw, as well as their emotional reactions to places and events. From the beginning Forbes was attracted to local customs, no matter where she went or how primitive or sophisticated the "natives." The evidence of that fascination in her travel writing served to increase the size of her reading audience and to attract well-known people of her day to write prefaces to her books.

Recognition came for Forbes in the winter of 1920–1921, when she crossed the Libyan Desert to the oasis at Kufara (Al-Kufrah), well beyond the frontiers of Italian occupation. The last European expedition to progress that far had occurred in 1879, when Gerhard Rohlfs (1831–1896), a German adventurer and former French Foreign Legionnaire, led an expedition to Al-Kufrah.

The journey to Al-Kufrah, which established Forbes's legitimacy as a serious world traveler, began in late November 1920. Rohlf's maps from the 1879 expedition had been taken from his tent during a hostile Bedouin raid. Therefore information concerning the desert route and the various oases proved seriously inadequate. In company with Ahmed Hassanein Bey, an Egyptian scholar and explorer, Forbes left Benghazi, then the capital of Italian Cyrenaica (now part of Libya); the expedition did not return to Alexandria until February. Forbes assumed the name and the guise of a Muslim, the "Sitt Khadija," to facilitate her ability to move about freely and to converse with all manner of natives. In addition she carried with her a letter from Mohammad Idris as Sanusi, the ruler of the area through which she would pass, expressing his willingness to meet and converse with her. As further protection Idris's brother, Said Rada, had provided Forbes with a passport. The expedition reached Al-Kufrah on 15 January 1921. By the time Forbes returned to

Forbes riding a camel during the expedition to Al-Kufrah that she described in The Secret of the Sahara *(1921)*

Alexandria she had produced an accurate set of maps of her entire route.

The published account of the expedition that appeared later in 1921 as *The Secret of the Sahara: Kufara* is a revision of the personal journal that Forbes maintained throughout the trip. The introduction was written by Sir Harry Hamilton Johnston (1858–1927), an explorer, colonial administrator, and linguist, who had been instrumental in adding nearly four hundred thousand square miles of Africa to the British Empire. Perhaps the most important experiences described in the book concern the arrival at Al-Kufrah and the entrance into the sacred city of Taj, the center of the Psenes (Sanusi) brotherhood, which had been denied to Rohlfs:

> To the east where the cliffs ran out a little, the sacrosanct village of Taj perched clear-cut against the sky, high above the oasis it guarded. The massive block of the zamia rose above the group of strong, dark houses, square, solid, all built of blocks of black stone with red sand mortar. The endless blind walls gave way no secrets, but here and there within the courts rose the triple arched porches of some big dwelling and already there were blotches of white that told of watchers for our arrival.

Forbes in Arab dress (Fox Photos)

Forbes made friends with Idris (later King Idris I of Libya), which allowed her to practice her Arabic–and to sprinkle Arabic phrases liberally throughout her narrative. Because of her attention to specifics in her book, readers can easily experience her frustrations with the Italian military officials who tried to confine her to the areas that they actually controlled, her discomfort from a long journey across the desert on the backs of assorted and temperamental camels, and her excitement and fear while sneaking about Taj in clandestine attempts to acquire as many photographs as possible. Forbes did not detail fully the invaluable assistance provided by Hassanein, who carried his resentment of Forbes well beyond the publication date of her book.

During 1922–1923 Forbes produced three novels in quick succession: *The Jewel in the Lotus* (1922), *Quest: The Story of Anne, Three Men and Some Arabs* (1922), and *A Fool's Hell* (1923). The second is as much a volume of travel literature as fiction. Its rather thin plot revolves around Anne Clevedon, an English beauty whose husband has been killed in World War I. Seeking a change of scenery to soften her loss, she travels to the Near East, where she entangles herself in espionage. After several adventures, she has satisfied her unsettled spirit and returns to England for a life of work and love. The novel includes vivid descriptions of Damascus, Cairo, Beirut, and Jerusalem–as well as the surrounding countryside. Forbes's knowledge of the Near East, particularly its history and its politics, overshadows her heroine's romantic adventures and lessens the redundant and overly sentimental plot.

In *El Raisuli, The Sultan of the Mountains: His Life Story* (1924) Forbes struck a reasonable balance of biography, adventure narrative, and travel writing. Undertaken in 1923, the book chronicles the life of Ahmad ibn Mohammad Raisuli, the Moroccan bandit and kidnapper whose exploits reached wide public notice between 1900 and 1905. Despite Raisuli's tendency toward cruelty and what one might term "wickedness," Forbes, who had a series of direct interviews with him, presented him as a pre–World War I Robin Hood who committed crimes for apparently noble purposes. To that extent he remained loyal to the political interests of his people, going to war in an endeavor to keep them isolated from what he feared as the overly ambitious schemes of modern Europe.

The essential argument between Raisuli and his attractive visitor from the West began and ended with his contention that "your ways are not ours." When Forbes tried to impress upon him the benefits of civilization, Raisuli countered, "You give a man safety . . . but you take away hope. In the old days everything was possible. There was no limit to what a man might become. The slave might be a minister or a general, the scribe a sultan. Now a man's life is safe, but for ever he is chained to his labour and his poverty." With the photographic eye of the traveler but also with the quick imagination of a fiction writer, Forbes attempted to capture the political struggles of a modern human soul who had to carve his own path to historical recognition through the wilderness of a primitive and barbaric culture.

After writing her Raisuli biography Forbes spent the winter of 1923–1924 on a lecture tour of the United States: eighty-eight lectures in ninety-one days. "It was enormously interesting and far more exhausting than any amount of desert travel," she wrote in *Gypsy in the Sun* (1944). "Unfortunately, it was the moment of the 'Sheek' [Rudolph Valentino's 1921 movie *The Sheik*]. So I arrived in New York with one purpose and Americans welcomed me with another. They wanted romance. I wanted a United States of Arabia." She confused the American popular press, "who expected a combination of whipcord and leather. I wore vermilion under a pencil-slim fur coat. When my unassuming figure was pointed out to the representative of the [New York] *Herald,* he exclaimed, 'That girl ride camels? Smokes them, you mean!'" Further complications arose when newspaper editors refused to publish a series of her articles on Palestine because they considered Forbes's prose too florid and unintelligible for American tastes.

In late 1924 Forbes joined the explorer, orientalist, and writer Harry St. John Bridger Philby (1885–1960). She had extracted a commission from the *Daily Telegraph* of London to accompany him on his crossing of the Rub 'al-Khali, the then-unexplored Empty Quarter of Southern Arabia. The British authorities at Aden refused to issue the necessary travel permits to the expedition, however, because of what they viewed as civil unrest in the region.

Forbes turned her attention to a 1925 journey to Ethiopia, accompanied by a motion-picture photographer, Harold Jones. That excursion resulted in a movie and Forbes's next book, *From Red Sea to Blue Nile: Abyssinian Adventures* (1925). In her foreword Forbes identified the volume not as a travel book about Abyssinia (as Ethiopia was then called) but as a careful and accurate record of a three-month arduous journey on the backs of several temperamental mules: "It is a tale of adventures, serious and frivolous, of what we saw and heard and did between the Red Sea and the Blue Nile, but it is only an impression of Abyssinia as she appeared from tent and saddle." For approximately eleven hundred miles she and Jones traversed mountains, forests, rivers, and deserts in their search for worthwhile scenes to film. Forbes included sixty-one of her photographs in the volume and appended a detailed foldout map of her route as well as a "Table of Marches," showing date, starting time, time of arrival, camping place, actual traveling hours, approximate miles covered, and remarks on the events of the day. On 2 March 1925, for example, they left their camp on the Gota River at 7:15 A.M., traveled eighteen miles in eight and one-half hours, and arrived at the village of Mahadera Maryam at 3:45 P.M. "Up same valley by Gota River," read the cryptic remarks. "At 2 1/2 miles Zaboaia village on left. Valley narrowed to point at 4 miles and Burra village left. Crossed ridge. Donder village 9 3/4 miles left. 11 1/4 miles crossed Gomara River (first of names), 11 3/4 miles Makalge village. Crossed Alakt Wons River 15 1/2 miles. Came up rift in wooded cliff by stream to Mahadera Maryam village. Chiefly wooded hilly country."

Despite the many photographs in *From Red Sea to Blue Nile,* Forbes's vivid language and concise style are essential vehicles by which she conveyed to her readers the sights and the sounds of the journey, as well as her own reactions to them:

> The Cocha is a peninsula of rock, shaped like an octopus. It is joined by one tentacle to the table-land beyond, and all the others just out into the crevasse which surrounds it. Why any route should choose to attack such an obstacle I do not know, but with painful perseverance the path we sought twisted up and down and round every one of these jagged rock-strewn hills. Sunset found us bewildered by the manifold turns, and aghast at the prospect of no water for the horses after a ten hours' march.

In an age of silent film Forbes's written narrative served well as the "sound track" for Jones's motion picture.

For the next five years (1925–1930) Forbes devoted the major portion of her time to writing mediocre fiction. These novels draw on her travel experiences. For example, *Sirocco* (1927), written with the help of her friend Noel Coward, portrays the journey to Morocco of Anne, a young English girl, and her friend Lillian, an older woman whose life has been clouded by romantic unhappiness. Both women attempt to evade the clutches of unwelcome suitors who arrive in the Moroccan desert, where they encounter a childhood friend of Anne and a man from Lillian's past. Forbes wove into this melodrama the specifics of a desert setting, complete with the French Foreign Legion, hostile Arabs, a series of raids, and a sirocco wind that blows continuously and drives men and women into physical and emotional frenzy.

In *Account Rendered, and King's Mate* (1928) Forbes again produced a fast-paced narrative with a wide geographic range. Beginning in Deauville, France, on the English Channel, and terminating in North Africa, the novel includes Forbes's usual corps of adventurers and adventurous activities.

Forbes at the India-Afghanistan border in the Khyber Pass during the long journey she described in her 1937 book Forbidden Road: Kabul to Samarkand *(photograph by Major Yeats-Brown)*

Sheiks and sultans rub their mysterious shoulders with an assortment of English types within a fictional environment of political intrigue, sudden death, love, and adventure. Although the actions and thoughts of Forbes's fictional North African characters may not have been believable to Western imaginations, she based her descriptions on her observations.

The plot of *The Cavaliers of Death* (1930) is also fantastic, but again Forbes employed her experiences as a traveler to advantage, particularly in depicting the local color of an unfamiliar region. The title characters are a group of Europeans who form a secret organization to combat a sect of Syrian devil worshipers. Between those two factions roams a young English girl who unconsciously becomes the central figure in a life-and-death struggle.

In 1928 Forbes combined travel literature and autobiography in *Adventure, Being a Gipsy Salad–Some Incidents, Excitements and Impressions of Twelve Highly-Seasoned Years.* The opening two chapters serve as Forbes's raison d'être for wanting to travel, beginning with her juvenile years as a collector of maps, through her postwar search for employment, to her convincing a Paris editor that she could write a series of articles, on site, relative to the French colonization of North Africa. With the exception of two chapters about Forbes's American lecture experience, the book is firmly anchored in the Middle East.

Perhaps the most fascinating aspect of Forbes's travel writing is her tendency to anticipate her readers' reactions to her experiences within the context of their stereotypical images of and notions about women. For example, she called chapter 10 of *Adventure* "Which Is the Braver?" and carried the question into the opening sentence: "Well, which is the braver, man or woman?" The substance of Forbes's response, while not entirely vintage 1928, demonstrates her willingness to strike a reasonable balance. Forbes's answer also allows the reader to observe her social and political acumen:

> On the whole, a woman's courage is instinctive or impulsive. A man's is reasoned and objective. A woman is perhaps more hopeful than logical. She may see "ways out" where none exist, but she is never weighed down by consequences.
>
> To some women any risk is a stimulant; to most men it is a responsibility. Therefore, if I were going into danger, I would rather have a woman with me. When I was well in the middle of it, I would rather have a man.

Forbes then proceeds to a series of short narrative episodes that chronicles the adventures of "brave" women in northern Australia, India, Mesopotamia, Ethiopia, Japan, China, and Turkey. In the end she concludes that "there is more courage in the world than we think. We hear about it only when it is spectacular. It belongs, in a different measure, to every country; it belongs to men and women. But perhaps the balance is in favour of women, for they have to put up the hardest fight against nerves, health, and circumstance; in fact, against the centuries-old heritage of Eve." As a traveler Forbes confronted the spectacular; she could, however, see through and around spectacle and stare hard at the mundane, discerning the potential for courage in both.

In *Conflict: Angora to Afghanistan* (1931) Forbes detailed her most extensive journey to that date. In 1930–1931 she trekked through Turkey, Iraq, Syria, Palestine, Persia (which became Iran in 1935), and Afghanistan. Essentially she wanted to underscore the struggles and contrasts predominating in the area: between medievalism and industrialization, feudalism and socialism, ancient religions and the new Soviet idealism, the Koran and the Talmud, and superstition and science. To add credence to her description and analysis, Brig. Gen. Sir Percy Molesworth Sykes (1867–1945), author of a two-volume study of Afghanistan, wrote the introduction. As Forbes noted later in *Gypsy in the Sun,* "he has always been ready to help travelers and writers at the beginning of their careers. So many of us have profited by his learning and made shameless use of his time."

In addition to the vivid details, the real value of Forbes's *Conflict* lies in her extensive, intelligent, clearly written commentary on the social, economic, and political conditions of those countries through which she traveled. On the surface her account appears picturesque and entertaining; yet she also sought to probe the Middle Eastern mind, realizing that the people would yield the initial clue to the origins of problems confronting the diverse races of Asia Minor and the Middle East.

Conflict also provided her readers significant knowledge about the government and commerce of Afghanistan, Turkey, Syria, Iran, and Arabia. As such, the volume rises above the usual level of the popular travel book to compete with textbooks and encyclopedias of the day as a storehouse of practical information. The nations of Syria, Transjordan, and Iraq did not exist prior to World War I, and during the years between the war and 1930, the political and cultural contexts of those states changed radically because of the intrusion of Western ideas and Western invention on their ancient customs. For example, Forbes noted contrasts between the new towns in the midst of the Persian oil fields–which she likened to new settlements in the midwestern United States–and the relatively primitive villages of Luristan (Lorestan), then still under the influence of bandit tribes dating back to ancient times. In Palestine, although continuing to demonstrate her love for Arab peoples and cultures, she expressed openly her appreciation for the agricultural and economic innovations being instituted by Jewish colonists from Europe.

Following another plunge into fiction with *Ordinary People* (1931), Forbes and her husband undertook a 1931–1932 tour of South America, a journey that resulted in *Eight Republics in Search of a Future: Evolution and Revolution in South America* (1933). The narrative discusses life in Brazil, Uruguay, Paraguay, Argentina, Chile, Bolivia, Peru, and Ecuador, devoting eleven chapters each to Brazil and Argentina, five to Chile, and between two and three to each of the other nations.

Eight Republics appears to be written with the assumption that Forbes's contemporary readers had no knowledge of South America or the importance of English political and economic interests there. In the majority of instances she was probably correct. In addition to describing the places she visited, she informed her readers about economics and politics, even being so forward as to predict the future of the region. For example, she wrote, "the only other source [other than farming immigrants] by which foreign wealth is likely to come into [Peru] . . . is by means of tourists. . . . The liners of the Pacific Steam Navigation Company or the Grace Line link England and America in delightful fashion with the west coast of South America. Excellent railways connect Lima or Mollendo with the unrivalled tropical beauty of the Chanchamayo Valley or with Cuzco, gem of the colonial period and centre of Incan ruins."

Unlike the majority of the travel narratives Forbes wrote between 1921 and 1931, in which she clearly demonstrated her extensive knowledge of and familiarity with the areas she visited, *Eight Republics* reveals that she knew relatively little about the language and customs of South America. To promote the legitimacy of her observations and comments, she (or her publishers) recruited Sir Edgar Vincent, sixteenth Baronet and Viscount D'Abernon (1857–1941), to write a preface for *Eight Republics.* Not only could he claim an international reputation as an overseas bank administrator and diplomat, but he had also led a 1929 British economic mission to South America, where he had seen most of what Forbes saw less than two years later. "There are two reasons for writing a preface to this book," Lord D'Abernon began, "a belief that Rosita Forbes is one of the acutest observers that England possesses to-day, and a conviction that the development of cultural and commercial relations with South America is one of the most urgent tasks before British statesmanship." That preface sets the tone for *Eight Republics,* which is indeed the most political of Forbes's travel narratives.

From left to right, H.H. The Rajah of Patna, Prince Bujinara (sons-in-law of the late Maharajah of Patiala), H.H. The Raj Kumar of Patiala, H.H. The Maharaj Rana of Dholpur and the author on the terrace of the palace at Patiala.

Elephants wrestling within the royal castle at Udaipur.

Illustrations from India of the Princes *(1939)*

Forbes's journey through South America covered approximately twenty-three thousand miles and omitted only Colombia and Venezuela. During most of her travels she conversed with patriots, rebels, politicians, and simple folk, finding that they cared less for politics than for maintaining their often-precarious states of existence. Indeed, during 1931–1932, Chile alone had witnessed no fewer than six military and civilian revolutions; Peru and Ecuador had a rebellion each; and Brazil a revolution that developed into a full-scale civil war.

In writing *Eight Republics* Forbes added the true qualities of first-rate journalism to her lively and witty prose style, realizing the value of pure statistical information to complement what she saw and thought. In discussing the economics of the coffee industry in Brazil, for example, she informed her readers that prior to 1902 average production amounted to nine million bags; in 1902 that figure rose to sixteen million, while the total world consumption stood at only thirteen million. As a result,

> Prices dropped forty per cent, and in September, 1905, the excessive flowering, promising an even vaster yield, produced something like panic. . . . The world consumption of coffee has increased to twenty-two million bags of a hundred and thirty-two pounds each. Of this Brazil supplies sixty-seven per cent, but she grows seventy per cent, and every year more land is planted with coffee, so that she is likely to be faced with an additional surplus every twelve months unless she undersells her rivals.

Journalism, however, with or without statistics, was not the reason for Forbes's popularity. People bought and read *Eight Republics* because they wanted to be transported away from their mundane existences by passages such as graphic descriptions of a herd of llamas or the bloody remains of a person murdered by machete and the details of an encounter between a steer and tiger fish (piranha):

> The water was smooth as tea and the same colour. Suddenly, when the steer was well away from the bank, a series of flickers cut the surface. The animal began to bellow and thresh with its fore-legs. In less than a minute it was the centre of a whirlpool. There was a flash of fin and metallic back as the pressure of a mob fighting-mad for blood forced some of its component parts out of the water. The steer's head went back. Its quarters sank. Red stained the river, yet except for an occasional gleam of silver, nothing could be seen but a few square yards of churning water in the middle of the vast placid stream.

Whether on the ground or in the air (she flew her own plane some fourteen thousand miles over Central and South America), Forbes directed her attention toward such natural phenomena as the beautiful South American sunsets while at the same time recognizing the need to communicate information about cultural tendencies and social, economic, political, and even natural problems within the eight republics.

Forbes also used her South American experiences in a mystery novel, *The Extraordinary House* (1934), which a book critic for *The New York Times* (31 March 1935) pronounced inferior to "its author's travel books." In 1935 Forbes published an updated and revised version of *From Red Sea to Blue Nile: Abyssinian Adventures,* with a new subtitle, *A Thousand Miles to Ethiopia.* This edition also has an introduction by Edmund Henry Hynman, first Viscount Allenby (1861–1936), the British field marshal who had gained considerable recognition for his military successes in the Middle East during World War I. Forbes had known Allenby since spring 1921, when he and his wife entertained her at a Cairo dinner party. Allenby's introduction described current conditions in Ethiopia, while Forbes suggested possible outcomes from the 1935 invasion of that nation by Benito Mussolini's Italian army, as well as an updating of Ethiopian economic conditions and lifestyles. Forbes expressed doubt over the Ethiopian question. On one side she pointed to the immorality of Mussolini's aggression, complete with bombs and mustard gas. Nonetheless his forces represented modern Italy, bearing with them efficiency and potential prosperity that fascism had (to that date) brought to the land of the Caesars. On the other side she had seen and known well the filth, disease, cruelty, and corruption that had long dominated Ethiopia.

Forbes next turned her literary attention to a book devoted entirely to women, a subject that she had considered at varying lengths in each of her preceding volumes. The result proved as unconventional as the writer herself. Forbes of course did not settle for a mere reexamination of the conventional subjects from the traditions of Western history. In *Women Called Wild,* published in 1935 with illustrations by Isobel R. Beard, Forbes paraded before her readers a collection of half-civilized women from remote sections of the world. Her route wound its way from the ancient, but then still extant, slave markets and harems of Abyssinia and Arabia to troglodyte women of Tripolitania (now part of Libya), who lived in caves and came out at night like foxes. Forbes also wrote about the revolutionary women of Russia and China, the mysterious women of Azerbaijan and Kurdistan, and the "people of the flame" of Dutch Guiana (now Suriname): "Rumour has it that these human salamanders are impervious to the effects of fire, but nobody

Arthur McGrath and Rosita Forbes arriving in Antofagasta, Chile, during the South American tour that she described in Eight Republics in Search of a Future *(1933)*

has yet explained whether it is due to the thickness of their epidermis, or to some spell which enables them to treat a bonfire as a nettle." Other "wild women" existed in Amazonia, Cochin China (now part of Vietnam), Lyons in France, Haiti, Turkey, and Tibet. Through Forbes's eyes, readers viewed women camp followers of the French Foreign Legion in Morocco and harem women of Tunisia, Syria, and Tripolitania. From there she transported them to Buenos Aires and Shanghai and finally to Java to meet women who dealt in witchcraft, assorted poisons, and opium.

Forbes did not write *Women Called Wild* simply to frighten or to entertain her readers. Certainly, as with all of her travel writings, she sought to enlighten those unfamiliar with remote sections of the globe. Yet in this work she had a more important goal: to create a Western awareness of those women whose status, goals, and earthly rewards lacked the compensations of their more modern and more socially and economically advanced contemporaries. Thus, Forbes described

> the condition and destination of the [Arabian slave] girls who walked sturdily through the bush in spite of the unaccustomed sandals on their feet. They wore the usual fatah, a knee-length skirt, with a strip of dirty calico slung cape-wise across their shoulders, and they possessed necklaces of bone, or strips of hide. Serious, they extracted thorns. Smiling, they stuck leaves into their nostrils. And sometimes, in the evening, they huddled together, singing in a monotonously nasal rhythm which reminded me of wind in dry grass.

Her subjects may have been considered "wild," but they were also human beings. She viewed them as possessed of a kind of quiet strength that allowed them to cope with extreme conditions not of their own making.

The striking unconventionality of *Women Called Wild* provoked negative criticism from those who challenged the believability of Forbes's accounts, particularly because she did not always bother to set down dates, either for her various journeys or for the incidents that she described. Indeed, Forbes's frequent journeys into the realm of romantic travel fiction caused detractors and skeptics to cast doubt on the validity of the entire book. Forbes remained popular with readers, however. Reviewing *Women Called Wild* for the *Saturday Review of Literature* (30 January 1937), J. W. Feiss summarized her technique and its appeal: "Scramble the seventeen volumes of [Sir Richard Francis] Burton's translation of 'The Arabian Nights' [1885–1888]. Mix with this the three volumes [*sic*] of [Sir James George] Frazer's 'Golden Bough' [1890–1915] and add a dash of Rosita Forbes to the result, condense into a single volume, and digest the product. . . . Irrespective of the accuracy of her observations, 'Women Called Wild' is a fascinating account written by a remarkable woman." In their search for vicarious pleasures Forbes's readers never concerned themselves with possible gaps between reality and imagination. In a world clouded by war and dampened by economic depression, they readily submitted themselves to the intoxication of travel to any place Forbes would lead them.

Following the publication of her last novel, *The Golden Vagabond* (1936), Forbes turned her attention to northern Russia, specifically Leningrad (St. Petersburg) and Moscow, in company with a group of researchers inquiring after the state of education in the Soviet Union. She entered Russia from the southeastern corner, heading northward from Afghanistan to the Caspian Sea and the Volga River. Although government officials informed her that the Soviet central Asian republics lacked adequate facilities for travelers, she proceeded on her journey, traversing Afghan territory, visiting those republics, and reaching her ultimate destination, Samarkand (Samarqand), in what is now part of Uzbekistan. The record of her experiences, highlighted by a traumatic but entertaining journey from Termez to Tashkent, was published in 1937 as *Forbidden Road–Kabul to Samarkand,* a work of forty-eight varied and detailed chapters, dedicated "To all fellow travelers who 'for lust of knowing what should not be known' have taken the road to Samarkand." The long road passed through such places as Peshawar, the Kohat Pass, Jellalabad (Jalalabad), Kabul, Kandahar (Qandahar), Bamyan, the Hindu Kush, Doab, the Mazar Pass, Tadjikistan (Tajikistan), Bokhara (Bukara), Samarqand, and Tashkent. It twisted and turned its way through the mountains and rugged terrain of India, Afghanistan, and Turkestan.

Perhaps the principal attraction of *Forbidden Road* is Forbes's fusion of that dedicatory statement into her own passionate interest in meeting the people of the regions through which she journeyed. "Six years ago in Meshed, in a holy city of the Shias, which lies in the North-East corner of Persia," she recalls in the opening chapter, "I stood in the middle of one of the wildest streets in Asia and watched fugitives from Turkmenistan drive by in their high-wheeled covered wagons. Women and children were heaped among household goods, but what I remember most clearly is the succession of men's faces, dark and hard with flat cheekbones, and the enormous sheepskin hats like halos." She came into contact with a wide range of social and economic classes, from lowly but honest laborers to skilled technicians and highly educated scientists. She traveled from town to town by motor car, plunging directly into the company of those same types of people, recording their conversations and taking close note of their personal experiences.

No doubt excited about what she saw, Forbes nonetheless tempered her enthusiasm with a strong tone of responsible control, separating the traveler from the travel writer. Thus she described the beautiful relics of Samarqand without being overwhelmed by them:

> The Mausoleum of Tamerlane stands bereft of walls, but the surrounding houses have withdrawn to give space to the still beautiful building. A few acacias, faintly flushed with blossom, cast shadows over the crumbling material evolved from Central Asian mud and rapidly reverting to its origin. The ribbed pumpkin dome rises proudly–and still flecked with blue–above the four-square mausoleum. . . .

She did not, however, ignore the undercurrent of excitement among young physicians, technicians, and managers who recognized their opportunities to contribute to the creation of what they thought would become a truly modern Soviet Uzbekistan society: "'The [silk] factory [at Bukhara] is not yet two years old,' explained the Russian manager, 'but already I have 300 workers, earning up to 400 rubles a month. Yes, they are nearly all women. What an escape it is from their homes! At first they were as frightened of light as of a man and they would scarcely even whisper, one to another. Now look at them.' His voice was proud and some of the workers glanced up at him, laughing." Yet Forbes did not attempt to idealize or patronize the women or their work. During the 1930s the possibility that Soviet economic philosophy could bring "ancient" nations into the twentieth century held a degree of attraction for her, but she remained cautious. Through the same approach to her subjects, Forbes worked hard to explicate Zoroastrianism without passing judgment on the religion or its followers.

Forbidden Road is a highly informative, readable, and thoroughly enjoyable travel book. For both Forbes and her audience "there . . . was no hurry. Everybody seemed willing to wait for endless hours, however unimportant the objective, and nobody showed any resentment at being forced to waste time, so plentiful and unimportant."

Forbes's twenty-first book, *These Are Real People* (1937), could be viewed as a companion piece of sorts to *Women Called Wild.* During 1937 she traveled with her husband through the Congo; when Arthur McGrath flew home to England, Forbes established herself in the residence of the game warden at Entebbe, Uganda, to write. In the preface to *These Are Real People* she wrote what seems to be a response to the critics who questioned the veracity of *Women Called Wild:* "For seventeen years I have traveled the length and breadth of the world and I have seen much that is inexplicable, but I am now prepared to believe a good deal that in more ignorant years I would have discredited without a second thought." As a traveler Forbes had little patience with the un-

Four cartoonists' impressions of Forbes (from Appointment with Destiny, *1946)*

imaginative among her critical readers. She usually devoted little attention to reviewers and cared even less about what they thought of her work.

True to its title, *These Are Real People* comprises accounts of individuals, mostly men, whom Forbes had met during her travel experiences, from her pre–World War I journey through Africa to her 1936 trek from Kabul through Afghanistan to Samarqand. Forbes introduced to her readers people such as a French idealist in Sumatra who committed murder because he despised everything that he considered ugly. She unfolded the story of "the Zebra man," one of the few convicts who had engineered a successful escape from Devil's Island. Another "real" person, a Mexican priest, murdered a man and then delivered himself to the Penitentes for crucifixion. A bootmaker from Northampton, England, fell in love in Ecuador and finalized the affair in central Asia.

The stories in *Women Called Wild,* when combined with those in *These Are Real People,* cause one to reflect on an aspect of Forbes's travel literature that sets it apart from other writers in that genre. Essentially she chose to write about people and places that ordinary travelers could not (or chose not to) see. She then filtered them through the fire of her imagination, and when they emerged upon the printed page, they often appeared larger than they perhaps ought to have been. Those same enlargements, when viewed through the negative lens of critics who understood neither her motivation for travel nor her narrative art, became distortions of reality. If her critics experienced problems distinguishing fact from fiction, however, Forbes did not.

World War II naturally placed limitations and restrictions upon travelers and travel writers, but Forbes managed to compensate somewhat. She devoted a significant amount of time supporting the Allied efforts by lecturing in Canada, the United States, and throughout Great Britain. She and Arthur McGrath also turned their attention to the Caribbean. In late 1939 and early 1940 they built an estate, Unicorn Cay, on four hundred acres of the nearly uninhabited island of Eleuthera in the Bahamas, some sixty-four miles from Nassau.

Some clues about the McGraths' activities in the Caribbean appear in *A Unicorn in the Bahamas* (1939), a 244-page description of the Bahama Islands. This work is more than an exciting travel narrative. It represents the end of one phase of Forbes's life and the beginning of another. In January 1939, she informed her readers in *Appointment with Destiny* (1946), "I decided–after eighteen years of serious and at times dangerous travel–that it was time that I embarked upon one journey for pleasure." Simply put, she would realize the fulfillment of a childhood dream:

> When I was very small I used to stare at a picture of a naked girl riding a unicorn. It hung above a mantelpiece laden with inherited chaos. In the background there was a forest. Along the edge of it–in the picture–pricked a figure dipped in coffee-gold upon a great white beast with a horn in its forehead. The girl's hair was a paler gold and wild in the wind. The unicorn's mane and tail were silken smooth, but they also trailed like a pennon in an Atlantic gale. The rider had neither reins nor spur. . . . It is years and years since I saw that picture. But always I have held to my intention–to find and tame a unicorn.

Instead of another journey to Africa, India, or the Middle East, Forbes responded to the call from the land of constant summer. She had been asked by the Bahama Government Development Board to write a book that would attract settlers to the islands. After more than twenty years as a traveler and travel writer, Forbes had little difficulty in satisfying both her own needs and theirs.

Forbes wrote about Bahama Islands such as New Providence, Harbour Island, Eleuthera, Exuma, Long Island and Cat Island, Andros, San Salvador, and Bimini. Organizing the first third of the work in loose chronological and historical fashion, she devoted the major portion of the book to the islands as she viewed them and as they affected her. In the opening chapters she demonstrated a deep sensitivity toward the historical background of the islands, tracing the history of the Bahamas from the time of their discovery, writing about the English and Spanish pirates of the sixteenth, seventeenth, and eighteenth centuries and the slavery and blockade running of the seventeenth, eighteenth, and nineteenth centuries. In the end she rented a house in Nassau that "stood with its toes on the rocks and its eyebrows, in the shape of a porch, hanging over the sea. There, with the colours which had become necessary to me, spread in changing splendour under my windows, I began to write this book. It is, I confess, about myself, as well as about the Bahamas." For Forbes *A Unicorn in the Bahamas* had become an exercise in the discovery of the self.

Forbes's road to self-discovery did not lead entirely away from the turbulence of world politics. As she reconstructed the relations of the Bahamas with Great Britain and the treatment of the islands by the League of Nations following World War I, Forbes openly challenged those political opportunists whose arrogance, contempt for the local inhabitants, legal manipulation, and blatant self-interest did little to improve the social and economic conditions of the islands. Unfortunately, however, her views toward people of color remind one of Rudyard Kipling's imperialistic notions about the need for Great Britain to "Take up the white man's burden."

Perhaps, in her eagerness to air her opinions about the Caribbean, Forbes did not investigate the facts and the subtleties of its history as thoroughly as she should. That fault, seen in combination with her relative unfamiliarity with the area (as opposed to her thorough knowledge of and commitment to the Middle East), creates almost a sense of detachment in *A Unicorn in the Bahamas.* In her defense Forbes may have found the West Indies a bit dull after more than twenty years of romantic adventure in Arab nations. Nonetheless, whatever its rhetorical or even factual shortcomings, *A Unicorn in the Bahamas* aroused the interest of readers and provided a useful guide for potential travelers to the Caribbean islands.

In 1939 Forbes also published *India of the Princes,* yet another attempt to fuse description and travel, personal narrative, historical fact, and contemporary opinion. At the outset of the book she announced, "Counting every small fief ruled by a semi-independent chieftain there are six hundred and seventy-five States [in India, which then included Pakistan]. Among these only seventy-three

Unicorn Cay, the house Forbes and McGrath built on the island of Eleuthera, Bahamas, in 1939–1940

of the Princes are entitled to salutes of more than eleven guns and to the prefix of Highness." Whether Forbes visited all these states cannot be determined, but she described them in a tone that proved both entertaining and authentic.

Before taking her readers on the tour, Forbes devoted a chapter to the Indian federation established by the British in 1935 with the eventual goal of Indian independence, and other chapters cover the three major political parties, public political opinion, and the relationship between Mohandas Gandhi and the Indian princes. Histories of the states, biographical sketches of the rulers, descriptions of the interiors and exteriors of their palaces as well as their domains and holdings, commentary on the rulers' wealth (including specific items in their jewelry collections), and exciting accounts of tiger and boar hunts constitute the substance of the volume, beginning in the states of Patiala, Kapurthala, and Dholpur, going through Jodhpur and Cochin, and ending with "the Big Five": Hyderabad, Mysore, Baroda, Kashmir, and Bhopal.

In 1940 Forbes published *These Men I Knew,* her impressions of more than two dozen men (and one woman) whom she had met or interviewed: Adolf Hitler, Hermann Göring, Joseph Goebbels, Joseph Stalin, Marshal Kliment Voroshilov (Soviet commissar for defense), Adm. Miklos Horthy de Nagybánya (regent of Hungary), Boris III of Bulgaria, George II of Greece, Alexander I of Yugoslavia, Russian-born banker and armaments contractor Sir Basil Zaharoff, Presidents Kemal Atatürk and Ismet Inönü of Turkey, Reza Shah Pahlavi of Iran, Faisal I of Syria (1920) and then Iraq (1921–1933), Leopold III of Belgium, Queen Wilhelmina of the Netherlands, Franklin Delano Roosevelt, Henry Ford, Benito Mussolini, Zog I of Albania, Emperor Haile Selassie of Ethiopia, Finnish field marshal and politician Baron Carl Gustaf Emil von Mannerheim, Prime Minister Jan Christian Smuts of the Union of South Africa, and Mohandas Gandhi.

To write *These Men I Knew* Forbes reached back into the farthest recesses of her memories as a traveler. Since 1915 she had met and formed impressions of people who played significant roles in world history, and her sketches yield more opinion than biographical fact. Contemporary events created a need for such a book, and the majority of Forbes's subjects were key players in World War II.

Almost four years passed before Forbes published another book, *Gypsy in the Sun* (1944), an autobiographical account of her travels during 1920 through 1934. She announced the work as the first of two volumes of memoirs. As usual Forbes stamped her lively, engaging personality on her narrative, flitting from one place to another as though challenging the reader to maintain the same breathtaking pace. She began the book with a statement that constitutes a summary of her life and purpose and an introduction to a quarter-century of travel and adventure:

> If there is one thing I love, it is the sun. If there is one thing I hate, it is a storm at sea. Yet searching for the beginning of me–as an individual, not as the daughter of a brilliant and much troubled father or the wife of a good looking Highlander with whom for three preposterous

> years I was miserable–I find it aboard a tramp between Massawa and Suez.

In *Gypsy in the Sun* and its companion volume, *Appointment with Destiny,* Forbes spared her reader little detail as she retraced her journey through an extremely active life. In the second volume of her memoirs, covering the years 1935 through 1943, Forbes felt obliged to fuse her adventures with keen, incisive surveys of political history and contemporary political events. Those times, with the world at war, proved most traumatic for Forbes. She continued, as in *Gypsy in the Sun,* to search for meaning in her life, to achieve a final destination following a lifetime of travel. Early in *Appointment with Destiny* she noted, "Somewhere I knew I must find a fragment of earth fresh as the first morning in Eden. I did not want comfort or intellectual intercourse. I wanted an old-fashioned and primitive condition dependent on my own brain and hands." Little wonder, then, that once Forbes and her husband found their Eden in the Bahamas, she removed herself almost entirely from the literary scene and the lecture circuit. By that time, however, she had seen most of the world.

During the thirty years in which Forbes published travel literature, she received several salvos of negative commentary from reviewers who neither accepted nor attempted to understand her prose style. The personality traits that drove her to seek adventure and the company of venturesome people produced a lively and witty style that seemed too light to serious critics. Reviewing *Secret of the Sahara* for the London *Times Literary Supplement* (4 August 1921), one writer complained about Forbes's "purple patches," while a review of *From Red Sea to Blue Nile* in the *New York World* (20 December 1925) accused her of trying "to force an atmosphere of excitement" into her observations and reactions. Writing for the *New Statesman and Nation* (19 August 1933), novelist and critic V. S. Pritchett referred to Forbes's style of the 1920s as "her early Wurlitzer manner," and a critic for *The New York Times* (31 January 1937) called *Women Called Wild* a product of Forbes's "adventure-dyed pen."

Other reviewers saw Forbes as trying to stretch too many points too far, particularly one in the *Saturday Review* (29 April 1933), who thought that in *Eight Republics in Search of a Future* "there are moments when she becomes rather a bore. The book is, in fact, rather too long." Perhaps the unkindest cut came from John Mavrogordato, whose review of *Women Called Wild* for the *New Statesman and Nation* (7 December 1935) asked: "How much of all this can we believe when most of it is treated in such a manner as to be indistinguishable from the worst fiction? How many of these 90,000 words could be spared? It would be kinder not to say."

One must declare, however, that Forbes's writing attracted far more followers than detractors among reviewers. Those who understood her objectives as traveler and travel writer assessed her work reasonably and accurately. Katherine Woods, writing about *These Are Real People* for *The New York Times* (29 January 1939), summarized the positive literary qualities that predominate in all Forbes's works:

> Rosita Forbes sees things that travelers cannot see easily and are not expected to see at all. She has an intense and imaginative curiosity about her fellow-humans, makes friends with them everywhere, shares the most appalling living conditions with a gay heart. And she writes of all this with cleverness and a vibrant personal quality of vividness and wit. By and large, this collection of far-flung adventure tales is exceedingly interesting. It is a book which probably no one but Rosita Forbes would have been able to write.

The words "intense imaginative curiosity" identify exactly the aspect of Forbes's personality that she managed to transfer so easily and so successfully to each page of her prose. Those who criticized her failed, perhaps, to see beyond her language and into her personality. A definite air of excitement and anticipation exists in Forbes's travel books, and thus they sold well. Obviously, her readers paid little notice to her critics.

Forbes died in Warwick, Bermuda on 30 June 1967, five years after the passing of her husband, Arthur McGrath. By then she had gained significant recognition for her writing. She received gold medals from the Royal Antwerp Geographical Society (1921) and the French Geographical Society (1923) and a silver medal from the Royal Society of Arts in London (1924) for her paper "The Position of the Arabs in Art and Literature." She was also named a fellow of the Royal Geographical Society.

In her travel writings Forbes climbed over simple description and observation to the consideration of world politics and social awareness. Equally important, she demonstrated to women they could contribute meaningful activity and significant thought to a male-dominated world.

References:

Thomas Charles Bridges and Hubert Hessell Tiltman, *Heroes of Modern Adventure* (Boston: Little, Brown, 1927), pp. 101–115;

Margaret Cole, *Women of To-Day* (London: Nelson, 1938), pp. 291–311.

E. M. Forster

(1 January 1879 – 7 June 1970)

Elizabeth A. Ford
Westminster College

See also the Forster entries in *DLB 34: British Novelists, 1890–1925: Traditionalists; DLB 98: Modern British Essayists, Second Series; DLB 162: British Short-Fiction Writers, 1915–1945; DLB 178: British Fantasy and Science-Fiction Writers Before World War I;* and *DLB Documentary Series 10: The Bloomsbury Group.*

E. M. Forster in India, circa 1921

BOOKS: *Where Angels Fear to Tread* (Edinburgh & London: Blackwood, 1905; New York: Knopf, 1920);

The Longest Journey (Edinburgh & London: Blackwood, 1907; New York: Knopf, 1922);

A Room with a View (London: Arnold, 1908; New York & London: Putnam, 1911);

Howards End (London: Arnold, 1910; New York & London: Putnam, 1910);

The Celestial Omnibus and Other Stories (London: Sidgwick & Jackson, 1911; New York: Knopf, 1923);

The Story of the Siren (Richmond: Leonard and Virginia Woolf at the Hogarth Press, 1920);

The Government of Egypt, Recommendation by a Committee of the International Section of the Labour Research Department, with Notes on Egypt by E. M. Forster (London: Labour Research Department, 1920);

Alexandria: A History and a Guide (Alexandria: Whitehead Morris, 1922);

Pharos and Pharillon (Richmond: Hogarth Press, 1923; New York: Knopf, 1923);

A Passage to India (London: Arnold, 1924; New York: Harcourt, Brace, 1924);

Anonymity: An Enquiry (London: Hogarth Press, 1925);

Aspects of the Novel (London: Arnold, 1927; New York: Harcourt, Brace, 1927);

The Eternal Moment and Other Stories (London: Sidgwick & Jackson, 1928; New York: Harcourt, Brace, 1928);

Goldsworthy Lowes Dickinson (London: Arnold, 1934; New York: Harcourt, Brace, 1934);

Abinger Harvest (London: Arnold, 1936; New York: Harcourt, Brace, 1936);

What I Believe (London: Hogarth Press, 1939);

England's Pleasant Land, a Pageant Play (London: Hogarth Press, 1940);

Nordic Twilight, Macmillan War Pamphlets, volume 3 (London: Macmillan, 1940);

Virginia Woolf: The Rede Lecture (Cambridge: Cambridge University Press, 1942; New York: Harcourt, Brace, 1942);

The Collected Tales of E. M. Forster (New York: Knopf, 1947); republished as *Collected Short Stories of E. M. Forster* (London: Sidgwick & Jackson, 1948);

Two Cheers for Democracy (London: Arnold, 1951; New York: Harcourt, Brace, 1951);

Billy Budd: Opera in Four Acts, music by Benjamin Britten and libretto by Forster and Eric Crozier, adapted from the story by Herman Melville (London, New York, Toronto, Sydney, Capetown, Buenos Aires, Paris & Bonn: Boosey & Hawkes, 1951);

The Hill of Devi (London: Arnold, 1953; New York: Harcourt, Brace, 1953);

Marianne Thornton (1797–1887): A Domestic Biography (London: Arnold, 1956; New York: Harcourt, Brace, 1956);

Maurice (London: Arnold, 1971; New York: Norton, 1971);

Albergo Empedocles and Other Writings, edited by George H. Thomson (New York: Liveright, 1971);

The Life to Come and Other Stories (London: Arnold, 1972); republished as *The Life to Come and Other Short Stories* (New York: Norton, 1972);

The Lucy Novels: Early Sketches for "A Room with a View," edited by Oliver Stallybrass (London: Arnold, 1973; New York: Holmes & Meier, 1973);

The Manuscripts of "Howards End," edited by Stallybrass (London: Arnold, 1973; New York: Holmes & Meier, 1973);

Aspects of the Novel and Related Writings, edited by Stallybrass (London: Arnold, 1974; New York: Holmes & Meier, 1974);

The Manuscripts of "A Passage to India," edited by Stallybrass (London: Arnold, 1978; New York: Holmes & Meier, 1979);

Commonplace Book [manuscript facsimile] (London: Scolar Press, 1978);

Arctic Summer and Other Fiction, edited by Elizabeth Heine and Stallybrass (London: Arnold, 1980; New York: Holmes & Meier, 1980);

The Hill of Devi and Other Indian Writings, edited by Heine (London: Arnold, 1983; New York: Holmes & Meier, 1983);

Commonplace Book, edited by Philip Gardner (London: Scolar Press, 1985; Stanford: Stanford University Press, 1985; revised edition, Stanford: Stanford University Press, 1987).

Collection: *The Abinger Edition of E. M. Forster,* 14 volumes to date, edited by Stallybrass and Heine (London: Arnold, 1972–1983; New York: Holmes & Meier, 1972–1983).

OTHER: Eliza Fay, *Original Letters from India (1779–1815),* edited by Forster (London: Hogarth Press, 1925).

In a 1959 lecture, "Three Countries," E. M. Forster called himself "a confirmed globetrotter," but the impact of travel on his life and work cannot adequately be suggested by that light phrase. What Forster learned as a traveler reinforced his belief in the ultimate importance of personal relationships, especially those that ignored traditional boundaries of gender, class, race, and culture. The egalitarian vision that set him apart from the more elitist writers among his contemporaries makes all his work, not just his novels, central to increasing multicultural understanding.

Forster's travel writings illustrate the cohesiveness of his creativity. The themes that dominate *Alexandria: A History and a Guide* (1922), *Pharos and Pharillon* (1923), *The Hill of Devi* (1953), and many letters and essays also resonate in his six novels: *Where Angels Fear to Tread* (1905), *The Longest Journey* (1907), *A Room with a View* (1908), *Howards End* (1910), *A Passage to India* (1924), and *Maurice* (1971). In his writings about the countries central to his experience–England, Italy, India, and Egypt–Forster's meticulous sense of place evokes more than setting. In his fiction and nonfiction he used travel as a metaphor for self-understanding.

Edward Morgan Forster was born on 1 January 1879. His father, also named Edward Morgan Forster, died before his son was two. His mother, Alice Clara Whichelo Forster (called Lily), made a series of uneasy odysseys between relatives' homes and boardinghouses before she leased Rooksnest, a country house in Hertfordshire, in 1882. Forster loved Rooksnest, which was the inspiration for *Howards End.* An only child, articulate and impetuous, he thrived at the center of a loving circle composed of his mother, two doting grandmothers, and several lively aunts.

Propelled from this nurturing environment into preparatory school at Kent House, Eastbourne, in 1890, Forster suffered the derision of his classmates, who found him weak and poor at sports. In his biography of Forster, P. N. Furbank recounts Forster's first inkling of his homosexuality, which occurred during these early school years and surely escalated his sense of difference. In 1893 bullying at Forster's next school, The Grange in Eastbourne, compelled his mother to move to Tonbridge, where she enrolled her son as a day boy at Tonbridge School. Forster's solace during these years came from his mother, and in 1895 he shared his first taste of travel with her when they toured churches in Normandy during a holiday he had planned. While they traveled Forster began jotting down his observations, a practice he continued for the rest of his life.

Forster's intellect eventually established him as a scholar at Tonbridge but did not grant him the easy popularity he admired. On entering King's College, Cambridge in 1897, he found a place that offered him intellectual fulfillment and satisfying personal relationships. His tutor Nathaniel Wedd

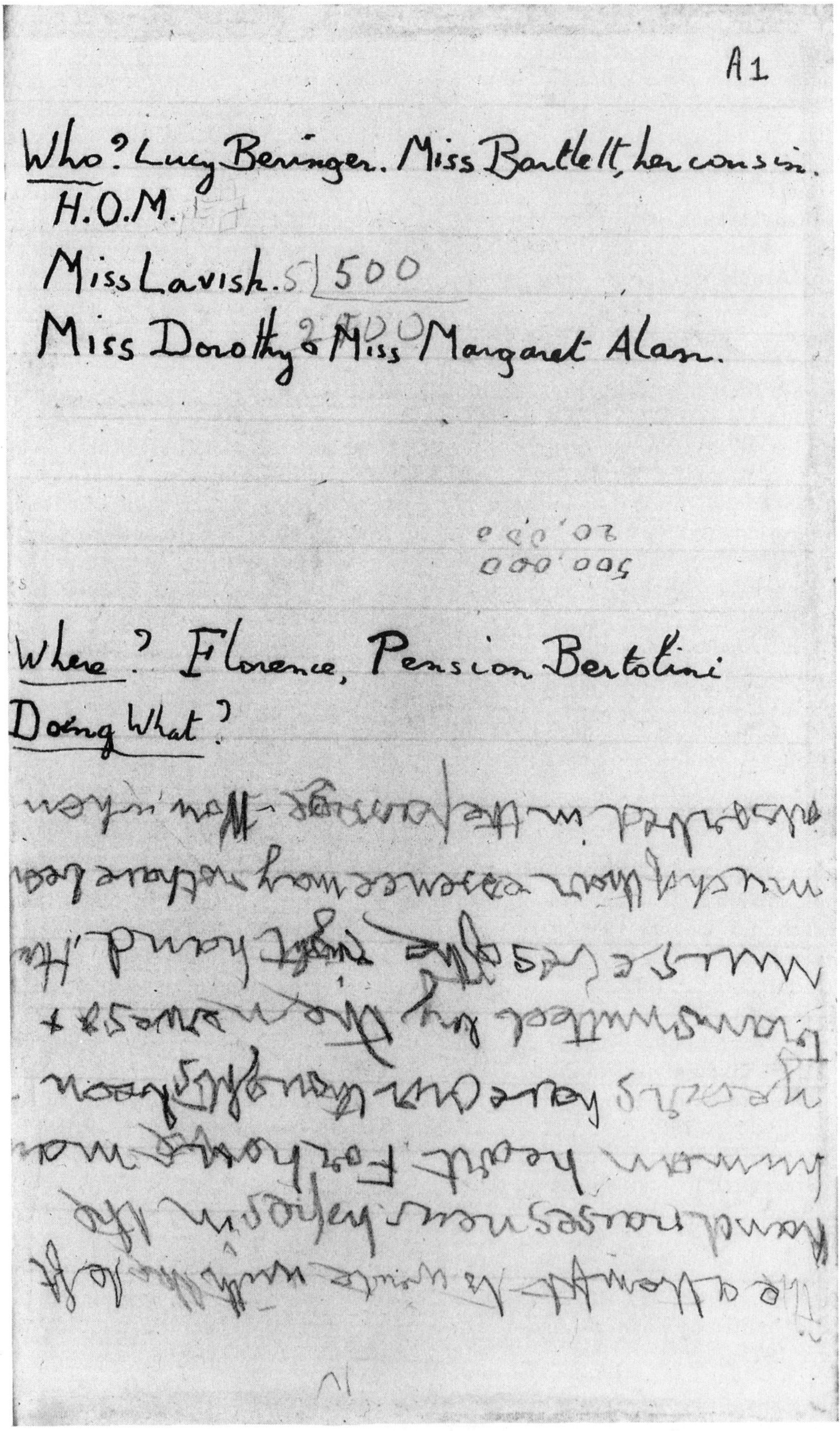
A1
Who? Lucy Beringer. Miss Bartlett, her cousin.
H.O.M.
Miss Lavish.
Miss Dorothy & Miss Margaret Alan.
Where? Florence, Pension Bertolini
Doing What?

Early plan for Forster's "Lucy" novel, the first draft of A Room with a View *(1908). Made in Naples in 1902, these notes mention a pension that Forster based on the Pensione Simi in Florence, where he and his mother stayed in 1901 (King's College, Cambridge)*

Forster, circa 1902–1903, wearing a cloak he bought in Italy

and the eccentric, scholarly Goldsworthy Lowes Dickinson influenced and encouraged Forster. As a member of the Apostles, an exclusive intellectual society, he met and befriended other young writers and thinkers such as Leonard Woolf and H. O. Meredith. At Cambridge Forster learned that others shared his homosexual feelings. Heavily involved in the creative life of Cambridge, he wrote for several university publications, and in 1900–1901 he began a novel, "They Are Nottingham Lace," which remained unfinished.

In October 1901, after receiving a disappointing second-class degree in history, Forster and his mother set off on a year of travel through Italy and Austria, to forestall Forster's decision about his future. After the initial shock of lodging in a Florentine pension so filled with other British travelers that it seemed chillingly like an English suburb, Forster felt thawed by Italian art and life. He had hoped to write during the trip, and he began by creating characters based on his fellow travelers for a work he first called his "*Lucy*" novel, which after revision became *A Room with a View*.

Moved by the beauty of the Italian landscape, Forster wrote "The Story of a Panic" (*Independent Review,* August 1903), which sets up the opposition between two types of travelers: those who can and those who cannot spiritually enter the places they visit physically. The characters in "The Story of a Panic" are English tourists too fearful to surrender to the living spirit of Pan, who first manifests himself as an unsettling silence and then as a gust of wind. Only one of them, the sullen young Eustace, gives himself to the spirit of the place and does not run in panic. Transfigured by his experience, Eustace can no longer live in a diminished real world, and the story ends with his "shouts and laughter" as he runs off.

The imaginative insight in this story and in notes Forster was making for his novel show that he was getting inspiration from his relative freedom, from the other travelers, and from Italy. His mother, however, found him to be a terrible traveler. She despaired at his constant misplacing of necessities, such as his Baedeker travel guide, and she bemoaned his clumsiness. (Furbank notes that Forster did indeed sprain his ankle and break his arm on the steps of Saint Peter's.) At the same time Lily Forster was calling her son vague and incompetent, however, Forster was developing competence as a writer. Her wish to perpetuate his helplessness foreshadowed the lifelong tension between mother and son.

The Greek cruise Forster took with Cambridge friends in April 1903 included a gradual separation from his mother, who went only as far as Florence. "The Road from Colonus" (*Independent Review,* June 1904), written on this trip, revisits the territory Forster marked out in "The Story of a Panic." Mr. Lucas, a bored British tourist, comes alive in the tiny Greek town of Plataniste when he experiences a magical stream of water flowing from an ancient tree. After resting beside the stream, he sees that every object, every motion has meaning. Mr. Lucas insists on remaining in this town, but his daughter, Ethel, laughingly dismisses his declaration, and they leave. Back in England, Mr. Lucas and Ethel read an account of a disaster that took place the night they passed through Plataniste: the tree fell, killing everyone at the hotel. Mr. Lucas pays little attention to this disaster because he is absorbed in trivialities. A single day of vibrant life, Forster suggests, would have had more value than eternally marking time.

Forster (second from right) in Rhodes during his April 1903 trip to Greece

"The Story of a Panic" and "The Road from Colonus," well received by friends and critics and still among his best stories, mark Forster's start as a serious author. As Paul Fussell points out in *Abroad* (1980), describing or defining travel writing is "hazardous." These short travel fictions provide no tips to ease a journey and identify no mandatory sights. Yet they do introduce travel themes that Forster revisited in fiction and nonfiction: the insight travel can offer, the battle between passion and convention, and the danger of merging oneself with the journey.

In his first published novel, *Where Angels Fear to Tread,* Forster alternated English and Italian settings to illustrate the distance between analytical and emotional approaches to life. Mrs. Herriton, a middle-class matriarch, sends Lilia, the exuberant widow of her eldest son, to Italy in the company of the admirable Caroline Abbot. Mrs. Herriton hopes the combination of Caroline and Italy will improve her daughter-in-law. Despite resistance from the Herritons and Caroline, Lilia marries Gino, a young Italian peasant. Their union is as grim as Mrs. Herriton has predicted, and Lilia dies giving birth to a half-Italian, half-English baby.

The battle for the baby sparks a crucial travel sequence. Mrs. Herriton sends her son and daughter, Philip and Harriet, to retrieve it, and Caroline Abbot attempts the same mission. Philip and Caroline respond positively to Italy and to Gino's love for his child, but Harriet, who sees Italy only as alien ground, wants to pick up the baby as if it were a parcel. Her persistence overrides Philip and Caroline's sensitivity, and she kidnaps the baby, deciding its fate. The child dies in a carriage accident. After making peace with Gino, Philip, Caroline, and Harriet return to Sawston, Philip and Caroline changed by glimpses of a real life.

Mishaps that Forster and his mother suffered on their trip to Italy found their way into Philip and Harriet's trying journey, and there are other correspondences between Forster's life and his first published novel. Like Forster, Philip is the intelligent, intuitive son of a dominant mother and finds Italy liberating. Philip, however, cannot act. Forster fought to link his external and internal realities by continuing to travel and to write.

In 1905 Forster visited Germany, not as a tourist, but as tutor to Elizabeth von Arnim's three daughters. Germany did not enchant him as Italy

Syed Ross Masood and Forster during a summer 1911 visit to Italy

had, but he liked von Arnim, her daughters, and the way he fit into the household. Von Arnim, remembered for her novel *The Enchanted April* (1922), reacted to proofs of *Where Angels Fear to Tread* with admiration, as did most critics, one of whom found the novel "startlingly original" and a "grotesque tragedy" (*Manchester Guardian,* 4 October 1905). In 1907, the year in which Forster published his next novel, *The Longest Journey,* von Arnim invited her daughters' former tutor to join a party of her friends on a caravan trip around Kent. Forster enjoyed this brief period of rugged living. He must have also reveled in the freedom, as he did when he traveled again to Italy in 1908, this time with a Cambridge friend instead of his mother, paying for the trip with profits from his writing. Travel fueled his imagination, and his imagination allowed him the luxury of travel.

Von Arnim wrote to Forster that *The Longest Journey,* set in Cambridge, was "a wonderful book." Contemporary critics complained about its harshness and its sudden deaths but saw the book as proof of Forster's potential. In *The Longest Journey* Forster began to link passion, direct experience, and intellect, using the metaphor of a journey toward self-knowledge. *A Room With a View* (1908), his next novel, relies on a literal travel motif and again on the opposition between the warmth of Italy and the chill of England.

A reviewer for the *Morning Leader* (30 October 1908) hailed *A Room with a View,* as "one of the best novels of the season," and most others reviewed it favorably. Forster feared that this novel, begun on his first Italian trip, was too sweet, too dated. Yet its sweetness does not preclude its seriousness.

Traveling in Italy, Lucy Honeychurch finds herself in a viewless room in Florence, feeling–as Forster did before her–that she might as well have stayed at home. Drama occurs when Lucy and George Emerson, another dissatisfied young tourist, witness a murder in the Piazza della Signoria. The moment of shared horror links them, and during a picnic in the Italian countryside George sweeps Lucy into his arms and kisses her. Refusing to acknowledge the passion she feels because she knows that George and his father are not of her class, Lucy flees to England where she agrees to marry the effete Cecil Vyse, a man who is "right" by every materialistic standard but agonizingly wrong by every human measure. Eventually, Lucy is

The Royal Palace at Chhatarpur, which Forster visited during his 1912–1913 travels in India

forced to acknowledge the truth. She marries George and returns with him to Florence.

A summary of the final states of Forster's fictional travelers suggests an upward path. In "The Story of a Panic" Eustace is rudely changed by a living Greek myth. In "The Road from Colonus" Mr. Lucas rejects the truth revealed to him on his trip and might as well be dead. In *Where Angels Fear to Tread* Philip Herriton sees Gino's love for the baby but cannot act upon his insight. Yet Lucy realizes her love for George and crosses class barriers to act on her realization.

A Room with a View includes its share of shadows along with its positive ending. There is the ugly possessiveness of the professional tourist, such as pulp novelist Eleanor Lavish, who feels she owns the country she visits; the limited understanding that Italophile Cecil Vyse recognizes in himself; and the numbing loneliness of Lucy's cousin and chaperone Charlotte Bartlett. Not everyone can make the journey toward self-actualization, Forster cautions; some will remain tourists, never travelers.

Similar distinctions between the characters occur in *Howards End* (1910), which asks whether idealists or realists will inherit England. This tragic novel depends on the quest motif, not actual travel. Forster asks that travelers making the longest journey through life "only connect" passion and intellect.

Because Forster and his mother were firmly ensconced in the suburban routine of Weybridge, it might seem as if Forster were not following his own formula–passion plus intellect–for living a meaningful life. London, however, provided what the suburbs could not. There Forster socialized with the Bloomsbury Group–avant-garde artists, writers, and thinkers including Virginia and Leonard Woolf, Lytton Strachey, Vanessa and Clive Bell, Maynard Keynes, Duncan Grant, and Roger Fry. Forster's London life also gave him a link to the working class. For twenty years, beginning in 1902, he taught at the Working Men's College.

Forster's Cambridge associations were the catalyst for a friendship that broadened his worldview. In 1906 he met Syed Ross Masood, an intelligent, charming young Indian who was studying at Cambridge and seeking a tutor. Forster first tutored Masood and then became his friend. Masood changed Forster's life by placing India in the center of his imagination.

In 1912 Forster went eagerly to visit India and Masood. He traveled with a group of Cambridge friends, including Goldsworthy Lowes Dickinson and Robert Trevelyan. According to Furbank, Forster's goal was not to "see" India as a British tourist but to "get to know Indians." He planned not to spend time with Anglo-Indians, although he visited with Malcolm and Josie Darling, friends who were "unusual," Nicola Beauman notes in her biography of Forster, because they socialized with Indians. During his yearlong visit Forster saw Masood in his natural context and met his family. Because of his connec-

Entrance to Lomas Rishi Cave, one of the seven Barabar Caves, which Forster visited in 1912 and later used as the model for the Marabar Caves in A Passage to India *(1924)*

tion with Masood, Forster entered India in a personal way closed to most tourists. He reveled in its scenery, from the cities of Aligarh and Delhi to the Vale of Kashmir, the caves of Ellora, and the Barabar Hills, whose caves became the model for the Marabar Caves in *A Passage to India.* He observed celebrations such as a nautch (a party with female dancers) and a Muslim wedding. He met Vishnwarath Singh Bahadur, Maharajah of Chhatarpur, and the charming Tukoji Rao III, Maharajah of Dewas Senior, who was later to figure prominently in his life. Attempting to become as Indian as possible, Forster sometimes wore Indian dress, including a turban of "scarlet and gold." He learned to relish Indian food and refused English food that was offered him. His rich and lively letters to his mother and aunts are full of keen insight; yet, when his trip ended in 1913, Forster felt he had not really seen India and that its ambiguity and ambivalence could not be described or perceived as a whole. His first trip to India increased his desire to return and to write about it.

While in India Forster had begun work on a novel set there. He had also written informative and evocative letters and had kept a journal. After his return to England stagnation set in, and he could neither finish the Indian novel nor commit himself to another. His reluctance to write about heterosexual love contributed to his writer's block. In 1914 to free himself Forster wrote the novel *Maurice,* which treats the topic of homosexuality. Its protagonist, Maurice Hall, tries to "cure" his difference, as if it were a disease, but finally realizes that loving men is good and right for him.

Forster's homosexuality is connected to his reliance on the traveler motif. His outsider status in his own society, much like that of a traveler walking through a foreign landscape, seems to have increased his sensitivity to other types of difference. Writing *Maurice* provided catharsis, but Forster could circulate the manuscript only among sympathetic readers. Because of the harshness of British law and Forster's insistence that his mother not be troubled, he suppressed *Maurice* and all his short stories that treated homosexual love. These works were published only after his death. Nonetheless Forster supported writers who chose to challenge the definition of "acceptable" material. In 1928 he defended Radclyffe Hall's lesbian novel *The Well of Loneliness* (1928) during legal actions that led to its withdrawal from publication, and in 1960, at the age of eighty-one, he was a witness at the trial in which Penguin Books was found not guilty of obscenity for publishing an unexpurgated version of D. H. Lawrence's *Lady Chatterly's Lover,* first published in Italy in 1928. After writing *Maurice* Forster wondered whether he would write another publishable novel.

In 1914 the international crisis of World War I overshadowed his personal angst. When England entered the war, Forster, like many of his Bloomsbury friends, felt that seeking conscientious-objector status was an appropriate response to carnage and horror. Forster wanted, however, to be useful to those who did serve. In 1915 he became a Red Cross searcher, a position similar to one held by Walt Whitman in the American Civil War. Stationed in Alexandria, Egypt, Forster located men listed as missing, visited ill and lonely invalids, and tried to lift morale. He performed his tasks ably and remained in Alexandria until 1919, a year after the war ended.

While Egypt never charmed Forster, he enjoyed this prolonged period of freedom. He was not a tourist here. He had important work and a passionate love affair with Mohammed el Adl, a young Egyptian tram conductor; the two corresponded until Adl's death in 1922. Forster also met poet Constantine Cavafy, whose work he championed.

According to Furbank, Alexandria became most alive to Forster while he was researching the history section of *Alexandria: A History and a Guide* (1922), his first extended piece of nonfiction travel writing. *Alexandria* is more than an objective guide to historical sites. In *A Room with a View* Lucy Honeychurch clings to her Baedeker, and *Alexandria* echoes the conversational tone of that guidebook. The history section is arranged chronologically and thematically to trace the progress of civilizations through the city, examining art, philosophy, science, religion, mathematics, literature, and warfare. Forster's voice animates the informative history, interrupting a paraphrase from Theocritus's Fifteenth Idyll about the way Greek women were afraid of Egyptians to comment "(just like Greek ladies today)," or pausing to highlight what he finds interesting, such as Plotinus and Neoplatonism. Like Percy Bysshe Shelley before him, Forster had Neoplatonic leanings and must have found personal satisfaction in linking Neoplatonism and Indian thought: "The Christian promise is that a man shall see God, the Neo-Platonic–like the Indian–that he shall be God."

The guide section of *Alexandria* connects with the history section. Forster's instructions to potential museum visitors reinforce his belief that to "see," one should know what has come before; thus, a traveler "should not visit the collection until he has learned . . . something about the ancient city." The work is pervaded with Forster's belief that Alexandria's "links with the past have been wantonly broken."

Forster in Alexandria, 1916

Literary scholars such as Frances B. Singh find *Alexandria* as important as *Maurice* in the development of Forster's canon. Certainly *Alexandria* demonstrates Forster's wish to "only connect" passion and intellect. The book traces both strains through the cultural history of the city. He does not try to "own" the city by demonstrating that he understands it; Forster's sensitivity to the mystery inherent in Alexandria also connects the book with *Maurice*. He does not use his insider status as Adl's lover to claim the city is somehow his. He knows it belongs to its past and to its present inhabitants.

Soon after Whitehead Morris, an Alexandria publishing house, brought out the first edition of *Alexandria* in December 1922, they reported to Forster that most copies of the book had been destroyed in a warehouse fire. Having received an insurance settlement, they sent him a check to cover his loss. Later the publishers sent Forster a second letter saying

The guest house in Dewas Senior, where Forster stayed in 1912 and 1921

that *Alexandria* had not been destroyed but that because the insurance money had already been paid, they had burned the books themselves. The company published a second edition of *Alexandria* in 1938.

Forster's response to the destruction of *Alexandria* was *Pharos and Pharillon* (1923), a series of sketches inspired by the research he had done on Alexandria. He dedicated the book to Mohammed el Adl. Again Forster lamented that ancient Alexandria no longer exists: "Alas! The modern city calls for no enthusiastic comment." The short, evocative pieces in *Pharos and Pharillon* tie glimpses of the past to the present. Forster calls Alexander the Great a "young tourist" and examines the history of the Jews in the city, who have survived hundreds of years of "rebuffs" but "are traveling first [class]" today. He describes the beauty of the Suez Canal, which "has never received full appreciation from the traveler. He is in too much of a hurry to arrive or depart, his eyes are too much bent on England or on India for him to enjoy that exquisite corridor of tinted mountain and radiant water." In this passage Forster seems to chide himself for remaining a tourist in Egypt. A "serious history" of Alexandria, he says, has yet to be written. While *Pharos and Pharillon,* which most critics liked, may not be a "serious history," it is a serious exploration of form. The sketches are an effective montage of myth, history, memory, and poetry. Forster's next piece of travel writing depended on its significant form.

When his two Egypt books appeared, Forster was in India. In 1921 he had been presented with a tantalizing reason to revisit that country. The maharajah of Dewas Senior, a native state in Hyderabad, invited Forster to be his temporary secretary, a substitute for the British colonel who held that post. Forster quickly agreed to take the job. As a British subject working under an Indian prince, he would be making an anticolonial, antiracist statement. As an insider in the royal court of Dewas, he would "see" Indians more intimately than most non-Indians had ever done. As a writer, he would have new material and, he hoped, ample time to finish his Indian novel.

Fascinated frustration replaced the euphoria present in Forster's early letters home from Dewas as he began to perceive the muddles that surrounded "Bapu Sahib," as the maharajah was affectionately called. Many aspects of daily Indian life seemed incomprehensible to Forster, including an expensive watering system that had no water source and two "unplayable" grand pianos Forster found "cracked by the dryness" in an empty room. His responsibilities were never specified, so he rarely knew on which problem to focus. Living through the hot season was more stressful than Forster had imagined, and the heat escalated his passion. He was alternately consumed by lust and embarrassed by it. Perhaps worst of all, he wrote little.

Yet Forster often gained exactly the kind of insight into India that he had anticipated. The maharajah invited him to family celebrations, includ-

Forster in 1921, while he was serving as secretary to Tukoji Rao III, Maharajah of Dewas Senior

ing the gift-giving that followed the birth of a new princess. Bapu Sahib also included Forster in the complex preparations for religious ceremonies such as Gokul Ashtami. Forster found this festival honoring the Hindu god Krishna surrounded by "bad taste" but intensely meaningful. The maharajah's exhausting role especially impressed Forster, who felt the pervasive power of Bapu Sahib's spirituality. Forster, who "dressed like a Hindu," did not believe that he understood what had taken place.

Forster described his stay in Dewas Senior in *The Hill of Devi* (1953). The book is not a memoir or a journal or a collection of letters, but a composite of the three. The preface apologizes for the touristy tone of the letters to his mother and his aunts, but these letters underscore his progress from curious onlooker to truth seeker. The materials Forster selected for the book combine to complete a portrait of the maharajah and Forster himself. *The Hill of Devi* is a monument to their relationship, continuing Forster's emphasis on personal connection.

The title refers to a sacred site in Dewas, and the work traces an upward path toward Forster's recognition of Bapu Sahib's spirituality. "Letters of 1912–1913" describe Forster's first meeting with the maharajah and give his early impressions of the state. "The State and Its Ruler" expands the description and analysis of Dewas, and the section called "Letters of 1921–1922" includes parts of the journal Forster kept during his stay in Dewas as well as letters. The "Catastrophe" section details the maharajah's troubled exile, precipitated when his eldest son ac-

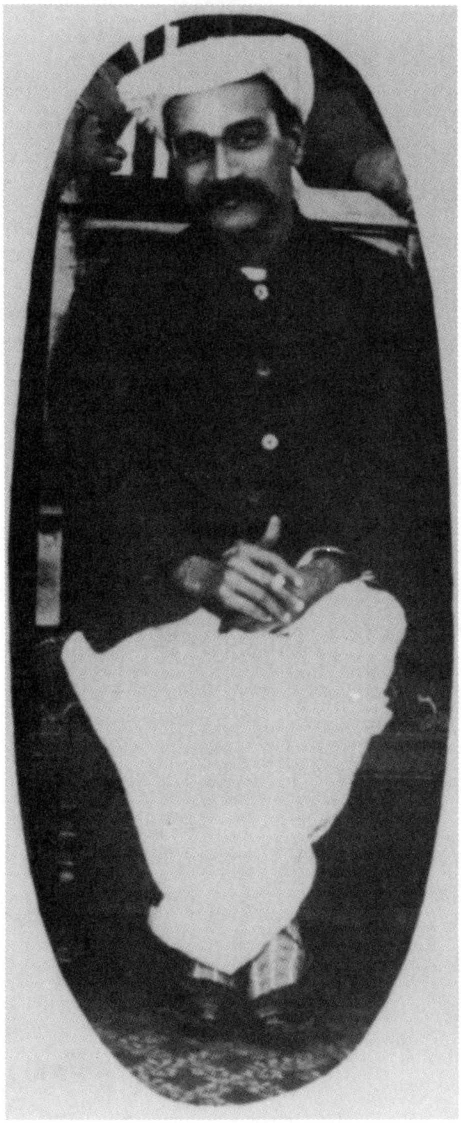

Tukoji Rao III, Maharajah of Dewas Senior

cused his father of attempted murder, and Bapu Sahib's death in Pondicherry in 1937. Forster felt the murder charge could not be true but concluded that it is ultimately less important to clear the rajah's reputation than it is to recognize his spirituality and sweetness. Contemporary reviewers of *The Hill of Devi,* including Richard Hughes, who reviewed it for *The Spectator* (16 October 1953), were "grateful for anything" from Forster's "golden" pen but suggested that this contribution was less important than a novel.

Forster's tribute to Bapu Sahib may have been an attempt to give him in death the reverence Forster felt he had not made clear in life. *The Hill of Devi* also illuminates a confused stretch of Forster's life; he left Dewas feeling less than successful. After six months little progress had been made on the construction of a new palace, and the maharajah's finances were still hopelessly entangled. Forster's predecessor was returning, and he and Forster had exchanged terse, unpleasant letters. It was not possible for either Englishman to untangle the muddle that enveloped Dewas Senior, but Forster had anticipated such accomplishment that he was dissatisfied.

Forster took his mother rolls of exquisite sari cloth from India. (After Lily Forster's death, Beauman notes, Forster found the unused material "rotted away.") His initially festive arrival had a correspondingly dismal downturn. At forty-three, back in England and back with his mother in Weybridge, Forster despaired that he would not or should not finish his Indian novel, or any other. He as well as his critics seemed to have valued his fiction more than his nonfiction. Though he had written *Alexandria* and *Pharos and Pharillon* and many essays and radio broadcasts, he felt unproductive. Virginia and Leonard Woolf raised Forster from his torpor and encouraged him to complete *A Passage to India.* Leonard Woolf had read the manuscript and felt it was an important work in the making, and Forster acknowledged the Woolfs' contribution in 1924, when he wrote to Leonard Woolf, "I have this moment written the last words of my novel, and who but Virginia and yourself should be told about it first." Forster initially felt little enthusiasm for the work most critics consider his masterpiece. As he added to and revised his manuscript, he worried, as he had about *A Room with A View*, that the material was dated.

Some contemporary readers, such as E. A. Horne, validated his worry, complaining in a letter to the *The New Statesman* (16 August 1924) that Forster's Anglo-Indians were "puppets, simulacra" and that their attitudes were "hopelessly out of date." Yet the lively discussion that followed the publication of *A Passage to India* showed that the novel tweaked some international nerves. Several Anglo-Indians protested the nature of the creator as well as his creation, asking how any artist could hope to understand and correctly portray the political reality of colonialism. In contrast one anonymous Indian reader applauded Forster's Indian characters because they were "human beings" (*Times of India,* 23 July 1924). Literary critics such as J. B. Priestley, who reviewed *A Passage to India* for the *London Mercury* (July 1924), hailed the novel as "an event," Forster's triumphant return to fiction, and felt that the aesthetics, not the politics, mattered most.

Yet the dialectic between the critics who deplored Forster's politics and those who applauded his vision may be more revealing than any static view. *A Passage to India* insists on intellectual mo-

Forster speaking at the International Congress of Writers in Paris, 1935

tion. Its title evokes a journey, as do its three sections: "Mosque," "Caves," "Temple." Travel through the novel begins in a place of worship, moves through an enclosed, dark space, and finishes in an overarching dome.

Forster's familiar disgruntled traveler motif dominates "Mosque." Two female travelers, the elderly Mrs. Moore and the youthful Adela Quested, visit India, determined to understand it. Of the two, the intuitive, innately spiritual Mrs. Moore is better equipped to do so. Adela Quested is dangerously curious, a quality that manifests itself in her reason for visiting India. She is trying to decide whether or not she should marry Ronnie Heaslop, Mrs. Moore's son and the city magistrate of Chandrapore. Since she cannot examine her own heart, it seems unlikely that her quest for the real India will bring her anything but dissatisfaction.

Adela's search disrupts the lives of everyone around her after she accuses a charming, intelligent Indian, Dr. Aziz, of attacking her in a cave outside Chandrapore during an outing. Her accusation ignites the divided city into two vocal camps: anti-British Indians and anti-Indian British. Dr. Aziz's subsequent trial threatens to spark violence, but the spirit of Mrs. Moore, who has died on the way back to England, pervades the courtroom, and through her mystical mediation, the trial uncovers the truth. Adela relives the experience in the cave, realizing that Aziz did nothing. What did happen in the cave never becomes clear, but Adela's threat permanently scars Aziz and ruins his developing friendship with the British head of education, Cyril Fielding. Years pass before they meet again.

Forster allows his characters a "climax, as far as India admits of one," but during a concluding conversation between Aziz and Fielding "even the earth" seems against their coming together. Yet the conclusion may be less negative than it seems. During their final ride, Fielding and Aziz speak to one another almost harshly but with complete honesty. The language of connection, so hard to achieve, cannot afford a mask of civility. It speaks truth. In Forster's earlier travel fiction, "Britishers abroad" take the inspiration they need from "alien" landscapes and transport it to England. *A Passage to India* reveals weaknesses in English and Indian characters and insists that both rethink their perceptions.

Forster's travels helped to give him insider status in other cultures, but he did not exploit his position. In his nonfiction travel works he denies full understanding, therefore ownership, of either India or Egypt. In *A Passage to India* he refuses the colonial imperative. Forster may have reached his goal as a novelist in Aziz and Fielding's concluding conversation; to bring two travelers from different cultures to such intimacy is no small feat. Nations can only hope such conversations will occur. Forster wrote no more novels.

He did continue to write, travel, and speak. At age forty-six he took a flat in London, conclusively separating his intimate life from his suburban life with his mother, and in London he formed friendships and sexual relationships, the most important of which began as a love affair with Robert Buckingham, a young policeman. When Buckingham married in 1931, his liaison with Forster became a lasting friendship that included Bob's wife, May.

After *A Passage to India* Forster focused on nonfiction. He edited a collection of letters by Eliza Fay, a nineteenth-century British travel writer; he wrote a biography of his mentor and friend Goldsworthy Lowes Dickinson; and he collected his own essays for publication in *Abinger Harvest* (1936) and *Two Cheers for Democracy* (1951). Forster's travel insights surface in his collected essays. Many reflect his fictional treatment of travel. He is rarely willing to generalize about a country, and he is resolutely personal. In "The Last Parade," on the Paris Exposition of 1937, Forster wrote that "at a little distance boundaries and disputes are indistinguishable," and it is "our clouds and our snows that show" (*New Writing,* Autumn 1937; collected in *Two Cheers for Democracy*).

In 1927 Cambridge named Forster the Clark Lecturer, giving him a prominent pulpit from which to speak about literature. In Forster's series of talks, published as *Aspects of the Novel* (1927), he imagined great authors of various times in a room together, linked by theme and concern. Their country is creativity, their time imagination.

A 1929 trip to South Africa with his friends George and Florence Barger made Forster sure that he did not want to profit from the exploitation he saw there. He divested himself of South African stocks on his return. As Furbank comments, Forster rediscovered his distaste for group travel on this trip. He most enjoyed a visit to Egypt after the rest of the group had returned to England. In 1945 Forster traveled to India again and to the United States for the first time. "India Again" (1946) emphasizes the contrast between the gray cold of England and the sunny warmth of India, but mentions being intensely troubled by India's poverty. Now an internationally recognized writer, Forster's purpose remained the same as on his 1912 trip to India: "I wanted to be with Indians, and was, and that is a very little step in the right direction" (first published as "India after Twenty-Five Years," *Listener,* 31 January and 7 February 1946; collected in *Two Cheers for Democracy*).

The response to Forster on his American trip demonstrated his international appeal. American literary critic Lionel Trilling's insightful analysis *E. M. Forster* (1943) had sparked interest in his work, and Forster enjoyed his stay, which inspired the essay "The United States" (first published as "Impressions of the United States," *Listener,* 14 September 1947; collected in *Two Cheers for Democracy*). He felt his visit to be a "complete success" and liked seeing "the faces of strangers lighting up everywhere, compassionate, respectful, anxious to help." *A Passage to India* had given Forster a global audience, and he accepted the status of world citizen when he spoke at the International Congress of Writers in Paris in 1935, when he spoke over the BBC during World War II, and when he spoke at the 1945 P.E.N. international conference for writers held in India.

After Forster's mother died in 1945, he returned to Cambridge, where Kings College had offered him rooms and a permanent position as a lecturer. Forster remained in Cambridge almost until his death. Literature-loving Cambridge undergraduates visited Forster's rooms for insight, and from his rooms he continued to create, collaborating with Eric Crozier on a musical adaptation of Herman Melville's *Billy Budd: Opera in Four Acts* (1951), compiling the material for *The Hill of Devi,* and reworking many of his earlier short stories. He died on 7 June 1970 at the home of his friends Bob and May Buckingham.

In "Tourism vs. Thuggism" (*Listener,* 17 January 1957) Forster lamented "the graciouness and the gravity . . . of the earlier travel . . . the precious possibilities of friendship between the visitor and the visited." The "precious possibilities" survive in Forster's writings. Artistic and moving when he created them, his travel writings now resonate even more emphatically in a world desperate to "only connect" divisions that Forster spent his life examining.

Letters:

Selected Letters of E. M. Forster, 2 volumes, edited by Mary Lago and P. N. Furbank (Cambridge, Mass.: Harvard University Press, 1983, 1985);

Calendar of the Letters of E. M. Forster, compiled by Lago (London & New York: Mansell, 1985).

Interviews:

John Farrelly, "Distinguished Visitor," *New Republic,* 117 (28 July 1947): 28–29;

Harvey Breit, "Talk with E. M. Forster," *New York Times Book Review,* 19 June 1949, p. 19; republished as "E. M. Forster" in his *The Writer Observed* (Cleveland: World, 1956), pp. 53–56;

P. N. Furbank and F. J. R. Haskell, "E. M. Forster: The Art of Fiction I," *Paris Review,* 1 (Spring 1953): 27–41; republished as "E. M. Forster," in *Writers at Work: The Paris Review Interviews,* edited by Malcolm Cowley (New York: Viking, 1958), pp. 23–35;

K. W. Gransden, "E. M. Forster at Eighty," *Encounter,* 12 (January 1959): 77–80;

David Jones, "E. M. Forster on His Life and His Books," *Listener,* 61 (1959): 11–12;

Stephen Watts, "Forster on 'India'–Author Talks about Novel into Play," *New York Times,* 28 January 1962, II: 1, 3;

Gilbert A. Harrison, "The Modern Mr. Forster," *New Republic,* 110 (11 January 1964): 15–16.

Bibliographies:

Frederick P. W. McDowell, *E. M. Forster: An Annotated Bibliography of Writings about Him* (DeKalb: Northern Illinois University Press, 1976);

B. J. Kirkpatrick, *A Bibliography of E. M. Forster,* second edition, revised (Oxford: Clarendon Press, 1985);

Claude J. Summers, *E. M. Forster: A Guide to Research* (New York & London: Garland, 1991).

Biographies:

P. N. Furbank, *E. M. Forster: A Life, Volume One: The Growth of a Novelist, (1870–1914)* (London: Secker & Warburg, 1977); *E. M. Forster: A Life, Volume Two: Polycrates Ring* (1914-1970) (London: Secker & Warburg, 1978); republished as *E. M. Forster: A Life,* 1 volume (New York: Harcourt Brace Jovanovich, 1978);

Francis E. King, *E. M. Forster and His World* (London: Thames & Hudson, 1978; New York: Scribners, 1978);

Nicola Beauman, *E. M. Forster: A Biography* (London: Hodder & Stoughton, 1993; New York: Knopf, 1994).

References:

James R. Baker, "Forster's Voyage of Discovery," *Texas Quarterly,* 18 (Summer 1975): 99–118;

J. B. Beer, *The Achievement of E. M. Forster* (London: Chatto & Windus, 1962; New York: Barnes & Noble, 1962);

Kathleen Collins Beyer, "Two Forster Novels and an Indian Prince," *International Fiction Review,* 13 (1986): 27–29;

Elizabeth Bowen, "A Passage to E. M. Forster," in *Aspects of E. M. Forster: Essays and Recollections Written for His Ninetieth Birthday, 1 January 1969,* edited by Oliver Stallybrass (London: Arnold, 1969; New York: Harcourt, Brace & World, 1969), pp. 1–12;

Bowen, "Where the Pharos Stood," *Reporter,* 24 (27 April 1961): 49–51; republished as "Alexandria," in her *Afterthought: Pieces on Writing* (London: Longmans, 1962), pp. 159–162;

Malcolm Bradbury, ed., *Forster: A Collection of Critical Essays* (Englewood Cliffs, N.J.: Prentice Hall, 1966);

Kenneth Burke, "Social and Cosmic Mystery: A Passage to India," in his *Language as Symbolic Action: Essays on Life, Literature, and Method* (Berkeley & Los Angeles: University of California Press, 1966), pp. 223–239;

James Michael Buzard, "Forster's Trespasses: Tourism and Cultural Politics," *Twentieth Century Literature,* 34 (1988): 155–179;

John Colmer, *E. M. Forster: The Personal Voice* (London & Boston: Routledge & Kegan Paul, 1975);

Richard Cronin, "*The Hill of Devi* and *Heat and Dust,*" *Essays in Criticism,* 36 (1986): 142–159; republished in his *Imagining India* (London: Macmillan, 1989), pp. 161–176;

G. K. Das, *Forster's India* (London: Macmillan, 1977; Towata, N.J.: Rowman & Littlefield, 1978);

Das and Beer, eds., *E. M. Forster: A Human Exploration, Centenary Essays* (London: Macmillan, 1979; New York: New York University Press, 1979);

D. J. Enright, "Tales of Alexandria," *New Statesman,* 62 (26 August 1961): 244–45; revised as "Too Many Caesars: The Poems of C. P. Cavafy," in his *Conspirators and Poets* (London: Chatto & Windus, 1966), pp. 160–166;

Peter Firchow, "Germany and Germanic Mythology in E. M. Forster's *Howards End,*" *Comparative Literature,* 33 (1981): 50–68; republished as "E. M. Forster's Rainbow Bridge," in his *The Death of the German Cousin; Variations on a Literary Stereotype, 1890–1920* (Lewisburg, Pa.: Bucknell University Press, 1986), pp. 61–76;

Paul Fussell, *Abroad: British Literary Traveling Between the Wars* (New York: Oxford University Press, 1980);

Phillip Gardner, ed., *E. M. Forster: The Critical Heritage* (London & Boston: Routledge & Kegan Paul, 1974);

Elizabeth Heine, Introduction to *The Hill of Devi and Other Indian Writings,* edited by Heine, The Abinger Edition of E. M. Forster, volume 14 (London: Arnold, 1983), pp. vii–lviii;

Judith Scherer Herz, "E. M. Forster and the Biography of the Self: Redefining a Genre," *Prose Studies,* 5 (December 1982): 326–335;

F. R. Leavis, "E. M. Forster," *Scrutiny,* 7 (September 1938): 188–202; republished in his *The Common Pursuit* (New York: Stewart, 1952), pp. 261–267;

Robin Jared Lewis, "E. M. Forster: The Indian Diary," in *Approaches to E. M. Forster: A Centenary Volume,* edited by Vasant A. Shahane (New Delhi: Arnold-Heinemann, 1981), pp. 127–137;

Frederick P. W. McDowell, *E. M. Forster* (New York: Twayne, 1969; revised, 1982);

Jeffrey Meyers, *Fiction and the Colonial Experience* (Towata, N.J.: Rowman & Littlefield, 1973);

K. Natwar-Singh, ed., *E. M. Forster: A Tribute* (New York: Harcourt, Brace & World, 1964);

Benita Parry, *Delusions and Discoveries: Studies on India in the British Imagination 1880–1930* (Berkeley: University of California Press, 1972);

Jane Lagoudis Pinchin, *Alexandria Still: Forster, Durrell and Cavafy* (Princeton, N.J.: Princeton University Press, 1977);

John Crowe Ransom, "E. M. Forster," *Kenyon Review,* 5 (Autumn 1943): 618–623;

Santha Rama Rau, "Introduction: Indian Entries from a Diary by E. M. Forster," *Harper's,* 224 (February 1962): 46–47;

S. P. Rosenbaum, ed., *The Bloomsbury Group: A Collection of Memoirs, Commentary and Criticism* (Toronto & Buffalo: University of Toronto Press, 1975);

Barbara Rosencrance, *Forster's Narrative Vision* (Ithaca & London: Cornell University Press, 1982);

Frances B. Singh, "The Centrality of Alexandria: A History and Guide to Forster's Fiction," in *Approaches to E. M. Forster: A Centenary Volume,* edited by Vasant A. Shahane (New Delhi: Arnold-Heinemann, 1981), pp. 118–126;

Wilfred Stone, *The Cave and the Mountain: A Study of E. M. Forster* (Stanford: Stanford University Press, 1966);

Lionel Trilling, *E. M. Forster* (Norfolk, Conn.: New Directions, 1943; London: Hogarth Press, 1944);

Alan Wilde, *Horizons of Assent, Modernism, Postmodernism, and the Ironic Imagination* (Baltimore & London: Johns Hopkins University Press, 1981);

Virginia Woolf, "The Novels of E. M. Forster," *Atlantic Monthly,* 140 (November 1927): 642–648; republished in her *Death of the Moth* (New York: Harcourt, Brace, 1942), pp. 104–112.

Papers:

The E. M. Forster Archive is at King's College Cambridge. The Harry Ransom Humanities Research Center, University of Texas at Austin, has the largest American archive, including the manuscript for *A Passage to India.* The Berg Collection at the New York Public Library and the Pierpont Morgan Library each have a few documents.

Robert Gibbings

(23 March 1889 - 19 January 1958)

Keith C. Odom
Texas Christian University

BOOKS: *The Zoo,* by Gibbings and Moira Gibbings (London: Bayard Press, 1930?);

Iorana! A Tahitian Journal (Boston & New York: Houghton Mifflin, 1932; London: Duckworth, 1932);

Coconut Island or the Adventures of Two Children in the South Seas (London: Faber & Faber, 1936);

John Graham (Convict) 1824: An Historical Narrative (London: Faber & Faber, 1937; New York: Barnes, 1957);

Blue Angels and Whales: A Record of Personal Experiences Below and Above Water (Harmondsworth, U.K.: Penguin, 1938; revised and enlarged edition, London: Dent, 1946; New York: Dutton, 1946);

Sweet Thames Run Softly (London: Dent, 1940; New York: Dutton, 1941);

Coming Down the Wye (London: Dent, 1942; New York: Dutton, 1943);

Lovely Is the Lee (London: Dent, 1945 [i.e., 1944]; New York: Dutton, 1945);

Over the Reefs (London: Dent, 1948); republished as *Over the Reefs and Far Away* (New York: Dutton, 1949);

Sweet Cork of Thee (London: Dent, 1951; New York: Dutton, 1951);

Coming Down the Seine (London: Dent, 1953; New York: Dutton, 1953);

Trumpets from Montparnasse (London: Dent, 1955; New York: Dutton, 1955);

Till I End My Song (London: Dent, 1957; New York: Dutton, 1957);

The Wood Engravings of Robert Gibbings, edited by Patience Empson (London: Dent, 1959; Chicago: Quadrangle, 1959).

OTHER: "Glory to God," in *Sermons by Artists* (N.p.: Golden Cockerel Press, 1934), pp. 21-27;

Owen Chase, Thomas Chappell, and George Pollard, *Narratives of the Wreck of the Whale-Ship Essex of Nantucket,* introduction by Gibbings (London: Golden Cockerel Press, 1935);

Robert Gibbings, 1948 (photograph by Oluf Nissen)

"Autumn Night," in *The Saturday Book,* no. 10, edited by Leonard Russell (London: Hutchinson, 1950), pp. 283-288;

"Well-Heads of Venice," in *The Saturday Book,* no. 14, edited by John Hadfield (London: Hutchinson, 1954), pp. 116-120;

"Thoughts on Fish" and "Thoughts on Wood," in *The Saturday Book,* no. 16, edited by Hadfield (London: Hutchinson, 1956), pp. 54-60, 207-213.

SELECTED PERIODICAL PUBLICATIONS–UNCOLLECTED: "They Built a Tower," *Beacon,* new series 1 (March 1925): 55;

"The Golden Cockerel Press," *Woodcut,* no. 1 (February 1927): 13–26;
"The Art of the Book: The Golden Cockerel Press," *Studio,* 97 (February 1929): 98–101;
"The Golden Cockerel Press," *Colophon,* part 7, no. 6 (September 1931): 1–12;
"Supplement," *Mercury* (London), 25 (November 1931): 1–8;
"A Revival in Wood Engraving," *Discovery,* 14 (October 1933): 319–322;
"A Garment for Sunbathing," *Sun Bathing Review,* 1 (Winter 1933–1934): 7;
"Exploring a Coral Reef," *Discovery,* 15 (May 1934): 140–142;
"A Holiday under the Sea," *Listener,* 19 (25 May 1938): 1114;
"Sharks Permitting–An Artist under the Sea," *Listener,* 20 (17 November 1938): 1046–1048;
"Under the Coconut Palm," *Listener,* 21 (30 March 1939): 689;
"The Rock Pool," *Sun Bathing Review,* 7 (Summer 1939): 57;
"Peace on the River," *Listener,* 22 (19 October 1939): 768–769;
"River Reverie," *Listener,* 22 (14 December 1939): 1168–1169;
"River Memories," *Listener,* 23 (22 February 1940): 356–357;
"Paradise Lost," *Sun Bathing Review,* 8 (Spring 1940): 8–9;
"Ducks Is Just Ducks," *Listener,* 23 (2 May 1940): 895–896;
"The English Society of Wood-Engravers," *Carnegie Magazine,* 14 (June 1940): 85–86;
"Fleet Street to Tahiti," *Penrose Annual,* 42 (1940): 34–36;
"Drawing Fish on the Sea Bottom," *Art in New Zealand,* 13 (September 1940): 26–29;
"My Best Friend," *John O'London's Weekly,* 51 (25 January 1952): 90;
"Lost in the Loneliest Ocean," *Everybody's,* 42 (6 September 1952): 14, 24;
"The Story behind Kon-Tiki," *Sphere,* 210 (27 September 1952): 455–457;
"With Prince Tungi," *Overseas* (March 1953): 37, 39;
"Rivers Are Roads," *John O'London's Weekly,* 62 (25 September 1953): 845;
"My View of the Irish R. M.," *Everyman* (November 1953): 16;
"Memories of Eric Gill," *Book Collector,* 3 (1953): 95–102;
"Throwing Away the Cork," *Everybody's,* 44 (24 April 1954): 22–23;
"A Finger of Friendship," *Ireland of the Welcomes* (May-June 1954): 11–13, 40;
"Backcloth to the Dolphin," *Folio* (Autumn 1954): 8–11;
"Winter in Britain," *Time and Tide,* 35 (2 October 1954): 1304–1305;
"Along the Valley of the Wye," *London Calling,* no. 782 (28 October 1954): 14–15;
"My Career in Medicine," *Medical World,* 85 (July 1956): 76, 79–80;
"The Country of the Wye," *London Calling,* no. 908 (28 March 1957): 14–15.

Robert Gibbings began writing books set in interesting and exotic places in the early 1930s and published his last in 1957, the year before he died. Nine of his twenty-one books are travel accounts, providing vivid impressions of the places he visited, not only details about the locale but also about the people and their lives. His travel books describe the journey, the setting, and the culture through his own anecdotes and those of the residents, who recount stories both present and past. He stayed anywhere from three months to two years in each country he visited and involved himself in the lives of the residents, learning their history and culture and joining in their work and play. While he planned his itineraries carefully, he often digressed in his narratives. His travels down the Thames, for example, led him to talk about Venezuela (which he had never visited) and other incidents from the past.

Gibbings's books were favorably reviewed in *The Times Literary Supplement* (London) and *The New York Times.* Well-known American critics, such as Clifton Fadiman, Orville Prescott, and Christopher Morley, and British critics, such as Richard Church, Sir Hugh Walpole, and Phillip Day, commented on the charm of Gibbings's text and wood engravings. Gibbings's biographers and bibliographers consider him one of the most creative people of the twentieth century.

Robert John Gibbings was born in Cork, Ireland, on 23 March 1889 to the Reverend Edward Gibbings, Anglican canon of Cork Cathedral, and Caroline Rouviere Day Gibbings, daughter of Robert Day, a Cork businessman who was internationally known for his interest in archaeology. Day's house overlooked the River Lee and was full of beautiful artifacts from Ireland to Polynesia. At first Gibbings's wish to study art was vetoed by his father, who said his son would starve and "would have to look at naked women." Acceding to his father's wish that he become a doctor, he attended University College, Cork, but failed to pass his medical examinations. He then went to London, where he studied art at the Slade School and after-

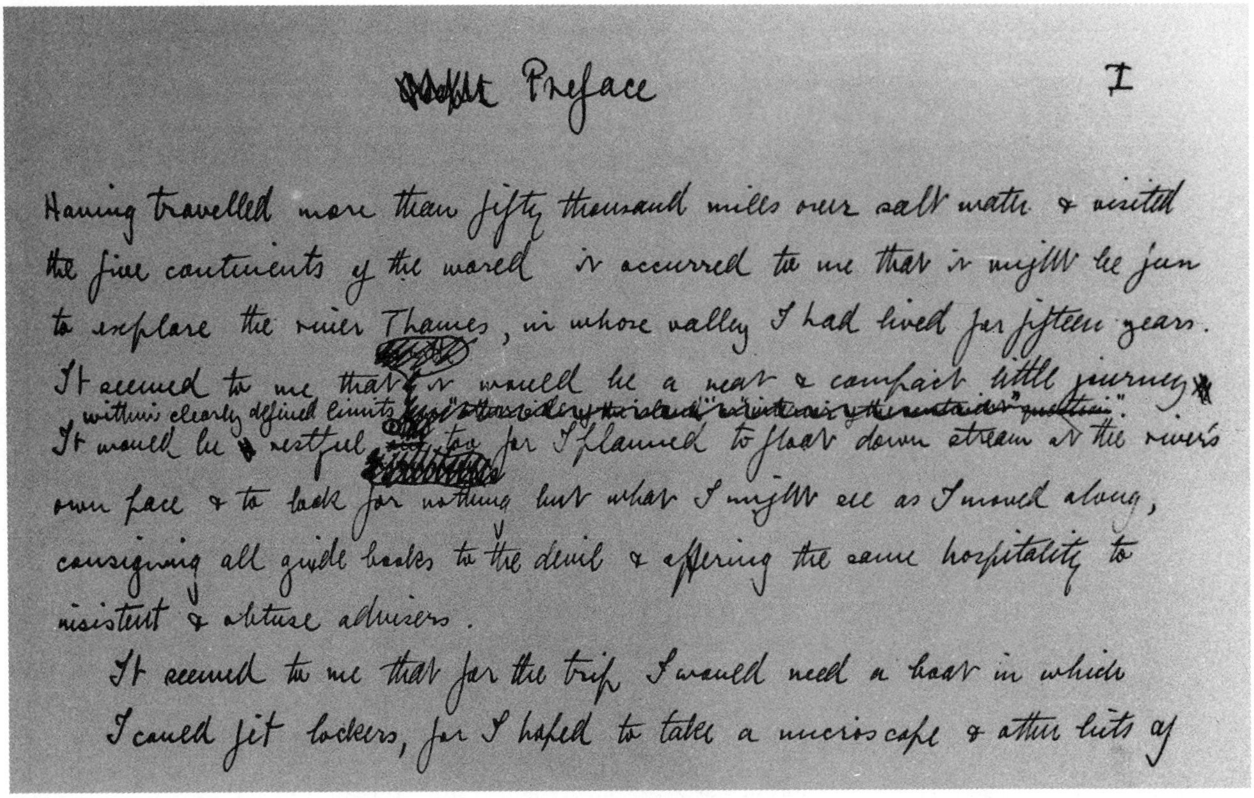
Preface I

Having travelled more than fifty thousand miles over salt water & visited the five continents of the world it occurred to me that it might be fun to explore the river Thames, in whose valley I had lived for fifteen years. It seemed to me that it would be a neat & compact little journey within clearly defined limits. It would be restful, too, for I planned to float down stream at the river's own pace & to look for nothing but what I might see as I moved along, consigning all guide books to the devil & offering the same hospitality to insistent & obtuse advisers.

It seemed to me that for the trip I would need a boat in which I could fit lockers, for I hoped to take a microscope & other bits of

Beginning of the manuscript for Gibbings's preface to his 1940 book, Sweet Thames Run Softly *(from A. Mary Kirkus,* Robert Gibbings: A Bibliography, *1962)*

ward at the London County Council Central School of Arts and Crafts, where Noel Rooke introduced him to wood engraving. During World War I he served in the Royal Munster Fusiliers (1914–1918), rising to the rank of captain. He was in the disastrous Gallipoli campaign until a wound in the throat on 28 June 1915 sent him home.

After World War I Gibbings began his artistic career, and in 1920 he helped to found the Society of Wood-Engravers, serving as its first honorary secretary. In January 1924 he bought the Golden Cockerel Press in Waltham St. Lawrence, Berkshire, from its previous owner, Harold Midgley Taylor, who was too ill with tuberculosis to carry on. Gibbings illustrated scores of books, most not his own, published by the press.

During the time he owned the press Gibbings lived in Waltham St. Lawence and kept a hands-on attitude from concept to press work. Books published by the Golden Cockerel Press during those years are creative productions because Gibbings developed harmony between type and illustration. Often he illustrated the books himself or had a talented colleague, such as Eric Gill or Denis Tegetmeier, create appropriate wood engravings. Gibbings's own engravings are so fine that some readers seek out his illustrated travel books just for his mastery of the art. In August 1933 the Great Depression forced Gibbings to sell the Golden Cockerel Press. During the years 1936–1942 he was a lecturer in typography and book production at the University of Reading, and on 8 February 1938 he was given an honorary M.A. degree by the National University of Ireland.

Gibbings began his travel-writing career in 1929, when he went to Tahiti under a contract with Houghton Mifflin to provide illustrations for a projected work by James Norman Hall. After three months of work on the wood engravings, Gibbings's progress was halted because Hall asked for a release from his book contract, citing too many other commitments. In 1932 Gibbings took the engravings he had made for the Hall book, wrote some text to accompany them, and published *Iorana! A Tahitian Journal.* He dedicated the book to James Norman Hall, whom he admired. Reviews of the book were positive, though sales were modest, and the book went through three small editions in Great Britain and the United States.

Encouraged by this modest interest, Gibbings wrote and illustrated with wood engravings a children's book, *Coconut Island or The Adventures of Two Children in the South Seas* (1936), and an historical narrative set in Australia, *John Graham (Convict)*

Gibbings's engraving of the bridge over the Thames above Shillingford (from Sweet Thames Run Softly)

1824 (1937). His next book was a travel narrative, *Blue Angels and Whales: A Record of Personal Experiences Below and Above Water* (1938), for which he drew on his experiences in Tahiti, Bermuda, and the Red Sea. Some of the sketches for his wood engravings were produced twenty feet underwater on xylonite (roughened celluloid sheets). Gibbings claimed to be the first person to make pencil sketches under the sea. Penguin Books published the book first as a Pelican Special, and it was republished in a hardback edition in 1946, after the paper rationing of World War II had been lifted in Great Britain.

Blue Angels and Whales established Gibbings's methods of writing–research in authoritative works and three months to two years of firsthand exploration. Not only did he describe the islands and the seas, and their flora and fauna, but he also visited the people and recorded their lives, traditions, and attitudes. While Gibbings was working on *Blue Angels and Whales,* the skipper of his launch, a Captain Whitfield, told Gibbings of his first disaster-fraught attempts to sail from England to Bermuda. The book conveys the feelings of exhilaration Whitfield experienced sailing on the open sea for the first time while also reporting how the unseaworthy craft began coming apart far away from the coast of Cornwall and how they made it back to port through mountainous waves and gale-force winds. Whitfield minimized the danger of his sinking ship. All he could remember was the supreme thrill of all-out sailing in such a wild wind. Gibbings conveyed that thrill to his readers, who bought up two printings of *Blue Angels and Whales* before World War II and several afterward.

During World War II Gibbings, like most Britons, was unable to travel beyond the islands of Great Britain. Thus, he sailed the length of the River Thames from its source, exploring its banks and depths and interviewing those who lived along it. In order to carry a microscope and an aquarium for some scientific investigation, Gibbings designed and built his own flat-bottomed boat with the aid of the shop at the University of Reading. He was almost always a solitary traveler, and in this instance he provided space in the boat for only himself.

The title of *Sweet Thames Run Softly* (1940) comes from a line in Edmund Spenser's *Prothalamion* (1596): "Sweete Thammes! runne softly, till I end my Song." Gibbings refers to the history of places located on the river banks, including Windsor Castle, Eton, and Runnymede; he also digresses to remark on such topics as the fatal Antarctic explorations (1910–1913) of Captain Robert Falcon Scott. He describes also the history of the river habitat and the "whole pageant of river scenery."

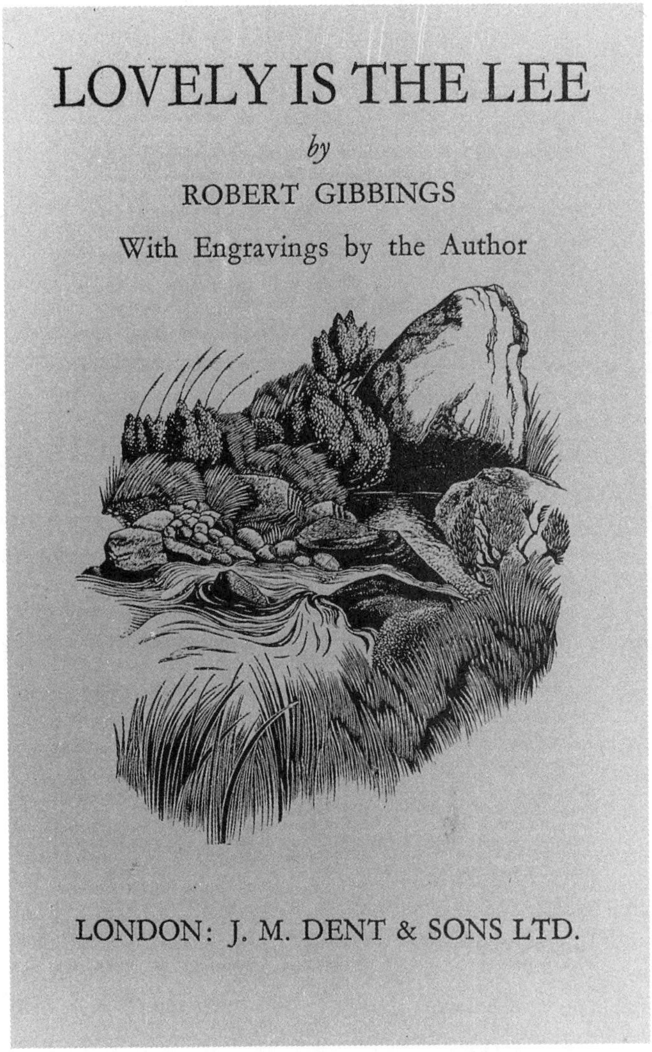
LOVELY IS THE LEE

by

ROBERT GIBBINGS

With Engravings by the Author

LONDON: J. M. DENT & SONS LTD.

Title page, with engraving by Gibbings, for his 1945 book, in which he traced the course of an Irish river, the Lee, from Killarny to Cork

As the war continued, Gibbings turned his attention to one of the most storied rivers of Wales, and beginning his journey at the source, he wrote and illustrated *Coming Down the Wye* (1942). Portions of the Wye run through hilly, rural, forested country that is not only wild and scenic but also, unlike the more placid, urban English rivers, is strewn with rapids. While Gibbings salted the narrative with tales about his Welsh hosts (such as a Mr. Harris who kept giving him fountain pens, handkerchiefs, and other unwanted items), he also digressed to the memory of his friend and fellow artist Eric Gill, who lived for several years along the Wye at Llanthony Abbey and whose favorite saying was "The artist does the work, the critic gets the inspiration." Reaching the mouth of the Wye, Gibbings rented a lake cottage for a season and visited the local pub with villagers who, in true Welsh custom, frequently burst into songs such as "Myfawny" and "Land of My Fathers." In spite of paper rationing, the book went through at least five printings during the war and two more after the war ended.

After his travels in Wales, Gibbings returned to the land of his own fathers and wrote about tracing the River Lee, which runs in Eire from south of Killarny to Cork. True to his digressive methods of travel writing, Gibbings began his trip with a visit to Galway. Standing on the shore of Galway Bay and looking out toward the remote Aran Isles, he could not see them. As a local commented, "If you see the Arans, it's a sign of rain, and if you can't see them it's raining." Gibbings also related the story of a peer with a double-barreled name who was crossing the square rather inebriated: "'Isn't that Lord Clare and Galway?' said one farmer to another. 'It is,' said the other, 'and both of them's drunk.'" *Lovely Is the Lee* went through several large printings in Great Britain, and the Book-of-the-Month Club made the book part of the December 1945 dual selection.

When World War II ended, Gibbings resigned from the University of Reading and returned to the South Pacific for two years. During a trip that led him from New Zealand to Fiji, then back to New Zealand, he collected material that led to the creation of his best sea volume, *Over the Reefs* (1948), in which he related his adventures in sailing, diving, and eating with his many native hosts throughout the South Pacific. Their cultures were so different that each visit became a new learning experience. For example, the doctor Gibbings accompanied to Tokelau wanted to collect insects, so he offered a cigarette for every spider the children brought him. The natives responded with amazement:

> The children were incredulous. "And tell them," he added, "that I'll give two cigarettes for every rat they bring me." This was too much even for the composure of the chiefs. They, too, burst out laughing. "I want to see what fleas they are carrying," said the doctor. That was funnier still. And because I had come ashore with the doctor, and because I seemed to understand what he was doing, I was classed as a potential lunatic. I couldn't move without being followed by a crowd of hopeful children. . . . I might at any moment do something sensational.

Gibbings arrived with relief at the Tahiti home of his friend James Norman Hall, which Gibbings had not visited since his 1929 trip, though Hall had a house prepared for him any time he returned. Hall was in the United States when Gibbings arrived but provided him with full access to his huge library and classical phonograph record collection. "In Polynesia, where life is tranquil," Gibbings wrote, "there is only the twanging of the guitar; but in the turmoil and agony of other civilizations exquisite music is brought into being." The first large British printing of *Over the Reefs* was well received by a readership that had been unable to travel abroad during the war. The American edition was increased in size by the requirements of the Readers Union and the Travel Book Club.

On his return to Great Britain, Gibbings established a base of operations on Warwick Road in London, which he kept until 1955. Consistent with his solitary journeying to faraway places or down familiar rivers, Gibbings recalled that he had not completed his trip down the Lee all the way to the city of Cork. He called *Sweet Cork of Thee* (1951)

> in a sense a continuation of *Lovely Is the Lee*. I began where I left off, with only a gap of five years. And what is five years in Ireland? A few young people had grown taller and a few of the old people had grown a little bent, but for the most part, from that night when I sat in Batty Kit's cottage in 1944 until the evening when I sat in it again in the spring of 1949, it might have been no more than a night's sleep with a few heavy dreams.

In *Sweet Cork of Thee* he tells more stories about local traditions than about scenery, including one about the vacant house on the hill where one night the devil came down the chimney, chains and all, and flew out the window. The family was so frightened that they left the house the next day never to return. Gibbings's narrative ranges from the Dingle Peninsula and Great Blasket Island in County Kerry back to Cork, his native city.

Next Gibbings turned his attention to the European continent, and, after two years of travel and research, he wrote and illustrated *Coming Down the Seine* (1953), starting at the source near Dijon and traveling through Paris to Le Havre, a distance of four hundred miles. Mostly he followed the river, boating, camping on the banks, and meeting people. The book also refers to historical landmarks, such as a castle built by Richard Coeur de Lion, and the Bayeaux Tapestry. Some of his digressions mention Napoleon, ancient history, England, and the South Seas. His landmarks for the seven miles of river that traverse Paris are familiar to Parisians and Francophiles throughout the world and are appropriate subjects for his descriptions and woodcuts from the Left Bank to Notre Dame, beginning with the statue to the Seine–a naked maiden. Mostly he describes the islands in the river at Paris and more than thirty bridges of Paris. "To follow a river," Gibbings wrote, "is like watching the growth of a child: only at intervals is one conscious of the increase in its strength, from brook to brook, from weir to weir, as from week to week." This book was reprinted twice in its first year of publication, including for the Readers Union.

Gibbings's second book set on the Continent is *Trumpets from Montparnasse* (1955); the title was taken from the last line of *Coming Down the Seine*. This book includes anecdotes about searching for an affordable Paris studio to rent, exploring the city, and meeting the people. Having traveled in Italy as well, he also wrote about his journey from France through Italy to Naples, where he was more successful in renting an artist's studio than he was in Paris. For the first time Gibbings's illustrations include color plates of oil paintings as well as black-and-white wood engravings. While well received, neither of Gibbings's continental books achieved the popular reception of his British river and Pacific island books.

In autumn 1955 Gibbings bought Footbridge Cottage in Long Wittenham, Berkshire, and then turned to finishing his aborted journey down the River Thames, no longer interrupted by wartime blackouts and bombing raids. In his last travel book he followed the Thames through London to the sea and explained his interest in travel along rivers. "There is nothing unusual in this love of water," he wrote. "Poets throughout the ages have sung of the peace of gently running streams. In the sacred writings a river is used constantly as a symbol of peace." Thus he finished his career with a book whose title completed the line from Spenser's *Prothalamion: Till I End My Song* (1957).

Gibbings died in Oxford on 19 January 1958 and was buried at Long Wittenham. According to Patience Empson, "At the time of his death he had work begun and planned that would have filled many years to come." He had married twice, first to Mary Pennefather, by whom he had three sons and one daughter, and second to Elisabeth Empson, by whom he had a son and two daughters.

Friends generally described Gibbings as an imposing, bearded man, 5'9" tall and three hundred pounds at his heaviest. In an article on the Thames for *National Geographic* (July 1958), Willard Price included a photograph of Robert Gibbings, "looking like Father Thames himself." As Patience Empson and John Harris have said, about both his engravings and his travel writing, "Robert Gibbings was . . . both versatile and prolific."

Bibliography:

A. Mary Kirkus, *Robert Gibbings: A Bibliography,* edited by Patience Empson and John Harris (London: Dent, 1962).

Biography:

F. J. Wallace, "Biographical Sketch of Robert Gibbings," *Wilson Library Bulletin,* 22 (January 1948): 356.

References:

Thomas Balston, "The River Books of Robert Gibbings," *Alphabet and Image,* no. 8 (December 1948): 38–49;

John Brodie, "First Impressions of Literary People: Robert Gibbings and the Lure of Water and the South Seas," *Books of Today,* 3 (October 1948): 8–9;

[Richard Church], "One Man in a Boat," *John O'London's Weekly,* 62 (11 September 1953): 801–802;

J. W. Davidson, "Happy Traveller: Robert Gibbings in the South Seas," *New Zealand Listener,* 22 (22 April 1949): 16–18;

John Hadfield, Note on Gibbings, *The Saturday Book,* no. 18 (London: Hutchinson, 1958), p. 5;

"An Irishman Sees the Islands," *New Zealand Listener,* 16 (24 April 1947): 16–17;

Charles Moorman, "Five Views of a Dragon," *Southern Quarterly,* 16 (1978): 139–150;

"More Readings by Robert Gibbings," *New Zealand Listener,* 17 (3 October 1947): 14–15;

Willard Price, "The Thames Mirrors England's Varied Life," *National Geographic,* 114 (July 1958): 45–93;

Eric Ramsden, "Robert Gibbings: Famous Illustrator-Author Goes to Samoa," *Pacific Islands Monthly,* 16 (19 November 1945): 30;

Alan R. Warwick, "An Appreciation of Robert Gibbings," *Sun Bathing Review* (Spring 1958): 9–10, 16;

J. D. Watson, "Robert Gibbings Loved Rivers," *Otago Daily Times* (Dunedin, New Zealand), 1 February 1958;

Montague Weekley, "A Red-headed Bohemian: Montague Weekley on Robert Gibbings and the Art of Wood-engraving," *Listener,* 62 (19 November 1959): 892.

Papers:

The Reading Public Library has an almost complete collection of Gibbings's work at the Golden Cockerel Press. Some of Gibbings papers are at the University of Reading. An extensive collection on Eric Gill, Gibbings's chief wood-engraving collaborator, is at the Clark Library in Los Angeles.

Louis Golding
(19 November 1895 – 10 August 1958)

Brian D. Reed
Case Western Reserve University

BOOKS: *Sorrow of War* (London: Methuen, 1919);
Forward From Babylon (London: Christophers, 1920; New York: Moffat, Yard, 1921; revised edition, London: Gollancz, 1932; New York: Farrar & Rinehart, 1932);
Shepherd Singing Ragtime, and Other Poems (London: Christophers, 1921);
Prophet and Fool: A Collection of Poems (New York: Dutton, 1923);
Seacoast of Bohemia (London: Christophers, 1923; New York: Knopf, 1924);
Sunward (London: Chatto & Windus, 1924; New York: Knopf, 1924);
Day of Atonement (London: Chatto & Windus, 1925; New York: Knopf, 1925);
Sicilian Noon (London: Chatto & Windus, 1925; New York: Knopf, 1926);
The Miracle Boy (London: Knopf, 1927; New York: Knopf, 1927);
Store of Ladies (London: Knopf, 1927; New York: Knopf, 1927);
Those Ancient Lands: Being a Journey to Palestine (London: Benn, 1928);
The Prince or Somebody (London: Knopf, 1929; New York: Knopf, 1929);
Adventures in Living Dangerously (London: Morely & Mitchell Kennerley Jr., 1930);
Give Up Your Lovers (London: Heinemann, 1930; New York: Cosmopolitan Book, 1930);
A Letter to Adolf Hitler (London: L. & V. Woolf, 1932);
Magnolia Street (London: Gollancz, 1932 [i.e., 1931]; New York: Farrar & Rinehart, 1932);
James Joyce (London: Butterworth, 1933);
The Doomington Wanderer: A Book of Tales (London: Gollancz, 1934); republished as *This Wanderer* (New York: Farrar & Rinehart, 1935);
Five Silver Daughters (London: Gollancz, 1934; New York: Farrar & Rinehart, 1934);
Terrace in Capri: An Imaginary Conversation with Norman Douglas (London: Centaur, 1934);
The Camberwell Beauty (London: Gollancz, 1935; New York: Farrar & Rinehart, 1935);

Louis Golding (portrait by Edward Wolfe; from Those Ancient Lands, *1928)*

The Pursuer (London: Gollancz, 1936; New York: Farrar & Rinehart, 1936);
The Dance Goes On (London: Rich & Cowan, 1937; New York & Toronto: Farrar & Rinehart, 1937);
In the Steps of Moses the Lawgiver (London: Rich & Cowan, 1937; New York: Macmillan, 1938); republished with *In the Steps of Moses the Conqueror* as *In the Steps of Moses* (Philadelphia: Jewish Publication Society of America, 1943);
The Song of Songs (Newly Interpreted and Rendered as a Masque) (London: Privately printed, 1937);
In the Steps of Moses the Conqueror (London: Rich & Cowan, 1938; New York: Macmillan, 1938); republished with *In the Steps of Moses the Lawgiver* as *In the Steps of Moses* (Philadelphia: Jewish Publication Society of America, 1943);

The Jewish Problem (Harmondsworth, U.K.: Penguin, 1938);
Hitler Through the Ages (London: Sovereign Books, 1939);
Mr. Emmanuel (London: Rich & Cowan, 1939; New York: Viking, 1939);
The World I Knew (London & Melbourne: Hutchinson, 1940; New York: Viking, 1940);
Who's There Within? (London & New York: Hutchinson, 1942);
No News from Helen (London & New York: Hutchinson, 1943; New York: Dial, 1943);
Pale Blue Nightgown: A Book of Tales (London & New York: Hutchinson, 1944);
The Vicar of Dunkerly Briggs, and Other Short Stories (London: Vallancey, 1944);
The Glory of Elsie Silver (London: Hutchinson, 1945; New York: Dial, 1945);
Louis Golding Goes Travelling (London: Vallancey, 1945);
Memories of Old Park Row, 1887–1897 (Brookline, Mass.: Privately printed, 1946);
Three Jolly Gentlemen (London & New York: Hutchinson, 1947);
The Dark Prince: A Short Novel (London: Findon, 1948);
Boxing Tales, A Collection of Thrilling Stories of the Ring (London: Findon, 1948);
My Sporting Days and Nights (London: Findon, 1948);
Honey for the Ghost (London & New York: Hutchinson, 1949; New York: Dial, 1949);
The Dangerous Places (London & New York: Hutchinson, 1951);
The Bare-Knuckle Breed (London & New York: Hutchinson, 1952; New York: Barnes, 1954);
The Loving Brothers (London: Hutchinson, 1952);
To the Quayside (London: Hutchinson, 1954);
Good-bye to Ithaca (London: Hutchinson, 1955; New York: Yoseloff, 1958);
Mario on the Beach, and Other Tales (London: Hutchinson, 1956);
Mr. Hurricane (London: Hutchinson, 1957);
The Little Old Admiral (London: Hutchinson, 1958; New York: Vanguard, 1958);
The Frightening Talent (London & New York: Allen, 1973).

OTHER: Alan Porter, Richard Hughes, and Robert Graves, eds., *Oxford Poetry 1921,* includes poems by Golding (New York: Appleton, 1923);
We Shall Eat and Drink Again: A Wine and Food Anthology, edited by Golding and André L. Simon (London: Hutchinson, 1944);
J. J. Lynx, ed., *The Future of the Jews: A Symposium,* includes an epilogue by Golding (London: Drummond, 1945).

A popular novelist best-known for *Magnolia Street* (1932) and *The Glory of Elsie Silver* (1945), Louis Golding was an avid traveler who wrote important travel narratives about the Mediterranean region and the Middle East. He was also a spokesperson for British Jews and principal opponent of anti-Semitic behavior. In addition to writing fiction and travel books, he was a poet, a lecturer, a Hollywood scriptwriter, a sportswriter, and an essayist.

Louis Golding was born in Manchester on 19 November 1895, the third son of Phillip and Yetta Golding. Golding described his early school days at Waterloo Road Elementary School in his novel *The Pursuer* (1936) and his later education at Manchester Grammar School in his first novel, *Forward from Babylon* (1920). During his schooldays he became known as a clever young poet. He wrote for the school magazine and won literary awards. In 1914 he received a scholarship from Manchester Grammar School to attend Queen's College, Oxford, but his studies were interrupted by World War I. In October 1914 Golding attempted to enlist in the Officers' Training Corps, but he was denied admittance because, as he wrote in *The World I Knew* (1940), "The authorities disliked my eyes, my tonsils, and my lungs." Still determined to serve his country in some capacity, Golding had a short stint as a hospital orderly in York before enrolling as a YMCA worker in the war efforts.

A few months later Golding began his life as a traveler when the YMCA dispatched him to their station in Salonica (Thessaloníki), Greece. He could hardly contain his excitement. In *The World I Knew* Golding wrote: "I was going to France, including Paris certainly, to Greece, including Athens as likely as not. Had I propounded such ideas to myself but a short year earlier, I would have run to the looking-glass to see if I had straws in my hair and if my mouth was drooling." His service was cut short because of a bout with malaria that forced him to return to England.

After the signing of the Armistice, Golding returned to Oxford, published his first novel, and began work as editor of the *Queen's College Miscellany.* After graduation he began his extensive travels and established a regimen of producing at least one book per year while spending half his time in London and the other half touring the world.

At first, on the advice of his physicians, Golding went on short trips to ward off another serious illness. As time progressed, he began traveling to es-

Photographs of Jewish settlers in Palestine, from Those Ancient Lands, *Golding's 1928 account of a journey from Cairo to Nazareth*

cape the distractions of London: "I went abroad to this city or that, by no means because it was the background of the book in process of composition, but because it was cheap to live there, or because that was the country in which, at that time, I felt I might find the sort of happiness in which the book could get itself discharged."

After writing *Seacoast of Bohemia* (1923), a satirical novel based on his early travels, Golding began his "Mediterranean period," spending much of his time in Capri and Sicily in the company of friends such as Norman Douglas and D. H. Lawrence. During this period he wrote novels and poetry as well as three travel narratives describing his adventures in the region: *Sunward* (1924), *Sicilian Noon* (1925), and *Those Ancient Lands* (1928).

Sunward, the first of Golding's Italian travel sketches, is remarkably personal and engaging. Golding had gone to Italy to "become a fit man again" after a new bout of sickness. Instead of choosing restful recuperation, he set out on a rambling tour of Venice, Verona, Bologna, Naples, Capri, and finally Sicily. Part of his intent was to write a travel book, but *Sunward* is not just the travel guide that he originally intended to produce. Instead, to the delight of his publishers and critics, *Sunward* is a remarkable collection of poetry and prose humor that captures the mood of Italy and the essence of its people. On his travels Golding shunned comfortable hotels as "the least common denominator of Western civilization" so that he could live with real Italians. Thus he encountered a delightful mixture of characters, including a clever smuggler headed to Innsbruck, a colorful barge captain with whom he shared a flask of Chianti, and myriad others. His descriptions of these people make his narrative read like Laurence Sterne's *A Sentimental Journey* (1768).

As he wrote about traveling the length of Italy, Golding included stories from his past. One humorous account describes "the divine moment" when he began to feel less uncomfortable as a downhill skier:

> I grew to understand that snow may be more sticky than treacle and wooden skis may develop a demon pliability and roll themselves about your neck like leather thongs. I learned how to endure humiliations . . . as the lissome youths swooped like eagles upon the pit of my despondency.

On occasion Golding's mood affects his perception of the countryside. For example, near the end of the book Golding describes how he boarded a seemingly demonic train to "escape" toward Sicily. His somber mood at the end of his journey is reflected in his description of the train ride from Battipaglia: "Probably no stretch of railway in Europe passes under so many and such malodorous tunnels, and when the train was not howling in the belly of one tunnel it was screaming as it emerged from another, or shrieking as it entered a third." His nightmarish ride with a loudly snoring and gaseous old man and a nervous, wailing old woman in mourning is quickly followed, however, by a joyous celebration as the train leaves the mountains and crashes into the "astounding blue" sky over Sicily. The countryside has transformed the writer's emotions as his "journey sunward was ended."

Golding's next travel narrative, *Sicilian Noon,* picks up where *Sunward* leaves off. His humorous digressions and vivid descriptions again impressed the critics. In writing about how he wandered Sicily on foot and by train, noting the influences of the ancient Greek and Arabic cultures, he captured the warmth and spirit of the island people. Starting in Messina and passing through Tindari and Cefalù, Golding alighted in Palermo and saw danger and excitement all around him, as if the whole city were a theatrical event. He imagined old men as Mafia dons and a Palermo girl as a wholesome young Lancashire maid. A pagan Easter celebration and a performance of a marionette show provided "less than half the general action" of the performance.

The center of the spectacle of Palermo was the Fiera di Pasqua, a carnival-like celebration complete with freak shows, gluttony, and vivid sexuality. Golding and most of the men of Palermo bought tickets to watch the "sexual pantomime" of a young woman dancing "in time to the pulse of the blood." Golding was concerned that "men should not be herded together when their blood's burning," and, as if to confirm his foreboding, a scuffle between two admirers of a dancer climaxed with the pulling of a knife. Golding was enraptured by the unfolding of the drama.

In Sicily, Golding's passion for the *Odyssey* took hold of him as he made Homeric connections with the landscape. His travels became an intentional quest to follow Samuel Butler's earlier trek to find the geographic sources of the *Odyssey*. In Trapani, which Butler "so conclusively proved was the domain of Nausicaa," Golding hoped to gather information for his growing file on the travels of Odysseus. Golding employed a peasant guide who had some hazy recollections of "Signor Butler" but did not understand why Golding had so little interest in the present noble gentlemen of the region. While he left with little new information, Golding succeeded in renewing his enthusiasm for Homeric study.

Golding traveled through Girgenta (Agrigento), Casrogiovanni, and Catania, where he witnessed with horror a fascist parade. By the time he reached the island of Lipari, off the northern coast of Sicily, he yearned for the safety of England. Standing on the brim of a volcanic crater, at the moment in his travel when he was farthest from home, he dreamed of picking blackberries in the "greenery" of Devon, momentarily transporting the reader to "God's bounty" in the English countryside. As the ground beneath his feet quaked with volcanic power, it seemed as if the hot passions of Sicily jarred him from his dream and caused him to depart.

Golding's final Mediterranean travel narrative, *Those Ancient Lands,* received mixed reviews because of his perceived Jewish biases and did not sell as briskly as his first two travel narratives. Golding had a particular purpose for writing the book. He hoped to rebut much of the modern anti-Semitic ignorance he witnessed around him by going to the land of his fathers and tracing the roots of Judaism. Describing himself as a "wandering Jew" on a quest to understand anti-Semitism, Golding made a pilgrimage to Zion through the Egyptian "land of bondage" toward the holy city of Nazareth. He toured the Jewish ghettos in the company of a Protestant, a Muslim, a Greek Orthodox churchman, and a Catholic and was shocked when he found he had little in common with the local Jews and much in common with the three Christians.

Because of this experience Golding's journey became as much a quest to find his Jewish identity as it was a crusade to combat anti-Semitism. On board a ship for Egypt he refreshed his knowledge of the Torah, stating he must know "the Book first, and then the Land of the Book." He disembarked at Port Said and excitedly smelled "the air of Egypt, as my people did once." At this point in his journey he remained hopeful that he would find some answers to the growing "Jewish problem" in Europe and make some sense of his own history.

Golding decided to walk in the steps of his ancestors because he hoped to assimilate his past culture with his present Western interests. When he finally reached Nazareth and encountered a beautiful maiden drawing water from the Well of Mary, his quest came to a reverential end. In some mystical way she pulled together the conflicting images of his journey: "An Arab maiden she was in her blood and a Christian maiden in her creed. But a Jewish maiden by the virtue of the symbol she was, and the incarnation her flesh had yielded to, little Mary of the Jews of Nazareth." For Golding she alone synthesized the "ancient meaning" of the area and "its present sweetness."

From the late 1920s through the mid 1950s Golding traveled widely. In 1927 he set out on a lec-

Soldiers aboard a ship headed for Troy and young women going to draw water from Nausicaa's stream on Corfu, photographs from Good-Bye to Ithaca *(1958), in which Golding described his 1953 attempt to retrace the wanderings of Odysseus*

ture tour. He toured America and Asia while writing novels, including his most successful book, *Magnolia Street* (1932), which gained him worldwide renown.

In *The World I Knew* (1940) Golding told of his travels in the New World and his enchantment with all things American. He watched with awe as Babe Ruth sent a ball "careening beyond the roof of Yankee Stadium towards the foot-hills of the Rockies." He thrilled at the gangster setting when "a Chicago millionaire" invited him "to lunch with him in his vast deep-carpeted tapestry-hung room." He was fascinated by "a dancer in a Negro cabaret in New Orleans" who danced "up and down a flight of stairs" while "his feet pattered like poppy-seeds."

Golding spent the summer of 1928 in Morocco, and the next two years he traveled between Spain and Paris while writing *The Prince or Somebody* (1929) and *Give Up Your Lovers* (1930). In 1929 and later in 1931 Golding also made short visits to Germany to gather information for *Magnolia Street.* During his 1931 stay in Berlin he sensed impending doom as he imagined the city perched above an active volcano. While Golding inhaled the pleasing odors of "baked meats and rich beer," he also smelled "the stink of sulphur thrust up from the crevices" and heard "the thump of lava." At the movies in Charlottenburg, Golding watched a propaganda film about Russian workers building a railroad to Siberia. He described the effect as disturbing, as if "the skin had been flayed off the bodies of all those polite ones that sat there. Enemy shrieked defiance against enemy across the black chasm which had already riven Germany apart. . . ."

After a pleasant trip to Russia in summer 1932 Golding continued to produce books at an astounding rate. In 1933 his important critical work *James Joyce* went to press, followed by a string of popular novels, including *Five Silver Daughters* (1934), *The Camberwell Beauty* (1935), and *The Dance Goes On* (1937). He also published two collections of short stories, a book of poetry, and some other scholarly works and articles before undertaking his next major journey.

In 1935 Golding's publishers suggested that he make a trek "in the steps of Moses, from the beginnings among the Nile bulrushes to his death on Mount Pisgah." Though Golding was reluctant to go at first, his memories of his father reading him bedtime stories from the Talmud made him accept the challenge. Thus Golding returned to travel writing with *In the Steps of Moses the Lawgiver* (1937), which may be the work that best displays his many talents. Golding composed a travel book and a biography that traces the life of Moses by following his journey from Egypt through the desert to Mount Sinai, where he received the Ten Commandments. Thinking it was of utmost importance to begin the journey at the exact place where Moses was born, Golding enlisted two friends to accompany him on his quest for Moses's origins. He thought that their search would not be too difficult because certainly Moses's mother "dared to go no more than a short distance" with her baby before she placed him in the Nile, so Moses must have been born somewhere along the river. With an old Egyptian postcard depicting "the tree showing the place where Moses was found by Pharaoh's daughter," Golding set out with his friends to Cairo. They planned to ask "old men in synagogues and churches and mosques, waiters in cafes, old women in markets," and whomever else they encountered to point them the way.

Their task turned out to be the most difficult part of the journey. Golding and his companions wasted time wandering the streets of Cairo to no avail. Finally, they had a mysterious encounter with a Professor Nesib, who gave a detailed account of his supposed scholarship on the subject, but he failed to show up at a later meeting. They decided to ask the area church leaders but discovered that organized religion had "never devoted a thought" to Moses's birthplace. After having no better luck with the scholars at the Cairo museum, they decided to "dig out the oldest man in the place" and show him the postcard. When he saw the card, a particularly elderly man quickly led them to a boat and took them up the Nile to an island, where they saw what was possibly the tree on the postcard. Most likely concerned with the time they had lost, Golding decided to accept this tree as their starting point. The exact site of Moses's birth might never be found. Golding exclaimed, "that is enough . . . we can go forward now," and their journey in the steps of Moses commenced.

Soon, however, the group began to disintegrate as they chose sides in petty quarrels and started to lose interest in the journey. After starting near the great pyramids and heading through Memphis and back through Cairo by car, the party stopped in Heliopolis for a meal. Finding a café, they entered, asked for "food," and were brought trays of Syrian sweets that were both unfamiliar and sickeningly rich to them. They attempted to wash their meal down with a hot beverage, but they were served an extremely sweet substance that was "thicker than any porridge." Unsatisfied with their meal, they soon began a quarrel about which path they should follow. The argument was repeated throughout most of the rest of the trip. In Zagazig, after another disagreement about where they should be going, they decided to continue for only "ten minutes more" unless they received a sign that they were on the right path. Luckily they immediately encountered an excavation party at the ruins of Tanis and were shown "the skeleton of a child" that was buried in a way that "was not in the least an Egyptian Custom." They felt they had been given the appropriate signal and decided to continue their journey.

Golding kept his eyes peeled for additional signs. He was rewarded in Midian with an epiphany. Citing the burning bush as the first miracle of the Moses story, Golding wondered if miracles can "be explained away in terms of natural rather than supernatural phenomena." Shortly thereafter he witnessed what he felt to be his own revelation:

> The thing happened "in the back of the wilderness" . . . under the flank of Sinai. . . . the winds met and, joining forces, became a cyclone, a tall pillar of air violently rotating on its axis. . . . In the center of this arena was a large thorny acacia, the only tree that grows in these regions. . . . The whole tree went up in flame. The smoke of it soared in golden gusts. . . . The bush burned with fire but was not consumed.

This vision unified the group and spurred them on.

After a particularly difficult day of travel by river barge, car, and donkey, the travelers settled in Ismailieh (Ismailia), where Golding tried to make additional connections between their journey and that of their biblical counterparts: "It was not without a sense of guilt that we splashed in a hot bath in the Palace Hotel, remembering the Israelites, who had made so long a stage that day, and had fallen asleep . . . too tired even to take their sandals off." Golding continued to look for connections during his journey, at one time seeing a marvelous "pillar of cloud" and at another time proclaiming it a miracle that they were saved from an uncomfortable night in the car by some friendly passersby.

As if transformed by their time in the desert, the three men seemed to have a different view of reality by the end of their journey. They felt that the many biblical mirages they had seen were divinely inspired. By the time they got to Sinai and their driver pointed and exclaimed "Nebi Musa" (there is Moses), Golding thought that if his "eyes had not been so enfeebled by books and city-smoke," he also could have seen the prophet.

In the Steps of Moses the Conqueror (1938) is a continuation of the same journey; yet "it was not the second part of a journey we were making, but a new journey" that was "different in mood." When they left Mount Sinai, Golding felt they were no longer tracing the steps of a lawgiver: "if the promise was to be fulfilled and the heritage won, he must be Moses the Soldier, the Conqueror." Heightened tensions just before the outbreak of World War II had made travel much more limited and troublesome, and thus Golding and his fellow travelers had to become "the conquerors" themselves. They used the Book of Numbers as their guide and planned to set out for the "wilderness of Paran." They were told the best way to get there was by camel, but Golding, who disliked traveling on camel back, was happy when camels could not be found. They bypassed the "desert of Wandering" and headed straight for Suez by "the cars that brought" them.

The impending war continued to make their journey difficult. When Golding's group arrived in Suez, they found they could hire cars to take them only as far as Akaba (Aqaba). The entire area was rather volatile, and most drivers would go no further than Aqaba without a police escort. They spent a few fruitless nights in Suez hotel bars trying to locate a driver who would take them further into Jordan and finally enlisted the services of the British residency in Amman to provide them with the necessary vehicle and a guide who would take them as far as they wanted to go. With this important piece in place, they left for Ain Kadeis, the biblical Kadesh, where the Hebrews spent "many days" before their forty years of wandering in the wilderness. The land was so inhospitable and barren that Golding wondered "what kept them there all that time."

Golding and his traveling companions climbed to the plateau of Et Tih (Al-Tih) and held a ceremony of remembrance to give meaning to their arrival: "we stood up and walked forty paces [to symbolize the years of wandering], . . . and we kept our eyes shut for forty seconds, and came back again to where we had been standing." Their Arab guides whispered in astonishment "it is their religion" and turned away respectfully.

As the party continued on their way they encountered anti-Semitism. Retracing part of the journey again, as Moses had before them, they traveled past beautiful "rust-red cliffs and cornflower sea" along the route to Aqaba. Their reception in the city was not so wonderful. As in much of the region, it was inadvisable to reveal one's Jewish heritage in Aqaba. Traveling Jews were routinely harrassed by the authorities and often deported. Golding's party kept a low profile. After a long and uncomfortable stay they left for Maan (Ma 'an), which Golding described as "a few mud houses, and then a few more and at last a street." The residents of Ma 'an let visitors know "that strangers are not loved" and that Jews were not welcomed. Turning over their passports to the local police, Golding and his friends were asked if there were any Jews among them. Fearing for their safety, a member of the party answered for Golding, saying "English! English!" Following a short stay in Ma 'an, Golding's party departed for the next stop on Moses's journey, Petra.

They were rewarded for their difficult journey by the splendor of this ancient capital of Edom, famous for its Hellenistic tombs, which are carved out of solid rock. In Petra, Golding was transported by the beauty and history of the region. Encountering the fabulous temple of Isis that Hadrian had built during the reign of the Romans, Golding attempted to squelch his enthusiasm, saying "it will be wildly easy in Petra to stray wildly far from Jehovah and Moses." After six pages of some of the most "wildly" colorful descriptions in the book, Golding continued to Amman. Exhausted by the journey, Golding concluded, "since we stood upon Mount Nebo, on the roof of the sepulchre, our imaginations were too worn to go on further journeys. . . . We knew that Moses was dead, that our journey was over."

In some ways *Good-bye to Ithaca* (1955) was the book Louis Golding had been preparing to write for his entire career. As a Homeric scholar who had already sailed the seas of Odysseus, eaten lotus on Djerba (Jerba), and been to the land of the Trojans, he wanted to conquer the *Odyssey* entirely. Using Homer as his guide to trace the supposed route of Odysseus, Golding set out on a journey of research and personal fulfillment.

Golding had been collecting information for his final travel narrative since his first voyages to Greece and Macedonia in 1916. Throughout his career, he made plans and drew maps. It was not, however, until 1953 that Golding finally set foot in Ithaca.

Much of *Good-bye to Ithaca* details the differences between a modern traveler going on an odyssey and the hardships that the ancients must have encountered. While making enlightened speculations such as "it is beyond belief that on his voyage from Ithaca to Aulis Odysseus did not disembark for supplies and water at Athens," Golding drew humorous comparisons that bridge the gap between the ages: "Odysseus disembarked, then, from his ship. Edward and I disembarked from our aeroplane." Likewise, when he and his companion went from Athens to Aulis by way of Thebes, Golding compared their car problems to Odysseus's trials at sea, and later while relaxing aboard a cruise liner headed for Troy, he remarked that "Odysseus and Telemachus would have endless trouble with their visas." These seemingly humorous connections help Golding to achieve a sense of timelessness. With his creative and active imagination he was able to fill in the gap that exists between the reader and Odysseus.

Golding made an almost metaphysical connection with Odysseus that brings him to life. As he recollected his past Greek island journeys, including "hunting Sirens in sirenland" in the early 1920s with Norman Douglas, Golding tied his journey to Odysseus. Likewise, while in Sicily, Golding saw "more than one cavern . . . where Odysseus had poked out the eye of the Cyclops" and "more than one rock which Polyphemus . . . had sent hurtling after the hero's ship." Later, while entering Corfu, Golding saw "a wrecked ship red and rusty wedged upon the rocks" and convinced himself that it is "all that was left of the vessel Odysseus had built for himself." When Golding reached Ithaca, his career as a travel writer both climaxed and concluded. He later wrote that "Troy and Ithaca were the two pinnacles" of his journeys. He had been "thinking of them, and striving toward them, for many years," and having reached them, he could face his later years with "a certain measure of fulfillment."

In 1956, the year following the publication of *Good-bye to Ithaca,* Golding married his childhood friend Annie Wintrobe. He continued to write, publishing three more works of fiction before a six-week illness ended in his untimely death in 1958.

Golding spent most of his life traveling and writing. His many trips to the Holy Land and his love for the classical world make him an important travel writer with an uncanny ability to bring the past to life. While his empathy for the masses and his concern about anti-Semitism have led some critics to consider his work overly polemical, his hope for future cultural understanding makes his ideological musings effective. It is no wonder that the Royal Air Force chose to drop works by Golding during a raid on Berlin during World War II. His writings are truly powerful.

Reference:

J. B. Simons, *Louis Golding: A Memoir* (London: Mitre Press, 1958).

Papers:

Some of Golding's letters and papers are at the London Archive Manuscript Control.

Helen Cameron Gordon, Lady Russell

(1867 - 2 February 1949)

Lisa Colletta
Claremont Graduate University

BOOKS: *A Woman in the Sahara* (New York: Stokes, 1914; London: Heinemann, 1915);
Love's Island (Nicosia, Cyprus: Archer, 1925);
Spain As It Is (London: Methuen, 1931);
My Tour in Portugal (London: Methuen, 1932);
The Sunwheel: Hindu Life and Customs (London: King, 1935);
Syria As It Is: The Republic of Lebanon, The Republic of Syria, The Government of Latakia, The Government of the Djebel Druze, The Autonomous Sandjak of Haytay (London: Methuen, 1939);
West Indian Scenes (London: Robert Hale, 1942).

Traveling in the wake of intelligent and intrepid women travelers such as Isabella Bird and Mary Kingsley, Helen Cameron Gordon spent most of her life wandering the globe and writing about her experiences in a publishing career that spanned almost thirty years. From her first travel book, *A Woman in the Sahara* (1914), to her last, *West Indian Scenes* (1942), readers are witness to the changes that travelers and travel writers encountered during the first half of the century as technology altered the world and the way it was experienced. Throughout her long career Gordon revealed herself as a natural traveler, disregarding discomforts and unexpected mishaps with unassuming friendliness, curiosity, and humor. Well-educated and a talented linguist, Gordon was also a keen observer, fascinated by the myths, legends, and languages of different cultures. Incorporating aspects of travel memoir, popular history, and ethnographic study, Gordon's works transcend traditional genres and create composite portraits of each place she visited.

Helen Cameron Gordon left only her travel books to bear witness to her extraordinary life, and there is almost no information about her outside them. Born in Scotland in 1867, she was the youngest daughter of James Gordon and spent some of her childhood in India, according to references made in *The Sunwheel: Hindu Life and Customs* (1935). On 11 October 1916 she married Sir Alison Russell, attorney general for Cyprus, whom she presumably met while traveling on the island. In 1924, when her husband was named chief justice of Tanganyika territory (now part of Tanzania), she moved with him to Dar es Salaam. When she was elected to the Royal Geographical Society on 10 January 1927, she listed among her qualifications for membership her travel books *A Woman in the Sahara* and *Love's Island* (1925) and her travels in India, Ceylon (now Sri Lanka), Algeria, Egypt, the Sudan, Kurdestan, Tanganyika, Uganda, Syria, Palestine, and Cyprus. Between the years 1932 and 1937, she became an honorary corresponding member of the Institut de France, which awarded her a silver medal in 1937; an honorary member of the Institute University of Coimbra, Portugal; and a member of the Folk-lore Society. When her husband died unexpectedly on 19 September 1948, *The Times* (London) reported that she was unable to attend the funeral because she was in Barbados. She died some five months later, on 2 February 1949, most probably in the West Indies.

A Woman in the Sahara begins with the epigraph "Hail to thee, O Sun! Not the pale reflexion of thyself that fitfully illumines the blue skies of Northern Europe or glooms, a ball of dusky red, through grey cold mist and fog; but thou indeed!" This paean to the sun is not only an appropriate introduction to Gordon's first travel book but to the rest of her writings as well, for Gordon, like many British travel writers of the period, seems to have spent her life in search of sunshine and warmth. Paul Fussell in *Abroad* (1980), his study of British travelers between the world wars, suggests that sun "worshiping" is an important new aspect of twentieth-century travel literature, separating it from nineteenth-century travel accounts. Gray skies and bland food had become emblematic of everything that was wrong with modern industrial life in the north, and, like many moderns, Helen Cameron Gordon was drawn to sun-drenched lands with ancient cultures that had not yet succumbed to the inexorable march of modernity. Perhaps her childhood years in India gave Gordon her taste for travel and hot climates, for she often wrote of the sun as if it were a long-lost friend.

Gordon's most autobiographical–and one might say best–travel book, *A Woman in the Sahara,* is organized like a travel diary, describing Gordon's experiences in North Africa from September 1912 to November 1913. Her longing for the sun drew her to the Sahara, and on her arrival in Algiers she was at first disappointed with the cloudy, damp weather and wondered if her "quest in search of the sun was, after all, fruitless–if, perhaps, he were on strike here as he had been in Europe throughout the whole of a miserable summer." Her fears were quickly allayed, however, as the motor car in which she and her friend Lisette were traveling dropped down to the plains of the Sahara, past Arab villages and caravans of dromedaries to a landscape of biblical wilderness. Instantly, she was reminded of passages in the history of the patriarchs and paintings illustrating Bible stories, none of which could possibly reproduce "*these* colours, or *this* light."

Color and light prove to be important for more reasons than their salutary effects on a traveler's psyche. Referred to by only her first name throughout the book, Gordon's traveling companion was a painter, and several interesting experiences stem from her attempts to persuade local women to pose for her, entranced as she was with the vibrant colors of their native costumes. This task was not easy because villagers feared that their portraits would make them vulnerable to evil spirits, and mothers of daughters knew that no future husband would want his wife's portrait to be in the hands of a stranger. The chapter "A 'Numéro,' " which describes how a young beauty called Nakhla agreed to pose, is one of the most charming in the book. (Lisette's painting of Nakhla illustrates the chapter.) Because Nakhla's mother refused to allow her to go Lisette's studio, the portrait was painted in Nakhla's home under cover of night so that gossiping neighbors would not see Lisette and Gordon carrying easel and brushes into the house. This episode is particularly fascinating because it affords a view of Arab life not usually allowed to travelers. In many travel narratives the "locals" are generally portrayed as petty annoyances for the traveler or as greedy innkeepers, rude government officials, and obsequious waiters. Because Gordon was allowed "behind the veil" and taken into the confidence of Nakhla, her family, and other women in the village, her representations of them are not caricatures. Instead they are full of genuine warmth.

As Gordon traveled through the villages of the Hauts Plateaux and along the the caravan routes of the M'Zab (Oued M'Zab) river and the Saharan Atlas mountains, she befriended many women. At a time when some women travelers disguised themselves as men to explore Islamic countries, Gordon drew attention to the fact that she was a woman in the Sahara. She was fascinated by the rich and passionate life of the women she encountered, for she found that they were the keepers of legends and the practitioners of magic. Many chapters are named for the women she met, or the chapters recount legends of women who were great prophets, warriors, or lovers. *A Woman in the Sahara* tells all of their stories with admiration and delight.

However privy Gordon may have been to the lives of the people of the Sahara, she never abandoned the visitor status that is the hallmark of most travel literature. She was always aware that she was a stranger, dutifully calling out *"Roumya"* (stranger or Christian) before entering any Arab dwelling. Of course, this sense of being a stranger, of being away from home, is the background against which travel experiences are put into relief, and Gordon used her position to add depth and dimension to her observations. At a meeting in Mélika with a government official and his interpreter, who spoke English "more wonderfully than intelligibly," she was escorted through the town by "four of those wonderful beings whom the Koran says God elevated above women by reason of the superior qualities with which he had endowed them." The interpreter bragged about a new school being built for boys, prompting Gordon to respond,

> "This is splendid for the future of your men, and what are you doing for the women?"
>
> *"Nothing!"* he responded shortly, *"and never will.* Our women must stay here. If they were taught to read, they would want to go away. Look at you, how you go about all over the world. We would never permit such a thing."
>
> I maintained a discreet silence but turned away to hide an involuntary smile! How often that idea had been expressed in every language, and in all lands had proved equally futile in the face of that inevitable law of evolution, which no man can arrest.

As Gordon ruminated on the better future that awaits Arab women, she was sure that "civilization" would put an end to oppressive traditions, relegating them "to the dust heap of other worn out creeds, injustices, and superstitions." These thoughts highlight the paradox inherent in her books, as well as in most twentieth-century travel writing. Travelers seek the charm of exotic places precisely because of their ancient "creeds and superstitions"; yet they are frequently appalled by them. The attempt to reconcile a nostalgic longing for the past and an anxious anticipation of the future is at the heart of many good travel books.

A Woman in the Sahara was well received by reviewers in the United States. *The New York Times* (10 January 1915) described it as "an interesting account," and the reviewer for the *Boston Transcript* (9 January 1915) called it "interesting in a hundred ways: a delightful tale akin to the *Arabian Nights*." This reviewer also admired Gordon's "welcome sense of humor" and her "sympathetic interest in Arab life of every form, except the debasement of women." *A Woman in the Sahara* was the only one of Gordon's books published and reviewed in the United States, and neither it nor any of her subsequent works appear to have been reviewed in the major British newspapers.

Love's Island (1925) is a disappointing successor to *A Woman in the Sahara*. Dedicated to Alison Russell, as a *souvenir* of their marriage, it includes little autobiography, and the work lacks the eccentric style of personal witness that usually makes travel narrative so compelling. The title seems to suggest an exploration of the mythological birthplace of Aphrodite through the eyes of one recently pierced by Cupid's arrow, but instead the book is a retelling of the violent history of Cyprus, from its geological severing from the continental land mass to its then-current state of British occupation.

There are, however, occasional moments of romance and reflection, beginning with the description of the island "anchored beneath a glowing sun in a sapphire sea, touched with broad lines of purple where foam flecked wavelets ripple melodiously over the reefs." Throughout the book Gordon's descriptions of the landscape are luminous, and she is clearly enchanted with the intermingling of Eastern and Western cultures on the island, remarking with wonder on the "shrouded Moslem women" who decorate their homes with the ruins of Gothic churches. Though the contrast between the two cultures is responsible for the distinctive beauty of the island, it is also responsible for its long history of violence and bloodshed: "On its plains has been spilt the red blood of both hemispheres: a huge graveyard, its shores are lined with tombs, their soil fertilized with the mingled dust of conquerors and conquered." Gordon intimates that the history of Cyprus is a microcosm of all mankind's history in which "all the accepted canons of civilization, of suitability, of art, seem to have been broken" in an endless succession of victors and vanquished.

Divided into two parts, the book begins with an examination of Cypriot monuments. Part one, "The Book of Stones," discusses well-known sites on the island dating from the ancient culture of the Phœnicians through the early Christian era and the Crusades to the end of the sixteenth century. Gordon personalized the legends associated with each of these monuments, telling the stories of St. Paul, St. Catherine, and Queen Caterina Cornaro with great passion and romance. The second part, "The Book of the People," retells Cypriot fables and folk songs with no attempt to contextualize them within Gordon's experiences on the island. Stories such as "The Three-Eyed Monster," "The Born Thief," and "The Tale of the Travelling Tinker," read, appropriately enough, like a combination of the *Arabian Nights* and *Aesop's Fables,* and many of them are quite engaging.

The Giralda in Seville, photograph from Spain As It Is *(1931), by Helen Cameron Gordon, Lady Russell*

In *Spain As It Is* (1931) Gordon recovered a bit of the narrative voice that was absent in *Love's Island.* In the remainder of her books, however, she was never as insistently autobiographical as she was in *A Woman in the Sahara.* Clearly, her interests rested more in ethnography and social history than in memoir and autobiography. In Spain she visited well-known cities and historical sites, recounting the legends associated with them, much as she did in Cyprus. Gordon's writing remains revealing, however, in the eccentric way in which these stories are told, and her books are marked by a decidedly romantic view of history, as if the characters in these legends had told her their stories in whispered confidence.

She began her journey in Mallorca (Majorca), where she was enchanted by the sunlight playing on the towers and spires of the forty-eight churches that encircle the city of Palma and by the medieval pageantry of Easter celebrations. To her delight little had changed over the centuries, but the specter of modern uniformity loomed in the background, and Gordon, much like D. H. Lawrence in his travels to Mediterranean islands, lamented that the Majorcans were abandoning their native costumes in favor of "the fashion of the Paris boulevard." From Majorca she journeyed to Ibiza before heading to Valencia on the Spanish mainland, where she immediately recalled the legend of the Holy Grail and how the Cathedral at Valencia came to be in possession of it, wryly noting that there are also Holy Grails in Jerusalem, Genoa, and Glastonbury. In Toledo she visited more cathedrals, and her narrative includes an amusingly idiosyncratic biography of El Greco.

The remainder of the book describes her visits to Barcelona, Pamplona, Santiago de Campostela, Salamanca, Madrid, Granada, and Seville. Each has its own "impressive" cathedral and accompanying legends, all of which, even for Gordon, become oppressive in their "medieval piety and antiquity." Despite her "intense love of colour," she could not paint these cathedrals because the "brilliant sun cast only heavy black shadows" on the buildings, and they "are not scenes for the brush." Indeed, the intensity of Spain–in its art, religion, and festivities–often seemed overwhelming to Gordon, and she complained that in Spain, "no one, except myself, goes to bed at a reasonable hour." She concluded her visit with the Christmas and New Year festivities in Barcelona, Granada, and Seville. It seems appropriate that she began and ended her journey with the two holiest celebrations on the Catholic calendar, considering how important a role the Church has played in Spanish history. The book finishes on a characteristically paradoxical note, with Gordon's elegiac comments on the passing of traditional customs: "Old-world ceremonies of the Catholic faith are, evidently, passing from out of the church to the theatres and concert halls, so secularized as to border on irreverence"; yet she approvingly noted that the income from these festivals has resulted in a fine new hospital, with "care of such a costly and highly scientific nature that could only be obtained elsewhere in the homes of the wealthy." In the end her hope for the future supplants her longing for the past.

My Tour in Portugal (1932), published just a year after *Spain As It Is,* might be viewed as a continuation of Gordon's trip to Spain, although she seems to have gone back to England for a few months between the two journeys. The book is written half as a travel diary, half in a nearly epistolary style, never fully adopting the letter-writing form but nonetheless using an intimate form of address. Her lifelong love of the sun manifests itself early in her description of leaving England for Portugal: "When you bade me farewell on board the Royal Mail-boat bound for 'the least known country of Europe' on a cold grey day of early June–it had been raining in Liverpool–you toasted me: 'Here's luck, Oporto, bright skies and *warmth!*' " Unfortunately, Gordon arrived in Oporto (Porto) during unseasonably cold weather, and in an unusual example of grumbling complained that the weather was "of the sort that only happens once in forty years, but of which, for some unknown reason, I often chance to be a victim." She quickly regained her good humor, although her arrival in Porto was somewhat chaotic. She found herself abandoned on the dock, not having made arrangements for anyone to meet her with a car and expecting to find the "usual array of hotel touts" to shuttle her into the city. Emerging from the customs house, she was alone on an empty road with only a private car vanishing around the corner at full speed and "with a derisive hoot." With British heartiness and aplomb, she plucked up her courage to inquire at a few villas near the quay and found herself entertained in true English fashion, with afternoon tea and a big armchair in which to repose until a car arrived "from somewhere or other" to take her to town.

In her previous two books Gordon had declined to discuss insignificant, personal experiences of this kind, so typical of most travel narratives. *My Tour in Portugal,* however, is again refreshingly self-revealing, more satisfactorily combining historical information with personal observation. As in *A Woman in the Sahara,* she describes fewer "famous" sites and more genuine adventures. *My Tour in Portugal* relates in a bemused tone the vagaries of Portuguese transportation and food, finding both at times a bit distasteful. The national dish, *bacalhau,* a salted cod, is found everywhere, "even met with in the street . . . carried over men's shoulders in flattened masses of string-grey fish, flat and floury looking." Nevertheless, with her usual good nature her discussions of local customs end on a positive note, asserting in this instance that "the beef in Portugal is good."

From Tobias Smollett to Osbert Sitwell, British travelers have been lured to the Continent to participate in the harvesting of the vintage, and Gordon is no exception. The countryside near the Douro is famous for its port wine, and Gordon was captivated by the "vine-culture" of the people there. The vintage was everything Gordon imagined it would be, though she was not so romantic as to ignore the backbreaking labor of the men and women harvesting the grapes or of the hostess who catered the delicious picnic for the British "pleasure-party in that out-of-the-way region." With the work done for the day the entire party returned to the sheds where the grapes were stomped. Though the work was strenuous, the men and women sing and dance, "merrily footing through the wine." Gordon herself took up the guitar and played a tune for them, delighted with the age-old ritual filled with "what no machine can ever give–the essence of humanity."

My Tour in Portugal is distinguished by its nostalgia for a passing way of life, and throughout her travels in the country Gordon was charmed by the rituals still practiced by the people, finding them far superior to machine-age advancements. On the last day of her stay Gordon was invited to a bullfight that was part of the Easter festivities. Judging them to be an outmoded, "disgusting spectacle," she had refused to attend bullfights in the past–even at the risk of offending her Spanish friends–just as she had refused to attend foxhunts in England. In Portugal, however, she came to realize that blood sport might satisfy some deep need in man, "that to satisfy the lust to kill is a specific and a vent to a type of humanity, and that it may serve to lessen some greater evil." The bulls were magnificent and majestic, respected by the men in the ring who battled with them on equal footing, and she found the bullfight "infinitely more desirable than a circus, where animals, so self-conscious and sensitive, are robbed of their dignity and subjected to ridicule and laughter by the performance of silly, odious tricks." Yet she was aware of the passing of the old ways and noted that the days of bullfighting were drawing to a close, the game being "too archaic for modern youth," who prefer the wild excitement of a football match. Gordon's account of her tour closes under the heading "On Board–and at Sea," evoking the wistfulness that accompanies the traveler's return home. She was still flush with the excitement of the bullfight, which seems emblematic of her experience in Portugal: "pleasantly human; ofttimes quite sudden, spontaneous and unexpected."

In *The Sunwheel: Hindu Life and Customs* (1935) Gordon returned to her peculiar sort of ethnographic study. She was again escaping "the dark days of an English winter to revel in the sunshine," and the book opens with an illustration of the Hindu god Arjuna driving the chariot of the sun. Given the political climate of the time–as Great Britain was about to lose the Indian jewel in its imperial crown–*The Sunwheel* is fascinating for modern readers. One of the primary features of the book is the impression of the utter inability of the British to fathom the Indian way of life: "Nowhere else than in India is it more possible for the European to live a life of splendid isolation from the people of the country." When Gordon lived in India as a girl, she "had no Indian neighbors. . . . I had never met, nor thought of visiting, a high caste Hindu lady, nor any Muslims . . . nor even Parsees, who were noted for their foreign education and intellectual attainments." This book attempts to be a corrective, by explaining the life and customs of the Hindu people to the British reader, but its charm (and at times its irritation) lies in following the observations–sometimes marveling and sensitive, sometimes churlish and judgmental–of an aging British aristocrat.

Gordon clearly had a genuine interest in her subject, and her retelling of Hindu legends is often vivid and lively, but far more interesting are her frequent comments on current political events and her recurring attacks on Mohandas Gandhi, of whom she was particularly disdainful. An entire chapter, "An Extraordinary Popular Delusion," is devoted to deriding Gandhi as a hypocrite and a charlatan, hoodwinking the lower castes of India and the gullible press in Britain. India is a complicated place for the British, and, like many before her, Gordon's attempts to make sense of her experiences occasionally left her overwhelmed and confused. On a visit to a deserted Siva shrine she was bewildered as she found herself alone in the dimly lit chamber: "An eerie feeling took possession of me, that I had been brought there for some purpose: had been commanded that the gods (Siva and Parvati) might look at the white woman from the West. . . . Utterly taken aback, confused at being thus confronted by them, . . . I stood transfixed by the stony, hard stare that met my eager gaze." Motoring away in her car, she was confused by the event and retreated into a more objective description of the landscape and Hindu mythology, much like the rest of the book.

Gordon began *Syria As It Is: The Republic of Lebanon, The Republic of Syria, The Government of Latakia, The Government of the Djebel Druze, The Autonomous Sandjak of Haytay* (1939) with an Arab proverb: "The mind said: 'I shall go and live in Syria,' and the spirit of discord hastened to add: 'I'll come with you.' " Probably written after Gordon accompanied her husband on a fact-finding trip on the partition of Palestine, the book supports her use of the saying. As the full title suggests, this region has experienced more than its share of division and strife, and few of the regions she visited still exist as autonomous political units. Like *The Sunwheel,* this book fascinates the modern reader because it reports on places in the midst of cataclysmic historical change.

Syria As It Is sketches the complicated and turbulent past of the region, expressing amazement at how quickly things change in this part of the world. Gordon had been in Syria just fifteen years before, but on her second arrival in the harbor at Beirut she was astonished at the modern houses built along the water, the airplanes winging overhead, and motor boats racing out to sea. Searching the city from the balcony of her hotel, Gordon realized, "There is nothing left of my remembrance," and, as she left the hotel to mail a few letters, she learned, to her great surprise, that she is not in Syria–as she had thought–but in the Republic of Lebanon, created by the French in 1925. Indeed, *Syria As It Is* is marked by a sense of rapid change and technological advancement, seeming in some ways to belong to another era of travel writing. Gone are the references to old master paintings; when Gordon stood in front of the ruins of the great stadium at Antioch, she was reminded of its "reconstruction" in the movie *Ben-Hur* (1926), and her shopping in Beirut was once interrupted by a terrorist attempt to blow up the palace of the Sérail. Gordon's style of representing place remains constant, however, and her tales of warriors, lovers, and prophets are still exuberant and eccentric. Traveling through Lebanon, Syria, and other independent areas, she wove a colorful tapestry of the region using the threads of Muslim, Druze, and Christian legends.

Appropriately Gordon's last travel book is steeped in warmth and color, praising the blue waters and the brilliant sunshine of the Caribbean and contrasting the fog and dreariness of the "Mother Country" with the blues, purples, greens, crimsons, and yellows of the tropics. *West Indian Scenes* (1942) is the record of about a year spent voyaging around the string of islands that make up the Antilles and Lesser Antilles, focusing on the islands of Barbados, Dominica, Antigua, Haiti, Puerto Rico, St. Thomas, and Trinidad. As with most of Gordon's other works, *West Indian Scenes* emphasizes history and ethnography, examining the past of the region and exploring the variety of influences–African, Indian, English, French, Spanish, and Dutch–that have created the culture of the islands.

The mingling of cultures had been a constant fascination throughout Gordon's long career, and in the Caribbean she seems to have been particularly curious about Creole languages and the variety of religious influences in the practice of voodoo. Though a glossary of foreign words is a standard component of all of her works, in this work she also included a glossary of West Indian sayings, most of which have legends attached to them, which she explains in the text. One such saying, "z'affe mouton pas z'affe cabrite"–which is literally translated as "the affairs of the sheep are not those of the nanny-goat" (that is, "it's none of your business")–is the standard response she received whenever she inquired into the practices of voodoo. Much to her disappointment, she was never allowed to witness any voodoo ceremonies, but her book includes many voodoo folktales. Though *West Indian Scenes* is not particularly autobiographical, there is a delightful episode near the end of the book in which Gordon is on the island of Trinidad for carnival. The locals presented her with a song written in her honor:

> Lady Russell we welcome heartily
> To our beautiful shore of La Trinity
> And we can assure her we are proud and glad
> For her presence with us in La Belle Trinidad.
> She is one of those lady authors of high repute
> That is a fact no one can refute
> Traveling extensively all will agree
> Collecting Datas very carefully . . .
> Those who have met her with one voice say
> That she is polished and cultured in every way.

Though Helen Cameron Gordon occupies only a small niche in the travel-writing genre, her career is remarkable for its longevity and breadth. Her work appeals primarily to readers interested in ethnographic questions and in investigating the ways in which one culture reports on another, particularly within the context of colonialism. Yet the fascination of travel writing lies in its heterogeneity, both in its form and its content, and Gordon's writing presents an unusual figure whose responses to adventure are never predictable. Exhibiting a certain flexibility throughout her travels, Gordon remained consumed with the desire to know, as well as to teach, and she found a pithy West Indian fable as adventurous as a trek over the caravan routes of the Sahara. She shared many characteristics with her fellow modernists: love of the sun, sadness at the passing of the old ways of life, and an intense desire to make sense of new experiences in a rapidly changing world.

Stephen Graham

(16 March 1884 - 15 March 1975)

Marguerite Helmers
University of Wisconsin Oshkosh

BOOKS: *A Vagabond in the Caucasus, with Some Notes on His Experiences among the Russians* (London & New York: John Lane, 1911);

Undiscovered Russia (London & New York: John Lane, 1912);

A Tramp's Sketches (London: Macmillan, 1912);

Changing Russia (London & New York: John Lane, 1913);

With the Russian Pilgrims to Jerusalem (London: Macmillan, 1913);

With Poor Immigrants to America (London: Macmillan, 1914; New York: Macmillan, 1914);

Russia and the World: A Study of the War and a Statement of the World-Problems That Now Confront Russia and Great Britain (London: Cassell, 1915; New York: Macmillan, 1915; revised and enlarged edition, London: Cassell, 1917);

The Way of Martha and the Way of Mary (London: Macmillan, 1915; New York: Macmillan, 1915);

Christmas in the Heart (London: A. T. Stevens, 1916);

Through Russian Central Asia (London & New York: Cassell, 1916; New York: Macmillan, 1916);

Priest of the Ideal (London: Macmillan, 1917; New York: Macmillan, 1917);

Russia in 1916 (London: Cassell, 1917; New York: Macmillan, 1917);

The Quest of the Face (London: Macmillan, 1918; New York: Macmillan, 1918);

A Private in the Guards (London: Macmillan, 1919; New York: Macmillan, 1919);

Children of the Slaves (London: Macmillan, 1920); also published as *The Soul of John Brown* (New York: Macmillan, 1920);

The Challenge of the Dead: A Vision of the War and the Life of a Common Soldier in France, Seen Two Years Afterwards between August and November, 1920 (London & New York: Cassell, 1921);

Europe–Whither Bound? (Quo Vadis Europa?) Being Letters of Travel from the Capitals of Europe (London: Butterworth, 1921; New York: Appleton, 1922);

Pencil drawing by Vernon Hill, from Changing Russia *(1915)*

Tramping with a Poet in the Rockies (London: Macmillan, 1922; New York: Appleton, 1922);

In Quest of El Dorado (New York: Appleton, 1923; London: Macmillan, 1924);

Under-London (London: Macmillan, 1923);

Life and Last Words of Wilfrid Ewart (London & New York: Putnam, 1924);

London Nights (London: Hurst & Blackett, 1925; New York: Doran, 1926);

Russia in Division (London: Macmillan, 1925); also published as *The Dividing Line of Europe* (New York: Appleton, 1925);

The Gentle Art of Tramping (New York: Appleton, 1926; London: Holden, 1927);
Midsummer Music (London: Hurst & Blackett, 1926; New York: Doran, 1927);
New York Nights (New York: Doran, 1927; London: Benn, 1928);
The Lay Confessor (London: Benn, 1928; New York: Knopf, 1929);
Peter the Great: A Life of Peter I of Russia (London: Benn, 1929; New York: Simon & Schuster, 1929);
The Death of Yesterday (London: Benn, 1930);
St. Vitus Day (London: Benn, 1930; New York: Appleton, 1931);
A Modern Vanity Fair (London: Benn, 1931);
Stalin: An Impartial Study of the Life and Work of Joseph Stalin (London: Benn, 1931);
Everybody Pays (London: Benn, 1932);
Ivan the Terrible: The Life of Ivan IV of Russia (London: Benn, 1932; New Haven: Yale University Press, 1933);
Twice Round the London Clock and More London Nights (London: Benn, 1933);
Boris Godunof (London: Benn, 1933; New Haven: Yale University Press, 1933);
One of the Ten Thousand (London: Benn, 1933);
Lost Battle (London: Nicholson & Watson, 1934);
The Padre of St. Jacobs (London: Nicholson & Watson, 1934);
Balkan Monastery (London: Nicholson & Watson, 1935; New York: Stokes, 1936);
A Life of Alexander II, Tsar of Russia (London: Nicholson & Watson, 1935); also published as *Tsar of Freedom: The Life and Reign of Alexander II* (New Haven: Yale University Press, 1935);
Characteristics (London: Rich & Cowan, 1936);
African Tragedy (London: Rich & Cowan, 1937);
Alexander of Jugoslavia, Strong Man of the Balkans (London: Cassell, 1938); republished as *Alexander of Yugoslavia: The Story of the King Who Was Murdered at Marseilles* (New Haven: Yale University Press, 1939);
The Moving Tent: Adventures with a Tent and Fishing-rod in Southern Jugoslavia (London: Cassell, 1939);
From War to War: A Date-Book of the Years Between (London & Melbourne: Hutchinson, 1940);
Liquid Victory (London & Melbourne: Hutchinson, 1940);
Thinking of Living (London: Benn, 1949);
Summing-Up on Russia (London: Benn, 1951);
Pay as You Run (London: Benn, 1955);
Part of the Wonderful Scene: An Autobiography (London: Collins, 1964).

OTHER: *Constable's Russian Library,* 6 volumes, edited by Graham (London: Constable, 1915–1918);
Vladimir Solovyov, *War and Christianity, from the Russian Point of View,* introduction by Graham (New York: Putnam, 1915);
Fedor Kuzmich Teternikov, *The Sweet-Scented Name, and Other Fairy Tales, Fables and Stories by Fedor Sologub,* edited by Graham (New York: Putnam, 1915);
Nikolay Gogol, *Dead Souls,* introduction by Graham (London: Unwin, 1915; New York: Stokes, 1916);
Vlas Doroshevich, *The Way of the Cross,* introduction by Graham (London: Constable, 1916);
Alexandr Kuprin, *A Slav Soul and Other Stories,* introduction by Graham (New York: Putnam, 1916);
Olga Novikova, *Russian Memories,* introduction by Graham (London: Jenkins, 1916);
The Tramp's Anthology, edited by Graham (London: Davies, 1928);
Vladimir Bogoraz, *Sons of the Mammoth,* translated by Graham (New York: Cosmopolitan Book, 1929);
Great Russian Short Stories, edited by Graham (London: Benn, 1929; New York: Liveright, 1929);
Roman Gul, *General B.O.,* edited by Graham (London: Benn, 1930);
Panteleimon Romanov, *Without Cherry Blossom,* translated by L. Zarine, edited by Graham (London: Benn, 1930);
Great American Short Stories, edited by Graham (London: Benn, 1931);
Gul, *Provocateur, a Historical Novel of the Russian Terror,* translated by Zarine, edited, with an introduction, by Graham (New York: Harcourt, Brace, 1931);
Romanov, *Three Pairs of Silk Stockings,* translated by Zarine, edited by Graham (London: Benn, 1931);
Yury Frolov, *Fish Who Answer the Telephone, and Other Studies in Experimental Biology,* translated by Graham (London: Kegan Paul, 1937);
One Hundred Best Poems in the English Language, edited by Graham (London: Benn, 1952).

Stephen Graham was a prolific writer of travel literature, fiction, and biography, as well as a translator of Russian literature and an interpreter of Russian culture. His reputation rests on a handful of travel volumes and his wartime exposé *A Private in the Guards* (1919). His early works were travel narratives. Graham made his journeys on foot, developing a rugged and aggressive style of travel that he

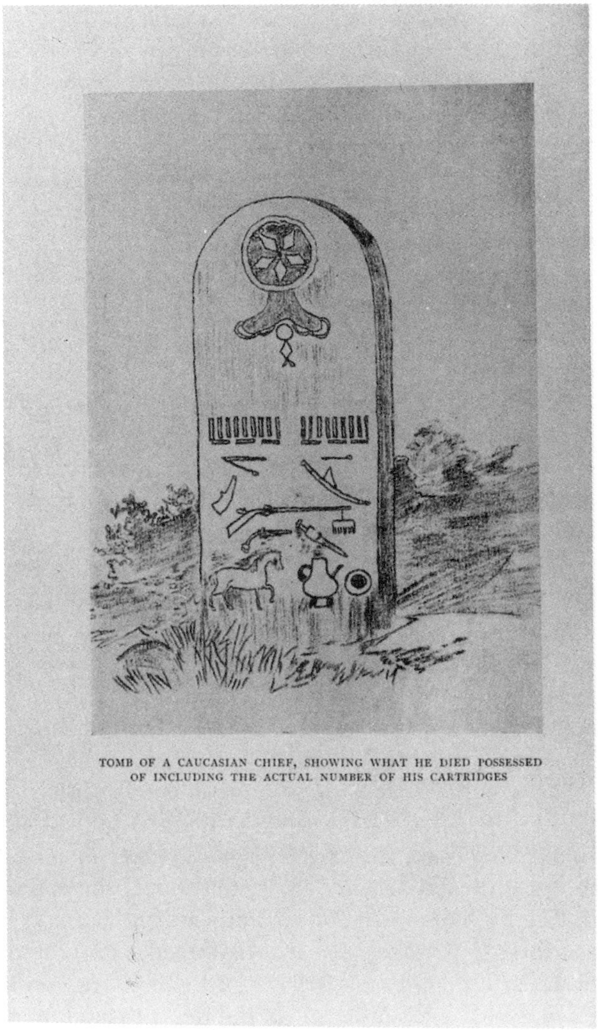
TOMB OF A CAUCASIAN CHIEF, SHOWING WHAT HE DIED POSSESSED OF INCLUDING THE ACTUAL NUMBER OF HIS CARTRIDGES

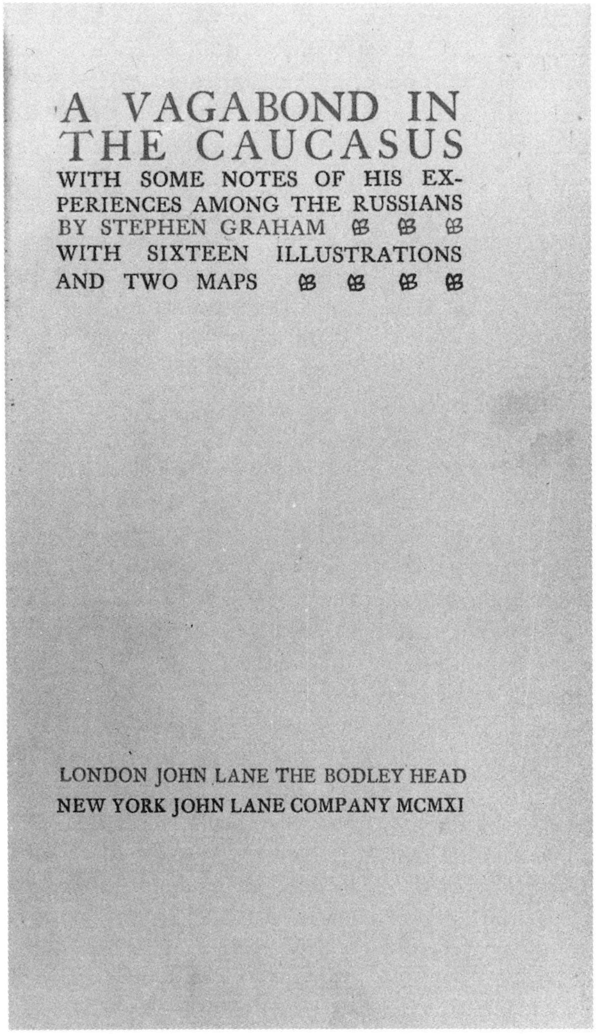
A VAGABOND IN THE CAUCASUS
WITH SOME NOTES OF HIS EXPERIENCES AMONG THE RUSSIANS
BY STEPHEN GRAHAM
WITH SIXTEEN ILLUSTRATIONS AND TWO MAPS

LONDON JOHN LANE THE BODLEY HEAD
NEW YORK JOHN LANE COMPANY MCMXI

Frontispiece and title page for Graham's first book, an account of his solitary wanderings through Russia in 1910

described as tramping. As a vagabond he was not interested in a fixed destination, but in the trip itself. He was a roving commentator, a "tramp" who produced picturesque descriptions, studied character types, and offered insights on contemporary political situations and history. In *A Tramp's Sketches* (1912), he called tramps "rebels against modern life," who are concerned more with people than with places. Graham translated the vagabond's dependence on people for food and a dry bed into his own socio-anthropological method for examining and characterizing national types. Three of his books–*A Tramp's Sketches, Tramping with a Poet in the Rockies* (1922), and his essayistic guidebook *The Gentle Art of Tramping* (1926)– describe the art and philosophy of vagabondage.

Graham continues to be regarded as an authority on aspects of prerevolutionary Russian culture. Remembered by *The Times* (London) in his obituary as enthusiastic, if "idiosyncratic and misleading," Graham was nonetheless responsible for the cult of "Holy Russia" and the idealization of the Russian peasant that swept England before World War I. Alfred Harmsworth, Lord Northcliffe, and Prime Minister Lloyd George both consulted Graham on Russia, and Graham frequently lectured on the subject throughout the United Kingdom. After the Russian Revolution of 1917, however, Graham's vision of Holy Russia seemed limited. He was prevented from traveling to Russia by both the British and Russian governments, and his influence on British foreign policy waned.

Graham was born on 16 March 1884 in Edinburgh to P. Anderson Graham, essayist, editor of *Country Life* magazine, and writer for the *Edinburgh Courant.* Shortly after Stephen's birth, the family moved to Cheltenham, where the senior Graham became editor of the *Cheltenham Echo.* Graham later recalled that his father wished him to be a success in school and to develop his writing skills. He was bribed with six pence a week to get to the top of his class, which he did, becoming school captain. He further credited his father with the foundation of his writing style. When the young Stephen Graham was writing an essay on Robert Louis Stevenson's *Kidnapped* (1886), his father warned him to avoid sentences longer than fourteen words and to limit paragraphs to five sentences. Graham compared this editing task to abbreviating telegrams, but he recollected that it gave him an interest in "the quantitativeness of style."

At the age of fourteen Graham quit school, and the following year he was employed at the Bankruptcy Court in Carey Street, London. Several years later he became staff clerk at Somerset House, where with his fellow employees he cultivated an interest in books and plays. He began to study the Russian language with Nikolai Lebedev, a Ukrainian who was the son of a deacon in the Orthodox Church. Lebedev invited Graham to spend Christmas at Lisichansk, a village north of the Sea of Azov and south of Kharkiv. It was the first time that Graham had been abroad. Many adventures on the train and with his companion sparked a lifelong love of Russia that was to sustain Graham for the rest of his writing career. Attracted to the spirit of Russia, he abandoned his London job and his respectable home in Berkeley Square and began a series of tramps through the Caucasus and Ural Mountains. As he said, he "never worked again."

Austin Harrison, editor of the *English Review,* encouraged Graham to write professionally. Graham's early writing appeared in *Country Life,* and his travel works were originally published as articles in British and American newspapers and magazines, including *The Times, Harper's,* and *The New Yorker.* The journals sustained him financially, and much of his early writing bears a journalistic stamp. The books appear to have been written hastily, with many chapters seeming like sketches and suffering from want of editing.

In 1910 Graham was invited to submit vignettes on London life to the *Evening Times,* edited by Charles Watney. Graham's articles focused his interest on "characteristics," the manners and customs of individuals and societies. He wrote about cases in the police court, striptease artists, and football matches. In *Part of the Wonderful Scene: An Autobiography* (1964) he reported that he "was said to have a gift for lurid realism," a trait that later became evident in his descriptions of the evils of American slavery in *Children of the Slaves* (1920) and in his account of Ivan the Terrible's massacre at Novgorod.

Through his connections at newspapers, Graham was introduced to Lloyd George and gained such a reputation that Lord Northcliffe, owner of both *The Times* and the *Daily Mail,* told him, "My papers are at your disposal. Go where you like and write what you like. I'll look after the financial side." Graham was given a contract for twenty-six two-column signed articles in *The Times,* becoming the first writer to have a byline in the paper. And he went where he liked: Russia.

Traveling in Russia, Graham met his first wife, Rosa Savory, a teacher fifteen years his senior. They married in Russia in 1909, when he was twenty-five and she was forty. Reminiscing in *Part of the Wonderful Scene,* he reported that they were deeply in love, "spell-bound by mutual inspiration" They moved into a seventeenth-century flat designed by Christopher Wren at 60 Frith Street, London, which was to remain Graham's home until his death in 1975.

Rosa Graham rarely accompanied her husband on his travels, and in the year following his marriage Graham made his first solo tramp through Russia. Inspired by Hillair Belloc's *The Path to Rome* (1902), he produced *A Vagabond in the Caucasus* (1911), a collection of articles originally published in the *St. James's Gazette. A Vagabond in the Caucasus* captures the initial sense of wonder that Graham felt in Russia. A breathless book, immersed in discovery and highly picturesque, it introduced Russia and Stephen Graham to a British audience. Graham's later works embroidered its themes and included less introductory material, fewer explanations of geography or customs. *A Vagabond in the Caucasus* encompasses the peculiarities of daily life in Russia, providing details of religious ceremonies and social customs such as tea drinking or wine drinking and reporting concerns of the locals about their crops, their herds, and their politics. The book describes in lavish detail what people wear and say, what stories they tell, how they toast one another, and how they treat foreigners and the homeless.

A Vagabond in the Caucasus is interesting for its autobiographical elements as well. Graham details his life with Nicholas Lebedev in Moscow, where the two rented a series of small, sparsely furnished rooms and lived in near poverty while teaching and occasionally enjoying the theater. Always sympathetic to and curious about the underprivileged, Graham and Lebedev often dressed themselves in their worst clothing to explore the crowded charitable shelters of Moscow. The book describes a night spent in a stinking, unventilated, and "fearsome den," where they and the other temporary residents were served cabbage soup and kasha (a kind of

Russian peasants outside a beerhouse in a Moscow slum (photograph from A Vagabond in the Caucasus)

buckwheat porridge), slept on straw that barely covered the black slime upon the floor, and rested their heads next to huge rat holes.

Graham left Lebedev in the spring to tramp through the Caucasus. The appendix to his book includes "a chapter for prospective tourists" called "how to get about," in which Graham asserts that there is "every reason why Englishmen should visit the Caucasus." It includes advice on hotels, train fares, and outfitting–being well-dressed assures a traveler respect. It also includes an itinerary of train routes:–"It is a long and tiring journey"–and the advice that travelers should hire a stagecoach or a horse, even though horses might be stolen by Ingooshi tribesmen, "expert horse thieves."

In *Part of the Wonderful Scene* Graham recalled his disappointment with *A Vagabond in the Caucasus,* sensing that it was a juvenile effort with only a few pages of which he could be proud. Yet the book demonstrates the style that was to be his hallmark: brief chapters written as quick impressions or sketches and pages filled with anecdotes and word drawings of those encountered along the road. For Graham the rewards for *A Vagabond in the Caucasus* far exceeded monetary reimbursement. His publisher, John Lane, held many parties for him, through which Graham became acquainted with the sculptor Vernon Hill, who was to remain a lifelong friend and who illustrated one of Graham's later works, *Tramping with a Poet in the Rockies* (1922). *A Vagabond in the Caucasus* also brought him an introduction to the fantasy writer Algernon Blackwood, who became a close friend until a misunderstanding with Rosa Graham divided the two men.

Between 1910 and 1912 Graham returned to tramp the Crimea, the coast of the Black Sea, the Urals, Vladikavkaz, and Moscow. The three interests that occupied Graham as he traveled and wrote are evident in *A Tramp's Sketches* (1912). The book exemplifies a convergence of his love of undisturbed nature, his fascination with the manners and customs of the people he encountered, and his pervading sense of spirituality. The descriptive passages show Graham at his best; he was a fine nature writer. Early in the book he describes how, after weeks of solitary tramping through forests and along the seashore and sleeping out of doors, he became almost wild, responding only to sensory impulses:

> All my days from dawn to sunset I hunted for food. My life was food-hunting. I certainly wrote not a line and thought less. In my mind formed only such elementary ideas as "Soon more grapes," "These berries are not the best," "More walnuts," "Oh, a spring; I must drink there."
>
> Something from the ancient past was awakened.

These observations contribute to the reader's sense that while on a tramp Graham lived by chance. In *A Vagabond in the Caucasus* he listed the spare contents of his kit: a waterproof sleeping sack, a camel-hair blanket, a pair of boots, a flannel hood, two suits of clothes, an overcoat, and a revolver–which he was more likely to use on the mastiffs that attacked him than on a human being. *A Tramp's Sketches* details how he spent several fine days by the sea, washing clothes, writing, and napping. In all his books he noted that he sought high ground when he slept, lining his bed with dead leaves or curling up in a cave with a rock for a pillow. He ate wild berries and other fruits and treated himself to a hot dinner whenever he came to a town. A fine dinner might consist of a boiled chicken and a bottle of wine, a poor one of a slab of dry black bread. In remote areas where no bridges forded rivers, Graham was forced to strip himself of his clothes to cross and pack them in his knapsack to avoid traveling wet. In *A Tramp's Sketches* he recalled a time when, seeking shelter from a gathering storm, he was invited by a peasant to sleep among the haystacks, where he buried himself to his neck to remain warm and dry.

A Tramp's Sketches roughly follows the chronology of Graham's trip, but subordinates that sequence to thematically organized impressions. The book abounds in humor. A portrait of Christ in the lonely and spare monastery of Pitsoonda resembles Robert Louis Stevenson, "a Christ with a certain amount of cynicism, one who might have smoked upon occasion." There is a freshness and innocence about the writing in this book that was overshadowed later in Graham's career by jaded cynicism and a tendency toward moralizing. This early work captures the wonder and awe of becoming intimate with a new country: wild men of the Caucasus thunder through towns in full armor, and in a coffee shop Graham discusses politics with a Turk who wears a straw fez swathed in green silk on his head and slippers with toes that curl upward like the shoes of a prince in a fairy tale.

A Tramp's Sketches becomes increasingly spiritual as it progresses toward its culminating description of Graham's travels to Jerusalem with Russian peasants, a story that he later amplified in *With the Russian Pilgrims to Jerusalem* (1913). Here are common themes for Graham: a lament over materialism, despair over inhospitality, and faith in the enormous spiritual power of the Russian peasant.

Changing Russia (1913) is one of Graham's finest works. The book follows a chronological pattern, charting his course from St. Petersburg south to the Black Sea and then moving north to the Urals. Graham's route took him to several monasteries and to the resorts of Gelendzhik, Tuapse, Sotchi (Sochi), Gagri (Gagra), and Sukhum (Sukhumi). Interspersed with descriptions of the scenery and inhabitants are observations on Russian literature and journalism, contemporary civic culture, the landscape, peasant culture, politics, and religion. An enemy of materialism and a friend of Christianity, which he saw as unequal and incompatible poles on a moral scale, Graham believed that "if the Tsar and his advisers are not wise enough to save their people from commercialism, they will certainly bring ruin on their own heads." Amplifying this point throughout the book, he painted a picture of Russians obsessed with fine clothing, gramophones, imported French horror films, and English goods.

The Russia that emerges from Graham's picture presages the contemporary in its Balkanization, decay, and neglect. The book describes resorts by the Black Sea as pestilential swamps in which local inhabitants die of malaria daily; tribes of the Caucasus speak entirely different languages; mining towns have streets a foot deep in dust and filth:

> No one asks whether the Urals are healthier and happier for the British and German firms exploiting the treasures of the rocks there; no one asks which it is better to produce, corn or gold?–which yields the nobler national life, which even yields the more profit for labour? For my part, having wandered in almost every corner of Russia, I am certain that every step which Russia takes away from being a corn-producing land to being a mineral-producing one, is a step towards national perdition.

While Graham found the illiterate and wild tribes of the outlying territories both frightening and picturesque, he was struck by the possibilities for Christianity to unite and enlighten. He concluded that "whenever the peasant lives simply as his fathers have done on the land, with the Church, before God and the Tsar, there is Russia."

In addition to being a reflection of Graham's pervading spirituality, the book reveals many colorful and entertaining details about daily life in Russia. For example, Graham's account of Russian journalism describes a tabloid for semiliterate peasants, the *Universal Panorama,* a compendium of photographs from newspapers around the world that offers a wide opportunity for misinformation, and the respectable *Russkoe Slovo,* including emotive, part-literary columns. Graham spent some time thinking about the power of ellipses in Russian prose: "the journalist uses dots to imply that he has no more words; that his ire, or his contempt, or his wonder

Holy Russia, *a painting by Russian artist Mikhail Nesterov, whose works Graham admired as expressions of his own idealized views about the pious Russian peasant (from* Undiscovered Russia, *1914)*

has passed out of the river of language and lost itself in an ocean."

Graham's colorful description of a ride in the peasant class of a Russian train brings the experience to life, especially in its portrait of the "hares," stowaways who lay flat under the wooden seats of the third-class carriages. The chapter "Adventures in Abkhasia" recounts how Graham was captured by three mounted and armed Caucasian tribesmen. He eluded them by buying them several bottles of wine and several boiled chickens at a wine dealer's cottage. Moving his pack ever closer to the door as they ate and drank, he eventually slipped into the night.

The book also provides some insight into Graham's feelings about traveling, revealing a particular loneliness that is not evident in later essays: "Despite all the romance of the road, there is something very hard about the beginning. . . . I parted with all my comforts in detail–my friends, my unblistered toes and heels, my comfortable soft indoors bed, my regular meals and the plenty of them, my town-bred laziness."

While in Russia, Graham learned of the thousands of peasants who left Russia each year to travel to Jerusalem, a story that had been neglected by European newspapers. This exodus prompted him to join their travels from Russia to the Middle East and resulted in *With the Russian Pilgrims to Jerusalem* (1913). The immense demonstration of the Russians' faith was exemplified in their willingness to endure cramped traveling conditions and discrimination and exploitation from those of other faiths and nationalities. For Graham the story was a testament to the power of Christianity to inspire and unite the Russian people.

Russia and the World (1915) and *Through Russian Central Asia* (1916) were inspired by experiences on the Russian eastern front during the early months of World War I. While *Through Russian Central Asia* is a travel narrative, *Russia and the World* is primarily political commentary. Subtitled *A Study of the War and a Statement of the World-Problems That Now Confront Russia and Great Britain, Russia and the World* is an attempt to uncover the reasons why various nations were fighting.

Although the two works represent sequential experiences, the chronology of Graham's travels and the eventual publishing dates of the two books are somewhat misleading. Although it was published before *Through Russian Central Asia, Russia and the World* actually covers later events. The journeys discussed in *Through Russian Central Asia* were taken in 1914. Begun as a series of articles for *The Times, Through Russian Central Asia* is the last of Graham's books to record actual travels through the country. Graham started on foot from Vladikavkaz in European Russia and traveled eastward to Central Asia, Bokhara (Bukhara), Samarkand (Samarqand), Tashkent, and then north through Siberia to a small village on the eastern borderlands, where news of World War I reached him. Although he continued to travel after hearing this news, he was eventually forced back to St. Petersburg by the fighting along the Russian Front. *Russia and the World* takes up the story from the point at which Graham learned of the war.

Through Russian Central Asia is a striking example of Graham's narrative ability and his ample powers of description. It is a highly descriptive and colorful narrative, with the rare power to transport readers to a different time and place. Some reviewers called his fabulous descriptions of costumes, music, fruits, market bazaars, prayers, tents and stone dwellings, carpets, and baskets as vivid as images from the *Arabian Nights*. The richness of the life Graham encountered is summed up in his comment that "Central Asia is necessarily one of the most interesting districts of the world, and its inhabitants are like living specimens in a great ethnological museum." The juxtaposition of this richly apparent past with the materiel of modern warfare is startling. Two appendices discuss the prospects of Russia in the war, then only just declared.

Interspersed with trips to Russia and Europe were Graham's travels to America. His 1912 pilgrimage to Jerusalem with Russian peasants had inflamed Graham's desire to embark on a further pilgrimage with them, that of their immigration to America. In 1913 he obtained passage to America on an immigrant steamer from a suspicious London agent who demanded a letter of introduction from "a revolutionary anarchist, a militant suffragette." The agent feared that Graham might be a political spy and that the Russian passengers might be victimized by the czar even at the great distance of America. Joining the boat train at London and departing from Liverpool, Graham found himself among a stream of all nationalities eager to make their fortunes in New Jerusalem. On Easter Day 1913 he and his fellow travelers arrived in New York City. The journey is recorded in *With Poor Immigrants to America* (1914).

The boat journey and his subsequent tramping through the American countryside afforded Graham the opportunity to study Russian Jews as well as Flemish and British passengers aboard ship and various types of Americans on the road in the United States. He fell in with laborers and farmers, many with stories to tell, and these stories compose much of the volume. Beyond tracing the paths and the fortunes of the immigrants, Graham wanted to see the United States from the point of view of a tramp. He set aside his literary connections to tramp the country from New York City to Chicago. His thesis was that Russia and America represented opposite poles of thought, with Russia embodying the *podvig*, the turning away from the world, and America embracing the ideal of "making good." He asked himself three questions as he traveled: "What *is* America? What *is* this new nation? How are they [the American people] different from us at home in England?"

Graham was skeptical about the promise of the American Dream. Early in the book, he tells of Russians who gazed at the Statue of Liberty but failed to understand its significance or to be stirred by its majesty. One told another that it was the tombstone of Christopher Columbus. The book denounces Ellis Island as "an insult to Europe," the screening of immigrants representing American ambition to accept only those who are clean, healthy, and fit for work. Rather than embracing the American spirit of entrepreneurship, Graham indulged in a common critique, seeing America as a country that buys a future through the exploitation of the weak and helpless.

Critical reception of the book was mixed, with American reviewers finding Graham's moralizing unsound and his reasoning untrustworthy, but his anecdotes and descriptions received praise. One reviewer attested to Graham's slipshod editorial habits by noting that the book includes a mistaken version of Abraham Lincoln's Gettysburg Address, which Graham included as the text of a speech given during Decoration Day celebrations in the town of Clearfield, Pennsylvania. Perhaps some of the poor reviews were engendered by wounded national pride. Graham was called "cavalier" for merely tramping through the country; his sketches were dismissed as "flimsy and unimportant." Rural Americans are painted unflatteringly, as rude in their treatment of wanderers. If the dialogue recorded in his book is accurate, however, Graham wasted no opportunity to chastise them immediately for their lack of hospitality. A particular arrogance about British national superiority emerges from this work, one encountered less frequently in Graham's later books. The obvious sympathy with the destitute in this book alerts the reader to Graham's capacity for compassion; yet it is also true that much of his sympathy for tramps and immigrants is limited to those who are Russian.

Largely anecdotal and rhapsodic in form, *The Way of Martha and the Way of Mary* (1915) is a series of sketches recorded almost without sequence. Here, as in other of Graham's works, is represented his tendency to string together incidents, images, and cursory impressions. Graham avoided framing incidents or conversations, dropping in names without explanation and moving from one incident to the next without transition.

The Way of Martha and the Way of Mary is an interpretation of Eastern Christianity. The title alludes to the biblical sisters Martha and Mary, Martha who dedicated herself to a life of service and Mary who devoted herself to meditation. While Christianity in the West has followed the way of Martha and emphasizes good works, Christianity in the East has followed the way of Mary, the way of faith. Russian Christianity seems to embody both ideals. Graham found a resonance in a Mikhail Nesterov fresco of the sisters at the convent of St. Martha and St. Mary in the Bolshaya Ordinka in Moscow and began to carry a small reproduction of the wall painting with him on his tramps to keep him from harm. He wrote that "in a remote Moslem town on the fringe of the desert, I had a strange experience of adventure and terror, when, as it seems to me, I was literally saved by looking at the picture."

Incorporated in the Russian spiritual idea is the *podvig,* here defined as "a denial of the reality of misery on earth," a religion that teaches the avoidance of suffering. Representing devotion to an altruistic goal, the *podvig* involved self-sacrifice, suffering, and martyrdom. Ironically, by the time that Graham was idealizing Holy Russia, the *podvig* was already appropriated by revolutionaries who interpreted it as a secular spiritualism that would provide a meaningful context for terrorist activities. Revolutionaries had murdered the abbess of the convent of St. Martha and St. Mary, the former Grand Duchess Elizaveta Federovna, and her husband.

The Way of Martha and the Way of Mary was written in Russia and Egypt during 1914 and 1915. In May 1915 Graham obtained a letter to the abbot of a monastery in the Egyptian desert where the bodies of sixteen patriarchs of the Christian Church were buried. The resulting study of Christian shrines in Egypt emerges in a fascinating third section to the book, "The Desert and the World."

Graham's return sojourns in England brought invitations for public speaking engagements. His first was at the National Liberal Club, where he delivered an extemporaneous talk on the subject of Russian idealism. His views were denounced by a group of audience members led by Israel Zangwill. Graham held to his belief in "the new and living Christianity emerging from Russia" and maintained the same opinion through many lecture assignments: in his birthplace of Edinburgh, in Manchester (where he addressed five thousand people), at St. Margaret's in Westminster (where he gave a special sermon to the members of Parliament who were parishioners), and in the drawing rooms of society hostesses. Following his exploits, the press eventually shortened the recurring theme of his talks to "Holy Russia," the name by which it has been known ever since.

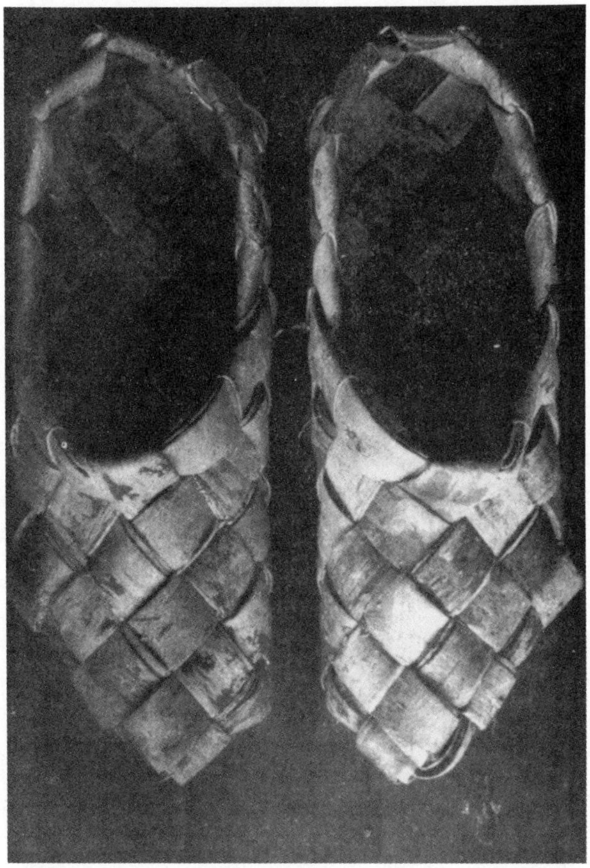

Birch-bark boots that Graham wore during part of one tramp through Russia

Graham sought to interpret Russia for Great Britain, hoping that the example of Russia would dissuade Britain from its ardent materialism. Russia was "yea," Britain "nay," as he wrote in *A Vagabond in the Caucasus.* Throughout his life Graham maintained an adamant dislike of materialism, seeing it as the downfall of the West. The West attempted to solve human problems through money, he argued, but Russia did so through love. This idealization of Russia did not survive the ravages of the 1917 revolution and eventually led to Graham's discredit as a primary Russian authority.

Although Graham's works record six years of travel in Russia, they reuse material and reformulate similar questions. Many of the books are intensely spiritual and reflective. He was a man with strong faith, and his travels tested it. Yet, in the case of his Russian travels, Graham's concern with the essence of Holy Russia was neither original nor personal enough to sustain the number of works he developed around that theme. Furthermore, while his Christianity enabled him an extraordinary sympathy with peasants, it blinded him to the contemporary political reality of the country. Following the Russian Revolution of 1917, Graham received official confirmation that his views of "Holy Russia" were no longer tenable. The British government, which supported the revolution, informed Graham that his viewpoint was unhelpful. Subsequently, Graham's lectures on Russia became infrequent and were frustrated by prorevolutionaries. Many of Graham's Russian friends had disappeared in the revolution. When he applied for a visa to return to Russia to study the effects of war and revolution, the British government acted on advice from their ambassador in Petrograd (as St. Petersburg had come to be called), and Graham was refused. Graham viewed the decision as a personal betrayal by Lord Robert Cecil, who had promised assistance if Graham were ever in need, but who, in denying the request for a visa, called Graham a "reactionary." Graham was invited to lecture on Russia in the United States, but he was denied passage again because of his perspective on Russia, this time by John Buchan, director of propaganda for the British.

It was an ignominious end to the Russian chapter of Graham's life. Russia was the country that he thought of as home. Despite his antirevolutionary stance, he was surprisingly in sympathy with the antimaterialistic goals of Communism, often excoriating the British for their reliance on capital and material wealth.

Following World War I the nature of Graham's tramps changed significantly. Before the war Graham had been able to discover the undisturbed beauty of wilderness in a way that he could not after 1918, when tragedy spurred the need to discover human life–the displaced in European capitals, the oppressed in America–and to recover the lives of the dead. Graham turned his focus to life in cities, places where he could examine his distrust of materialism and its corrupting influence on human existence.

Graham described the first of his political commentaries, *Russia in 1916* (1917), as a "little book of the hour." Intended as a rapprochement between Great Britain and Russia, the book reveals his interest in national characteristics. Mixed with a study of mundane topics such as the cost of living, the price of vodka, and the status of Russian literature is a commentary on the mood of the Russian people during World War I. During this period Graham also began writing fiction. Influenced by Russian character and spiritual belief, he produced *Priest of the Ideal* (1917), an insightful and spiritual novel that advocates the renunciation of worldly goods. Richard Hampden, the lay priest of the title, is, like Graham himself, a gifted British orator. He is also a Christ figure and an inspiration to many in his country. Although the book gained Graham a popular following, his tendency toward philosophizing was generally not well received by contemporary critics, who found it shallow and distracting.

Although he had come close to the fighting on the Russian front in 1914, Graham did not write about the war that stopped his travel to Russia until his postwar book *A Private in the Guards* (1919). Graham was not drafted until 1917, and his early memories of the war years in Britain included parties, editing manuscripts, and incidental war work. During this time, he wrote, "I was sleepwalking, talking in canteens, visiting the wounded in hospitals, addressing Princess Christian's needlework school, discussing Russian literature with Ponsonby at Lady Maud Parry's, getting a translation of Valery Brussov's stories published, dancing attendance upon Mme Novikov, amusing myself with Maya and Blackwood, having parties to read poetry aloud at Frith Street."

He was then drafted. Although offered the chance to join an officers' training corps, he turned it down in favor of being a member of the ranks. He wanted to see the war from the "inside" and enlisted in the Second Battalion of the Scots Guards as a private in 1917, at the point when the war was in its final stages. Never without connections, Graham received a letter at the front from Walter James Hore-Ruthven, eighth Baron, encouraging him to write of the war. Graham later quoted from the letter in *Part of the Wonderful Scene:*

> It is seldom we have had a man of your calibre who can tell us, from first-hand knowledge, about the life and thoughts of a private soldier on active service. However much we officers may admire and sympathize with our men and do our best to help them and make them comfortable, we all realize how little we really know about them. I am looking forward to learning from you their real thoughts and feelings, which are so often carefully hidden from *us*.

The charge from Lord Ruthven sums up the import of Graham's work. Graham combined his compassion for the lower classes and his training as an investigative journalist to create a work that not only articulated the concerns of the enlisted men but was critical of the demeaning assumption of inequality that informed relationships between officers and their men. In particular, *A Private in the Guards* reflects unflatteringly on the demeanor of superior officers. Although it lacks the richly descriptive narrative style of other war memoirs, Graham's work is an insightful and scathing journalistic inquiry, significant because it led to a parliamentary inquiry on the conditions under which soldiers were trained and instructed to perform in battle. Ironically, Graham's enlistment concluded when the exertion of a person of influence in Britain allowed Graham to remove himself from Cologne in early 1919 while his regiment remained.

Graham's genuine sympathy toward the destitute also extended to African Americans. At the front he had been introduced to several black American soldiers; impressed by their service, he became curious about the future of blacks in the United States and Africa. He was outraged by abuses of slavery and continuing prejudices, and in his efforts to understand the predicament of African American culture he interviewed American workmen, teachers, doctors, and preachers, and he visited southern schools, churches, and theaters. The result was *Children of the Slaves* (1920), published in the United States as *The Soul of John Brown.* Unfortunately, *Children of the Slaves* reads today as a facile work, filled with inaccurate and now outdated assumptions about race. This book reveals the limits of Graham's method of searching for essential types: his judgments of the personal dispositions of black people as innately and primitively simple, innocent, and shiftless are superficial at best. At their worst they recall nineteenth-century scientific and moral pronouncements.

In 1920 Graham returned to France to visit the battlefields and wrote *The Challenge of the Dead* (1921), a collection of word pictures intended to raise the reader's emotions. Graham was at his best when describing the details of this pilgrimage to the western front, where the smell of gunpowder still lingered over the blasted land. Nonetheless this book is a perplexing work, permeated with battle anecdotes drawn from someone else's histories, as Graham did not see battle until 1917. Too many re-created battles and comments on strategy overcast the poignancy of the empty present: fields of already decaying and toppled wooden crosses, callous and exhaustive exhumation of war dead, and resigned French villagers sorting rubble. Yet the pattern of the book underscores his point that in 1920 the present in France is almost wholly absorbed by the past. A hill is not significant because it is picturesque but because a battle was fought on its slopes, because the dead lie in its soil. Graham's slender book hints that World War I was a war virtually designed for poetry and that there is even poetry in its horrible aftermath: instead of crops in France, there are crosses.

Graham (right) and Vachel Lindsay in 1921, just before the two men set out on the hike through Glacier National Park that Graham described in Tramping with a Poet in the Rockies *(1922)*

The Challenge of the Dead includes thoughtful comments on the relentless process of reburying the war dead. Identification of specific individuals was difficult: Germans, French, Americans, and British fell side by side; each country wanted its dead to be treated differently. Americans insisted that bodies be shipped home; Germans relinquished the tending of grave sites; British employed caretakers of cemeteries. To whom did the remains belong? Graham speculated that they belonged to the war, to the death that leveled them all equally, regardless of nationality, personality, religion, or cause. As war dead, Graham wrote, they should lie where war left them, perpetually signifying the waste of war.

With travel to Russia forbidden by the British government Graham pursued his interest in Russian culture by following Russians elsewhere. After World War I he undertook a rapid tour through European capitals, hoping to gain an impression of the progress each country was making toward the creation of a unified Europe. The book that resulted from these journeys is *Europe–Whither Bound?* (1921), a collection of essays originally published in *Country Life* (London) under the general title of *Quo Vadis Europa?* Graham added afterthoughts to the book in the form of "extra leaves." The essays cover a zigzag route around Europe from east to west, moving through Constantinople (now Istanbul), Sofia, Belgrade, Budapest, Vienna, Prague, Warsaw, Munich, Berlin, Rome, Monte Carlo, London, and Paris. Taken together the sketches form more of a general impression than a continuous, chronological record of a journey.

That overall impression is one of destitution and discomfiture. Bitterness, hatred, and distrust abound among nations and peoples. Graham supported his thesis that Europe was endangered by recording images of poverty and destruction. In the eastern countries he saw the imminent fall of European civilization; in the west he found euphoria, nostalgia, and a decided obliviousness to the troubles of the east. In the underbelly of each city he saw children orphaned by the war sleeping in the streets, former members of the privileged classes waiting tables or turning to prostitution, and bureaucratic entanglements ensnaring the traveler. Rather than the peasants of Russia, Graham encountered displaced and impoverished nobility. Overall, however, *Europe–Whither Bound?* is a dispassionate, political monologue, unfortunately written so exclusively for an audience of Graham's contemporaries that entire passages are unintelligible without a rather extensive knowledge of postwar European history. With *Europe–Whither Bound?* as with other works Graham neglected larger themes, choosing to dwell on the temporal rather than the transcendent.

While in the United States in 1919, Graham met poet Vachel Lindsay through Christopher Morley of the *New York Evening Post.* Graham admired Lindsay's style of oral recitation, the way he intoned his poems to audiences in his full voice, and he was drawn to Lindsay as a friend because Lindsay's ideas were similar to his own. "I have rarely met such a rebel against vulgarity, materialism, and the modern artificial way of life," Graham wrote. In 1921 the two tramped through Glacier National Park in Montana, a trek that resulted in Graham's *Tramping with a Poet in the Rockies* (1922). In this book the voices of Graham and Lindsay combine in dialogue and diverge as Graham describes the Montana wilderness and the particulars of their journey through it. Etchings by Vernon Hill appear at the head of each chapter. The work compares favorably with the later writings of John Muir, capturing the mingled sense of awe and respect for the wild with a certain boyish enthusiasm at being able to make a journey without maps. Graham led the way, often far ahead of Lindsay, who paused frequently to discuss politics or literature or to write couplets and hide them in hollow trees and under stones, calling them rewards for future hikers. They encountered bears and were daunted by waterfalls and sheer rock precipices, but they were determined to encircle the park. Originally Lindsay had asked John Masefield to accompany him on the trip, but Masefield, who was older than Lindsay and fearful that he would not have the strength, refused. Graham, who was only five years younger than Lindsay, exhausted Lindsay on the trip: Graham's long legs and martial stamina enabled him to cover more ground, and as Eleanor Ruggles wrote in her biography of Lindsay, Lindsay was either terrified by their mad adventuring or lagged behind calling, "Stee-ven, wait for little Vachel!"

Some of Graham's best writing occurs in this book, perhaps because of Lindsay's influence. In fact much of what is literary in the book is taken from Lindsay, who inspired the poetic epigrams that Graham wrote to close each chapter. Graham's control over narrative, his ability to write a compelling adventure story, and his powers of description are at their finest in *Tramping with a Poet in the Rockies.* He achieved a level of writing that is finally more than journalism.

Lindsay attributed his London success to Graham, who arranged readings and social gatherings that introduced Lindsay to influential people. Graham also arranged for his American publisher, D. C. Appleton, to publish Lindsay's reply to *Tramping with a Poet in the Rockies,* a volume of drawings and poems, *Going-to-the-Sun* (1923). Letters reveal that Lindsay considered Graham a good Christian, "red-blooded, open-hearted and jolly."

In 1922 Lindsay tried to interest Graham in a second tramp, possibly in the spring of 1923. Lindsay proposed that the two harvest wheat from Texas to Canada or Alaska, posing as migrant farmhands. Their tramp would develop Lindsay's idea of "American Hieroglyphics," cultural signs created through drawings and text, and Graham would write a book with wheat as the hero, capturing the thoughts of Ralph Waldo Emerson and "the Russian Sages" on wheat. Lindsay and Graham never made the trip, nor did they make a trek they considered in 1923, a tramp through the Indian reservations of western Canada.

In 1923 Graham embarked on a journey that followed the route of the Spanish conquistadors. *In Quest of El Dorado* (1923) traces the routes of Christopher Columbus and other Spanish explorers, passing through Puerto Rico, Haiti, Cuba, the Bahamas, New Orleans, New Mexico, and Mexico. He made the trip from Spain with his wife, Rosa, and was joined in Mexico by Wilfrid Ewart. Graham traveled alone to Panama and the peak of Darien.

HAIL TO ALL MOVING THINGS

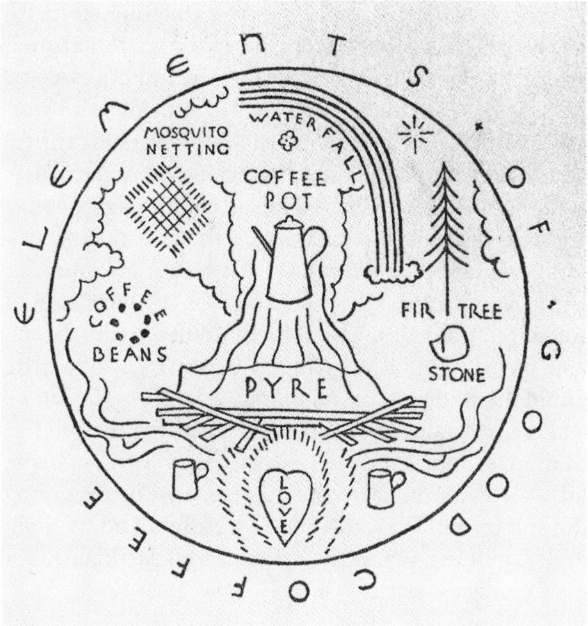

THE CHRISTIAN BECOMES SUN-
WORSHIPPER ALSO

FROM THE FIRE TO THE DARK GOES THE TINY SPARK

Emblems by Vernon Hill in Tramping with a Poet in the Rockies

In Quest of El Dorado is a picturesque, colorful travelogue filled with scenes that illustrate national character. Graham's sketches are limited, however. The Pueblo Indians are depicted as ferocious and warlike in their festival dress. Costume, chant, and movement are described without attempt to discern their meaning, as if the dance had no sacred significance and the words of the chant were merely savage guttural inflections. To Graham it is all picturesque; his Christian idealism allowed no serious consideration of pagan religions. It is also difficult to determine the extent of his sympathy with the Spanish. In Spain he found them to be cruel and shabby. In New Mexico he commented impassively that the Spanish missionaries of the Catholic Church failed to convert the natives fully. In Panama he seems overcome with emotion at the thought of Vasco Nuñez de Balboa and his men dancing in the sea as they discovered the Pacific for the Western world.

Ewart, who had befriended Graham during the war, was eager to write, and he wanted to be initiated into Graham's methods of observation. Tragedy struck on Old Year's Eve in Mexico City. As the night progressed, celebrations in the street grew wilder and guns were fired in the air in excitement. Ewart, who was shaving by an open window, was struck by a stray bullet and killed. It was the end of the brief and promising friendship. Graham eulogized Ewart in *Life and Last Words of Wilfrid Ewart* (1924).

Recalling the postwar period in his autobiography, Graham reflected that his poetic imagination had faded. He had become objective, critical, and committed to solving social problems. During the 1920s Graham was speaking in prisons, volunteering as a prison visitor, and lecturing in Toynbee Hall, a settlement house in the East End of London. Graham's 1923 novel, *Under-London,* captures his growing interest in the middle and working classes. A story of teenage struggle for identity, the novel foreshadows the impact of the dispossessed and unemployed on British culture. Also resulting from Graham's new ethic, *London Nights* (1925) is rooted in the British literary tradition of self-investigation, a tradition of which George Orwell's *Down and Out in Paris and London* (1933) and *The Road to Wigan Pier* (1937) are perhaps the most notable examples. In his *Culture and Society, 1780–1950* (1958) Raymond Williams has commented that reports on local culture emphasize either the "curious or the exotic" or "when the class or society is nearer the reporter's own, the perceptive critique." Prompted by his visits to the incarcerated at Pentonville Prison in London, Graham embarked on a quest to discover the curious and exotic in the lives of London tramps.

London Nights is a sketchy and ephemeral journalistic chronicle. Graham seems to have been interested in providing local-color word-pictures and in examining specimens of the underclass such as "the prison inmate." Yet Graham was sympathetic to the homeless and the underdog in principle, and he paused from time to time to reflect ruefully on either their extreme youth or their advanced age and to imagine better lives for them. The book describes a Christmas when he and his wife took port and Dundee cake to the Embankment and offered cheer to those sleeping on the park benches.

Graham's book is more thorough than Orwell's *Down and Out in Paris and London* in its presentation of types, but it lacks a complex narrative and developed characterization. In both books the disposition of the authors is clear: Orwell was the advocate of working-class rights, whereas Graham was critical of workers' strikes, blind to the economic forces leading to the Russian Revolution, and unsympathetic to safety and productivity disputes in British factories. His conviction that strong Christian faith could empower the individual and cure social ills was as limiting in his discussion of life at home as it was in his assessments of Russia. Because Graham was constrained by his moral, political, and religious biases, *London Nights* fails to lead readers to an understanding of the conditions that create urban poverty. It is not a study of the hypocrisy of religious philanthropists and public officials in dealing with the situation. *London Nights* is often critical of poor people's dirty clothes and slovenly habits without seeking to understand the reasons behind them. At one point the book attributes the hopeless conditions in which many of the homeless lived to a lack of self-respect. Graham often railed against immorality, perhaps because of his disgust at the prostitutes who swarmed along the streets of his neighborhood in Soho. He also neglected an important discussion on the status of World War I veterans, many of whom became beggars on the streets of London.

The Gentle Art of Tramping (1926) recovers the ironic sense of humor of *Tramping with a Poet in the Rockies.* The book is arranged as a guide for travelers, with chapters covering footwear, knapsacks, clothing, food, coffee, sleeping arrangements, tobacco, books, maps, marching songs, keeping a notebook, making a fire, carrying money, and having a proper attitude for hiking. The book entertains and instructs. The work is so detailed and so comprehensive that it would be difficult for any but the most seasoned hiker to heed all of Graham's advice. The chapter on starting a fire cautions travelers to remember scraps of dry paper, then goes on to instruct future tramps on where to set their knapsacks, how to arrange stones around the fire, where to place the coffeepot, how to choose the correct type of stones to encircle the fire, how large the bits of tinder should be. A later chapter details how one can use the fire to dry blankets and clothing. This advice is intertwined with anecdotes and lengthy descriptive passages, many of which recall Graham's extensive experience tramping in Russia. His observations also offer a picture of the United States unspoiled by tourism.

Graham defined tramping as a humble and simple activity to be undertaken by inquisitive members of the leisure class. Tramps are distinct from hoboes because they have more money and choose to leave that money at home; they are distinct from hikers because they usually take to the open road rather than difficult terrain; and they are distinct from day-trippers because they neither set goals in miles nor return in evening to a comfortable bed in a cozy inn. A tramp is almost certainly a gentleman, soundly dressed in army boots and a tweed cap and coat and carrying a pipe in the pocket and a volume of John Keats's poems in the rucksack. Those the tramp meets along the trail are noble savages: heavily romanticized, honest farm laborers willing to part with some coffee and fruit pie, and golden-hearted highwaymen, susceptible to losing at arguments.

In a chapter useful for the modern travel critic Graham detailed "emblems of tramping," three motifs that readers of travel literature recognize as essential to the plot and theme of many narratives: the road, the river, and the wilderness. Graham found them to be universal motifs of life. "The road," he wrote, "is the simplest of these emblems–with its milestones for years, its direction posts to show you the way, its inns for feasting, its churches for prayer, its crossroads of destiny, its happy corners of love and meeting, its sad ones of bereavement and farewell; its backward vista of memory, its forward one of hope." He compared the river to the River of Time, or man's life, or Eternity. The wilderness is a representation of the tangle and symmetry of the human mind; to be lost spiritually is like being lost physically.

Graham's novel *Midsummer Music* (1926) is a nostalgic and somewhat embittered work, recalling Graham's prewar tramps through eastern Europe. Like Graham its protagonist, Felix Morrison, is a thoughtful English writer who enjoys adventure. Morrison and two friends travel to Dalmatia in Yugoslavia, a mountainous, sparsely populated region where the people have encountered few strangers. Morrison feels acutely his difference from the odd and backward villagers, who are suspicious of Morrison and his friends.

Graham made several trips to New York during the 1920s, and his impressions of Prohibition, the variegated nightlife of New York society, and the urban underworld create a vivid picture of the city in *New York Nights* (1927). A tall, handsome man who somewhat resembled Douglas Fairbanks, Graham seems to have found the companionship of women easy to find in any country, and New York proved no exception. Although the book remains decorous on the subject of his behavior, it does reveal that it is possible to "bring your dancing partner from the night club to give her a drink at three in the morning" without raising the interest of the neighbors. He dedicated the book to one of his female companions in New York, Patricia, a woman of the type he seemed to prefer: a well-educated, talented career woman, who was not necessarily physically attractive. She and a friend named Helen set the stage for a new, refreshing frankness in this work. *New York Nights* marks Graham's abandonment of Victorian and Edwardian prudishness and the commitment to extracting a moral ideal from his surroundings. *New York Nights* has a more worldly tone than Graham's previous books, with the exception of *A Vagabond in the Caucasus,* which was frank in its youthful exuberance. *New York Nights* includes Graham's recollection that a man in a bar tried to kiss him. The book also notes the extent of political corruption: he saw the mayor of New York in a nightclub and policemen completing reports as they sipped beer at a bar. The style of *New York Nights* captures the free atmosphere of the 1920s.

Whereas in *London Nights* Graham walked with the underclass, he walked in New York with the upper class. Graham's adventures typically began after dinner. He dined, attended the theater, visited nightclubs or speakeasies, or wandered alone on foot through the streets of the city until dawn. He passed through Chinatown, the Bowery, Little Italy, Greenwich Village, and tramps along Broadway. He was present at the burning of the Sherry Netherland Hotel and recorded the event in detail. Commenting that the street of Broadway is itself theater, he anticipated architectural and cultural critics of the late twentieth century, and he extended his metaphor to a description of the desire of New Yorkers to play like children in the frivolous and extravagant decor of the clubs. His style reveals an obvious familiarity with the images of the time: throughout the book there is a fascination with technology and the worker that captures some of the art, excitement, and pathos of Charlie Chaplin's *Modern Times* (1936). Together these observations and insights reveal Graham at his most astute.

The book is marred, however, by the same sort of sophomoric phrasing and idiosyncratically spiritual commentary that scar other works by Graham. His

Illustrations of Little Italy and a burlesque show in Graham's New York Nights *(1927), his impressions of social life in Manhattan during Prohibition*

fascination with speakeasies made him devote too many pages to discussions of how he obtained various entry passwords and aliases. Repeated references to his charming female companions, to the unspoken rule about bringing one's own bottle of liquor to a high-toned club, or to the "half-naked" girls of the chorus are tedious by the end of the book.

While enjoying the nightlife of New York and London, Graham nostalgically re-created prerevolutionary Russia in his 1928 novel, *The Lay Confessor.* The title refers to the character, Serge Epiphanov, a devout and holy man who listens to people confess their troubles. As he counsels them as a lay priest,he searches for his own epiphany. Graham's sympathies are with Serge, who represents the ideal of czarist and Holy Russia that Graham so often espoused in his lectures and essays. The main characters, Sasha and Serge, find themselves divided by their loyalties at the time of the revolution, with Sasha in sympathy with the revolutionaries and Serge supporting the czar. Early in the tale Sasha is jailed for his revolutionary sentiments but is released as the revolution begins. Later Serge is jailed for being a czarist and dies in prison. The setting is bleak: the novel opens during the dark and frigid Russian winter of 1910 and closes as prison guards kill Serge. Even they cannot help mourning for Serge as a good man with simple ideals.

Continuing Graham's fascination with city life, the travel sketches collected in *Twice Round the London Clock* (1933) register a patient sensibility. The degradations of Soho that seemed to anger Graham in *London Nights* are here represented as inevitable features of urban life. The tone of *Twice Round the London Clock* is distanced, serious, and somewhat amused. The book records the life of the city with a practiced eye for detail, even down to a notice announcing "all-in" boxing "without effeminate gloves." Whereas in 1911 Russia was the "yea" and Britain the "nay," by 1933 Graham was able to proclaim London the finest city in the world.

In the 1930s Graham concentrated less on tramping and more on biography, historical commentary, and fiction. Graham's travels took him to South Africa, where he lived on a farm on the Bushveld. He was also in Yugoslavia, where he and Rebecca West were awarded the Order of St. Sava. While some of Graham's fiction from the 1930s relies on exotic settings, he primarily worked with themes that can be detected in his travel narratives, including the conflicts of personal faith with religious doctrine, the quest for spiritual and physical love, the test of character by circumstance, and the relationship of life to material wealth.

In the novel *Lost Battle* (1934), for example, Graham explored the themes of fidelity and passion. The main character, John Rae, an agricultural writer who must travel to rural locations throughout England, abandons his wife and four children for life in London with a younger woman and starts a new family. The moral dilemma of the story is that John Rae continues to love his wife, with whom he shares a love of literature.

Balkan Monastery (1935) is a fictionalized account of the life of Vera Mitrinovich, who eventually became Graham's second wife and appears in the novel as Desa Georgevitch. The story follows Desa's extraordinary adventures from the age of eight, just before the outbreak of World War I, when she is enrolled in a Yugoslavian convent school. At the start of the war all the children are removed to an isolated monastery, and then when food and supplies become scarce they are auctioned to temporary shelter with good families in neighboring villages. Vera escapes from the tyrannical wealthy woman who had adopted her and returns to the monastery, where she hopes to be discovered by her brother Sava, a Serbian soldier. The book exemplifies Graham's capacity for description in its rich re-creations of the harsh conditions from which the children scraped an existence. It celebrates the character of Desa, who is painted as thrifty, intelligent, and good-tempered. Vera Mitrinovich was slightly associated through her brother Dmitri with the student activists who surrounded Gavrilo Princip, Danilo Ilitch, Nedielko Cabrinovic, and Trifko Grabezh, the Serbian nationalists who plotted and executed the assassination of Archduke Francis Ferdinand of Austria in 1914. Graham had told their story in *St. Vitus Day* (1930).

Graham's novel *African Tragedy* (1937) chronicles the adventures of a British World War I veteran, Tom Anderson, who stows away on a ship to the United States on the day after the Armistice and realizes his dream of a journey to Africa. He tramps from New York to Mississippi, with occasional commentary on American characteristics, eventually taking a boat to Brazil and moving on to southern Africa. His life is complicated by the frequent appearances and disappearances of Lady Charters, who is married to another man but finances his house in Africa, promising to join him there. Captivated by the lives of the Africans, who treat him sociably, Anderson finds kinship in their peaceful, uncomplicated carpe-diem philosophy. His dream of a natural, unspoiled life is shattered by the arrival of Lady Charters, who is horrified by uncivilized life in the bush. The novel closes with her departure and Anderson's search for a new adventure, out of Africa.

Graham's final travel book, *The Moving Tent* (1939), describes his adventures in Yugoslavia, where he was fishing rather than tramping. Graham traveled from Prespansko (Prespa) and Ochrid (Ohrid) Lakes in the south of the country along the Greek border, up the Drim (Drin), a river that flows north from Ohrid Lake forming part of the border with Albania, and then to Prizren. From there he traveled by horseback to Naked Mountain, one hundred miles north; he also fished the Rama River near Sarajevo. Graham was joined on his angling vagabondage by Zeichar, an odd but apparently loyal straggler with a criminal past. Vera Mitrinovich was also a companion and guide and at times a nurse to the peasants. She is described as "a dark, handsome girl with uncut black hair, merry eyes and one of those aquiline noses which the ancient Romans left behind on the Balkan peninsula." Graham offers no details about their relationship. The narrative abounds in the lush detail of the tramp itself: smells of coffee, Turkish delight, fish, moss, rain, bread, tobacco; sounds of thunder, river, market, campfire; sights of copper kettles, blackened skillets, Gypsy women, peasant weavers, untrustworthy merchants–men and women either richly clad in colorful local costume or drab and matted by poverty.

The contemporary critical reception of Graham's work was mixed. He was often faulted for writing too hastily, for naïveté, for an exaggerated prose style. In its obituary of Graham *The Times* of London asserted that his works were "over coloured in style and often naïve in historical argument." Reviewers criticized his superficial philosophizing, lack of insight when dealing with political situations, poor poetical style, and the Anglo-Saxon perspective that he relentlessly applied in comparing every country with England.

Graham's works are too topical, often written with shorthand references to recent events. Yet his contemporaries also found his books entertaining, charming, and vividly descriptive. His works were aptly described as "romances," revealing his literary tastes for Keats, Robert Browning, and George Gordon, Lord Byron. Graham's romantic proclivities resulted at times in sentimentalized reveries and archaically stylized phrasings that recall his attraction to Thomas Carlyle, as when he wrote in *Europe–Whither*

Bound?: "this thing which we call 'charity' faileth, it vanisheth away." References to Friedrich Nietzsche dot Graham's early works. In *A Vagabond in the Caucasus* he discussed at length his attraction to the writing of Carlyle, whom he calls "a true friend." Under the influence of Carlyle, he became "a puritan, serious, intolerant and heroic." He then sought the company of other literary greats, John Ruskin, Robert Browning, and Henrik Ibsen, all of whom confirmed "the heroism of achieving impossible tasks." Among Russian writers, he found a model in Maksim Gorky.

Throughout his writings Graham attempted to re-create the essence of a place in prose through an integration of visual impressions and historical background. The desire to capture essences extended to Graham's writing about people, and his narratives are filled with brief studies of representative types such as "the Russian," "the Negro," and "the Spaniard." This method achieved fruition in *Characteristics* (1936), a volume in which he attempted to mark national traits and preferences for everything from food and clothes to newspapers, gossip, and secrets. In his autobiography Graham commented that collecting human characters "is like collecting moths or beetles and pinning them in your mind." Unfortunately his method of seeking essences ultimately prevented him from realizing his potential as a writer. His writing demonstrates a considerable gift for narrative, and he was at his best when he told the tale of an adventure.

Graham's works are frequently marred by a passive anti-Semitism, in which direct quotations revealing Russian biases against Jews are passed along without comment. This racism is perhaps not surprising, given Graham's intense Christianity. As he wrote of Christianity in *The Way of Martha and the Way of Mary,* "Its stories are our stories. Its Word is the living Word. The other stories are not our stories. . . . Christianity is the *Word.*" The Turks were also frequent objects for Graham's attack, even more so than the Jews. In *Changing Russia* he calls the Turk "stupid and ugly . . . strong as a bull, and brutal."

From 1941 to 1949 Graham served with the BBC Foreign Service, and in 1949 he became councillor of the Poetry Society. He was elected a fellow of the Royal Society of Literature in 1950. After the death of Rosa Graham in 1956, he married Vera Mitrinovich at Westminster on 18 October of the same year. Graham's autobiography, *Part of the Wonderful Scene* (1964), sheds no new light on his life or adventures. Instead it summarizes his writings and travels with a liberal dose of name-dropping. (It was originally titled "Pictures of My Friends".) Graham died at his London home on 15 March 1975, one day before his ninety-first birthday.

No single travel work of Graham's has emerged as his masterpiece. Annie Dillard listed *The Gentle Art of Tramping* among her favorite nature works, tacitly recommending the book to readers of *Antaeus* in 1987. *With Poor Immigrants to America* has been of some interest to scholars studying the Jewish experience in America. *With the Russian Pilgrims to Jerusalem* is consulted as the first English-language work to describe the experience of these pilgrims.

Although he was a popular figure in his time, the ambitious tramping expeditions, colorful public life, and prolific literary career of Stephen Graham were overshadowed by the accomplishments of a later generation of literary travelers, including Christopher Isherwood, W. H. Auden, Evelyn Waugh, and Graham Greene. Graham's life was so rich in experience that even he seemed unable to fully comprehend its significance. His works provide documentary evidence of the customs, costumes, and conversations of a generation of anonymous, peasant-class eastern Europeans. Critical reconsideration is often aided by historical distance: decades after his death the achievements of Stephen Graham and not the total of his literary works prove most absorbing.

Papers:

A collection of Graham's manuscripts, working papers, correspondence, and memorabilia is available at the John D. Strozier Library, Flordia State University at Tallahassee. The Harry Ransom Humanities Research Center at the University of Texas, Austin, has speeches, articles, letters, notes, reviews, and manuscripts for *Part of the Wonderful Scene, Stalin, The Lay Confessor, Peter the Great, The Death of Yesterday, A Modern Vanity Fair,* and *A Private in the Guards.* In London individual letters can be found at the Imperial War Museum, the India Office Library and Records, the House of Lords Record Office, the Garrick Club Library, the British Library of Political and Economic Science, the British Library, and the Royal Society of Literature. Other small collections are at the Bodleian Library in Oxford, the University of Reading Library, the National Library of Scotland in Edinburgh, the University of Nottingham Library, and the Eton College Library.

Aldous Huxley

(26 July 1894 – 22 November 1963)

Scott R. Christianson
Radford University

See also the Huxley entries in *DLB 36: British Novelists, 1890–1929: Modernists; DLB 100: Modern British Essayists, Second Series;* and *DLB 162: British Short-Fiction Writers, 1915–1945.*

Aldous Huxley, 1920s

BOOKS: *The Burning Wheel* (Oxford: Blackwell, 1916);
Jonah (Oxford: Holywell, 1917);
The Defeat of Youth and Other Poems (Oxford: Blackwell, 1918);
Limbo (London: Chatto & Windus, 1920; New York: Doran, 1920);
Leda (London: Chatto & Windus, 1920; New York: Doran, 1920);
Crome Yellow (London: Chatto & Windus, 1921; New York: Doran, 1922);
Mortal Coils (London: Chatto & Windus, 1922; New York: Doran, 1922);
On the Margin: Notes and Essays (London: Chatto & Windus, 1923; New York: Doran, 1923);
Antic Hay (London: Chatto & Windus, 1923; New York: Doran, 1923);
Little Mexican & Other Stories (London: Chatto & Windus, 1924); republished as *Young Archimedes, and Other Stories* (New York: Doran, 1924);
Those Barren Leaves (London: Chatto & Windus, 1925; New York: Doran, 1925);
Along the Road: Notes and Essays of a Tourist (London: Chatto & Windus, 1925; New York: Doran, 1925);
Selected Poems (Oxford: Blackwell, 1925; New York: Appleton, 1925);
Two or Three Graces and Other Stories (London: Chatto & Windus, 1926; New York: Doran, 1926);
Jesting Pilate (London: Chatto & Windus, 1926; New York: Doran, 1926);
Essays New and Old (London: Chatto & Windus, 1926; New York: Doran, 1927);
Proper Studies (London: Chatto & Windus, 1927; Garden City, N.Y.: Doubleday, Doran, 1928);
Point Counter Point (London: Chatto & Windus, 1928; Garden City, N.Y.: Doubleday, Doran, 1928);
Arabia Infelix, and Other Poems (London: Chatto & Windus / New York: Fountain Press, 1929);
Holy Face and Other Essays (London: Fleuron, 1929);
Do What You Will: Essays (London: Chatto & Windus, 1929; Garden City, N.Y.: Doubleday, Doran, 1929);
Brief Candles: Stories (London: Chatto & Windus, 1930; Garden City, N.Y.: Doubleday, Doran, 1930);

Vulgarity in Literature: Digressions from a Theme (London: Chatto & Windus, 1930);
Apennine (Gaylordsville, Conn.: Slide Mountain Press, 1930);
The World of Light: A Comedy in Three Acts (London: Chatto & Windus, 1931; Garden City, N.Y.: Doubleday, Doran, 1931);
The Cicadas and Other Poems (London: Chatto & Windus, 1931; Garden City, N.Y.: Doubleday, Doran, 1931);
Music at Night and Other Essays (London: Chatto & Windus, 1931; Garden City, N.Y.: Doubleday, Doran, 1931);
Brave New World (London: Chatto & Windus, 1932; Garden City, N.Y.: Doubleday, Doran, 1932);
Texts and Pretexts: An Anthology with Commentaries (London: Chatto & Windus, 1932; New York: Harper, 1933);
Rotunda: A Selection from the Works of Aldous Huxley (London: Chatto & Windus, 1932);
T. H. Huxley as a Man of Letters, Imperial College of Science and Technology, Huxley Memorial Lecture (London: Macmillan, 1932);
Retrospect: An Omnibus of Aldous Huxley's Books (Garden City, N.Y.: Doubleday, Doran, 1933);
Beyond the Mexique Bay (London: Chatto & Windus, 1934; New York: Harper, 1934);
What Are You Going to Do about It? The Case for Constructive Peace (London: Chatto & Windus, 1936; New York: Harper, 1937);
Eyeless in Gaza (London: Chatto & Windus, 1936; New York: Harper, 1936);
1936 . . . Peace? (London: Friends Peace Committee, 1936);
The Olive Tree and Other Essays (London: Chatto & Windus, 1936; New York: Harper, 1937);
Ends and Means: An Enquiry into the Nature of Ideals and into the Methods Employed for Their Realization (London: Chatto & Windus, 1937; New York: Harper, 1937);
Stories, Essays, and Poems (London: Dent, 1937);
The Most Agreeable Vice (Los Angeles: Ward Ritchie, 1938);
The Gioconda Smile (London: Chatto & Windus, 1938);
After Many a Summer (London: Chatto & Windus, 1939); republished as *After Many a Summer Dies the Swan* (New York: Harper, 1939);
Words and Their Meanings (Los Angeles: Ward Ritchie, 1940);
Grey Eminence: A Study in Religion and Politics (London: Chatto & Windus, 1941; New York: Harper, 1941);
The Art of Seeing (New York: Harper, 1942; London: Chatto & Windus, 1943);
Time Must Have a Stop (New York: Harper, 1944; London: Chatto & Windus, 1945);
Twice Seven: Fourteen Selected Stories (London: Reprint Society, 1944);
The Perennial Philosophy (New York: Harper, 1945; London: Chatto & Windus, 1946);
Science, Liberty, and Peace (New York: Harper, 1946; London: Chatto & Windus, 1947);
Verses and a Comedy (London: Chatto & Windus, 1946);
The World of Aldous Huxley: An Omnibus of His Fiction and Non-Fiction over Three Decades, edited by Charles J. Rolo (New York: Harper, 1947);
Ape and Essence (New York: Harper, 1948; London: Chatto & Windus, 1949);
The Gioconda Smile: A Play (London: Chatto & Windus, 1948; New York: Harper, 1948);
Prisons, with the "Carceri" Etchings by G. B. Piranesi (London: Trianon, 1949; Los Angeles: Zeitlin & Ver Brugge, 1949);
Themes and Variations (London: Chatto & Windus, 1950; New York: Harper, 1950);
The Devils of Loudun (London: Chatto & Windus, 1952; New York: Harper, 1952);
Joyce, the Artificer: Two Studies of Joyce's Method, by Huxley and Stuart Gilbert (London: Privately printed, 1952);
A Day in Windsor, by Huxley and J. A. Kings (London: Britannicus Liber, 1953);
The Doors of Perception (London: Chatto & Windus, 1954; New York: Harper, 1954);
The French of Paris (New York: Harper, 1954);
The Genius and the Goddess (London: Chatto & Windus, 1955; New York: Harper, 1955);
Heaven and Hell (London: Chatto & Windus, 1956; New York: Harper, 1956);
Adonis and the Alphabet, and Other Essays (London: Chatto & Windus, 1956); republished as *Tomorrow and Tomorrow and Tomorrow, and Other Essays* (New York: Harper, 1956);
Collected Short Stories (London: Chatto & Windus, 1957; New York: Harper, 1957);
Brave New World Revisited (London: Chatto & Windus, 1958; New York: Harper, 1958);
Collected Essays (New York: Harper, 1959);
On Art and Artists, edited by Morris Philipson (London: Chatto & Windus, 1960; New York: Harper, 1960);
Island (London: Chatto & Windus, 1962; New York: Harper, 1962);
Literature and Science (London: Chatto & Windus, 1963; New York: Harper & Row, 1963);
The Crows of Pearlblossom (New York: Random House, 1967; London: Chatto & Windus, 1968);

The Collected Poetry of Aldous Huxley, edited by Donald Watt (London: Chatto & Windus, 1971; New York: Harper & Row, 1971).

MOTION PICTURES: *Pride and Prejudice,* scenario by Huxley and Jane Murfin, M-G-M, 1940;
Madame Curie, treatment by Huxley, M-G-M, 1943;
Jane Eyre, scenario by Huxley, 20th Century-Fox, 1944;
A Woman's Vengeance, adaptation by Huxley from his *The Gioconda Smile,* Universal-International, 1948.

OTHER: Thomas Humphry Ward, ed., *The English Poets: Selections with Critical Introductions,* introductions by Huxley to poetry by John Davidson, Ernest Dowson, and Richard Middleton (London: Macmillan, 1918);
Rémy de Gourmont, *A Virgin Heart: A Novel,* translated by Huxley (New York: Brown, 1921; London: Allen & Unwin, 1926);
Mrs. Frances Sheridan, *The Discovery: A Comedy in Five Acts,* adapted by Huxley (London: Chatto & Windus, 1924; New York: Doran, 1925);
Oliver Simon and Jules Rodenberg, *Printing of Today,* introduction by Huxley (London: Davies, 1928; New York: Harper, 1928);
Maurice A. Pink, *A Realist Looks at Democracy,* preface by Huxley (London: Benn, 1930; New York: Stokes, 1931);
Douglas Goldering, *The Fortune,* preface by Huxley (London: Harmsworth, 1931);
The Letters of D. H. Lawrence, edited, with an introduction, by Huxley (London: Heinemann, 1932; New York: Viking, 1932);
Samuel Butler, *Erewhon,* introduction by Huxley (New York: Limited Editions Club, 1934);
Alfred H. Mendes, *Pitch Lake: A Story from Trinidad,* introduction by Huxley (London: Duckworth, 1934);
Norman Haire, *Birth-Control Methods (Contraception, Abortion, Sterilization),* foreword by Huxley (London: Allen & Unwin, 1936);
An Encyclopedia of Pacifism, edited by Huxley (London: Chatto & Windus, 1937; New York: Harper, 1937);
Barthélemy de Ligt, *The Conquest of Violence: An Essay on War and Revolution,* introduction by Huxley (London: Routledge, 1938; New York: Dutton, 1938);
Knud Merrild, *Knud Merrild, A Poet and Two Painters: A Memoir of D. H. Lawrence,* preface by Huxley (London: Routledge, 1938; New York: Viking, 1939);
Maksim Gorki, *A Book of Short Stories,* edited by Avram Yarmolinsky and Baroness Moura Budberg, foreword by Huxley (London: Cape, 1939; New York: Holt, 1939);
Joseph Daniel Unwin, *Hopousia; or, The Sexual and Economic Foundations of a New Society,* introduction by Huxley (London: Allen & Unwin, 1940; New York: Piest, 1940);
Ashley Montagu, *Man's Most Dangerous Myth: The Fallacy of Race,* foreword by Huxley (London: Columbia University Press, 1942);
Bhagavadgita: The Song of God, translated by Swami Prabhavananda and Christopher Isherwood, introduction by Huxley (Hollywood: Marcel Rodd, 1944; London: Phoenix House, 1947);
William Law, *Selected Mystical Writings,* edited by Stephen Hobhouse, foreword by Huxley (New York: Harper, 1948);
Ramakrishna, *Ramakrishna: Prophet of New India,* translated by Swami Nikhilananda, foreword by Huxley (New York: Harper, 1948; London: Rider, 1951);
Jiddu Krishnamurti, *The First and Last Freedom,* introduction by Huxley (New York: Harper, 1954; London: Gollancz, 1954);
Hubert Benoît, *The Supreme Doctrine: Psychological Studies in Zen Thought,* foreword by Huxley (London: Routledge & Kegan Paul, 1955; New York: Pantheon, 1955);
Frederick Mayer, *New Directions for the American University,* introduction by Huxley (Washington, D.C.: Public Affairs Press, 1957);
Alvah W. Sulloway, *Birth Control and Catholic Doctrine,* preface by Huxley (Boston: Beacon, 1959);
Danilo Dolci, *Report from Palermo,* introduction by Huxley (New York: Orion, 1959).

Aldous Huxley earned widespread attention in the 1920s as a promising young fiction writer who wrote brilliant and scathing stories about British writers and intellectuals gathered around socialite Ottoline Morrell. He soon became widely recognized as a literary and cultural critic, a polymath able to range over social, historical, scientific, and aesthetic matters with intelligence and aplomb. In 1932 Huxley published *Brave New World,* his best-known novel–which, with Arthur Koestler's *Darkness at Noon* (1940) and George Orwell's *Nineteen Eighty-Four* (1949), is among the most important dystopian novels of the twentieth century. *Brave New World* has been continuously in print since its first publication, and it put Huxley in the forefront of the socially and politically engaged writers of the 1930s. By the 1940s and 1950s Huxley was firmly estab-

The Huxleys in the 1890s: (seated on ground) Aldous, Trevenen, and Julian Huxley; (seated in chairs) Ella Salkovski (governess), Julia Huxley, Arnold Ward, Mrs. Humphry Ward, Mrs. Thomas Arnold, and Thomas Arnold; (standing) Miss Churcher (secretary to Mrs. Ward), Dorothy Ward, and Janet Ward

lished among educated, intelligent, "middle-brow" readers; his books ranked above best-sellers if not among the most "serious" or critically acclaimed literature. Following Huxley's death on 22 November 1963 (the day on which President John F. Kennedy was assassinated), the critical establishment placed him comfortably among the second rank of modern writers. He earned a sort of cult status in the late 1960s because he had written *The Doors of Perception* (1954) about his experiments with hallucinogenic drugs and because *Brave New World* and its sequel, *Brave New World Revisited* (1958), seemed politically relevant in that unsettled decade. In the 1990s, however, Huxley's works are less known and less read than in earlier decades. Yet a respectable body of criticism on Huxley exists and grows steadily.

Other belletristic writers have traveled as much as Huxley, and some have written about their travels at much greater length or more profoundly than Huxley. For few of them, however, has travel been as fundamental to their writing and their lives as it was for Huxley. His traveling spirit was nurtured by his family and their privileged status in British society. It developed from the necessities of love and fortune, and it was facilitated financially by his generous and regularly renewed contract with the publishing house of Chatto and Windus.

Born on 26 July 1894 in Surrey, Aldous Leonard Huxley was the scion of two of the best-known intellectual families of Victorian England. His father, Leonard Huxley, was the son of the renowned biologist Thomas Henry Huxley, and his mother, Julia Arnold Huxley, was the niece of poet Matthew Arnold and the sister of novelist Mrs. Humphry Ward. Aldous Huxley's birthright, therefore, included such entitlements as stimulating intellectual company and the best education England could offer. Leonard Huxley was a schoolmaster at Charterhouse, and Julia Huxley ran an unconventional girls' school. According to Sybille Bedford, Huxley "was born into a particular and self-conscious enclave, a class within a class, the governing upper middle–an elite, an intellectual aristocracy made up of a handful of families–Trevelyans, Macaulays, Arnolds, Wedgwoods, Darwins, Huxleys–who had produced extraordinarily and diversely gifted individuals whose influence, although they never confused themselves with the actual nobility, upon nineteenth-century England had been tremendous." This intellectual aristocracy traveled, sustaining and being sustained by the British Empire to which they were thoroughly committed.

Three losses marked Huxley's early life. The first was the death of his mother of cancer at age forty-five. Huxley was fourteen, in his first term at Eton. Always close to his mother, he internalized a permanent sense of "the vanity, the transience, the hopeless precariousness of all merely human happiness"–as he later described the loss of a parent in *Grey Eminence* (1941), his biography of François Leclerc du Tremblay.

Huxley's second loss was of his eyesight at age sixteen, following keratitis punctata, an inflamation of the cornea. According to Bedford, Huxley "was nearly blind. He could just distinguish light from darkness; he was unable to go out by himself. He could not read." Forced to leave Eton, he taught himself to read Braille and spoke of the particular tedium of reading Thomas Babington Macaulay by that method. Huxley eventually recovered some of his eyesight, facilitated by eyeglasses and a magnifying glass for reading. Bedford attributes his phenomenal memory to the necessity of reading slowly and extracting as much as possible from a single reading. After studying French in France for the summer, he entered Balliol College, Oxford, in October 1913.

Huxley's third loss was the suicide in August 1914 of his elder brother Trevenen, with whom he had lived while he recovered from his blindness and prepared for entry into Oxford. According to their sister, Margaret, Trevenen Huxley had been "the hub of the family wheel" after their mother's death. These two deaths, as well as the second marriage in 1912 of Leonard Huxley to a woman younger than some of his children, meant that Aldous Huxley's childhood home and family circle effectively no longer existed. He lived most of his life as a nomad, traveling often and for extended periods; yet even when he was not traveling he was not fixed to a place or a home.

The deaths of his mother and brother literally cut Huxley loose on the world, removing not only the actuality but perhaps even the sense of a home base. Rather than inhibiting his lust for knowledge, his temporary blindness and permanent eye damage confirmed his desire for learning. Moreover his disability prohibited him from joining most of his contemporaries in military service during World War I. Huxley spent the war years continuing his studies at Oxford. Sir George Clark, who was Huxley's tutor at Oxford, told Bedford that Huxley was "impaired" by his losses and his isolation at Oxford.

In *The Defeat of Youth and Other Poems* (1918) Huxley wrote:

> I look abroad, and all I see
> Is my creation, made for me:
> Along my thread of life are pearled
> The moments that make up the world.

These lines from "Scenes of the Mind" forecast Huxley's personal and professional future, characterizing him perhaps more than any other writer of the twentieth century.

Huxley began his writing career at Oxford, where he wrote poems that appeared first in Oxford periodicals and then in three slim volumes of poetry in 1916, 1917, and 1918. A fourth, slightly larger collection, *Leda* (1920), was submitted to T. S. Eliot, who was not enthusiastic about Huxley's verse, nor were most subsequent readers.

Except for certain verbal formulations that assert his ability to command style, this poetry is unremarkable; yet it provides early glimpses of the dynamic that shaped his literary career. The title poem of *The Burning Wheel* (1916) employs the metaphor of the burning wheel, which possesses "its own busy restlessness" and is "dizzy with speed." This metaphor describes Huxley's sense of his own life as circling yearningly around a motionless center that bursts into passionate flame as the wheel fulfills "its will in fixity," only to start turning once again. The metaphor is complex, even contradictory, but in the movement of the wheel, the fixity of its center, and the passion of the flame that starts and restarts the cycle of "busy restlessness" and "the anguish of fixity," the poem details Huxley's homelessness. It also foreshadows a lifelong practice of travel and return, Huxley longing to be "along the road" and desiring to get back home, with home as any place–in Italy, England, or America–from which to begin and end his travels.

Huxley's early writings parallel and mirror his travels: he went abroad to write and wrote as he traveled. After graduating from Oxford in June 1916, Huxley served the war effort by chopping wood at Garsington, the country estate of Philip and Lady Ottoline Morrell, whom Huxley had met and visited for the first time in December 1915. At Garsington, Huxley met the literary set gathered around Lady Ottoline Morrell–the British modernist writers, artists, and thinkers including T. S. Eliot, D. H. Lawrence, Virginia Woolf, Desmond McCarthy, Bertrand Russell, and others. A cosmopolitan enclave in a provincial English world, Garsington provided a locale and character types for Huxley's first novel, *Crome Yellow* (1921).

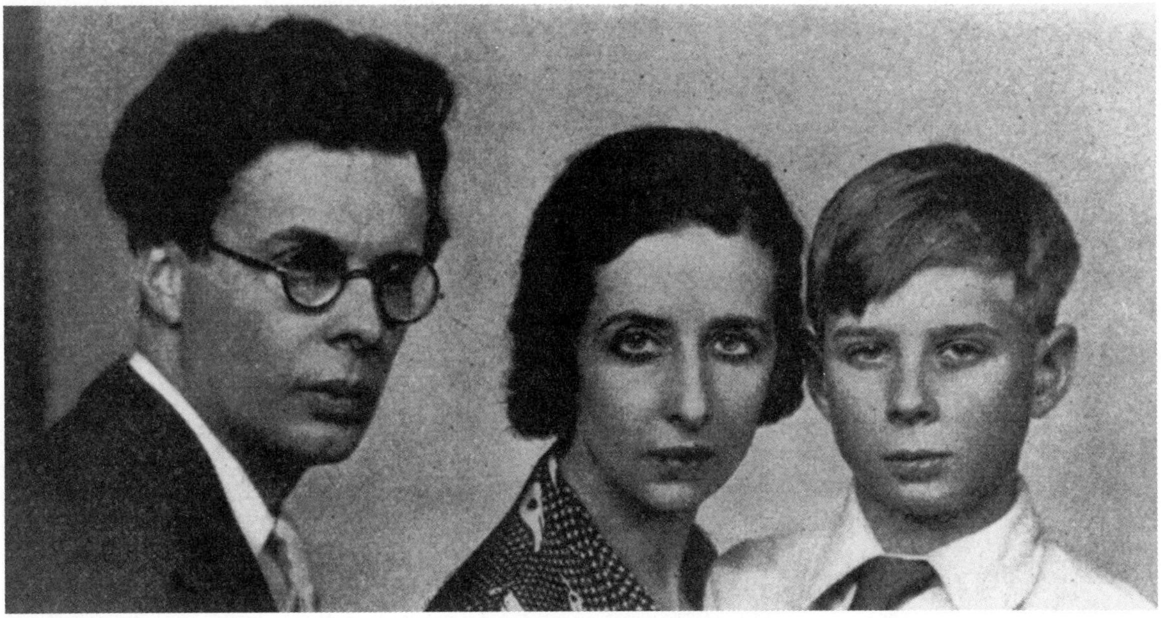

Aldous, Maria, and Matthew Huxley, 1920s

Huxley also worked as a temporary schoolmaster at Repton (July–August 1916) and as a clerk at the Air Board (April–July 1917) before becoming a master at Eton in January 1918. He resigned in April 1919 to begin editorial work for *The Atheneum,* the first of several jobs in journalism. He also traveled occasionally to Europe to meet with his fiancée, Maria Nys, a young Belgian woman whom he had met at the Morrells. The two were married on 10 July 1919. The Huxleys and their young son, Matthew (born 1920), spent several months of 1921 in Italy, where Huxley wrote *Crome Yellow*. This dynamic–travel to earn experience, followed by travel to a pleasant place to write–marks Huxley's whole career.

The state of publishing and of contracts between publishers and writers at the time at once enabled and constrained Huxley. *On the Margin* (1923), a collection of essays written primarily for *The Atheneum,* includes a potpourri of literary, social, and travel essays written under pressure. *On the Margin* also satisfied part of his new and generous contract with Chatto and Windus for two books a year for three years, and the book marks the last time Huxley had to produce essays for the periodical market. The contract with Chatto and Windus, which paid five hundred pounds a year over three years, allowed the Huxleys to settle in Florence, which they made their home base for a little more than four years, beginning in August 1923.

The travel essays in *On the Margin* establish that travel is an essential metaphor for Huxley's wide-ranging mind and interests. Huxley's essays are forays into territory new and old. His reflections on Percy Bysshe Shelley in "Centenaries" led him to a comparison between English and Italian celebrations. His meditations on English depression in "How the Days Draw In" is followed by an attack on Tibet, in a review of a recent book on Tibetan travels; Huxley found an antidote for English depression in the contemplation of a place "where stupidity reigns even more despotically than in Western Europe."

On the Margin was followed by *Antic Hay* (1923), a novel set in Italy but which transports much of the Garsington experience to that locale, which was favored by the English of a certain class who had figured out they could live abroad more cheaply than in England. The novel was a critical success, particularly among Huxley's "Jazz Age" contemporaries, but its close parallels to the Garsington circle angered or irritated many in the Morrell set.

Bedford has commented on the enormous importance of Italy for Huxley. To him it represented the hallmark of Western culture, and the climate and living conditions attracted many English people of his own class–as well as writers of many classes. Huxley completed *Antic Hay* in Italy at the beginning of the period that Bedford calls "perhaps the most easy of their lives." Bedford also notes that Huxley was enamored of the motor car; he bought a Citroën as soon as he could afford it and read avidly "the motoring papers, technical brochures, reports of Grand Prix racing." Huxley was no race-car driver;

Huxley and D. H. Lawrence in the Tuscan Hills near Florence, 28 October 1926 (photograph by Maria Huxley)

Maria did the driving. He appreciated the speed and the mobility, as well as the opportunity to witness "the landscapes whizzing by." "The Journey," part four of his third novel, *Those Barren Leaves* (1925), written in Italy, features a motor-car excursion through Italy that conveys Huxley's love of speed and travel.

Bedford describes Huxley's travel writing as "breathing space before his next go at fiction." That his travel writing afforded Huxley a change of pace does not belie the thought and care with which it was written, as Bedford makes clear in her discussion of *Along the Road* (1925), Huxley's first "travel book" that did not come from occasional writing produced for periodicals. Many critics have noted that *Along the Road* is rare among travel books in its avowed purpose of dissuading readers from travel. Huxley opens the first section of the book, "Travel in General," with the essay, "Why Not Stay at Home?" Huxley voiced the "genuine" traveler's disdain for would-be travelers–what Paul Fussell calls "tourists"–who invariably complain that the problem with "abroad" is that it is not enough like home. "Why Not Stay at Home?" ironically links traveling with reading, claiming that we do not read to "broaden and enrich our minds, but that we may pleasantly forget they exist." Traveling, like reading, is a substitute for thought. In "Wander-Birds" Huxley likens driving a car through a variety of countries to time travel "through art, through many languages and customs, through philology and anthropology." He devotes some time to discussing travel guides and books to be taken on one's travels (Friedrich Nietzsche was among his favorite travel reading). As Bedford notes, *Along the Road* demonstrates Huxley's enthusiasm for travel, works of art, and places. She also observes that while his novels often "read like essays," Huxley's essays exhibit the "novelist's latitude" taken in "a form that suited him–a form which he refreshed and of which he became a master."

In late 1925 the Huxleys began a journey around the world that Maria Huxley had dreamed of since she was a girl. The tour took them through India, Malaya, Japan, and across the Pacific to the United States. The Huxleys undertook the tour because they wanted to and could afford to. On completion of the tour and delivery of *Jesting Pilate* (1926), Huxley's second major travel book, Chatto and Windus renegotiated Huxley's already lucrative contract with more favorable terms. He agreed to produce two books a year, one of which would be fiction, and "possibly three other books during the said three years." Huxley's contracts with Chatto and Windus enabled the Huxleys to travel and assured that the resulting travel writing would be published and paid for; and travel supplied Huxley with knowledge and experiences that he incorporated into the fiction that made his reputation.

Two books were the result of Huxley's world tour: the travel book *Jesting Pilate,* written during the tour, and his most critically acclaimed novel, *Point Counter Point* (1928), begun after the Huxleys' arrival in London. Just as critics proclaim *Point Counter Point* the pinnacle of Huxley's novelistic achievement, they also point to *Jesting Pilate* as the best of Huxley's travel writing. The two books deserve to be considered together. The contrapuntal theme and method of *Point Counter Point* are at the heart of *Jesting Pilate.* In writing the novel Huxley conceived of the diversity of human experience as an elaborate composition in contrapuntal style–not "theme and variations" but multifarious and individual human and cultural melodic lines counterpointing each other in complex harmony. The travel book counterpoints the multiple experiences of British colonists and the colonized, of the colonies and former colonies, and of allies and enemies of the British Empire in an attempt to voice the complex harmony of global human experience. *Jesting Pilate* documents the oppressive power of colonialism–to which Huxley was, in principle, opposed–even as it displays how colonialism enabled, constrained, and ultimately shaped the ideas and even being of British writers such as Huxley.

In spite of his liberal-humanist critique of colonialism Huxley revealed in *Jesting Pilate* his inability, common to many, to get truly outside the colonialist perspective. The book "counterpoints" the various existing perspectives on British colonialism. Deploring the colonial apparatus and its oppressive effects, extolling Mohandas Gandhi's vision and political efforts, and trying to understand from inside the Indian spiritual perspective (Muslim and Hindu), Huxley applied what he understood to be universal standards of value (such as aesthetics) and bravely came to some politically incorrect conclusions (against the "tourists" who extol the Taj Mahal or the overly enthusiastic who endorse anything Indian over anything British). Yet Huxley reasoned himself into the neoconservative conclusion, well documented by Edward Said, that the British colonies and former colonies could not govern themselves as well on their own as the British Empire governed them. Huxley arrived at this conclusion not by way of the conservative devotion to empire or the "white man's burden" but through a seemingly rational and pragmatic analysis that accepted, without question, that the progress of Western civilization is inexorable. In other words colonialism might be reversible through decolonization, but the "civilization"–progress through technology–that colonialism has advanced is irreversible, and the formerly colonized world needs to face that inexorable fact.

Jesting Pilate engages with the "Indian Question" that had occupied and preoccupied the English for so long. For centuries India had been the "pearl" or cornerstone of the British Empire. An "Indocentric" conceptualization of that empire is omnipresent in British writing. At its height and before "decolonization" the empire was conceived as radiating, not from a center in the British Isles but from India. The British tenaciously held the rock of Gibraltar for access to the Mediterranean and the ports of the Middle East; in turn British efforts there and in Egypt were concerned with keeping open their direct land routes to India. South Africa was crucial to safeguard the sea route around the Cape of Good Hope to the Indian Ocean. China and other parts of the Far East were contiguous with the Indian subcontinent, and British efforts in those areas were part of its Indian policies as well as crucial to the burgeoning opium trade. India was "the Jewel in the Crown" of Queen Victoria and subsequent rulers of England. The importance of India to the British worldview cannot be overestimated. It is fitting, then, that Huxley began his account of his world tour in *Jesting Pilate* at Port Said in Egypt and within a scant three pages arrived in Bombay.

In drawing a telling analogy between the devaluation of British currency in Europe and the value of British human "currency" abroad, Huxley suggested that it was only a matter of time before "our 'inferiors'" in the empire would "refuse to regard us as anything more precious than waste paper," and he asserted that "merely by refusing to accept the white man at his own valuation," Indians might end their period of involuntary servitude and colonization. As few as the British were in India–compared to the teeming millions of Indians–India might achieve self-rule when enough of its 320 million people chose to ignore the English. The subsequent "passive resistance" of the movement inspired by Gandhi was verification of Huxley's prescience. Yet Huxley seriously wondered if the Indians would govern themselves as well as the British did. His reflection that it was the majority of uneducated Indians still acquiescing in British rule who stood in the way of home rule conveys his skepticism that Indians would rule India any better, if as well, as the British.

Aldous and Maria Huxley with their Bugatti in the South of France, 1930s

However "liberal" Huxley seemed at the time, he loathed India–as D. H. Lawrence observed after visiting with the Huxleys in autumn 1926, shortly after their return to Italy from their world tour. Bedford observes that Huxley's first encounter with the East produced mainly the emotion of "horror." In *Jesting Pilate* he inveighed against Indian scholarship (slavish adherence to traditional authority), against Indian eating customs ("discomfort and protracted starvation," which are "very painful to Western limbs and loins, Western hams, and Western stomachs"), against Gandhi's lack of political abilities (in spite of his evident admiration for the Indian leader and his own prediction as to the success of passive resistance), and against the caste system, which in Huxley's estimation placed Indian cultural development at the medieval stage.

The viewpoint that Indians were at a medieval stage of cultural development marks Huxley's travel writing as "colonialist" despite his sympathizing with colonized peoples wherever he traveled. Said and other critics of colonialist discourse affirm that inherent in the colonialist view is the twofold perspective that colonized peoples are culturally retarded, arrested in development at some point in the distant past, and childlike, arrested at an early stage of human development. For all his liberal opinions, in professing this twofold cliché of "Orientalist" or colonialist discourse Huxley revealed how his mind-set depends on the colonial and imperial economic system that enabled his travel and his writing. Although he admitted that, thanks to the empire, he could carry his "privileges of comfort, culture, and wealth in perfect safety," even in the heart of Bombay, Huxley was not aware that colonialism not only made his travel possible but also formed his mind and opinions. Only in *Brave New World* did Huxley expose the colonialist apparatus, but even in that novel he provided only a wild caricature of "the Savage" living outside of the World State. He could not conceive of a viable alternative to colonialism and the spread of Western civilization, even as he exposed and deplored their major tendencies.

The questions Huxley asked himself about Indian democracy and home rule–and his answer–reveal how Huxley believed that his liberal and cultured British perspective was the best:

> Do I mean anything whatever when I say that democracy is a good thing? Am I expressing a reasoned opin-

> ion? Or do I merely repeat a meaningless formula by force of habit and because it was drummed into me at an early age? I wonder.
>
> . . . Born an Indian or brought up in the slums of London, I should hardly be able to achieve so philosophical a suspense of judgment.

That Huxley was even able to pose such questions is admirable; that he ratified his philosophical detachment, however much a product of his upper-middle-class upbringing, exemplifies his containment within colonialist discourse and perspectives.

However colonialist he may have been, Huxley in Malaya offered the following reflections (in telling parentheses) on empire:

> Examined in detail and at close quarters, our far-flung Empire is seen to consist of several scores of thousands of clubs and golf courses, dotted at intervals, more or less wide, over two-fifths of the surface of the planet. Large blond men sit in the clubs, or swipe the white ball down clearings in the jungle; blackamoors of various shades bring the whiskey and carry round the niblicks. The map is painted red. And to the casual observer, on the spot, that is the British Empire.

Jesting Pilate concludes with Huxley's travels in the United States. If the British Empire was painted red on maps to signify the many British golf courses and clubs, the United States was painted all in gold, signifying the utmost fulfillment of imperial tendencies in the material wealth of "Joy City." Stunned by American opulence, Huxley perceived it as the future already present–a view analogous with his colonialist belief that colonized peoples were backward in time and intellectual and emotional development. Compared to the present of the British Empire, the United States was futuristic in its wealth, leisure, and lifestyle.

Perhaps the most telling observation in *Jesting Pilate* is one Huxley made after his departure from India and his discovery of a copy of Henry Ford's *My Life and Work* (1922) in the ship's library. He read the book and commented: "In these seas, and to one fresh from India and Indian 'spirituality,' Indian dirt and religion, Ford seems a greater man than Buddha."

Having entertained the possibility while in Europe that the "way of the Gautama" might be the "way of salvation," Huxley, fresh from India, counterpointed this feeling with the notion that Ford looked a whole lot better than Buddha. If India was the past and the empire was the present, Henry Ford and America were the future. Huxley's intention is thoughtful inquiry; his method contrapuntal; but his conclusion colonialist. In the spirit of "counterpoint," Huxley announced, "To travel is to discover that everybody is wrong." The irony or facetiousness latent in this comment notwithstanding, the inbred colonialist perspective rises to the surface in Huxley's remark. Yet one can respect the goal of *Jesting Pilate,* which is announced by its title and the two quotations to which it alludes: "Pilate saith unto him, What is truth?" (John 18:38); "What is truth? said jesting Pilate, and would not stay for an answer" (Francis Bacon, "Of Truth," in *Essays* [1625]). However conditioned, enabled, and constrained he was by colonialism, Huxley was passionately concerned with the pursuit of truth.

In *Point Counter Point* the contrapuntal method–the interweaving of differing and even contradictory perspectives, ideas, and opinions–provides the structural and thematic principle for the novel. As he counterpointed the various attitudes toward India, the Empire, the East, and the United States in *Jesting Pilate,* so in *Point Counter Point* Huxley juxtaposed a variety of attitudes toward life and truth in the actions and opinions of a large cast of characters. Woven into the contrapuntal complexity of the novel is a world tour, which takes the main characters–Philip Quarles (based on Huxley) and his wife, Elinor–away from their young son and their home base in England. Following their trip to India, the Quarleses return to England to find their son, young Phil, seriously ill with meningitis. After the child dies a rather horrible death, the hedonistic intellectual Spandrell voices an opinion about Philip Quarles that applies equally well to Huxley: "Settling down in the country in England wasn't at all like you. Travelling about, being unfixed, being a spectator–that was like you. You're being compelled to do what's like you." (Huxley's son, Matthew, did not get ill during the Huxleys' world tour, nor did he die upon their return.) The illness and death of Quarles's son signifies Huxley's awareness of the potentially dire consequences of his own wanderlust. As Philip Quarles had to learn the lesson of his traveling nature, Huxley grappled with his own compunction to be always on the move, "along the road."

Huxley's travel experiences and his commitment to "the novel of ideas" came together in *Brave New World,* his most popular, if not his most critically acclaimed, novel. *Brave New World* carved a rather large niche for itself among "educated" readers in the 1930s. Yet critical contempt made itself heard from the first. Huxley's dystopian novel of ideas was too much of the 1930s to qualify as a "well-wrought urn" of the modernist tradition.

Considered from the perspective of his travel writing, Huxley's *Brave New World* can be understood as a powerful indictment of the institutions of power that enforced colonialism even as it shows how knowledge of the world is only attainable through travel made possible by colonization: "dark" and "wild" places of the world are made accessible through the technology of travel brought into being by imperialism and colonialism. Everything from the private realm to the entire geophysical globe has been colonized by the World State. Areas considered unusable or unredeemable are designated as "Reservations" and are populated by "Savages" who are not subjected to mass eugenics and lifelong biochemical engineering, as are the "civilized" people. The Savages of the Reservations are Huxley's extrapolation of southwest Native Americans (mainly Hopi or Zuni). The Savages, who live in abject poverty in "pueblos," have elaborated and amalgamated the religious beliefs of southwest Indians and Catholicism and enjoy a kind of freedom unknown within the boundaries of the World State. Privileged citizens of the World State may receive permission to travel to the Reservations for vacations. The protagonist, Bernard Marx, director of hatcheries and conditioning at the London Hatchery and Conditioning Centre (for the propagation of World State citizens), returns to the Southwest Reservation and finds the female companion who was lost during his first visit years earlier. The lost woman, Linda, has borne Marx's son, who becomes known as the "Savage." Bernard brings Linda and the Savage back to London and achieves social notoriety by introducing the Savage to the elite citizens of the World State, but instead of effecting the dramatic social change for which he dimly hopes, Bernard gets himself exiled to an island for individuals whose antisocial attitudes threaten the "COMMUNITY, IDENTITY, STABILITY" of the World State.

In *Brave New World* the uncivilized or exotic places of the world are controlled and made accessible by an imperial mechanism that promotes the travel of its citizens, just as the expansion of the civilized world through technology and travel enabled British writer Huxley to travel over the world to earn his living, at least in part, by writing about his travels and to experience people and places that he incorporated into his major fiction. Critical of the British Empire and colonialism, Huxley nevertheless formed his view of the world under the influence of the travel that the colonialist apparatus made possible.

As Said points out throughout his *Culture and Imperialism* (1993), the relation of English writers to British imperialism is seldom noted. When viewed as a travel book *Brave New World* becomes an important literary document of the global tensions and the concerns about colonization and decolonization that dominated the first half of the twentieth century. These tensions and concerns were often effaced or obscured by the critical aesthetic formalism of modernism, which itself was an attempt to articulate an alternative to the emphasis on technology and progress that was making the World State seem increasingly imminent. As high modernism tried to distance itself from the disillusioning legacy of technological progress, colonialism, and decolonization, Huxley grappled with those issues directly–through his literary, critical, and travel writings. In *Brave New World* he sacrificed critical acclaim for the sake of disseminating his ideas; the widespread popularity of his books among "middle-brow" readers is an indication that they spoke the concerns of his time. For that reason alone they demand attention in this fin de siècle time of reassessing and reevaluating twentieth-century literature.

Huxley in the mid 1930s (photograph by Bassano and Vandyke Studios)

In 1932 the Huxleys traveled to the remote regions of Central America and Mexico. Thanks to *Point Counter Point* and *Brave New World*, Huxley was one of the best-known living British writers. Thanks to another, still more lucrative contract with Chatto and Windus publishers, Huxley could afford the

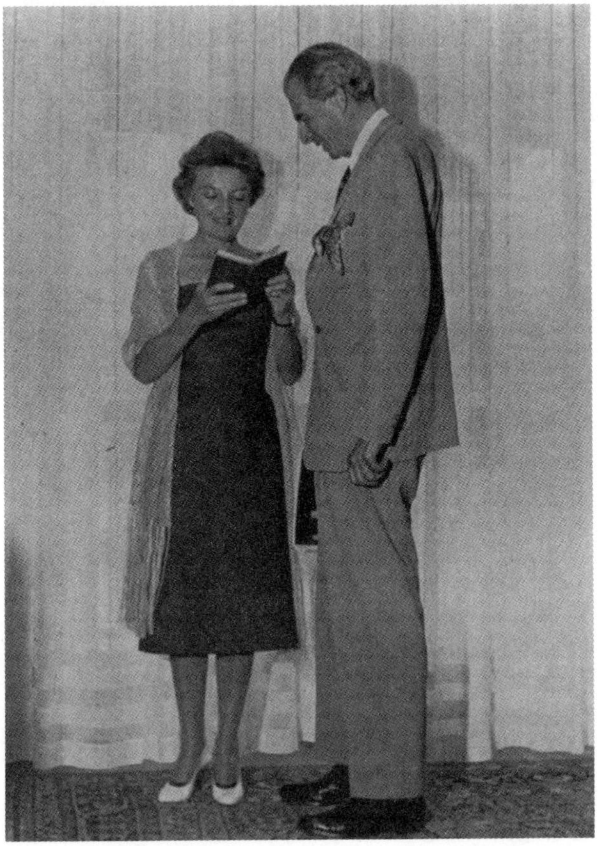

Huxley and his second wife, Laura, in Italy, 1958

time and expense to travel to the Caribbean, Central America, and Mexico. Why he did so is unclear. He may have been influenced by the fact that his close friend D. H. Lawrence, whose letters Huxley edited in 1932, had traveled to Mexico and the southwestern United States in pursuit of his dream of forming the ideal human community. Roughly one-third of the way into *Beyond the Mexique Bay* (1934), the book he wrote about his journey, Huxley admits, "Frankly, try how I may, I cannot very much like primitive people. They make me feel uncomfortable." This quite remarkable book–beautifully written and illustrated–finally is testimony to the intractability of the colonialist mind. *Beyond the Mexique Bay* conveys Huxley's complex yet ultimately colonialist perspective, misrepresenting Central American and Mexican politics and cultures in its persistence in the colonialist attitudes that "primitive peoples" are at once childlike and arrested in an evolutionary past, in its sensitive response to the art and culture of the great dead civilizations of Central America and Mexico, and in its socio-cultural-political analyses of the Central American nation-states, in which Huxley seems completely oblivious to the impact of colonial "gunboat" diplomacy. As in his analysis of the "Indian Question," Huxley took the neoconservative posture that the Central American countries were largely to blame for their impoverished and chaotic conditions.

Published a scant two years after his warning of an imminent World State in *Brave New World, Beyond the Mexique Bay* displays Huxley's inability to think beyond the technological progress of civilization. Despite–or even because of–the growing national socialism in Germany, Italy, and Japan of the early 1930s, Huxley could only perceive the nation-states of Central America as primitive forebears of fascism. His comments about the phenomenon of national socialism, or fascism, are courageous and prophetic. Huxley was a minority voice in opposing fascism during the early 1930s; his concerns about the dogma of racial purity disseminated by Adolf Hitler, Benito Mussolini, and their fascist followers placed him among the first voices to oppose mass genocide. Yet as much as he deplored the nationalism and accompanying racialism of emerging fascist regimes, Huxley applied the same racial stereotyping and reductionism to his experience of Central America and Mexico. In drawing an analogy between Central American regimes and the fascist regimes of Germany and Italy, Huxley evinced the same racialist doctrines he meant to indict.

In *Beyond the Mexique Bay* Huxley developed his cultural theory of the "Local Pavlov." According to this theory, local or indigenous cultures condition their members in a manner analogous to Ivan Pavlov's psychological experiments. Although in places Huxley's theorizing about cultures sounds remarkably like Michel Foucault's emphasis in his early works on disruption and discontinuity in the unfolding of history, Huxley finally resorted to the "Great Man" theory of history: the belief that idiosyncracies and individualities across diverse cultures are the product of a handful of great men whose ideas were either adopted by or enforced on the masses. Huxley advanced this theory in explicit opposition to the "blood and soil" politics and racial theories disseminated by the fascist regimes of Europe. Yet Hitler and Mussolini were employing this same "Great Man" theory to their own advantage. Furthermore, in responding to the propaganda efforts of the fascists–whose messages of hatred, racism, and nationalism seemed to have primary appeal to the emotions of the masses–Huxley directly denied the Marxist explanation that economic factors are at the structural base of any society. He completely ignored the fact that during a decade of worldwide economic depression the fascist governments were putting bread on their peoples' tables through their massive industrial and military effort of rearmament.

In one revealing passage Huxley compared the Mayan art of Central America with the art and culture of India. Huxley was a brilliant art critic. His knowledge of art and architecture and his ability to articulate the forms and achievements of the plastic arts are perhaps unparalleled. Yet the importance of Italy in forming Huxley's tastes and opinions everywhere colors his analyses. Similarly the centrality of India, not only to the British Empire but also to the formation of the British mind or worldview, clearly inserted itself in Huxley's comparison of Mayan and Indian art. Why Mayan art should be compared with Indian art rather than that of any other civilization is never addressed. The "naturalness" of such a comparison was evidently so obvious for Huxley that no rationale was necessary. Colonialism was such an essential part of the fabric of British existence that Huxley compared Mayan and Indian art because the empire had brought them into contiguity.

Huxley lived and wrote for another thirty years after the publication of *Beyond the Mexique Bay.* In 1937 the Huxleys decided to settle in the United States. It was less of a "new start" than another example of Huxley's fundamental homelessness, a temporary fixation of abode in a country he had already found to be somewhat unreal, even futuristic. Maria Huxley died on 12 February 1955, and on 19 March 1956 Huxley married a younger woman, Laura Archera. He died peacefully on 22 November 1963 while Laura Huxley tended him and watched the news of John F. Kennedy's assassination on television. Other than a handful of travel essays written over that period, Huxley did not produce significant travel writings. He continued to travel, and he continued to explore the vast terrain of human experience in novels and essays.

In May 1961 the house in Los Angeles where the Huxleys had lived for some time burned to the ground, destroying a lifetime of papers and the draft for a new novel. The man whose adolescence had been marked by the destruction of any sense of home or family center, who had adapted to and even come to prefer a nomadic existence, was homeless again. Unlike many writers Huxley marked no place by his presence.

Letters:

The Letters of Aldous Huxley, edited by Grover Smith (New York: Harper & Row, 1969).

Bibliographies:

Claire John Eschelback and Joyce Lee Shober, *Aldous Huxley: A Bibliography 1916–1959* (Berkeley & Los Angeles: University of California Press, 1961; London: Cambridge University Press, 1961);

Thomas D. Clareson and Carolyn S. Andrews, "Aldous Huxley: A Bibliography 1960–1964," *Extrapolation,* 6 (December 1964): 2–21;

Philip Thody, *Aldous Huxley: A Bibliographical Introduction* (London: Studio Vista, 1973);

Dennis D. Davis, "Aldous Huxley: A Bibliography 1965–1973," *Bulletin of Bibliography,* 31 (April-June 1974): 67–70.

Biographies:

George Heard, "The Poignant Prophet," *Kenyon Review,* 27 (Winter 1965): 49–93;

Julian Huxley, ed., *Aldous Huxley, 1894–1963: A Memorial Volume* (London: Chatto & Windus, 1965; New York: Harper & Row, 1965);

Ronald W. Clark, *The Huxleys* (London: Heinemann, 1968; New York: McGraw-Hill, 1968);

Laura Archera Huxley, *This Timeless Moment: A Personal View of Aldous Huxley* (New York: Farrar, Straus & Giroux, 1968);

Sybille Bedford, *Aldous Huxley: A Biography* (2 volumes, London: Chatto & Windus, 1973, 1974; 1 volume, New York: Harper & Row, 1974);

David King Dunaway, *Huxley in Hollywood* (New York: Harper & Row, 1989).

Christopher Isherwood

(26 August 1904 - 4 January 1986)

Thomas Dukes
University of Akron

See also the Isherwood entries in *DLB 15: British Novelists, 1930-1959* and *DLB Yearbook, 1986.*

BOOKS: *All the Conspirators* (London: Cape, 1928; New York: New Directions, 1958);

The Memorial: Portrait of a Family (London: Hogarth Press, 1932; New York: New Directions, 1946);

Mr. Norris Changes Trains (London: Hogarth Press, 1935); republished as *The Last of Mr. Norris* (New York: Morrow, 1935);

The Dog Beneath the Skin or Where Is Francis? A Play in Three Acts, by Isherwood and W. H. Auden (London: Faber & Faber, 1935; New York: Random House, 1959);

The Ascent of F 6, a Tragedy in Two Acts, by Isherwood and Auden(London: Faber & Faber, 1936; New York: Random House, 1937);

Sally Bowles (London: Hogarth Press, 1937);

Lions and Shadows: An Education in the Twenties (London: Hogarth Press, 1938; Norfolk, Conn.: New Direction, 1947);

On the Frontier: A Melodrama in Three Acts, by Isherwood and Auden (London: Faber & Faber, 1938; New York: Random House, 1938);

Journey to a War, by Isherwood and Auden (London: Faber & Faber, 1939; New York: Random House, 1939);

Goodbye to Berlin (New York: Random House, 1939; London: Hogarth Press, 1939);

The Berlin Stories (New York: New Directions, 1945);

Prater Violet (New York: Random House, 1945; London: Methuen, 1945);

The Condor and the Cows: A South American Travel Diary (New York: Random House, 1948; London: Methuen, 1949);

The World in the Evening (New York: Random House, 1954; London: Methuen, 1954);

Down There on a Visit (New York: Simon & Schuster, 1962; London: Methuen, 1962);

An Approach to Vedanta (Hollywood: Vedanta Press, 1963);

Christopher Isherwood

A Single Man (New York: Simon & Schuster, 1964; London: Methuen, 1964);

Ramakrishna and His Disciples (New York: Simon & Schuster, 1965; London: Methuen, 1965);

Exhumations: Stories, Articles, Verses (New York: Simon & Schuster, 1966; London: Methuen, 1966);

A Meeting by the River (New York: Simon & Schuster, 1967; London: Methuen, 1967);

Kathleen and Frank: The Autobiography of a Family (London: Methuen, 1971; New York: Simon & Schuster, 1972);

Frankenstein, the True Story, by Isherwood and Don Bachardy (New York: Avon, 1973);

Christopher and His Kind, 1929-1939 (New York: Farrar, Straus & Giroux, 1976; London: Eyre Methuen, 1977);

My Guru and His Disciple (New York: Farrar, Straus & Giroux, 1980; London: Eyre Methuen, 1980);
October (Los Angeles: Twelvetrees Press, 1980; London: Methuen, 1980);
People One Ought to Know, by Isherwood and Sylvain Mangeot (Garden City, N.Y.: Doubleday, 1982; London: Macmillan, 1982);
Where Joy Resides: A Christopher Isherwood Reader, edited by Bachardy and James P. White (New York: Farrar, Straus & Giroux, 1989; London: Methuen, 1989).

OTHER: Charles Baudelaire, *Intimate Journals,* translated by Isherwood (London: Blackmore, 1930; revised edition, Hollywood: Marcel Rodd, 1947);
Bertolt Brecht, *A Penny for the Poor,* translated by Isherwood (London: Hale, 1937; New York: Hillman-Curl, 1938);
Vedanta for the Western World, edited by Isherwood (Hollywood: Rodd, 1946; London: Allen & Unwin, 1948);
Shankara's Crest-Jewel of Discrimination, translated by Isherwood and Swami Prabhavananda (Hollywood: Vedanta Press, 1947);
Vedanta for the Modern Man, edited by Isherwood (New York: Harper, 1951; London: Allen & Unwin, 1952);
How to Know God: The Yoga Aphorisms of Patanjali, translated by Isherwood and Swami Prabhavananda (New York: Harper, 1953; London: Allen & Unwin, 1953);
Great English Short Stories, edited by Isherwood (New York: Dell, 1957).

Christopher Isherwood was considered a major British writer of the 1930s and 1940s, and much of his writing continued to be well received until the end of his life. Following his critically praised second and third novels, *The Memorial* (1932) and *Mr. Norris Changes Trains* (1935), Isherwood began producing the works for which he received his first great acclaim, the novella *Sally Bowles* (1937) and the parts of what became *Goodbye to Berlin* (1939). These works were based on his experiences in Nazi Germany during the 1930s, and Isherwood was praised for his prescience and imagination. That travel was important to Isherwood's life and work is evident in the titles of his fiction as well as his nonfiction, and he is known for using fact in his fiction. His two travel books–*Journey to a War* (1939), written with W. H. Auden, and *The Condor and the Cows* (1948)–were published at the height of his renown, a time when many believe he was at the peak of his ability as a writer. These works are significant for their individual contributions to the historical record and for what they reveal about Isherwood's views on the politics of his time, a concern reflected in his fiction of the period.

Christopher William Bradshaw-Isherwood was born at Wyberslegh Call in Cheshire on 26 August 1904, the elder son of a professional soldier, Frank Bradshaw-Isherwood, and the daughter of a successful wine merchant, Kathleen Machell-Smith Bradshaw-Isherwood. Isherwood's father was killed in World War I. After graduating from Repton School, near Derby, Isherwood entered Corpus Christi College, Cambridge, in October 1923. He left in 1925 without earning a degree, his undistinguished academic career having culminated by giving mischievous and wrong answers to the questions on his final exams. At this time Isherwood admitted to his mother and himself that he was homosexual.

After the poor reception of his first novel, *All the Conspirators* (1928), and a half-hearted attempt to study medicine at King's College, London, in 1928–1929, Isherwood joined his Cambridge friend W. H. Auden in Berlin. There Isherwood began teaching English and formed his first long-term romantic liaison, with a young man he called Bubi in his autobiography *Christopher and His Kind, 1929–1939* (1976). He spent most of the 1930s in Germany and other European countries. In 1939, the year in which *Goodbye to Berlin* and *Journey to a War* were published, he immigrated to the United States.

Journey to a War describes Isherwood and Auden's visit to China in 1938, during the Sino-Japanese War, which had erupted in August 1937 and represented a grim foreshadowing of World War II in the Pacific just as the Spanish Revolution did in Europe. The volume comprises a "Travel Diary" by Isherwood, poems by Auden, and photographs taken mostly but not exclusively by Auden. The book is at once a travel diary and a war chronicle that deserves a place in the war literature of the period. While Isherwood and Auden were not experts on China, as Isherwood's foreword frankly acknowledges, Isherwood's observations during their travels do give a sense of the Chinese people at the time.

Isherwood's "Travel Diary" records each leg of their often dangerous journey, starting with the voyage from Hong Kong to Canton. The narrative voice is objective in detailing the travelers' experiences, but it also offers commentary on people and battles. At the beginning, Isherwood wrote, "One's first entry into a war-stricken country as a neutral observer is bound to be dream-like, unreal." Soon,

Isherwood and W. H. Auden leaving for China, 1938

however, his consciousness became sensitive to its surroundings, and he was able to describe them realistically. Almost at once the travelers were plunged into the absurdity of war. While having tea at a mission they heard the "dull, heavy thuds" of bombs, and Isherwood asked, "as conversationally as I could manage, 'Isn't that an air-raid?'" His hostess replied, "'Yes, I expect it is. They come over about this time, most afternoons. . . . Do you take sugar and milk?'" At this early stage of his travels Isherwood forced himself to see

> that those noises, these objects are part of a single, integrated scene. Wake up. It's all quite real. And, at that moment, I really did wake up. At that moment, suddenly, I arrived in China.

Isherwood and Auden met and interviewed many kinds of people in what might be called their journey *through* a war. Isherwood was never sentimental about them, but he was always empathetic. During the tea at the mission, Isherwood noted his hosts' disappointment at the Cantonese theological students who had advocated war with Japan but did not want to serve in the trenches, claiming they were saving themselves for the rebuilding afterward. Their hypocrisy seems obvious, but Isherwood observed in his diary entry, "China can ill afford to sacrifice her comparatively small educated class. And it must be remembered that, for the Cantonese, the land warfare was taking place in an area hundreds of miles distant, inhabited by a people whose language they could not even understand."

At dinner the next evening Isherwood and Auden learned of the Chinese resourcefulness against the much stronger Japanese. A Chinese colonel described how Chinese citizens tried to shoot down Japanese fighters, making "anti-aircraft defense . . . a local sport, like duck-shooting." One Japanese pilot was downed by a one-hundred-year-old mortar fired from a Chinese junk. Isherwood's connection of China's fight for its life with a leisure sport at once contrasts life in the East and the West and highlights the absurdity of war.

Isherwood and Auden's interview with Madame Chiang Kai-shek (Chiang Mei-ling) is one of the most effective portions of the book. Although Madame Chiang Kai-shek was one of the most photographed and written about women of her time, Isherwood's description of his impression is unmatched in its accuracy, brevity, and grace: "She is a small, round-faced lady, exquisitely dressed, vivacious rather than pretty, and possessed of an almost terrifying charm and poise. . . . She could be terrible, she could be gracious, she could be businesslike, she could be ruthless; it is said that she sometimes signs death-warrants with her own hand." In a few sentences Isherwood created an idea of how the woman looked and acted, and illustrated how a rumor can attach itself to a famous person and become part of his or her character. Madame described how she tried to enforce the New Life Movement, a program to reform moral and social behavior that Isherwood suspected, correctly, was of dubious worth. Isherwood was also astute in his evaluation of her husband, Gen. Chiang Kai-shek, who entered the room at the end of the interview. When his wife led the general to the balcony for a photograph, Isherwood observed, "Under the camera's eye he stiffened visibly, like a schoolboy who is warned to hold himself upright."

Isherwood painted a less exalted picture of his servant, Chiang, who "has the manners of a perfect butler. His English leaves much to be desired, and he does not even pretend to be able to cook." Yet Chiang was soon able to "exhibit his powers" by getting Isherwood and Auden through bureaucratic confusion at a train station. Chiang was serving, not servile. When he bowed to let Isherwood and Auden through, "This, his unctuous gesture seemed to say, is how Big Shots board a train." Chiang proved valuable many times as Isherwood and Auden showed themselves to be innocents abroad, and the two Englishmen were not above taking advice. Isherwood and Auden always had to bargain and hire as best they could and were dependent on the good, or ill, will of other people.

While Isherwood admitted that Auden and he were perhaps incapable of making fully informed judgments, he attempted to assess the war situation, writing that the Chinese deprecate their own trenches at the front. He explained, "In Europe one is so accustomed to cocksureness and boasting that the reticence of a Chinese officer seems positively defeatist." Admiring the Chinese spirit, which held them firm in the face of vastly superior armaments and medical services, Isherwood believed that European troops fighting in such conditions "would probably all mutiny within a fortnight."

Isherwood and Auden were not immune to the sort of European attitudes and needs that Isherwood implied were the reason for the inferior character of European soldiers. While traveling on a train, Isherwood observed,

> Meals were our greatest solace. Constipated though we were we could still eat, and the food provided by the kitchen-truck was, considering the circumstances, excellent. Our chief luxury was the American coffee which we had brought with us from Hankow in tins.

Forced by a power failure to dine by candlelight, they expelled Chiang from their train compartment because he tried to make music with a flute that he could not play. He then astonished them by returning with whiskey they had facetiously asked him to find. This passage shows at once the problems of the travel (their constipation) as well as the romanticism created by the unexpected appearance of home pleasures. Their treatment of Chiang also indicates that Isherwood was unable to avoid acquiring the Western imperialist attitudes he disdained. Yet his observations about the meeting of European and Chinese cultures can also be moving, as in his description of how the wife of a Chinese professor, a Madame Chen, gave Auden and him a box holding a lovely carved ivory skull to take to Virginia Woolf.

As their journey progressed, Isherwood and Auden encountered what might be expected under the circumstances: trains delayed, dirty, and overcrowded; tracks destroyed; bombs falling in seemingly random attacks; and the material deprivations inflicted on civilians who have little in the first place. Isherwood's specificity of description distinguishes this work from similar ones, and his fine sense of irony is served by letting facts and events speak for themselves. For example, the book recounts how European and American missionaries often live by rules that seem ludicrous under the circumstances: a missionary might be sent home for drinking a glass of wine. Yet even the missionaries approached life with humor; one trained his dog to eat a piece of cake when it was asked if it were an American Baptist but not when it was asked if it belonged to another denomination.

Throughout his journey Isherwood remained unsentimental about history. On one occasion, having gotten into an argument with two Germans about Germany in the Far East during World War I, Isherwood lost the argument–noting "I am never much good at defending the British Empire, even when drunk"–thus summing up his ironic sense of himself, his country, and his distaste at the British history of conquering other nations. Isherwood's contempt for such events, for all war, is summed up in a passage quoted by many critics:

> War is bombing an already disused arsenal, missing it, and killing a few old women. War is lying in a stable with a gangrenous leg. War is drinking hot water in a barn and worrying about one's wife. War is a handful of lost and terrified men in the mountains, shooting at

Auden in the Chinese trenches, photograph from Journey to a War *(1937)*

> something moving in the undergrowth. War is waiting for days with nothing to do; shouting down a dead telephone; going without sleep, or sex, or a wash. War is untidy, inefficient, obscure, and largely a matter of chance.

Isherwood was hardly the first to note the insanity of war, but his contempt for it takes on special meaning in his recording of the hell it visited on China.

China had internal political struggles throughout the war, and the book shows how the Communists, led by Mao Tse-tung, and the Nationalists, under Chiang Kai-shek, wanted one another's defeat as much as they wanted the defeat of the Japanese. Perhaps the most absurdly realistic part of Isherwood's narrative is his account of a luncheon with four Japanese civilians in occupied Shanghai. The victors justified their occupation in the language of all wartime occupiers, provoking Isherwood to confront them with accounts of the atrocities the Japanese inflicted on the Chinese. Toward the end of the luncheon, "the gun-turrets of H.M.S. Birmingham slid quietly into view, moving upstream. In this city the visual statements of power-politics are more brutal than any words." Once more Isherwood employed a few well-selected words, this time to show how war and empire can create strange allies and enemies. The final pages of the book offer an analysis of the Chinese internal political situation and the lives of the peasants that now seems prescient in showing why the Communists ultimately triumphed.

Reviews of *Journey to a War* tended to be essentially positive, but Mildred Boie of *The Atlantic* (November 1939) scolded the book for being at times not as "original and profound" as she would have liked. Reviewing *Journey to a War* for the *Manchester Guardian* (19 May 1939), J.M.D.P. offered the opinion that Auden and Isherwood "were frankly tourists–and tourists in a war are always slightly indecent," a curious criticism given Isherwood and Auden's great sympathy for the suffering around them. Lincoln Kirsten offered possibly the most accurate summation of what Isherwood and Auden achieved when he called the book "perhaps the most intense record of China at war yet written in English" (*The Nation,* 5 August 1939).

Journey to a War is less an exposé of the all-too-familiar results of battle than an account of a specific people's response to war. More good-humored and less ironic than, say, the travel writing of Paul Theroux, *Journey to a War* is written in much the same voice as Isherwood's fiction collectively known as *The Berlin Stories–Mr. Norris Changes Trains, Sally Bowles,* and *Goodbye to Berlin*–dispassionate, curious, and interested. Book-length studies on Isherwood have focused on his fiction and have characterized the plays Isherwood wrote with Auden as heavy-handed political melodrama with little to offer posterity. *Journey to a War* is usually dismissed in a page or two, if that. Yet it merits attention because it offers the distinctive viewpoint of outsiders who were writers but not strictly journalists.

Written a decade later, *The Condor and the Cows: A South American Travel Diary* (1948) is also about a place in political and social crisis. Once again Isherwood had a traveling companion, this time Bill Caskey, a young photographer whose work appears in the book. Isherwood's title refers to the fact that "the Condor is the emblem of the Andes and their mountain republics, while the Cows represent the great cattle-bearing plains, and, more specifically, Argentina–no offense intended." Again Isherwood made clear that his narrative is no way an expert account of the land or its people. He acknowledged that Caskey and he missed stopping in several countries: Uruguay, Brazil, Chile, Paraguay, and the Guianas–French Guiana, British Guiana (Guyana), and Netherlands Guiana (Suriname). Isherwood and Caskey spoke about as much Spanish as Auden and Isherwood spoke Chinese. Even if they had possessed knowledge of the language, the dialects would have often left them at a loss. As is true in *Journey to a War,* and perhaps in much good travel writing, the author's foreignness enables the reader to identify with the narrative voice. Once more, the reader seems to travel with Isherwood, and his impressions seem to be those of the reader.

The book covers the period from September 1947 through March 1948. From the beginning Isherwood's best writing is in his descriptions of people. Of an American traveler Isherwood wrote, "For him, as for so many Americans of his kind, a pleasure-journey is just another sort of investment–a sound one, most likely, but he has got to watch it." Isherwood was equally perceptive in describing a little Ecuadoran boy "who is fat and squat with an archaic Inca face. . . . He has two pleasures; gorging food and bullying his sisters." Caskey and Isherwood voted the boy "Most Loathsome Child on Board."

As in *Journey to a War* Isherwood recognized that he was indeed a traveler in a foreign place: "This morning, very early, I went up on deck–and there was South America." His submersion into a different experience seems direct: "Its mountains rose up sheer and solemn out of the flat sea, thrown into massive relief by tremendous oblique shafts of light from the rising sun." Traveling through Colombia over a miserable road, Isherwood and Caskey laughed when their driver told them the good road had just ended, but then they discovered "What followed was much worse." They also learned the necessity of bribes:

> A racket? Naturally. The Government is being cheated. What do we care. We are being blackmailed. What does the Government care?

Isherwood noted that the drama of collecting the bribe entertained the driver as well. These experiences introduced the travelers to the rituals of South American travel. Typically, Isherwood took it all in with good humor.

As Isherwood and Caskey moved deeper into the countryside by boat, they found, "The vegetation has become much thicker and wilder. Often, though the stream may be half a mile wide, the steamer is obliged to hug the bank so closely that the branches scrape our sides and we look right into the jungle, as if through the windows of a hothouse."

Perhaps because South America still felt the effects of colonization, the Europeans and Americans whom Isherwood encountered seem more a part of the landscape than the visiting Europeans in China. For example, the book describes an oilman who has survived in the wilderness during his long stays by taking a specific interest in the flora and fauna of the region. Isherwood noted, however, that the British are "essentially . . . schoolmasters" while the Americans, even the government officials, are essentially businessmen. Supper with an American army major and his wife showed Isherwood that the attitude of expatriate military people "hasn't changed since the days when my father was stationed with a British regiment in Ireland thirty-five years ago." Yet Isherwood tried to be objective in his assessment of foreign workers in South America. In Peru he observed that "foreigners bring money and technical skills, and very few of them could honestly be called exploiters." While Americans and Europeans also bring better work conditions and better pay for the local workers, however, Isherwood noted that they are by definition intruders, "bossy or at best benevolently schoolmasterish."

Isherwood became sensitized to class differences and prejudices, but he did not orate about injustice. Carmen, a pretty girl he met early in his journey, took pride in being an upper-class Antiqueño and expressed indignation when a black man put his arm around her. Isherwood also discovered that she and other members of her social class were anti-Semitic; yet he adds that "you can't condemn her, despite her prejudices. She is frank and cheerful and very friendly. I always enjoy being with her." Isherwood tended to describe people without passing judgment, observing that her brother, a student at an American college, had become thoroughly Americanized. On another occasion he met a young local man who was "anxious to show himself as a blend of a tough young businessman and sophisticated Latin lover." Isherwood also recounted visits with well-known South American writers, who expressed their admiration for William Faulkner and John Dos Passos. As was typical with Isherwood, famous people and ordinary folk register equally.

Some of the best prose in the book is in the section about a visit to a bullfight. After describing how dressing Paco Lara, one of the star matadors, "takes a long time and a lot of care," Isherwood undercut the elaborate preparations by noting that the event itself was a letdown. The bulls were inferior, and another matador got more glory than Lara. With typical honesty Isherwood wrote:

> I hope I shan't go to any more bullfights. Not because they are cruel or because they disgust me. Actually, I find them very exciting. But I would die of terror if I had to face a bull myself, and therefore I have no right to demand this spectacle.

"Paco Lara entering the bullring: Bogatá" and "Prisoners making shoes: the García Moreno," photographs taken by William Caskey for The Condor and the Cows *(1948), Isherwood's account of his 1947–1948 visit to South America*

Isherwood was more comfortable at a fiesta in another country, where a bullfight was acted out by people in costume.

The most quoted passage in the book sums up Isherwood's attitude toward traveling:

> That is the irony of travel. You spend your boyhood dreaming of a magic, impossibly distant day when you will cross the equator, when your eyes will behold Quito. And then, in the slow prosaic process of life, that day undramatically dawns–and finds you sleepy, hungry and dull. The equator is just another valley; you aren't sure which and you don't much care.

What Isherwood wanted on that day in November 1947 were the creature comforts provided at a pension run by Czech immigrants. Yet his narrative shows that in retrospect he cared about crossing the equator, or he would not have written about the moment, if only to recall his exhaustion.

Meeting people was far more meaningful to Isherwood than any line on a map. Visiting a Shell oil-drilling camp after a hard and dangerous journey, he found that the managers had created a small suburb outside the camp and realized that there are "people who will grow up remembering this place as their childhood home." He also recorded the tale of a missionary who staggered into a nearby mission station after an airplane crash; a search party found his companion eleven days later in the jungle. The oil men commented about the missionaries: "They trusted in the Lord, so they didn't bother to clean their spark plugs." As always, Isherwood enjoyed the irony.

Isherwood is not immune to the effect of seeing great poverty juxtaposed with wealth, graciousness beside barbarity. Witnessing an engagement party at a hotel, he wondered how people can drink champagne with such ease while so many of the guests' fellow citizens live in wretchedness. Caskey and he visited a prison that seemed humane, but a few days later they learned of a fight at the prison in which one prisoner killed another. "Maybe," Isherwood speculated, "we actually saw and spoke to both of them." He heard of barbarity in nature as well. Prentice Cooper, the U.S. ambassador to Peru, described how friends traveling by pack train in a remote part of the country were set on by three condors. They fired at the birds, which retreated but returned with about twenty-five reinforcements and drove two horses off a mountain precipice. Still, Isherwood recognized contradictions in nature and society were a part of the history of the continent, and he devoted several pages to the beauty and barbarity of the Inca civilization.

Despite his ability to accept a place and its people on its own terms, Isherwood was unsentimental and unsparing in his judgments. He was harsh in noting the failures of the Catholic Church, even when allowing that half the horror stories are hyperbole. He is equally firm with the "prudery of the average Protestant" missionary, who makes no attempt to understand the beauty of the Catholic liturgy and its psychological value in South America. Nor does Isherwood have patience with the "Left Wing" who have "removed the whole spiritual basis of consent." As is true in most of Isherwood's writing the individual is celebrated for surviving against the odds, but the governing agency, whether political, religious, or familial, is deplored for not serving its people better.

Isherwood's judgments of the United States are not overly harsh, but *The Condor and the Cows* does express his concern about the U.S. role in South America. The politics of the countries to which Isherwood and Caskey traveled were so tumultuous that Isherwood had to update the fates of various political figures when he wrote the introduction. He also acknowledged that many more changes would occur by the time his book was published. He viewed the various armies of the countries he visited as monoliths that sucked the life out of the people. In Argentina he observed the great psychological hold of the army over the people because of the sentiment against colonialism, fueled by the Argentines' desire for the British-controlled Malvinas, or the Falkland Islands. His astute analysis of Eva Peron explains convincingly how a demagogue could acquire power because of the psychological need of the people for someone who is at once one of them and above them:

> She is their Evita–just a working-class girl–one of themselves, their mother, their sister, their truest friend . . . . And . . . She is also the First Lady, the dazzling representative of their Party's wealth and power, the shining exemplar of what any one of them might become, the projection of their dearest dreams.

Isherwood ended his account by expressing confidence in South America. He found it a land of "contrasts–the strongest I can find" and "a land of violence"; yet he foretold "a new race and a new culture."

The Condor and the Cows received mixed reviews. A *Kirkus* review (15 July 1949) said its "impressions of South America . . . are at once sharply witty, sometimes wicked and at all times fresh-eyed." Writing for *The New Statesman and Nation* (19 November 1949), V. S. Pritchett called it "irresistible," and the book was praised by reviewers for *The Times Literary Supplement* (11 November 1949) and *The New York Herald Tribune Book Review* (4 December 1949) as well. Reviewers for *The New Republic* (7 November 1949), *The Spectator* (9 December 1949), and *The Manchester Guardian* (6 December 1949) were disappointed by what they felt was a shallow treatment of South American issues. Other reviewers were divided along similar lines.

Isherwood's other major travel writings are several short essays collected in *Exhumations* (1966). For a twenty-five-page section called "Places," Isherwood selected his best travel journalism and wrote a brief introduction telling how the pieces came to be written. "Escales" is a short, selective account of his 1938 journey to Hong Kong, where *Journey to a War* begins. The essay again shows Isherwood's gift for selecting an anecdote that confirms his impression of a place. "Coming to London" describes his 1947 return to London from the United States and begins with his speculation that he probably came first to London as a child, which might well have made it his first travel destination of any distance in his life. The essay describes how for the first time Isherwood felt he was an American, a claim this essay on London makes suspect. In "Los Angeles," written for Cyril Connelly's *Horizon* in 1947, Isherwood's sympathy for the place that would be his home until death is obvious; yet he also recognized how development and expansion would damage the sun-drenched place he loved. The essay ends with the observation that the topography prevents feelings of security and home. "The Shore," a short description of the Santa Monica-Venice area, is a romantic account of the place before contemporary life destroyed much of its charm. The essay is loving, as only an outsider can make it, despite Isherwood's claim that he thought of this part of the world as home.

Isherwood's travel writing is a valuable addition to his work. Like his best novels it includes astute, unsentimental observations about people and places situated in a particular time. *Journey to a War* and *The Condor and the Cows* are valuable historical documents and illustrate Isherwood's talent for making his point through the meaningful anecdote.

Isherwood maintained his popularity with the public during the 1950s with the best-selling but poorly reviewed novel *The World in the Evening* (1954). His critical reputation recovered with *Down There on a Visit* (1962), arguably his most stylistically and thematically complex novel, and *A Single Man* (1964), the novel in which he most successfully combined the themes of religion and homosexuality which preoccupied him during the second half of his life and career. *A Meeting by the River* (1967), his last novel, deals with his religious faith and was a disappointment. During the 1970s and 1980s Isherwood concentrated on writing nonfiction, including *Kathleen and Frank* (1971), a biography of his parents, and *Christopher and His Kind* (1976), a memoir of the years in Berlin that inspired *The Berlin Stories.* He also continued to write about his religious experiences, as in *My Guru and His Disciple* (1980). Isherwood died in 1986.

In *Journey to a War* and *The Condor and the Cows* Isherwood was at the peak of his writing powers, a first-rate observer of the international scene and a skilled writer who could find the detail that reveals much more than itself. Isherwood's fiction and travel writing of the late 1930s and 1940s show the reader how the unsettled world looked to a sensitive observer in the years just before and soon after World War II.

Interviews:

George Wickes, "An Interview with Christopher Isherwood," *Shenandoah,* 16 (1965): 22–52;

Clifford Solway, "An Interview with Christopher Isherwood," *Tamarack Review,* 39 (1966): 22–35;

Nicola Thorne, "Christopher Isherwood: In Conversation with Nicola Thorne," *Vogue* (British edition, November 1971): 154–155;

Arthur Bell, "An Interview with Christopher Isherwood," *Fag Rag,* 5 (1973): 4–5;

Daniel Halpern, "A Conversation with Christopher Isherwood," *Antaeus,* 13–14 (1974): 366–388;

Sarah Smith and Marcus Smith, "To Help Along the Line: An Interview with Christopher Isherwood," *New Orleans Review,* 4 (1975): 307–310;

Heywood Hale Broun, *An Interview with Christopher Isherwood,* Audio-Forum Sound Seminars, no. 40263 (Guilford, Conn.: Jeffrey Norton, 1977);

Mark Thompson, "Double Reflections: Christopher Isherwood and Don Bachardy on Art, Love and Faith," *Advocate,* 20 March 1984, pp. 32–36.

Bibliographies:

Selmer Westby and Clayton M. Brown, *Christopher Isherwood: A Bibliography 1923–1967* (Los Angeles: California State College at Los Angeles Foundation, 1968);

Stathis Orphanos, "Christopher Isherwood: A Checklist 1968–1975," *Twentieth Century Literature,* 22 (October 1976): 354–361;

Robert W. Funk, *Christopher Isherwood: A Reference Guide* (Boston: G. K. Hall, 1979);

James White, and William White, eds., *Christopher Isherwood: A Bibliography of His Personal Papers* (Austin: Texas Center Writers, 1987).

Biography:

Brian Finney, *Christopher Isherwood: A Critical Biography* (Oxford & New York: Oxford University Press, 1979).

References:

Jonathan Fryer, *Isherwood* (Garden City, N.Y.: Doubleday, 1978);

Carolyn G. Heilbrun, *Christopher Isherwood* (New York: Columbia University Press, 1970);

Linda Mizejewski, *Divine Decadence: Fascism, Female Spectatorship, and the Makings of Sally Bowles* (Princeton, N.J.: Princeton University Press, 1992);

Paul Piazza, *Christopher Isherwood: Myth and Anti-Myth* (New York: Columbia University Press, 1978);

Claude J. Summers, *Christopher Isherwood* (New York: Ungar, 1980);

Stephen Wade, *Christopher Isherwood* (New York: St. Martin's Press, 1992);

Alan Wilde, *Christopher Isherwood* (New York: Twayne, 1971).

Papers:

The University of Texas, the University of California at Los Angeles, New York University, and Cambridge University have collections of Isherwood's papers.

D. H. Lawrence

(11 September 1885 – 2 March 1930)

D. R. Swanson
Wright State University

See also the Lawrence entries in *DLB 10: Modern British Dramatists, 1900–1945; DLB 19: British Poets, 1880–1914; DLB 36: British Novelists, 1890–1929: Modernists; DLB 98: Modern British Essayists, First Series;* and *DLB 162: British Short Fiction Writers, 1915–1945.*

D. H. Lawrence, 1913 (photograph by W. G. Parker)

BOOKS: *The White Peacock* (New York: Duffield, 1911; London: Heinemann, 1911);

The Trespasser (London: Duckworth, 1912; New York: Kennerley, 1912);

Love Poems and Others (London: Duckworth, 1913; New York: Kennerley, 1913);

Sons and Lovers (London: Duckworth, 1913; New York: Kennerley, 1913);

The Widowing of Mrs Holroyd (New York: Kennerley, 1914; London: Duckworth, 1914);

The Prussian Officer and Other Stories (London: Duckworth, 1914; New York: Huebsch, 1916);

The Rainbow (London: Methuen, 1915; expurgated edition, New York: Huebsch, 1916);

Twilight in Italy (London: Duckworth, 1916; New York: Huebsch, 1916);

Amores (London: Duckworth, 1916; New York: Huebsch, 1916);

Look! We Have Come Through! (London: Chatto & Windus, 1917; New York: Huebsch, 1918);

New Poems (London: Secker, 1918; New York: Huebsch, 1920);

Bay: A Book of Poems (London: Beaumont Press, 1919);

Women in Love (New York: Privately Printed for Subscribers Only, 1920; London: Secker, 1921);

The Lost Girl (London: Secker, 1920; New York: Seltzer, 1921);

Touch and Go (London: Daniel, 1920; New York: Seltzer, 1920);

Psychoanalysis and the Unconscious (New York: Seltzer, 1921; London: Secker, 1923);

Movements in European History, as Lawrence H. Davidson (London: Oxford University Press, 1921);

Tortoises (New York: Seltzer, 1921);

Sea and Sardinia (New York: Seltzer, 1921; London: Secker, 1923);

Fantasia of the Unconscious (New York: Seltzer, 1921; London: Secker, 1923);

Aaron's Rod (New York: Seltzer, 1922; London: Secker, 1922);

England, My England and Other Stories (New York: Seltzer, 1922; London: Secker, 1924);

The Ladybird, The Fox, The Captain's Doll (London: Secker, 1923); republished as *The Captain's*

Doll: Three Novelettes (New York: Seltzer, 1923);

Studies in Classic American Literature (New York: Seltzer, 1923; London: Secker, 1924);

Kangaroo (London: Secker, 1923; New York: Seltzer, 1923);

Birds, Beasts and Flowers (New York: Seltzer, 1923; augmented edition, London: Secker, 1923);

The Boy in the Bush, by Lawrence and M. L. Skinner (London: Secker, 1924; New York: Seltzer, 1924);

St. Mawr: Together with The Princess (London: Secker, 1925); republished in part as *St. Mawr* (New York: Knopf, 1925);

Reflections on the Death of a Porcupine and Other Essays (Philadelphia: Centaur Press, 1925; London: Secker, 1934);

The Plumed Serpent (London: Secker, 1926; New York: Knopf, 1926);

David: A Play (London: Secker, 1926; New York: Knopf, 1926);

Sun (expurgated edition, London: Archer, 1926; unexpurgated edition, Paris: Black Sun Press, 1928);

Glad Ghosts (London: Benn, 1926);

Mornings in Mexico (London: Secker, 1927; New York: Knopf, 1927);

Rawdon's Roof (London: Elkin Mathews & Marrot, 1928);

The Woman Who Rode Away and Other Stories (London: Secker, 1928; New York: Knopf, 1928);

Lady Chatterley's Lover (Florence: Privately printed, 1928; Paris: Privately printed, 1929; expurgated edition, London: Secker, 1932; New York: Knopf, 1932; unexpurgated edition, New York Grove, 1959; Harmondsworth, U.K.: Penguin, 1960);

The Collected Poems of D. H. Lawrence, 2 volumes (London: Secker, 1928; New York: Cape & Smith, 1928);

The Paintings of D. H. Lawrence (London: Mandrake Press, 1929);

Pansies (London: Secker, 1929; New York: Knopf, 1929);

My Skirmish with Jolly Roger (New York: Random House, 1929); revised as *A Propos of Lady Chatterley's Lover* (London: Mandrake Press, 1930);

Pornography and Obscenity (London: Faber & Faber, 1929; New York: Knopf, 1930);

The Escaped Cock (Paris: Black Sun Press, 1929); republished as *The Man Who Died* (London: Secker, 1931; New York: Knopf, 1931);

Nettles (London: Faber & Faber, 1930);

Assorted Articles (London: Secker, 1930);

The Virgin and the Gipsy (Florence: Orioli, 1930; London: Secker, 1930; New York: Knopf, 1930);

Love Among the Haystacks & Other Pieces (London: Nonesuch Press, 1930; New York: Viking, 1933);

Apocalypse (Florence: Orioli, 1931; New York: Viking, 1931; London: Secker, 1932);

Etruscan Places (London: Secker, 1932; New York: Viking, 1932);

Last Poems, edited by Richard Aldington and Giuseppe Orioli (Florence: Orioli, 1932; New York: Viking, 1933; London: Heinemann, 1935);

The Lovely Lady (London: Secker, 1933; New York: Viking, 1933);

The Plays of D. H. Lawrence (London: Secker, 1933);

A Collier's Friday Night (London: Secker, 1934);

A Modern Lover (London: Secker, 1934; New York: Viking, 1934);

Phoenix: The Posthumous Papers of D. H. Lawrence, edited by Edward D. McDonald (New York: Viking, 1936; London: Heinemann, 1936);

The First Lady Chatterley (New York: Dial, 1944);

Le Tre "Lady Chatterley" (Verona: Mondadori, 1954);

The Complete Short Stories, 3 volumes (London: Heinemann, 1955);

The Complete Poems of D. H. Lawrence, 2 volumes (London: Heinemann, 1957);

The Symbolic Meaning: The Uncollected Versions of Studies on Classic American Literature, edited by Armin Arnold (Fontwell, U.K.: Centaur Press, 1962);

The Complete Poems of D. H. Lawrence, 2 volumes, edited by Vivian de Sola Pinto and Warren Roberts (London: Heinemann, 1964; New York: Viking, 1964);

The Complete Plays of D. H. Lawrence (London: Heinemann, 1965; New York: Viking, 1966);

Phoenix II: Uncollected, Unpublished, and Other Prose Works, edited by Roberts and Harry T. Moore (New York: Viking, 1968; London: Heinemann, 1968);

John Thomas and Lady Jane (New York: Viking, 1972; London: Heinemann, 1972);

Mr. Noon, edited by Lindeth Vasey (London & New York: Cambridge University Press, 1984).

Collection: *The Cambridge Edition of the Works of D. H. Lawrence,* 25 volumes to date (Cambridge: Cambridge University Press, 1980–) –*Apocalypse and the Writings of Revelation,* edited by Mara Kalnins (1980); *The Lost Girl,* edited by John Worthen (1981); *The Trespasser,* edited by Elizabeth Mansfield (1981); *The*

The farmhouse in Taormina, Sicily, where the Lawrences lived in 1920

Prussian Officer and Other Stories, edited by Worthen (1983); *St. Mawr and Other Stories,* edited by Brian Finney (1983); *The White Peacock,* edited by Andrew Robertson (1983); *Mr Noon,* edited by Lindeth Vasey (1984); *Study of Thomas Hardy and Other Essays,* edited by Bruce Steele (1985); *The Plumed Serpent,* edited by L. D. Clark (1987); *Women in Love,* edited by David Farmer, Vasey, and Worthen (1987); *Aaron's Rod,* edited by Kalnins (1988); *Reflections of the Death of a Porcupine and Other Essays,* edited by Michael Herbert (1988); *Movements in European History,* edited by Philip Crumpton (1989); *The Rainbow,* edited by Mark Kinkead-Weekes (1989); *The Boy in the Bush,* by Lawrence and M. L. Skinner, edited by Paul Eggert (1990); *England, My England, and Other Stories,* edited by Steele (1990); *The Fox, The Captain's Doll, The Ladybird,* edited by Dieter Mehl (1992); *Sketches of Etruscan Places and Other Italian Essays,* edited by Simonetta de Fillipis (1992); *Sons and Lovers,* edited by Helen Baron and Carl Baron (1992); *Lady Chatterley's Lover & A Propos of Lady Chatterley's Lover,* edited by Michael Squires (1993); *Kangaroo,* edited by Steele (1994); *Twilight in Italy and Other Essays,* edited by Paul Eggert (1994); *The Woman Who Rode Away and Other Stories,* edited by Mehl and Christa Jansohn (1995); *Sea and Sardinia,* edited by Kalnins (1997).

D. H. Lawrence had a special gift for portraying what he called the spirit of place. Landscape is an essential character in his narratives, but often it is more a spiritual than a physical landscape, one that incorporates the physical facts of the place with the people who inhabit it and who have been formed by it. "I am not Baedeker," Lawrence said, referring to the popular tourist guidebooks. His friend Aldous Huxley called him "a kind of mystical materialist." Lawrence's travel writing is more about his own reactions to people and places than descriptions of the places he visited. The places are physically there, but the reader travels mainly inside Lawrence's feelings about the places and the people. For example, his essay "Christs in the Tirol," first published in the 22 March 1913 issue of the *Saturday Westminster Gazette,* does not actually describe the land through which he passed but rather the feeling he derived from the experience of the crucifixes he saw along the way, allowing him to look into the hearts of their artists. Lawrence had a strong sense of the spiritual continuity between the past and the present and between one person and another. "My great religion is a belief in the blood, the flesh, as being wiser than the intellect," he wrote in an early letter. This sense is as apparent in his travel essays as in his fiction and poetry. His belief in the primacy of "blood consciousness" over "mind consciousness" became stronger as his experience grew.

Lawrence is one of the most controversial English writers of the twentieth century: his works were praised and condemned, his novels censored and banned, and his paintings seized by the authorities. During World War I he was suspected of being an enemy spy, partly because of his marriage to a German woman, and their movements were restricted until well after the war. Yet he has had a profound influence on the course of literature. His novels, especially *The Rainbow* (1915) and *Lady Chatterley's Lover* (1928), have provided test cases in the battle over literary censorship. In the decades following his death in 1930 from tuberculosis, Lawrence's reputation grew until his works have come to stand among the classics of twentieth- century literature. He produced nearly fifty volumes of novels, stories, plays, essays, and an enormous number of personal letters to a vast number of friends, including some of the most important and influential writers, critics, philosophers, and patrons of the arts of the early part of the century. He traveled around the world, from England to Italy to Ceylon (Sri Lanka) to Australia to the United States and Mexico, and back to Europe to complete the circle.

Though the essays that are specifically labeled travel literature are collected in only four volumes, one of which was published after his death, many of his novels and stories could also be read as travel literature. In these works the reader enters the houses of the living and tombs of the long-dead, whose lives the author imagined. Lawrence's family, early life, and education profoundly influenced his writing, and the people and places of his English midlands provide models for comparison with the people and places of his later travels.

David Herbert Lawrence was born in Eastwood, Nottinghamshire, in the English midlands, on 11 September 1885. Lawrence's mother, Lydia Beardsall Lawrence, had been a teacher in Kent, had written poetry, and was fond of reading. She wanted her children to improve their lot in life, which meant first of all that they should have as good an education as possible. She was also extremely religious. Lawrence's father, Arthur Lawrence, was a handsome, strong, jovial young miner who loved singing and dancing. The two were married in December 1875 and had two daughters and three sons. David Herbert was the youngest son and next-to-youngest child.

He followed his next older brother, William Ernest, at Beauvale school in Eastwood. Though he did not equal his brother's physical stamina or athletic ability, he surpassed him by becoming the first pupil at Beauvale to win a scholarship to Nottingham High School, which included a stipend of twelve pounds a year. When he left school in 1901 he was employed as a clerk at a surgical-appliance factory. In this year–the year of the death of Queen Victoria–William Ernest Lawrence, age twenty-three, died suddenly, and Lawrence himself also became seriously ill with pneumonia. After he recovered from this illness he did not return to the surgical-supply factory.

During the summer of 1901 Lawrence became friends with the Chambers family of Haggs Farm (the model for Willey Farm in *Sons and Lovers,* 1913), where he became a regular visitor and virtually a member of the family. Lawrence delighted in the life of Haggs Farm, and became attracted to Jessie Chambers, the daughter of the family. Together they read and discussed all the books they could borrow from the Mechanics' Institute in Eastwood, ranging widely over literature and philosophy.

In 1902 Lawrence became a pupil teacher (an apprentice or student teacher) at the British School, Eastwood, and he attended a course for pupil teachers at Ilkeston, where Jessie Chambers and Louie Burrows (to whom Lawrence would later be engaged) were also pupil teachers. In 1904 he sat for a King's Scholarship examination, which he passed with high marks, qualifying him for a free place at a teacher-training college, but he did not take it. In the following year, during which he also wrote his first poems, he passed the London Matriculation examination, which qualified him for entrance to Nottingham University College. After teaching for another year at Eastwood to save the money for his expenses, Lawrence entered Nottingham University College in 1906 for a two-year teacher training course. In 1907, during his second year at college, he submitted three stories in a Christmas competition to the *Nottinghamshire Guardian,* which offered a prize of three pounds for stories in each of three categories. Since the rules limited each competitor to one entry, he submitted two of the stories under the names of Jessie Chambers and Louie Burrows, with their permission. The story entered under Jessie Chambers's name won one of the prizes. This story was the first by Lawrence to appear in print.

Illustrations by Jan Juta for "To Nuoro" in Sea and Sardinia *(1921)*

After completing his university course in June 1908, with distinction in all subjects except English, Lawrence got a job at the newly opened Davidson Road School at Croyden, in the south suburbs of London, where he remained until 1912. Here he taught with some success though without great enjoyment. He worked steadily on a novel that he first called "Laetitia," then "Nethermere." He sent parts of this novel, as well as some poems, to Jessie Chambers for criticism. In June 1909 she sent some of his poems and the short story "Odour of Chrysanthemums" to *The English Review,* then under the editorship of Ford Madox Hueffer (later Ford Madox Ford). In due course Jessie received a letter from Hueffer inviting the author to London, where Hueffer introduced Lawrence to the literary world of that city. In 1910 Lawrence completed his novel, by then called *The White Peacock,* which was published in January 1911. Because his mother was dying of cancer and he did not expect her to live to see its official publication, Lawrence had a copy especially bound for her. She died shortly after, in December 1910, having endured five months of great pain.

Earlier in 1910 Lawrence had become engaged to Louie Burrows and began writing the book that became *The Trespasser* (1912). While *The White Peacock* was well received, it did not do well enough financially for Lawrence to live on earnings from his writing. In the year it was published he began work on a novel he called "Paul Morel." This work, after many rewritings, became his great early novel, *Sons and Lovers.* He was becoming more and more dissatisfied with teaching, which was a distraction from his writing and a serious strain on his health.

Until 1912 Lawrence's whole experience was of a small part of England. He had received a good education, both formally and through his extensive reading, and he had an acute sense of place, an awareness of his physical surroundings and his relationship to them. The experiences of this year vastly expanded Lawrence's world. Early in 1912 Lawrence was still on the staff of Davidson Road School, but he was looking for a more congenial way of making a living. A relative who was married to a German scholar invited him to join them on holiday in Germany, with a view to Lawrence's finding a job as a lector in a German university. To get help in his search Lawrence first visited his former teacher of French, Ernest Weekley, Professor of Modern Languages at Nottingham University College. At Weekley's home in Nottingham he met the professor's wife, Frieda, who was a daughter of Baron Friedrich von Richthofen, formerly a German army officer, who was now a civilian bureaucrat in Metz.

Frieda Weekley was disappointed in the life of a housewife in the English midlands and had little to occupy her time except her children and household routines. She was strongly attached to her son and two daughters, but she needed an intellectual and physical life denied her by her position. When they met she was thirty-two years old and Lawrence was twenty-seven, but the difference in their sophistication and in their stations in life was considerably greater than the difference in their ages.

Although Lawrence was strongly interested in physical sex, he was not as "liberated" in these matters as Frieda. He fell in love with this extraordinary woman and agreed to go to the Continent with her. She had already planned to visit her family in Metz, so her husband was apparently not surprised at her going away. She left her son at home and took the girls to stay with their paternal grandparents, neglecting to tell Lawrence that she had not told her husband that they were going together. She had no intention of getting a divorce, and at the time neither she nor Lawrence expected their relationship to lead to marriage. Frieda had a profound influence on Lawrence's ideas and on the final revision of "Paul Morel" as *Sons and Lovers.*

At that time travel was much less officially complicated. Not until World War I, with the growing obsession with military security and with the suspicion of foreigners, were passports and other travel documents required. Thus in 1912 they could travel freely and without documents.

Lawrence met Frieda's family and then went to his relative's home near Bonn, where he continued to work on "Paul Morel," while Frieda stayed with her family in Metz. When it was completed, Lawrence sent the manuscript to Heinemann in London, but the publisher rejected it because, according to Lawrence, it was considered a dirty book. After this rejection Lawrence sent the manuscript to Edward Garnett at another London publishing house, Duckworth. A skilled and conscientious editor, Garnett returned it with detailed suggestions for revision.

By the time Lawrence and Frieda met again according to plan in Munich, Frieda had informed her husband of her relationship with Lawrence and suggested divorce. Weekley denied her request and also refused to allow Frieda to see the children. By this time Lawrence had given up his attempt to get a teaching post in Germany and determined to make his living as a writer. Wanting to see Italy, he and Frieda began a journey by foot–a popular way to travel at the time for the more adventurous. They set out in August with only twenty-three pounds in cash between them. Having sent most of their luggage on ahead of them, they carried backpacks and a small spirit stove. After a three-week hike across the Alps, they arrived at Riva, Austria, near the Italian border at the northern tip of Lake Garda. (In the aftermath of World War I, Riva became part of Italy.) They traveled into Italy, taking a boat down Lake Garda to the then isolated village of Gargnano (now a popular resort), and rented a flat in a villa, where they lived until the following April. Lawrence spent most of his time in Gargnano writing and doing some painting, while gathering experiences and observing the people who would lend substance to *Twilight in Italy* (1916). The word *twilight* has many connotations, not only the literal meaning of the vague division between day and night but also a similar place between sun and moon, intellectual and spiritual, mind consciousness and blood consciousness, and the modern industrial world and a more primitive world of feeling.

Twilight in Italy, Lawrence's first book of nonfiction prose, consists of a series of more-or-less connected essays, some of them heavily revised versions of articles he sent from Italy to *The English Review* and the *Westminster Gazette* during his travels in 1912 and 1913. The first, "The Crucifix across the Mountains," which serves as an introduction to the volume, is nevertheless self-contained. It is followed by a group of essays under the general title "On the Lago di Garda": "The Spinner and the Monks," "The Lemon Gardens," "The Theatre," "San Gaudenzio," "The Dance," "Il Duro," and "John." This group is followed by "Italians in Exile" and finally "The Return Journey." These essays were essentially fugitive pieces that were revised and brought together during the summer of 1915. Lawrence did not consider these pieces as "serious" as his fiction or poetry, but when *Twilight in Italy* was unfavorably reviewed in the *Times Literary Supplement* (15 June 1916) Lawrence wrote to a friend, "Really, I do object to being treated like that." The reviewer wanted a travel book that simply described

Frieda and D. H. Lawrence (seated second and third from right) on an outing with friends to the Disappearing River, near Thirroul, Australia, 1922

places; Lawrence provided a view that linked a physical place to what he felt was the spirit of the place.

A comparison of the first and the later version of the first essay in the volume sheds light not only on Lawrence's travel writing but on his writing methods as a whole. Lawrence revised almost all his works extensively, especially his novels. Yet even a short essay such as "Christs in the Tirol" was carefully polished and redesigned. Written in September 1912 and published in the *Saturday Westminster Gazette* on 22 March 1913, "Christs in the Tirol" is more highly personal than "The Crucifix across the Mountains," the version published in *Twilight in Italy*. Foreign travel was still new to Lawrence in September 1912, but he already saw things and places as part of a broader "spiritual" experience.

The first version begins by describing not the landscape Lawrence saw during his walk south through the Alps but a defining experience: what he felt about the crucifixes he encountered. The essay begins conventionally enough, as if it were an entry in a guidebook: "The real Tirol does not seem to extend far south of the Brenner, and northward it goes right to the Starnberger See." It turns quickly, however, to what Lawrence saw as the most significant objects along the way, the roadside crucifixes. As he followed the track south, he says, "one must walk, as it seems, for miles and endless miles past crucifixes, avenues of them. At first they were mostly factory made, so I did not notice them . . . except just to observe that they were there. But coming among the Christs carved in wood by the peasant artists, I began to feel them. Now, it seems to me, they create almost an atmosphere over the northern Tirol, an atmosphere of pain." As the essay develops, the figures on the crosses reflect both the nature of the land in which they are found and the rustic artists who fashioned them.

The changes from "Christs in the Tirol" to "The Crucifix across the Mountains" introduced a less personal element. In the revised version of July 1915, published in *Twilight in Italy,* the opening is historical (or pseudohistorical) rather than personal: "The imperial road to Italy goes from Munich across the Tyrol, through Innsbruck and Bozen to Verona, and over the mountains. Here the great processions passed as the emperors went South, or came home again from rosy Italy to their own Germany." Suddenly the reader is no longer traveling with Lawrence on foot but with the Holy Roman (that is, German) emperors on horseback. The experience is historical, not immediate. "And how much has that old imperial vanity clung to the German soul?" the essay continues. "Did not the German kings inherit the empire of bygone Rome? It was not a very real empire, perhaps, but the sound was high and splendid." After placing the scene in this frame-

Frieda and D. H. Lawrence at Chapala, Mexico, 1923 (Harry Ransom Humanities Research Center, University of Texas at Austin)

work, Lawrence got back to the present: "The imperial procession no longer crosses the mountains, going south. That is almost forgotten, the road has passed almost out of mind. But still it is there, and its signs are standing." Thus the essay introduces the crucifixes in the context not of his immediate personal experience of them but of the historical past that has informed the natures of the artists who crafted them.

Symbols are often explicit in *Twilight in Italy.* First published with "The Lemon Gardens" and "The Theatre" as "Italian Studies: By Lago Garda" in *The English Review* (September 1913), "The Spinner and the Monks" begins with a discussion of Christian symbols: "The Holy Spirit is a Dove, or an Eagle. In the Old Testament it was an Eagle; in the New Testament it is a Dove." The essay goes on to divide Christian churches into two kinds, those of the Dove and those of the Eagle. In passing it also mentions churches of another kind, "which do not belong to the Holy Spirit at all, but which are built to pure fancy and logic; such as the Wren Churches of London." Such churches had no interest for Lawrence.

Churches of the Dove are "shy and hidden"; those "of the Eagle stand high, with their heads to the skies, as if they challenged the world below." This distinction leads to descriptions of two

Lawrence sitting by the adobe oven at Kiowa Ranch, New Mexico, where the Lawrences stayed for five months in 1924 (Harry Ransom Humanities Research Center, University of Texas at Austin)

churches: the Church of San Francisco, a church of the Dove that he passed frequently in the village almost without noticing it; and the Church of San Tomasso, a church of the Eagle on a hill towering over the village, always clearly present but apparently impossible to approach. In this essay Lawrence wrote as a first-person fictional character who sets out on a quest to find the Church of San Tomasso. As he follows backstreets, "Women glanced down at me from the top of the flights of steps, old men stood, half-turning, half-crouching under the dark shadow of the walls, to stare." The watching people, the local population, have souls that are "dark and nocturnal." Their eyes follow him as he passes through a "labyrinth made by furtive creatures" as he attempts to find the church but keeps coming out again and again on the piazza. After days of searching, he finally finds "a broken stairway" that leads to "another world, the world of the eagle, the world of fierce abstraction" and the church he has been seeking. The church hangs suspended above the village: "the terrace of San Tomasso is let down from heaven, and does not touch the earth." His experience inside the church is both physical sensation and brooding delight. Leaving the church, he comes on a woman who is spinning in the old way, with distaff and bobbin, and has a brief and cryptic conversation with her. She also represents something mysterious and timeless. The experience takes place in a magic "twilight" world: "Then I remembered that it was Saturday afternoon, when a strange suspension comes over the world. And then, just below me, I saw two monks walking in the garden between the naked, bony vines. . . ." Though he could not hear their voices, he says, "I was one with them," feeling the world as they felt it. The vivid physical description in this essay has an overlay of the mystical, and it ends with a poetic evocation of the ecstasy of the unity of the senses, showing Lawrence the "mystical materialist" at work.

"The Lemon Gardens" begins in the middle of an action, like a short story: "The padrone came just as we were drinking coffee after dinner. It was two o'clock. . . ." The tone and method are quite different from those of the previous essay; the essay is more matter-of-fact, focused on the events and conversations of the ordinary physical world. The appearance and manner of the padrone are described, as well as an important character trait: he loves to speak French, which he does badly. He approached Lawrence because he needed assistance in interpreting instructions, written in "laconic and American" English, for installing a patent door spring. Besides explaining how Lawrence solved the door-spring problem, the essay describes the place, as well as "the soul of the Italian since the Renaissance." The story line is mixed with historical elements, leading to the description of the enclosed lemon plantations, a source of pride for the padrone and the district. The essay explains that their culture is sadly in decline because it costs more to produce these lemons than they sell for in England–and they can be grown more cheaply in the warmer south of Italy. Most of "The Lemon Gardens" deals with Christianity and art, "the soul of the Italian since the Renaissance," and the nature of God, lamenting the influence of industrialization and consequent destruction of old ways and old institutions. The end of the essay expresses ambiguity about such changes: "I thought of England . . . the black, fuming laborious Midlands and north-country. It seemed horrible." Yet "It is better to go forward into error than to stay fixed inextricably in the past." Lawrence's view darkened later.

"The Theatre" is like a little drama. The padrone of the previous essay, who had his own box in the local theater, a "cast-off church" that is ideally suited for the purpose, lent Lawrence the key to this box, and he and Frieda (neither of whom is named in this volume) went the next day to see *I Spettri,* which they expected to be a local entertainment, "some good, crude melodrama." The suspense of the essay builds as it might in such a play. The people in the audience provided Lawrence an occasion for describing social distinctions and divisions, especially the separation of men and women, both at the theater and in the society as a whole. The play turned out to be an almost unrecognizable Italian version of Henrik Ibsen's *Ghosts,* astonishingly different from the German version, "which I have just seen in Munich, perfectly produced and detestable." The robust actor who portrayed the main character was indeed oppressed by a "secret sickness," but "it was no taint in the blood, it was rather a kind of debility in the soul." The play "was so different from Ibsen, and so much more moving." The essay goes on to compare northern and southern theater and sensibilities, discussing several plays and performances and expressing delight at Italian actors' transformations of plays for local audiences, especially *Amleto,* their version of *Hamlet.* Lawrence was still the teacher in spite of himself and later wrote his textbook, *Movements in European History* (1921), in a style something like that of the travel essays.

"San Gaudenzio" opens with a portrayal of the passage of the seasons in terms of their signifying flowers, beginning with the "little rosy cyclamens" of late winter (associated with Grecian mythological figures of the Bacchae, Phaedra, and Helen), followed by the orchids and hyacinths (which announce the spring and signal that it "was time to go up, to climb with the sun"). Lawrence and Frieda went to San Gaudenzio, three miles from their winter quarters, high on "a headland that hung over the lake." The pink farmhouse–inhabited by Paolo Fiori, his wife, Maria, and their children, Giovanni, Marco, and Felicina–is surrounded by a high wall on the land side and by a cliff toward the lake. Lawrence and Frieda lived here for a time, becoming close to the family. The Fiori family considered Lawrence ("I") and Frieda ("la Signora" or an "English woman") noble and rich as compared to themselves. Though they owned their farm, the Fioris were peasants and poor. Paolo was a man of the mountains and "was strangely like the pictures of peasants in the northern Italian pictures, with the same curious nobility, the same aristocratic, eternal look of the motionless, something statuesque." His values were of the past, and he respected the upper classes as naturally superior. In contrast Maria was from the lowlands, broad, dark-skinned, "slow in her soul." Unlike Paolo she did not believe in natural superiority but rather in a superiority based on money. Having been a housekeeper in the city, she had been accustomed to eating bread, whereas on their farm she ate polenta at noon and soup in the evening. Bread, elsewhere the food of the poor, was a luxury.

Paolo had gone to the United States, where he worked for five years as a laborer in a gold mine in a "wild valley" in California, leaving Maria and the two boys at home; Felicina was born after his return. Even with this experience he "had never really left San Gaudenzio," and he "never grasped the fact of money." To him wealth was land and olive trees. Maria understood more clearly where power lay in the modern world. She "wanted her sons to be freer, to achieve a new plane of living." The ending of the essay, obviously written during the dark days of World War I, shows how Lawrence's experiences had changed the way he saw his experiences of 1912–1913: "Giovanni is in America, unless he has come back to the War"; afterward he and Marco will make new lives elsewhere, "that is–if they do not kill him in this War."

ıe Dance" portrays a group of men who came San Gaudenzio to drink wine, sing, and dance with each other. The only females present were Maria, who officiated over wine and food (making sure the men paid), and two "English women," who danced with several of the men. The men were divided into two groups: the men from the village, who constituted a special class because they had money, and the peasants. By tradition local women did not attend such occasions, and the Englishwomen were the butt of obscene songs until Maria realized that Lawrence understood the dialect of the lyrics and put a stop to them.

"Il Duro" and "John," which portray two men who had been to America, reveal Lawrence's interest in the shabbiness and innocent poverty of northern Italian peasant life. The man known as Il Duro returned to Italy and the only work he knew and did well–grafting the shoots of the grapevines. Giovanni–called John because of his hope to escape to an English-speaking world–was marginally more successful abroad and returned to Italy only to pay his duty to his father and to complete his military service (if he did not he could not return until he was forty). The end of the essay describes his setting out again, having performed the duty of seeing his father and leaving his young wife and child behind: "his face was set outwards, away from it all–whither, neither he nor anybody knew, but he called it America."

"Italians in Exile" is set in Switzerland and portrays Lawrence as traveling alone on foot. The time is indicated only in the casual mention that he has lived on Lake Garda. Without any indication of how this account is related to the foregoing parts of the book, "Italians in Exile" begins "When I was in Constance the weather was misty and enervating and depressing, it was no pleasure to travel on the big flat desolate lake." The essay makes clear that Lawrence did not like Switzerland or the German Swiss people he met. He was, however, attracted to a group of Italians, an amateur theatrical group, who lived in a local Italian community and worked in a silk factory. More open and free than the Swiss, they loved Italy but did not intend to return there because, as dreary as their lives were in Switzerland, they could live better there than they had in Italy. What is most significant about this essay is its portrayal of people and their characteristic surroundings. It is as if Lawrence were writing notes and sketches that might be used later in fully developed stories.

The title of "The Return Journey" is misleading: Lawrence was not returning "home" but rather to Italy, in which he was himself a transient. The essay gives successive character sketches of several people Lawrence met on his walking tour from Switzerland south to Italy (parallel to his walk south at the beginning of the volume) and ends with several observations concerning the "process of disintegration" through which Lawrence saw the world passing. It is worth noting that this book was published in 1916, at a time when World War I had reached a degree of horror previously impossible to imagine. Lawrence at first intended to call this collection "Italian Days," which is both misleading and unimpressive; his publisher "hated" that title. The title *Twilight in Italy* suggests both the end of the old Italy that Lawrence was describing and the mysterious atmosphere that overlays much of the book. As a whole the parts of *Twilight in Italy* do not hold together. Yet the individual essays have an interest as sketches of characters, places, and events and as drafts of Lawrence's personal and social philosophy.

The Lawrences aboard the SS Resolute, *leaving the United States in September 1925*

Several major events took place between Lawrence's return to England in 1913 and the publication of *Twilight in Italy*. *Sons and Lovers* was published in May 1913, and he began work on "The Sisters," which eventually became two novels, *The Rainbow* (1915) and *Women in Love* (1920). He made another trip to the Continent, but was back in England in 1914. On 28 May of that year Frieda was finally divorced from Ernest Weekley, and on 13 July she married Lawrence. The outbreak of World War I

The Lawrences at Villa Mirenda, in the Tuscan Hills near Florence, 1926 (photograph by Arthur Wilkinson)

on 4 August forced them to remain in England until 1919 under especially harrowing conditions, trapped not so much by the war as by a complex of war paranoia and bureaucratic regulations. In November 1914 *The Prussian Officer and Other Stories* was published. Lawrence had at first called the title story "Honour and Arms," an ironic reference to the military mind. The editorial decision to change the title to "The Prussian Officer" made the story specifically anti-German in the context of the war hysteria.

When *The Rainbow* was published at the end of September 1915, it received almost universally hostile reviews. The novel was called "vicious," "obscene," and "pornographic." Within three weeks the book was seized by the police. At the trial the publishers apologized for having published the book, and the magistrate ordered all copies destroyed. The central character's antiwar sentiments probably contributed to the antagonism toward the book. The rest of the war years were no better for Lawrence, who was rejected for military service for health reasons but was called up for medical examinations on at least three occasions. During that time Lawrence worked on *Women in Love* and several short works, including the essays collected in *Studies in Classic American Literature* (1923).

In 1919 the Lawrences left England for good, except for brief visits, escaping from a world that had become intolerable to him. Lawrence was briefly at Florence, Rome, and Capri (which he characterized as "a stewpot of semi-literary cats") before he crossed to Sicily, where he rented the upper story of a farmhouse in Taormina. Frieda joined him there and they went briefly to Malta, where

Lawrence worked on *Aaron's Rod* (1922) and *The Lost Girl* (1920). Frieda then went to Germany while Lawrence returned to Italy, staying in San Gervasio, near Florence. They met again later in Florence, and in January 1921 they went on a ten-day visit to Sardinia. Less than two months later Lawrence finished writing *Sea and Sardinia* (1921), which he claimed to do from memory without any notes. As in his earlier travel book, he was able to capture the "spirit of place," even of those he visited only briefly.

Sea and Sardinia (1921) is an account of the Lawrences' journey and a characterization of the people and places they saw, into which Lawrence sometimes injected philosophical and social judgments based on his observations of people. The book also gives a delightful characterization of Lawrence as narrator-character, and of Frieda, who is referred to as "queen-bee" (one of Lawrence's nicknames for her), or simply as "q-b." The book is divided into eight chapters, which, unlike the essays in *Twilight in Italy*, constitute a continuous narrative. "As Far as Palermo," the prologue in Sicily, is followed by "The Sea," "Cagliari," "Mandas," "To Sogorno," "To Nuoro," "To Terranova and the Steamer," and finally "Back." Two chapters were first published in *The Dial:* "As Far as Palermo" (October 1921) and "Cagliari" (November 1921). The book begins with the comment, "Comes over one an absolute necessity to move. And what is more, to move in some particular direction. A double necessity then: to get on the move, and to know whither." After describing Sicily's attractions, the opening chapter catalogues the possible directions one might go from there, finally settling on "Sardinia, which is like nowhere." The nothingness of Sardinia attracted Lawrence.

Sea and Sardinia is a much darker book than *Twilight in Italy*, owing in part to the cold weather, the poor accommodations, the frequently disgusting food, and the often unfriendly people. Lawrence was also more knowledgeable about the world, no longer an innocent on his first trip abroad but the bitter survivor who saw around him everywhere the effects of the war so recently past. He needed to move on, but the places to which he moved, including Sardinia, were mostly disappointing. There are, however, touches of humor and even momentary joy in this book, and Lawrence created a self that is more various in mood and temperament than the one he crafted in *Twilight in Italy:* more crabby, more delighted, more self-satirizing.

Lawrence portrayed himself as an English eccentric traveling not with a suitcase but with a knapsack, while q-b carried the "kitchenino," a sack that contains food, drink, a spirit stove for making their tea, and a thermos flask. They were up at half past one on a January night preparing breakfast and filling the kitchenino. "Why does one create such discomfort for oneself!" Lawrence mused. "'It's fun,' she says, shuddering. 'Great,' say I, grim as death." This passage sets the tone for what is to follow. The crossing is described in detail, including the beauty of the sea, the general unpleasantness of the passengers, and the rapaciousness of the crew–whose food, Lawrence discovered, was infinitely better than what was served to the passengers. There is also an encounter with a Sicilian military veteran who resents Italy's former allies the English because of their wealth and admires Italy's former enemies the Germans. Lawrence was disgusted that "to an Italian I am a perfected abstraction, England–coal–exchange. The Germans were once devils for inhuman theoretic abstracting of human beings. But now the Italians beat them." Lawrence wanted to be seen as an individual, and in his portrayal of people he tried to show them as individuals, but even he could not escape such abstractions as "Italian." In the course of their brief journey the anti-English (and generally antiforeigner) theme was repeated, something absent in *Twilight in Italy*. The war had changed people, including Lawrence.

A focus of Lawrence's description of Cagliari is a children's ball, a carnival at which children were dressed in costumes of the eighteenth century, "the last bright reality" for Cagliari. The children attracted Lawrence's attention; the poor were barefoot urchins, "gay and wild in the narrow dark streets," while the well-to-do "promenade with Papa and Mama with such alert assurance." He also wrote about the cathedral, in which "St. Joseph must be a prime saint," his altar bearing an inscription invoking him as "true potential father of Our Lord." "What can it profit a man," Lawrence wondered, "to be the potential father of anybody! For the rest I am not Baedeker."

Perhaps he was not Baedeker, but he was a meticulous describer of the people, the livestock, the markets, including the prices of all sorts of commodities. As for the livestock, Sardinia had been denuded of its flocks of donkeys and cattle, not so much by the war as by "the wanton, imbecile, foul lavishness of the war-masters. . . . It was the deliberate evil wastefulness of the war-makers in their own countries. Italy ruined Italy." This observation is echoed in *Lady Chatterley's Lover* (1928), in which Lawrence described the destruction of centuries-old oak forests on the Chatterley estate to make trench-props in France. England ruined England.

From Cagliari they traveled by train in third-class coach. The land through which they traveled

Lawrence in the Tuscan Hills near Villa Mirenda, circa 1926–1927

seemed like Cornwall. The traditional peasant clothing had all but vanished; instead everyone including children wore Italian khaki left over from the war. The dominant images are of dirt, poverty, hunger, lack of sanitation, bad food, poor roads and railways (compared to those of mainland Italy), and the suspicion of strangers. Old ways were disappearing, though some of the worst of the old remained. The travelers finally arrived at Terranova (Olbia), where they boarded a steamer to Italy. It was "quite a small ship" and sexually segregated. Lawrence had to share a cabin with three other men; Frieda shared another with three women. All the cabins were inside without portholes or any ventilation. Other passengers included a contingent of soldiers who set up tents on deck and shared the food they had brought with them–fowl, legs of lamb, kid, bread, and wine. "We envy them their good food." The Lawrences arrived in Cività Vecchia (Civitavecchia) after a night passed in "inside cabin airlessness." The last chapter, "Back," takes them from Civitavecchia by train to Rome and then, after a few hurried words with the friends who were to meet them, by train to Naples and on an extraordinarily luxurious ship to Palermo and "home," completing their circular journey.

A need to travel soon took Lawrence away from Italy altogether, partly because of the changes he saw taking place, including the spread of Fascism. In 1922 he thought of going to America at the invitation of Mabel Dodge but was enticed by other American friends, Earl and Achsah Brewster, to travel eastward to visit them in Ceylon. At first Ceylon pleased him, but in six weeks, oppressed by the heat and ill, he and Frieda left for Australia, where they spent three months. There Lawrence was able to gather material for and write a draft of his novel *Kangaroo* (1923), which also drew on his experience in England during the war and on what he saw of Fascism before he left Italy. From Australia the Lawrences traveled by way of New Zealand, the Cook Islands, and Tahiti to San Francisco. By 11 September 1922, Lawrence's thirty-seventh birthday, they were in Taos, New Mexico, visiting Dodge and her future fourth husband, Tony Luhan. Thus Lawrence finally arrived in America by traveling eastward around the world.

On 14 September, Luhan took Lawrence on a trip to an Apache reservation, about which he wrote, "It is all an experience. But one's heart is never touched at all–neither by landscape, Indians or Americans. Perhaps it is better so. Time, I suppose, that one left off feeling, and merely began to register.–Here I register." He kept busy writing stories and poems, reading, and gathering impressions. He revised *Kangaroo,* traveled to Mexico, and began work on the novel "Quetzalcoatl," which was eventually published as *The Plumed Serpent* (1926). Lawrence spent almost three years in America, mainly in New Mexico and Mexico, with two interim visits to Europe. His last sojourn in America ended in September 1925, when he was forty years old.

Lawrence's literary production during this period was extensive. Among his works were many periodical publications, several of which were later collected in *Mornings in Mexico* (1927), his third volume of travel essays. Unlike *Sea and Sardinia, Mornings in Mexico* is not a continuous narrative. The collection resembles *Twilight in Italy* in that the essays are loosely connected by geography and there is a core group of related essays. *Mornings in Mexico* (1927) is about selected experiences in Mexico and the American Southwest in the way that *Twilight in Italy* is about selected experiences in Italy and Switzerland. In both books Lawrence commented on the philosophical and religious life of the people.

Mornings in Mexico was put together by Lawrence's English publisher Martin Secker. Lawrence devised the title not for this volume but for a group of interconnected essays that are the first four pieces in the collection: "Corasmin and the Parrots" was originally published as "Friday Morning" in the December 1925 issue of *The Adelphi*; "Walk to Huayapa" (originally "Sunday Morning") was published in the November 1925 issue of *Travel* as "Sunday Stroll in Sleepy Mexico" and in the March 1927 issue of *The Adelphi* as "Mornings in Mexico, Walk to Hayapa"; "The Mozo" (originally "Monday Morning") was published in the February 1927 issue of *The Adelphi* as "Mornings in Mexico, the Mozo" and in the 1 April 1927 issue of *Living Age* as "Sons of Montezuma"; "Market Day" (originally "Saturday Morning") was published as "The Gentle Art of Marketing" in the April 1926 issue of *Travel* and as "Mornings in Mexico, Saturday" in the June 1926 issue of *The New Criterion.* The next three essays–"Indians and Entertainment" (first published in the 26 October 1924 issue of *The New York Times Magazine*), "The Dance of the Sprouting Corn" (*Theatre Arts Monthly,* July 1924), and "The Hopi Snake Dance" (*Theatre Arts Monthly,* December 1924)–portray Indian festivals of New Mexico and Arizona that Lawrence witnessed at various times, with his philosophical comments on their mystical and religious significance. The eighth essay, "A Little Moonshine with Lemon" (first published in *Laughing Horse,* April 1926), is an epilogue set in Italy. Only half of the essays have to do with Mexico. They all portray the people, places, and customs of Lawrence's aboriginal America. As a whole *Mornings in Mexico* is the least satisfactory of Lawrence's travel books. Lawrence at first objected to the collection but consented after Secker convinced him that he would not have to write anything new for the book. By the time Secker began to assemble the book, Lawrence was engaged in other projects, and Mexico was part of a receding past for him.

During his last years Lawrence was involved in continuing controversy. He began the story that was to become *Lady Chatterley's Lover* after a short visit to England in 1925. While staying in Ravello, Italy, with his friends the Brewsters, he wrote a second version of that story as well as some essays about the Tuscan countryside, and he visited the nearby Etruscan tombs. He rewrote *Lady Chatterley's Lover* again, finishing it by January 1928. At this time he considered calling the novel "Tenderness." His articles about his visits to the Etruscan tombs were published in *Travel* from November 1927 through February 1928 and were not brought together as the book *Etruscan Places* (1932) until after his death. Like his other travel pieces it combines an account of his physical experiences in visiting particular places, his reading, and his extracting from his experiences and his reading the feelings he has about the places.

In April 1926 Lawrence first mentioned in letters to several people the possibility of a travel book on Umbria and the Etruscans. In May he mentioned that he was reading Theodor Mommsen's *The History of Rome* (1854–1885), which was hostile to the Etruscans; Fritz Weege's *Etruskische Malerei* (Etruscan Painters, 1851), mainly for its illustrations; and

Pericle Ducati's *Etruria Antica* (1925). In June he read Roland Fell's *Etruria and Rome* (1925), but he found it difficult to discover many facts about the Etruscans. Thus when he wrote *Etruscan Places* Lawrence depended largely on his own impressions–the feelings that he derived from seeing the tombs. In an earlier letter about his attraction to Italy he had written, "We can go wrong in our minds. But what our blood feels and believes and says, is always true." Though he had found little about the Etruscans in the history books, he was able to see in their tombs evidence that they followed a "great religion" similar to his own.

Etruscan Places describes the tour of Etruria that Lawrence took on 6–11 April 1927 with Earl Brewster, who is referred to in the book as "B." Brewster's *D. H. Lawrence: Letters and Reminiscences* (1934) gives a detailed account of the trip from his perspective. One chapter of *Etruscan Places* is devoted to Cerveteri, the first place they visited, and Tarquinia is covered in another whole chapter, while two more are devoted to "The Painted Tombs of Tarquinia." Vulci and Volterra each get one chapter. By 29 April, Lawrence had begun writing his "Travel Sketches of Etruscan Places." In July, Lawrence wrote to Secker that he planned a further Etruscan tour to complete a book, but this trip never took place.

The book begins with a sarcastic attack on the Romans: "The Etruscans, as everyone knows, were the people who occupied the middle of Italy in early Roman days, and whom the Romans, in their usual neighbourly fashion, wiped out entirely to make room for Rome with a very big R." Since the Romans destroyed the living culture, "we know nothing about the Etruscans except what we find in their tombs." There are references to them in Latin writers, but the tombs do in fact provide the only first-hand information about them. Lawrence combined a conversational account of his experience with the few facts derived from what he read in histories of the Greeks and Romans and what he saw in museums.

Lawrence opposed the views he found in the books he had read, which generally approach the Etruscans from a Roman perspective. Frequently *Etruscan Places* draws parallels between the Romans and the modern Fascists, who had adopted the Roman salute. When some girls on the street in Volterra greeted Lawrence and Brewster with this salute, he felt that "in an Etruscan city which held out so long against Rome I consider the Roman salute unbecoming, and the Roman *imperium* unmentionable." He distrusted museums because they remove artifacts from their natural setting. Yet he was attracted to the Etruscan things he first saw in the museum at Perugia, and he was strongly drawn to what he saw in the museum in Volterra: "with all those hundreds of little sarcophagi, ash-coffins, or urns, as they are called, the strength of the old life begins to warm one up." Still, Lawrence did not quite like museums.

What struck Lawrence most about the artifacts in the tombs that have survived, especially the paintings depicting the drinking and dining of the dead, was their joyousness. While the mourners feast outside the tomb, the dead feast in a similar, perhaps better, place beyond. The theme of resurrection is a constant in the tomb paintings, and even slaves are apparently guaranteed life after death. Lawrence commented, "It is a relief to think that even the slaves–and the luxurious Etruscans had many in historical times–had their remains decently stored in jars and laid in a sacred place." Apparently the "vicious Etruscans" "had nothing comparable to the vast dead-pits which lay outside Rome, beside the great highway, in which the bodies of slaves were promiscuously slung." Throughout the book the Romans represent "brute force" while the Etruscans are characterized by their "delicate sensitiveness."

Published more than two years after Lawrence's death in March 1930, *Etruscan Places* is a fitting last travel book for Lawrence. If *Twilight in Italy* reflects Lawrence's fresh experiences while traveling in Italy for the first time, *Etruscan Places* rounds out his view of the past and present and summarizes his philosophy of life. At the time he wrote the pieces in the book his health was rapidly deteriorating and he was deep in controversies concerning an exhibit of his paintings in London and the difficulties associated with the publication of *Lady Chatterley's Lover*. His travel books are in no way among his major works, and they deal with only a few of his experiences in Italy and America. Most of what he had to say about travel appears in the immense body of his letters, published in seven volumes by Cambridge University Press (1979–1993). Lawrence's travel books show Lawrence in a more casual, less structured mode than in his novels, stories, and poems.

Letters:

The Letters of D. H. Lawrence, edited by Aldous Huxley (London: Heinemann, 1929);

The Collected Letters of D. H. Lawrence, 2 volumes, edited by Harry T. Moore (London: Heinemann, 1962);

The Cambridge Edition of the Letters of D. H. Lawrence, 7 volumes (Cambridge: Cambridge University Press, 1979–1993)–volume 1: September 1901–May 1913, edited by James T. Boulton; volume 2: June 1913–October 1916, edited by George J. Zytaruk and Boulton; volume 3: October 1916–June 1921, edited by Boulton and Andrew Robertson; volume 4: June 1921–March 1924, edited by Warren Roberts, Boulton, and Elizabeth Mansfield; volume 5: March 1924–March 1927, edited by Boulton and Lindeth Vasey; volume 6: March 1927–November 1928, edited by Boulton and Margaret Boulton with Gerald M. Lacy; volume 7: November 1928–February 1930, edited by Keith Sagar and Boulton;

The Selected Letters of D. H. Lawrence, edited by Boulton (Cambridge: Cambridge University Press, 1997).

Bibliographies:

Edward D. McDonald, *A Bibliography of the Writings of D. H. Lawrence* (Philadelphia: Centaur Book Shop, 1925);

John E. Stoll, *D. H. Lawrence: A Bibliography, 1911–1975* (Troy, N.Y.: Whitston, 1977);

Warren Roberts, *A Bibliography of D. H. Lawrence,* revised edition (London: Hart-Davis, 1982);

James C. Cowan, *D. H. Lawrence: An Annotated Bibliography of Writings about Him,* 2 volumes (De Kalb: Northern Illinois University Press, 1985);

Michael Squires, *D. H. Lawrence's Manuscripts* (New York: St. Martin's Press, 1991).

Biographies:

Keith Sagar, *The Life of D. H. Lawrence* (New York: Pantheon, 1980);

Harry T. Moore and Warren Roberts, *D. H. Lawrence* (New York: Thames & Hudson, 1988);

Jeffrey Meyers, *D. H. Lawrence: A Biography* (New York: Knopf, 1990).

References:

Earl Brewster, *D. H. Lawrence: Letters and Reminiscences* (London: Secker, 1934);

David Cavitch, *D. H. Lawrence and the New World* (New York: Oxford University Press, 1969);

L. D. Clark, *The Minoan Distance: The Symbolism of Travel in the Works of D. H. Lawrence* (Tucson: University of Arizona Press, 1980);

Paul Fussell, *Abroad: British Literary Traveling between the Wars* (New York: Oxford University Press, 1980);

Jeffrey Meyers, *D. H. Lawrence and the Experience of Italy* (Philadelphia: University of Pennsylvania Press, 1982);

Peter Preston, *A D. H. Lawrence Chronology* (New York: St. Martin's Press, 1994);

Keith Sagar, *D. H. Lawrence: A Calendar of His Works* (Austin: University of Texas Press, 1979).

Papers:

The extant manuscripts of Lawrence's works are widely scattered among libraries in the United States and Great Britain and private owners. The Harry Ransom Humanities Research Center at the University of Texas at Austin has corrected page proofs for *Twilight in Italy;* manuscripts for "The Spinner and the Monks," "By the Lago di Garda," and other fragments; a corrected typescript for *Sea and Sardinia;* a manuscript titled "Diary of a trip to Sardinia"; a manuscript and a corrected carbon typescript for "The Mozo"; a corrected typescript for "The Hopi Snake Dance"; and a corrected typescript for *Etruscan Places.* The University of California at Berkeley has a manuscript and a typescript for "Indians and Entertainment," as well as a one-page manuscript of notes for *Etruscan Places.*

T. E. Lawrence

(16 August 1888 - 19 May 1935)

Khani Begum
Bowling Green State University

BOOKS: *The Wilderness of Zin,* by Lawrence and Leonard Woolley (London: Palestine Exploration Fund, 1915; New York: Scribners, 1936);

Seven Pillars of Wisdom (8 copies, Oxford: Privately printed by the *Oxford Times,* 1922; revised edition, London: Privately printed by Manning Pike & H. J. Hodgson, 1926; New York: Doran, 1926; trade edition, London: Cape, 1935; Garden City, N.Y.: Doubleday, Doran, 1935); abridged as *Revolt in the Desert* (London: Cape, 1927; New York: Doran, 1927);

The Mint: A Day Book of the RAF Depot between August and December 1922, and at Cadet College in 1925, as 352087 A/c Ross (Garden City, N.Y.: Doubleday, Doran, 1936; revised edition, London: Cape, 1955; Garden City, N.Y.: Doubleday, 1955);

Crusader Castles, I: The Thesis (London: Golden Cockerel Press, 1936);

Crusader Castles, II: The Letters (London: Golden Cockerel Press, 1936; Garden City, N.Y.: Doubleday, Doran, 1937);

An Essay on Flecker (London: Corvinus Press; Garden City, N.Y.: Doubleday, Doran, 1937);

The Diary of T. E. Lawrence, MCMXI (London: Corvinus Press, 1937);

T. E. Lawrence to His Biographers Robert Graves and Liddell Hart: Information about Himself in the Form of Letters, Notes, Answers to Questions, and Conversations (London: Cassell, 1938);

Oriental Assembly, edited by A. W. Lawrence (London: Williams & Norgate, 1939; New York: Dutton, 1940);

Secret Despatches from Arabia, edited by A. W. Lawrence (London: Golden Cockerel Press, 1939);

Men in Print: Essays in Literary Criticism, edited by A. W. Lawrence (London: Golden Cockerel Press, 1940);

T. E. Lawrence

The Essential T. E. Lawrence, edited by David Garnett (London: Cape, 1951; New York: Dutton, 1951);

Evolution of a Revolt: Early Postwar Writings of T. E. Lawrence, edited by Stanley and Rodelle Weintraub (University Park & London: Pennsylvania University Press, 1968);

Lawrence of Arabia, Strange Man of Letters: The Literary Criticism and Correspondence of T. E. Lawrence, edited by Harold Orlans (Rutherford, N.J.: Fairleigh Dickinson University Press / London & Cranbury, N.J.: Associated University Presses, 1993).

OTHER: *Carchemish: Report on the Excavations at Djerabis on Behalf of the British Museum,* 3 volumes, includes contributions by Lawrence (London: British Museum, 1914–1952);
Charles M. Doughty, *Travels in Arabia Deserta,* introduction by Lawrence (2 volumes, London & Boston: Warner & Cape, 1921; new, definitive edition, 1 volume, London: Cape/Medici Society, 1926);
Richard Garnett, *The Twilight of the Gods and Other Tales,* introduction by Lawrence (London: Bodley Head, 1924);
Adrien Le Corbeau, *The Forest Giant,* translated by Lawrence, as L. H. Ross (London: Cape, 1924; New York: Harper, 1924; augmented edition, London: Cape, 1935; Garden City, N.Y.: Doubleday, Doran, 1936);
Catalogue of an Exhibition of Paintings, Pastels, Drawings, and Woodcuts Illustrating Col. T. E. Lawrence's Book 'Seven Pillars of Wisdom,' prefaces by Lawrence and Bernard Shaw (London: Leicester Galleries, 1927);
The Odyssey of Homer, translated by Lawrence, as T. E. Shaw (London: Printed and published by Sir Emery Walker, Wilfred Merton & Bruce Rogers, 1932; New York: Oxford University Press, 1932);
Bertram Thomas, *Arabia Felix: Across the Empty Quarter of Arabia,* foreword by Lawrence (London: Cape, 1932);
Simon Jesty, *River Niger,* prefatory letter by Lawrence (London: Boriswood, 1935);
Minorities, collected by Lawrence, edited by J. M. Wilson (London: Cape, 1971; Garden City, N.Y.: Doubleday, 1972).

SELECTED PERIODICAL PUBLICATIONS–UNCOLLECTED: "Release of Damascus," *Palestine News* (Cairo), 10 October 1918, p. 6;
"The Arab March on Damascus," *Times* (London), 17 October 1918, p. 5;
"Campaign of the Caliphs for Damascus: Story of the Desert Fighting from Mecca to Damascus under the King of the Hedjaz," *Current History,* 9 (February 1919): 348–357;
"Four Pledges to the Arabs," *Times* (London), 11 September 1919, p. 11;
"The War of the Departments," *Daily Express* (London), 29 May 1920, p. 4;
"The Middle East. How We Are Losing Prestige, Vacillating Policy," *Sunday Times* (London), 30 May 1920, p. 11;
"To the Editors," *Times* (London), 22 July 1920;
"Arab Rights: Our Policy in Mesopotamia," *Times* (London), 23 July 1920, p. 15;
"France, Britain and the Arabs," *Observer* (London), 8 August 1920;
"Ferment for Freedom," *Daily Herald* (London), 9 August 1920, p. 2;
"With Feisal at Court and Afield: 1. Adventures in Arabia with the Prince of the Hedjaz and the Desert Tribes," *World's Work,* 42 (July 1921): 277–288;
"Arabian Nights and Days: A Second Chapter from the Hitherto Unpublished Personal Record of the Arabian Revolt and Conflicts with the Turk," *World's Work,* 42 (August 1921): 381–386;
"Arabian Nights and Days: 3. A Camel Charge and Other Adventures in the Desert," *World's Work,* 42 (September 1921): 516–520;
"Adventures in Arabia's Deliverance: The Turkish Army Passes," *World's Work,* 42 (October 1921): 617–621;
"Massacre: Being a Chapter from the History of the Arab Revolt," *Winter Owl,* 3 (1923): 5–13;
"Col. T. E. Lawrence Tired of Beastly Arabian Affairs," *Daily News* (London), 29 October 1923;
"Mixed Biscuits," as C.D. (Colin Dale), *Spectator* (London), 20 August 1927, pp. 290–291;
"Hakluyt–First Naval Propagandist," as C.D. (Colin Dale), *Spectator* (London), 10 September 1927, pp. 390–391;
"Among the Bedouins," *Empire News* (Manchester), 9 June 1935, p. 7.

Widely known as "Lawrence of Arabia," T. E. Lawrence is best known for *Seven Pillars of Wisdom* (1922), an account of the successful Arab revolt that he led against the Turks in 1917–1918. He also wrote several other books, reports, and newspaper articles, both under the name T. E. Lawrence and under various other names, including John Hume Ross and T. E. Shaw. While his government reports and personal accounts of expeditions might not be taken as travel literature by some casual readers of the genre, they are incisive, sympathetic explorations of culture and geography that throw as much light on the complexities of the Arab world as they do on the European mind and politics of the time.

Thomas Edward Lawrence was born at Tremadoc, in Caernarvonshire, Wales, on 16 August 1888. He was the illegitimate son of Sir Thomas Chapman, who had left his wife and legitimate children in 1885 for their governess, Sarah Junner (who also used the name Sarah Lawrence). Chapman took Lawrence as his last name, and the two lived together as husband and wife, eventually having five sons, of whom T. E. Lawrence was the second.

Lawrence and Leonard Woolley at Carchemish, 1913

Lawrence did not learn his father's true identity until 1919.

The family lived briefly in Wales; Scotland; Dinard, Brittany; and elsewhere before moving to a house on the edge of New Forest, in southern England, in 1894. In 1896 they settled in Oxford, where Lawrence attended Oxford City High School from September 1896 until July 1907. Even at a young age Lawrence was interested in travel and other cultures and spent the summers of 1906, 1907, and 1908 studying medieval castles in northern France.

Lawrence attended Jesus College at Oxford from 1907 to 1910, achieving his degree with first-class honors in modern history. To research his thesis on medieval architecture Lawrence traveled in the Middle East during the summer of 1909, mostly in Syria. His first substantial piece of writing analyzed castles he had visited in Europe and the Middle East and included 127 photographs and drawings. His argument that the Syrian castles were modeled on those in Europe contradicted the current view on the subject. Oxford University Press would have published the thesis in 1910 if Lawrence had been willing to cut some of the expensive illustrations, but Lawrence, who was often critical of his own writing, felt that the thesis was "an elementary performance" and "Not worth printing." After his death the thesis was published as *Crusader Castles* (1936).

In 1910 Dr. David George Hogarth invited Lawrence to join him as an assistant at the archaeological excavation of the ancient Hittite city of Carchemish on the west bank of the Euphrates River, near the border between Turkey and Syria. Lawrence's expenses were covered by a senior demyship (or research fellowship) from Magdalen College, Oxford, which ran from December 1910 until summer 1914. While working at these archaeological excavations and traveling in the region he learned to live like an Arab.

Early in 1914 the Palestine Exploration Fund sent Lawrence and another archaeologist at Carchemish, Leonard Woolley, to survey the Sinai, then under Turkish rule. Their report, *The Wilderness of Zin* (1915), was the first published work bearing Lawrence's name. As with much of his writing, Lawrence was critical of this book. Yet his reports and other government writings are forceful and incisive, revealing his genius for identifying technical and political courses of action. His reports were written rapidly with little revision while he sometimes worked and reworked his literary writings over several years.

Lawrence wanted to be a great writer and more than once felt that he had failed and would write no more. He saw writing as a craft and worked on perfecting his sentences and paragraphs. Often his creative impulse and his desire for technical control were in conflict. Francis Yeats-Brown, the literary editor of *The Spectator,* called Lawrence's prose "the standard of modern descriptive English" and George Bernard Shaw called Lawrence "one of the greatest descriptive writers in English literature."

After the outbreak of World War I, Lawrence, who was at Oxford completing work on *The Wilderness of Zin,* was commissioned an officer in the British Army, and in late 1914 he arrived in Cairo to serve as an intelligence officer. In April and May 1916, while still posted there, he was on special duty to Mesopotamia (now Iraq), where he assessed the potential for an Arab revolt against the Turks in that region. In October 1916 he met Faisal, a leader of the rebellion and the future king of Iraq (1921–1933). By December, Lawrence had become officially attached to the staff of the expeditionary force sent to the Hejaz to support the Arab rebels and temporarily served as a liaison to Faisal. In 1917, after the success of the Hejaz campaign, Lawrence was promoted to major and permanently assigned to serve with Faisal's troops. He participated in the successful expeditions at Aqaba in May–July 1917 and at Dar'a in November 1917 (where he experienced a homosexual rape, which left him with an abhorrence of any sort of physical contact). He was present at the official entry into Jerusalem in December 1917 as well as at the Arab victory in the battle of Tafila in January 1918. In March, soon after his transfer to General Edmund Allenby's staff, Lawrence was promoted to lieutenant colonel. After the capture of Damascus in October 1918, Lawrence returned to England, where he addressed the Eastern Committee of the War Cabinet and then left for Paris, where he served as a member of Faisal's delegation to the Paris Peace Conference from January through September 1919. In Paris, Lawrence began the first draft of *Seven Pillars of Wisdom.*

Lawrence originally planned to use this title for an earlier book that he was working on in 1913 and probably never completed, a travel book on seven eastern cities–Cairo, Smyrna (Izmir), Constantinople (Istanbul), Beyrouth (Beirut), Aleppo, Damascus, and Medina. He later claimed that he had burned this book, retaining only the title, *Seven Pillars of Wisdom,* for his book about the war. In a 1923 letter to Robert Buxton he explained that this title comes from Proverbs 9:1: "Wisdom hath built a house: she hath hewn out her seven pillars."

Even before *Seven Pillars of Wisdom* was published, American journalist Lowell Thomas was giving lectures and slide shows that were making Lawrence widely known in Europe and America. His fame gained momentum because of the romantic picture the desert war presented, especially in contrast to the trench warfare in Europe. As a result Lawrence, who did not want this publicity, began to receive unwelcome invitations to social functions and public events. By the end of 1919 he had almost finished a draft of *Seven Pillars of Wisdom,* only to lose the sole copy–along with most of his notes for the final chapters, photographs, and negatives–in a train station. He was persuaded to rewrite the book from memory, and by mid 1920 he had completed a new version of the book with the help of his surviving notes and his copies of the *Arab Bulletin* that included his war reports, later collected in *Secret Despatches from Arabia* (1939).

Seven Pillars of Wisdom focuses on two years of desert war, October 1916 to October 1918, and expresses Lawrence's belief that the Arabs had been betrayed by British and French plans to divide the Middle East into mandates under their influence rather than granting the Arabs the outright self-rule promised them during the war. He tried hard to make the document historically accurate. Referring to himself in the third person, he wrote to his friend and biographer Robert Graves in 1927: "He founded his strategy on an exhaustive study of the geography of his area; of the Turkish Army; of the nature of the Beduins, and the distribution of their tribe-masses. So he founded his desert tactics on the raiding parties of the Arabs." Despite his concerted effort to be historically accurate, *Seven Pillars of Wisdom* reflects his concern about French ambitions in Syria and takes on a political role, seeking to support Faisal's claims to self-government and to win sympathy for the Arabs. Official documents show that Lawrence glossed over some politically damaging information, and the whole truth is not revealed. He downplayed the role of non-Arab personnel and emphasized the Arab achievement in the revolt. While redrafting *Seven Pillars of Wisdom* Lawrence became involved in the ongoing Middle East negotiations at the Paris Peace Conference and in writing articles to support the Arab cause. Meanwhile, having bought some land, he needed money.

In October 1920 he wrote an introduction to a new edition of Charles Doughty's *Travels in Arabia Deserta* (1921; first published in 1888), an invaluable source of information during the Middle East campaign. In his introduction Lawrence praised Doughty's book as "a necessity to any student of Arabia, . . . one of the greatest prose works in the English language, and the best travel book in the world." Claiming that Doughty had told the "full and exact truth of all that he saw," Lawrence revealed his fascination with Arabia:

> here you have all the desert, its hills and plains, the lava fields, the villages, the tents, the men, the animals. They are told of to the life, with words and phrases fitted to

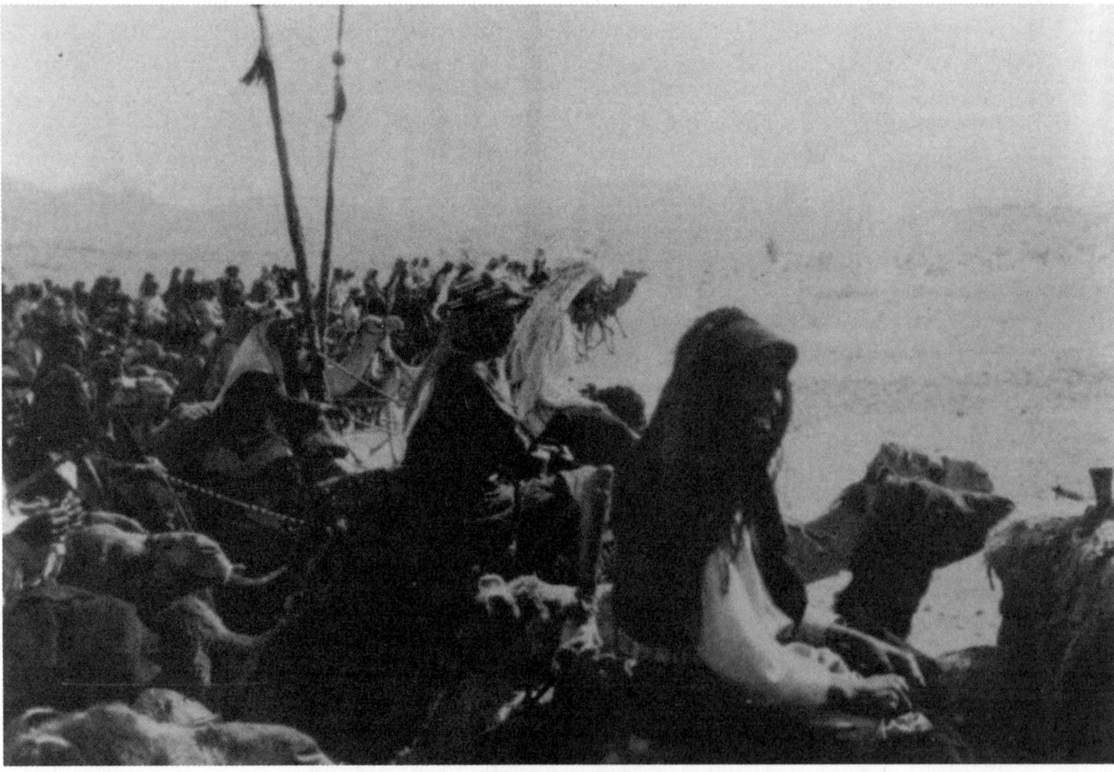

Faisal's camp at dawn and Faisal setting out from Wejh, photographs taken by Lawrence in January 1917

> them so perfectly that one cannot dissociate them in memory. It is the true Arabia, the land with its smells and dirt, as well as its nobility and freedom.

Even though he was occasionally critical of Doughty's work, he appeared to agree with several of Doughty's generalizations regarding Bedouins and Semites and their way of life, commenting, for example, "Semites are black and white not only in vision, but in their inner furnishing; black and white not merely in clarity, but in apposition. Their thoughts live easiest among extremes." Lawrence's introduction also points to the changes in the Arab world since the Hejaz railway and how the Arabia of Doughty had adapted to the resulting political changes.

Toward the end of 1920 Winston Churchill became colonial secretary, and in January 1921 he invited Lawrence to join him as an adviser on Arab affairs. After his disappointment with the Paris Peace Conference, Lawrence had decided not to take a personal role in Arab politics and to concentrate mostly on writing. Churchill, however, brought the reluctant Lawrence back into the diplomatic negotiations with Faisal. Lawrence was sent on several missions to Aden, Jidda (in present-day Saudi Arabia), and Transjordan (Jordan), feeling increasingly disillusioned with British foreign policy toward the Arabs. By the end of 1921, Faisal having become king of Iraq and his brother Abdullah having been established as ruler of Transjordan with both nations under British mandate, Lawrence felt his work had been completed. Early in 1922 he wrote to Sir Hugh Trenchard that politics "wearied me out, by worrying me over-much. I've not got a coarse-fibred enough nature for them: and have too many scruples and an uneasy conscience."

Lawrence's main focus became his ongoing ambition to be a respected writer. He continued revising *Seven Pillars of Wisdom,* and in reliving those wartime experiences he also became depressed, particularly over his sometimes morally ambiguous wartime role with the Arabs. In 1922 he had the *Oxford Times* print eight copies of the completed second draft. He had no strong family relationships or dependents, and, as his popularity with the public grew, he increasingly sought isolation. His desire to hide his identity came from his "itch to make myself ordinary in a mob of likes." Lawrence had often sought to live among those who did not share his advantages and at times confessed to a desire for subservience and self-abasement. Yet he had also manipulated his superiors and gotten what he wanted. By 1922, however, his desire for self-abasement and his recollections of the homosexual rape he had experienced in 1917 at Dar'a had begun to affect his emotional state, bringing him close to a nervous breakdown.

He chose to resign from the Colonial Office in July 1922 and, having decided to write a book about the RAF from the viewpoint of an enlisted man, he signed up as A/c John Hume Ross in September 1922. With the help of the authorities he was able to do so without anyone recognizing his identity. Life in the RAF, especially basic training at Uxbridge, was not what he had expected, but he could not bear to leave. At the same time, however, he seemed to be inviting exposure of his true identity. On 27 December 1922 an article in the *Daily Express* revealed Lawrence's secret, and after some months of uncertainty he was discharged at the end of January 1923. Even though he had been considering leaving the RAF, his pride was wounded, and he appealed for a reinstatement more than once.

In February 1923 the War Office agreed to let Lawrence enlist in the Tank Corps as Private T. E. Shaw, a pseudonym Lawrence selected from the *Army List* index, and he found himself at Bovington Camp in Dorset. Later that year he acquired a cottage at Clouds Hill, near the camp, and continued as a private in the Tank Corps until August 1925, when he was allowed to transfer to the RAF as Aircraftsman Shaw. He remained in the RAF until February 1935.

The *Oxford Times* circulating copies of *Seven Pillars of Wisdom* brought favorable comments from their handful of readers, and during the 1920s Garnett tried to get Lawrence to revise and cut the book for publication. Lawrence meanwhile was spending a lot of literary energy on his letters, many of which include detailed descriptions of his trips and are almost like essays. He did some translations to make money. In autumn 1923 Lawrence agreed to a plan to publish *Seven Pillars of Wisdom* in an expensive subscription edition, which meant cutting the book considerably. In the process of revision Lawrence became aware of problems with his style and was grateful to E. M. Forster for detailed and lengthy comments and suggestions.

Lawrence was suffering from a malaise. Revising *Seven Pillars of Wisdom* and worrying about the additional expenses for reproducing pictures and for a possible American edition did not help his depression. The book remains his major literary effort; yet when it was finished, he felt he had failed. Praise from writers such as Thomas Hardy, George Bernard Shaw, H. G. Wells, and Winston Churchill failed to convince him that the work was not "muck," "longwinded and pretentious, and dull," "perverse," "a stodgy mess of mock-heroic ego-

Arab delegation and advisers at the Paris Peace Conference, January 1919: Faisal is standing in front with Rustum Haidar (Faisal's secretary), Nuri Said, Captaine Pisani of France, Lawrence, and Capt. Hassan Kadri behind him; the man in the background is Faisal's slave.

tism." The British edition comprised some two hundred copies, and twenty-two copies were published in the United States, largely to secure the American copyright.

Though Lawrence's *Seven Pillars of Wisdom* has most frequently been examined as autobiography, Lawrence placed himself and his work in the "great tradition of 'Arabian' writers," a point Stephen Tabachnick supports through citations from the foreword Lawrence wrote to Bertram Thomas's *Arabia Felix* (1932) and from various letters to literary and political figures and to his mother. As a great admirer of Doughty's writing, Lawrence distinguished between Doughty and Thomas, whom he considered a great explorer only. For Lawrence there were the Arabian writer-explorers–Wilfred Blunt, Charles Doughty, and William G. Palgrave; and there were the Arabian explorers–Richard Burton, Bertram Thomas, and St. John Philby. Using the phrase "autobiography of travel" (which Tabachnick borrows from Doughty's biographer David G. Hogarth) to apply to Lawrence is apt. As is true for a select group of travel writers before and after Lawrence, Lawrence sought to combine the life of the man of action, testing himself against the elements and identifying himself with the primitive and the life of the intellectual. He carefully set forth his literary forebears in a tale of a journey as much inwardly alien and tumultuous as outwardly foreign and dangerous. As with much great travel literature, both aspects are worthy of attention, although in Lawrence's case the emphasis has too often fallen on the man.

While interest in Lawrence the man continues, *Seven Pillars of Wisdom* is also discussed for its literary craft. The beauty and precision of the language strikes the reader immediately in the opening paragraph:

> Some of the evil of my tale may have been inherent in our circumstances. For years we lived anyhow with one another in the naked desert, under the indifferent heaven. By day the hot sun fermented us; and we were dizzied by the beating wind. At night we were stained by dew, and shamed into pettiness by the innumerable silences of stars. We were a self-centered army without parade or gesture, devoted to freedom, the second of man's creeds, a purpose so ravenous that it devoured all our strength, a hope so transcendent that our earlier ambitions faded in its glare.

> As the time went by our need to fight for the ideal increased to an unquestioning possession, riding with spur and vein over out doubts. Willy-nilly it became a faith. We had sold ourselves into its slavery, manacled ourselves together in its chain-gang, bowed ourselves to serve its holiness with all our good and ill content. The mentality of ordinary human slaves is terrible–they have lost the world–and we had surrendered, not body alone, but soul to the overmastering greed of victory, by

our own act we were drained of morality, or volition, of responsibility, like dead leaves in the wind.

The veracity of the tale, disputed by some (such as Richard Aldington) who sought to discredit Lawrence, is no longer an issue, and the work is accepted as classic of military history and adventure as well as of travel literature.

While work on the subscription edition was coming to a close, talk of an abridged, trade edition of *Seven Pillars of Wisdom,* which Garnett had been proposing for some time, was revived. Extracts from an earlier, incomplete abridgement that Lawrence had undertaken in 1920 had been published in an American magazine, *The World's Work,* in 1921. Now Lawrence cut the 1926 version to less than half its length, and this abridgement was published in March 1927 as *Revolt in the Desert.* He made over the copyright of *Revolt in the Desert* to a charitable trust.

In late 1926, just as the subscription edition came out in England, the RAF posted Lawrence to India, and in early 1927 the trustees of *Revolt in the Desert* arranged an exhibit of the originals for the illustrations in *Seven Pillars of Wisdom* at the Leicester Galleries. Glad to be away during the publicity surrounding the books, Lawrence considered India an "exile, endured for a specific purpose, to let the book-fuss pass over." Yet India overwhelmed him, and he wrote, "I shall be happy only when they send me home again." On reading reviews sent him by Charlotte Shaw, the wife of George Bernard Shaw, Lawrence responded with puzzlement at the superlative praise and the comparisons of his style to Doughty's.

Wanting to exploit the public interest in Lawrence's life after the enthusiastic reception of *Revolt in the Desert,* the publisher of that book, Jonathan Cape, proposed a biography of Lawrence. Lawrence agreed reluctantly, in part because he wanted to preempt an unauthorized version that Thomas planned to publish. Feeling that his friend Robert Graves was a suitable choice, Lawrence sent him detailed notes and letters from his post in Karachi (now in Pakistan). Lawrence also gave Graves permission to contact his friends and associates, including Charlotte Shaw, a good friend and frequent correspondent. Offended that Lawrence had asked her to make his letters available to Graves, she was not cooperative. Graves's work was also hampered by publisher's deadlines and by the fact that Lawrence's copious notes rarely revealed anything personal. When the book was completed, Lawrence expressed his disappointment, especially with Graves's fairly extensive use of material from *Revolt in the Desert.* He wrote to Graves, "I had hoped to find someone who would retell the story of the Arab Revolt from the available eye-witness, leaving the 'I' of *Revolt in the Desert* out of it: whereas you only turned the first person to third person."

While in Karachi, Lawrence worked on *The Mint* (1936), his book about the RAF, completing it in spring 1928. By this time Lawrence had settled into life in Karachi and was relatively happy, but after hearing a rumor that an officer was "laying to jump on me," he requested a transfer to another post. He was sent to Peshawar in late May, and after two days was moved to Miranshah, on the Afghan border. There Lawrence began work on a translation of *The Odyssey* that he had been commissioned to undertake for a special edition of the work designed by American typographer Bruce Rogers. On 26 September the London *Evening News* reported that Lawrence was on a secret mission to counter Soviet covert activities in the Punjab. This report was followed by more absurd reports claiming that Lawrence was "in Amritsar, posing as a Mohammedan saint, and investigating Communist activities" (*Sunday Express,* 28 September 1928). After much discussion the India Office and the Foreign Office decided to ignore these allegations. Lawrence remained unaware of the trouble.

In December more rumors about Lawrence appeared in the press, including the claim that Lawrence intended to go to Afghanistan and take part in the Afghan revolt. In January 1929, because of anxiety expressed by the India Office over the rumors and because of Lawrence's actual presence so near the border of Afghanistan, Lawrence was flown to Lahore, where he chose to return home after denying all the allegations.

On his return to England he was besieged by the press because rumors about his alleged involvement as a spy were still running rampant. A group of friends gave him a motorcycle, and he started to work as a clerk at an RAF station in Plymouth. Eventually he was involved in testing and working on new designs of marine craft. The press continued to hound him, and in late 1929 Cape suggested that a military historian, Capt. Basil Henry Liddell Hart, write another biography of Lawrence. Liddell Hart was more thorough than Graves in pursuing Lawrence for information and in obtaining access to relevant military documents. After reading drafts of Liddell Hart's military chapters Lawrence responded:

I was not an instinctive soldier, automatic with intuitions and happy ideas. When I took a decision, or adopted an alternative it was after studying every relevant–and many an irrelevant–factor. Geography, tribal

Lawrence during his final years in the Royal Air Force

structure, religion, social customs, language, appetites, standards–all were at my finger-ends. The enemy I knew almost like my own side. I risked myself among them a hundred times, to *learn*.

Despite his praise for Liddell Hart's military analysis, Lawrence said the book "is heavy, and contains little criticism." More publicity followed the publication of this biography in 1934, including questions about Lawrence's real name. Lawrence was also disturbed by publicity in April 1934, when there was talk of making a movie version of *Revolt in the Desert.*

By August 1931 the effects of the worldwide economic depression resulted in a 10 percent decrease in RAF pay. Lawrence had chosen to live on his salary and found it hard to make ends meet. In 1933 he decided to request an early discharge, which was granted on 6 April. With money from his translation of *The Odyssey* to meet his immediate financial needs, he settled in his cottage at Clouds Hill. On 19 April, however, the Air Ministry called him back and offered him a post at the RAF Marine Aircraft Establishment at Felixstowe. By the end of the month Lawrence was back in the RAF, and within weeks he was sent to Manchester and then traveled frequently to various boatyards. He began making improvements on the cottage at Clouds Hill, where he planned to spend his retirement in February 1935. Since news of his retirement had leaked out before the actual date, it became a news event, and he was met by a throng of journalists and photographers at Clouds Hill.

Lawrence intended to continue writing and to travel around England during the summers. Though he heard that he might be offered work for the government, he remained determined to stay at Clouds Hill. On 13 May, while driving home from the post office, he swerved to avoid two boys on bicycles and was thrown from his motorcycle. He died on 19 May without regaining consciousness and was buried at Moreton, Dorset, on 25 May 1935.

Despite the many biographical studies that have been published since Graves's *Lawrence and the Arabs* (1927), Lawrence remains an enigma. His public image reached mythic proportions during his own lifetime, making him, next to Churchill, one of the most famous and memorable Englishmen of his generation.

The largest problem plaguing Lawrence's many biographers has been distinguishing fact from fancy, especially before 1968. That is the year when scholars were able to gain access to official state documents previously unavailable because of the official secrecy embargo, which was changed from fifty years to thirty years at that time. Lawrence's papers, mostly letters, housed at the Bodleian Library at Oxford, will not be open to scholars until the year 2000, but in 1968 Lawrence's brother A. W. Lawrence granted Phillip Knightley and Colin Simpson access to these papers for their *The Secret Lives of Lawrence of Arabia* (1969).

With the publication of Knightley and Simpson's *The Secret Lives of Lawrence of Arabia*, a new phase of interest in Lawrence was initiated. In its revelations about Lawrence's masochistic tendencies their book shed new light on Lawrence's emotional and psychological condition after the war. Like Aldington, Knightley and Simpson questioned Lawrence's role in the Arab revolt. A full biography of Lawrence had to wait until Jeremy Wilson agreed in 1974 to write *Lawrence of Arabia: The Authorized Biography of T. E. Lawrence* (1990). For this monumental work Wilson had access to materials that had not been available to previous biographers.

Another great difficulty in understanding Lawrence comes from Lawrence himself. Lawrence said that he did not understand himself and did not want to, and Graves claimed that Lawrence "fought coherence. I could not, and cannot do for him what he has set his face against doing for himself."

Letters:

Letters from T. E. Shaw to Bruce Rogers (London: Rudge, 1933);

More Letters from T. E. Lawrence to Bruce Rogers (New York: Privately printed, 1936);

The Letters of T. E. Lawrence, edited by David Garnett (London & Toronto: Cape, 1938; Garden City, N.Y.: Doubleday, Doran, 1939);

Shaw-Ede: T. E. Lawrence's Letters to H. S. Ede 1927–1935, edited by H. S. Ede (London: Golden Cockerel Press, 1942);

The Home Letters of T. E. Lawrence and His Brothers (Oxford: Blackwell, 1954);

T. E. Lawrence: The Selected Letters, edited by Malcolm Brown (London: Dent, 1988; New York: Norton, 1989).

Bibliographies:

Elizabeth W. Duval, *T. E. Lawrence: A Bibliography* (New York: Arrow Editions, 1938);

Guyla Bond Houston, *Thomas Edward Lawrence, 1888–1935: A Checklist of Lawrenciana, 1915–65* (Stillwater, Okla., 1967; first supplement, 1970; second supplement, 1975; third supplement, 1978);

Frank Condie Baxter, *An Annotated Check List of a Collection of Writings by and about T. E. Lawrence* (Los Angeles, 1968);

Frank Clements, *T. E. Lawrence: A Reader's Guide* (Newton Abbot, U.K.: David & Charles, 1972);

Philip O'Brien, *T. E. Lawrence: A Bibliography* (Boston: G. K. Hall, 1988);

Jeremy M. Wilson, *T. E. Lawrence: A Guide to Printed and Manuscript Materials* (Fordingbridge, U.K.: Castle Hill Press, 1990).

Biographies:

Robert Graves, *Lawrence and the Arabs* (London: Cape, 1927);

B. H. Liddell Hart, *T. E. Lawrence, in Arabia and After* (London: Cape, 1934); republished as *Colonel Lawrence: The Man behind the Legend* (New York: Dodd, Mead, 1934);

Charles Edmonds, *T. E. Lawrence* (London: Davies, 1935);

Vyvyan Richards, *Portrait of T. E. Lawrence: The Lawrence of the Seven Pillars of Wisdom* (London: Device, 1936);

Richard Aldington, *Lawrence of Arabia: A Biographical Enquiry* (London: Collins, 1955);

Flora Armitage, *The Desert and the Stars: A Biography of Lawrence of Arabia* (New York: Holt, 1955);

Anthony Nutting, *Lawrence of Arabia: The Man and the Motive* (London: Hollis & Carter, 1961);

Robert Payne, *Lawrence of Arabia: A Triumph* (London: Hale, 1966);

Suleiman Mousa, *T. E. Lawrence: An Arab View,* translated by Albert Butros (London: Oxford University Press, 1966);

Phillip Knightley and Colin Simpson, *The Secret Lives of Lawrence of Arabia* (London: Nelson, 1969);

Jeremy Wilson, *Lawrence of Arabia: The Authorized Biography of T. E. Lawrence* (New York: Atheneum, 1990).

References:

R. P. Blackmur, *The Expense of Greatness* (Gloucester, U.K.: Peter Smith, 1958);

Joel C. Hodson, *Lawrence of Arabia and American Culture: The Making of a Transatlantic Legend* (Westport, Conn.: Greenwood Press, 1995);

Lawrence James, *The Golden Warrior: The Life and Legend of Lawrence of Arabia* (London: Weidenfeld & Nicolson, 1990);

Jeffrey Meyers, *The Wounded Spirit: T. E. Lawrence's Seven Pillars of Wisdom* (New York: St. Martin's Press, 1989);

Thomas J. O'Donnell, *The Confessions of T. E. Lawrence: The Romantic Hero's Presentation of Self* (Athens: Ohio University Press, 1979);

Stephen E. Tabachnick, *T. E. Lawrence* (Boston: Twayne, 1978);

Tabachnick, *The T. E. Lawrence Puzzle* (Athens: University of Georgia Press, 1984);

Stanley Weintraub, *Private Shaw and Public Shaw: A Dual Portrait of Lawrence of Arabia and G. B. S.* (London: Cape, 1963);

Weintraub and Rodelle Weintraub, *Lawrence of Arabia: The Literary Impulse* (Baton Rouge: Louisiana State University Press, 1975).

Papers:

The T. E. Lawrence manuscripts housed in the Bodleian Library at Oxford are closed to public scrutiny until the year 2000. The Public Records Office in London holds Lawrence's official reports, state documents, and papers to the Foreign Office. Complementary materials are located at Durham University, the Scottish Record Office, St. Anthony's College at Oxford, and the Government of India archives in New Delhi.

Ella Maillart

(20 February 1903 - 27 March 1997)

Dennis M. Read
Denison University

BOOKS: *Parmi la jeunesse russe–de Moscou au Caucase* (Paris: Fasquelle, 1932);

Des Monts Célestes aux Sables Rouges (Paris: Grasset, 1934); translated by John Rodker as *Turkestan Solo: One Woman's Expedition from the Tien Shan to the Kizel Kum* (London: Putnam, 1934; New York: Putnam, 1935);

Oasis interdites de Pekin au Cachemire (Paris: Grasset, 1937); translated by Thomas McGreevy as *Forbidden Journey: From Peking to Kashmir* (London & Toronto: Heinemann, 1937; New York: Holt, 1937);

Gypsy Afloat (London & Toronto: Heinemann, 1942);

Cruises & Caravans (London: Dent, 1942);

The Cruel Way (London & Toronto: Heinemann, 1947);

'Ti-Puss (London & Toronto: Heinemann, 1951);

The Land of the Sherpas (London: Hodder & Stoughton, 1955).

Ella Maillart

Ella Maillart has been well known to British readers of travel writings since the 1930s. A member of the Royal Geographical Society for many years, she was awarded the Sir Percy Sykes Medal in 1955. Her books have been translated into German, Swedish, French, and Spanish. Maillart brought to travel writing an unflinching honesty and a singular seriousness of purpose. Her constant goal was to reach locations where the essential rhythms of life follow a pattern refined through thousands of years, and she achieved this aim among the shepherds and nomads of northern Asia. In chronicling her travels through these regions she hoped to offer a spiritual balm to Western readers, locating a fundamental quality of life that had been lost to them. Although her journeys were arduous and often dangerous (prompting one reviewer to call her "a dauntless lady"), she disdained heroics in her writing and used her journals and camera to record her experiences without exaggeration or false drama. Her forays across mountain ranges and into hidden valleys prompted Sir Denion Ross to place her "among the great travellers of the world."

Ella Katherine Maillart (known as Kini to all friends) was born in Geneva, Switzerland, on 20 February 1903 to a Swiss father, Paul M. Maillart, and a Danish mother, Dagmar Marie Kliim Maillart. She was their second child, six years younger than her brother, Albert. Paul Maillart ran a fur business, supplying shops in London and New York with pelts and coats. The business provided the family with a comfortable upper-middle-class life until the Great Depression of the 1930s.

As a child Maillart preferred solitude, delving deeply into her brother's library of adventure books. The one group activity she relished was holiday skiing with her family in the Alps. She continued to ski until she was in her late seventies. When she was ten her father secured a small house on Lake Geneva at the Creux de Genthod, five miles from the city, and the family lived there from May to September every year. There she learned to sail in a succession of boats borrowed from friends and relatives. She also enjoyed ballroom dancing and hockey, forming a girls' hockey club when she was sixteen.

In *Cruises & Caravans* (1942) Maillart wrote of these early years, fondly remembering her close friend Miette. With Miette she bought her first boat, *Perlette,* a three-top sloop, which they sailed from Marseilles to Corsica and Nice. There Maillart met Alain Gerbault aboard his ship, *Firecrest,* before he embarked on his solo sail around the world.

After attending school in Geneva, Maillart studied with a tutor for two years preparing for the university entrance exam. When she failed to pass the parts in mathematics and Latin, her formal education came to an end. She began an apprenticeship in her father's business, but finding her father too domineering and the work too stultifying, she soon quit. At nineteen she left home to teach French in a coeducational preparatory school in Wales. In his memoir, *Mount Ida* (1948), Monk Gibbon, who was also a teacher at the school, provided an extensive portrait of her. She had "fair, short hair" and "was not tall, but something lithe and active about her . . . gave the impression of height." Her arms and face were "bronzed like some young Atalanta." He failed to mention her brilliant blue eyes.

Overwhelmed by the crush of duties and the isolation of the school, Maillart left before the year was out for a similar post in a girls' school in Hertfordshire. There she found herself bored and seriously wondered for the first time what to do with her life. By twenty she had forsaken a conventional life to sail in a succession of crafts, more for the experience the sailing offered than for the pay she received.

In *Gypsy Afloat* (1942) Maillart recalled that these initial adventures began after she answered an advertisement in the London *Times* for crew members. She admitted in a postscript to her letter, "I am a girl" but added quickly, "I do not think it matters as everybody is so alike in sailors' kit, and I am a sailor first and only." After an interview with the boat owner, a rotund country squire she called the Colonel, she was hired as a cabin boy aboard the *Volunteer,* a flat-bottomed sailboat, and rose in rank to deckhand. While on night watch one evening, she warmed her hands over the bowl of her pipe and meditated on the serenity the sea induced in her:

> there was no more sense of time. Nothing but a friendly, regular smashing of seas by the bow. . . . Nothing but an all-pervading peace, the deep peace in which you forget what you are, you can't think any more, you are just lost in the whole with a rich feeling that some part of you is getting nourishment out of the silence. You feel unknown gigantic forces flowing near you in which your minute self is happily drowned.

Maillart left the *Volunteer* to join three other women, including Miette, aboard Miette's boat, the *Bonita.* They sailed the *Bonita* to Greece and then sold it to purchase a larger boat on which they hoped to sail to the South Seas, "where we would make our lives." The plan got as far as buying the *Atalante,* a yacht of more than fifty feet equipped with even "a small harmonium," and sailing it into the Atlantic Ocean, bound to New York. Only a few days into the voyage Miette became so ill that they turned back. The voyage was scuttled and with it their dream. Subsequent ships on which Maillart sailed included the schooner *La Françoise* and the yawl *Insoumise.* During these days of sea travel, however, she was overwhelmed by aimlessness:

> This life of mine, to what purpose had it been lived, free as it was from any tie? Did some constructive ideal exist which I could serve wholeheartedly? I longed to work with people who shared a single aim, and to feel the human warmth round me which created brave ideas, as well as the courage to realize them.

While Maillart found nothing to quell this sense of aimlessness, she did find some worthwhile diversions when not at sea: watching bullfights at San Sebastian, skiing in Switzerland, performing on the Jungfrau Joch for the movie *Sportrivalen,* and spending time in Trouville, France, where she enjoyed the company of her friend, Alain Gerbault, who had completed his solo sailing voyage around the world since she had last seen him. All the publicity surrounding his voyage and the publication of his book about it, *Seul à Travers l'Atlantique* (1924; translated as *Flight of the "Firecrest,"* 1926) had made him a celebrity.

Maillart's experiences at sea prepared her well to compete for Switzerland in single-handed women's sailing in the 1924 Paris Olympics. She was the youngest of the seventeen entrants, finishing ninth overall. She participated in other athletic competi-

Maillart in Moscow during her 1930 trip to the Soviet Union

tions well into the next decade. In 1931 she was captain of the Swiss Ladies' Hockey Team, and between 1931 and 1934 she was a member of the Swiss ladies' ski-racing club.

Between 1925 and 1928 Maillart held a variety of jobs, including a typist in a Paris office and an actress at the Studio des Champs Elysées. She was interested in making her own movies and tried to find backers for a documentary about life aboard the *Atalante*. When this endeavor came to nothing, she moved in 1929 to Berlin, then a major center for the motion-picture industry, supporting herself by giving English lessons and usually eating just one meal a day. She had no better luck there, and she was depressed by the city, which she described as "crowded with hawkers and beggars." When Charmian London, the widow of Jack London, visited Berlin, Maillart acted as her guide and interpreter. At the end of her stay, London gave Maillart fifty dollars so that she could go to the Soviet Union. The gift was half Maillart's total bankroll.

In 1930 Maillart traveled by train to Moscow, ostensibly to do research for a book on Russian silent films. After conducting an interview with the famous filmmaker Dziga Vertov in Kiev, however, she realized that the advent of sound had rendered any study of silent movies superfluous. She stayed in Moscow five months, then hiked with a group of students across the Caucasus Mountains. A serious dog bite caused her to remain behind at Sochi, a sea resort, while the group moved on, and after she recovered she visited Odessa and Kiev on her own. Returning to Berlin later that year, a Hearst Press correspondent asked her to write about her trip. Her sixty-page account was rejected, but she was not disappointed because, she wrote in *Cruises & Caravans,* "I have never nursed the illusion that I could write."

Maillart returned to Geneva to visit her ailing father, and then she went to Paris, where Gerbault introduced her to his publisher, Charles Fasquelle. Fasquelle encouraged her to rewrite and expand her account of her experiences in the Soviet Union and then bought the manuscript for sixty pounds, "more money than I have ever had before." *Parmi la jeunesse russe–de Moscou au Caucase* (Among Russian Youth–From Moscow to the Caucasus, 1932) was her first book and a major breakthrough in her writing career. It has never been translated into English.

From this time on Maillart traveled extensively and wrote about her experiences. The first of these trips was her return to the Soviet Union in July 1932. Her account of this trip, *Des Monts Célestes aux Sables Rouges* (1934; translated into English as *Turkestan Solo,* 1934), was her first book to reach an English-reading public. The book is an attempt to realize the "elemental laws" of life by traveling among "primitive, simple peoples" in the states of Kirgiziya (Kyrgyzstan) and Uzbekistan in the south-central Soviet Union, the region of ancient Turkistan. By the end of her journey in January 1933 she had traveled by an amazing variety of conveyances: train, bus, camel, horse, bicycle, paddle wheeler, arba (a kind of wagon), kayak, airplane, and skis. Perhaps even more amazing was her budget. She financed her entire trip on "rather less than £75."

At the beginning of the journey Maillart was traveling in the company of two Russian couples on their way to the T'ien Shan (Tian Shan) mountains to ski. She did, however, attend to certain matters on her own. She climbed alone to the summit of Sari Tor, an elevation of nearly sixteen thousand feet, and then skied down its slopes. And she observed the nomadic habits of the Kirghiz tribes, whose actions were largely in conflict with the policies of Soviet collectivization.

Maillart's companions left her at Alma Ata to return to Moscow, and she then ventured into the lands of the Kazakh tribes, encountering challenges in terrain (from deserts to mountains) and weather (from stifling summer heat to dangerous winter ice). She bore up well, suffering nothing more severe than a broken molar sustained while chewing a piece of bread. Ever resourceful, she at one point sacrificed her edition of Honoré de Balzac's works for toilet paper. She also took photographs with her Leica camera in spite of the vigilance of soldiers and officials; thirty-two of them are reproduced in the book.

In her travels throughout Turkistan, Maillart found widespread famine and desperate poverty, the result of droughts and the inability of the Soviet Union to advance production programs. The collective farms lacked equipment, trained workers, and coherent planning. The single exception Maillart found was Turt Köl (Turtkul') on the Amu Daria (Amu Dar'ya) River, which she described as "indeed a land flowing with milk and honey."

Although Soviet policy promoted equality between women and men, Maillart found that traditional attitudes continued to prevail among the natives. Because the tribesmen could not imagine "a woman traveling without her husband," one of her Russian companions advised her early in the trip to explain her traveling alone with the fiction that her husband had become ill and remained behind in Frunze (Bishkek). Later Maillart visited an embroidery factory in which all the workers were women. The female director of the factory reported, "The liberation of the women has created discontent in the home."

While Maillart was disappointed in her quest to find "elemental laws" among the Kirghiz and Kazakh peoples, she was impressed by a village of German Mennonites with well-ordered and flourishing farms. The forebears of these farming families had immigrated there during the previous century. The elders worried, however, about the specter of collectivization.

A *New York Times* review of *Turkestan Solo* gives a succinct summary of its qualities: "The entire book is written with very great detail, often picturesque and colorful, but so truthful that it does not spare the reader the filth, the vermin, the discomforts, the crudities of the daily life, none of which, however, did Miss Maillart seem to mind in the least, so keen was her constant enjoyment" (24 February 1935).

In *Cruises & Caravans* Maillart wrote of several incidents that she had not included in *Turkestan Solo.* One was watching barbers removing the *rishta,* or Guinea worm, from its victims in Bokhara. Because the Guinea worm can grow as long as a yard, the barbers had to extract it over a period of several days, "every day winding out an inch or two of the worm round a match stick. Great caution was necessary, otherwise the worm would break and one had to start all over again." Another incident was Maillart's being robbed. While she was sleeping, someone stole her boots, which she was using as a pillow. The robbery, she noted, "shows, at the same time, the cunning of the Kazaks and the quality of my sleep." When she returned to Berlin in January 1933, she was amazed to discover she had gained more than thirty pounds during her travels.

While she was writing *Turkestan Solo* Maillart gave lectures on her experiences in the Soviet Union, illustrating them with slides of her photographs. Two hundred of her photographs of Turkistan were exhibited in the Trocadéro Museum. She finished writing *Turkestan Solo* in Saléve, France (just south of Geneva), in November 1933.

Maillart immediately undertook her next travel assignment, as a correspondent in Manchuria for Elie J. Boise, who published her articles in *Petit Parisien.* Near the end of that trip, while making her way to the dining car on the Vladivostok-Harbin Express, Maillart was forced to run a gauntlet through a train car filled with Japanese soldiers, who slapped her face, kicked her in the stomach, and shouted derisive remarks. She attributed the incident to the prevailing Japanese belief that Western nations had inflicted many wrongs on Manchuria. In *Forbidden Journey* (1937) she wrote that the Japa-

"Trained hunting eagle on the fist of its master" and "Jocubai with an argali skull," photographs taken by Maillart for Turkestan Solo *(1934), her account of her 1932–1933 travels in the Soviet states of Kyrgyzstan and Uzbekistan*

nese hated all whites, "whether we be *émigré* Russians or Red Russians, Americans or Europeans, Catholic missionaries or Protestant missionaries." Peter Fleming came upon Maillart as she was reporting this incident in the Harbin office of the chief of the railway police. The atmosphere in the crowded office, Fleming wrote in *News From Tartary* (1936), was extremely tense. "The only person who appeared not only unruffled but definitely amused," he wrote, "was Kini." Perhaps Maillart's traveling unescorted had something to do with the brazen behavior of the soldiers. Nevertheless the incident did not shake Maillart's conviction that "a weak girl travelling alone through a difficult country has a better chance of success than anybody else."

By January 1935 Maillart had established herself in Peking (Beijing) and was considering how to reach and cross Sinkiang (the Chinese name for Turkistan) in the face of the Chinese government prohibition against foreigners taking such a route. A traveler there faced the possibilities of being murdered by bandits or of being imprisoned by local officials on suspicion of being a spy. Her first impulse was to "avoid the known routes." She carefully studied the routes taken by the successful expeditions of Owen Lattimore in the mid 1920s and André Citroën in 1931.

The success of Maillart's journey was in part owed to her decision to allow the experienced newspaper correspondent and accomplished traveler Peter Fleming to join her. The first of many ironies in this union is that both of them were unabashed solitaries. Her most recent book had been titled *Turkestan Solo,* and his was *One's Company* (1936). Each of them wrote an account of this thirty-five-hundred-mile journey. Fleming's *News From Tartary* was published in 1936, nearly a year earlier than Maillart's *Forbidden Journey.* Like the two companion travelers, the two books complemented one another.

Fleming, who was in Beijing as a special correspondent to *The Times,* was twenty-seven, four years younger than Maillart, who had met him in London in 1934. Maillart "appreciated Peter's brilliant intelligence, his faculty of being able to eat anything and sleep anywhere, and also his sure grasp of the kernel of any situation, of the essential point in any argument," as well as "his horror of any distortion of facts and the native objectivity with which he recounted them." Perhaps even more important to Maillart was her conviction that Fleming "had been born under a lucky star."

For his part Fleming saw much in Maillart to admire. As he wrote in *News From Tartary,*

> She had courage and enterprise and resource; in endurance she excelled most men. She was also what is known as "good with natives," and knew, when dealing with a proud but simple people whose language she did not speak, where to be formal and silent, and where to be mildly the buffoon. She could eat and sleep anywhere.

The ability of both travelers to "eat and sleep anywhere" indicates their compatibility. Fleming added, "We were both adaptable and fairly phlegmatic; and we were both fatalists, as all travellers, and especially travellers in Asia, ought to be."

The two had their differences, however. The major one was Fleming's incessant desire to travel quickly (Maillart nicknamed him "Galloper") while Maillart typically "wanted to dawdle in my usual fashion." Another was Fleming's refusal to regard anything or anyone seriously, while Maillart tended to the opposite extreme. Fleming specified other differences: Maillart's "certain contempt for him" versus his "sneaking respect for her," both perhaps deriving from Maillart's being "a professional" and Fleming's being "eternally the amateur." Maillart was systematic and neat, Fleming disorganized and messy. Furthermore, while Maillart took the position that one should attend to any job that needed to be done, Fleming far preferred inducing others to do it. In their division of labor Maillart did all the cooking, cleaning, sewing, mending, and medical and veterinary work, while Fleming did the hunting (he prided himself on his marksmanship), heavy work, and negotiating with officials and soldiers. Maillart was conversant in Russian, Fleming in Chinese and (by the end of the trip) Turki. Maillart and Fleming got along extremely well, for the most part enjoying one another's company during the long days of slow treks and the cold nights inside a custom-made pup tent.

Maillart's single misgiving about their traveling together concerned a diminution of the pleasure she felt when traveling alone. "I had lost," she wrote, "the intense joy, the intoxication, of blazing my own trail and the proud sense of being able to get through alone, to which I had become accustomed. Above all, a piece of Europe inevitably accompanied us through the mere fact of our association. That isolated us."

By mid February 1935 they had begun their journey together, traveling by train to Chengchow (Zhengzhou), Tungkwan (T'ung-hua), and Sian (Xi'an). Noticing the great number of Chinese soldiers on the trains, Maillart commented, "No matter where one went war seemed to be imminent." From Xi'an they traveled in the back of an overcrowded truck to Lanchow (Lanzhou). It was a bumpy ride, and at one point Fleming was violently thrown in the air. "I just managed to catch him in flight," Maillart wrote, "and plant him down beside us. I had saved his life. But he complained that I had hurt him." They rode mules from Lanzhou to Sining (Xining), where they traded them for horses.

They began a daily routine of traveling fifteen to eighteen miles in eight hours, stopping only for a breakfast and lunch of *tsamba,* a Tibetan staple prepared by mixing rancid butter with toasted barley meal. Dinner was whatever Fleming had been able to shoot. The fare included antelope, wild goose, hare, duck, and pheasant. Maillart was in her element:

> I loved the primitive way of living which gave one back that hunger that transforms every morsel one puts under one's tooth into solid satisfaction; the healthy weariness that made sleep an incomparable voluptuousness; and the desire to get on that found realization in every step one took. . . . I should have liked the journey to continue the rest of my life.

They shared various amusements to stave off boredom. While riding they tried to remember movies, books, writers, and friends. Once, after exhausting those categories, Maillart asked Fleming to expound on all the London clubs he knew. Alone, Maillart recited poems by Paul Valéry; Fleming read Thomas Babington Macaulay's *History of England* (1849–1855). During evenings in camp Maillart played records on the phonograph she had brought along. Since she had only three records, she and Fleming came to know them very well. Fleming played interminable games of patience and smoked his pipe.

Along the way Maillart captured various moments vividly. The bound feet of Chinese women were "like pointed stumps." After a particularly difficult day Maillart and Fleming consumed tsamba mixed with brandy and found, "The result was exactly like bad *baba au rhum.*" While cleaning a duck for dinner she found six eggs inside it. "I don't think," she wrote, "there were ever fresher or more

Maillart and Peter Fleming riding yaks during their 1935 travels in China, the subject of Maillart's Forbidden Journey *(1937) and Fleming's* News From Tartary *(1936)*

delicious eggs than those." At an elevation of sixteen thousand feet, searching alone for a lost tent pole, she found herself singing "I'm sitting on top of the world."

Yet Maillart was disappointed to learn that a simpler, more austere life did not bring fulfillment. Instead, "at the heart of Asia, where I expected to find myself amongst poor men but free, I found economic slavery and national antagonism as strong as in any part whatsoever of the present-day world." In Beijing she found the threat of Japan; in Xi'an, Communists menaced the Nanking (Nanjing) government; in Kansu (Gansu) there were Tungan uprisings; in Sinkiang (Xinjiang) the Chinese exploited the native Mongols.

Maillart and Fleming were able to make their way through all these politically tense areas with only a few close calls. The worst injury Maillart suffered, in fact, was a kick on her shin from a horse. Planning carefully, traveling light, using local guides, riding camels and donkeys, and maintaining easy relations with anyone they encountered enabled them to move steadily across the southern expanse of China.

When they arrived at Kashgar (Kashi) they were honored (along with two Soviet doctors who had flown in a serum for the plague) with a banquet hosted by the local Chinese and Turki officials. Much drinking occurred, and the evening culminated with Fleming's announcement to the assembly that Maillart "danced extremely well in the Turkish style." She had never done so before but found herself performing an approximation with a Chinese general. Then, turning the tables, Maillart announced that Fleming had a wonderful singing voice–something far from the fact. He, however, declined to sing. Maillart later admitted in *Cruises & Caravans* that "I had never been, and never again shall be, so drunk in all my life."

Maillart and Fleming crossed the Northwest Frontier into India and ended their odyssey together in Kashmir on 13 September 1935. Fleming boarded an Imperial Airways flight for England, and Maillart, after spending a week visiting the Taj Mahal, flew on Air France to Karchi, the Persian Gulf, Baghdad, and Damascus. She then drove to Beirut before flying to Greece, Lyons, and Paris. "It's an astounding contrast," she wrote, "to be going at fifteen miles a day one day and at fifteen hundred the next."

"By all the conventions of desert island fiction," Fleming wrote, "we should have fallen madly in love with each other; by all the laws of human nature we should have driven each other crazy with irritation." Neither occurred. Maillart said simply, "Peter was the best of comrades and I had found that I could be absolutely frank with him." Fleming added, "We had complete confidence in each other." Maillart claimed that they retained their autonomy throughout the journey; "it was only our egotisms that worked together, each helping the other." Yet Fleming suggested, "Perhaps we were less independent of each other than we felt."

The experience produced Maillart's most successful book, illustrated with sixty-four of the photographs she took during the journey. It was warmly received by critics and readers. Maurice Richardson's review in the *New Statesman and Nation* (4 September 1937) noted that Maillart's attitude, compared to Fleming's, "is perhaps more conventional and she may be more anxious to impart information. She is less selective and is inclined to treat each incident in the same way, but though she has not got Mr. Fleming's easy fluency, she is intensely readable and succeeds in presenting their journey as a running narrative." Richard Vaughan noted that Maillart's book "is always entertaining" and "gives a clear picture of the political drama now being played in Central Asia" (*Manchester Guardian,* 27 August 1937). George E. Sokolsky said that the book should be read "even by those who are weary of Far Eastern travel literature" (*Saturday Review of Literature,* 13 November 1937).

Maillart finished writing *Forbidden Journey* in Lebanon in September 1936. During the next several years she took several "lorry hops" between India and Turkey and wrote accounts of them for newspapers. She also lectured in England on her travels. From 6 June to the end of 1939 she drove from Switzerland to Kabul, Afghanistan, with a friend who is identified in Maillart's next travel book, *The Cruel Way* (1947), only as Christina. The purpose of their trip was to escape the threat of warfare in Europe and to overcome Christina's drug addiction and general malaise. Maillart's account of this journey is in many measures her most moving book. Their destination was a cherished valley of the Hindu Kush deep in Afghanistan, where Maillart hoped they would find sanctuary from the madness she saw in the world and relief for Christina's suffering.

The journey began when Maillart and Christina drove through the Simplon pass from Switzerland into Italy in Christina's new Ford V-8 roadster. Its eighteen-horsepower engine was often taxed by the steep climbs, and the rough Yugoslavian roads caused its body to begin opening "like an over-ripe melon." Most of the roads were dirt; some were no more than paths or trails. The trip was difficult; the terrain demanding. But the car sustained nothing more serious than three flat tires during the entire journey.

Inside the car was a bookshelf that contained about a dozen works on the history and culture of the areas Maillart and Christina passed through, as well as two still cameras (one with black-and-white film, the other with color film) and one movie camera. Christina was the expert driver; Maillart, of course, was the expert traveler. In fact she had already been to many of the places they visited and was familiar with much of their itinerary.

Christina was hardly the ideal traveling companion, especially for so arduous a journey. Thirty years old, she was driven by a supreme sense of suffering. "She worshipped it," Maillart wrote, "as the source of all greatness." This suffering had been self-consuming, resulting during previous years in a broken marriage, a nervous breakdown, and an addiction to drugs. Christina was extremely thin, ate poorly, and smoked incessantly. A friend had nicknamed her "Fallen Angel."

Maillart had embarked on this trip in part "to save my friend from herself." At the outset Christina vowed to Maillart that she would ski for exercise, smoke less, eat more, and generally take much better care of herself, as well as giving up drugs. Away from the temptations of cities and among simple, vital people, Christina believed she could begin a new life.

Maillart intended to conduct ethnological studies of the Kafirs in the Hindu Kush and to stop writing travel books. "What is the good," she asked Christina, "of sending people round the world? I have done it: it doesn't help. It only kills time. You return as unsatisfied as you left." She hoped her studies would enable her "to understand the deepest cause of our craziness. . . . I hope to grasp why my contemporaries have ceased to live from the core of their being."

They had gone only as far as Sofia, Bulgaria, however, when Maillart found the "brittle glass of an empty ampoule" in the bathroom, evidence that Christina "had succumbed once more" to her addiction. The tension between them grew, and Maillart decided she could not let Christina out of her sight until the end of the journey.

Adding to their difficulties was an injury Maillart sustained several weeks later in Iran. She spilled kerosene on one of her hands, and it ignited. Her hand "burned like a plum-pudding. I was so interested in watching every thought that rose in me that I had no time to feel anything." The clinical result was ugly: "The swollen back of my right hand looked like a glove filled with water to bursting point." Yet Maillart's psychological insight almost made the accident worthwhile: "Once more I had the proof that I can look at myself with detachment and that curiosity is uppermost in me. In my greatest moments, in danger, in love, I remain a spectator of myself." Maillart received medical attention for her burned hand in Tehran, and she recovered the use of it in a matter of weeks.

Maillart and Christina were making a journey that few people, and perhaps no unescorted women, had made before. Entering Iran, they found that they were only the second car to cross the border on that road. In Tehran the German minister invited them to stay in a guest house "Till you decide to go home, for you won't be allowed further East." They pressed on nevertheless. At the next border Afghan soldiers got into their car, and as they drove through the crossing one soldier, not convinced these two strangely dressed people were women, investigated: "very slowly his hand began to follow

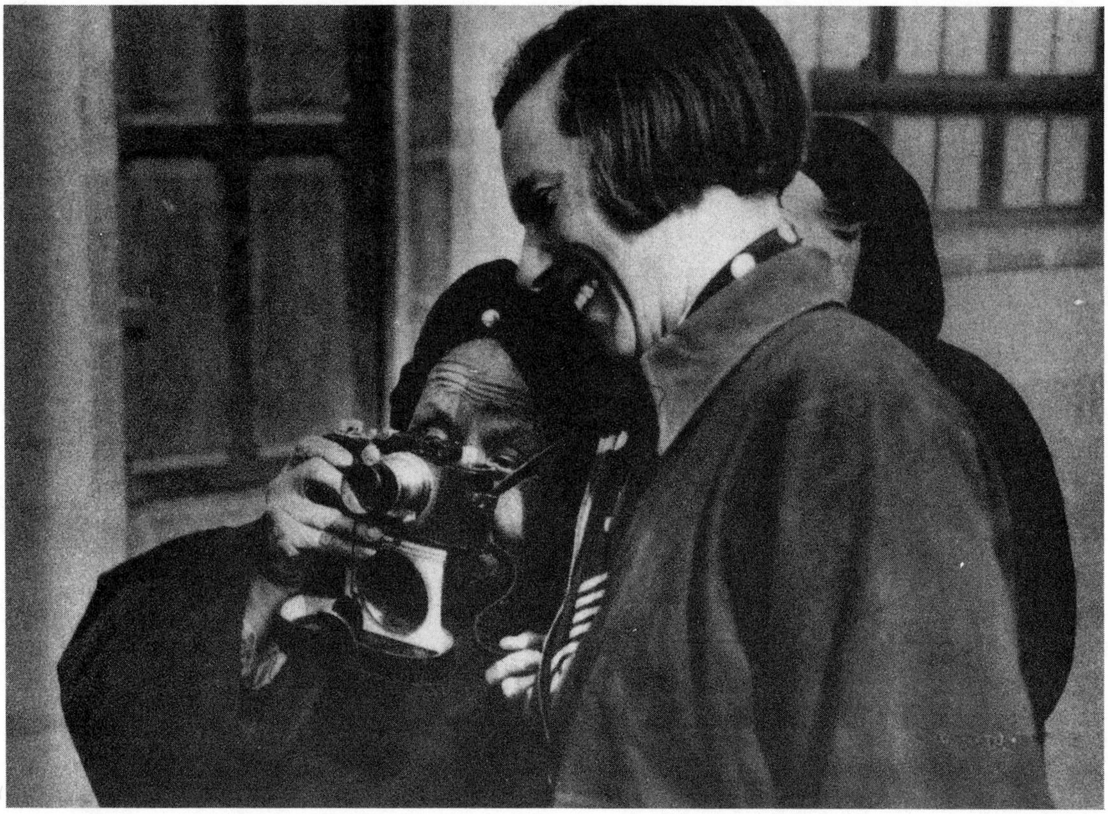

Maillart showing her camera to a Chinese woman, 1935

the curves of our ribs! . . . We could not afford to be offended and thus perhaps antagonize these feline soldiers because after all, we were at their mercy."

The investigation fortunately went no further. Perhaps it would not have even begun if Christina had been wearing the skirt Maillart had persuaded her to buy in Tehran, arguing, "when difficulties are encountered in Asia, women are more readily helped if they are seen to be without a man." But wearing skirts brought other concerns, since most Afghan men, they learned, had seen the faces of no more than four women in their lives: their mother, sister, wife, and daughter. Maillart and Christina had to be constantly on their guard against unwanted advances, and they had to discipline themselves to make no gesture that could be interpreted as provocative.

In Herat the completely covered Afghan women were a constant hazard as Maillart and Christina drove the streets of the city, for "they saw little and heard less. We had to be right upon them before they would jump aside, frightened like cackling hens." After the two Western women drove beyond Herat, Afghan women seemed to disappear entirely; they kept themselves hidden from public view.

The journey was punctuated by tombs, citadels, and mosques on the horizon; and they stopped to admire many of them and to contemplate the people who built them, fought over them, and lay dead in them. The modern residents along the way also provided engrossing, if not uplifting, moments, as well as food and shelter. *The Cruel Way* includes seventy-three photographs of the architecture and people they saw. One moment of the journey stood out in particular. At the Shahidan pass, ten thousand feet in elevation, Maillart felt unified with something immense and eternal:

> We were in the heart of an old, a very old world. Was it not already old sixteenth [*sic*] centuries B.C. (young were the forests of Europe then) when Aryan tribes speaking Vedic Sanskrit came from the North on their way to Kurdistan and India? In this great empty space there were now myself and the earth, a pair in good accord. Reduced to essentials, a skeleton of hills covered with the leanest flesh, for all the little it gave, the world pleased me as it was.

The feeling is momentary, however, and it competes with more-banal experiences. Earlier in the trip, near a fourteenth-century vault with walls twenty feet thick and more than one hundred feet high, Maillart found "a huge cinema screen" and "the fire-proof cabin of a cinema-projector, new god and bestower of oblivion to our mass civilization." At Pol-I-Khumri (Pol-e-Khomri) in Afghanistan, Maillart came upon a massive dam-building project which, when completed would produce electricity to power new industries and thereby bring about major changes for people who had lived the same way for centuries. She hardly regarded such a project as progress, for "to turn healthy peasants or independent shepherds into nerveless or up-rooted robots [that is, factory workers] is nearly a murder."

Some six months after they had begun, Maillart and Christina arrived in Kabul just as World War II was breaking out in Europe. The armed hostilities brought an end to free movement, making inaccessible the valley in the Hindu Kush, which Maillart was hoping to reach. She had to forgo her ethnographic study of the Kafirs. Instead she traveled on to India, arranging for Christina to return to France. Maillart saw Christina only one more time, in Tiruvannamalai, India, on New Year's Day 1940. During the two days of her stay Christina claimed to be free from her addiction and to be living a healthier life. She had little time to carry out that possibility, dying on 15 November 1942 of injuries suffered in a bicycle accident. Her life indeed followed the cruel way.

To support herself in India, Maillart wrote two books drawing on her earlier years. The first, *Gypsy Afloat* (1942), recounts her initial sailing adventures. It is the first book she wrote in English, explaining that she wanted to avoid "the small surprises I get when reading the work of even the best of my translators." Thirty-three photographs fill out the volume. The second, *Cruises & Caravans,* uses some material from *Turkestan Solo, Forbidden Journey,* and *Gypsy Afloat* but also adds much new material. The book, part of the Dent series of Travellers' Tales, includes twenty-seven photographs. In a postscript to *Gypsy Afloat* Maillart announced her shift to an inward course:

> I know I must turn away from the outside world which is not the ultimate reality, and listen to the strength which is hidden in me. I know that we have in us a spark of energy which cannot die. If we knew how to kindle it instead of unwillingly smashing it, we could create bonds linking all of us so strongly together that we could not hate or kill each other any more. . . . Our power would be limitless.

During World War II Maillart quietly looked for this "spark of energy" in herself by studying with Hindu holy men and visiting various shrines and temples throughout India.

Maillart described her years in India in her next book, *'Ti-Puss* (1951), named after her pet cat. The name is a diminutive form of "Brave petit pussy," Maillart's spontaneous effusion when the cat climbed the back leg of a deck chair and leapt into her lap. Later, after the cat had become an adult, Maillart renamed her Mrs. Minou Wildhusband, an apt description of her lustful proclivities. Maillart had decided long ago not to become a wife and mother, but her maternal feelings were hardly smothered by that decision, and she found an outlet for them in 'Ti-Puss. Her comparison of babies with cats shows something of this side of her personality (as well as her preoccupation with mystical matters):

> Indian babies are left to themselves; they live in their own silence, no one wrenching them from their vegetative contemplation in order to educate their curiosity; sometimes they show a slight reaction, a detail from the surrounding scene having entered their infinity; but their glance seldom goes out eager to meet the world of appearances. With an equal facility, a cat's perception can be centered alternatively outwards or inwards.

The companionship 'Ti-Puss offered brought many rewards, among them an insight into a state of simple bliss:

> It looked as if every time I managed to reduce my inner conflicts into a higher level of fact, thus reaching the "natural order of things," the cat felt in me that same peace and harmony which belongs to young children and animals, both of them devoid of "objectivation"; they are no rebels; they have not been sent away from the paradise. They live their own fulness, in pure spontaneity . . . which is happiness, though they don't know it. As for us, peace does not pass our understanding, and we know when we are happy; but it happens too rarely.

Maillart and 'Ti-Puss were hardly ever apart. Six months after 'Ti-Puss came into Maillart's life, however, the cat disappeared. Maillart searched for her daily, finally finding her fifteen days later, weak and with a broken collarbone. Maillart vowed not to part with 'Ti-Puss again, even when she traveled, but other misadventures occurred. Once, while a bus she was riding was parked at a station, she left 'Ti-Puss tied to a box on her seat and went to the coffee room to write a letter. When Maillart returned the bus had left. She found her box on the ground, but 'Ti-Puss was no longer attached to it. Maillart located her cat in a nearby sewer but could not entice her to come out and finally had to crawl into the sewer to retrieve her.

A caravan of gypsies going to India and an Afghan father and child, photographs taken by Maillart during her 1939 journey from Switzerland to Kabul, Afghanistan, the subject of her 1947 book, The Cruel Way

Not long after this incident 'Ti-Puss reached maturity, and in quick succession over the next several years she gave birth to five litters of kittens. Maillart kept one or two of them, killing the others. The act seems especially chilling in a country where life in all forms is so thoroughly venerated. The first time, when she drowned two kittens in a pail of water, she was overcome with grief. The second time she twisted the neck of a kitten "as quickly as possible before I had time to think about it." After killing two kittens from the next litter in the same way, she noted, "their limp necks fell down like the stems of thirsty flowers." Since the fourth litter yielded only two kittens, she was spared the exercise. But she kept only one of the four from the final litter and carried out her grim task with dispatch, noticing "that I had less repulsion in doing so than previously." She had tried to stop this relentless procreation by taking 'Ti-Puss to a Swiss surgeon practicing in India to get her spayed, but he did not have instruments small enough to do the operation.

'Ti-Puss also is about Maillart's experience in India, a country for which she clearly has great affection. She took great steps to adjust to the Indian ways, but she balked at wearing a sari because she found it too difficult to wash eight yards of material every day. Wearing slacks, however, once caused her to be mistaken for a man while she was riding a train, momentarily causing much embarrassment to all present. In Benares (Varanasi), because of the constantly burning funeral pyres along the Ganges, "the wind brought a fine sugary taste to one's mouth." On another occasion Maillart accepted an invitation to smoke some hashish, but it brought about "a colic, instead of the supposed hashish paradise."

When Maillart took a trip to Tibet, she left 'Ti-Puss at home because the journey was too arduous to take with a cat, even one as remarkable as 'Ti-Puss. On her return Maillart was told 'Ti-Puss had been frightened away by two terriers two weeks earlier. Maillart never again saw her cat.

The book, illustrated with nineteen photographs, is less about travel than it is about a disinterested, egoless love, the kind 'Ti-Puss displayed for Maillart. For her part Maillart realized that she could not both own and love 'Ti-Puss, but she never completely achieved this state of mind. She especially regretted their last moments together, before she left for Tibet, for of course she did not think at the time those were their last moments together. Such matters seem insignificant compared to the events of World War II during the early 1940s, but in Maillart's mind they did provide the best use of her time. In the midst of so much carnage and destruction, she believed, "Better to be scratching and scrimping but nourishing the soul."

Maillart's last travel book is *The Land of the Sherpas* (1955), a thin volume of forty-eight pages heavily supplemented with seventy-eight photographs. Nepal, the land of the Sherpas, opened its borders to foreigners for the first time in 1949. Maillart's descriptions of the people and their land are rhapsodic, calling the Nepalese "a race of gay and hospitable mountaineers, brave and incredibly hardy." Approaching Malemchi, she noticed a rhododendron tree "dotted with blood-red flowers standing out against the receding blue slopes tinged with purple by distance, under the dark indigo of the sky, whilst beyond shimmers the satin of the Himalayan snows."

Still on a spiritual quest, Maillart visited Bodhnath, "the most important Tibetan sanctuary outside Tibet," and secured an audience with the lama of Bodhnath. He did not make a good impression on her. She noted his "imperious manner," which seemed to befit his costume of "the traditional robe of yellow Chinese satin," but the image was shattered "when he crossed his legs" and inadvertently revealed "the grey flannel of European trousers."

The Europeanization of the lama's wardrobe was a symptom of outside civilizations threatening the Nepalese culture. Maillart worried specifically about democracy from India or communism from China overtaking Nepal, threatening an ancient civilization with the ways of the twentieth century. This concern, in fact, extends from her last book to her first.

While Maillart published no more books after *The Land of the Sherpas,* she continued to write articles for journals and magazines. In 1957 she started conducting group tours in Asia, and in 1965 she camped for two weeks at the base of Mount Everest during a long stay in Nepal. She died in Chandolin, Switzerland, on 27 March 1997.

In *Cruises & Caravans* Maillart commented on what kind of travel writer she was:

> People often expect to hear me describe thrilling escapes; but even at the cost of disappointing my readers I have to confess that neither at sea nor in the mountains, in deserts nor in towns, have I ever felt seriously endangered. No freezing blue hell in a crevasse, no rescue party, no ransom paid, no kidnapping, no track irremediably lost–all that could exist only is in my imagination, were I to give it rein.

The fact that none of these dire situations ever occurred in Maillart's travels indicates more the kind of woman she was than the degree of danger she faced. She went prepared; she exercised good judgment; she expressed a straightforward openness with native peoples; she was tremendously resourceful; and she had a tough, resilient, dauntless courage. People everywhere knew better than to try anything untoward with her.

But finally hers was an inner journey, one involved with a way of living that brings about a purity of feeling and a serenity. In her early travels she looked for people living simple lives, not unlike those of their medieval ancestors, who had refined the rhythms of existence to a natural clarity. She found that vision disturbed beyond repair by twentieth-century governments imposing a central authority on those peoples. In her later travels she concentrated on her own state of mind, conducting a spiritual journey. This journey has no beginning or end.

References:

Peter Fleming, *News From Tartary* (London: Cape, 1936);

Monk Gibbon, *Mount Ida* (London: Cape, 1948);

John Pilkington, "Kyrgystan: A Tale of Two Journeys," *Geographical Magazine,* 65 (April 1993): 8–12;

Mary Russell, Introduction to *The Cruel Way* (Boston: Beacon, 1986);

Stuart Stevens, *Night Train to Turkistan* (New York: Atlantic Monthly Press, 1988).

Ethel Mannin
(11 October 1900 – 5 December 1984)

Dana E. Aspinall
University of Montevallo

See also the Mannin entry in *DLB 191: British Novelists Between the Wars.*

Ethel Mannin in the 1920s (photograph by E. O. Hoppé)

BOOKS: *Martha* (London: Parsons, 1923; New York: Duffield, 1923; revised edition, London: Jarrolds, 1929);

Hunger of the Sea (London: Jarrolds, 1924; New York: Duffield, 1924);

Sounding Brass (London: Jarrolds, 1925; New York: Duffield, 1926);

Pilgrims (London: Jarrolds, 1927; New York: Doran, 1927);

Green Willow (London: Jarrolds, 1928; Garden City, N.Y.: Doubleday, Doran, 1928);

Crescendo, Being the Dark Odyssey of Gilbert Stroud (London: Jarrolds, 1929; Garden City, N.Y.: Doubleday, Doran, 1929);

Children of the Earth (London: Jarrolds, 1930; Garden City, N.Y.: Doubleday, Doran, 1930);

Confessions and Impressions (London: Jarrolds, 1930; revised edition, London: Hutchinson, 1936);

Bruised Wings, and Other Stories (London: Wright & Brown, 1931);

Common-Sense and the Child: A Plea for Freedom (London: Jarrolds, 1931; Philadelphia: Lippincott, 1932);

Green Figs (London: Jarrolds, 1931);

Ragged Banners: A Novel with an Index (London: Jarrolds, 1931; New York: Knopf, 1931);

The Tinsel Eden, and Other Stories (London: Wright & Brown, 1931);

All Experience (London: Jarrolds, 1932);

Linda Shawn (London: Jarrolds, 1932; New York: Knopf, 1932);

Love's Winnowing (London: Wright & Brown, 1932);

Dryad (London: Jarrolds, 1933);

Venetian Blinds (London: Jarrolds, 1933; New York: Knopf, 1933);

Forever Wandering (London: Jarrolds, 1934; New York: Dutton, 1935);

Men Are Unwise (London: Jarrolds, 1934; New York: Knopf, 1934);

Cactus (London: Jarrolds, 1935; revised, 1944);

The Falconer's Voice (London: Jarrolds, 1935);

The Pure Flame (London: Jarrolds, 1936);

South to Samarkand (London: Jarrolds, 1936; New York: Dutton, 1937);

Common-Sense and the Adolescent (London: Jarrolds, 1937; revised, 1945);

Women Also Dream (London: Jarrolds, 1937; New York: Putnam, 1937);

Darkness My Bride (London: Jarrolds, 1938);

Rose and Sylvie (London: Jarrolds, 1938);

Women and the Revolution (London: Secker & Warburg, 1938; New York: Dutton, 1939);
Privileged Spectator: A Sequel to "Confessions and Impressions" (London: Jarrolds, 1939; revised, 1948);
Christianity–or Chaos?: A Re-statement of Religion (London: Jarrolds, 1940);
Julie: The Story of a Dance-Hostess (London: Jarrolds, 1940);
Rolling in the Dew (London: Jarrolds, 1940);
Red Rose: A Novel Based on the Life of Emma Goldman–"Red Emma" (London: Jarrolds, 1941);
The Blossoming Bough (London & New York: Jarrolds, 1942);
Captain Moonlight (London & New York: Jarrolds, 1942);
Castles in the Street (London: Dent, 1942);
Commonsense and Morality (London & New York: Jarrolds, 1942);
No More Mimosa (London: Jarrolds, 1943);
Proud Heaven (London: Jarrolds, 1943);
Bread and Roses: An Utopian Survey and Blue-print (London: Macdonald, 1944);
Lucifer and the Child (London & New York: Jarrolds, 1945);
The Dark Forest (London: Jarrolds, 1946);
Selected Stories (Dublin & London: Fridberg, 1946);
Comrade O Comrade; or, Low-down on the Left (London & New York: Jarrolds, 1947);
Connemara Journal (London: Westhouse, 1947);
German Journey (London & New York: Jarrolds, 1948);
Late Have I Loved Thee (London: Jarrolds, 1948; New York: Putnam, 1948);
Every Man a Stranger (London: Jarrolds, 1949);
Bavarian Story (London: Jarrolds, 1949; New York: Appleton-Century-Crofts, 1950);
Jungle Journey (London & New York: Jarrolds, 1950);
At Sundown, the Tiger (London & New York: Jarrolds, 1951; New York: Putnam, 1951);
The Fields at Evening (London & New York: Jarrolds, 1952);
This Was a Man: Some Memories of Robert Mannin by His Daughter (London & New York: Jarrolds, 1952);
The Wild Swans, and Other Tales Based on the Ancient Irish (London: Jarrolds, 1952);
Moroccan Mosaic (London & New York: Jarrolds, 1953);
Lover under Another Name (London & New York: Jarrolds, 1953; New York: Putnam, 1954);
Two Studies in Integrity: Gerald Griffin and the Rev. Francis Mahony ("Father Prout") (London: Jarrolds, 1954; New York: Putnam, 1954);
So Tiberius (London: Jarrolds, 1954; New York: Putnam, 1955);
Land of the Crested Lion: A Journey through Modern Burma (London: Jarrolds, 1955);
The Living Lotus (London: Jarrolds, 1956; New York: Putnam, 1956);
The Country of the Sea: Some Wanderings in Brittany (London: Jarrolds, 1957);
Pity the Innocent (London: Jarrolds, 1957; New York: Putnam, 1957);
Fragrance of Hyacinths (London: Jarrolds, 1958);
The Blue-Eyed Boy (London: Jarrolds, 1959);
Brief Voices: A Writer's Story (London: Hutchinson, 1959);
Ann and Peter in Sweden (London: Muller, 1959);
Ann and Peter in Japan (London: Muller, 1960);
The Flowery Sword: Travels in Japan (London: Hutchinson, 1960);
Sabishisa (London: Hutchinson, 1961);
Ann and Peter in Austria (London: Muller, 1962);
Curfew at Dawn (London: Hutchinson, 1962);
With Will Adams through Japan (London: Muller, 1962);
A Lance for the Arabs: A Middle East Journey (London: Hutchinson, 1963);
The Road to Beersheba (London: Hutchinson, 1963; Chicago: Regnery, 1964);
Aspects of Egypt: Some Travels in the United Arab Republic (London: Hutchinson, 1964);
Rebel's Ride: A Consideration of the Revolt of the Individual (London: Hutchinson, 1964);
The Burning Bush (London: Hutchinson, 1965);
The Lovely Land: The Hashemite Kingdom of Jordan (London: Hutchinson, 1965);
Loneliness: A Study of the Human Condition (London: Hutchinson, 1966);
The Night and Its Homing (London: Hutchinson, 1966);
An American Journey (London: Hutchinson, 1967);
The Lady and the Mystic (London: Hutchinson, 1967);
Bitter Babylon (London: Hutchinson, 1968);
England for a Change (London: Hutchinson, 1968);
The Midnight Street (London: Hutchinson, 1969);
The Saga of Sammy-Cat (Oxford & New York: Pergamon, 1969);
Practitioners of Love: Some Aspects of the Human Phenomenon (London: Hutchinson, 1969; New York: Horizon, 1970);
England at Large (London: Hutchinson, 1970);
Free Pass to Nowhere (London: Hutchinson, 1970);
My Cat Sammy (London: Joseph, 1971);

Young in the Twenties: A Chapter of Autobiography (London: Hutchinson, 1971);
The Curious Adventure of Major Fosdick (London: Hutchinson, 1972);
England My Adventure (London: Hutchinson, 1972);
Mission to Beirut (London: Hutchinson, 1973);
Stories from My Life (London: Hutchinson, 1973);
An Italian Journey (London: Hutchinson, 1974);
Kildoon (London: Hutchinson, 1974);
The Late Miss Guthrie (London: Hutchinson, 1976);
Sunset over Dartmoor: A Final Chapter of Autobiography (London: Hutchinson, 1977).

Ethel Mannin, a prolific writer of novels, travel narratives, magazine articles, children's stories, short stories, educational treatises, and political manifestos, published more than one hundred books over half a century, incorporating into many of them her often-protean socialist political ideology. Mannin ardently voiced her opinions on politics and religion in nearly all her nonfiction, especially in her travel narratives. Mannin wrote poignantly on issues such as the Allied rebuilding of Europe and Japan after World War II, British colonial abuses, and Arab-Israeli tensions. She advocated pacifism during the Spanish Civil War; she remained throughout her life an unyielding anti-Zionist; and she scoffed at the British aristocracy. A socialist and later self-styled anarchist, Mannin received attention for her early work, but in later years she struggled for recognition and financial security. As she said in *Brief Voices* (1959), she recognized that she had "only a limited talent," but she had a passion for writing, deciding in 1930 to publish one novel and one nonfiction work annually.

The eldest of three children, Ethel Edith Mannin was born on 11 October 1900 to Robert and Edith Gray Mannin, in Clapham, England. Robert Mannin, a postal sorter at the Mount Pleasant General Post Office for forty years, was a Londoner of poor Irish descent who immersed himself in books, and Ethel Mannin once explained her penchant for writing as a manifestation of her "deep affinity" for her father's imagination. Edith Mannin was a farmer's daughter who taught her eldest child the "gift of happy living." Ethel Mannin, who began writing at seven years old, attended the local council school. During these early years she exhibited a "subjective fear in the feeling of things. It was of the feel of life that I was afraid and which drove me in upon myself from the time I was three years old." Her rather harsh and unimaginative teachers and her intense sensitivity to the thoughtless cruelties of other children kept her home writing stories. She particularly enjoyed her father's company when he returned from work.

In her stories Mannin wrote of what she would later call "real people," those who eluded class distinctions and were "respecters of persons." Her father, probably a major source for these "real people," also influenced her political leanings. Mannin later remembered that "from the time I was five years old I knew that a socialist was the proper thing to be." At fourteen she was reprimanded for an essay in which she derided patriotism. The attention she received from this incident, however, provoked her less-inhibited side to emerge. By the time she left the council school for a commercial school, she knew where her talents lay and expressed a self-confidence in them that later spread to nearly all areas of her personality: "When it came to a matter of essays I knew that I could write better than anyone, even in the forms above me."

At fifteen Mannin left commercial school for London to begin a career as a stenographer for the Charles F. Highman advertising agency, earning twenty-three shillings a week. She worked diligently and efficiently, taking her father's early advice to write as if it were her living. With the assistance of "J.S.," a man who furthered her training in socialist philosophy, she became assistant editor of the *Pelican,* a theatrical and sporting journal, just two years after going to work for Highman's.

In 1919, the year the *Pelican* ceased publication, she married John Alexander Porteous, a Scotsman thirteen years her senior, who wrote copy at Highman's and later became the general manager of the agency. Their marriage produced one child, a daughter, Jean, within its first year. After Jean was born, Mannin spent little time with Porteous, preferring the company of her more-libertine friends, who exhibited a lifestyle she associated with her budding socialist politics.

By the time she was married Mannin had begun selling articles to women's magazines as well as writing novels and children's stories. Her first publications, "tupenny yellow-backed" novelettes such as "Road to Romance," were published in serial form. "I cannot bear to look at them now" Mannin wrote in *Confessions and Impressions* (1930). Her first full-length published novel, *Martha* (1923), however, was runner-up in a competition for first novels. Her second novel, *Hunger of the Sea* (1924), about Sussex fishermen, was recommended for the Prix Femina.

Mannin's first financial success came with *Sounding Brass* (1925), a novel that bitterly satirized the advertising world she knew from Highman's. Mannin later called this book her best novel. The

Mannin and her daughter, Jean, preparing to board an airplane to Paris, 1925

money she earned from *Sounding Brass* provided her with the financial means to travel. Her first trip abroad was to New York City, which she later wrote about in *Confessions and Impressions:*

> There is something starkly incredible about New York City when one visits it for the first time. One has heard of skyscrapers, seen pictures of them; intellectually one knows all about them, but the reality is so much beyond one's imaginings that one is bewildered. . . . One feels in its streets that one has somehow arrived at the very heart of the Machine Age. One hears the roar of the machinery, frighteningly. It is there in the thunder of the overhead railway, in the din of the building and demolition going on all the time, in the clangour of those chasms of streets, where humanity surges black in its density, like swarming ants. There is no peace or friendliness anywhere in those streets, nothing but noise and the press of the crowds which seem to move in mass formation at the base of those monstrous buildings which go towering away like sheer vast cliffs above them.

Mannin's impressions of New York illustrate her already established aversion to capitalism and her growing disregard of elitist postures. She considered the United States the ultimate capitalist nation and "the country without a soul." She did not return there until 1966.

Shunning intellectual writers such as Virginia Woolf, Mannin wrote in a style that she thought much more accessible: "I wanted–and want–a language that will make meaning clear, that will speak with tongues of men and of angels, language that does not merely photograph actuality but interprets it." Mannin's experiences in New York and in social circles that included Noël Coward, William Butler Yeats, and Rebecca West are reflected in nearly all her early novels.

Published in 1930, *Confessions and Impressions* is equal parts autobiography, reminiscences, and travel narrative. The book, which includes intimate details of her extramarital affairs, created an immediate scandal and earned for her the label "angry woman." Reactions to remarks such as "Every woman of courage and intelligence has had numerous lovers" or "Religion is for the defeated, or those who lack courage" overshadowed her important political, social, educational, and religious insights. Mannin admitted that her overriding purpose in writing the book was to shock, particularly the older generation. She was "angry with the existing social system, angry with the humbug of conventional morality, angry with the anti-life attitude of orthodox religion and the futility of orthodox education." For all the controversy, the book was not without its supporters. The well-known anarchist Emma Goldman praised Mannin's "sincerity and frankness, adding, "I had never known an English writer so completely oblivious to censure and condemnation from English bigotry and prudishness." *Confessions and Impressions* describes not only Mannin's visit to New York but also her brief summer journeys to Europe with her daughter, Jean. Mannin's marriage to Porteous became progressively more turbulent during the

Mannin in the early 1930s (photograph © Paul Tanqueray; courtesy of Jean Faulks)

late 1920s and early 1930s, and they were divorced in 1938. Taking full responsibility for the breakdown of their marriage, Mannin apologized after Porteous's death in 1956 for the grief she had caused.

Mannin lived abroad, mostly on the Continent, from 1930 until 1935 and used the regions she visited as settings for novels. Her friendship with the well-known British educator A. S. Neill prompted her to write her first piece of nonautobiographical nonfiction, *Common-Sense and the Child: A Plea for Freedom* (1931), as well as *Common-Sense and the Adolescent* (1937).

In 1934 Mannin published her first book completely devoted to her travels. *Forever Wandering,* a collection of essays written while she was living in Paris, concentrates on her travels through Central Europe, her first trip to Soviet Russia, and various sojourns in the British Isles. The book displays the sort of precise details found in nearly all her later travel works: meticulous descriptions of her reasons for embarking on a particular journey, the arrangements and time spent getting to her destinations, and her arrivals in cities that seem to have a coldness and otherness before unfolding the beauty that originally compelled her to visit.

Mannin also had no reservations about expressing her feelings about events or situations. On arriving in the Soviet Union, she exclaimed, "At last . . . I am in Russia!" Her emotional fervor escalated as she compared what she saw with her political beliefs. At this point in her life Mannin fully embraced Russian socialism. As she tried to explain the difficult "period of transition" under Communist rule, she defended the Soviet Union as "the greatest experiment in the history of humanity."

After visiting Moscow–with the western architecture of recently constructed buildings all around the familiar onion domes and Orthodox churches–Mannin was relieved and excited to say about Soviet Russians,

> I believe they *are* happier, that they *are* benefiting. That the capitalist system is outworn is self-evident; I believe that we of this generation are witnessing the slow process of a bloodless revolution, the collapse of the capitalist system, and that in Russia we are witnessing the birth of a new civilization.

In *Forever Wandering* and in her later works Mannin often focused on contrasts. In describing the Soviet Union she juxtaposed the unrivaled beauty of the country with the government red tape that kept one waiting for hours to go through customs or to board a train. When she wrote about England she compared the lush greenery of London parks with landscapes defiled by capitalist industrialization.

Forever Wandering also includes Mannin's essays on her ancestral home, the area around Connemara and Mannin Bay, the site of many of her subsequent travel narratives and novels. Mannin was fascinated by western Ireland and its customs. She was especially fascinated by Irish inattention to time. Instead of surrendering themselves to strict daily schedules, Mannin noted, they embraced nonchalant yet charmingly habitual diurnal routines. For example, the most cherished social event in Connemara was the arrival of a train:

> "Going to meet the train" is rather like going to a London party. If you arrive late there's very little room; also you meet "everyone" there; and, just as at a party, you stand about and chat, and in a little while go home.

Also in the book is an account of Mannin's climb up an "easy mountain" in the Untersburg Range of the Austrian Alps, the setting for her 1934 novel, *Men Are Unwise.*

Mannin's early financial successes with her novels and magazine articles allowed her to buy

Mannin and her second husband, Reginald Reynolds, 1940s (courtesy of Jean Faulks)

Oak Cottage in Wimbledon, a house she had admired since youth. Oak Cottage was her home for forty years; here she entertained friends such as Sir Allen Lane, Christina Foyle, and Dame Daphne du Maurier. In her later years she also provided quarters for many visitors from overseas, especially those involved in the causes she championed.

In 1933 Mannin joined the Independent Labour Party, a Marxist/socialist organization with international ties. Because of the totalitarianism and notoriously inefficient bureaucracy of the Stalinist Soviet Union, however, Mannin soon became disenchanted with the organized political Left. By 1939, when her second autobiographical book, *Privileged Spectator,* was published, she was expressing her "bitter disappointment" with the Soviet Union.

In 1936 Mannin published what she considered her best travel narrative, *South to Samarkand,* which she later described as an account of her most difficult journey. During her arduous trip through the Soviet Union, much of it illegal, Mannin took along a friend, artist Donia Nachshen, a Marxist whom Mannin had met on her first trip to the Soviet Union. Nachshen made drawings that were intended to illustrate *South to Samarkand,* but she withdrew them after Mannin refused to include Nachshen's apology for Communism in the final chapters. After returning from the Soviet Union, Mannin expressed ardently anti-Communist feelings and did not want her "book to be in any way propagandist." In response the Soviet government declared Mannin persona non grata, and she never returned.

Mannin and Nachshen arrived in Moscow after a long boat journey, on which Mannin completed the last chapter of her novel *The Pure Flame* (1936). She hoped to end their journey in Samarkand (Samarqand), the burial place of

Tamerlane (Timur), but on their arrival in Moscow they found that foreigners were forbidden to travel there. Ignoring repeated warnings, the two women resolved to go anyway. Despite her anger at excessive Soviet bureaucracy, at the beginning of her journey Mannin hoped for the eventual success of the Soviet experiment:

> If Russia fails ultimately it will be the greatest tragedy that has happened to humanity since the failure of Jesus Christ to impose Christianity–and all that it stands for of a living socialism and selflessness–upon an innately selfish world, so that instead of getting the sweetening and enriching philosophy of Christ we get the repressive anti-life philosophy of Paul.

For Mannin, who denied the existence of God but respected the teachings of Christ, both Christianity and Soviet socialism had been distorted and abused by their various proponents. She had lost her previous optimism about the revolution in Russia, saying that "even I, who believe the overthrow of the capitalist system to be desirable in every country, even if it does not yield the full measure of revolutionary dreams, felt that the end was not justifying the bitter means. . . ."

From Moscow, which she described as grotesquely modern, like an "American" city, she traveled to Leningrad (Saint Petersburg), which "has escaped this insistent and aggressive modernization, though it is not without its fine new streets and its seemingly inevitably barrack-like blocks of workers' flats." While there Mannin toured the estates and municipal buildings of the czars and was aghast at their grotesque gaudiness. Nevertheless she felt pity at the cruel deaths of the last Romanovs even as she was angered by their "Imperialism."

Back in Moscow, Mannin pondered the predicament of the Russian common laborer, finding in a worker's dwelling the epitome of all Soviet Russia:

> The trouble is that in the majority of cases each flat in these fine-looking modern buildings houses several families, and the clean efficient appearance is confined to the outsides; enter one of these blocks and you will be confronted with dark dirty entrance halls, stone chairs covered with expectorations and as often as not excrement, never any lift, and the names on the front doors hard to make out.

In spite of the stark realities looming beneath the polished veneer of Russia, Mannin found in the Russian people an ever-present sense of optimism, a faith that she saw as a replacement for their belief in a Christian God. Ask any Russian about conditions in the Soviet Union, Mannin observed, and they will say that "things are getting better every day."

Mannin also noted that working-class dwellings were segregated according to the occupation of the particular factory worker: "thus in one part of the town you get blocks of apartments entirely inhabited by boot operatives, and in another pile of boxes live all the workers of some other vast factory." She doubted that such arbitrary segregation enhanced either the workers' productivity or their overall happiness. Suspecting an underlying despair in these workers, Mannin repeatedly noticed, sometimes with humor and sometimes in frustration, the Russians' severely limited topics of conversation: they spoke repeatedly of the need to love all humanity and then longingly asked, "What are the working class conditions in Britain?"

Her skepticism of Soviet policies concerning workers increased when she visited the workers' rest homes, or vacation sites. At first she seemed to have been impressed with their beauty, the intentions behind them, and effectiveness in promoting rest: "It is a pity that all the grand hotels of the French and Italian rivieras and Palm Beach, and all such luxury resorts, cannot be put to such good use, instead of to pampering the idle rich, the nouveau riche, and other parasites and vulgarians." Yet Mannin soon observed that the bulk of the vacationers were army officers and upper-level managers. She later lamented that the Red Army officers got the best of everything in Russia, including housing and food.

After noting still-prevalent class divisions, as exemplified in the people using the vacation homes, Mannin then criticized the never-ending drive for increased production impressed on the people for whom these homes were originally intended:

> It is a new form of record-beating. This passionate devotion to an ideal is admirable, but it can be horrifying too. When work becomes a mania, what happens to that thing in man which for want of a better name we call a soul? Every worker in Russia is a unit in the vast machine of production, and the machine is accelerating in a relentlessly unceasing speed-up.

The concept of man as machine, Mannin believed, stemmed from the Russian perversion of Marxism and permeated issues far outside the parameters of workers' conditions: "Your good Marxist is always concerned with social significance. In practical Communism, art and beauty must serve a social purpose, be the handmaidens of propaganda, otherwise they do not justify their existence. Beauty alone is no good *raison d'être*."

As Mannin traveled eastward, further away from the European part of the Soviet Union, her

Mannin on the Grand Bé in St. Malo, summer 1956, during the travels she described in her 1957 book The Country of the Sea *(photograph by F. W. Ziemsen; courtesy of Jean Faulks)*

disgust for the Russian form of travel replaced political discussions: "Trams stuffed with humanity that overflowed at the exits and swarmed on the steps and rode clinging to the sides, rocked and clattered past." As she continued east, she also noticed that the grip of the bureaucratic Soviet power structure, although still much in existence, was somewhat looser: "To live happily in Moscow you need to be either Russian or of the Communist faith; in Tiflis you do not feel this demand; there is not the insistent reminder of *Russia;* it is cosmopolis."

Farther east, "you lose the vast efficient machine of the U.S.S.R. in the centuries old Orientalism of Eastern bazaar and market." Mannin was angered at the eastern tradition of treating women as servants and property of men. She also lashed out at the dictatorial nature of Voks and Intourist, the two agencies that arranged her every move while she was in European Russia and forbade her travel to some areas. She jokingly blamed such outbursts on her Irish ancestry.

Mannin's account of Samarqand is less appealing than her description of how she reached her destination. It includes the usual historical background and anecdotes, along with often poignant descriptions of the landscape, but her obsession with the defilement and filth of the areas she visited becomes almost overwhelmingly oppressive: "The changed face of Asia, more enduring than the

Mannin at Oak Cottage in Wimbledon, circa 1956 (courtesy of Jean Faulks)

monuments of Tamerlane? Cinemas, hospitals, schools . . . aeroplanes, tanks, machine guns. A mechanised civilisation means . . . tanks as well as tractors, poison-gas as well as antiseptics. It means an existence of ruthless efficiency and an end of idling in the sun."

When Mannin returned from the Soviet Union, she spent time completing *South to Samarkand* and writing fiction. In 1938 she married Reginald Reynolds, whom she had known since 1935. A professional gardener, Reynolds was a Quaker, a lifelong pacifist, and a friend of Mohandas Gandhi, who had trusted Reynolds to carry his historic letter of ultimatum to the British Raj in the Civil Disobedience Campaign of 1930. Reynolds's spiritual influence may be seen in Mannin's subsequent works, but Mannin claimed to maintain a "materialist" skepticism about religious beliefs all her life. Reynolds was also a traveler, but he and Mannin rarely traveled together. When she wanted companionship on her travels, Mannin preferred the company of her daughter, Jean.

Partially because of the outbreak of World War II in 1939, Mannin retreated to Ireland, spending parts of 1940 through the winter months of 1945 at Connemara. She went to Connemara because of her love for Ireland and all things Irish as well as her haunting feeling that she must leave England for a while. The war curtailed her travel abroad for several years. While at her cottage in Connemara she wrote, repaired the ramshackle house, and gardened. *Connemara Journal* (1947) is an account of her activities at Connemara during the war years.

Mannin described *Connemara Journal* as a "love letter" to Ireland. Like *South to Samarkand,* the book is often a springboard for her protean anarchist/socialist views. Though Mannin was born and raised in England, *Connemara Journal* reveals her marked preference for Ireland over England, sometimes vehemently condemning the English for their past and present actions: "English soldiery laid waste Ireland; it was denuded of its forests and all that was planted in its stead was–Protestants." Mannin's conclusion states her desire for Irish sovereignty, expressing the hope that "out of my love for the country, and my passionate belief in its right to an unmutilated nationhood, I may in some measure serve the third person in the trinity, and that with an impassioned loyalty to the utmost of my power and to the end of my days."

Mannin worried over the future of Ireland, bemoaning the mass exodus of young people in search of employment. Yet her love for the Irish countryside and her political convictions led her to exclaim, "If the solution of the problem is the industrialisation of the country–God forbid! Let there be at least one place left sacred in the blasphemous world. Some other solution should be possible, other than emigration or industrialisation." Later in the book she linked her particular sort of socialism with Christianity, betraying the influence of Reynolds and her evolving conception of Christ.

At Connemara Mannin also began to see her city acquaintances and her loved ones in a different light. True to her lifelong estrangement from the intellectual elite, she abhorred anyone who romanticized the rural areas of England:

> Nothing is more nauseating than literary ladies and gentleman who live in cities, or in modernized country cottages, romanticizing about the Peasant and his alleged communion with the Good Earth. The soft white hands of these intellectuals wouldn't even know how to tend a few geraniums in a window-box.

Connemara Journal also tackles issues such as English censorship and literature (including lengthy digressions on Kate O'Brien and D. H. Lawrence), her husband's Quaker faith, the passage of time (and the western Irish conception of it), aging, diary keeping, painting, outhouses, and the war in Europe. Mannin kept her cottage in Connemara until 1962, when the "long love-affair with Ireland" was ended, as she wrote in *Stories from My Life* (1973).

Connemara Journal expressed Mannin's increasing depression not only with the war but with its hellish aftermath:

> Those of us who contend that war is the greatest evil that can befall mankind, more terrible than any evil it seeks to destroy, have always in mind that the evil of war is much more than the mass slaughter of the actual fighting, since the horror does not end with the cessation of hostilities but merely changes its form. Those who sanction war sanction, with it, the unspeakable after-war.

Her sense of loss may have influenced the recurrent discussions of death and dying in the book. Mannin also felt that she might not be capable of returning to the Continent. Her memories of prewar cities such as Paris and Salzburg compelled her to reflect in weary dejection on what might be left of their beauty and to consider that a return might destroy her precious memories.

Yet return she did. In 1948 she published *German Journey,* an account of her travels through ravaged postwar Germany and Austria. Her account of Germanic Europe is enlivened by histories of the Krupp factory and Dresden and by rich descriptions of the Autobahn (and her distaste for it), the postwar habit of tipping in cigarettes instead of money, the Viennese amusement park Prater, and Volkswagens. Yet, mostly because of the utterly defeated atmosphere of Germany, Mannin employed fewer of the typical travel-narrative devices she had used in earlier books: descriptions of local color, landscape, and people. Taking stock of postwar German attitudes and political inclinations, particularly those of the youth, Mannin was heartened by occasional hopeful comments, especially concerning politics: "If the people of Germany had free choice today . . . they would decide for democratic socialism or a liberal democracy rather than for totalitarian Communism." Mannin aptly asserted several times throughout the narrative that the political future of Germany depended almost entirely upon its youth, those too young for complete ideological indoctrination by the Nazi regime: "these were not 'the Fuhrer's children.'"

In large part *German Journey* is a plea to Mannin's readers for aid in eradicating the ineptitude of the victorious powers in their attempt at setting Germany in a democratic direction. She saw hunger as the major obstacle to rebuilding Germany and discovered that the problem was not lack of food but Allied bureaucracy. The book includes frequent observations about how hunger looms over the population: "It was in Hannover that I first literally looked starvation in the drawn, yellow face. I would find myself averting my eyes with a curious sense of shame." Throughout her journey Mannin lost her shame at her own nation's neglect of the needy. Late in the book she remarked that "the best way to get the miner to work 'all out' is to feed him properly all the time." For Mannin being fed "all the time" was the cure for Germany's poor emotional and physical health; proper diet would "get the wheels going again."

Mannin in Tokyo, 1960, during her first visit to Japan (courtesy of Jean Faulks)

The book also reveals Mannin's complete disillusionment with the Soviet system and her fears about Soviet actions and policies both in Russia and in the recently conquered eastern zone of Germany. There are several digressions on Russian atrocities during the final days of the war and on their brutal occupation of eastern Germany:

> Herr X began to speak of the Russians, how they had come to the houses and taken what they wanted–clothes, clocks, anything they fancied, including the women, young and old. His wife had been raped. She had been hiding with other women in a cellar but the Russian soldiers broke in. Afterwards she went, with other violated women, to hospital for examination for V.D.

In her almost desperate plea for "faith" regarding the future of Germany, the book displays further traces of Reynolds's Quaker influence:

> As never before in the history of mankind the world today needs faith–faith that "somehow good" will emerge from the chaos, that the spirit of good latent in mankind . . . will somehow triumph, out of universal will to survive. Only in such a faith is it possible to live creatively and constructively . . . and at peace.

Another distinguishing feature of Mannin's travel writing, one of its strongest attributes, is her thorough research into the politics, geography, and cultures of the regions in which she traveled. She conducted her research before and after her visits, testing others' accounts against her own insights, often disputing government-produced propaganda or enhancing the observations of her contemporaries. In *German Journey* Mannin employed her research to dispel some self-serving Western condemnations of the Soviet Union. Occasionally including glimpses of British, French, and American sometimes overzealous fears of the Soviets, Mannin cast the blame for Germany's wretched condition equally, regardless of ideology.

She saw in the Allied reluctance to speed up food distribution a compulsion to punish the German people further for the sins of the Nazis. She sympathized with the Germans who, for whatever reason, went along with Adolf Hitler's policies without ever fully realizing their ramifications until it was too late. In the various cities she visited she reacquainted herself with friends who were completely ashamed of German atrocities, but all claimed ignorance of those evils when they occurred.

Mannin was profoundly dispirited by the German people's predicament: "they are living abnormal lives in abnormal conditions." Her descriptions of once-beautiful German cityscapes and pastoral farmlands reflect her mournfulness: "Each side of the road there are the hills of rubble, and the hollow houses; not a house or building here and there, but each and every house, continuously. You were prepared for it, you remind yourself, you knew it would be like this. . . . You discover that you feel sick. Physically sick." The rubble horribly disfigured the German landscape, and it partially masked an even greater atrocity. Passing a heap of rubble immediately after a rainfall, Mannin noticed a terrible smell rising from the heap: "No one doubts that there are still bodies buried under the hill-high rubble and masonry."

Mannin wrote of Germany again in her novel *Bavarian Story* (1949). After that her travel destinations became areas of the world in which Reynolds had political and social interest, especially the Middle and Far East. Because of these travels, Mannin became an anti-Zionist, viewing the newly created nation of Israel (1948) as a terrorist state. All the passion she had expressed for Soviet workers, the oppressed and poor of Ireland, and the defeated Germans she now focused on the downtrodden of Asia. While sales of her books remained constant enough to keep her gainfully employed but nowhere near prosperous, she gained new notoriety in Great Britain and the United States as a vocal advocate of pro-Arab policies.

In 1950 Mannin published *Jungle Journey,* an account of her first trip to India. Accompanied by her husband Reginald and her daughter, Mannin traveled to India in 1949 by plane, ship, and train. Her distaste for these modes of transportation, however, seemed insignificant when compared to the harsh realities she encountered on Indian soil, including the poverty all around her: "There are a few beggars–mere bundles of dirty white rags they seem. Suddenly the words, 'the halt, the maimed and the blind,' have new meaning. It is the East all right–unchanged since Biblical times in many of its aspects–of which its beggar population is one."

Mannin felt the plight of India's lower castes and devoted much attention to describing the poverty she saw, describing scenes in which beggars and thieves, merchants and con men, homeless children and teenagers all interacted. She also noted that although the young Indian government maintained a remarkable stability, it had also helped to provoke instability in some surrounding countries. The refugee Hindus from Pakistan, who had "fled from their country" in droves because of recent political upheaval, added to the legions who "sleep out in the streets, on the window ledges of banks and offices and shops, and under arcades, in preference to overcrowded rooms."

As usual Mannin paid attention to everyday living conditions and customs, providing useful and interesting information on the Indian caste system, including this account of a lower tier:

> Begging is a profession; people are born into it, they rear their children to it. Some of the babies are mutilated at birth to equip them for their profession. Until then it had struck us as odd that so many people, and young children, should have missing fingers, and arms amputated–and roughly amputated at that, by the look of the stumps–above the elbow.

Mannin also described the untouchables and their emancipator, Gandhi, who attempted to change the centuries-old perceptions of the untouchables by living with them and renaming them "Harijans," or "Children of God." Gandhi's goals still wait for realization, however, especially in the rural areas, where tradition dies hard. Mannin called for patience until someone with Gandhi's compassion and diplomatic skills could help push India further along in humanitarian terms.

Mannin also recognized such impressive Indian achievements as the Taj Mahal, the modernization of Bombay's streets, apartments, and water facilities, and the thriving tourist trade. She emphasized that Indian poverty only partially stained her otherwise complete enchantment with the East. Even though "there is no splendour like the splendour" of Indian metropolitan areas, the chief purpose for Mannin's visit was to see the agricultural and forest regions of India. She had been invited by Reynolds's friend the chief conservator of forests to accompany him on his annual tour of the jungles to see the forest managers. Mannin and her daughter toured the principal forest of India and witnessed a tiger hunt. While describing the heat, dust, and various aridities of certain forests and jungles, Mannin also paid special attention to the circumstances of living there, including a vivid account of tourists' rest houses, complete with commodes, bedrooms, and ingeniously designed washing facilities. This trip also provided the background for Mannin's novel *At Sundown, the Tiger* (1951).

In 1953, after intense preparatory study and travel through Northern Africa and Europe, Mannin wrote *Moroccan Mosaic,* her first travel narrative set in the Arab regions of the world. The book is divided into descriptions of Tangier, Spanish Morocco, and French Morocco–which were united as the independent nation of Morocco in 1956. The book also includes an appendix with discussions of the nationalist movement, housing, education, emancipation of women, labor conditions, health issues, and civil liberties. As in all her travel narratives, Mannin thoroughly researched these topics and supported her claims by her eyewitness accounts. This book is less a travel narrative than an unabashedly propagandistic survey. Only in the

Mannin interviewing Gen. Abdul Kassem, prime minister of Iraq, during her research for A Lance for the Arabs *(1963)*

closing pages of *Moroccan Mosaic* does Mannin avoid her tendency to politicize.

Mannin explained that she chose the title because of the constituent qualities of a mosaic. Not only are there several different cultures, languages, and religions in Morocco, but also,

> There is much red in the mosaic; there is the red earth of the Rif, and of the *bled* round Marrakesh; there is the yellow of the "Golden Plain" of Ketama, and the gold and grey of the deep Valley of Asila with its Biblical, El Greco landscape of twisted olive trees and sun-warmed boulders; there is the brilliant blue of the sky emphasised by the intense whiteness of the High Atlas ranges; and at the very heart of the design a greyness of ancient walls encircling the secret white city of Fez, where the centuries are engulfed in a thousand years. And threading through all the close-packed colours are the wine-coloured streaks of bougainvillaea, the soft blue of jasmine, and the dark green of palms.

Mannin's trip to Morocco intensified her growing concern for the displacement of the Palestinians after the creation of Israel. She continued appearing at public lectures and symposia to advocate solutions to the Palestinians' plight. Her concern for the Arab world proved the longest-lasting and most heartfelt of her political causes.

Mannin's next extended trip was a 1954 journey to the Far East, another area in which she developed an interest because of its political urgency. She noted the parallels between Burma (now Myanmar) and India in their attempts to shake off the colonial influence of England. In *Land of the Crested Lion: A Journey through Modern Burma* (1955) Mannin explained Burma's pre- and postcolonial history, explaining its allegiances to Buddha, its different ethnic groups, and the political atmosphere of Rangoon (Yangon).

For Mannin this capital city eclipsed in splendor nearly every other locale she visited. She believed that the Shwe Dagon Pagoda, located just outside the city, was the finest building ever constructed: there is a "magic" in the "purity of its line against the flawless sky" that represented for her the pristine natural beauty of the entire country, a beauty that removed it from "everyday reality."

Mannin does not ignore "everyday reality" on her travels through Burma, however. *The Land of the Crested Lion* is replete with the everyday habits and customs of the Burmese people, including the treatment of pariah dogs and the prohibition of footwear into holy temples and homes. She also discovered that "Chinese" food ordered in American or British restaurants never compares with the authentic cuisine of Burma, and she marveled at the hospitality she received in nearly every Burmese home. Even in the most remote, poverty-stricken area, she was welcomed with the traditional green tea, bananas, or biscuits. She attributed much of the Burmese generosity to the people's sincere embracing of Buddhist philosophy.

After she had fully immersed herself in the several attractions of Yangon, Mannin visited other cities along the deltas of the Bay of Bengal. In Moulmein she noticed the same sort of stark contrasts that she found in Soviet Russia–poverty and wealth, wasteland and fertile plain. For Mannin

Burma was a land full of paradox. As in Yangon, there was something magical about Moulmein. From the hills above the city, "even the corrugated iron roofs lose their unsightliness in their thickly wooded setting, bounded by the wide island-studded river and the outlines of low shadowy hills beyond." Everywhere she saw thriving foliage, flowing rivers, and people struggling valiantly to eke out lives from nature. Mannin was amazed at the people's tolerance for the heat, which makes it "necessary to put blotting-paper under the hand when writing to keep the sweat off the paper." She was happy, for the moment, to leave the area for the cooler climes of Mandalay.

As she left Moulmein Mannin shifted her focus to British imperialism. On arriving in Mandalay she described the Mons people, who are indigenous to the region, as actually descending from the Mongols to the north. She then set her sights on what is left of Mandalay:

> Properly speaking Mandalay no longer exists. The old city, built just about a hundred years ago for king Mindon, when he moved his palace bodily from Amarapura, the Golden City across the river from Sagaing, was destroyed in one night by British bombers in May 1945, and only the high encircling red brick wall of that "miracle of rare device" remains. Burmans I talked to everywhere will not have it that the old city was a military objective; they say that "there was no one in it," that the Japanese had gone from it.

When Mannin presses them as to why the old city was destroyed so thoroughly, the people respond, "They wished to break our national spirit." Mannin was appalled.

The results of this unnecessary destruction became the focus of the rest of Mannin's tour of Mandalay. As she left the region for Maymyo she was still concentrating on the effects of British colonialism:

> In what the Burmese call "the English time" it was a very small popular hill-station, as indicated by the street-names–the Mall, Downing Street, Church Road, Club Road; a little way out there is the Harcourt Butler lake, named after the Governor. The houses are red brick, with vaguely pseudo-Tudor effects in the shape of nailed-on timber.

Mannin's admiration for Burmese urban life soured only when she entered areas of British influence or destruction. Her distaste for the imperialist policies of any nation intensified as she grew older. After completing *Land of the Crested Lion,* Mannin used Burma as the setting for her novel *The Living Lotus* (1956).

Mannin's next destination was Brittany in France, where she toured during the summer of 1956. Her account of these travels was published as *The Country of the Sea: Some Wanderings in Brittany* (1957). This book opens with a rare insight into what she attempted to do with all her travel books: "The difference between a guide book and a travel book is that the former is impersonal, a dispassionate presentation of facts, the latter coloured by the writer's temperament, an essentially subjective presentation of impressions." Although Mannin claimed that her reasons for traveling to Brittany were nonpolitical, politics nevertheless entered into her discussions. Mannin began her tour in the department of Finistère, thinking it "might prove to be a French Connemara. It has the same sort of shape on the map." What she found was that areas of Finistère, such as Brest, had been 80 percent destroyed by Allied bombers in 1944. She lamented the destruction of so beautiful a site.

Next she visited Côtes-du-Nord, where she found herself attracted to Lannion "because of a photograph of a street of steps leading up past old cottages to a church," a photograph she had seen many times in a friend's room. She visited several churches and cathedrals, some dating from the fifteenth century. All in all, she found Côtes-du-Nord far less exciting and less reminiscent of Connemara than she had anticipated. Visiting La Côte D'Emeraude, Mannin was enraptured with the "most truly emerald [color] on the lovely strip of coast west of Dinard the beauty of which culminates in the wild and splendid heights of the Cap itself." The book also discusses the castles of the Morbihan district and provides a detailed history of English and Danish sieges throughout the Dark Ages.

Although pleasantly entertained by all she saw, Mannin seems to have been neither interested in Brittany nor intent on interesting her readers. When she spoke of the destruction committed by the Allies while liberating this region in World War II, even her disgust seems artificial.

In 1959 Mannin published the first of a series of travel books for children, written partly for her new granddaughter and partly for financial reasons. Mannin's finances always seem to have been strained. Since the controversy surrounding *Confessions and Impressions* in 1930, her books had sold only modestly. Most never warranted second editions. Aimed at increasing sales and reaching a wider audience, the series eventually included three books: *Ann and Peter in Sweden* (1959), *Ann and Peter in Japan* (1960), and *Ann and Peter in Austria* (1962). Their sales did not reach Mannin's expectations.

Mannin talking to Izzat Atawnah, sheik of Beersheba, 1965 (courtesy of Jean Faulks)

The Flowery Sword (1960) describes Mannin's first trip to Japan, a country in many ways more ravaged by World War II than Germany. Dedicated to the memory of Reginald Reynolds, who died in 1958, the book retraces his steps on an anti-atomic bomb tour some years earlier. Mannin found herself unable to resolve what she called the "paradox" of Japanese culture: "I had been so often desperately lonely, yet so often complete strangers had been kind and helpful; I had been stared at and even laughed at, yet sometimes touched by friendliness. And with all that was ugly and vulgar there was so much that was beautiful."

Throughout her journey Mannin was distressed by crowded streets and trains, language barriers, seeming rudeness, mass-produced trinkets for tourists, Japanese dance, food, taxis, the "hostess system" in many taverns, and sanitary facilities. When discussing the litter problem in Enoshima, a city she used as an example for a problem pervasive throughout Japan, Mannin charged that the Japanese were trying "to vulgarize something naturally beautiful." She noted many parks and city vistas littered knee-high with garbage, but she concluded that Japan was "an extremely beautiful country in spite of all that its people have done to it."

Yet Mannin was committed to exploring Japan: "Arriving in a new country is like getting out of bed in the morning; once you have put foot to ground you are committed; you must begin to cope." Perhaps her heavy reliance on the *Official Guide to Japan* colored her expectations. Mannin also took a somewhat scornful view of the patrilineal nature of Japanese society, noting that it is not easy for Westerners, especially women, to get used to Japan. In fact Mannin could never "form a great attachment for it."

Mannin was also confused and disappointed by the Japanese people's lack of spirituality. They dutifully follow customs and rituals of marriage, child initiation, and death, but, unlike the Burmese, they never openly profess their faith in any religion, even the Buddhism that pervades their culture. They are a "people without religion," Mannin informed her readers several times. This opinion may stem from her lack of sympathy for Zen Buddhism, the teachings of which had been a major reason for her visit to Japan. She quickly learned, however, that its precepts stand quite counter to her thinking: "The Catholic Church requires that shutters be pulled down over the intellect; Zen requires its abolition."

As in *German Journey,* Mannin was critical of the slowness of the Allies' rebuilding efforts after World War II, and she implied that nearly all Japanese shortcomings were the result of the rapid Americanization of Japan since the end of the war. Furthermore, Mannin considered the U.S.-backed Land Reform Act, which split all arable land into small allotments and thus abolished feudalism, a measure that further impoverished farmers, resulting in an American destruction of Japanese life that wrought far more damage than the atomic bombs dropped on Hiroshima and Nagasaki.

When discussing the horrors caused by these bombings, Mannin accused the American government of destroying the two cities without considering an alternate solution to end the war. Her discussions with a doctor in Hiroshima revealed rarely discussed aspects of the disaster:

> I mentioned the shock of suddenly coming face to face with terribly scarred people; he replied that that was not the worst injury. I thought that he meant leukemia and the various other forms of cancer, but he went on to explain about the "deep inner injury," the invisible harm done to the psyche of the victims, who because of what has happened to them feel themselves a people set

apart–since few people would knowingly marry an A-bomb victim for fear of the genetic hazard . . . many who are not externally recognizable as victims keep quiet about it–even to the extent of keeping away from hospital when they know themselves to be ill, keeping their terrible secret to the point of death.

Mannin believed that her research had proved that Japan had been willing to surrender on the Allies' terms before the atomic bombs were dropped. Her anger at the United States was exacerbated by the Americans' construction of a facility in Hiroshima to research means of overcoming the consequences of nuclear war.

At times Mannin's mood lightens, however, especially on her many walks through the beautiful Shinto shrines and parks in every Japanese city. An avid gardener, Mannin joyfully described the flowers, shrubs, and cherry blossoms that beautify every city, even Hiroshima and Nagasaki. Her succinct yet detailed histories of national and local customs and architecture demonstrate her respect for this ancient but rapidly evolving culture. After *Ann and Peter in Japan,* Mannin wrote another children's book about Japanese culture and scenery, *With Will Adams through Japan* (1962).

Early in 1962 Gen. Abdul Kassem (or Qassim), prime minister of Iraq, invited Mannin to be his guest on a visit to his country. In addition to touring that oil-rich nation, she also traveled to other Arab countries, including Jordan, Kuwait, Syria, and Lebanon. The result was *A Lance for the Arabs* (1963), her most accomplished study of the Arab nations.

Mannin's purpose is apparent in her dedication: "To and For THE PALESTINIAN REFUGEES who in camps and cover, cities and towns, throughout the Middle East, wait to return home. . . ." She also made her intentions clear in the introductory chapter:

I would make a tour of the Arab states, with a view to writing a book which would present to the West a general picture of the Middle East, with special reference to the Palestinian tragedy. . . . I thought the majority of people in the West had no real understanding of the Palestine tragedy and the reason why of a million displaced and dispossessed Palestinians, more than half of them living out sub-human lives in camps and the wilderness, and a new generation growing up there had never known the land of their fathers.

In *A Lance for the Arabs* Mannin was determined to portray a region inhabited by gentle, kind, intelligent, and tragic people.

She began her tour in Iraq, where she described the recent revolution under Kassem as a "social revolution" that established an entirely new societal system and government infrastructure. During an interview with him Mannin learned that because of his humble beginnings, his first priority was the defeat of poverty, and he described to her his plan to redistribute land. He also hoped to keep Iraq free of political alignment with either the United States or the Soviet Union. Mannin was impressed by his manners, knowledge, and–most of all–his greeting her without the usual pomp and circumstance surrounding a national leader. She summed up Kassem by saying, "he gives an impression of sincerity."

While in Iraq Mannin witnessed the trial of a boy arrested for avenging his father's death, and her book successfully explains the complex conflict of ideologies surrounding the trial. She also visited a children's hospital and new living quarters constructed for nomadic peoples who were being forced to adapt to new lifestyles.

Mannin was not totally uncritical of the Arab mentality, especially in connection with the Palestinian cause. She heard a conversation in Baghdad that expressed an often-heard view of the Palestinian plight and was chilled by its violent overtones:

When two or three Arabs are gathered together the talk turns inevitably on Palestine and how it is to be liberated. The young man declared that only the Palestinians could affect this; that they should be trained as an army and wage guerrilla warfare, in the way that the Algerians had against the French. I was to hear this idea put forward many times in the months that were to follow, in Syria, Jordan, Lebanon, the United Arab Republic, and even in Kuwait, where there are many Palestinians.

She also heard Kassem echo these same sentiments. Later, after she had visited several Arab states, she noted their lack of unity concerning how to solve the Palestinian problem as well as other diplomatic issues: "Most Arabs, I felt . . . want Arab unity, yet it seemed to me that whenever twelve Arabs were gathered together there would be thirteen opinions."

After Mannin left Baghdad she visited ancient Iraqi sites holy to Christians and Muslims. At most times, however, her focus was on the present. In Basrah she was impressed with a housing project for nomads of the area, expressing admiration for the architects' close attention to people's needs. While in the desert Mannin went to see the reconstruction efforts at the ancient city of Ur, a joint undertaking of archaeologists from all over the world.

Mannin in the late 1960s (photograph © Paul Tanqueray; courtesy of Jean Faulks)

Mannin was much less impressed with Jordan. Believing that the creation of this nation had furthered the demise of the Palestinian state, she considered King Hussein of Jordan no more than a puppet for the British imperialists. Refusing a chance to meet Hussein, Mannin commented, "I always said that I was too much a dyed-in-the-wool Republican for any meetings with royalty, adding sometimes, with conscious inverted snobbery, that it would be rather distinguished to visit Jordan *without* meeting the King."

Mannin compared Jordan unfavorably with Iraq, commenting on finding "in Amman such a feeling of deadness, and armed police and soldiers with tommy-guns everywhere." She also noticed the poverty: "On the roads out of the town there are large shanty towns huddled at the foot of the hills and climbing up their sides, and nothing that I could see was being done about them; the building is all for the monied people." While in Jordan she also went to the Dead Sea, the Palestine refugee camps, the Arab portion of Jerusalem, Bethlehem, and Bethany.

Though she was slightly dismayed by its lack of "Arabness," Lebanon improved her mood immensely. She described Beirut as "Mediterranean," and its atmosphere as "French." Even the Beirut airport suggested a sense of cultural infiltration. In 1945 "Beirut airport had been a ramshackle place . . . all sheds and barbed wire; today it is European-smart–and the density of the shining cars is greater." She was unimpressed with the traditional "Cedars of Lebanon" because there were so few of them, but she enjoyed the beautiful drive to the cedars.

While describing meetings with several dignitaries in Lebanon, Mannin carefully emphasized the Arabs' mostly pacifist tendencies: "I never met any Moslems who expressed anti-Christian attitudes; on the contrary I met continually Moslems who expressed a live-and-let-live attitude as regards religion–urging did they not after all believe in the one God?" She remembered an Iraqi businessman who had confided to her that he did not hate the Jews, but that they certainly hated him and his Arabness. While in Syria, Mannin heard several other dignitaries express the same sentiments. She was pleasantly surprised at the beauty of Damascus, the oldest continually functioning urban area in the world. She also visited Syrian biblical landmarks such as Palmyra and Bosra (Busra).

In 1963 Mannin published *The Road to Beersheba,* a novel that, in her words, was

> Designed as an "answer" to the best-selling Zionist novel, *Exodus;* this novel, which set forth part of the story of the other exodus–the enforced exodus of a million Palestinian Arabs in 1948, following the creation of the Zionist state of "Israel," at the heart of the Palestinian homeland. . . .

Plans were made for a joint Jordanian/Egyptian movie version of the book, but filming was never undertaken because of the mutual distrust between Jordanians and Egyptians.

Having visited Egypt several times during 1962–1963, Mannin next wrote *Aspects of Egypt: Some Travels in the United Arab Republic* (1964). The book begins with an account of an interview with President Gamal Abdel Nasser, who had staged a bloodless coup against King Farouk in 1952. Nasser and Mannin agreed on condemning Israel for terrorist policies, such as the recent bombing of a plane and the disfigurement of an Arab minister's wife's face with a mail bomb. When the conversation shifted to Palestine, Nasser, like the Arab dignitaries Mannin had met earlier, said that the Palestinians must fight for themselves.

Mannin praised the Egyptians' nationalist and socialist venture, especially their progress with the poor, agrarian reform, democracy, woman's rights, and the High Dam. With the Arab states' increasingly united efforts against exploitation by American and British capitalists, Mannin had found a cause. She had even changed her views on Jordan by the time she wrote *The Lovely Land: The Hashemite Kingdom of Jordan* (1965).

In 1966 Mannin traveled to the United States for the first time since the 1920s. *An American Journey* (1967) includes paraphrases of radio and television spots she did there to defend the Arab states. Her opinions of the United States were not much different from the ones she expressed in *Confessions and Impressions.* Despite her derision of American capitalism, however, she appreciated the friendliness of the people and found goodness in much of what she saw, especially the wide-open spaces of nature just outside each city.

Beginning her cross-country journey via Greyhound bus from the Port Authority in New York City, Mannin at first viewed the United States as a land that "can seem all cars, in endless streams, and gas-stations, and eating places. As though all Americans ever did was drive and eat–mostly hamburgers." She then realized, however, that her mode of transportation might be influencing her observations.

As she traveled through Texas and into the Oklahoma Panhandle–once set aside as "Indian Territory"–she wondered, "What happened to the Indians of this erstwhile Indian Territory? Oh, most of them were cleared out, like the Arabs from Palestine in 1948." Later in the book she included further information on the Native Americans' plight:

> Average family income for Indians is 1,500 dollars a year. Only twenty-six per cent of Indian families on reservations have an income of 3,000 dollars a year, the minimum set for the poverty program.
>
> The homes of ninety per cent of Indians do not meet Public Housing Authority Standards.

Summing up European atrocities to Native Americans all over the continent, Mannin observed,

> Of all this I knew nothing the beautiful morning I drove through the fine city of Oklahoma, remembering the musical. I am glad not to have known; it would have taken the brightness out of the morning–as it has taken it out of it in recollection. Perhaps it was symbolic that later in the day a rough wind blew the red dust across the road and the sky became overcast.

Mannin's consuming interest in the Middle East and the plight of the Palestinians is apparent even in her descriptions of the American West. In Arizona she was "reminded of Jordan, with the wide horizons, the strange rock formations, and the vast sandy wilderness areas." She was also amused by the American obsession with mobility, especially in the West, commenting on the prevalence of mobile homes, recreational vehicles, and of course the omnipresent automobile.

In Los Angeles she noticed the lack of pedestrians, the outlandish architecture, abstract sculptures, "garish Sunset Boulevard," and death-defying driving on freeways. Mannin's westward journey was quick; she traveled from New York City to Los Angeles in less than a week. On her return journey she allowed herself time to stop in areas she had only passed through on the way west. On this leg of her trip her opinion of the landscape softened, but her disdain for American capitalism did not.

Mannin was impressed by the majesty of the Grand Canyon: "At the first confrontation one is, I think, stunned–simply." She admired the "very beautiful thousand acres" of the mostly man-made woods in Golden Gate Park. She was enthralled with the desert flowers of Arizona and New Mexico and by the "most amazing colours" of the Petrified Forest. Yet a sign she saw frequently throughout the Petrified Forest– "Lookee, Lookee, No Takee"–served to confirm her view of the motives behind American capitalism.

After *An American Journey,* Mannin's travel narratives became less political. *England at Large* (1970) and *England My Adventure* (1972) describe short travels in rural England, including the Lake District and the Welsh and Scottish borderlands, as well as in some cities. As she traveled her mind was filled with thoughts of her past, her experiences, and her acquaintances. With *Mission to Beirut* (1973) she attempted unsuccessfully to recapture the immediacy of her earlier accounts of Middle East life, while *An Italian Journey* (1974) is similar in style to her late accounts of her English travels, especially in the descriptions of the villages and snow-peaked mountains of north Italy.

In 1973 Mannin published *Stories from My Life,* vignettes about her experiences in Ireland and elsewhere, including the Middle East. Her discussion of Kuwait, some twenty years before the Gulf War, explains the tensions that continue to exist between Kuwait and Iraq:

> All the Arab countries except one, Iraq, and the Arab League, recognize the independent status bestowed on Kuwait by the British in 1961. General Qassim's claim to Kuwait as an integral part of Iraq rested on the fact that since 1775, and until the First World War and the occupation of Iraq by the British, it was part of Basrah province. Under the Ottoman Sultan the rulers of Kuwait were subject to the Governor of Basrah.

Ultimately Mannin considered Kuwait far too rich for its own good, providing the example that when cars were no longer considered useful, they were driven to the desert and abandoned. Other vignettes in *Stories from My Life* include reminiscences of Paris, her father, "My Burglar, Mr. Stanley," aging, England, racism, Athens, and her favorite cat, Sammy, who later became the subject of two books.

In *Sunset over Dartmoor: A Final Chapter of Autobiography* (1977) Mannin described the realization of age that set in when she sold Oak Cottage to live in Shaldon. Writing of her own long and eventful life, she observed,

> A certain shock, I think, attaches to one's seventieth birthday–the shock of the realization that one has had one's "allotted span," and anything that comes after that is a bonus. It seems so very far-away-and-long-ago that we were young-and-twenty, and yet, too, it has all gone so incredibly quickly. Well, but there you are; you've had your allotted span and you're still there–and for all you know there may be another ten, fifteen, or even twenty years of it, which is a daunting thought.

Mannin died in 1984 after falling at home. She is survived by her daughter, Jean, who lives in Devon, continues to travel to many of the areas once visited by her mother, and defends her mother's often vitriolic condemnations of British and American capitalism.

Ethel Mannin's writings reveal her remarkable devotion to the causes and ideals of peaceful coexistence as well as nonviolent means of settling disputes. Her criticism of Western capitalism in many ways foreshadows more recent postcolonial academic inquiries into travel writing. Finally, her interesting and full life, including her willingness to share it in books with any who would listen, should initiate further appraisals of her influence on the peace movement, feminism, and political non-conformance. She deserves a more respected place in discussions of the genre.

Reference:

Andy Croft, "Ethel Mannin: The Red Rose of Love and the Red Flower of Liberty," in *Rediscovering Forgotten Radicals: British Women Writers, 1889–1939,* edited by Angela Ingram and Daphne Patai (Chapel Hill & London: University of North Carolina Press, 1993).

Papers:

Mannin's papers, manuscripts, and letters are in the archives at Boston University.

W. Somerset Maugham

(25 January 1874 – 16 December 1965)

Stanley Archer
Texas A&M University

See also the Maugham entries in *DLB 10: Modern British Dramatists, 1900–1945; DLB 36: British Novelists, 1890–1929: Modernists; DLB 77: British Mystery Writers, 1920–1939; DLB 100: Modern British Essayists, Second Series;* and *DLB 162: British Short-Fiction Writers, 1915–1945.*

BOOKS: *Liza of Lambeth* (London: Unwin, 1897; revised, 1904; New York: Doran, 1921);

The Making of a Saint (Boston: Page, 1898; London: Unwin, 1898);

Orientations (London: Unwin, 1899);

The Hero (London: Hutchinson, 1901);

Mrs. Craddock (New York: Doran, 1902; revised edition, 1955; London: Heinemann, 1902);

A Man of Honour: A Play in Four Acts (London: Chapman & Hall, 1903); republished as *A Man of Honour: A Tragedy in Four Acts* (London: Heinemann, 1912 [i.e., 1911]; Chicago: Dramatic Publishing, 1912);

The Merry-Go-Round (London: Heinemann, 1904);

The Land of the Blessed Virgin: Sketches and Impressions in Andalusia (London: Heinemann, 1905; New York: Knopf, 1920); republished as *Andalusia: Sketches and Impressions* (New York: Knopf, 1920);

The Bishop's Apron: A Study in the Origins of a Great Family (London: Chapman & Hall, 1906);

The Explorer (London: Heinemann, 1908 [i.e., 1907]; New York: Baker & Taylor, 1909);

The Magician (London: Heinemann, 1908; New York: Duffield, 1909); enlarged as *The Magician: A Novel, Together with A Fragment of Autobiography* (London: Heinemann, 1956; Garden City, N.Y.: Doubleday, 1957);

Lady Frederick: A Comedy in Three Acts (London: Heinemann, 1912 [i.e., 1911]; Chicago: Dramatic Publishing, 1912);

Jack Straw: A Farce in Three Acts (London: Heinemann, 1912 [i.e., 1911]; Chicago: Dramatic Publishing, 1912);

W. Somerset Maugham, 1914

Mrs. Dot: A Farce in Three Acts (London: Heinemann, 1912; Chicago: Dramatic Publishing, 1912);

Penelope: A Comedy in Three Acts (London: Heinemann, 1912; Chicago: Dramatic Publishing, 1912);

The Explorer: A Melodrama in Four Acts (London: Heinemann, 1912; Chicago: Dramatic Publishing, 1912);

The Tenth Man: A Tragic Comedy in Three Acts (London: Heinemann, 1913; Chicago: Dramatic Publishing, 1913);

Landed Gentry: A Comedy in Four Acts (London: Heinemann, 1913; Chicago: Dramatic Publishing, 1913);

Smith: A Comedy in Four Acts (London: Heinemann, 1913; Chicago: Dramatic Publishing, 1913);

Of Human Bondage (New York: Doran, 1915; London: Heinemann, 1915);

The Moon and Sixpence (London: Heinemann, 1919; New York: Doran, 1919);

The Unknown: A Play in Three Acts (London: Heinemann, 1920; New York: Doran, 1920);

The Circle: A Comedy in Three Acts (London: Heinemann, 1921; New York: Doran, 1921);

The Trembling of a Leaf: Little Stories of the South Sea Islands (New York: Doran, 1921; London: Heinemann, 1921); republished as *Sadie Thompson, and Other Stories of the South Sea Islands* (London: Readers Library, 1928);

Caesar's Wife: A Comedy in Three Acts (London: Heinemann, 1922; New York: Doran, 1923);

East of Suez: A Play in Seven Scenes (London: Heinemann, 1922; New York: Doran, 1922);

The Land of Promise: A Comedy in Four Acts (London: Heinemann, 1922; New York: Doran, 1923);

On a Chinese Screen (New York: Doran, 1922; London: Heinemann, 1922);

Our Betters: A Comedy in Three Acts (London: Heinemann, 1923; New York: Doran, 1924);

The Unattainable: A Farce in Three Acts (London: Heinemann, 1923);

Home and Beauty: A Farce in Three Acts (London: Heinemann, 1923);

Loaves and Fishes: A Comedy in Four Acts (London: Heinemann, 1924);

The Painted Veil (New York: Doran, 1925; London: Heinemann, 1925);

The Casuarina Tree: Six Stories (London: Heinemann, 1926; New York: Doran, 1926); republished as *The Letter: Stories of Crime* (London & Glasgow: Collins, 1930);

The Constant Wife: A Comedy in Three Acts (New York: Doran, 1927; London: Heinemann, 1927);

The Letter: A Play in Three Acts (London: Heinemann, 1927; New York: Doran, 1927);

Ashenden: or, The British Agent (London: Heinemann, 1928; Garden City, N.Y.: Doubleday, Doran, 1928);

The Sacred Flame: A Play in Three Acts (Garden City, N.Y.: Doubleday, Doran, 1928; London: Heinemann, 1928 [i.e., 1929]);

The Gentleman in the Parlour: A Record of a Journey from Rangoon to Haiphong (London: Heinemann, 1930; Garden City, N.Y.: Doubleday, Doran, 1930);

Cakes and Ale: or, The Skeleton in the Cupboard (London: Heinemann, 1930; Garden City, N.Y.: Doubleday, Doran, 1930);

The Bread-Winner: A Comedy in One Act (London: Heinemann, 1930); republished as *The Breadwinner: A Comedy* (Garden City, N.Y.: Doubleday, Doran, 1931);

Six Stories Written in the First Person Singular (Garden City, N.Y.: Doubleday, Doran, 1931; London: Heinemann, 1931);

The Book-Bag (Florence: Orioli, 1932);

The Narrow Corner (London: Heinemann, 1932); Garden City, N.Y.: Doubleday, Doran, 1932);

For Services Rendered: A Play in Three Acts (London: Heinemann, 1932; Garden City, N.Y.: Doubleday, Doran, 1933);

Ah King (London: Heinemann, 1933; Garden City, N.Y.: Doubleday, 1933);

Sheppey: A Play in Three Acts (London: Heinemann, 1933);

Don Fernando; or, Variations on Some Spanish Themes (London & Toronto: Heinemann, 1935; Garden City, N.Y.: Doubleday, Doran, 1935; revised edition, Melbourne, London & Toronto: Heinemann, 1950);

Cosmopolitans (Garden City, N.Y.: Doubleday, Doran, 1936; London & Toronto: Heinemann, 1936);

Theatre: A Novel (Garden City, N.Y.: Doubleday, Doran, 1937; London & Toronto: Heinemann, 1937);

The Summing Up (London & Toronto: Heinemann, 1938; Garden City, N.Y.: Doubleday, Doran, 1938); republished in *The Partial View* (London: Heinemann, 1954);

Christmas Holiday (London & Toronto: Heinemann, 1939; Garden City, N.Y.: Doubleday, Doran, 1939);

France at War (London: Heinemann, 1940; New York: Doubleday, Doran, 1940);

Books and You (London & Toronto: Heinemann, 1940; New York: Doubleday, Doran, 1940);

The Mixture As Before (London & Toronto: Heinemann, 1940; New York: Doubleday, Doran, 1940);

Up at the Villa (New York: Doubleday, Doran, 1941; London & Toronto: Heinemann, 1941);

Strictly Personal (Garden City, N.Y.: Doubleday, Doran, 1941; London & Toronto: Heinemann, 1942);

The Hour Before the Dawn: A Novel (Garden City, N.Y.: Doubleday, Doran, 1942; Sydney & London: Angus & Robertson, 1945);

The Unconquered (New York: House of Books, 1944);

The Razor's Edge: A Novel (Garden City, N.Y.: Doubleday, Doran, 1944; London & Toronto: Heinemann, 1944);

Then and Now: A Novel (London & Toronto: Heinemann, 1946; Garden City, N.Y.: Doubleday, 1946); republished as *Fools and Their Folly* (New York: Avon, 1949);

Creatures of Circumstance (London & Toronto: Heinemann, 1947; Garden City, N.Y.: Doubleday, 1947);

Catalina: A Romance (London, Melbourne & Toronto: Heinemann, 1948; Garden City, N.Y.: Doubleday, 1948);

Here and There: Short Stories (Melbourne, London & Toronto: Heinemann, 1948);

Great Novelists and Their Novels: Essays on the Ten Greatest Novels of the World and the Men and Women Who Wrote Them (Philadelphia & Toronto: Winston, 1948); revised and enlarged as *Ten Novels and Their Authors* (London & Toronto: Heinemann, 1954); republished as *The Art of Fiction: An Introduction to Ten Novels and Their Authors* (Garden City, N.Y.: Doubleday, 1955);

A Writer's Notebook (London, Melbourne & Toronto: Heinemann, 1949; Garden City, N.Y.: Doubleday, 1949); republished in *The Partial View* (London: Heinemann, 1954);

The Writer's Point of View (London: Cambridge University Press, 1951);

The Vagrant Mood: Six Essays (London, Melbourne & Toronto: Heinemann, 1952; Garden City, N.Y.: Doubleday, 1953);

The Noble Spaniard: A Comedy in Three Acts, adapted from Ernest Grenet-Dancourt's *Les Gaîtés de veuvage* (London: Evans, 1953);

Points of View (London, Melbourne & Toronto: Heinemann, 1958; Garden City, N.Y.: Doubleday, 1959);

Purely for My Pleasure (London, Melbourne & Toronto: Heinemann, 1962; Garden City, N.Y.: Doubleday, 1962);

Seventeen Lost Stories, compiled by Craig V. Showalter (Garden City, N.Y.: Doubleday, 1969);

Marriages Are Made in Heaven: A Play in One Act (London: Blond, 1984);

A Traveller in Romance (London: Blond, 1984; New York: Potter, 1985).

Collections: *The Collected Plays,* 6 volumes (London: Heinemann, 1931–1934);

The Collected Edition of the Nondramatic Works of W. Somerset Maugham, 35 volumes (London: Heinemann, 1931–1969);

East and West: The Collected Short Stories of W. Somerset Maugham (Garden City, N.Y.: Doubleday, Doran, 1934); republished as *Altogether: Being the Collected Stories of W. Somerset Maugham* (London: Heinemann, 1934);

The Complete Short Stories of W. Somerset Maugham (3 volumes, London: Heinemann, 1951; 2 volumes, Garden City, N.Y.: Doubleday, 1952);

Selected Prefaces and Introductions (Garden City, N.Y.: Doubleday, 1963);

The Works of W. Somerset Maugham, 45 volumes (New York: Arno, 1977).

PLAY PRODUCTIONS: *Schiffbrüchig,* Berlin, Schall and Rauch, 3 January 1902;

A Man of Honour: A Tragedy in Four Acts, London, Imperial Theatre, 22 February 1903;

Mademoiselle Zampa, London, Avenue Theatre, 18 February 1904;

Lady Frederick: A Comedy in Three Acts, London, Royal Court Theatre, 26 October 1907;

Jack Straw: A Farce in Three Acts, London, Vaudeville Theatre, 26 March 1908;

Mrs. Dot: A Farce in Three Acts, London, Comedy Theatre, 26 April 1908;

The Explorer: A Melodrama in Four Acts, London, Lyric Theatre, 13 June 1908; revised version, London, Lyric Theatre, 19 May 1909;

Penelope: A Comedy in Three Acts, London, Comedy Theatre, 9 January 1909;

The Noble Spaniard, adapted from Ernest Grenet-Dancourt's *Les Gaîtés du veuvage,* London, Royalty Theatre, 20 March 1909;

Smith: A Comedy in Four Acts, London, Comedy Theatre, 30 September 1909;

The Tenth Man: A Tragic Comedy in Three Acts, London, Globe Theatre, 24 February 1910;

Grace, London, Duke of York's Theatre, 15 October 1910;

Loaves and Fishes: A Comedy in Four Acts, London, Duke of York's Theatre, 24 February 1911;

The Perfect Gentleman, adapted from Molière's *Le Bourgeois Gentilhomme,* London, His Majesty's Theatre, 27 May 1913;

The Land of Promise: A Comedy in Four Acts, New York, Lyceum Theatre, 25 December 1913; London, Duke of York's Theatre, 26 February 1914;

Caroline, London, New Theatre, 8 February 1916;

Our Betters: A Comedy in Three Acts, New York, Hudson Theatre, 12 March 1917; London, Globe Theatre, 12 September 1923;

Love in a Cottage, London, Globe Theatre, 26 January 1918;

Caesar's Wife: A Comedy in Three Acts, London, Royalty Theatre, 27 March 1919;

Home and Beauty, London, Playhouse, 30 August 1919; produced again as *Too Many Husbands,* New York, Booth Theatre, 8 October 1919;

The Unknown: A Play in Three Acts, London, Aldwych Theatre, 9 August 1920;

The Circle: A Comedy in Three Acts, London, Haymarket Theatre, 3 March 1921;

East of Suez: A Play in Seven Scenes, London, His Majesty's Theatre, 2 September 1922;

The Camel's Back, New York, Vanderbilt Theatre, 13 November 1923; London, Playhouse, 31 January 1924;

The Constant Wife: A Comedy in Three Acts, New York, Maxine Elliot's Theatre, 29 November 1926; London, Strand Theatre, 6 April 1927;

The Letter: A Play in Three Acts, London, Playhouse, 24 February 1927;

The Sacred Flame: A Play in Three Acts, New York, Henry Miller's Theatre, 19 November 1928; London, Playhouse, 8 February 1929;

The Breadwinner: A Comedy in One Act, London, Vaudeville Theatre, 30 September 1930;

For Services Rendered: A Play in Three Acts, London, Globe Theatre, 1 November 1932;

The Mask and the Face, adapted from Luigi Chiarelli's *La Maschere e il volto,* New York, Fifty-Second Street Theatre, 8 May 1933;

Sheppey: A Play in Three Acts, London, Wyndham's Theatre, 14 September 1933.

OTHER: *Traveller's Library,* compiled, with an introduction, by Maugham (Garden City, N.Y.: Doubleday, Doran, 1933); republished as *Fifty Modern English Writers* (Garden City, N.Y.: Doubleday, Doran, 1933);

Tellers of Tales: 100 Short Stories from the United States, England, France, Russia and Germany, compiled, with an introduction, by Maugham (New York: Doubleday, Doran, 1939);

Great Modern Reading: W. Somerset Maugham's Introduction to Modern English and American Literature, compiled by Maugham (Garden City, N.Y.: Doubleday, 1943);

Rudyard Kipling, *A Choice of Kipling's Prose,* compiled, with an introduction, by Maugham (London: Macmillan, 1952).

W. Somerset Maugham ranks among the most prolific, versatile, and successful British authors. Among his more than eighty books, five are usually classified as travel literature. The composition of these works spanned more than four decades, indicating his long-time interest in travel and travel literature.

Born at the British Embassy in Paris on 25 January 1874, William Somerset Maugham was the fourth son of Robert Ormond Maugham, an English solicitor, and his socialite wife, Edith Mary Snell Maugham. Maugham spent his early childhood in France. At age ten, following the death of his mother in 1872 and his father in 1874, he was sent to live with a married but childless elderly uncle, the Reverend Henry Maugham, vicar of Whitstable, near Canterbury. During his lonely days in the vicarage, Maugham found solace in reading his uncle's books. Owing to painful shyness, he found little relief for his solitude after entering the King's School, Canterbury, in May 1885. By then Maugham had developed a permanent stammer that made him unfit for the legal profession of his father and two of his older brothers. After completing the sixth form, he persuaded his uncle and German-born aunt to permit him to travel to Germany rather than enter an English university. Continuing his studies as a seventeen-year-old in Heidelberg, he fell under the influence of modernism in literature, art, and philosophy. Returning to England, he eventually enrolled in medical school at St. Thomas' Hospital, London, and received his M.D. in 1897. After completing his medical studies, he traveled to Spain, where he lived in Seville from December 1897 until April 1899.

Meanwhile he had tried his hand at writing, and the unexpected success of his first novel, the brief, naturalistic *Liza of Lambeth* (1897), encouraged him to become a professional man of letters. He began writing stories, novels, and dramas in profusion, but a decade passed before he encountered much success. Beginning with *Lady Frederick* (produced in 1907), a series of dramas written in the comedy-of-manners tradition brought him acclaim and financial success. He continued, nevertheless, to write fiction, most notably his Bildungsroman *Of Human Bondage* (1915), as well as nonfiction.

In 1916 Maugham began service with British Military Intelligence in Switzerland, and his varied experiences brought additional materials for his writing. In 1915 he had a daughter by Syrie Bernardo Wellcome, whom he married on 26 May 1917, after her divorce from Henry Wellcome became final. Maugham's basically homosexual nature brought an end to his marriage; they separated in 1927 and were divorced in 1929. In 1926 Maugham bought the Villa Mauresque on the French Riviera and made it his home for the remainder of his life, except during the German occupation of the early 1940s. He frequently traveled the world in search of materials for fiction. His health began to fail when he was in his late eighties, and he died at the Villa Mauresque 16 December 1965.

One result of Maugham's 1897–1899 sojourn in Spain was his first travel book, *The Land of the Blessed Virgin,* completed in 1899 but not published until 1905. Taken together, the forty sketches in the book suggest a continuous journey through southern Spain, beginning in Rhonda, then to Cordova (Córdoba), Seville, Ecija, Granada, and Jerez and concluding in Cadiz (Cádiz), whence the narrator departs to Tangier. In reality the experiences occurred over the entirety of Maugham's stay in Spain; he took many journeys from Seville and later arranged the accounts coherently. Initially, the book was not successful. Half the 1,250 copies in the first edition were remaindered, but the book fared better after Maugham had established his reputation. In 1920 and 1935 it was republished as *Andalusia.* Despite its poor sales, the first edition received the qualified praise of Virginia Woolf, who reviewed it for *The Times* (London, 26 May 1905), and the book was noticed in at least one other contemporary review.

The Land of the Blessed Virgin is in many ways the purest example of travel writing among Maugham's books. When he visited it in late 1897, Andalusia, the region of southern Spain near the Mediterranean, retained much evidence of Moorish influence. The Moorish art and architecture were especially captivating to Maugham. The brief sketches in *The Land of the Blessed Virgin*–depicting places, buildings, ceremonies, characters, natural scenery, and events–clearly exemplify the travel genre. Relying heavily on contrasts and irony, Maugham portrayed Spanish life and culture primarily through description. His tolerant, cosmopolitan outlook made him essentially nonjudgmental; he balanced his criticism of Spanish customs such as bullfighting with criticism of English customs.

The narrator, an example of the Maugham persona of fiction, is the only character who reappears consistently in *The Land of the Blessed Virgin.* True to Maugham, this persona identifies himself as a writer and describes medical problems in a way that demonstrates his medical training. He is clinical, detached, usually uninvolved, and nonjudgmental. His interests include dimly lit churches, works of art, eccentric people, and out-of-the-way places. He has a sincere interest in the land and makes an earnest effort to understand it. A well-informed traveler, he has studied the history of the region and has read the accounts of travel writers who preceded him. His interest inclines toward discovering the unusual in the familiar or in visiting and describing places not frequented by other travelers. For the most part he avoids typical tourist attractions and prefers to depict obscure persons instead of celebrities. He willingly accepts risks and endures hardships and privation to visit remote places where few outsiders have ventured.

Maugham in 1929

Most of the characters depicted in the book are not named. They are identified by their status, occupation, or profession, as, for example, the wine merchant, the poet, the swineherd. Among the few exceptions are historical figures, such as Pedro the Cruel (Peter I, fourteenth-century king of Castile) and Ferdinand and Isabella. The work includes a recurring hint of romance with a Spanish beauty named Rosarito, but the account is handled with so little passion and such scant detail that critics have generally considered Rosarito a creation of Maugham's imagination.

In Spain the narrator finds life more casual and hedonistic and the people more insouciant than in northern lands. He also discovers that beggars throng the streets and that most people are poor, a situation that stands in contrast to the opulence of the baroque church interiors, a reminder of vanished glory. Whether describing the architecture of the cathedrals at Seville and Granada or Moorish

Maugham (center) and Gerald Haxton (second from right) with friends in Austria, 1930s

structures such as the Giralda or the Alhambra, he turns from architectural details to the persons near or within the structures, adding dialogue, as if to introduce elements for a story. More straightforward description occurs in the sketches on bullfighting, which provide realistic detail punctuated by Spanish words, as when he describes the entry of the matadors and their entourage into the ring: "First come the three *matadors,* the eldest in the middle, the next on his right, the youngest on the left; they are followed by their respective *cuadrillas,* the *banderilleros,* the *capeadors,* the *picadors* on horseback, and finally the *chulos,* whose duty it is to unsaddle dead horses, attach the slaughtered bull to a team of mules, and perform other minor offices." Among other experiences, his account of a journey to Ecija on horseback furnishes an impression of the Spanish countryside. Accounts of Spanish song, theater, and art capture the major artistic elements of the culture. The discussion of religious art is devoted primarily to the paintings of Bartolomé Murillo, portraying him as the most characteristic painter of the region.

In the interim between *The Land of the Blessed Virgin* and his next travel work, *On a Chinese Screen* (1922), Maugham was exceptionally peripatetic. During World War I he was posted to Switzerland, the United States, and Russia and between assignments traveled to American Samoa and Tahiti. Before the war ended, he was in a Scottish sanatorium for treatment of tuberculosis. All these locales and experiences furnished a wealth of information for novels and short stories. By 1920 he had embraced the concept of the exotic story, one that deals with Caucasians, usually Anglo-Saxon, dwelling in an alien environment populated by different races and being shaped by it. His favorite subject for fiction was British colonials serving in the South Pacific or East Asia lands. In the winter of 1919–1920 Maugham spent four months in China, accompanied by his American secretary Gerald Haxton. *On a Chinese Screen* is based on his experiences there.

The fifty-nine sketches in *On a Chinese Screen* reveal a different approach from the book on Spain though the narrator has not changed significantly. He retains his identity as a writer trained in medicine, but he is more self-conscious and more selective about the subject matter. Instead of attempting to portray as much as he can about China, he frequently writes about Europeans who serve there, so the book reflects European attitudes about the Chinese. Two sketches of European officials from *On a Chinese Screen,* "The Consul" and "The Taipan," are included in the first volume of his *Complete Short Stories* (1951). For the most part the sketches have little plot, and the portraits of Maugham's fellow Europeans are ironic.

Maugham in London, 1940

In a preface written for the 1935 edition of *On a Chinese Screen,* Maugham called the work not a book but the materials for a book. Even while describing life in a strange land, he wrote as though gleaning materials for his fiction. The sketch "Dr. Macallister" is a good example. An American missionary physician goes to China expecting to serve heroically while enduring hardship and self-denial. When he discovers that missionaries have a higher standard of living in China than in their own lands, he grows disillusioned, leaves the position, and conducts his own desultory medical practice. In the course of explaining his actions, he draws the narrator's attention to a photograph of a young man. The narrator fails to recognize the photograph as an early likeness of his host. When the matter is clarified, he wonders what accounts for the dramatic change and adds, "That is the story I'd like to write."

In seeking the hidden and often incongruous qualities of transplanted Anglo-Saxons, Maugham depicted a rich gallery of types. There is the American Adventist missionary, narrowly intolerant of Chinese culture but a good enough companion unless his authority is questioned. A British socialist, who affects bohemian dress and manner, identifies with the lower classes but berates and kicks a rickshaw boy. A prim British ambassador with a supercilious manner seems polished until he gives away his bad taste. A missionary lady engages the narrator in a conversation that consists exclusively of platitudes. A desperately lonely official for the British Alcohol and Tobacco Company (B.A.T.) at a remote outpost attempts to stop an itinerant missionary for company and conversation, but the missionary, after discerning that the man's business involves alcohol and tobacco, presses on without pause. The only European who has made any attempt to understand Chinese civilization and culture has mastered the language and literature, but, the narrator concludes, he has missed the spirit of China.

When he described China and the Chinese, Maugham evinced sympathy with the Chinese character though he acknowledged that his understanding of the Chinese was limited. *On a Chinese Screen* conveys Maugham's genuine concern in its descriptions of anonymous coolies and their lives of endless drudgery. Sketches of an opium den and a baby tower (the site of infanticide) reveal the dark side of life in China though Maugham's rational, analytical perspective mitigates their inherent unpleasantness. When he described pleasant Chinese scenes such as a landscape or an expanse of rice paddies, he often

Maugham and Haxton in 1942 (photograph by Carl Van Vechten; by permission of Joseph Solomon, for the Estate of Carl Van Vechten)

drew comparisons to his prior European experience. A journey through an area of mixed woodland and fields reminds the narrator of the scenes of his boyhood in Kent. Viewing a large plain traversed by a river, he likens the view to the Rhine Valley near Heidelberg, the site of Maugham's sojourn as a student.

The workmanlike prose style of *On a Chinese Screen* reflects a maturity beyond that of *The Land of the Blessed Virgin.* Clichés and colloquial expressions are replaced by lucid, realistic narrative and description. In an effort at involving the reader, Maugham occasionally altered the point of view to the indefinite second person, even when the *you* clearly relates to the experiences of the narrator. The book was not popular, the first British edition being limited to two thousand copies.

Maugham's third travel book, a product of his trip to Southeast Asia in 1921, enjoyed greater success, in part because his stories and novels set in the Pacific and Asiatic regions had linked his art with the lands and peoples of the area. Borrowed from William Hazlitt, the main title of *The Gentleman in the Parlour: A Record of a Journey from Rangoon to Haiphong* (1930) suggests the secure status and the sort of anonymity enjoyed by the traveler who is aware that his meetings with others will be casual and temporary. The style achieves a subtlety unusual in Maugham, with lengthy, carefully crafted sentences effectively employing balance, antithesis, and climax as schemes of repetition. Although the style does not approach the baroque, it employs rich, concrete diction and an unusual number of similes; the reader even encounters an occasional passage of purple prose. The description of Angor Wat during a rainstorm represents Maugham's heightened style at its best. The passage concludes, "I stood in a doorway, not a little frightened, and as the lightning tore the darkness like a veil I saw the jungle stretching endlessly before me, and it seemed to me that these great temples and their gods were insignificant before the fierce might of nature. . . . For nature is the most powerful of all the gods."

Although he wrote lengthy accounts of selected subjects in the forty-four untitled chapters of *The Gentleman in the Parlour,* Maugham bound the narrative closely to the actual route of his journey. During the winter of 1921–1922 he traveled with Gerald Haxton up the Irrawaddy River from Rangoon (Yangon) to Pagan and Mandalay, a route that took him through modern Burma (now Myanmar), Thailand, Laos, Cambodia, and Vietnam. Before sailing back to Japan he visited cities such as Kengtung, Bangkok, Phnom Penh, Saigon (now Ho

Chi Minh City), Hanoi, and Haiphong. In addition to travel by steamship, this journey involved transportation by pack train, railway, motorcar, truck, and sampan. As a result Maugham's experiences in these remote and primitive lands were richly varied.

The book illustrates Maugham's technique of making private conversation with lonely colonial officials stationed at obscure outposts. They recount their stories over drinks with Maugham's narrator, who has learned to be a good listener and to elicit the speakers' innermost thoughts. As with Maugham's previous travel book, some of the accounts were altered only slightly to be included among his collected short stories: "Mabel," "Masterson," "The Princess and the Nightingale," "Mirage," and "A Marriage of Convenience." Apart from the fairy tale about Princess September, the stories are concerned with Europeans and might well have used another setting. The final chapter introduces a Jewish-American salesman named Elfenbein, whom the narrator finds offensive. Still, Elfenbein makes a magnanimous gesture and offers the final observation on human nature: "I'll give you my opinion of the human race in a nutshell, brother; their heart's in the right place, but their head's a thoroughly inefficient organ." The plot and characterization bear a strong resemblance to those of a later well-known Maugham story, "Mr. Know-All."

Among the sketches are many descriptions of life in the Orient, always from a narrator conscious that he remains on the outside. He imparts a feel for the jungles and rain forests, for the exotic birds that inhabit them, and for the diverse peoples of the regions. Among the man-made artifacts described are wats, pagodas, ramshackle living quarters, primitive roads, and rickety bridges. The book also describes what it was like to take the first motorcar ride over a primitive road and to see the people along the way staring in wonder, not knowing what to make of the machine. In addition, it makes an effort to clarify the intellectual outlook and character of the peoples, attempting to explain Buddhism, karma, and the relation between ethical thought and belief in transmigration, subjects that Maugham explored elsewhere as well. Writing primarily as an observer seeking to absorb and understand, Maugham portrayed incongruities in human beings less boldly than in his previous travel writing.

Don Fernando (1935), Maugham's second travel book on Spain, bears a resemblance to books of critical essays such as *The Vagrant Mood* (1952) and *Points of View* (1958). Further, the reflective material and aesthetic passages on writing and literature are repeated in Maugham's autobiographical book *The Summing Up* (1938). By the time *Don Fernando* was written Maugham claimed to have made a dozen trips to Spain, the last in 1934. In *Don Fernando* he wrote primarily of the Golden Age of Spanish culture, the sixteenth and seventeenth centuries. In a note on the 1950 edition Maugham explained that the book exploits themes and materials he had assembled for use in an unwritten novel on the subject of Spanish mysticism, but he had abandoned the project because he could not create a suitable hero.

The book begins with a recollection of a Seville tavern and its eccentric owner, Don Fernando, an avid collector of curios and artifacts. The episode is a legacy of Maugham's first trip to Seville in 1897, during which he haggled with the owner over the price of items such as books, trinkets, and crucifixes. Apart from recapturing the Seville setting, little else in the book resembles travel literature though it includes a detailed chapter on Spanish food that seems of interest to potential visitors. Maugham found the food uniformly oily, but the book explains how tourists can secure wholesome fare at reasonable prices (though not at hotels). The sections devoted primarily to essay and biography describe Spanish places such as Salamanca, Manresa, Montserrat, and Avila in such detail that it is clear he has visited them.

The most substantial portions of *Don Fernando* represent chapters on Spaniards who were typical of their age. Here, as elsewhere, Maugham wrote informal essays that essentially blend biography and criticism. For Spanish writers of literature he cited Lope de Vega, Pedro Calderón de la Barca, and Miguel de Cervantes, exploring and critiquing drama and picaresque novels, sometimes giving plot summaries. Further, as if to supplement his earlier extended treatment of Murillo in *The Land of the Blessed Virgin,* he assessed the paintings of El Greco, Diego Velázquez, and Francisco de Zurbarán, enriching the descriptions of their most important masterpieces with anecdotes about their lives and those of other painters. Among important Spanish religious leaders, he examined St. Ignatius Loyola, St. Teresa of Avila, and Fray Luis de Leon, largely in an effort to clarify his peculiar interest in mysticism. When Maugham turned to mysticism, he cast the subject under such a broad net that he denied much originality to Spain, or even to Christianity. Citing Ignatius Loyola's *Spiritual Exercises* (written 1522–1535), he noted that the founder of the Jesuit order was heavily indebted to mystical writers before him. Despite his admiration for Spain, Maugham nonetheless found Spanish life narrow, its culture derivative, and its genius limited, observing, for example, that Spain has produced no impor-

Maugham at his villa on the French Riviera

tant philosophers and few literary artists of the first rank.

The final chapter of *Don Fernando,* which reads like a valediction to Spain and its culture, concludes that the celebrated painting of Spain, as seen in the works of El Greco and Velázquez, had its origins elsewhere. From his birth and early schooling in Crete, El Greco had come to Spain by way of Rome. The celebrated architecture that Maugham so much admired was a legacy of the Moors, and the literature was of secondary importance. Spanish philosophy had made no enduring contribution to the world's intellectual legacy. What the Spaniards of the Golden Age achieved beyond other civilizations since Rome was nobility of character, as evidenced by their reserve, discipline, devotion, and self-denial.

Although Maugham often retitled his works and recycled portions of them, he seldom revised extensively, but *Don Fernando* represents a notable exception. When the book was republished in 1950, he heeded the comments of two reviewers, Desmond McCarthy and Raymond Mortimer, and made substantive changes, omitting reflections on the art of writing that he had previously reused in *The Summing Up* and an entire chapter made up primarily of a sample of dialogue in the Spanish manner by the obscure Elizabethan writer John Minsheu. He added several pages on roads, inns, and weather in Spain, material of a kind often encountered in travel writing.

Maugham's final work relating to travel, *France at War* (1940), is largely neglected by Maugham critics and remains little known. It is more accurately designated a collection of propaganda articles than travel writing. Following the defeat of Poland in 1939 the British Ministry of Information communicated with Maugham at his villa on the French Riviera, persuading him to tour military sites and write a series of articles on the French state of preparedness for war. The primary purpose was to boost British morale through a favorable account of the conditions in France, but Maugham admitted that a secondary and

Maugham in London, 1954, on the day Queen Elizabeth II named him a Companion of Honour

less obvious purpose was to transmit privately his own assessment of the situation as he observed it.

From his estate near Nice, he made semi-official trips to Nancy, Alsace, and Lorraine, to munitions plants near the front and around Paris, and to the naval base at Toulon. When he toured the Maginot Line, he reported that the state of readiness was excellent and morale high though the troops were not eager for war. The main danger to troop morale during the period known as the "Phoney War" was boredom. During his tour of munitions factories and a coal mine he praised the incessant and efficient labor, pointing out that many manufacturing jobs had been assumed by French women because so many men had been mobilized. On the whole he found the rate of production impressive. At Toulon, a major naval base, he boarded a cruiser for gunnery and torpedo exercises at night, finding naval maneuvers of interest. In Alsace and Lorraine he observed that the region was almost deserted because, expecting imminent attack, the French had evacuated a half million citizens and sent them to other cities.

Asked to report on the contribution of religious institutions to the war, Maugham dutifully visited two bishops and an English priest serving in France. He received assurance that priests in their hundreds had volunteered as clergy and as fighting men. The book leaves the impression that the war increased the sense of devotion among the French, not–as one bishop explained–because of fear of death but because duty to country naturally led young men to think of duty to God.

Although the Maugham persona is clearly recognizable in *France at War,* he intrudes less than in his other travel writings. When he does so, the persona is that of an Englishman attempting to explain differences between France and England to an English audience. Convinced that the French identify more deeply with their families than do the English, he explains why the French navy still functions effectively even though it is less formal and more democratic than its English counterpart. He pleads for gifts from England–small luxuries such as books for the bored soldiers and necessities for the suffering people of Alsace and Lorraine.

While Maugham accurately reported what he saw, it is clear from his autobiographical account of the period, *Strictly Personal* (1941), that he was less than candid about his misgivings. He knew of serious rivalries and feuds among the French high command and realized German intelligence had penetrated French political structures at all levels. Furthermore, he was aware that the evacuation of Alsace and Lorraine had been a minor disaster. The people were poorly cared for, and their homes were looted after their departure. Despite many doubts, what he saw seemed to reassure him about French determination and ability to withstand invasion.

France at War appeared in March 1940, the Ministry of Information having arranged to distribute several thousand free copies. It quickly sold more than a hundred thousand copies in an inexpensive, soft-cover edition priced at sixpence. After the German blitzkrieg of May 1940, distribution ceased, and the book was not republished during Maugham's lifetime.

Readers of Maugham's fiction and drama can readily detect the influence of travel on the entire range of his literary art. The South Pacific and Asiatic settings for some of his best-known novels and stories are legacies of his extensive travels. Among his stories, a few, notably "Salvatore" and "A Friend in Need," are little more than travel sketches. Maugham wrote other sketches that introduce or conclude early books of short stories, or set a mood, but they were omitted when the works were collected in later editions.

Taken together, his travel writings reflect two major characteristics of his writing. First, he was quite aware that travel literature as a genre would inevitably change after photography made illustrated articles and books more readily available. Instead of making use of illustration in his works, he sought to create interest by writing about remote places where few Englishmen had ventured; thus he avoided celebrities and famous sites to focus on subjects that would appear fresh and unusual to readers. Even in describing Angor Wat, he selects a portion of the massive stonework that had not been restored but was still partially claimed by jungle. Second, he subordinated travel writing to his art of fiction. A major purpose of his travels was the quest for new materials for dramas, stories, and novels. His early naturalism blended well with the assumption of the exotic story–that the environment shaped character, particularly of European colonials in remote settings. Just as he made use of the travel writing for fiction whenever possible, he used materials collected for fiction in his travel literature when it suited the genre better.

Letters:

The Letters of William Somerset Maugham to Lady Juliet Duff (Pacific Palisades, Cal.: Rasselas, 1982).

Bibliographies:

Charles Sanders, *W. Somerset Maugham: An Annotated Bibliography of Writings about Him* (De Kalb: Northern Illinois University Press, 1970);

Raymond Toole Stott, *A Bibliography of the Works of W. Somerset Maugham* (London: Kaye & Ward, 1973).

Biographies:

Robin Maugham, *Somerset and All the Maughams* (London: Longmans/Heinemann, 1966);

Frederic Raphael, *Somerset Maugham and His World* (London: Thames & Hudson, 1976);

Anthony Curtis, *Somerset Maugham* (London: Weidenfeld & Nicolson, 1977);

Ted Morgan, *Maugham* (New York: Simon & Schuster, 1980);

Robert L. Calder, *Willie: The Life of W. Somerset Maugham* (London: Heinemann, 1989).

References:

Stanley Archer, *W. Somerset Maugham: A Study of the Short Fiction* (New York: Twayne, 1993);

Laurence Brander, *Somerset Maugham: A Guide* (Edinburgh: Oliver & Boyd, 1963);

Ivor Brown, *W. Somerset Maugham* (New York: Barnes, 1970);

Forrest Burt, *W. Somerset Maugham* (Boston: Twayne, 1986);

Richard Cordell, *Somerset Maugham: A Biographical and Critical Study* (London: Heinemann, 1961; revised, 1969);

Anthony Curtis, *The Pattern of Maugham* (London: Hamilton, 1974);

Curtis and John Whitehead, eds., *W. Somerset Maugham: The Critical Heritage* (London & New York: Routledge & Kegan Paul, 1987);

John Whitehead, *Maugham: A Reappraisal* (London: Vision, 1987; Totowa, N.J.: Barnes & Noble, 1987).

Papers:

There are collections of Maugham's papers at the Humanities Research Center, University of Texas at Austin; the Berg Collection, New York Public Library; the Lilly Library, Indiana University; Stanford University; the Houghton Library, Harvard University; the Fales Collection, New York University; the Butler Library, Columbia University; the Olin Library, Cornell University; Beaverbrook Papers, House of Lords Records Office, London; and the University of Arkansas Library.

H. V. Morton

(25 July 1892 - 18 June 1979)

Carol Huebscher Rhoades

BOOKS: *The Heart of London* (London: Methuen, 1925);

London (London: Methuen, 1926; New York: McBride, 1926); revised as *London: A Guide* (London: Methuen, 1937);

The London Year: A Book of Many Moods (London: Methuen, 1926); republished as *When You Go to London* (New York & London: Harper, 1927); revised as *A London Year* (London: Methuen, 1933); republished as *The London Scene* (New York: McBride, 1935);

The Spell of London (London: Methuen, 1926);

The Nights of London (London: Methuen, 1926);

In Search of England (London: Methuen, 1927; New York: McBride, 1928; revised edition, London: Methuen, 1929; New York: Dodd, Mead, 1935);

May Fair: How the Site of a Low Carnival Became the Heart of Fashionable London (London: Marshalsea Press, 1927);

The Call of England (London: Methuen, 1928; New York: McBride, 1928; revised edition, London: Methuen, 1936; New York: Dodd, Mead, 1936);

The Land of the Vikings, from Thames to Humber (Bungay, Suffolk, U.K.: Richard Clay, 1928);

In Search of Scotland (London: Methuen, 1929; New York: Dodd, Mead, 1930);

In Search of Ireland (London: Methuen, 1930; New York: Dodd, Mead, 1931); republished in part as *The Magic of Ireland,* edited by Patricia Haward (London: Eyre Methuen, 1978; New York: Dodd, Mead, 1978);

In Search of Wales (London: Methuen, 1932; New York: Dodd, Mead, 1932);

Blue Days at Sea and Other Essays (London: Methuen, 1932; New York: Dodd, Mead, 1933);

In Scotland Again (London: Methuen, 1933; New York: Dodd, Mead, 1933);

What I Saw in the Slums (London: Labour Party, 1933);

In the Steps of the Master (London: Rich & Cowan, 1934; New York: Dodd, Mead, 1934; abridged edition, London: Methuen, 1941); abridged and simplified as *In the Steps of Jesus* (New York: Dodd, Mead, 1953; London: Methuen, 1954);

Our Fellow Men (London: Methuen, 1936; New York: Dodd, Mead, 1936);

In the Steps of St. Paul (London: Rich & Cowan, 1936; New York: Dodd, Mead, 1936);

Through Lands of the Bible (London: Methuen, 1938; New York: Dodd, Mead, 1938);

Ghosts of London (London: Methuen, 1939; New York: Dodd, Mead, 1940);

Women of the Bible (London: Methuen, 1940; New York: Dodd, Mead, 1941);

Middle East: A Record of Travel in the Countries of Egypt, Palestine, Iraq, Turkey and Greece (London: Methuen, 1941; New York: Dodd, Mead, 1941);

I, James Blunt (London: Methuen, 1942; New York: Dodd, Mead, 1942);

I Saw Two Englands; The Record of a Journey before the War, and after the Outbreak of War, in the Year 1939 (London: Methuen, 1942; New York: Dodd, Mead, 1943);

Atlantic Meeting: An Account of Mr. Churchill's Voyage in H.M.S. Prince of Wales, in August, 1941, and the Conference with President Roosevelt Which Resulted in the Atlantic Charter (London: Methuen, 1943; New York: Dodd, Mead, 1943);

In Search of South Africa (London: Methuen, 1948; New York: Dodd, Mead, 1948);

In Search of London (London: Methuen, 1951; New York: Dodd, Mead, 1951);

A Stranger in Spain (London: Methuen, 1955; New York: Dodd, Mead, 1955);

A Traveller in Rome (London: Methuen, 1957; New York: Dodd, Mead, 1957);

This Is Rome (Kingswood, U.K.: World's Work, 1960; New York: Hawthorn Books, 1960);

This Is the Holy Land (Kingswood, U.K.: World's Work, 1961; New York: Hawthorn Books, 1961);

A Traveller in Italy (London: Methuen, 1964; New York: Dodd, Mead, 1964);

The Waters of Rome (London: Connoisseur/Joseph, 1966); republished as *The Fountains of Rome* (New York: Macmillan, 1966; London: Connoisseur/Joseph, 1970);

A Traveller in Southern Italy (London: Methuen, 1969; New York: Dodd, Mead, 1969).

Editions and Collections: *H. V. Morton's London; Being The Heart of London, The Spell of London and The Nights of London* (London: Methuen, 1940; New York: Dodd, Mead, 1941);

H. V. Morton's Britain, edited by Gilbert Carter (London: Methuen, 1969; New York: Dodd, Mead, 1969);

H. V. Morton's England, edited by Patricia Haward (London: Eyre Methuen, 1975);

The Splendor of Scotland (London: Eyre Methuen, 1976; New York: Dodd, Mead, 1976);

In Search of the Holy Land, edited by Christopher Derrick (London: Eyre Methuen, 1979).

SELECTED PERIODICAL PUBLICATIONS–UNCOLLECTED: "Krak des Chevaliers: A Great Crusader Castle of Spain," *Country Life,* 90 (1 August 1941): 204–207;

"In the London of the New Queen," *National Geographic,* 104 (September 1953): 291–340;

"High Road in the Pyrenees," *National Geographic,* 109 (March 1956): 299–331;

"Lake District, Poets' Corner of England: Literary Landmarks Amid the Dales and Fells of 'Wordsworthshire' Draw Hikers and Climbers to a Favorite British Park," *National Geographic,* 109 (April 1956): 510–545;

"The Magic Road Round Ireland," *National Geographic,* 119 (March 1961): 293–332.

Henry Canova Vollam Morton, who wrote under the name H. V. Morton, was called "the greatest living British travel writer" for most of his career. His books, particularly the "In Search of . . ." series, were immensely popular in Great Britain and the United States, and three of his early books, on England, Ireland, and Scotland, were still in print in the 1980s. These books were popular because of his relaxed and vivid writing style and his enthusiasm for his subject matter. Many of Morton's early books were first published serially as daily columns in popular newspapers. Morton's perspective was not that of the discoverer or adventurer but that of a middle-class British citizen who unashamedly took advantage of his private motorcar and comfortable inns and hotels along the way while imaginatively and enthusiastically responding to the countryside and villages. Morton was not alone in his exploration of England by automobile. In fact quite a few travel books by writers motoring "off the beaten tracks" during the 1920s and 1930s popularized the notion that one need not leave one's own country to find interesting and stimulating travel destinations. Morton visited and described famous and well-frequented sites in his books, enlivening the experiences by presenting them imaginatively in the context of the historical and the legendary.

Morton summarized his approach to travel and explained the lasting appeal of his books in his introduction to *H. V. Morton's Britain* (1969): "Perhaps my desire, first expressed in the 'Search' books, to explain some of the historic events and processes which have shaped the countries of the British Isles may have kept these books alive, since the past does not date." Reviewers cited Morton's ability to relate the kinds of details that fill guidebooks in such a way that they are entertaining rather than tedious. Another source of Morton's popularity, especially during the 1930s, was his emphasis on Christian history, which he traced in three books on the Holy Land. Throughout his writings Morton mixed travel observations with essayistic interpolations of historical records and stories. Unlike many of the more literary travelers of his period, Morton did not portray himself as an adventurer into the unknown. Instead he showed his readers how, with some prior study and an open imagination, anyone could easily visit a country as a traveler rather than as a mere tourist.

Henry Canova Vollam Morton was born on 25 July 1892 in Birmingham, England. He was the son of Joseph Vollam Morton, editor of *The Birmingham Mail,* and Margaret Constance McLean Ewart Morton. Morton was educated in Birmingham and began his newspaper career at the age of seventeen, when he joined the staff of *The Birmingham Gazette and Express.* He became its assistant editor in 1912. In 1913 he moved to London and went to work at *The Empire Magazine,* but he stayed for only a few months before becoming the subeditor of *The Daily Mail,* working there until the beginning of World War I. During the war he served in France as an officer with the Warwickshire Yeomanry. In 1919 Morton joined the staff of *The Daily Standard* in London, and in 1921 he moved to *The Daily Express.* Morton's position as a descriptive writer was established in 1923 with his well-received reports on the discovery of the tomb of Tutankhamen in Egypt.

Morton's first book, *The Heart of London* (1925), is a compilation of vignettes about London life that were originally published in his columns for *The Daily Express.* This popular book, which went into

H. V. Morton with Bishop Fulton Sheen and photographer Yousuf Karsh, his collaborators on This Is Rome *(1960)*

four printings within a year, covers subjects ranging from a Roman bath and the layers of history buried beneath the streets to the Orientalism of Petticoat Lane and the psychology needed to sell designer dresses to women. It is clear that Morton not only studied his history books for information but, more important, walked through London with an open and observing eye. Morton was proud of the city in which he lived and saw in it evidence of the unchanging human heart and a democratic poetry and drama. Through his descriptions London becomes an exotic place, full of wonders to be discovered by anyone willing to look afresh at the city. After an excursion to Petticoat Lane, with its bazaar-like markets, Morton declared: "I caught a penny omnibus back to England with the feeling that I might have spent two hundred pounds and seen less of the East, less of romance, and much less of life." The book depicts London as the heart of the world, embracing the foreign and exotic, the past and the present, within its everyday life of children playing in the parks, women having tea, and workers arriving on early-morning trains.

Morton continued his romance with London in his first guidebook, establishing the imaginative narrative perspective that became his trademark. While *London* (1926) includes maps and practical information for the tourist, such as opening days and hours and a calendar of London events, it concentrates on providing the reader with a history of various London sites and traditions. In Morton's view contemporary London, with its large, flimsily built towers for flats and offices, is transitory and not part of the enduring London, which has roots in the Roman and medieval periods. The book was one of Methuen's Little Guide series and was produced in a small format so that the visitor to London could easily carry the book in a pocket. For the tourist interested in the background of the city, *London* offers a wealth of information concisely presented in short chapters divided by subject. The history of London from the Romans until after World War I is presented in just thirty-four pages and begins by engaging the reader with the past by imagining a tourist from Rome visiting that interesting outpost of the Empire called Londinium. This history explains the rise of London in connection with its commercial concerns and discusses the peoples and places important to cultural and religious development. A long section with alphabetized listings of churches, Inns of Court, museums, and art galleries follows the history, and the book also includes eight photographs of famous London sites and an appendix with tidbits of London history that would

"And in the village streets it is always England," photograph from the 1929 American edition of In Search of England

be of special interest to Americans. In a later edition of the guide Morton acknowledged the sources for much of his information, in particular the extensive listing of London's churches. Morton's enthusiastic and imaginative approach to history are apparent throughout the book.

Morton referred to his next book, *The London Year: A Book of Many Moods* (1926), as an "anti-guide book." An introduction to London through its social events, the book, most of which originally appeared in daily columns for *The Daily Express,* is a guide for visitors who want a sense of the rituals of London life. The book suggests that readers imagine they are in London for a whole year with plenty of money and then allows them to follow Morton as he begins the journey in the cold mists of January in London, when the only sensible thing to do is to enjoy cozy domestic tea times. February is still cold, but Parliament opens with the rituals and pomp of the centuries. Although March winds bring in the new ladies' fashions, the real social whirl begins in April and May. The Chelsea Flower Show, opening day at the Royal Academy, Covent Garden operas, and bluebell time at Kew Gardens entice residents and visitors alike. In May, American visitors begin to appear on the scene, amusing Morton with their slang and trivial interests. The summer months are packed with horse shows, boat races, air shows, and cricket. The family vacation in August is described from a left-at-home dog's point of view. The last months of the year are times for observing the exquisite shades and textures of London light. December ends the year rather forlornly with the damaged puddings, pies, and gifts that are stacked up at the post office.

While Morton may have felt that his book was an "anti-guide book," simply an amusing view of a year in London, he did include an appendix with useful details for tourists, especially Americans. The 1927 American edition, titled *When You Go to London,* is dedicated to "All Those Knowing Americans Who Prefer London to Paris." Indeed, the book proved popular with American visitors, and later editions feature foldout maps and photographs of famous sites rather than the humorous sketches that illustrated the original text. The book appeals to those who prefer the time-honored traditions and once exclusively upper-class pursuits and to those of a more democratic and irreverent spirit. The subject of Morton's book still appeals: Godfrey Smith covers many of the same events in *The English Season* (1995).

While he was producing his guides to London, Morton was also writing vignettes of London for *The Daily Express,* and in 1926 they were collected in *The Spell of London,* which begins with forays to the Tower of London, Big Ben, and Westminster Abbey. Then Morton's focus shifts to the human dramas around him, as in *The Heart of London.* While some of the scenes, such as that of the husband and wife fighting on the street about his mistress, could have occurred anywhere, other sketches seem more particular to British life. The distressed gentlemen housed and fed at Charterhouse are a holdover from Anthony Trollope's Barsetshire novels. The single women attending Sunday services in city churches are similar to those later described in Barbara Pym's novels. Hansom cabs cause Morton to imagine characters in a Victorian love story although the scene he presents about an old man asking for a young girl's agreement to marriage has a sense of the unsavory about it.

Morton's representations of women, not only in these vignettes but in his later works as well, are disturbing. The women are either pitiable or shrewish. Married women are sentimental and have no interests other than taking care of their men while workingwomen's only interest is their salaries, which will buy them silk stockings and cheap but good-quality clothing at the Berwick Street markets. It is important when reading Morton's works to recall the scenes of social change that he must have seen as he walked through London. While Morton focused his observations on genteel poverty and lovely, vacuous women, men and women were agitating for better living and working conditions. The General Strike of 1926 occurred not long after *The Spell of London* was published.

Social unrest does not appear in Morton's next book either. With the exception of "Our Last Inn," the short essays of *The Nights of London* (1926) were first published in *The Daily Express.* Morton approaches the nightlife of London as though it were a dark stage setting, which he illuminates with scenes of the life unseen by most Londoners. His tales of rich gentlemen and chorus girls seem somewhat Edwardian, and his visits to the Limehouse area with its Chinese residents bring the decadence of dangerous and exotic Victorian opium dens to the contemporary scene. Another nineteenth-century image, that of the muscular Christian, is evoked by Morton's dawn in London: "London, the most masculine city in the world, seems standing clean and stripped, like a boxer entering a ring, for another twenty-four rounds with Fate." For the most part the book focuses on the earnest people of the city: workers who attend institute courses to better themselves; hospital workers, policemen, and firemen who are always ready to save lives. In Peckham Rye, Morton found girls and boys meeting, women knitting, and discussions of cricket–in other words, utopian Britain. Morton avoided the less rosy aspects of London life, finding refuge, for example, at the last of the coach inns, the George

Morton's photograph of Leuchars Church in his In Search of Scotland *(1929)*

Inn in Southwark, where "this bed was a genuine escape from modern London; this room was insulated from the London we know."

When *The Heart of London, The Spell of London,* and *The Nights of London* were republished in one volume, *H. V. Morton's London* (1940), Morton reminisced about his youthful writings in the introduction, recalling his enthusiasm and vitality as he went around London to observe and interview for his daily newspaper articles. At the time he wrote them the articles were simply snapshots of London life; when they were republished during World War II, the essays became a record of a past that was rapidly being destroyed by enemy bombs and a tribute to the spirit of Londoners. The 1940 collection went through ten printings within four years.

Morton began his "In Search of . . ." series in the late 1920s. The daily walks in London that he described in his earlier books were a novel way of presenting new perspectives on both famous and little-known aspects of London. To explore outside the city Morton discovered another method: travel by motorcar. When *The Saturday Review* compared seven travel books on England that appeared in 1927, it welcomed the new class of literature in which the countryside was being rediscovered. Besides traveling by motorcar, the authors of these books shared a common attitude about traveling. As the reviewer noted in the 2 July 1927 issue of *The Saturday Review:* "it is an amusing illustration of the self-conscious modern attitude in the matter that they are all so anxious to explain that they are not intended for the ordinary tourist, but only for quite exceptional adventurers; that they are not guide-books–fatal word–but just amusing travelling companions; and, above all, that they are 'off the beaten track.'" Even though Morton visited several well-known sights on his journey, he was not connected with tourism because he saw them differently from the average tourist.

Morton had decided to take a tour around England some years before his journey. He reported that he thought he was dying in Palestine and longed for nothing more, should he live, than to be able to wander the byways of England and explore its essence in its villages and fields. Morton chose the ideal time for this journey, setting off from London in April and traveling around the country during the summer. *In Search of England* (1927) is infused with Morton's jaunty attitude, and it is not difficult to imagine the youthful reporter encountering the former and present inhabitants of the land. In this and in subsequent books on Great Britain, Morton fulfilled the promise that he made at the beginning of *In Search of England:*

> I will see what lies off the beaten track. I will, as the mood takes me, go into famous towns and unknown hamlets. I will shake up the dust of kings and abbots; I will bring the knights and the cavaliers back to the roads, and, once in a while, I will hear the thunder of old quarrels at earthwork and church door. If I become weary of dream and legend I will just sit and watch the ducks on a village pond, or take the horses to water. I will talk with lords and cottagers, tramps, gipsies, and dogs; I will, in fact, do anything that comes into my head as suddenly and lightheartedly as I will accept anything, and everything, that comes my way in rain or sun along the road.

Morton was at his best in calling up the ghosts and legends of the areas through which he passed. His landscape is that of the present overlaid by the past, and his village and countryside scenes are timeless. Although Morton appreciated the beauty of the English countryside, the book does not describe it at length. The Lake District receives only the briefest of mentions. In writing about the places and people of England as though they were unfamiliar, even to the English, Morton relied on his readers' familiarity with the idealized English countryside in the landscape paintings of Thomas Gainsborough and John Constable and in Romantic poetry.

A companion to *In Search of England, The Call of England* (1928) records another springtime journey, in the north of England. For many living in southern England, the northern counties were relatively unknown. Hull, commonly thought of as having nothing to offer the tourist, was the starting point for the adventurous part of Morton's journey. As Morton wandered through Yorkshire, he was more observant than usual of the contemporary situation, perhaps because he was aware that it would intrigue his readers as much as his historical accounts of the more familiar parts of the country. In York, for example, he explored the medieval city walls and the cathedral and wondered about the story of the well-known eighteenth-century robber Dick Turpin, but he also visited a modern chocolate factory, still an important industry in York.

Morton must have sensed that most of his readers would use his book for imaginative, rather than actual, travel. For their sake as well as his own he experienced a warm peat bath in a Harrogate spa, tried to gather gannet eggs over the side of a cliff, stole a bit of Virginia tobacco from a warehouse and a piece of medieval tilework from Jervaulx Abbey, and repeated typical jokes from Manchester as well as village conversations about the plague. Whether his readers followed his tour from the armchair or by train, Morton proposed two results for the English traveler: "I think that any man has done well if, on his return from a journey, he can truthfully say, 'I have had an exciting time–I have met myself' and there will come a time in any tour of England when most men . . . [will] have fought their way back to the country and have planted their feet in the splendid sanity of English soil." Morton's travels and writings were attempts to deepen the understanding of and feeling for England by the English.

One of Morton's least-known books came out shortly after the success of *In Search of England. The Land of the Vikings, from Thames to Humber* (1928) explores the eastern counties that formed the Danelaw of the Vikings: Essex, Suffolk, Norfolk, Cambridgeshire, and Lincolnshire. After giving a brief history of the names of the counties, Morton presented each county similarly in chapters titled: "How to Enjoy [county name]" and "Places to See in [county name]." The traveler using the book as a guide could enjoy each county by visiting churches and stately homes in the area, learning a bit about its

A bridge over the Sark and a view of Dumfries, photographs taken by Morton for In Scotland Again *(1933)*

history in Roman and Norman times, and viewing the landscape. The "Places to See" sections list the villages of each county with a quick paragraph on their interesting features. Some of the incidents are taken from *In Search of England,* but the landscape descriptions give more information about contemporary conditions than is usual in Morton's books. There is a sadness not normally seen in Morton's works in the contrast of the meal marshes of Norfolk "alive with waterfowl, herons, and light against various hues of sea heath, sea lavender, thrift, and starwort," with the dead and dying villages that have become separated from the sea as the marshes have filled in between sea and town.

When Morton motored to Scotland in 1928, he did so with the spirit of a traveler breaking new ground. *In Search of Scotland* (1929) cites several studies about Scotland but claims that records of personal journeys around Scotland are nonexistent. While Morton injected a great deal of Scottish history and some information about famous or intriguing places into his narrative, he emphasized that *In Search of Scotland* is a travel record, not a guidebook. Sections of the book were originally published as sketches in *The Daily Express,* and one senses in his interviews with fishermen, landladies, and steelworkers that he went searching for amusing anecdotes for his columns. Morton was immensely taken with Scotland, and his nature descriptions abound with superlative adjectives. The many castles and lochs of Scotland sent him into continual musings about the lives of Mary, Queen of Scots, and Bonnie Prince Charles. These were Morton's favorite historical figures, and he found stories about them in the most unexpected places.

Morton's description of one day in his journey encapsulates his attitude about himself and his ability to capture the essentials about a place. On a whim Morton decided to climb Ben Nevis. His city shoes impeded his progress along the hard, flinty paths, but he was exhilarated by the crisp air and the splendid views of lochs and distant islands. Near the summit a thin mist turned to sleet and snow, and he felt utterly alone. As he descended, he stumbled about and then came into brilliant sunshine and a panoramic view of Scotland. Of all the events in Morton's many books, this climb best portrays him as a traveler: he was spontaneous, impressionable, and perceptive about himself and the environment. *In Search of Scotland* was tremendously popular, quickly selling more than 135,000 copies. The critical reception of this book was similar to that of all Morton's travel books: the critics appreciated his easy and vivid style and emphasized the pleasure of books that were simply the records of entertaining journeys.

Before journeying to Ireland, about which he wrote next, Morton traveled to Italy, France, and the Middle East, and he occasionally referred to what he saw in Europe for comparative purposes in *In Search of Ireland* (1930). These Irish impressions were originally published as newspaper columns and then revised for publication in book form. What charmed Morton most about Ireland was its primitive state. The book briefly discusses the political and social implications of the recently created Irish Free State before describing Morton's journeys into the countryside to observe and meet a people he viewed as exotic and almost mythic. For Morton, Connemara seemed emblematic of exotic Irishness, its people superstitious, living in suspended time, and nobly poor. Morton even imagined that the people were so used to their condition that they did not notice their hunger or poverty. While he proposed at the beginning of the book that the English should look at the Irish in a new light, he drew on stereotypes and romanticized imagery to portray Ireland. Nevertheless, at the end of his journey Morton envisioned an Ireland departing from the Celtic twilight and entering a more modern world. The implication is, however, that the Irish should discard romanticized notions of an Irish nation, while still maintaining their romantic charms and quirks.

In 1931 Morton began working as a special writer for *The Daily Herald,* the Labour Party newspaper. The last two chapters of his next book, *In Search of Wales* (1932), describing the lives of the miners in South Wales, were first published serially in *The Daily Herald.* Perhaps because of the focus of the newspaper, Morton's book on Wales is much more descriptive of the daily lives of the people and their jobs than his usual travel books. The book supplies details on the workings of woolen and steel mills, coal mines, and sheepdogs. It does not, however, neglect the legends of Wales although it concentrates on the aspects of Welsh history that intersect with English history.

In the opening of the book Morton informed the reader that he had been to Wales twenty years earlier, when he was a "notorious prig" and in love with a girl whose family rejected him. On his second trip, recorded in this book, he felt almost as young as he was on the first. Starting out in May, his favorite time for beginning travels, he entered what was to him, and still is for many other English people, a foreign land. While in Wales, Morton participated in typical tourist pursuits. He climbed Snowdon, was guided around castles, attended the Eisteddfod, and bought Welsh tweed. Nevertheless, he disparaged such pursuits and advised other visitors to Wales against them. He was certain that most visitors were simply overwhelmed and bemused by what they saw while he had read his histories and had a journalist's instincts, which helped him draw out stories from the local people. *In Search of Wales,* which praises the Welsh spirit and working people's pride along with the mystic and poetic qualities of the Welsh mountains and language, won Morton the approval of the Welsh. He was crowned a bard at Wrexham on 8 August 1933.

The four "In Search of . . ." books ensured Morton's lasting renown as a travel writer. In a short time the books sold more than one hundred thousand copies each, and they were still in print in the mid 1980s. While the information in them is useful for tourists and travelers, much of it could be read in standard guidebooks. People continue to read the "In Search of . . ." books for Morton's charming and humorous observations and musings and for his curiosity and deep feelings for the people and traditions of Great Britain. While other travel writers of the period–such as W. H. Auden, Robert Byron, and Vita Sackville-West–were describing Iceland, Russia, Tibet, and Persia (now Iran) in terms of a modernist aesthetic emphasizing foreignness and disjunctures, Morton emphasized the familiar and secure. Other writers also interjected historical details and personal stories into their narratives, but they did so in the context of a specific time and place. Morton, however, re-created and heightened the ideal, sympathetic vision of the British Isles, sensing that his readers shared it with him. For this reason it is easy to see why some readers and reviewers of the "In Search of . . ." books suggested that Morton had not actually visited some of the places he described. Because so much of the narrative in these books is taken up with imaginative historical stories, there is a sense that Morton took only a quick jaunt to an area and then hurried back to his room in London to consult his books and imagination and to write undisturbed by British contemporary reality. In a later edition of *In Search of Ireland,* however, Morton asserted that all the vignettes in the books are literal reporting.

Sometime during the early 1930s Morton met a woman named Mary. *In Search of Wales* is dedicated to her, and they were married sometime between 1932 and 1934. Mary Morton traveled to the Middle East with her husband, and some of the photographs for *In the Steps of the Master* (1934) and *In the Steps of St. Paul* (1936) are credited to her. Photographs by Mary Morton also appear in her husband's later books, but Morton never indicated in any of his books that she traveled with him. He always portrayed himself as the lone traveler.

Blue Days at Sea and Other Essays (1932) collects observations that Morton evidently made in the Middle East and Europe before his trip to Ireland. Also including essays about life at home, the book is divided into three sections: "About Men," "About Women," and "About Places." The men are in the navy, and Morton likens their life on a battleship to that of a well-run public school. The women are lovely, silly, working in offices, looking for husbands, and fighting with husbands. The most interesting of these essays, most of which were originally published in *The Daily Herald, The Daily Express,* and *The Sunday Express,* are "About Places." Rome is presented in its early-morning splendor, and Egypt, which represents the dawn of humanity, inspired Morton to visions of twenty beautiful girls rowing a king's golden boat with ivory oars. Morton the traveler reported on tourists who could barely remember what they saw in Luxor, so they were not sure what to write on the postcards home. The book ends with an essay on the excitement and delights of being abroad, which somehow do not match the comfort and security of home. While Morton admitted that the glow of being back in London might not last long, it reminded him of what, should a war come, he would be fighting to preserve.

In 1933 Morton published as a booklet *What I Saw in the Slums,* a series of articles that he had written for *The Daily Herald.* Although Morton claimed that *What I Saw in the Slums* is not propaganda, he argued adamantly that the slums were a disgrace to the British nation and must be torn down and replaced, not with more expensive and distant corporation houses but with affordable and decent inner-city housing. Morton's work is primarily descriptive, reiterating sightings of insects, terrible or nonexistent sanitation, disintegrating interiors, and crowding in the large cities north of London. In contrast to his other works, the observations on this journey were starkly stated with the force of a deeply felt social conscience. When he described many of these same northern cities in *The Call of England,* Morton made no mention of the slums or difficult working lives of their residents.

Byzantine wall in Salonica, from In the Steps of St. Paul *(1937), with photographs by H. V. and Mary Morton*

A series of articles for *The Daily Herald* on the working lives of Scottish trawler fishermen were included in Morton's *In Scotland Again* (1933). Some of the same stories and territory are covered as in his previous book on Scotland, but on this autumn journey Morton traveled deeper into the countryside and onto the western isles. It is easy to sense his sheer enjoyment at the sights and smells of the land and sea, and the reader can empathize with Morton's reveries and aches as he ventured out on a twenty-mile walk in the Cairngorm hills. He also attested to one of the last thrills left in travel: leaving for the next destination in the stillness before dawn. The Scotland portrayed in this book commingles pagan and Norse gods with early Christian saints and the movements of the Stuarts and Jacobins with the journeys of intrepid English travelers. The pleasures of meeting these spirits along his way are heightened by the coziness of firesides, high tea, and friendly talk.

Morton next made a series of journeys to the Holy Land and produced three books that express his deeply felt religious beliefs. To illuminate the unbroken connections between contemporary life in the Near and Middle East, Morton traveled with the stories of the New and Old Testaments in mind. *In the Steps of the Master* (1934), which quickly became a best-seller, explores Palestine following the life and death of Christ. Clearly, the book is meant not only to record Morton's journey but also to inspire others to follow him. He stressed the ease of travel, even to the most remote areas, and mentioned the excellent European hotels in the major cities, recommending March, April, and May as the ideal months for the journey. Sections of the book originally appeared in *The Daily Herald* as "Through the Land of the Bible," and the book was later simplified for family reading as *In the Steps of Jesus* (1953).

Morton wrote *In the Steps of St. Paul* from a similar perspective, following the routes of the apostle around the Roman Empire. Pointing out that the roads that were once major thoroughfares are now byways, Morton encouraged those who would follow in his footsteps with the information that, except in Turkey, transportation and lodging could be arranged without undue difficulty. Morton, who made four trips within two years to the areas depicted in the book, placed himself and the reader into the persona of St. Paul: that of traveler. He envisioned St. Paul as both a saint and a man, and, in the interest of drawing direct connections between the Acts of the Apostles and history, he describes as accurately as possible the contrasts and similarities of the ancient and modern worlds.

Through Lands of the Bible (1938) again takes the perspective of the Christian traveler, but it is less exclusively centered on the study of Christian sites and peoples. Morton gathered materials for this book while on the journeys he made for the previous two books. Here he concentrated on Egypt and the Sinai, making a pilgrimage from the Euphrates to the Nile to examine the remains of early Christian communities and churches. He also met and drank tea with Arabs and explored Egyptian tombs and temples. He ended the journey in Rome, with visits to the places frequented by the apostles.

These books appeal to the Christian who wishes to read about or travel to the Holy Land in a spirit of adventure and reverence. Compared with the more literary accounts of travel to the area during that period, Morton's books suffer from too great a credulity and an unwillingness to take a critical distance. In *Abroad* (1980), a study of the travel literature of the 1930s, Paul Fussell dismisses Morton's books as naive but concedes that *In the Steps of the Master* was "an important bourgeois devotional classic and sold 210,000 copies the first two years. . . . The book is interesting here because it suggests the readiness of the 30's audience to receive essayistic views and improving exposition as long as they were attended by the décor of travel–the palm trees of the Holy Land can't have hurt–or seemed to issue harmlessly as an adjunct to geography." During the war British soldiers stationed in the Middle East wrote to Morton praising his books as useful but complaining that their size made them difficult to carry. For their sakes he selected and revised portions of *In the Steps of the Master, In the Steps of St. Paul,* and *Through Lands of the Bible* and added sections on Istanbul and Greece. This condensed version was published in 1941 as *Middle East: A Record of Travel in the Countries of Egypt, Palestine, Iraq, Turkey and Greece.*

Morton's empathy with bourgeois sensibilities and mores is also evident in *Our Fellow Men* (1936), which sketches the working lives of thirty people whom he interviewed as they worked. While not a travel book as such, the characters are presented as if they were colonial subjects: the invisible masses who support middle- and upper-class Britains. Morton affectionately described the "typical" lives of the working classes and their wages. While Morton included some disparaging remarks about working conditions by factory and piece-workers, he represented these people as hardworking, happy, and proud to be the backbone of England. These essays were originally published in *The Daily Herald.*

Morton published another book of portraits with a different perspective in 1940. The essays in *Women of the Bible* were inspired by an Arab girl whom Morton watched as she drew water from a well in Palestine. In this girl Morton saw the distinctive qualities of women that he felt had remained unchanged over the ages. His vignettes of Delilah the betrayer, devoted Sarah, and charming, then petulant Rachel stress their connections with women of the twentieth century. Morton's perspective typifies his attitudes toward women as well as his imaginative readings of the faces of the people he met on his many journeys.

After his travels in the Holy Land, Morton returned to London and produced a series of brief articles on the antecedents of some of London's traditions and rituals. He put the proofs of the book away as World War II began, but his publishers felt the book should go on the market to remind its residents of the continuity of London traditions. *Ghosts of London* (1939) chronicles more historically than imaginatively the background of such customs as the dinner and curfew horns for law students, the "Lion Sermon," Maundy money, and the ceremony of the keys at the Tower of London. (Morton occasionally broadcast this ceremony for the BBC.) Morton explained that he often did research at the College of Arms for information on heraldry and genealogy, and the reader discovers that Morton was made uneasy by those who were even more enthusiastic than he about London history.

Two journeys around England are recorded in *I Saw Two Englands* (1942). In May 1939 Morton left his home in Chelsea for an early-summer tour of England. On his last prewar look at the country he saw two divisions: "the bright, vulgar, crowded England of the main roads and the quiet, lovely England of the side roads and the lanes." He motored on the side roads and visited castles, stately homes, cathedrals, thatched houses, and Roman ruins. Imbued with the spirits of the past in Sussex, he bought several sprigged Georgian waistcoats. That June, sitting at a restaurant in Peterborough and admiring the sixteenth-century columns of the town hall, he noticed that the people quietly waiting for a bus were all carrying their gas masks. Morton knew then that the England he had been touring and writing about for so long was about to change irrevocably.

Four months later, in October, Morton set out with petrol coupons and letters of introduction from various ministries and the War Office to see the changes brought on by the war. He visited armament factories, a prison camp for German officers, shipyards, land girls, and postal censors. By the time the book was published, Morton was serving in the Home Guard, watching and protecting his bit of England.

In 1941 Morton and best-selling novelist Howard Spring were invited to accompany Prime Minister Winston Churchill on board the HMS *Prince of Wales* to meet President Franklin D. Roosevelt for discussions that led to the Atlantic Charter. At that time Morton was living in Hampshire and serving in the Home Guard. While his tone in *Atlantic Meeting* (1943) is jaunty, he stressed the risks Churchill took by traveling on the open seas to Newfoundland for the secret rendezvous with Roosevelt. Neither Morton nor Spring was privy to the negotiations, and Morton's reporting focuses on shipboard life and relaxed evenings spent watching movies with Churchill. The experience of the foreign came twice during the trip. In Newfoundland Morton was surprised by the abundance of a peacetime economy: silk stockings, butter, cheese, and meat were all available without rationing. In Iceland he expected to find reindeer in the streets but saw elegantly dressed Icelandic women and well-stocked bookstores instead. Because of the secret nature of the trip, Morton was not allowed to publish anything on it for eighteen months. Yet there is nothing in the text that seems dangerous to the security of the nation. The book was deemed "instant history," but its value is more anecdotal than analytical. Not long after his journey with Churchill, Morton resigned from *The Daily Herald,* later writing for it occasionally as a special correspondent. For the rest of his life he worked as an independent traveler and writer.

"A Girl of Siwa," an illustration in Through Lands of the Bible *(1938), with photographs by H. V. and Mary Morton*

While Morton was keeping the manuscript of *Atlantic Meeting* on hold, he wrote his only published fictional work, *I, James Blunt* (1942), the fictional diary of an older man who records, over a period of seven months, the horrors of life in Britain after its capitulation to the Germans. The book was written as a warning to the British people that they should not remain complacent in their war efforts. The American publisher of the book extended the warning to the American people. The village in which the story is set represents Britain's virtuous and glorious past, and the true British are worn down and destroyed by those who are only too willing to serve their new masters, the Germans. Blunt's final despair comes as he watches the village children and even his own grandchildren become entranced by their German language lessons. The unintended irony of this story is that, while the narrative is graphic and emphatic in its depiction of the horrors of colonization of the British, it is oblivious to the horrors of colonization by the British.

After World War II, Morton flew to South Africa for a stay of about four months. In his introduction to *In Search of South Africa* (1948) he emphasized that the book should be read as an account of his pleasures as he traveled and not as an exposition of either the problems of or possible solutions to the question of race relations in that country. For those interested in a more in-depth study, Morton provided a bibliography of historical and recent accounts. As was his wont, Morton began with surmises as to how South Africa might have fitted into the Roman and Greek classical periods, but he knew there were no actual connections. With the dismembering of his usual framework for viewing a country, Morton saw South Africa from a perspective that is usually absent from his other travel accounts.

Morton wrote that on arrival in South Africa he was "declimatised and unreal," warning the reader immediately that he was faced with a country that could not be described with his typical overlay of the past upon the present. While Morton included historical accounts in the narrative, these accounts are directly pertinent to an understanding of the contemporary scene. The Boers reminded him of Oliver Cromwell and the Puritans, but they are clearly depicted in the homes and occupations of the mid twentieth century. Morton liked to spot the familiar while he traveled, but in South Africa his delight in finding a "typical" Irish or Scottish face was deflated by responses in Afrikaans. Because South Africa did not conform to the tropes of his imagination, Morton presented much more of what he saw. The reader learns a great deal about the varied landscapes of the country and its flora and fauna. Morton did not tell much about himself in his writings, but he did occasionally let slip that he was a gardener. As such, he was amazed at the rapid maturation of plants in the South African climate, and he marveled at how, given proper watering, so many English plants could be grown there. When Morton immigrated to, and later became a citizen of, South Africa, he built himself an English-style house with English furnishings.

The reader is also presented with both verbal and photographic representations of the major South African cities, and there is information about social structures, educational systems, and families. Unable to comprehend the position of the blacks in the country, Morton took the attitude of other whites and thought of native Africans as animal-like or childlike. He associated civilization and culture only with white South Africans, and he did not even consider the blacks as part of the history of the country: "The story of South Africa is that of two fine European peoples, as alike as two races can be, who have established their civilisation at great cost and with courage upon the tip of Africa. In spite of their unhappy schism they have managed to exert their sway over, and to accept responsibility for, a greater number of servants than any nation has been blessed or cursed with. . . ." Although Morton reiterated throughout the book that one could understand the relations between all the races in South Africa without a long-term stay in the country, clearly he viewed the black population as inferior, and, while they could be given better educations and economic opportunities, he never suggested that they should be allowed to amass the political power to overwhelm the white minority. In this light Morton's book becomes more serious than he perhaps intended, but his attitudes and depictions represent more clearly and accurately than any of his other books a picture of a country as it was when he traveled through it.

Morton's next book, *In Search of London* (1951), explores much of the same territory he described in his previous books about the city, augmented with observations of war damage and the rebuilding. In many cases Morton simply updated information from earlier books. The book does reveal, however, that in his youth he wrote a novel about two London lovers who are so desperate to be alone that they climb all the way up into the Monument. In his wanderings about the city over the years, Morton found that there are, in fact, many quiet and out-of-the-way places for desperate lovers and tourists alike.

As *A Stranger in Spain* (1955), Morton was less sure of himself as a traveler. His essays on Spanish history, with particular emphasis on its intersections with British history, assure the reader that he did not simply wander about and unimaginatively stare at cathedrals and landscapes. On this journey, however, Morton was more often content with following tour guides and taking tours by bus.

A Roman animal-welfare woman feeding stray cats in Trajan's Market, photograph by Morton in his A Traveller in Rome *(1957)*

When he was on his own in a new city, Morton took advantage of letters of introduction rather than exploring by himself. He was not beyond making gentle fun of other tourists, but he followed up a sneer at those Americans who think they have seen the "real Spain" with a list of the famous places he visited and checked off his list. He even admitted to a decided preference for American breakfasts, although he enjoyed local food for other meals. Morton was ill for some time during this journey, and perhaps that dampened his enthusiasm. In his previous books Morton could even make his moments of boredom seem lighthearted, but here, for instance, when he is disappointed by the Alhambra, the reader senses a feeling of real letdown that is only partially alleviated by the later delight at the mosque of Córdoba. Sometimes a too-bookish knowledge cannot be enlivened. Morton also revealed that in his youth he had gathered the materials for a novel about the Catholic exiles from England who were attempting to reclaim the country for their religion, but he was unable to make the narrative work as a novel. Perhaps in Spain his historical imagination was not sufficient to see the country fully.

For the next decade Morton concentrated on writing about Italy. Although he had visited Italy during the 1920s, he did not begin writing about it until later in his life. The books that he produced are based on several visits, each lasting a few months.

One would scarcely know from reading *A Traveller in Rome* (1957) that Morton had been there during the twentieth century. The book asserts that Rome is many cities: ecclesiastical, business, diplomatic, archaeological, artistic, tourist, the American enclave, and an everyday Rome. Of these Morton chose the ecclesiastical and archaeological for his focus. His five-month stay in the city was taken up with visits to its many churches, cathedrals, fountains, and Roman ruins. As he walked through Roman streets, Morton walked through its history and recorded it in his book. Rome of the 1950s is represented only by nonfunctioning elevators, Vespas, and buses that require considerable forethought and strategic planning if one is to exit at the correct stop without severe personal injury. Morton's Rome is essentially the city of the Caesars and the Roman Catholic Church. Though he was intensely curious and reverential about both, he could also take a humorous view. He could not resist a pun about papal bulls when he visited the Pope's dairy farm, and when he was given a private audience, he was most impressed with the Pope's red velvet shoes.

Almost everything Morton saw in Rome took him into the past, which he presented imaginatively, as though he were a witness to the slaying of Julius Caesar; the rituals of the Vestal Virgins; the eventful journey of Clementina Sobieski from Poland to Rome so that she might marry James, the pretender to the British throne; and the arrival of the British on the Grand Tour in search of classical inspiration. The landscape of Morton's Rome is crowded with ghosts of the past, and residents of his own time were pushed aside. As usual, Morton revealed little about himself, but he did confess to disliking spaghetti and to having an interest in miniature photography. He must also have enjoyed exterior photography as he took several of the photographs in the book.

In *A Traveller in Italy* (1964) Morton ended his tour in Rome. The book covers the months preceding his arrival there. Morton's route through northern Italy took him through the major cities and historical towns: Milan, Mantua, Parma, Modena, Bologna, Verona, Venice, Florence, and Perugia. In many of these places he followed guides with groups of tourists and used their questions as the springboards for the historical and anecdotal narratives that fill the text. As usual, Morton was more taken with past residents than with present inhabitants. His narrative is crowded with stories about saints, the Borgias, and English expatriates. In Italy, Morton even found a precedessor for himself: Thomas Coryate toured Italy by foot in the early seventeenth century and, like Morton, traveled abroad "out of sheer curiosity to see the world and its people," returning home to write the first modern travel book in English.

Most of Morton's travel books give the impression of him as someone who wandered through streets and buildings, his images of what he saw vastly augmented by thoughts of history and legend. In northern Italy he appreciated his hotel rooms and wonderful dinners in small cafés and restaurants. He wandered about, especially during the early-morning hours, to glimpse cities waking up, but there seems more of a distancing between the interpolated narratives and Morton's observations than in the earlier works. The people around Morton–city dwellers, villagers, and tourists–are simply people of his own time and not evocations of earlier peoples. Morton even admitted that the tourists in Venice add vitality to the city. In a way the history and stories seem to be included as expected parts of a Morton travel book; they are separated from Morton's unmediated enjoyment of the sunshine, lakes, crowds, and food. Reading *A Traveller in Italy* before traveling there would allow one to enjoy the country as a relaxed, comfortable, and knowledgeable traveler and not as a harried tourist.

For the tourist wanting a specialized guide to Rome, Morton's *The Waters of Rome* (1966) offers a wealth of information to lovers of architecture, history, and hydraulic engineering. Of all Morton's books, this one synthesizes his sensibilities most felicitously, for in the 1960s Rome began reconstructing some of the ancient aqueducts while building new ones. In describing the intricacies of providing Rome with water and the artistic impulses behind the construction of the fountains around the city from which the water was distributed, Morton could indulge in his pleasure at fixing works of art in time without giving the reader the sense that the present has been quite erased. The ingenuity and engineering skills of the ancient Romans are still useful and often surprising. Steam was used to open temple doors automatically, and compressed air moved figures and caused bronze birds to sing in fountains. After a general history of the ancient aqueducts and fountains, the book is divided into chapters on each of the six modern Roman aqueducts and the fountains into which each feeds. The book is lavishly illustrated with color and black-and-white photographs.

In *Abroad* Fussell lists the images that constituted the new pastoral view of the Mediterranean that cropped up in British travel books during the 1920s and 1930s: beaches, sun, shellfish, olive oil, cheap-but-good local wines, street noise, Vespas, colorful fishermen, Catholic processions, blessings of the fishing fleet, and a discreet eroticism. Morton only barely hinted at the eroticism he found and described in southern Italy during the 1960s. (The most erotic he ever got in his books is a wistful appreciation of young women's legs.) While *A Traveller in Southern Italy* (1969) has the flavor of a 1920s travel book, it extracts its essence from much earlier periods. The back endpapers have a chart of the rulers of southern Italy, from the eleventh to the mid nineteenth centuries. On this journey Morton seemed rather disconcerted with the evidence of twentieth-century life. He came to see women clad in colorful traditional costumes and happy peasants at one with the land. He did, however, appreciate the improved roadways and the clean hotels with private bathrooms.

Over a long summer Morton traveled by car through the mountains and along the coastal roads of Italy south of Rome. He set out to discover the medieval world that still clung to southern Italy. Morton bridged the perspective between his and the earlier time by invoking the works of his predecessors: Norman Douglas, Edward Hutton, and Estella Canziani, who visited the area in the early twentieth century, when southern Italy was much less accessible. In effect Morton saw the area through their eyes and through his historically fired imagination.

Morton's books on Italy have not been forgotten. In her *Italian Days* (1989) Barbara Grizzuti Harrison, for example, acknowledges Morton as an indefatigable traveler and scholar. But when she quotes him in her book, it is to contrast what she sees in modern Italy with what seems to be Morton's distant and vanished past.

Morton's earlier works are remembered by David W. McFadden, who used *In Search of Ireland* as the guide for his trip to Ireland in the early 1990s. McFadden was amazed to discover that many of the traditions Morton noticed are still intact, but he was also surprised that Morton, who was usually so interested in history, bypassed so much evidence of pre-Celtic and Celtic societies on the island. McFadden's assessment of Morton in *An Innocent in Ireland* (1995) is mixed: "Morton was a nice man, people responded well to him, and, if they hadn't, he wouldn't have noticed. He was a well-wisher, an optimist, a Pollyanna, a rank sentimentalist, a gladhander, a promoter of peace and goodwill, a schmoozer, and he always seemed to be on the lookout for a free meal. He was funnier than he realized. He was a certifiable Everyman." All and all McFadden finds Morton an interesting but rather unreliable guide.

The last books published under Morton's name were lavish books of photographs accompanied by texts compiled from Morton's earlier works. Selections for *H. V. Morton's Britain* (1969) were made by Gilbert Carter and taken from a dozen of Morton's works on the British Isles. The photographs– mostly of cathedrals, castles, and famous London scenes–were taken during the 1960s. In the introduction to the book the publisher noted that the popularity of Morton's books on Britain had been unabated since their original publication. Morton suggested that they were popular because they created a mood and the sense of a period in which one could unhurriedly and without planning motor along less-traveled roads and lanes. In other words the books appeal to nostalgia for a simpler life. This appeal to nostalgia is again apparent in *The Splendor of Scotland* (1976), which draws its text from Morton's two previous books on Scotland to accompany 160 pages of photographs. The text focuses on the imaginative manner by which Morton "can project himself back into history and capture distant events and the actors on stage at a particular place he visits. And when the people he meets are contemporaries, of the twentieth-century, he understands them and their work with a sympathy they repay." Readers who meet Morton through his books understand him through his love of history, curiosity about place-names, indulgence in spa treatments, occasional regional recipes, and love of travel during the summer months. Although Morton defined himself as a traveler, he maintained his affinity with less knowledgeable tourists, encouraging them to give vent to imagination and enthusiasm in visiting well-known and little-known places.

In 1937 Morton was honored as Commander, Order of the Phoenix (Greece), and in 1965 he became Cavaliere, Order of Merit (Italy). Sometime after his initial visit to South Africa he immigrated there and purchased a grape-producing farm in the wine district outside Cape Town. He later became a citizen of South Africa and died there on 18 June 1979. He was survived by his wife, Mary, as well as three sons and a daughter.

References:

Paul Fussell, *Abroad: British Literary Traveling Between the Wars* (New York: Oxford University Press, 1980);

Barbara Grizzuti Harrison, *Italian Days* (New York: Weidenfeld & Nicolson, 1989);

David W. McFadden, *An Innocent in Ireland: Curious Rambles and Singular Encounters* (Toronto: McClelland & Stewart, 1995).

Papers:

Morton's correspondence with members of the staff of the BBC from 1934 to 1962 is in the BBC Written Archives Centre, Radio Contributors section, in Reading, England. An editorial correspondence file relating to the publication of *In Search of England* is at the University of Bristol Library. Morton's letters to Cecil Roberts (1957–1976) are housed in the Churchill Collection Archives Centre in Cambridge, England.

George Orwell
(Eric Arthur Blair)

(25 June 1903 - 21 January 1950)

Bill V. Mullen
Youngstown State University

See also the Orwell entries in *DLB 15: British Novelists, 1930-1959* and *DLB 98: Modern British Essayists.*

BOOKS: *Down and Out in Paris and London* (London: Gollancz, 1933; New York: Harper, 1933);

Burmese Days (New York: Harper, 1934; London: Gollancz, 1935);

A Clergyman's Daughter (London: Gollancz, 1935; New York: Harper, 1936);

Keep the Aspidistra Flying (London: Gollancz, 1936; New York: Harcourt, Brace, 1956);

The Road to Wigan Pier (London: Gollancz, 1937; New York: Harcourt, Brace, 1958);

Homage to Catalonia (London: Secker & Warburg, 1938; New York: Harcourt, Brace, 1952);

Coming Up for Air (London: Gollancz, 1939; New York: Harcourt, Brace, 1950);

Inside the Whale, and Other Essays (London: Gollancz, 1940);

The Lion and the Unicorn: Socialism and the English Genius (London: Secker & Warburg, 1941);

Animal Farm (London: Secker & Warburg, 1945; New York: Harcourt, Brace, 1946);

Critical Essays (London: Secker & Warburg, 1946); republished as *Dickens, Dali and Others* (New York: Reynal & Hitchcock, 1946);

Nineteen Eighty-Four (London: Secker & Warburg, 1949; New York: Harcourt, Brace, 1949);

Shooting an Elephant, and Other Essays (London: Secker & Warburg, 1950; New York: Harcourt, Brace, 1950);

England Your England and Other Essays (London: Secker & Warburg, 1953); republished as *Such, Such Were the Joys* (New York: Harcourt, Brace, 1953);

A Collection of Essays (Garden City, N.Y.: Doubleday, 1954);

The Orwell Reader: Fiction, Essays, and Reportage (New York: Harcourt, Brace, 1956);

The Collected Essays, Journalism, and Letters of George Orwell, 4 volumes, edited by Sonia Orwell and Ian Angus (London: Secker & Warburg, 1968; New York: Harcourt, Brace & World, 1968);

Nineteen Eighty-Four: The Facsimile of the Extant Manuscript, edited by Peter Davison (London: Secker & Warburg / Weston, Mass.: M & S Press, 1984);

Orwell: The War Broadcasts, edited by W. J. West (London: Duckworth/British Broadcasting Corporation, 1985);

Orwell, The Lost Writings, edited by West (New York: Arbor House, 1985);

Orwell: The War Commentaries, edited by West (London: Duckworth/British Broadcasting Corporation, 1985; New York: Pantheon, 1986).

George Orwell's three major books of travel writing–*Down and Out in Paris and London* (1933), *The Road to Wigan Pier* (1937), and *Homage to Catalonia* (1938)–revived the tradition of excursionary literature as social and political analysis. "Into Unknown England" books were initiated by reform-minded Victorian and Edwardian authors. In his three travel books Orwell, who casts himself as a representative of English "lower-upper-middle-class" and as an imaginary social conscience, ventured into the slums of Paris and London, the mining towns of northern England, and the battlefront of the Spanish Civil War, addressing what he saw as a largely conservative and apathetic English readership. Orwell sought to prove that class inequality and the corruption of progressive political ideals were, in his evolving socialist estimation, damning England and the Western world to social division, provincial bigotry, and eventually world war. Yet Orwell's deep acculturation in traditional middle-class British mores and patriotic sentiments clashed with his sensitivity to class and racial bias. In particular Orwell's travel essays on Marrakech and Burma (now Myanmar) are ambiguous but important examples of how literature that seeks sympathy with or advocacy for other cultures and

George Orwell, 1943 (BBC Photograph)

groups also demonstrates how the identities of writers, their subjects, and those who read their work are constructed by intercultural exchange. These complications, coupled with the political inconsistencies within Orwell's worldview over the course of his lifetime, have led to warring interpretations of his legacy. Recent critical debate has focused on Orwell's reliability as an observer, his idiosyncratic views on socialism, and the degree to which his reputation for fairness, decency, and common sense are attributable to his insistence on empirically verifiable political and moral "truths."

George Orwell was born Eric Arthur Blair on 25 June 1903 in Bengal, India, where his father, Richard Walmesley Blair, was an administrator in the Opium Department of the government of India. Though Orwell left India when still a young boy, his father's involvement with the British colonial project determined Orwell's later decision at age nineteen to return to the country that became the subject for his first novel, *Burmese Days* (1934), and essays. When he was three Orwell returned to England with his mother, Ida Mabel Limouzin Blair, to be raised in what he called a "shabby-genteel family" at Henley-on-Thames. The modest pleasures of his upbringing, which Orwell recorded in the posthumously published essay "Such, Such Were the Joys" (written in 1947), were a touchstone for Orwell's lifelong sympathy for the durability of British middle-class values, against which he often compared the culture and castes of non-English societies while abroad.

In 1911 Orwell entered St. Cyprians, an elite private school, and in 1917 he enrolled at Eton Col-

Orwell (standing third from left) at the Police Training School in Mandalay, 1923

lege, the most distinguished preparatory school in Great Britain. There Orwell began to question the values of privilege and upward mobility that his upbringing seemed destined to fulfill. His rebellion was most obvious in his decision to leave Eton in 1921 and apply to join the Indian Imperial Police rather than attending college. This impulse toward the "road not taken" recurred throughout Orwell's career and is a perfect metaphor for his travel writing. The decision to go to India was not only a naive denial of personal privilege and class status but also the first of many impulsively chosen explorations of the structural causes of political and social inequality.

Orwell was accepted into the Indian Imperial Police in 1922. In October he began serving as assistant superintendent of police in Rangoon (Yangon), Burma. There Orwell quickly became uncomfortably self-conscious of his role as intruder, alien, and symbol of British authority and of the ways in which these aspects of position obscured and prejudiced understanding of the indigenous population. "A Hanging" (*Adelphi,* August 1931), his first published work of real travel writing, is a report of the execution of a Hindu prisoner to which Orwell, in the role of British police officer, was both inactive bystander and symbol of authority. The detached exposition of the event–and the conspicuous absence of political commentary by the author–stands in for Orwell's disquieting implication in the death of one whose anonymity is defined as his invisibility to the abstract system of rule under which he lives. The essay implies what Orwell stated much more overtly in "Marrakech," an essay published in the Christmas 1939 issue of *New Writing:* "People with brown skins are next door to invisible. . . . All colonial empires are in reality founded upon that fact. The people have brown faces–besides, there are so many of them! Are they really the same flesh as yourself? Do they even have names?" "A Hanging" is the first ambiguous evidence of Orwell's recognition of what contemporary criticism calls the "Orientalist" construction by Western cultures of the identities of non-Western persons. Recent criticism has noted, for example, that Orwell's portrait of the Hindu prisoner reinforces the anonymity of Indian culture to Western eyes even as it critiques colonial domination.

As a literary text "A Hanging" reveals Orwell's early reliance on the realistic and naturalistic technique he encountered in reading the works of William Makepeace Thackeray, Charles Dickens, and others. This influence partly informs Orwell's naive early faith–one complicated by his later work–in the ability of empirical observation to render intercultural experience truthfully. The "meticulous descriptive quality" of "A Hanging" reflects an aesthetic Orwell developed in part through the jolting experience of being culturally dislocated. Orwell's self-conscious role as outside observer in another culture and the desire to eliminate subjective bias that was part of his journalistic orientation inform his best-known declaration of his own writing method as expressed in "Why I Write" (*Gangrel,* Summer 1946): "one can write nothing readable unless one constantly struggles to efface one's own personality. Good prose is like a window pane." In "A Hanging" he adhered to this aesthetic of impersonality; yet it is strained by Orwell's temptation to draw negative conclusions about colonialism and his role in it, a role he was not confident or certain enough to voice.

The subject of "Shooting an Elephant" (1936), Orwell's other well-known and widely anthologized essay on his Burma experience, is the impossibility of either objectivity or the effacement of the writer's own political role in the events he describes. The essay explodes a paradox particular to nearly all Orwell's travel writings, his participation in the events he describes as a first-person test of political conscience. While serving as a subdivisional police officer in Lower Burma, Orwell was called on to kill an escaped elephant rampaging through the small town of Moulmein. As "the white man with his gun" standing before an unarmed native crowd, Orwell suddenly saw himself as he imagined the natives did. While "seemingly the leading actor of the piece . . . in reality I was only an absurd puppet pushed to and fro by the will of those yellow faces behind." Orwell's self-consciousness threw into relief the conventional relationships of colonialism and allowed him to interpret his participation as part of an allegory of political power: "I perceived in this moment that when the white man turns tyrant it is his own freedom that he destroys."

Orwell's Burma experience heightened his suspicions of social inequities and his sympathy for oppressed peoples. On his return to England in 1927 he aggressively transferred this suspicion and sympathy to the British class structure. In 1928 Orwell wedded these newfound ideas to a strong desire to become a full-time writer. He abandoned his apartment and set out for the East End of London to document the lives of the poor and homeless. He lived first for several months in and around the London slums and then went to Paris, where he lived among the poor for a year and a half. His mixed motives behind the book that eventually became his first, *Down and Out in Paris and London* (1933), indicate a crossroads in his career. In 1936 Orwell wrote that his desire to "submerge myself, get right down among the oppressed" reflected the "bad conscience" he had acquired from the Burma experience. Yet in the preface to the French edition of *Down and Out in Paris and London,* published in 1935, Orwell wrote that he went to France "so as to live cheaply while writing two novels. . . . and also to learn French." The confusion of these two tasks delayed composition of the book and its publication. A first version, titled "A Scullion's Diary," was completed in 1930 and included only the Parisian experiences. After it was rejected, Orwell expanded and revised it, adding the more documentary section on London, only to have it rejected again in 1932 by T. S. Eliot, representing Faber and Faber. When Victor Gollancz finally agreed to publish the book, Orwell requested that it be done pseudonymously, and came up with the name George Orwell. Published in January 1933, the book sold out its first printing.

Though in large part social documentary, *Down and Out in Paris and London* is called a "novel" because Orwell had set out to write one. Its narrator is not named–part of Orwell's strategy of personality "effacement"–and the first part of the book has the dramatic momentum and anecdotal power of fiction. As a piece of travel writing, the first half is characterized by enthusiastic curiosity for the marked bohemianism of Paris that must have struck Orwell as very un-English. Somewhat exoticized vignettes of Paris street life, prostitution, and thievery nearly eclipse Orwell's more characteristic anthropological analysis of alien cultures. Almost as if to make good on a forgotten promise early in the book to write about "poverty," *Down and Out in Paris and London* focuses toward the end on the caste system among employees in the Hotel X, where the narrator is employed as a dishwasher. Here Orwell reverted to a favorite strategy: illustrating through analogy so that British readers might apprehend a lesson about class structure. Hotel cooks, he noted, are the most "workmanlike class" among the employees; plongeurs (dishwashers) are "one of the slaves of the modern world" and are compared to English coal miners; waiters, whose skills are "chiefly in being servile," are closer to snobs than socialists, with the exception of a friendly Italian who "looked just like an Eton boy." The book reveals a fundamental strategy of virtually all Orwell's

Orwell in the late 1920s, while he was living among the poor and homeless people who became the subject of his first book, Down and Out in Paris and London *(1933)*

travel writings: to consider the English social situation in light of the international picture.

Indeed, the second half of *Down and Out in Paris and London* is a grim-faced documentary of Orwell's London street experiences that is in marked contrast to the ribaldry of the Paris section. Fragments of these London experiences were initially published as "The Spike" in *Adelphi* (April 1931) and later reshaped to become chapters 27 and 35 of the finished book. "Spikes" were British poorhouses where Orwell lodged as he traveled. Their despicable conditions moved him to write in increasingly dark and prescriptive tones about the conditions of the underclass, describing the marginalization of the poor as resulting from characteristically royalist British fear of the mob. Orwell also assaulted British vagrancy laws for contributing to the squalor. In the tradition of Henry Mayhew, Orwell added a "glossary" of words used among the street poor and ended with a plea to make lodging houses cleaner and safer for the "tramps."

What is finally most significant about *Down and Out in Paris and London,* however, is its tentative formation of Orwell's method of social inquiry and the vague discerning of principles that would soon make him turn socialist. "At present I do not feel that I have seen more than the fringe of poverty," he wrote near the end of the book, chastening himself by insisting he would never again "enjoy a meal at a smart restaurant. That is a beginning." *Down and Out in Paris and London* closes with an admission that, while no temporary excursion into poverty equals social change, it does provide a necessary perspective from which to live and write, a point of view that may be carried back to one's "lower-upper-middle-class" and intellectual life. Recent criticism, however, has challenged Orwell's achievement of his purpose, noting that he never overcame a middle-class detachment from the poor and that the book lacks formal coherence and a decisive political point of view.

Down and Out in Paris and London earned Orwell a reputation as a champion of the underdog and made him a writer for good. Over the next three years he published *Burmese Days* (1934), *A Clergyman's Daughter* (1935), and *Keep the Aspidistra Flying* (1936). During this period he married Eileen O'Shaughnessy on 9 June 1936, and, influenced by the course of world events in Germany, Italy, and particularly in Spain, he moved closer to becoming a socialist. In 1934 he began an affiliation with the British Independent Labour Party (ILP), a left-wing democratic and pacifist party, officially joining in 1938. Gollancz's offer in 1937 to have Orwell write a book about the unemployed of northern England precipitated his permanent commitment to socialist principles and his engagement with literary strategies explicitly designed to promote socialist thinking.

In *The Road to Wigan Pier* (1937) Orwell wrote that he went to Lancashire and Yorkshire in northern England "partly because I wanted to see what mass-unemployment is like at its worst, partly in order to see the most typical section of the English working class at close quarters. This was necessary to me as part of my approach to Socialism." His findings are delivered in two parts. The first half of the book is close reportage of the domestic and work conditions of the miners, and the second is an autobiographical account of Orwell's path to socialism. The two halves are connected by Orwell's larger purpose of explaining how the experience of visiting the miners solidified his growing conviction that class and provincial inequalities in England were microcosms of pressing global disparities between rich and poor, haves and have nots, capitalists and victims of capitalism. Orwell found that official ignorance and neglect of the conditions of British miners

Orwell (second from left) at the Aragon front in 1937, during the Spanish Civil War

were emblematic of a bigoted national will and a failed political resolve: "the English regional snobberies are nationalism in miniature."

A practical goal of *The Road to Wigan Pier* was to prick the conscience of English politicians into recognizing the struggle of the National Unemployed Workers' Movement to counsel workers facing the government Means Test, which was used to determine the needs of the indigent. Orwell supported his plea for consideration of the hardships of miners with some of his best descriptive prose. Most memorable is a long account of a descent into the mines, where the body-breaking labor performed under dangerous, claustrophobic, and at times deadly conditions is rendered with a restraint that is itself harrowing. Typically, and in ways reminiscent of his Burma essays, Orwell foregrounded his intellectual and class differences from the miners as a strategy to convince middle-class or intellectual readers to empathize with the miners. He admitted to his phobic reactions, cultivated in grade school, to the dirt, smell, and disease of poor manual laborers, and he stressed the regional stereotypes southerners such as himself brought to northern industrial life, attitudes that must be smashed to allow for political and class sympathy. As in *Down and Out in Paris and London,* Orwell sought to illustrate and explode the fear of being poor that he said is the worst nightmare of his class (the bourgeoisie). Facing this fear, he suggested, provides the necessary catharsis that allows interclass affiliation: "you feel that you have seen the worst and the worst has no terrors for you."

The second half of the book, Orwell's declarations on what he perceived as weaknesses of left-wing politics and contemporary socialism, is the most important and controversial legacy of *The Road to Wigan Pier*. There Orwell made his well-known, cranky pronouncement on left politics as a lure for both reputable and, according to his own chauvinistic version of socialism, eccentric causes: "One sometimes gets the impression that the mere words 'Socialism' and 'Communism' draw towards them with magnetic force every fruit-juice drinker, nudist, sandal-wearer, sex-maniac, Quaker, 'Nature Cure' quack, pacifist and feminist in England." In a veiled reference to Joseph Stalin, Orwell also lamented the influence of the "stupid cult of Russia" over socialists in England, whom he accused of failing to undertake truly revolutionary aims. The formal split in *The Road to Wigan Pier* between an empirical demonstration of why one must be a socialist and a condemnation of socialism as practiced is emblematic of Orwell's lifelong political struggle to reconcile moral outrage at everyday fact with his disdain for systemic politics and ideology. Orwell condemned any socialist or communist politics that failed to retain identification with the "common man" and with the principles of decency and equality that were fundamental to his mix of liberal humanism and democratic socialism. Thus, the book ironically confirms Orwell's socialist commitment while distancing him from mainstream left movements.

Gollancz wrote an introduction to *The Road to Wigan Pier,* warning readers against what he felt were Orwell's peevish and narrow interpretations of socialist and communist practice. The choice of the book as a main selection of the Left Book Club met with strenuous objections from communists. The contemporary controversy over Orwell's interpretation of socialism was recast as vigorous debate in the 1940s and 1950s between socialists, communists, and anticommunists, all of whom found material for their political position. Over time, the controversy solidified Orwell's reputation as an outsider and independent critic of the left. This view was reinforced by the despairing view of all state politics Orwell displayed in *Animal Farm* (1945) and *Nineteen Eighty-Four* (1949).

In December of 1936 Orwell went to Spain to report on the Civil War and to test his socialist sympathies once again. He arrived in Barcelona with letters of introduction from the Independent Labour Party in London and was enrolled by the ILP office there in the militia of its sister party in Spain, the POUM (Party of Marxist Unification). Typically, exposure to the drama of political events led Orwell to move from the position of witness to participant. His naive enthusiasm for the populist comradeship of the Spanish peasants fighting Francisco Franco's antidemocratic forces convinced him to take up arms on behalf of the POUM. Badly armed and uniformed with the peasant army on the Aragon front, Orwell still found an almost utopian

> foretaste of Socialism. . . . Many of the normal motives of civilized life–snobbishness, money-grubbing, fear of the boss, etc.–had simply ceased to exist. The ordinary class-division of society had disappeared to an extent that is almost unthinkable in the money-tainted air of England; there was no one there except the peasants and ourselves, and no one owned anyone else as his master.

Against these communal brigades of mainly working-class peasants Orwell identified the "enemy" in Spain as fascists and the Spanish Communist Party. The Communists' strategy of separating the Civil War from the aim of revolutionary overthrow of the Spanish government and of casting the POUM as reactionary "Trotskyites" and "fifth column" fascists (both distortions) convinced Orwell that this relatively small guerrilla war was the best test case for the future of socialism worldwide. In "Spilling the Spanish Beans," published in the 29 July and 2 September 1937 issues of *New English Weekly,* Orwell first articulated what he felt was the underriding political imperative of the war: "The real struggle is between revolution and counterrevolution; between the workers who are vainly trying to hold on to a little of what they won in 1936, and the Liberal-Communist bloc who are so successfully taking it away from them."

Like *The Road to Wigan Pier, Homage to Catalonia* (1938) is fractured, reflecting Orwell's desire to both tell and explicate his story. The first two-thirds of the book is a vivid chronicle of his arrival in Barcelona, his activity at the Aragon front, and the quotidian frustrations of fighting a guerrilla war. Orwell wrote a meticulous, detached account of peasant-army struggles against lice, food-and-fire shortages, and the general tedium of inaction. (His division saw little fighting.) These sections climax with Orwell's stoical description of being shot through the neck by a sniper. The wound altered his vocal ability permanently and hastened the furlough that returned him to Barcelona in spring 1937. The section that describes his furlough reports on the attempted pogrom against POUM members by the state secret police, which forced Orwell to live an absurd underground existence: "By night we were criminals, but by day we were prosperous English visitors–that was our pose, anyway." These chapters also recount Orwell's attempts to stay in contact with POUM colleagues, many of whom were rounded up and imprisoned by the Spanish police.

Orwell prefaced two intervening chapters of analysis of the ideological and strategic split between Spanish socialists, anarchists, and communists with the complaint that "So much political capital has been made out of the Barcelona fighting that it is important to try and get a balanced view of it." He complained that "nine-tenths" of the published accounts of the war were probably "untruthful," singling out the liberal British press and Communist press in particular for distortions aimed at discrediting the socialist and anarchist forces or stopping them short of a complete revolution. Orwell cited and rebuked articles from *The Daily*

Worker, whose propagandistic intent was to portray the POUM as a group of counterrevolutionary fascists. The seeds of Orwell's obsession with historical revision, agitprop, "newspeak," and political hypocrisy leading to totalitarian strategies of absolute rule are embedded in these chapters. Orwell's exaggerated perception of an internal war among Spanish socialists, anarchists, and communists prepared the way for his increasing skepticism about the ability of ideological movements to avoid corrupting or short-circuiting their own revolutionary aims.

The legacy of *Homage to Catalonia* is complex. Many regard it as Orwell's best nonfiction book, and Lionel Trilling, among others, argued that it is the best document available on the Spanish Civil War. This assessment is complicated by the relative commercial failure of the book: only nine hundred copies had been sold by the time of Orwell's death in 1950. Because it was published late in the United States (in 1952), it was also marketed and received not just as an history of the war but as an example of the genre of "confessional" literature popularized in the 1940s by former Communists and socialists, who were critical of their past political affiliations. In addition contemporary historians and participants in the war have challenged Orwell's lack of deeper understanding of party politics in Spain, as well as his superficial generalizations about the "fascist" nature of Franco's regime. Feminist critics have noted a masculinist romanticizing of combat consistent with Orwell's almost complete exclusion or ignorance of female lives and politics in his writings. A balanced appreciation of the book and Orwell's Spanish experience must take all of these perspectives into account. *Homage to Catalonia* should also be remembered as the book that committed Orwell to his most activist position regarding socialism and the role of the intellectual. "It is not possible for any thinking person to live in such a society as our own without wanting to change it," he wrote in "Why I Joined the Independent Labour Party" (*New Leader,* 24 June 1939), two months after the publication of *Homage to Catalonia.* "The tempo of events is quickening; the dangers which once seemed a generation distant are staring us in the face. One has got to be actively a Socialist, not merely sympathetic to Socialism, or one plays into the hands of our always-active enemies."

As a literary text *Homage to Catalonia* is by far Orwell's most mature and most complete book of reportage. More successfully than *Down and Out in Paris and London* or *The Road to Wigan Pier,* it integrates experience and analysis, and more convincingly than either it demonstrates political engagement as a process of observation and reaction. Finally, what stands out from the book is Orwell's unflagging resolve on two matters crucial to his intellectual life and character: his conviction after contact with Spanish guerrillas that he is left "with not less but more belief in the decency of human beings" and his concomitant frustration with the failure of the Western world to move beyond its provincial interests into real internationalist fraternity. The final words of *Homage to Catalonia* imply the distance of his intellectual and political journey throughout the 1930s, away from middle-class provincialism and into internationalist socialism, as rendered in an ambivalent and defamiliarizing return "home":

Orwell in Marrakech, 1939

> Down here it was still the England I had known in my childhood: the railway-cuttings smothered in wild flowers, the deep meadows where the great shining horses browse and meditate, the slow-moving streams bordered by willows, the green bosoms of the elms, the larkspurs in the cottage gardens; and then the huge peaceful wilderness of outer London, the barges on the miry river, the familiar streets, the posters telling of cricket matches and Royal weddings, the men in bowler hats, the pigeons in Trafalgar Square, the red buses, the blue policeman–all sleeping the deep, deep sleep of

A recording sesssion for the poetry magazine Voice: *(standing) Orwell, Nancy Barratt, William Empson; (sitting) Venu Chitale, J. M. Tambimuttu, T. S. Eliot, Una Marson, Mulk Raj Anand, C. Pemberton, and Narayana Menon (BBC Photograph)*

England, from which I sometimes fear that we shall never wake till we are jerked out of it by the roar of bombs.

The Spanish War was Orwell's last prolonged excursion abroad. After his return home in 1938, in a kind of reversal of his prior role, he became correspondent about contemporary political events from England to the rest of the world. From 1941 to 1943 Orwell worked in the Indian Section of the Eastern Service of the BBC, producing and writing literary shows and weekly war commentaries for radio broadcast abroad. He also used his wartime diaries as the basis for his "London Letter to *Partisan Review*," published in that American magazine between January 1941 and summer 1946. In this column Orwell translated his firsthand apprehensions of European political struggle into analysis of its implications for international socialism and democracy.

In 1945 Orwell took one of his last trips abroad, visiting a prisoner-of-war camp in southern Germany. "Revenge Is Sour," his account of that visit, published in the 9 November 1945 issue of *The Tribune,* describes his tour of the camp with a Viennese Jew who had enlisted in a branch of the American army. The essay singles out a moment when the guide stopped to berate a physically ravaged German SS officer. The bespectacled German, Orwell noted, "Could have been an unfrocked clergyman, an actor ruined by drink, or a spiritualist medium. I have seen very similar people in London common lodging houses, and also in the Reading Room of the British Museum." Typically, Orwell considered the act a kind of morality tale that links the particular atrocities of war to the mundane injustice of life everywhere.

His wife having died on 29 March 1945, Orwell spent most of the last ten years of his life in England raising his adopted son, Richard Horatio, and writing letters, essays, and the novels that solidified his international reputation. Domesticity, war, age, and the long bout with tuberculosis that ended his life on 21 January 1950 curtailed his desire or ability to travel. On 13 October 1949 he married Sonia Brownell in a ceremony conducted at his bedside in a tuberculosis sanatorium.

An illuminating coda to his career as traveler is the essay "Pleasure Spots," published in the 11 January 1946 issue of *The Tribune*. Orwell began by discussing some paragraphs written in a "shiny magazine" by a journalist describing the "pleasure resort of the future." The resort is an entrepreneur's dream of an antiseptic utopia under a series of sliding plastic roofs, where vacationers enjoy climate-controlled leisure in pools heated by sunlight lamps, piped-in music, "uniformed male attendants," and cocktail waitresses in "white satin slacks." Orwell wryly compared the builder's vision to that of Samuel Taylor Coleridge in his poem "Kubla Khan," but then he noted that the resort builder's banal commodification of all things natural makes it "difficult not to feel that the unconscious aim in the most typical modern pleasure resort is a return to the womb," a return which "in the name of pleasure is simply an effort to destroy consciousness."

Against this satirical view of modern life as a longing for the convenient and familiar, it is easier to understand Orwell's lifelong quest to travel and report on pressing problems of his time as an attempt to complicate his own comfortable "lower-upper-middle-class" perspective so that he might create a more radical political and intellectual consciousness. Ultimately it is the moral and political stance of the traveler that is put to the test in his work. Orwell seemed to sense that a reversal of the traditional focus in travel writing from the object to the viewing subject represented a politically necessary shift in Western liberal humanism if it hoped to understand the changing racial, cultural, and political lines of a rapidly destabilizing modern world. By turning the traveler's eye to the complex interrelation of empirical observation, writing, and political engagement, Orwell helped to prepare a postwar England and a postwar world for the contentious, polyvalent perspectives about global power and literary meaning that his writings perceptively foretold.

Biographies:

Peter Stansky and William Abrahams, *The Unknown Orwell* (New York: Knopf, 1972);

Stansky and Abrahams, *Orwell: The Transformation* (New York: Knopf, 1980);

Bernard Crick, *George Orwell: A Life* (Boston: Little, Brown, 1980);

Michael Shelden, *Orwell: The Authorized Biography* (New York: HarperCollins, 1991);

Stephen Ingle, *George Orwell: A Political Life* (Manchester, U.K. & New York: Manchester University Press, 1993).

References:

Keith Alldritt, *The Making of George Orwell: A Literary History* (New York: St. Martin's Press, 1969);

Gordon Beadle, "George Orwell and the Spanish Civil War," *Duquesne Review,* 16 (Spring 1971): 3–16;

Peter Buitenhuis and Ira B. Nadel, eds., *George Orwell: A Reassessment* (Basingstoke, U.K.: Macmillan, 1988);

Mark Connelly, *The Diminished Self: Orwell and the Loss of Freedom* (Pittsburgh: Duquesne University Press, 1987);

Philip Dodd, "The Views of Travellers: Travel Writing in the 1930s," *Prose Studies,* 5 (May 1982): 127–138;

Irving Howe, "Orwell: History as Nightmare," in his *Politics and the Novel* (New York: Horizon, 1956), pp. 235–251;

Jeffrey Meyers, ed., *George Orwell: The Critical Heritage* (London: Routledge & Kegan Paul, 1975);

Christopher Norris, ed., *Inside the Myth: Orwell, Views from the Left* (London: Lawrence & Wishart, 1984);

Daphne Patai, *The Orwell Mystique: A Study in Male Ideology* (Amherst: University of Massachusetts Press, 1984);

Alok Rai, *Orwell and the Politics of Despair: A Critical Study of the Writings of George Orwell* (Cambridge & New York: Cambridge University Press, 1988);

John Rodden, *The Politics of Literary Reputation: The Making and Claiming of 'St. George' Orwell* (New York: Oxford University Press, 1989);

Edward Said, *Orientalism* (New York: Pantheon, 1978);

Paras Mani Singh, *George Orwell as a Political Novelist* (Delhi: Amar Prakashan, 1987);

Lionel Trilling, Introduction to *Homage to Catalonia* (San Diego: Harcourt Brace Jovanovich, 1980), pp. v–xxiii;

Raymond Williams, *George Orwell* (New York: Viking, 1971);

George Woodcock, *The Crystal Spirit: A Study of George Orwell* (Boston: Little, Brown, 1966);

Alex Zwerdling, *Orwell and the Left* (New Haven: Yale University Press, 1974).

Papers:

The most important collection of Orwell's papers is the George Orwell Archive at University College, London.

H. St. John B. Philby

(3 April 1885 – 30 September 1960)

M. D. Allen

University of Wisconsin Fox Valley

BOOKS: *The Heart of Arabia: A Record of Travel and Exploration,* 2 volumes (London: Constable, 1922; New York & London: Putnam, 1923);

Arabia of the Wahhabis (London: Constable, 1928);

Arabia (London: Benn, 1930; New York: Scribners, 1930); revised as *Sa'udi Arabia* (London: Benn, 1955; New York: Praeger, 1955);

The Empty Quarter: Being a Description of the Great South Desert Known as Rub 'al Khali (London: Constable, 1933; New York: Holt, 1933);

Harun al Rashid (London: Davies, 1933; New York: Appleton, 1934);

Sheba's Daughters: Being a Record of Travel in Southern Arabia (London: Methuen, 1939);

A Pilgrim in Arabia (London: Golden Cockerel Press, 1943);

The Background of Islam: Being a Sketch of Arabian History in Pre-Islamic Times (Alexandria: Whitehead Morris, 1947);

Arabian Days: An Autobiography (London: Hale, 1948);

Arabia Highlands (Ithaca, N.Y.: Published for the Middle East Institute, Washington, D.C., by Cornell University Press, 1952);

Arabian Jubilee (London: Hale, 1952; New York: Day, 1953);

The Land of Midian (London: Benn, 1957);

Forty Years in the Wilderness (London: Hale, 1957);

Arabian Oil Ventures (Washington, D.C.: Middle East Institute, 1964);

The Queen of Sheba (London: Quartet, 1981).

H. St. John B. Philby, 1945

When H. St. John B. Philby died in Beirut in 1960, his son had inscribed on his tombstone the words "Greatest of Arabian Explorers." Few would quarrel with this claim. His biographer Elizabeth Monroe wrote in *Philby of Arabia* (1973) that no other explorer "had covered half so much as he of the huge surface of Arabia. None had drawn attention to so many of its antiquities; none had equalled his spread of maps." Robin Bidwell in *Travellers in Arabia* (1976) observed, "None of the writers we have discussed saw so much of the Peninsula, visited as he did practically every corner of it nor traversed it so many times in so many ways." Bidwell went on to say that no other Arabian explorer had spent more than twenty months in the region, but Philby lived there for most of forty years. If his friendship with Ibn Sa'ud, the first king of Saudi Arabia, and his conversion to Islam in some ways facilitated Philby's travels, they did not lessen the dedication and physical hardihood these journeys demanded, and

Philby at the end of his 1917 journey across central Arabia

they helped increase his wide and deep knowledge of the topography, history, and mores of the area, a knowledge made available to a Western audience in fifteen books that are still read by specialists. It must be admitted, however, that Philby's turgid and long-winded style has always denied him a more popular audience and the approbation of readers who judge books in literary terms.

Harry St. John Bridger Philby's second Christian name commemorates the Ceylon tea estate where he was born, and his third comes from his paternal grandmother's respectable family of merchants. He came of solid middle-class stock on both his father's and his mother's sides of the family. Henry Montague Philby, his father, became a tea planter in Badulla (or Badula), Ceylon (now Sri Lanka), and in 1883 he married Queenie, the eldest daughter of Col. (later Lt. Gen.) John Duncan of the Dublin Fusiliers. Harry, nicknamed "Jack," was the second of the Philbys' sons. Queenie Philby eventually left her unfaithful and debt-ridden husband for a financially precarious life in London, where in 1898, at the age of thirteen, Jack Philby won a scholarship to the prestigious Westminster School. He was elected a Queen's Scholar (a King's Scholar after Victoria's death in 1901) and took part in the coronation ceremonies of Edward VII in 1902 in neighboring Westminster Abbey, as was a Westminster schoolboy's right. Successful both academically and at games, Philby ended his time at Westminster as school captain. A contemporary later remembered that "autocracy was his aim and autocratic rule his avowed intention." In October 1904 he enrolled at Trinity College, Cambridge, where again he did well: disappointed at the second-class pass he gained in the first part of the Classical Tripos, he switched to modern languages and got a first in 1907.

Philby's life continued to run along conventional upper-middle-class lines as he entered the Indian Civil Service after completing his elite education. During the seven years he spent in India (1908–1915), he showed characteristic strengths and typical weaknesses. Among the former were his appetite for work, his attraction to Muslim culture, and his intellectual abilities, especially at languages: he added tens of thousands of rupees to his income as rewards for passing examinations in Urdu, Hindi, Punjabi, Persian, and Baluchi, the last of which he learned in six weeks. During his Indian years Philby began to study Arabic, hoping to win more than £300 and be appointed to the political department of the Civil Service. Among the strikes against him were his marriage and several instances of tactless treatment of Indians. On 20 September 1910, after fewer than two years in India, Philby

Philby at Jidda in 1930, just before leaving on his first pilgrimage to Mecca

had married Dora Johnston, the lively and attractive daughter of a senior railway engineer, a union for which he suffered official disapproval because the Civil Service discouraged marriage as too expensive for those in the first years of their careers. Philby had also made the mistake of improperly refusing bail to two Indians accused of perjury, and in a separate incident he had angrily struck an Indian who was impertinent to him. His manifest talents notwithstanding, Philby had three black marks against his name.

The ups and downs that followed, however, sank into insignificance in comparison with Philby's desire to help defeat Germany after the outbreak of World War I, a feeling strengthened by his brother's death in the trenches in 1914. He had to wait until November 1915 for the opportunity he coveted: a need for Arabic-speaking civilian administrators was anticipated as an Allied army advanced toward Baghdad. "My greatest ambition," wrote Philby to his wife as he traveled toward Baghdad, "is to take some part in the war coupled with work among the Arabs." He was about to enter that part of the world and culture with which he was indissolubly linked for the rest of his life: his work for the British government and Saudi Arabia, his explorations and writings about his travels, and his longstanding friendship with an emerging Arab leader who made some of these travels possible.

Philby spent two years (1915–1917) in what was then known as Mesopotamia (now Iraq) administering financial and revenue matters. As in India he established a reputation for being difficult. On one occasion he made what Monroe has called "the classic remark that was for years quoted against him." In Philby's version, given in his autobiography, *Arabian Days* (1948), a colleague "was prosing away and suddenly, my attention being arrested by a remark of his, I was actually heard to say: 'I didn't hear what you said–but I entirely disagree with you.' Of course there was a roar of laughter, and it was no use trying to explain that, in the split second represented by the dash, the purport of his remark had reached my brain, which had reacted instantly." Monroe's version of the remark runs, "I can't hear what you say, Edmonds, but I join issue with you." Both forms of the comment illustrate the combative contrariness that many saw as the hallmark of Philby's character, but the biographer's version is perhaps more reliable than that of her subject. A few years later British diplomat Reader Bullard wrote home of Philby, "I never met such a fellow. Any scheme that anyone else puts up he disagrees with. His great phrase is 'I join issue with you,' and he spends his life joining issue with someone."

Philby's readiness to disagree with others helped get him assigned to a mission in the deserts of central Arabia, from which he could no longer dictate to his colleagues in Mesopotamia. There he met Ibn Sa'ud, who in 1932 became the king of the new country to which he gave his family's name. He was then an obscure desert chieftain who had to be persuaded not to attack Husayn ibn 'Ali, Sharif of Mecca, leader of the Arab revolt against the Turks, who were Germany's allies, and, if possible, to mount instead an expedition against the pro-Turkish chieftain Ibn Rashid. Appointed leader of the mission, Philby remained in central Arabia for nearly a year with only a short break. He returned having acquired his first fame as an explorer and material for his first two travel books, *The Heart of Arabia* (1922) and *Arabia of the Wahhabis* (1928). In Ibn Sa'ud, Philby had found a friend "beyond all price." The desert leader Philby was sent to manipulate in Britain's war interests had so beguiled Philby that the course of his life and opinions were irrevocably changed.

Ibn Sa'ud had spent much of his childhood in exile in Kuwait after his family's military defeat at the hands of the Rashidis, and he returned to capture Riyadh in a daring raid in 1902. Eleven years later he ejected the Turks from what is now eastern Saudi Arabia. In 1919 he defeated the Rashidis again, for the last time, and in 1925 he was victorious over the forces of the sharif of Mecca. The Kingdom of Saudi Arabia was proclaimed in 1932. In his *Arabia,* published in Benn's Modern World Series in 1930, Philby described Ibn Sa'ud as "the Great Wahhabi himself, the hero of my tale."

Philby's first great achievement as a traveler, for which he was awarded the Founder's Medal of the Royal Geographical Society in 1920, was a journey across central Arabia from east to west, a journey only once before accomplished by an Englishman, nearly a century previously. Philby crossed almost half of the Arabian peninsula as part of a prearranged mission, riding on camelback to Riyadh to meet Ibn Sa'ud. Their conversation necessarily turned on the relations between the Saudi and his hated rival to the west, the sharif of Mecca. Using the situation to assuage his thirst for adventure and primacy, Philby suggested that he ride on to Taif, only sixty miles from the Red Sea coast, and bring back a senior British official to Riyadh so that he could witness the extent of Ibn Sa'ud's sway in central Arabia, thus enabling British authorities to make informed judgments about the relative claims to greatness of the British-sponsored sharif and the neglected Ibn Sa'ud. When Philby and his Arab guides arrived at Taif, they discovered that no British official was present or expected. They were directed to proceed to Jidda on the west coast.

Philby thus made a journey that no one had accomplished in the last ninety-eight years because of the harshness of the climate and terrain, and, even more, the hostility of the inhabitants. Later, when Ibn Sa'ud asked him to remove his obviously English presence while the expedition against Ibn Rashid was organized, Philby obtained permission to explore the Jabal Tuwaiq, south of Riyadh. In his journeys he collected data that enabled the Royal Geographical Society to prepare accurate maps of territory hitherto unknown to the West.

Philby described his trips of 1917 and 1918 in *The Heart of Arabia,* which focuses on his journeys across the peninsula and south of Riyadh, and *Arabia of the Wahhabis,* which deals with an abortive journey toward Ha'il and the abrupt termination of his mission by the British government. Ibn Sa'ud, afraid of the complications Philby's death in battle would cause, had refused to let him travel beyond the town of Buraydah. (The last word in the title is a reference to the puritanical sect led by Ibn Sa'ud.) Contemporary expert reviewers lauded Philby's contributions to Western knowledge of Arabia. In a statement quoted in an advertisement for *Arabia of the Wahhabis,* D. G. Hogarth described *The Heart of Arabia* as "packed with novel experience fully and faithfully set down, and with information about the heart of Arabia more comprehensive and exact than any Briton has collected except Doughty." *The New Statesman* reviewer, however, complained of an excess of information, "detailed almost to weariness. He does not give the atmosphere of desert life as Doughty has done so vividly. The great and first fault of the book is that it is extremely hard to read" (20 January 1923). In *Arabian Days* Philby observed wryly, "Many readers, desiring only a glimpse at Arabia, may have found my works heavy going and laid them aside with a sigh of despair, duly reflected in my royalties."

Even readers desiring more than a "glimpse" may be pardoned for finding in Philby's works a sort of literary equivalent of the demanding journeys across arid wastes that they narrate. ("All those damned wadis. . . !" an anonymous reader once exclaimed.) Philby's verbose and sometimes ludicrously cliché-ridden style, only occasionally enlivened by a felicitous phrase, prevents anyone but the specialist in Arabian lore from reading Philby for pleasure. Not a great, or even by many standards a good, writer, he wrote his books as a means to an end. Philby wrote to his wife in 1928 that "my chief aim [is] to secure the immortality to be gained by the accomplishment of some great work." His books reported his achievements to a Western audience.

Philby wanted Western fame for exploits performed in the East and specialist status with regard to that region. Yet, because of his friendship with Ibn Sa'ud, he was no "orientalizing" tool of imperial Britain. Philby's admiration for the leader neglected by Britain helped bring about his resignation from his next two jobs.

Philby's mission to central Arabia was succeeded by stints as adviser to the Ministry of the Interior in Mesopotamia (1920–1921) and chief British representative in Transjordan (1921–1924). Philby withdrew from the former position when he realized that Britain was intent on placing the British client Faisal, rather than the local candidate, on the throne. A son of the sharif of Mecca, Faisal had fought alongside T. E. Lawrence in the Arab revolt and was the beneficiary of his formidable propagandizing abilities. Nevertheless, Philby agreed to work with Abdullah, another of the sharif's sons, who was made ruler of Transjordan (now Jordan). Succeed-

The Green Palace in Jidda, which became Philby's home in 1933

ing Lawrence, about whom he was later to write an admiring essay, Philby hoped to foster the independence of at least some Arabs by consolidating the administration and curbing the financial excesses of Abdullah's precarious desert kingdom. The difficulties of the latter task and increasing tension between Philby and the British high commissioner in Palestine eventually led to his resignation.

There followed half a dozen frustrating years. No longer a conventional upper-middle-class servant of the Crown, Philby resigned from the Indian Civil Service in 1925 in order "to serve my country after my own fashion." He made speeches and wrote articles attacking British policy in Arab countries, but his resignation necessitated another regular source of income. In 1926 Philby became a resident of Jidda and received permission from Ibn Sa'ud to start a branch of Sharqieh Ltd, an import business, in that city. Returns were meager and unpredictable for some years.

Having resigned from government service and settled in Arabia, Philby had yet to take the step that eventually led to his great achievements in exploration: conversion to Islam. He had already conceived the idea of becoming the first European to cross the great southern deserts, the so-called Rub 'al-Khali or "Empty Quarter." This journey would be the "great work" of which he wrote to his wife in 1928, an achievement that would give him "immortality." Converting to Islam in 1930, he gained increased access to Ibn Sa'ud, whose permission and support were essential to the expedition. His new religion also made him a more effective businessman in Arabia and bound him more fully into the life of the Saudi theocracy. He wrote to his friend Donald Robertson, "My future is irrevocably bound up with that of Arabia and Ibn Sa'ud, and I have perhaps delayed unnecessarily long not in recognising that fact (for I have long realised it and its inevitable consequence) but in publicly admitting it."

Permission to venture into the Rub 'al Khali was not immediately forthcoming, and Philby had the bitter disappointment of learning that another Arabist, Bertram Thomas, had accomplished the feat in February 1931 without Ibn Sa'ud's leave. Philby could not be the first, but he could be the best. He decided to satisfy "this beastly obsession which has so completely side-tracked me for the best years of my life" not by crossing the Empty Quarter as quickly as possible but by exploring it as thoroughly as possible. Eventually obtaining permission, he left Hofuf (Al Hufuf) in the east on 7 January 1932 and entered Mecca ninety days later, after journeying south, then east, and then west, zigzagging northwest to describe a triangle, and next proceeding west to Sulayyil (As Sulayyil). This part of the journey, most of it in the Rub 'al-Khali proper, took sixty-eight days. The last twenty-two days he spent traveling northwest to Mecca.

There can be no denying the magnitude of his accomplishment. As Leslie McLoughlin, an Arabist and the biographer of Ibn Sa'ud, wrote in a 1991 article:

> To note the direction and distance involved gives little idea of the immense hardship which Philby and his companions endured. In many areas there had been drought for 8–10 years, and in Sulayyil for 12–13 years. Nor can the map show the great contributions in many branches of science which this journey made. In many areas into which he led his group not only was he the first non-Arab to penetrate there but it seems clear from the evidence of his companions that he was the first human being to have trodden there.

McLoughlin also gave a selective list of the "many branches of science" to which Philby contributed: "topography, palaeography, zoology, entomology, history, geology, mineralogy, botany, meteorology, to name a few." Thomas had crossed the Empty Quarter before Philby, and Wilfred Thesiger later crossed it twice (in 1946 and 1948), but Philby added more to Western knowledge than either man.

One result of Philby's journey was *The Empty Quarter* (1933), in which his inability to select or to write with freshness and originality is again evident. Bertram Thomas was among those who reviewed it generously, calling the book "an epic narrative of Arabian exploration" (*The Spectator*, 2 June 1933). A more critical and perceptive verdict came from David Garnett, later the editor of T. E. Lawrence's letters. Reviewing Philby's book for *The New Statesman and Nation* (24 June 1933), Garnett noted that "Mr. Philby is not naturally a good writer"and went on to lament that Philby "half-heartedly attempts" to employ the "very rich vocabulary full of rare and ancient words" used by Charles Doughty in his *Travels in Arabia Deserta* (1888) and by Lawrence in his *Seven Pillars of Wisdom* (1926). While Garnett considered such language suitable to and evocative of "simpler ages and . . . a primitive mode of life," he pointed out that in Philby's book it "often breaks down absurdly." One of the most distinguished members of the group of Britons who worked in the Middle East, Philby must be denied all but a minor place in the Anglo-Arabian literary tradition, despite his awareness of it and ambition to join it. (His choice of vocabulary for example, can be traced back to his first book.). In *Ibn Saud: Founder of a Kingdom* (1993) McLoughlin is blunt:

> The book is, like so many of Philby's works, over large tracts quite unreadable but it is a treasure-house of information which is still used by experts in many scientific fields making comparative studies of Saudi Arabia. This is its true significance, for it was the first book published in English to describe, however imperfectly, the extent of the dominions of Ibn Saud.

Its lame style notwithstanding, *The Empty Quarter* won Philby the fame he had so ardently desired. Although the Empty Quarter expedition was neither his longest nor even perhaps his most physically demanding, it captured the imagination of the educated public in a way that his earlier and later journeys did not. It helped fill in a famous blank space on the world map, one of the few remaining. On his visits to London Philby was invited to lecture to the Royal Geographical Society and the Royal Central Asian Society; he found himself a success in drawing rooms.

Philby's life also became easier financially. He always enjoyed what he called "spacious living and the instinct of hospitality" and wanted the same expensive education for his son, Kim (later to become notorious as a Soviet agent), that he had had. Beginning in 1932 he played an eventually profitable role in negotiations between Saudi Arabia and Western oil companies, supporting what he saw as the anti-imperialist Americans rather than his manipulative countrymen and advising Ibn Sa'ud accordingly. In 1934 he obtained for Sharqieh Ltd the monopoly on Ford car sales in Saudi Arabia. Both Philby and the country with which he had thrown in his lot were becoming richer.

Philby's next expedition was his longest, lasting nine months, from May 1936 to February 1937. It was his ambition to fill in yet another blank on the Arabian map, perhaps the last of all: he wished to explore in the southwest from Najran to the Hadhramaut and hoped to travel as far southwest as Shabwa, which he identified with the legendary Sheba. The expedition was a success. He not only reached Shabwa but also got to Mukalla (Al Mukalla) on the south coast, becoming the first European to cross Arabia from north to south by car. The trip, however, had unfortunate consequences for both Philby and the Arabs whose independence from foreign control he wished to maintain. Because his explorations were also an official Saudi mapping of Ibn Sa'ud's southwest frontier, Philby had traveled with armed Saudi soldiers. In reaching as far south as he did, Philby had entered what the British considered the Aden Protectorate, and the acting British resident asked him to withdraw his Saudi soldiers from British territory. On his return, when Philby gave a lecture to the Royal Central Asian So-

Philby and his wife in Kuwait, 1935

ciety, he claimed that the British "wanted to shoot me," the room erupted in indignant cries of "Nonsense!" and "Rubbish!" Philby's reputation as irrationally anti-British was further strengthened in official circles. In addition, the British authorities took steps to administer more closely the Arabs in the hinterland of the Aden Protectorate.

On 7 March 1937, shortly after Philby's return to Mecca from Aden, Sir Reader Bullard, the British minister to Jidda, wrote "that Philby is staying in Mecca because he is ill, but hopes to be down in a few days. His nine months journey of exploration and the fever would have killed a less obstinate man, and it shook even him. His next book should have much interesting matter in it, but whether he will be able to make it interesting is another matter. He is a pedestrian writer." Bullard's fears were fulfilled in *Sheba's Daughters* (1939). Philby's account of the mapping of the Saudi-Yemen frontier did not see print until 1952, when Cornell University Press published it as *Arabia Highlands.*

Of the 1952 book Samuel C. Chew wrote gently but justly in the *New York Herald Tribune,* "the narrative of such a journey must perforce, if it is accurate and sincere, partake of something of the harsh monotony of the actual experience. . . . Brevity is sacrificed to exactness, and if the reader sometimes tires he will the more sympathize with the courageous explorer who was often weary" (6 July 1952). E. A. Speiser in the *Yale Review* (June 1952) made a sociological observation increasingly relevant to Philby's life in Arabia and central to the experience of all later travelers in the Middle East, writing that *Arabia Highlands* "constitutes a record which was taken down on the eve of the penetration of the country by the motorcar. The land will not change appreciably, to be sure, but the people are not likely to remain the same much longer."

After his 1936–1937 journeys Philby had more difficult years. His attempts to mediate in the growing problem of Palestine, although not dismissed out of hand by all parties, were unavailing. Furthermore, his pacifist and anti-British observations seemed almost mentally unsound to many during the early stages of World War II. Arrested under the Defence of the Realm Act in August 1940, he was imprisoned in England until March 1941 and remained in Britain until the end of the war. He spent a fruitless and wasted four years, working on verbose books that still remain unpublished. In 1945 he sailed back to a Saudi Arabia that, thanks in part to Sharqieh and Philby himself, was becoming more and more mechanized and modernized.

Philby was sixty years old at the end of the war, but there remained more major exploring projects and another major row. His scholarly interest in his adoptive country had caused him to write *The Background of Islam: Being a Sketch of Arabian History in*

Philby in Alexandria, 1937 (portrait by Elisabeth Ada Montgomery)

Pre-Islamic Times (1947), which he had privately printed in Alexandria, Egypt, after it was rejected by the English publisher to whom the work was submitted. (Philby, who was living isolated in wartime England, had been using out-of-date sources.) In 1950, planning to do what he could to confound the specialist reviewers, Philby headed north to explore the land of Midian in the hope of establishing a reputation as a historian of pre-Islamic Arabia by finding rock inscriptions to help elucidate the vexed history of the development of Semitic scripts. At Khaibar, which he reached in December, Philby found some rock drawings; at Taima (Tama) he found actual inscriptions. In early 1951 he located Rawafa, a temple with yet more inscriptions, and later the Nabatean ruins (Al Quraiya) that Sir Richard Burton and Doughty had known about but not seen. Philby's real coup came in 1951–1952, when he persuaded the distinguished epigraphist Gonzague Ryckmans of Louvain University in Belgium to visit Saudi Arabia under his guidance with Ibn Sa'ud underwriting the expedition. According to Monroe, "they reached Riyadh in mid February, 1952, well content, for they had in all collected 13,000 new inscriptions, rock drawings and graffiti; they had travelled 3,000 miles without mishap, and virtually without illness, along a route two-fifths of which had never been mapped before." *The Land of Midian* (1957) deals in typical Philby style with the first part of his travels in the northwest. On another major expedition to explore Midian, in 1952–1953, Philby mapped to the Jordanian frontier. He reported the existence of twenty-five hundred inscriptions previously unknown to the West.

In November 1953 Ibn Sa'ud died and was succeeded by his son Sa'ud. For a while Philby held in check his increasing dissatisfaction with the ostentation and extravagance of the court, hoping that the new king would work against moral and accounting looseness, but it was not to be. Philby had already annoyed the Saudis by hinting at princely decadence in *Arabian Jubilee* (1952), the biography of Ibn Sa'ud he had written for the king's Golden Jubilee. His *Sa'udi Arabia* (1955), a revision of *Arabia* (1930), went further, criticizing misadministration, lack of financial planning, and hypocrisy about alcohol. After giving a series of frank talks to mixed audiences of Saudi and American employees in the oil industry, Philby was asked to leave Saudi Arabia. On 15 April 1955 he left the country he had made his primary home for nearly three decades.

Following a period of banishment in Beirut, Lebanon, he was eventually readmitted to Saudi Arabia, going to live in Riyadh in November 1956, while continuing to shuttle from place to place even in his seventies. He happened to be in Beirut when, in June 1957, he learned of the death of his wife in England. Although he had been open with her about his love affairs, she had discovered the existence of his two Saudi sons and their mother in the chaos caused by his ejection from Arabia two years before her death. He was also in Beirut for the winter of 1957-1958, teaching at the American University, and he was there when he died, on 30 September 1960, after complaining of difficulty in breathing.

Large claims have been made for Philby the man. "In his hunger for power and fame," wrote Mark Cocker in 1992, "in his persistent need to speak his mind whether to Briton or Arab, in his ultimate lack of allegiance, except to a highly personal version of reality, one senses a figure of almost Faustian proportions. At times it seemed that Philby was in revolt against the limitations of life itself." Few would deny that Philby was a vivid figure in the history of twentieth-century Anglo-Arabian relations, certainly in revolt against the prevailing orthodoxy of his time as represented by T. E. Lawrence and others in their support for the sharif of Mecca and his sons. If, as Philby wrote in the preface to *Arabian Days*, Lawrence and those of his party "drove me into the desert," they helped him to find unique literary material. It was the Sharifian Lawrence, but it might have been the Saudian Philby, who wrote, "The story I have to tell is one of the most splendid ever given a man for writing." Lawrence made an epic, *Seven Pillars of Wisdom*, of his two years in the desert. Philby did not make epics of the rise of Ibn Sa'ud or the crossing of the Empty Quarter. Vastly knowledgeable, immensely detailed, covering nearly all areas of the Arabian peninsula and contributing to many scientific disciplines, Philby's books will be a primary source for students of Arabia for years to come. Over the last twenty-five years professional scholars have made claims for the literary value of Lawrence's, Doughty's, and Thesiger's writings, but no champion has come forward to advance the literary merits of Philby's books.

Biographies:

Elizabeth Monroe, *Philby of Arabia* (London: Faber & Faber, 1973; New York: Pitman, 1973);

Anthony Cave Brown, *Treason in the Blood: H. St. John Philby, Kim Philby and the Spy Case of the Century* (Boston: Houghton Mifflin, 1994; London: Hale, 1995);

John Halperin, *Eminent Georgians: The Lives of King George V, Elizabeth Bowen, St. John Philby, and Nancy Astor* (New York: St. Martin's Press, 1995).

References:

Robin Bidwell, *Travellers in Arabia* (London: Hamlyn, 1976), pp. 96-115;

Peter Brent, *Far Arabia: Explorers of the Myth* (London: Weidenfeld & Nicolson, 1977), pp. 208-218;

Mark Cocker, *Loneliness and Time: The Story of British Travel Writing* (London: Secker & Warburg, 1992; New York: Pantheon, 1992), pp. 38-51;

R. H. Kiernan, *The Unveiling of Arabia: The Story of Arabian Travel and Discovery* (London: Harrap, 1937; New York: AMS Press, 1975), pp. 327-339;

Leslie McLoughlin, "Abdullah Philby's Crossing of the Empty Quarter," *Asian Affairs*, 22 (June 1991): 142-151;

G. Ryckmans, *H. Saint John B. Philby: Le "Sheikh Abdullah": 3 avril - 30 septembre 1960* (Istanbul: Nederlands Historisch-Archaeologisch Institute in Het Nabije Oosten, 1961);

Richard Trench, *Arabian Travellers: The European Discovery of Arabia* (London: Macmillan, 1986; Topsfield, Mass.: Salem House, 1986), pp. 201-210.

Papers:

The Middle East Centre at St. Antony's College, Oxford, holds some of Philby's correspondence, memos, travel diaries, engagement books, and published and unpublished manuscripts, dating from circa 1915 to 1957. The unpublished manuscripts are "Stepping Stones in Jordan," "Arabian Mandates, Mesopotage," "Mines of Midian," "More Arabian Days" (two chapters), "The Legend of Lijman," and "Simon Peters Out." The Middle East Centre also has route maps of Philby's journeys in Arabia. The Royal Geographical Society in London holds miscellaneous papers, correspondence, and notebooks, including the diary Philby kept on his journey across the Empty Quarter in 1932 and a corrected typescript for *Arabia Highlands*.

Peter Quennell

(9 March 1905 - 27 October 1993)

Doris H. Meriwether
University of Southwestern Louisiana

See also the Quennell entry in *DLB 155: Twentieth-Century British Literary Biographers.*

BOOKS: *Masques and Poems* (Waltham Saint Lawrence, U.K.: Golden Cockerel Press, 1922);

Poems (London: Chatto & Windus, 1926; New York: Cape & Smith, 1930);

Inscription on a Fountain-head (London: Faber & Faber, 1929);

Baudelaire and the Symbolists (London: Chatto & Windus, 1929; revised edition, London: Weidenfeld & Nicolson, 1954);

The Phoenix-Kind (London: Chatto & Windus, 1931; New York: Viking, 1931);

A Letter to Virginia Woolf (London: Leonard & Virginia Woolf, 1932);

A Superficial Journey through Tokyo and Peking (London: Faber & Faber, 1932);

Sympathy and Other Stories (London: Faber & Faber, 1933);

Byron (London: Duckworth, 1934);

Byron: The Years of Fame (London: Faber & Faber, 1935; New York: Viking, 1935; revised edition, London: Collins, 1967; Hamden, Conn.: Archon, 1967);

Somerset: Shell Guide, by Quennell and C. H. B. Quennell (London: Architectural Press, 1936);

Victorian Panorama: A Survey of Life and Fashion from Contemporary Photographs (London: Batsford, 1937; New York: Scribners, 1937);

Caroline of England: An Augustan Portrait (London: Collins, 1939; New York: Viking, 1940);

Byron in Italy (London: Collins, 1941; New York: Viking, 1941);

Four Portraits: Studies of the Eighteenth Century (London: Collins, 1945); republished as *The Profane Virtues: Four Studies of the Eighteenth Century* (New York: Viking, 1945); revised as *Four Portraits: Studies of the Eighteenth Century* (London: Collins, 1965; Hamden, Conn.: Archon, 1965);

John Ruskin: The Portrait of a Prophet (London: Collins, 1949; New York: Viking, 1949);

Spring in Sicily (London: Weidenfeld & Nicolson, 1952);

The Singular Preference: Portraits and Essays (London: Collins, 1952; New York: Viking, 1953);

Hogarth's Progress (London: Collins, 1955; New York: Viking, 1955);

The Sign of the Fish (London: Collins, 1960; New York: Viking, 1960);

Shakespeare: The Poet and His Background (London: Weidenfeld & Nicolson, 1963); republished as *Shakespeare: A Biography* (Cleveland: World, 1963);

Alexander Pope: The Education of Genius (London: Weidenfeld & Nicolson, 1968; New York: Stein & Day, 1968);

Romantic England: Writing and Painting, 1717–1851 (London: Weidenfeld & Nicolson, 1970; New York: Macmillan, 1970);

The Colosseum, Wonders of Man Series (New York: Newsweek, 1971; London: Reader's Digest Association, 1973);

Casanova in London (London: Weidenfeld & Nicolson, 1971; New York: Stein & Day, 1971);

Samuel Johnson: His Friends and Enemies (London: Weidenfeld & Nicolson, 1972; New York: American Heritage Press, 1973);

Who's Who in Shakespeare, by Quennell and Hamish Johnson (London: Weidenfeld & Nicolson, 1973; New York: Morrow, 1973);

A History of English Literature, by Quennell and Johnson (London: Weidenfeld & Nicolson, 1973; Springfield, Mass.: G. & C. Merriam, 1973);

The Marble Foot: An Autobiography, 1905–1938 (London: Collins, 1976; New York: Viking, 1977);

The Wanton Chase: An Autobiography from 1939 (London: Collins, 1980; New York: Atheneum, 1980);

Customs and Characters: Contemporary Portraits (London: Weidenfeld & Nicolson, 1982; Boston: Little, Brown, 1982);

The Last Edwardians: An Illustrated History of Violet Trefusis and Alice Keppel; selections from an exhibition prepared by and held at the Boston Athenaeum November 4 through December 6, 1985, and at the Henry Morrison Flager Museum, Whitehall Mansion, Palm Beach, Florida, March 11 through April 13, 1986, by Quennell, John Phillips, and Lorna Sage (Boston: Boston Athenaeum, 1986);

The Pursuit of Happiness (London: Constable, 1988; Boston: Little, Brown, 1988).

OTHER: *Oxford Poetry 1924,* edited by Quennell and Harold Acton (Oxford: Blackwell, 1924; New York: Appleton, 1925);

Buzurg ibn Shahriyar, *The Book of the Marvels of India,* translated by Quennell and Marcel L. Devic (London: Routledge, 1928; New York: McVeagh, 1929);

Anthony Hamilton, *Memoirs of the Comte de Gramont,* translated by Quennell (London: Routledge, 1930; New York: Dutton, 1930);

Aspects of Seventeenth Century Verse, edited, with an introduction, by Quennell (London: Cape, 1933; revised edition, London: Home & Van Thal, 1947);

Jane Austen, *Sense and Sensibility,* edited, with a preface, by Quennell (London: Cape, 1933);

The Private Letters of Princess Lieven to Prince Metternich, edited and translated, with a biographical foreword, by Quennell (London: Murray, 1937; New York: Dutton, 1938);

George Paston (Emily Morse Symonds), *"To Lord Byron": Feminine Profiles Based upon Unpublished Letters, 1807–1824,* completed and edited, with an introduction, by Quennell (London: Murray, 1939; New York: Scribners, 1939);

Cecil Beaton, *Time Exposure,* edited, with commentary, by Quennell (London: Batsford, 1941);

Lithographs of Toulouse-Lautrec, edited by Quennell (London: De La More Press, 1943);

Charlotte Brontë, *Villette,* edited, with an introduction, by Quennell (London: Pilot Press, 1947);

Novels by the Brontë Sisters, edited, with an introduction, by Quennell (London: Pilot Press, 1947);

The Pleasures of Pope, edited by Quennell (London: Hamilton, 1949; New York: Pantheon, 1950);

Byron: Selections from Poetry, Letters and Journals, edited by Quennell (London: Nonesuch, 1949);

Henry Mayhew, *Mayhew's London,* edited by Quennell (London: Pilot Press, 1949);

Charles Baudelaire, *My Heart Laid Bare & Other Prose Writings,* translated by Norman Cameron, edited, with an introduction, by Quennell (London: Weidenfeld & Nicolson, 1950);

Byron: A Self-Portrait, edited by Quennell (London: Murray, 1950; New York: Scribners, 1950);

Mayhew, *London's Underworld,* edited by Quennell (London: Kimber, 1950);

Mayhew, *Mayhew's Characters,* edited, with a note on the English character, by Quennell (London: Kimber, 1951);

Jonathan Swift, *Gulliver's Travels,* edited by Quennell (London: Collins, 1952; New York: Norton, 1952);

Selected Writings of John Ruskin, edited, with an introduction, by Quennell (London: Falcon Press, 1952);

Marjorie and C. H. B. Quennell, *A History of Everyday Things in England,* sixth edition, volume 4, revised by Peter Quennell (London: Batsford, 1958; New York: Putnam, 1958);

George Borrow, *The Bible in Spain,* edited, with an introduction, by Quennell (London: Macdonald, 1959);

Selected Verse and Prose Works, Including Letters and Extracts from Lord Byron's Journals and Diaries, edited by Quennell (London: Collins, 1959);

Byronic Thoughts: Maxims, Reflections, Portraits from the Prose and Verse of Lord Byron, edited by Quennell (London: John Murray, 1960; New York: Harcourt, Brace, 1961);

Memoirs of William Hickey, edited by Quennell (London: Hutchinson, 1960);

De Montherlant, *Selected Essays,* translated by John Weightman, edited, with an introduction, by Quennell (London: Weidenfeld & Nicolson, 1960);

The Past We Share: An Illustrated History of the British and American Peoples, edited by Quennell and Alan Hodge (London: Weidenfeld & Nicolson, 1960; New York: Prometheus, 1960);

Thomas Moore, *Journal, 1818–1841,* edited by Quennell (London: Batsford, 1964; New York: Macmillan, 1964);

De Montherlant, *Chaos and Night,* translated by Terence Kilmartin, edited, with an introduction, by Quennell (London: Weidenfeld & Nicolson, 1964);

Marcel Proust, 1871–1922: A Centenary Volume, edited by Quennell (London: Weidenfeld & Nicolson, 1971; New York: Simon & Schuster, 1971);

The Day before Yesterday: A Photographic Album of Daily Life in Victorian and Edwardian Britain, edited, with an introduction, by Quennell (London: Dent, 1978);

Vladimir Nabokov, His Life, His Work, His World: A Tribute, edited, with an introduction, by Quennell (London: Weidenfeld & Nicolson, 1979; New York: Morrow, 1980);

Genius in the Drawing Room: The Literary Salon in the Nineteenth and Twentieth Centuries, edited by Quennell (London: Weidenfeld & Nicolson, 1980); republished as *Affairs of the Mind: The Salon in Europe and America from the 18th to the 20th Century* (Washington, D.C.: New Republic Books, 1980);

A Lonely Business: A Self-Portrait of James Pope-Hennessy, edited, with an introduction, by Quennell (London: Weidenfeld & Nicolson, 1981);

The Selected Essays of Cyril Connolly, edited, with an introduction, by Quennell (New York: Persea Books, 1984);

John MacDonald, *Memoirs of an Eighteenth-Century Footman,* edited, with an introduction, by Quennell (London: Century, 1985).

Eminent biographer, esteemed literary and cultural historian, essayist, reviewer, and editor, Peter Quennell was called "probably the last genuine example of the English man of letters" by the obituary writer for the London *Times* (29 October 1993). He was also a world traveler. Though he wrote only two books properly classified as travel writing, his lifelong practice of engaged attention to the many places he visited, his habit of reflective analysis of persons and customs, and his innate desire to study human expressions of beauty found along the continuum linking the present with the past all enriched his works, particularly his biographies. His success as a biographer, the foundation of his literary reputation, owes much to his travels. For Quennell the appeal of writing biography was the charm of visiting the past to imagine the social fabric of a former age and to give renewed life to one of its luminaries. Familiarity with his subjects' haunts, for example, enabled Quennell to write with convincing detail of Charles Baudelaire walking the night streets of Paris or George Gordon, Lord Byron, in exile in Venice. Through the life he gave to his subjects in his imagination, Quennell's writings draw the reader into re-created time and place.

The New York Times obituary for Quennell (31 October 1993) identified him as a "Man About Town" as well as "a wit, gossip, world traveler, and hedonist." Not born into wealth or social position, Quennell earned literary renown by the hard work of refining his prose style and by a large measure of personal charm. Naturally gregarious, a master of the amusing anecdote, tall and strikingly handsome, he played the perfect guest in the fashionable drawing rooms of London and in the great country houses and villas of England, France, and Italy.

Peter Courtney Quennell was born on 9 March 1905 in Bromley, Kent, a south London suburb, the first child of artistic parents. His father, Charles Henry Bourne Quennell, was a young architect with a promising career, and his mother, Marjorie Courtney Quennell, an art student before her marriage, had already established a modest reputation as a watercolorist. The family soon moved to nearby Bickley. A daughter, Gillian, was born in 1909, and a second son, Paul, was born in 1915. Talented and ambitious, Charles and Marjorie Quennell reared their children in an atmosphere heavy with the Victorian virtues of industry and self-improvement. Peter Quennell's love of architecture and architectural detail derived from his admiration for his father's work, while his love of the past and his sense of history–as a record of human activity, of human goals and desires, successes and failures–was a trait fostered by his parents' consuming interest in social history.

When his architectural career faltered during World War I, Charles Quennell supplemented the family's income by starting a project he had long delayed for want of time. Having been an active participant in the post-Ruskinian arts-and-crafts fervor that gripped industrialized England in the late nineteenth century, he mobilized his wife and son to help him produce a highly successful and much-imitated series of books for schoolchildren, *A History of Everyday Things in England.* The first two volumes, published in 1918, cover the years from 1066 through 1799 and chronicle the design and craftsmanship of English laborers before the machine destroyed their creativity and pride of workmanship. Marjorie Quennell provided the copious illustrations of clothing, tools, and implements; Charles Quennell did the architectural drawings; and Peter Quennell did the drawings at the beginnings of each volume–spirited renditions of a medieval knight in combat astride a spotted horse that might have escaped from the nursery toy box–a whimsical blending of fact with humor that characterizes much of his mature writing.

Near the end of World War I the family moved to Berkhamsted, northwest of London, where Peter Quennell sporadically attended the grammar school, then under the guidance of headmaster Charles Greene, father of novelist Graham Greene. Not a diligent pupil, Quennell preferred exploring the town and neighboring countryside, which was rich in reminders of English history dating from the Stone Age. These early forays into the English past were valuable preparation for his writing career. His first biography of an historical figure, *Caroline of England: An Augustan Portrait* (1939), grew from his discovery of a tombstone in a churchyard marking the burial place of the "Wild Boy," a human freak who was part of Princess Caroline's collection of "curiosities." His early immersion in English history bore other fruit later in his career. In 1951 Quennell and Alan Hodge founded *History Today,* a popular monthly journal aimed at the general reader. Quennell edited the magazine until his retire-

Peter Quennell and his fifth wife, Marilyn, in 1967 (Hulton Deutsch Picture Collection)

ment in 1979, often surprising contributors with pieces of information likely to have come from his schoolboy store of knowledge.

Quennell began his long writing career as a poet, writing his first poem before the age of ten. In the first volume of his autobiography, *The Marble Foot* (1976), he recalls making his "earliest attempt to become a modern poet" while returning across the English Channel after a brief holiday with his parents in Rouen. When he was fifteen, his poems were selected to appear in *Public School Verse* (1920, 1921), anthologies edited by Richard Hughes, and when he was seventeen, a selection of his poems was included in Edward Marsh's *Georgian Poetry 1920–1922* (1922).

Through his associations with Hughes and Marsh, Quennell found doors to London literary life opening to him. In *The Sign of the Fish* (1960), a collection of autobiographical sketches, he recalls how, late on a summer afternoon, Hughes led him along a dusky London street to visit Edith Sitwell, the ruling presence of "the enchanted realm [he] longed to enter." Though the other guests assembled on that day were not then known to him, their eccentricities of manner and dress charmed Quennell utterly: "At last I had entered the literary world, in which beauty, lunacy and genius were woven together into the pattern of everyday life."

This early introduction to the Sitwell set was soon followed by friendships with members of the Bloomsbury circle, positioning Quennell among the leading and often contending camps of mid-twentieth-century tastemakers in art and literature. His contacts with these figures of influence, together with the friendships he formed at Oxford, gave Quennell a source of intellectual stimulation and the opportunity to mingle with many legendary British writers, who later became subjects of his essays and memoirs. *The Wanton Chase* (1980) and *Customs and Characters* (1982), the second and third volumes of his memoirs, are reflective excursions into that lost world.

Going up to Oxford in 1923 with a scholarship to Balliol College, Quennell went as a published poet whose works had received considerable critical attention and had prompted the *Evening Standard* reviewer to warn poets in general to "look to their laurels. They have been outdone by a schoolboy." In his memoir *Another Part of the Wood* (1974), Kenneth Clark recalled a luncheon invitation from the dean of Balliol to meet Quennell, "who had arrived in Oxford with the reputation of the most gifted schoolboy poet since Rimbaud."

At Oxford, Quennell soon fell in with the Hypocrites, the social group of Oxford bohemians then dominated by the wealthy Harold Acton. Finding Oxford tradesmen eager to extend credit, Quennell ran up large debts in order to keep up with his newfound friends. This pursuit of hedonistic pleasures soon became an established habit. Though he knew he should economize between terms by returning to the family fold, Quennell believed that "whatever the cost," he must "shun Berkhamstedian imprisonment" and the "spiritual suicide" sure to follow. Twice, at spring vacations, he crossed Europe to Italy and Greece. During one holiday, he was the houseguest of the Sitwells for most of the summer at Renishaw, their ancestral home in Derbyshire. Another invitation took him to Garsington Manor as a houseguest of Lady Ottoline Morrell, a member of the Bloomsbury set.

Quennell gained little formal education during his two years at Oxford. Avoiding lectures and attending tutorials erratically, he spent his time reading English and French poetry and novels, as well as the great Russian novels. Torn between indulging his literary interests and enjoying the pleasures of a rich social life, Quennell tried to satisfy both urges. In pursuing these impulses he found himself part of an Oxford set that included future historians, novelists, and art critics such as Robert Byron, David Cecil, Kenneth Clark, Cyril Connolly, Graham Greene, Anthony Powell, Evelyn Waugh, Edward Sackville-West, and Henry Green–a group immortalized in Evelyn Waugh's *Brideshead Revisited* (1945).

Dismissed from Oxford in 1925, Quennell was forced to consider in earnest the life of a professional writer, and he gladly accepted an invitation from the Sitwells to spend a literary vacation with them at their favorite wintertime haunt in Amalfi on the Italian coast. Here he learned firsthand the rigorous routine of the serious writer–day-long, solitary labor until evening and dinner released hosts and guests from their work. While the others wrote productively, Quennell despaired over his inept prose style, as well as his ill-conceived project. Departing in defeat, he set out for England at a leisurely pace, traveling north through Italy with a guidebook in hand.

Quennell called the days following his return to Berkhamsted "the darkest in [his] whole existence." Unqualified for suitable employment and longing to escape the family household, Quennell persuaded his father to support him in London until he found a job. Starting with hackwork as a reviewer, and all the while striving to improve his prose style, he moved steadily upward. Though his friends scoffed at journalistic writing, Quennell accepted it as a practical means of earning his living. A spendthrift and bon vivant, he held no scorn for money earned as a freelance

Quennell's drawing for volume one of his parents' History of Everyday Things in England *(1918)*

magazine journalist and later as a book critic for *The Daily Mail* (1943–1956) and as editor of *Cornhill Magazine* (1944–1951) and *History Today* (1951–1979). Throughout his life Quennell contributed essays and articles to major journals on both sides of the Atlantic, often using material drawn from the people he knew and the places he visited.

Not long after his move to London in 1926 Quennell offered his translation of Jules Laforgue's *Moralités Légendaires* (1887) to T. S. Eliot, then editor of the prestigious magazine *The Criterion.* Eliot suggested that Quennell give up this unprofitable exercise and try his hand at a book on the Symbolists instead. The result was *Baudelaire and the Symbolists* (1929), Quennell's first published volume of prose. While writing this book Quennell discovered that he was as interested in the complexities of Baudelaire's private life as in the poet's literary achievements. As a result, Quennell noted later, "I became a biographer; and . . . a biographer I have ever since remained." His reputation as a literary biographer was secured with the appearance of his highly acclaimed studies *Byron* (1934), *Byron: The Years of Fame* (1935), and *Byron in Italy* (1941). These works, plus *Four Portraits* (1945)–biographical studies of James Boswell, Edward Gibbon, Laurence Sterne, and John Wilkes–and his full-length biographies of William Shakespeare, Alexander Pope, Samuel Johnson, William Hogarth, and John Ruskin form a literary and cultural history of a major portion of English literature, revealing the breadth of Quennell's learning and the depth of his insights into the workings of the creative mind. Given his propensity for examining the impulses of both the living and the dead, and for celebrating the human spirit in its creative and imaginative achievements, Quennell had found his career. Except for a teaching stint at Bunrika Daigaku, a Tokyo university, in 1930–1931 that resulted in his first travel book, *A Superficial Journey through Tokyo and*

Peking (1932), Quennell spent the rest of his life in the service of English prose.

In hindsight Quennell concluded that the most valuable part of his time in the Far East was traveling to and from Japan. He admitted that a major reason for accepting a position in Tokyo was the opportunity to spend time in Saigon and the neighboring Angkor region of Cambodia. *The Marble Foot* describes the memorable days he spent exploring the fabled architectural treasures of Angkor Wat, the remnants of the palace structures of Angkor Thom, and the Bayon with its ruined towers displaying the smiling, carved-stone faces of Hindu gods.

His arrival in Japan, however, struck a sour note. Quennell sensed immediately that he was unacceptable to the department head, being neither old enough nor distinguished enough for the eminent position. This inauspicious beginning perhaps accounts for the often peevish tone of the chapters devoted to Tokyo in *A Superficial Journey through Tokyo and Peking*. Quennell found the country, its customs, and its inhabitants perplexing, frustrating, and bewildering to a stranger reared in the West. For him the atmosphere was stifling and suffocating. China, which he visited between university terms, offered breathing room. Its sprawling plains and endless vistas of landscape signified an openness of spirit, an unperturbed and even casual acceptance of outsiders not extended to him in the closely ordered scheme of Japanese life.

A prefatory note to *A Superficial Journey through Tokyo and Peking* warns the reader not to expect the usual travel book and asks the reader to view the work "as a kind of travel film, a sequence in which image suggests image." Thus, the work follows no temporal or spatial order. The chapters of the first two parts deal with his often-troubled impressions of Tokyo and university life. The third and fourth parts treat enthusiastically the time Quennell spent in Peking and his return to Tokyo via Kyoto, the ancient capital of Japan, where he discovered a visual and spiritual feast of temples and public buildings that bear comforting traces of Western origin, residue of the contact of early Japanese inhabitants with India and her Greek connections.

Despite the lapse of more than sixty years since its first publication, *A Superficial Journey through Tokyo and Peking* speaks eloquently to the reader of the 1990s, especially one facing a lengthy stay in a foreign culture. In describing what is strange and alien, Quennell referred repeatedly to images of the familiar, playing image against image. The book opens with his impressions of an earthquake that occurred soon after his arrival in Tokyo. Awakened in the darkness of his hotel room by creakings and lurchings that ended as abruptly as they had begun, he compared the sensation to "the rumbling retreat of a heavy vehicle which through the London night rushes ominously beneath your window and dwindles back again into the nowhere from which it has sprung." The other hotel residents, roused from their sleep, came twittering to life "like a tree-load of awakened starlings," a reminder of an English landscape. Summing up this tendency to nostalgia that besets the traveler, Quennell wrote: "Alas, that to set out on any journey is to start the Romantic upon its travels in the opposite direction, due to pass one in mid-career toward one's goal." The reader can also identify with Quennell's frustration with getting around Tokyo while going about the business of daily life–shopping and meeting social obligations–in a city devoid of street names and house numbers. (Taxi drivers relied on the passengers to show the way.) More than once the book refers to Quennell's Tokyo experience as living in "a dream-world" from which he may awaken at any moment.

The university experience offered no respite from Quennell's sense of unreality. Though the Japanese seemed inherently curious and inquisitive, Quennell could not engage his students in the intellectual questioning and debate common among university students in the West. He despaired of any success as a professor expected to saturate his students with facts, nor could he overcome his bewilderment at the students' polite but passive hold on pure selflessness. No talk of individualism and the Westerner's sense of self could penetrate their serene facades.

Reviews of *A Superficial Journey through Tokyo and Peking* were mixed. Plainly annoyed that Quennell had not expressed enjoyment of his experiences in Tokyo, the anonymous reviewer for *The Times Literary Supplement* (21 July 1932) placed the fault on the author's lack of sympathy for his subject. On the other hand, the reviewer for *The Times* (22 July 1932) hailed the book as "an artistic achievement," calling it "the record of a vivid poetic mind working on what it saw, rather than an account of what the eye lights upon." A reader in the 1990s is likely to recognize that what appeared to the *TLS* reviewer as hostility was no more than Quennell's lack of preparedness for the essential differences between West and East. While Quennell was bewildered by Japanese life, his observations are never mean-spirited, and he often resorts to humorous self-mockery at his own inability to cope with this alien culture.

Like *A Superficial Journey through Tokyo and Peking*, Quennell's second travel book, *Spring in Sicily* (1952), is not an ordinary travel narrative. Taking the reader on a clockwise tour of coastal towns and villages on the island, the book includes little autobiography, but the reader is aware from the opening paragraph that the book is the account of a return visit to the island.

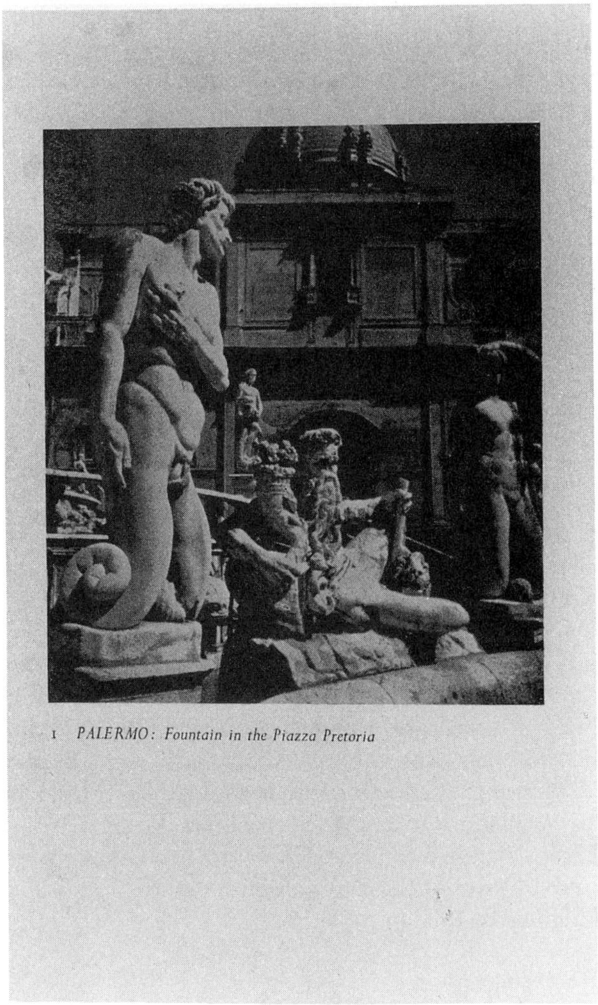

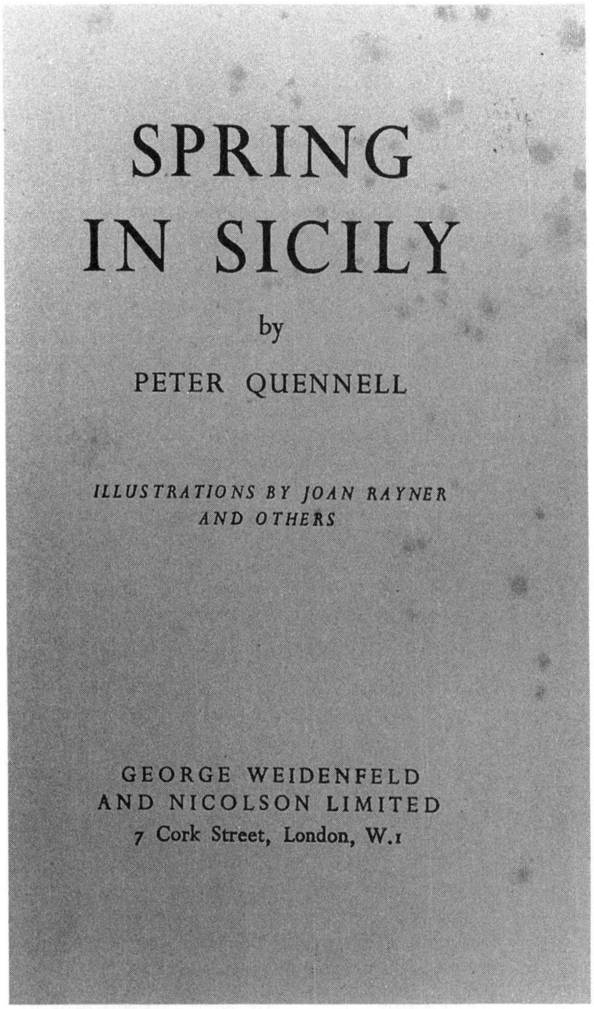
SPRING
IN SICILY
by
PETER QUENNELL

ILLUSTRATIONS BY JOAN RAYNER
AND OTHERS

GEORGE WEIDENFELD
AND NICOLSON LIMITED
7 Cork Street, London, W.1

Frontispiece and title page for Quennell's 1952 book, about his second visit to Sicily

Quennell had, in fact, visited Sicily in spring 1923, when a photograph of the ruins of the Greek theater at Taormina "had filled me with a passionate desire . . . to spend an hour among those broken columns." According to *The Marble Foot,* the eighteen-year-old Quennell had sold some pen-and-ink drawings for funding and convinced his parents to allow him to travel alone to Sicily.

On his later visit to Sicily, as the descending plane cast its shadow on the land below, Quennell recollected the melancholy atmosphere that pervaded the Sicilian landscape, calling up from his memory the image of "black-cloaked and black-shawled . . . figures against grey or yellowish masonry." The people of Sicily remain dark and insubstantial shadows stored in Quennell's mind. What does come alive for the reader is the rich past of this Mediterranean culture, as seen through the eyes of a man deeply imbued with a knowledge of history, architecture, and art.

Avoiding personal anecdotes about himself and his unidentified traveling companion and descriptions of travel from site to site, Quennell captures the reader's attention by sharing his pleasure at seeing again the remnants of successive periods of Greek, Carthaginian, and Roman domination in Sicily. Present structures, artworks, and landmarks provided him with opportunities to evoke the past. His descriptions avoid the dry accounts one finds in history books, focusing instead on the human impulses that made the past. The reader becomes aware that Quennell studied these ruins for what they could tell of men and manners in the past. His appreciation for beauty created by the human hand and heart is a hallmark of his writing.

The reviewer for *The Times Literary Supplement* (6 June 1952) expressed disappointment in the work as a travel book, regretting that Quennell's impersonal approach "gives his reader no great sense of being there at this precise moment in time." He did, however, praise the play of Quennell's poetic imagination, which dwells on an object in order to "delve deep into antiquity or into the Renaissance" to reveal the accretions of time that "make up the present." He also lauded the work as the effort of "a man of taste and style." A few months later the anonymous author of a review essay titled "The Younger Travel Writers" (*TLS,* 29 August 1952) noted that, while the Mediterranean and Italy had long appealed to English travel writers, these sites had fallen from favor between the wars. Following World War I the travel writer tended to seek out destinations more distant and exotic–Africa, South America, Asia, the Orient–"as if he wished to assure himself that parts still remained in the world where natural life had remained intact, and he could bring news of it to Europe." After World War II, the reviewer saw a pattern emerging among the new generation of travel writers that suggests "the old northern necessity for a return to the womb of European culture on the shores of the Mediterranean." Noting that Quennell belonged to an older generation, he nevertheless included *Spring in Sicily* in this trend, observing that Quennell "has never before written such beautiful and supple prose." The late-twentieth-century reader whose taste runs to an appreciation of the past as it informs the present will still find *Spring in Sicily* rewarding.

While not a travel book, *The Sign of the Fish* (1960) illustrates how Quennell's travel experiences enriched his prose. This series of meditative, autobiographical essays examining the problems of authorship interweaves allusions to places and objects known from his travels as it ranges from Quennell's experiences as a writer to those of his contemporaries and of great writers of the past. The prologue opens with his memories of writing tools he bought in Japan, soft-paper tablets and fine brushes complete with an inkstone. They are useless to his Western fingers but have a parallel in the blank sheet of paper that urges a writer onward. A chapter titled "The Traveller" discusses travel as potentially "a powerful stimulant" for the writer, describing at length his exhilarating return trip from Japan on the Trans-Siberian railway and contrasting the natural beauty he found in the tropics on a later excursion to Jamaica.

Three decades of the writing life remained when Quennell completed *The Sign of the Fish,* and his closing paragraph is an affirmation of his chosen profession as well as a statement of the principles that guided his career to the end. His years of writing "enriched and enlightened the experience of living" for him, and he expressed the belief

> that the life of the writer is greatly preferable to any other form of life, and that the smallest scintilla of art, if the artist can apprehend it and, having apprehended it, can impose it on his raw material, will always shine out from the disorder of the present and the accumulated rubbish of the past.

The artist "is acutely conscious of the vital link that connects the works of the past with the works of the present day, and has discovered how little humanity changes through all the changes of our temporal setting." When he wrote these words, some of Quennell's finest works were yet to come, including his final book, *The Pursuit of Happiness* (1988), an inquiry into the varying ideas of happiness found in literature and art through the ages. The common thread that runs through Quennell's work is his abiding appreciation for human expressions of beauty.

Quennell was married five times during his long life and had two children. He was named Commander of the Order of the British Empire in 1973 and was knighted in 1992.

References:

Geremie Barme, Introduction to *A Superficial Journey through Tokyo and Peking* (Oxford: Oxford University Press, 1986);

Humphrey Carpenter, *The Brideshead Generation: Evelyn Waugh and His Friends* (Boston: Houghton Mifflin, 1990);

Paul Fussell, *Abroad: British Literary Traveling Between the Wars* (New York: Oxford University Press, 1980);

David Pryce-Jones, *Cyril Connolly: Journal and Memoir* (London: Collins, 1983).

Papers:

Quennell's papers are at the Harry Ransom Humanities Research Center, University of Texas at Austin. His letters to Clive Bell are at the King's College Modern Archive Centre, Cambridge University.

Vita Sackville-West

(9 March 1892 - 2 June 1962)

Linda J. Strom
Youngstown State University

See also the Sackville-West entry in *DLB 34: British Novelists, 1890–1929: Traditionalists.*

BOOKS: *Chatterton: A Drama in Three Acts* (Sevenoaks: Privately printed by J. Salmon, 1909);

Poems of East and West (London & New York: John Lane, 1917);

Heritage (London: Collins, 1919; New York: Doran, 1919);

The Dragon in Shallow Waters (London: Collins, 1921; New York & London: Putnam, 1922);

Orchard and Vineyard (London & New York: John Lane, 1921);

The Heir: A Love Story [one story] (London: Privately printed, 1922);

The Heir: A Love Story [five stories] (London: Heinemann, 1922; New York: Doran, 1922);

Knole and the Sackvilles (London: Heinemann, 1922; New York: Doran, 1922; revised edition, London: Benn, 1958);

Challenge (New York: Doran, 1923);

Grey Wethers: A Romantic Novel (London: Heinemann, 1923; New York: Doran, 1923);

Seducers in Ecuador (London: Leonard & Virginia Woolf, 1924; New York: Doran, 1925);

The Land (London: Heinemann, 1926; Garden City, N.Y.: Doubleday, Doran & Coy, 1927);

Passenger to Teheran (London: Leonard & Virginia Woolf, 1926; New York: Doran, 1927);

Aphra Behn: The Incomparable Astrea (London: Howe, 1927; New York: Viking, 1928);

Twelve Days: An Account of a Journey across the Bakhtari Mountains in Southwestern Persia (London: Hogarth Press, 1928; Garden City, N.Y.: Doubleday, Doran, 1928);

King's Daughter (London: Leonard & Virginia Woolf, 1929; Garden City, N.Y.: Doubleday, Doran, 1930);

Andrew Marvel (London: Faber & Faber, 1929);

The Edwardians (London: Leonard & Virginia Woolf, 1930; Garden City, N.Y.: Doubleday, Doran, 1930);

Vita Sackville-West, 1910

Sissinghurst (London: Leonard & Virginia Woolf at the Hogarth Press, 1931);

Invitation to Cast Out Care (London: Faber & Faber, 1931);

All Passion Spent (London: Leonard & Virginia Woolf at the Hogarth Press, 1931; Garden City, N.Y.: Doubleday, Doran, 1931);

The Death of Noble Godavary and Gottfried Kunstler (London: Benn, 1932);

Thirty Clocks Strike the Hour and Other Stories (Garden City, N.Y.: Doubleday, Doran, 1932);

Family History (London: Leonard & Virginia Woolf at the Hogarth Press, 1932; Garden City, N.Y.: Doubleday, Doran, 1932);

Collected Poems (London: Leonard & Virginia Woolf at the Hogarth Press, 1933; Garden City, N.Y.: Doubleday, Doran, 1933);

The Dark Island (London: Leonard & Virginia Woolf at the Hogarth Press, 1934; Garden City, N.Y.: Doubleday, Doran, 1934);
Saint Joan of Arc (London: Cobden-Sanderson, 1936; Garden City, N.Y.: Doubleday, Doran, 1936);
Joan of Arc (London: Leonard & Virginia Woolf, 1937; New York: Stackpole, 1938);
Pepita (London: Leonard & Virginia Woolf at the Hogarth Press, 1937; Garden City, N.Y.: Doubleday, Doran, 1937);
Some Flowers (London: Cobden-Sanderson, 1937);
Solitude: A Poem (London: Hogarth Press, 1938; Garden City, N.Y.: Doubleday, Doran, 1939);
Country Notes (London: Joseph, 1939; New York & London: Harper, 1940);
Country Notes in Wartime (London: Hogarth Press, 1940; New York: Doubleday, Doran, 1941);
Selected Poems (London: Hogarth Press, 1941);
English Country Houses (London: Collins, 1941);
Grand Canyon: A Novel (London: Joseph, 1942; Garden City, N.Y.: Doubleday, Doran, 1942);
The Eagle and the Dove, A Study in Contrasts: St. Teresa of Avila. St. Thérèse of Lisieux (London: Joseph, 1943; Garden City, N.Y.: Doubleday, Doran, 1944);
The Women's Land Army (London: Joseph, 1944);
The Garden (London: Joseph, 1946; Garden City, N.Y.: Doubleday, Doran, 1946);
Nursery Rhymes (London: Dropmore Press, 1947);
Devil at Westease: The Story as Related by Roger Liddiard (Garden City, N.Y.: Doubleday, 1947);
In Your Garden (London: Joseph, 1951);
In Your Garden Again (London: Joseph, 1953);
The Easter Party (London: Joseph, 1953; Garden City, N.Y.: Doubleday, Doran, 1953);
More for Your Garden (London: Joseph, 1955);
Even More for Your Garden (London: Joseph, 1958);
A Joy of Gardening: A Selection for Americans, edited by Hermine I. Popper (New York: Harper, 1958);
Daughter of France: The Life of Anne Marie Louise d'Orleans, Duchesse de Montpensier, 1627–1693, La Grande Mademoiselle (London: Joseph, 1959; Garden City, N.Y.: Doubleday, 1959);
No Signposts in the Sea (London: Joseph, 1961; Garden City, N.Y.: Doubleday, 1961);
Faces: Profiles of Dogs, text by Sackville-West and photographs by Laelia Goehr (London: Harvill, 1961).

OTHER: *The Diary of the Lady Anne Clifford*, introduction and notes by Sackville-West (London: Heinemann, 1923);
Preface to Walther Berendsohn, *Selma Lagerlof: Her Life and Work*, translated by George Timson (London: Nicholson & Watson, 1931);
Rainer Maria Rilke, *Duineser Elegien: Elegies from the Castle of Duino*, translated by Sackville-West (London: Hogarth Press, 1931);
"Street Music," in *Essays of the Year 1931–1932*, edited by F. J. Harvey Darton (London: Argonaut, 1932);
"George Eliot," in *The Great Victorians*, edited by H. J. Massingham and Hugh Massingham (London: Nicholson & Watson, 1932; Garden City, N.Y.: Doubleday, Doran, 1932);
"Vita Sackville-West," in *Beginnings*, by Adrian Alington and others, edited by L. A. G. Strong (London: Nelson, 1935);
Another World Than This, edited by Sackville-West and Harold Nicolson (London: Joseph, 1945);
Introduction to *Prose and Poetry*, by Alice C. Meynell (London: Cape, 1947);
Ernest Raymond, *The Brontë Legend: Its Cause and Treatment*, foreword by Sackville-West (London: Cassell, 1953).

SELECTED PERIODICAL PUBLICATIONS–UNCOLLECTED: "Women Poets of the 'Seventies," *Royal Society of Literature of the United Kingdom*, 9 (1929): 111–132;
"In the Highlands," *Travel*, 56 (May 1930): 18;
"The Future of the Novel," *Bookman*, 72 (December 1930): 350–351;
"Impressions of a Traveler," *Times* (London), 5 January 1931, p. 16.

Vita Sackville-West began *Passenger to Teheran* (1926) by suggesting that because "travel is the most private of pleasures," writing about that pleasure is suspect: "There would seem to be something definitely wrong about all letters of travel, and even about books of travel. . . . There would seem, going a step further, to be something wrong about travel itself. Of what use is it, if we may communicate our experience neither verbally nor on paper?" For Sackville-West travel was a pleasure that eluded reason; it had to be described in a language that appeals to the senses rather than the intellect.

Readers of Sackville-West's two travel books will not find historical facts or discussions of local customs or cultures. Instead they encounter a world of impressions that reveals more about the writer's vision than it does about the country she is describing: "But for my part, I would not forgo the memory of an Egyptian dawn, and the flight of herons across the morning moon." In her travelogues, as in so much of Sackville-West's writing, personal experience translates into the sensual prose of a woman who approached life as if it were an adventure that she, as the hero of her story, had to explore and exploit. Unlike many other nineteenth- and twentieth-century travel writers, who focused attention on the factual and anthropological nature of travel, Sackville-West saw travel writing as a creative act.

Sackville-West's romantic vision of life was inspired in part by her ancestral background. She was born Victoria Mary Sackville-West on 9 March 1892, the only child of Victoria Josepha Dolores Catalina Sackville-West and Lionel Sackville-West. As the daughter of Lord Lionel Sackville-West, she was a direct descendent of Sir Thomas Sackville (1536–1608), a renowned poet and politician. Vita Sackville-West was born and grew up at Knole, the estate in Sevenoaks that Thomas Sackville was given in 1556 as a wedding present from Queen Elizabeth. Vita's mother, who was born in Paris in 1862, was the daughter of Pepita (Josefa Duran y Ortega de la Oliva), a well-known Spanish dancer. Vita Sackville-West believed that her personality was shaped by her mixed blood, inheriting rationality from her English ancestors and passion from her Spanish ancestors. The effects of such a dual nature became a theme for many of her early works of fiction, such as *Heritage* (1919), *The Dragon in Shallow Waters* (1921), *Grey Wethers* (1923), and *Pepita* (1937).

By her own description Sackville-West was an "insufferable child." In *Beginnings* (1935), a collection of essays by postwar fiction writers, she recalled her first public reading at age twelve: "Thus, I remember that my earliest ambition was to appear at a dinner-party of thirty people in the banqueting hall at home, dressed in a sheet representing a ghost, in order to recite an epic poem composed by myself on the various exploits of my ancestors." By age fourteen she was writing a five-act tragedy that combined "both the poetical romanticism of Rostand and the historical romanticism of Dumas." Her parents indulged their daughter's writing ambitions, treating her "with creditable intelligence" and "neither injudiciously" encouraging "nor unkindly" snubbing her. Her only complaint against her parents "is that they taught me neither Latin nor Greek, and never thought of sending me to school or to a university." Like most women growing up in the late nineteenth and the early twentieth centuries, Sackville-West was expected to marry and to have children. Thus, she was educated to prepare her for the role of upper-class wife and mother. Through her early writings she circumvented domestic training, exploring feelings and actions that took her beyond the enforced social boundaries of her gender.

When Sackville-West was seventeen her romantic belief in the vocation of writing led her to publish privately *Chatterton* (1909), a verse drama dramatizing the life and death of eighteenth-century poet Thomas Chatterton. In her play the struggling poet is encouraged by a friend to devote his life to writing. After a critic characterizes his poetry as worthless, Chatterton destroys his work and commits suicide. In her biography of Sackville-West, Victoria Glendinning writes that Sackville-West hid a pair of black trousers in order to act out the role of Chatterton in the privacy of the attic at Knole. The play allowed the young writer to explore her doubts and fears about her literary talent and to cast herself in the role of hero–a role she cultivated in her writing and her life.

Sackville-West on board the SS Rajputana, *sailing from Port Said, Egypt, to Bombay, India, during her 1926 travels to Tehran (Estate of Vita Sackville-West)*

During her formative years Sackville-West traveled throughout Europe, spending summers in Paris with her family. In 1909 she traveled to Russia, Poland, and Austria, and in 1910, the year of her social debut, she met Harold Nicolson. They married three years later, on 1 October 1913. After a honeymoon in Italy and Egypt, they set up housekeeping in Constantinople (now Istanbul), where Nicolson worked as a diplomat in the Foreign Office. With the outbreak of World War I in 1914, Nicolson was called back to England.

Sackville-West's photograph of her car and other travelers during her four-day journey from Baghdad to Tehran in 1926 (Estate of Vita Sackville-West)

From 1914 to 1925, Sackville-West and Nicolson lived together in England. During that time Sackville-West gave birth to two sons, Benedict in 1914 and Nigel in 1917. In 1925 Nicolson was posted to Tehran, Persia (now Iran). Refusing to be "just" the wife of a diplomat, Sackville-West did not initially accompany Nicolson to Persia, but she did visit him in 1926 and in 1927. The visits were the occasion for her two travel books: *Passenger to Teheran* (1926) and *Twelve Days* (1928).

Passenger to Teheran traces Sackville-West's trek from England to Tehran through Egypt, India, and Iraq. She began writing the book on the boat to Iraq while recovering from a sprained ankle and a high fever. Even the description of her suffering reveals her sense of adventure. After four days of having a "temperature, which fluctuated wildly" and watching her ankle develop "all the colours of a stormy sunset," she grew tired of being sick. She smashed her thermometer, dressed, limped on deck, fetched "a deck-chair, pen, and paper," and began her first travel book.

Although Sackville-West spent most of her introduction to the book explaining why writing about travel is impossible, she overcame her doubts by arguing that travel is an "irrational passion" that takes the traveler out of his or her own country into the "unknown," where "the wise traveller" is "perpetually surprised." From this sense of wonder, passion, and adventure Sackville-West structured a narrative that takes the reader from the security of England to "an unexploited country whose very name, printed on my luggage labels, seemed to distill a faint, far aroma in the chill air of Victoria Station."

Sackville-West emphasized that her book was not an "odious . . . informative book of travel" but rather a "frankly personal" travel log, "reflecting the weakness, the predilections, even the sentimentalities, of the writer." Asking her reader to surrender preconceived notions of travel writing in order to experience her distinctive approach to the genre, Sackville-West made it clear that her intention was to entertain. Traveling with Sackville-West via her writing is pleasurable and, in spite of her warning, informative. Readers soon learn that their guide avoids the well-traveled road, showing instead the back roads of a part real and part imagined world.

Sackville-West's first side trip occurred in Egypt, which she was visiting for the second time. Though she does not tell her reader that her previous visit took place during her honeymoon, she does say that she then felt "very young, very shy, and very awkward." Although she claimed to be writing a personal account, she also omitted other biographical information, including her gender and her reason for traveling to Tehran. These omissions allowed Sackville-West to construct a literary identity that freed her from her traditional roles of wife and of mother, allowing her to become the sole hero of her adventure.

A woman traveling and then writing about those experiences faced the challenge of describing in a new way a place that had been seen already and was being domesticated. Sackville-West met the challenge by showing what men had not seen in places they had already been. Once she left England, she left behind the responsibility of home, family, and country to embark on an adventure that explored the inner geography of feelings and imagination rather than the unexplored territories of the British Empire: "How exhilarating it is, to be thus self-contained; to depend for happiness on no material comfort; to be rid of such sentimentality as attaches to the dear familiar; to be open, vulnerable, receptive!"

In this receptive state Sackville-West visited sites that reflect her personal vision of what is significant about a culture and a country. In Egypt, for example, Howard Carter was excavating the tomb of Tutankhamen while Sackville-West was in Luxor. She visited the Valley of the Kings, but instead of describing the splendor of Tutankhamen's tomb or Carter's discoveries, she expressed regret at trading "the pleasure of the imagination" for "the dreary fact of knowledge." She built excitement in her narrative by describing her feelings about visiting such a spectacular sight, explaining that on her first trip to Luxor she did not visit the Valley of the Kings because she was suffering from a sunstroke. This missed opportunity made her 1926 visit even more poignant: "Full of energy I took the dazzling, naked road that leads to the Valley of the Kings." As she traveled down this road, she thought of the lush landscapes of home, seen in contrast to the "silence and lifelessness" that surrounded her. Before she arrived at the sight, she felt a growing anticipation: "There is a keen excitement in not knowing what one is going to see next; the mind, strung up, reaches forward for an image to expect, and finds nothing." With a sleight of hand, the Valley of the Kings disappears, and the reader is left wondering what Sackville-West saw. It is a clever gesture. Sackville-West traveled to one of the most famous places in history and then refused to do the expected thing, to describe in great detail what she saw.

Leaving the Valley of the Kings to the imagination of the reader, she turned her vision to less sensational sights: "I like getting away from the roads, into the region of country life." What fascinated Sackville-West was the timeless rhythm of everyday life: "Husbandry is of all ages and all countries. Nothing dates." *Passenger to Teheran* lavishly describes the beauty of the land and the people who cultivated it. Sackville-West was captivated by the peasants' simple lifestyle and their close connection to the land. As she described the work of a group of peasants laboring at the excavations, she romanticized their oppressive working conditions, calling them "beasts of burden" who seemed hardly to notice the whippings they received for not working fast enough. She saw her task as not to critique but to present the scene as a timeless picture of tranquillity and continuity, the symmetry of past and present: the peasants cleaning out tombs that their ancestors were forced to dig centuries earlier.

Sackville-West may have glossed over the peasants' suffering, but her respect for their work– whether they be day laborers, potters, or farmers– and the land on which they live is genuine. One of her finest literary works is the long poem *The Land* (1926)–a poem she began while traveling in Persia. Celebrating the timelessness of agricultural life in England and the craftsman as artist, it is peppered with references to her travels in Egypt and Persia. As an upper-class English woman, Sackville-West lived in a world apart from the people she celebrated in her poem and the peasants she described in her travel log. Yet despite this gap she connected with their lives through her love of tradition and the apparent simplicity of country life.

Sackville-West in the garden of the British Legation in Tehran (Estate of Vita Sackville-West)

Before leaving Egypt, Sackville-West visited Karnak, the northern half of the ruins of ancient Thebes. Seeing the ruins by moonlight, she was transfixed by their beauty, and in describing them she painted a canvas of words on which architecture and nature combined in breathtaking beauty: "the colossal aisle soared, its base plunged in the deepest shadow, its head lifted to the moon; shafts of light struck the columns, lay in silver druggets across the floor."

Sackville-West traveled through India and Iraq, neither of which held much interest for her, and devoted the remainder of the book to her travels in Persia. To reach Tehran she had to travel through the desert by car for four days. Leaving Baghdad was a dramatic moment for her because she left behind what she considered "a last shout of civilization." For Sackville-West the Persian desert represented a vast undomesticated space that filled her with tranquillity. As she motored with her driver across the desert and over the mountains, the past colored the present, revealing "the secrecy of days when no traveller passed that way, but only the nomads of Kurds driving their flocks." Sackville-West imagined for the moment that

Benedict, Harold, and Nigel Nicolson with Sackville-West, 1927

she was breaking new ground on the arduous journey to Tehran.

Once Sackville-West arrived at her destination, she announced that she was "no longer a traveller, but an inhabitant" and spent her time strolling through the streets of Tehran, shopping at bazaars, searching for gardens, and exploring the sights surrounding the city. She avoided her fellow Europeans, opting instead for her solitary wanderings: "For, personally, I prefer the bazaars to the drawing room." Although Sackville-West spent her childhood and the early years of her marriage in a whirl of social activity, she was never comfortable in social gatherings and disdained society and its trappings. She was critical of the Europeans in Tehran who recreated the culture they had left behind, giving tea parties, playing cards, and spending the day making social calls. They would be happier, she asserted, if they would cast off their "European preconceptions"; then they would be "at liberty to turn around and absorb an entirely new set of conditions."

Sackville-West heeded her own advice, realizing, of course, that she could never completely bracket her cultural preconceptions, choosing instead to show how her position as an outsider affected her observations. This perspective is one of the many strengths of her travel writing, reminding the reader that her perceptions are subjective and perhaps even slightly distorted by her social and cultural background. For example, while observing a street scene, she first described the crowd as mysterious and threatening: "one imagines these separate, hurrying people coagulated suddenly into a mob, pressing forward with some ardent purpose uniting them, and the same intent burning in all those dark eyes." In the next sentence, she revised her first impression, pointing to her own ignorance as the reason for her lapse in judgment: "But a life of which one knows nothing, seeing only the surface, does suggest something cabalistic and latent."

Sackville-West continues to pay tribute to artisans, praising the weavers, spinners, potters, and farmers that she encountered as she traveled to Isfahan (Esfahan) and to Kum (Qom). As she herself acknowledged, the result of her enthusiasm for what she called "primitive labor" is an idyllic portrait of Persia–one that ignores "the physical disease and political corruption." The health and politics of the country were not her concern; instead, she focused her keen eye on the beauty of the rugged terrain and the splendor of daily life, filtering out what did not please her. Sackville-West's first travel book ends with an account of her return home through Russia, Poland, and Germany.

In her second travel book, *Twelve Days: An Account of a Journey across the Bakhtiari Mountains in South-western Persia* (1928), Sackville-West described her second visit to Persia, during which she and four other Europeans, including her husband, Harold Nicolson, made a trek through a remote mountainous area of Persia inhabited by nomadic tribes. The group first motored from Esfahan to Shalamzar, where they met their caravan and began their long and difficult journey through the Bakhtiari mountains.

The area was isolated, making it difficult to acquire any information about the best travel routes and what to expect along the way. For Sackville-West this remoteness made the journey more exciting and appealed to her desire to explore the unknown: "I know, somewhere in my heart, that I want to be where no white man has ever been before, far from any place that has ever been heard of." This desire, of course, was impossible, and she lamented, "The globe is too small and too well mapped, and cinema too active." Her initial enthusiasm for adventure soon faded as she began the physically taxing hike.

Twelve Days is a less interesting travel book than *Passenger to Teheran.* The prose is flatter, and the charm and wit of the first book are absent. The first chapter alludes to the difficulty Sackville-West had in writing this book. She could not see a "shape" to her experiences–"no pleasing curve; nothing but a series of anti-climaxes, and too much repetition of what I had done, and written down, before." The book reads like a travel journal in which Sackville-West noted the group's daily progress and the problems that occurred along the way. As in her previous travel book, she described the surrounding scenery; yet the descriptions are less colorful and the language less lyrical. Toward the end of the book, she presented a plan for improving the political and social conditions in Persia without the country falling victim to European modernization. Having spent twelve days in the pristine Bakhtiari mountains, Sackville-West was shocked by the sight of the Persian oil fields: "From constant contact with life reduced to its simplest elements, we walked straight into a hell of civilisation."

The book ends with Sackville-West questioning the value of progress. Persia is a country of contrast–she concluded–a country in which two different communities collide, "the one weary, ignorant, and poor; the other energetic, scientific, and prosperous." Her romantic vision of a nomadic pastoral life was spoiled by the sight of the oil fields, and she indicted not only the Persians who have become rich from the oil but also the British who also prospered: "now it is time to see what becomes of empires as arrogant as the British."

The Persia that Sackville-West cherished is the one she created in *Passenger to Teheran.* For her it was a romantic country existing outside the twentieth century–a country made up of hustling bazaars, creative artisans, nomadic tribes, and picturesque landscapes that captured her imagination. In *Twelve Days* she wrote that Persia "is an anachronism in our eyes, and therefore romantic; the double elements of space and time, geographical and chronological, necessary to romance are amply satisfied."

Sackville-West found it difficult to reconcile this image of Persia with the reality of modernization, and *Twelve Days* suffers from this failure. Her prose is lively and engaging when it describes what she saw and what she felt as she trekked through the Bakhtiari mountains, and her writing is stilted when she turned to social and political commentary, which, as she pointed out in *Passenger to Teheran,* are not her areas of expertise. Her gifts are her enthusiasm for adventure and her ability to convey that energy in her writing. *Passenger to Teheran* and *Twelve Days* testify to that passion.

Sackville-West continued to travel and to write throughout her life. Her two travel books were well received by critics and the public; both have been republished so that contemporary audiences can enjoy her lively prose. Critic Michael Stevens notes that the period between 1913 and 1927 marked the most dramatic growth for Sackville-West as a writer. *Passenger to Teheran* and *Twelve Days* contributed to that growth by allowing the insatiable adventurer to combine her talent as a writer with her passion for travel.

Letters:

Dearest Andrew: Letters from V. Sackville-West to Andrew Reiber, 1951–1962, edited by Nancy MacKnight (New York: Scribners, 1979);

The Letters of Vita Sackville-West to Virginia Woolf, edited by Louise DeSalvo and Mitchell A. Leaska (New York: Morrow, 1985).

Biographies:

Nigel Nicolson, *Portrait of a Marriage* (New York: Atheneum, 1973);

Victoria Glendinning, *Vita: The Life of Vita Sackville-West* (New York: Knopf, 1983).

References:

Suzanne Raitt, *Vita and Virginia: The Work and Friendship of V. Sackville-West and Virginia Woolf* (Oxford: Clarendon Press, 1993);

Michael Stevens, *V. Sackville-West: A Critical Biography* (London: Joseph, 1973);

Sara Ruth Watson, *V. Sackville-West* (New York: Twayne, 1972).

Papers:

Sackville-West's papers are at Sissinghurst Castle and at the Lilly Library, Indiana University.

Osbert Sitwell

(6 December 1892 - 4 May 1969)

Doris H. Meriwether
University of Southwestern Louisiana

See also the Sitwell entry in *DLB 100: Modern British Essayists, Second Series.*

BOOKS: *Twentieth Century Harlequinade, and Other Poems,* by Osbert and Edith Sitwell (Oxford: Blackwell, 1916);

The Winstonburg Line: Three Satires (London: Hendersons, 1919);

Argonaut and Juggernaut (London: Chatto & Windus, 1919; New York: Knopf, 1920);

At the House of Mrs. Kinfoot; Consisting of Four Satires (Kensington: Favil Press, 1921);

Who Killed Cock Robin? Remarks on Poetry, on Its Criticism, and, as a Sad Warning, the Story of Eunuch Arden (London: Daniel, 1921);

Out of the Flame (London: Richards, 1923; New York: Doran, 1925);

Triple Fugue (London: Richards, 1924; New York: Doran, 1925);

C. R. W. Nevinson, as O. S. (London: Benn, 1925; New York: Scribners, 1925);

Discursions on Travel, Art and Life (London: Richards, 1925; New York: Doran, 1925);

Poor Young People, by Osbert, Edith, and Sacheverell Sitwell (London: Fleuron, 1925);

Before the Bombardment (London: Duckworth, 1926; New York: Doran, 1926);

England Reclaimed: A Book of Eclogues (London: Duckworth, 1927; Garden City, N.Y.: Doubleday, Doran, 1928);

All at Sea: A Social Tragedy in Three Acts for First-Class Passengers Only, by Osbert and Sacheverell Sitwell, with a preface by Osbert Sitwell (London: Duckworth, 1927; Garden City, N.Y.: Doubleday, Doran, 1928);

The People's Album of London Statues (London: Duckworth, 1928);

The Man Who Lost Himself (London: Duckworth, 1929; New York: Coward-McCann, 1930);

Miss Mew (Stanford Dingley, U.K.: Mill House Press, 1929);

Dumb-Animal, and Other Stories (London: Duckworth, 1930; Philadelphia: Lippincott, 1931);

Osbert Sitwell, 1942

The Collected Satires and Poems of Osbert Sitwell (London: Duckworth, 1931);

Three-quarter Length Portrait of Michael Arlen, With a Preface: The History of a Portrait, by the Author (London: Heinemann / New York: Doubleday, Doran, 1931);

A Three-quarter Length Portrait of the Viscountess Wimborne (Cambridge: Cambridge University Press, 1931);

Dickens (London: Chatto & Windus, 1932);

Winters of Content: More Discursions on Travel, Art, and Life (London: Duckworth, 1932; Philadelphia: Lippincott, 1932); revised and enlarged as *Winters of Content and Other Discursions on Mediterranean Art and Travel* (London: Duckworth, 1950);

Miracle on Sinai: A Satirical Novel (London: Duckworth, 1933; New York: Holt, 1934);

Brighton, by Sitwell and Margaret Barton (London: Faber & Faber, 1935; Boston & New York: Houghton Mifflin, 1935);

Penny Foolish: A Book of Tirades & Panegyrics (London: Macmillan, 1935);

Mrs. Kimber (London: Macmillan, 1937);

Those Were the Days: Panorama with Figures (London: Macmillan, 1938);

Trio: Dissertations on Some Aspects of National Genius, Delivered as the Northcliffe Lectures at the University of London in 1937, by Osbert, Edith, and Sacheverell Sitwell (London: Macmillan, 1938);

Escape with Me! An Oriental Sketch-Book (London: Macmillan, 1939; New York: Harrison-Hilton, 1940); republished as *Escape with Me! A Travel Book* (London: Pan, 1948);

Open the Door!: A Volume of Stories (London: Macmillan, 1941; New York: Smith & Durrell, 1941);

A Place of One's Own (London: Macmillan, 1941);

Gentle Caesar: A Play in Three Acts, by Sitwell and Rubeigh James Minney (London: Macmillan, 1942);

Selected Poems, Old and New (London: Duckworth, 1943);

Left Hand, Right Hand! (Boston: Little, Brown, 1944); republished as *Left Hand, Right Hand! An Autobiography. Vol. 1: The Cruel Month* (London: Macmillan, 1945);

Sing High! Sing Low!: A Book of Essays (London: Macmillan, 1944);

A Letter to My Son (London: Home & Van Thal, 1944);

The True Story of Dick Whittington: A Christmas Story for Cat-Lovers (London: Home & Van Thal, 1945);

The Scarlet Tree (Boston: Little, Brown, 1946); republished as *The Scarlet Tree, Being the Second Volume of Left Hand, Right Hand: An Autobiography* (London: Macmillan, 1946);

Alive–Alive Oh! and Other Stories (London: Pan, 1947);

Great Morning! (Boston: Little, Brown, 1947); republished as *Great Morning, Being the Third Volume of Left Hand, Right Hand! An Autobiography* (London: Macmillan, 1948);

The Novels of George Meredith and Some Notes on the English Novel (London: Oxford University Press, 1947);

Laughter in the Next Room (Boston: Little, Brown, 1948); republished as *Laughter in the Next Room, Being the Fourth Volume of Left Hand, Right Hand! An Autobiography* (London: Macmillan, 1949);

Four Songs of the Italian Earth (Pawlet, Vt.: Banyan Press, 1948);

Demos the Emperor: A Secular Oratorio (London: Macmillan, 1949);

Death of a God, and Other Stories (London: Macmillan, 1949);

England Reclaimed, and Other Poems (Boston: Little, Brown, 1949);

Noble Essences; or, Courteous Revelations, Being a Book of Characters and the Fifth and Last Volume of Left Hand, Right Hand! An Autobiography (London: Macmillan, 1950); republished as *Noble Essences: A Book of Characters* (Boston: Little, Brown, 1950);

Wrack at Tidesend: A Book of Balnearics, Being the Second Volume of England Reclaimed (London: Macmillan, 1952; New York: Caedmon, 1953);

Collected Stories (London: Duckworth, 1953; New York: Harper, 1953);

The Four Continents: Being More Discursions of Travel, Art and Life (London: Macmillan, 1954; New York: Harper, 1954);

On the Continent: A Book of Inquilinics, Being the Third Volume of England Reclaimed (London: Macmillan, 1958);

Fee Fi Fo Fum! A Book of Fairy Stories (London: Macmillan, 1959);

A Place of One's Own, and Other Stories (London: Icon, 1961);

Tales My Father Taught Me: An Evocation of Extravagant Episodes (London: Hutchinson, 1962; Boston: Little, Brown, 1962);

Pound Wise (London: Hutchinson, 1963; Boston: Little, Brown, 1963);

Poems about People, or England Reclaimed (London: Hutchinson, 1965);

Queen Mary and Others (London: Joseph, 1974; New York: Day, 1975).

OTHER: "Biographical Memoir," in *The Works of Ronald Firbank,* volume 1 (London: Duckworth / New York: Brentano's, 1929);

Sober Truth: A Collection of Nineteenth-Century Episodes, Fantastic, Grotesque and Mysterious, edited by Sitwell and Margaret Barton, with a preface by Sitwell (London: Duckworth, 1930);

Ifan Kyrle Fletcher, *Ronald Firbank: A Memoir,* includes a contribution by Sitwell (London:

Duckworth, 1930; New York: Brentano's, 1932);

Victoriana: A Symposium of Victorian Wisdom, edited by Sitwell and Barton (London: Duckworth, 1931);

Two Generations, edited by Sitwell (London: Macmillan, 1940);

Walter Sickert, *A Free House! Or, The Artist as Craftsman,* edited by Sitwell (London: Macmillan, 1947).

In the introduction to *Great Morning!* (1947), the third book of his widely acclaimed five-volume autobiography, Osbert Sitwell referred to himself as "novelist, poet, satirist, and writer of essays," a hierarchical ordering of his literary efforts reflecting his personal valuation of his attainments as a man of letters. Travel writing is subsumed under "writer of essays," for his several travel books are generally collections of essays previously published in periodicals. In relegating his essay writing to last place Sitwell showed fashionable scorn for mere journalistic pursuits and a loathing to admit the necessity during much of his life to write for money to supplement his allowance from his miserly father.

Osbert Sitwell has earned a place in the pantheon of twentieth-century British writers for his role in a well-known literary trio–joining his sister, Edith, and brother, Sacheverell, in ushering in modernism in British poetry–and for his autobiographical memoirs, which give a panoramic view of his family life up to 1930 and reflect an epoch of English history. Enjoying the privileged life of the upper class from the Victorian era into the modern, Sitwell derived much of the material for his writing from his many opportunities for extensive travel and his experiences of living abroad, especially in Italy.

The Sitwells' contribution to English letters can be measured by the dramatic change that overtook poetry in the 1920s. John Pearson calls the three Sitwells "a self-contained literary and artistic movement" and places Osbert in the leadership role in their drive to achieve power over the direction of English arts and letters. Aiding him in this endeavor was the general disarray of London's artistic life after World War I as well as Sitwell's favored position in aristocratic London society and his anger at the sacrifice of art and artists to war. In 1923 their combined efforts to mount the first public performance of *Façade,* a fusion of Edith Sitwell's experimental poetry and the young William Walton's music, assured the trio's place in literary history. Together they sounded the death knell of Georgian poetry and showed how to use language in a way comparable to modern, abstract art.

Francis Osbert Sacheverell Sitwell was born on 6 December 1892 in London, where his father had taken a house while Parliament was in session. Osbert was the elder son and middle child of Sir George Reresby Sitwell and his wife, Lady Ida Denison Sitwell. Their marriage had merged two ancient and aristocratic English families. The Sitwell ancestors had amassed large tracts of land in coal-rich Derbyshire and began building Renishaw, one of the grand stately homes of England, in the early seventeenth century. Ida Sitwell was the second daughter of Henry, first Earl of Londesborough, one of the largest landholders in England, and granddaughter of Henry Somerset, seventh Duke of Beaufort, a direct descendant of John of Gaunt.

In the first volumes of his autobiography, *Left Hand, Right Hand!* (1944) and *The Scarlet Tree* (1946), Osbert Sitwell dealt at length on growing up amid the tensions between his hopelessly incompatible parents. His cold and distant father was absorbed in his passion for Sitwell genealogy, medieval studies, and renovations to Renishaw and its gardens while his emotionally unstable mother gave in to uncontrollable rages and frequent tantrums. The birth of their first child, Edith, in 1887 had strained an already unstable union. Not being the anticipated son, she had thwarted her father's ambitions, and her mother judged her first child both ugly and unwanted. Osbert, born five years later, rekindled Sir George's dreams of building a distinguished lineage and aroused Lady Ida's motherly instincts to a level of adoration for her son. Even Edith, still an outcast from her parents' affections, found joy in loving her baby brother and, in another five years, a second brother, Sacheverell. The bond the young Sitwells formed in childhood sustained them in future years against their parents' failure to understand the needs of their gifted children and against a disparaging public unprepared for the new direction in which they were moving the arts.

For Osbert the idyllic years ended when he was sent to school in 1901 as a day pupil at a private school in Scarborough. In 1903 he was enrolled at Ludgrove, a fashionable boarding school, and he entered Eton College in 1905. With no pleasant memories of school years and having achieved no distinction as a student, Sitwell still hoped to attend Oxford; instead, after he left Eton in 1910, his father decided to send him to a military "crammer" in preparation for Sandhurst and a brilliant military career. The pattern of contentious relations between father and son was firmly fixed in these early years. Disappointed at being denied the opportunity to attend Oxford, Osbert deliberately failed the Sandhurst examination. In response his father forced

Osbert, Edith, and Sacheverell Sitwell with William Walton and a friend, 1926

him to accept a commission in the Sherwood Rangers. A year later he was transferred to the Grenadier Guards, stationed in the Tower of London. As a handsome young guardsman–tall and aristocratic in bearing, witty and elegant in manner, a splendid figure in his regimental uniform–Sitwell soon found himself caught up in the fashionable world of Edwardian London.

These brief years in London, before the outbreak of World War I, established firmly in Sitwell's mind the primacy of the arts as the highest expression of the human. In *Great Morning!* Sitwell described attending a 1912 Covent Garden performance of Igor Stravinsky's ballet *L' Oiseau de Feu* (*The Firebird,* 1910), which showed him the power of art to transform reality. He discovered his personal mission to "support the artist in every controversy, on every occasion" and consciously set about immersing himself in a world of art and artists. In the drawing rooms of Margot Asquith (wife of Prime Minister Herbert Henry Asquith), Mrs. George Keppel, and others, "belles of the Edwardian summer," young Sitwell found a glittering world of pleasures where people "lived for amusement and for things of the mind, eye, ear." There he met such notable figures of music and ballet as Claude Debussy, Richard Strauss, Vaslav Nijinsky, Fyodor Chaliapin, Frederick Delius, and Sergey Diaghilev. In the clubs he frequented he mingled with promising artists and writers as well as London theater people. Wartime service in the trenches in Flanders confirmed for Sitwell the folly and futility of armed conflict and provoked his most satirical literary outbursts. For the remainder of his life Sitwell fostered the arts in a relentless personal war against the philistine taste of his times.

Sitwell had his first experience at foreign travel as a schoolboy, when he was taken to the Italian Riviera to escape the harsh English winter while recovering from an illness. In *The Scarlet Tree* he recalled the delight he felt as a ten-year-old looking out of his window on his first Italian morning: "I

Osbert Sitwell and David Horner with their house servants in Beijing, 1934

knew that this was how I had always hoped the world would appear." For the rest of his life Italy remained a place of refuge. Between the world wars he often escaped to Amalfi, near Naples, to spend working holidays in a Capuchin monastery turned hotel, where he and artistic guests spent their days laboring in isolated cells before meeting in the evenings for dinner and conversation. Other times Italy offered a haven from middle-class English eyes and the freedom to explore less-frequented Italian sites, gathering material for his travel essays. Italy became his final home. After World War II he settled at Castle Montegufoni, near Florence, inherited on the death of Sir George Sitwell in 1943.

Sitwell came to travel writing almost accidentally. Having escaped his father in the winter of 1922 by going to the monastery-hotel in Amalfi, he found the pleasures of prose writing. In a letter to his publisher, Grant Richards, Sitwell confided that he was "busily engaged on completing a book of travel sketches." The resulting volume, *Discursions on Travel, Art and Life* (1925), set the pattern for his subsequent travel books. The sketches are digressive and the order in which he recounted his memories of travels in Italy, Sicily, and Germany is arbitrary. In the preface he defended the unusual form of his book as a means of describing what is seen and of freeing "the mind to voyage . . . backward and forward through time as well as in space."

Discursions on Travel, Art and Life is not a conventional travel book. It offers little sense of a setting out place, a direction of movement, or a destination reached. The book is divided into four parts, three of which are groups of essays relating to southern Italy, Sicily, and southern Germany. Tucked between the parts on Sicily and Germany is a tribute to Gabriele d' Annunzio, the radical poet-ruler of the principality of Fiume near Venice. Sitwell's habit of juxtaposing descriptions of striking scenery and tenuously connected digressions pulled from memory produces a close equivalent in words to the scraps arranged on canvas in the early collages of Pablo Picasso and Georges Braque as modern art entered its Cubist phase.

The opening essay describes the approach to Lecce through a surreal and barren coastal landscape of olive trees with their "grey shapes," which contrast to "the cactus and prickly-pear that stand out in menacing staccato attitudes." In Lecce the sight of a bulky old bus leads to a digression on old cabs and other public conveyances Sitwell has known—"jockey-carts" of his boyhood days in Scarborough, a three-wheeled London hansom cab, horse-drawn coaches plying the road between London and Hampton Court, and a relic chariot-coach in provincial France. Returning to his Italian subject, Sitwell focuses on the shape and color of villagers' dwellings near Lecce, completing his montage with a scene stark in its "blinding whiteness" and the straight lines and cubes of its "square white houses," seemingly "fashioned from snow, or carved from salt."

Perhaps the most satisfying piece is "The Miracle," a tour of Amalfi and the Capuchin hotel that Sitwell knew so well. Set in the spring during the Feast of St. Andrew, the patron saint of Amalfi, the essay describes sights and local customs. Sitwell was obviously pleased to share these memories despite his acerbic asides about the annual invasion of tourists, "old English ladies abloom with bugles and jet" or tiresome Americans filling the hotel sitting room with endless talk of plumbing. He painted in loving detail the feast day itself, its carnival atmosphere, with crowds of local peasants and tourists mingling among fruit sellers, sweets stalls, fortune tellers, and bagpipers. He also captured the solemnity and pageantry of the procession to the cathedral before returning to the hotel high above the sea for an eye-level view of the fireworks that closed the day.

Contemporary reviewers found little merit in *Discursions on Travel, Art and Life*. *The Times* (London) critic (20 May 1925) found Sitwell, "like the rest of his generation," obsessed with modern artists. This reviewer was disgruntled with Sitwell's failure to take either a classicist's or a romanticist's approach to his travel accounts. For him "eclectic" describes Sitwell's mood as he "oscillates between the discursionist and the excursionist." The reviewer for *The Times Literary Supplement* (*TLS,* 21 May 1925) was equally offended, objecting to Sitwell's "friendly attitude" to Rococo and Baroque art and architecture but conceding that the pursuit of such examples "lends a certain unity to Mr. Sitwell's rambling reflections." He was bothered most by Sitwell's unfriendly attitude to other travelers, observing that Sitwell too frequently resorted to "tart" expressions of "that dislike of other tourists which distinguishes the superior person." Sitwell, he concluded, was "too peevish" to be "an altogether agreeable travelling companion."

In his next travel book, *Winters of Content: More Discursions on Travel, Art, and Life* (1932), Sitwell heeded some of the critics' objections and curbed his belittling of other travelers. The volume reveals Sitwell in a holiday mood as he invites readers to revisit with him favorite and often overlooked sights in Venice, Bologna, and Parma. Though Sitwell never acknowledged a travel companion, Pearson records that the source of pleasure in this "happiest book he ever wrote" was Sitwell's newly established friendship with the young and handsome David Horner, who remained his companion for the next thirty years.

On the train carrying him to his Christmas rendezvous with Horner in Venice, a genial Sitwell refined his aesthetics of travel writing. Addressing the critics' objections to the digressions in *Discursions on Travel, Art and Life,* Sitwell claimed that the technique was a necessary agreement between reader and writer, asserting that the writer who transports readers to "unknown and distant lands" must have their permission "to break the journey where and when he may determine, to conceive of travel in a metaphorical as well as a physical sense, and to descant on the mood during the journey as much as of the journey's end." In his view the aim to communicate "a sense of holiday" requires this bargain.

In *Winters of Content* Sitwell crossed the line dividing traveler from tourist. With the plan to revisit familiar places he forfeited the traveler's commitment to exploration and discovery as well as the sense of adventure inherent in seeking out the unknown and the elevated status of the traveler, who often scoffs at mere tourists. In addressing his "gentle reader" with an invitation to share his holidays, Sitwell assumes the role of tour guide. As the train goes "swinging and jangling along" toward Venice, Sitwell passes the time with "remembrances" of that familiar and well-loved city, "the proudest, most challenging city that man has attempted." He compares Venice, rising from the sea in "flower-like shapes of buildings" under a nurturing sun, to the work of generations of coral polyps "piling one corpse upon another, until they build a world which ends in a swirl of palm trees and tropical blossoms." The reader may also take pleasure in his reflections on Christmas. Despite the Scrooge-like claim that he "was sure that Venice was a good place to bury Christmas," Sitwell is soon caught up in the nostal-

Sitwell visiting Renishaw, 1950s (photograph by Hans Wild)

gia of family Christmases of his childhood in England, memories rendered in the superb style of *Left Hand, Right Hand!* (1944).

Sitwell is a reliable, if eccentric, guide to the neglected treasures of northern Italy. While his taste in art and artists deviates from mainstream taste, *Winters of Content* offers much that satisfies. Sitwell sometimes turned in his memories to earlier visits to tell of instances of discovery that remained epiphanies for him. Though Parma had declined to the point of being the city of "cheese and violets," he recalls a time when he had been mysteriously drawn to enter an old, seemingly abandoned, public garden. Anticipating little, Sitwell had been so moved by the unexpected beauty of the walled enclosure and by the ancient gardener who tended it that he sensed the moment held "some magic that made the whole scene vibrate for ever in the memory." Such moments of discovery, he noted, lie behind the urge to travel, "the wish to see new lands and works of art or nature."

The reviewers of *Winters of Content* were less hostile toward this book than Sitwell's previous travel book, but they did not offer generous praise. The reviewer for *The Times* (7 June 1932) called the book eccentric, observing that Sitwell "travels in order to assist and nourish his fancy" and "treats monuments and works of art cavalierly" as occasions for digressions. He recommended this "characteristic and worthy specimen" to readers "who enjoy Mr. Sitwell's peculiar imagination" and are not put off by his looking at his subject as "a rather perverse still-life" or by "his stiff and ornamental prose." The *TLS* reviewer (9 June 1932) echoed the idea that, for Sitwell, travel provided "much matter for discourse and many props for his fancy." Reminding readers of Sitwell's "particular mode of sensibility," this critic catalogued the eccentricities of art, artists, and architecture that Sitwell singled out for admiration and cautioned against any expectations of pleasure unless readers "understand how these diverse objects appeal inevitably and as if by

Sitwell at Montegufoni (photograph by Reresby Sitwell)

some fixed rule of feeling, to Mr. Sitwell." The reviewer finally dismissed the volume as "a curious and fascinating chapter in the history of taste."

When *Winters of Content* was republished in 1950, the work was expanded to include parts of *Discursions on Travel, Art and Life* and the short story "Echoes," originally published in *Dumb-Animal, and Other Stories* (1930). Though the book attracted little critical attention, a lapse of twenty years had brought a changed perspective on Sitwell and his travel writing, and critics treated Sitwell less harshly. By 1950 *Noble Essences,* the last volume of his monumental autobiography, had firmly established him as a man of letters in England and in the United States. Citing "its full flavour of a pre-war richness in art and architecture," the reviewer for *TLS* (8 December 1950) praised the new edition of *Winter of Content* as "an alluring descriptive work for the traveller or aesthete, having all the distinction of its author's critical outlook and imaginative prose."

Escape with Me! An Oriental Sketch-Book (1939) is an account of Sitwell's travels in the Far East from the winter of 1933 through the spring of 1934. Despite the rumblings of war in Europe and the signs of worldwide economic depression, Sitwell was in a happy mood. Once more traveling with Horner, his purpose was "escapist," as he admitted in the opening sentence of the preface. Sitwell had given up the angry, activist stance that had propelled his satiric essays and poems throughout the 1920s for a resigned pessimism in the face of human folly. In reiterating his aesthetic he justified any apparent abnegation of his responsibility to work toward changing the world, claiming that an author's "chief duty . . . was—and still is—to use his eyes, to record what he sees, and what, because of them, he feels." He also reminded the reader that the author had the privilege of including "passing thoughts and reflections, as well as memories" and the "right" to move through time and space to strengthen "a visual image."

The introductory section, "The Cherry Tree," is an engaging contemplation of the magnetic hold China had had on him since boyhood. Aboard the ship to Saigon, from which he made his way to Angkor Wat and then Peking (Beijing), Sitwell explored his memory for clues to explain this urge to travel to so distant a part of the world. Apart from hereditary and cultural leanings, he attributed the impulse to the times he spent as a young child with his paternal grandmother in Surrey, where he discovered in her garden an exotic, flowering cherry tree that he knew instinctively to be oriental in origin. The book is a storehouse of what Sitwell saw, whether the fabulous ruins of the ancient city of Cambodia, the treasures of the Forbidden City in Beijing, or features of English and Italian art and landscape seen through the eye of memory. The present-day reader can appreciate the richness of Sitwell's descriptions, the interweaving of historical details gleaned from earlier travelers' accounts, and the privilege of seeing through his eyes a part of a world now vanished.

Published only two months after Great Britain had declared war on Germany, *Escape with Me!* met with resentment. The reviewer for *The Times* (10 November 1939) was unsympathetic with Sitwell's "latest attack of *Wanderlust,*" calling his journey "an artistic escapade." Yet he admired Sitwell's description of Bayon, more beautiful than Angkor Wat "and possessing the same elusive beauty that often lies between the lines of a great poem." Sitwell fared less well for his effusive appreciation of Chinese landscape and his idealized view of Chinese faces, overstatements attributable to his "acute sense of colour and poetic feeling" that results from his relying on his eyes for understanding. The reviewer for *TLS* (11 November 1939) saw affectation in Sitwell's describing a river scene in Indochina in terms of "the wooded canvases of Fragonard." He further found fault with Sitwell's habit of writing as a traveler "overcome with wonder at strange sights and events, though often not grasping their causes or implications." Granting that Sitwell was "a skilful artist in words," the reviewer implied that, given his lack of understanding of the complex political and social conditions in China, Sitwell should have limited himself to describing "landscapes, architecture, and art" and left aside "the world of men and mundane affairs."

During World War II Sitwell retreated to Renishaw. Though still unfit for year-round occupancy, lit by ancient oil lamps and without adequate heating, the house nonetheless proved a sanctuary for the duration of the war. Among memories of childhood summers in this ancestral home, the legends of his ancestors, and other events of his life from late Victorian times to the present, Sitwell wrote the five volumes of his autobiography: *Left Hand, Right Hand!* (1944), *The Scarlet Tree* (1946), *Great Morning!* (1947), *Laughter in the Next Room* (1948), and *Noble Essences* (1950).

At the end of the war Sitwell was eager to resume his traveling life, yet he was hampered by ill health, a condition eventually diagnosed as Parkinson's disease. After several painful trips in the late 1940s and early 1950s lecturing across the United States, Sitwell turned his attention to writing his last travel book, *The Four Continents: Being More Discursions on Travel, Art and Life* (1954), determined to keep his mind alive as his physical deterioration progressed. Searching for a title as he planned the work, he thought of calling it "Round the World in Sixty Years," indicating that the material in the book is drawn from memories of a lifetime of travel in Europe, Asia, northern Africa, and America. He also hit upon the device of building his free-ranging memories, impressions, and opinions around the four elements of air, water, fire, and earth. The finished volume appeals to the reader as a sustained example of Sitwell's verbal virtuosity and his skill in weaving together imagery, anecdotes, and history to display through the prism of his imagination the beauty and grandeur of a world intimately known.

Contemporary reviewers praised this work dutifully, apparently used to the fact that Sitwell was an anomaly. *The Times* reviewer (17 July 1954) maintained that the reader was led around, not four continents, but "a new continent, the continent of Sitwellia." He pictured Sitwell as a neoclassical nobleman who opened to the public for its pure enjoyment "the avenues and lakes, gardens and galleries, secret grottoes and shadowy caverns of his mind." The review of *The Four Continents* in *TLS* (20 August 1954) is titled "Sitwellian Purple," perhaps a double-edged allusion to a prose that "makes no concession to the resurgent fashion . . . for the plain style" and to the regal lifestyle that Sitwell had assumed in his Italian castle. The reviewer might well be charged with mean-spiritedness in his consideration of the origins of Sitwell's style. Certainly aware of the low regard in which Sitwell held John Ruskin, the critic speculated that "this great neglected Victorian writer, with his passion for landscape, and clouds, and architecture, with his fervour and his irascibility and his excitable eloquence, has been one of Sir Osbert's masters."

Readers of Sitwell's prose continue to share the sentiments of readers in his time–frustration with a style that often lapses into endless rococo phrases that are convoluted one into another, finally burying the soul of the sentence, or irritation with the posturing snobbery that demeans Sitwell more than the objects of his scorn. Yet these infractions can be forgiven when they are weighed against the pleasure the reader gains from seeing much of the world's beauty through the eyes of a connoisseur. Sitwell left a record of places and times now forever lost, written in a style that captures that past.

Though he began his writing career with the intention of arousing the English public to an awareness of its ignorance and folly, Sitwell soon abandoned polemics in favor of indulging his private and personal tastes in what he found both beautiful and good. In this mode, serene and self-assured, he offered objects of beauty to a world torn by class struggle, labor disputes, and two devastating world wars. Whether they came from his memories of a happy childhood in a lavish and graceful bygone age or whether they were collected during his travels, Sitwell's souvenirs, displayed for admiration in his eloquent prose, remind the reader of the need to seek out what is beautiful to nourish the human spirit. As one reviewer said in appreciation of Sitwell's final travel book, "One of the writer's central duties of all times is to praise the wonders of creation." For Sitwell such wonders included landscapes, works of art and architecture, flowers single and massed, and fellow humans who espoused the eternal verities.

Sitwell spent most of his last years at Castle Montegufoni, returning briefly to England to be named a commander of the Order of the British Empire in 1956. He died on 4 May 1969, and his ashes were buried in the Allori Protestant cemetery near Montegufoni. In accordance with his wish, a copy of *Before the Bombardment* (1926), his first novel and his personal favorite among his books, was buried with his ashes. Sitwell cherished this work, which first brought him critical acclaim, to the end of his days as a symbol of his dream of making his mark as a novelist.

Bibliography:

Richard Fifoot, *A Bibliography of Edith, Osbert and Sacheverell Sitwell,* second edition, revised (Hamden, Conn.: Archon, 1971).

Biographies:

Rodolphe Louis Mégroz, *The Three Sitwells: A Biographical and Critical Study* (London: Richards, 1927);

John Lehmann, *A Nest of Tigers: Edith, Osbert and Sacheverell Sitwell in Their Times* (London: Macmillan, 1968);

John Pearson, *Façades: Edith, Osbert and Sacheverell Sitwell* (London: Macmillan, 1979); republished as *The Sitwells: A Family Biography* (New York: Harcourt Brace Jovanovich, 1979).

References:

Roger Fulford, *Osbert Sitwell* (London: Longmans, Green, 1951);

Paul Fussell, *Abroad: British Literary Traveling Between the Wars* (New York: Oxford University Press, 1980).

Papers:

Osbert Sitwell's papers are at the Harry Ransom Humanities Research Center, University of Texas at Austin, and at the Washington State University Library.

Francis Sydney Smythe

(6 July 1900 - 27 June 1949)

Pratul Pathak
California University of Pennsylvania

Francis Sydney Smythe, 1931

BOOKS: *Climbs and Ski-Runs: Mountaineering and Ski-ing in the Alps, Great Britain and Corsica* (Edinburgh: Blackwood, 1929);
The Kangchenjunga Adventure (London: Gollancz, 1930);
Kamet Conquered (London: Gollancz, 1932);
An Alpine Journey (London: Gollancz, 1934);
The Spirit of the Hills (London: Hodder & Stoughton, 1935);
Over Tyrolese Hills (London: Hodder & Stoughton, 1936);
Camp Six: An Account of the 1933 Mount Everest Expedition (London: Hodder & Stoughton, 1937);
The Mountain Scene (London: Black, 1937);
The Valley of Flowers (London: Hodder & Stoughton, 1938; New York: Norton, 1949);
Peaks and Valleys (London: Black, 1938);
A Camera in the Hills (London: Black, 1939);
Edward Whymper (London: Hodder & Stoughton, 1940);
The Adventures of a Mountaineer (London: Dent, 1940);
Mountaineering Holiday (London: Hodder & Stoughton, 1940);
My Alpine Album (London: Black, 1940);
The Mountain Vision (London: Hodder & Stoughton, 1941);
Over Welsh Hills (London: Black, 1941);
Alpine Ways (London: Black, 1942);
British Mountaineers (London: Collins, 1942);
Secret Mission (London: Hodder & Stoughton, 1942);
Snow on the Hills (London: Black, 1946);
Again Switzerland (London: Hodder &Stoughton, 1947);
The Mountain Top: An Illustrated Anthology from the Prose and Pictures of F. S. Smythe (London: St. Hugh's Press, 1947);
Rocky Mountains (London: Black, 1948);
Swiss Winter (London: Black, 1948);
Mountains in Colour (London: Parrish, 1949); republished as *Behold the Mountains: Climbing with a Color Camera* (New York: Chanticleer Press, 1949);
Climbs in the Canadian Rockies (London: Hodder & Stoughton, 1950; New York: Norton, 1950).

OTHER: J. H. B. Bell, *A Progress in Mountaineering*, foreword by Smythe (London: Oliver & Boyd, 1950).

SELECTED PERIODICAL PUBLICATIONS–UNCOLLECTED: "Peak of Terror," *Blackwood's Magazine*, 223 (May 1928): 596–602;
"Bivouac on the Aiguille du Plan," *Cornhill Magazine*, 65 (August 1928): 229–239;

"Night Adventure in the Dolomites," *Cornhill Magazine,* 65 (December 1928): 721–729;
"New Route Up Mont Blanc without Guides," *Blackwood's Magazine,* 224 (December 1928): 719–742;
"Winter Tussle with the Ogre," *Blackwood's Magazine,* 225 (April 1929): 452–465;
"Bad Weather on Mont Maudit," *Blackwood's Magazine,* 226 (November 1929): 687–712;
"Stone That Moved," *Cornhill Magazine,* 68 (February 1930): 155–161;
"Near Thing in the Dolomites," *Blackwood's Magazine,* 227 (March 1930): 408–416;
"Unconquered Kangchenjunga: A Panorama of the Himalaya," *Times* (London), 21 June 1930, p. 16;
"The Conquest of Jonsong: Climber's Own Story: Great Wind Storms," *Times* (London), 23 June 1930, pp. 14–16;
"The Himalaya Expedition: Another Peak Climbed," *Times* (London), 30 June 1930, p. 13;
"Kangchenjunga: Lessons of the Expedition: A Law unto Itself," *Times* (London), 9 August 1930, pp. 11–12;
"Kangchenjunga: Porterage of The Peaks: Future of Himalayan Climbing," *Times* (London), 16 August 1930, pp. 11–12;
"British Expedition To Mount Kamet," *Times* (London), 4 April 1931, p. 14;
"Difficulties of Kamet: The Climbing Party," *Times* (London), 11 April 1931, p. 11;
"The Readiness for Kamet: Equipment and Food," *Times* (London), 25 April 1931, p. 11;
"The Advance on Kamet: British Party on the Move: World's Finest Panorama," *Times* (London), 1 June 1931, pp. 15–16;
"High Camps on Kamet: 22,500 Ft. Up," *Times* (London), 27 June 1931, p. 12.

Frank S. Smythe was a sickly child who as an adult had his military career ended by a heart condition. Defying medical advice, he turned to climbing mountains and writing about his exploits. Smythe became one of the foremost advocates of travel to mountainous regions around the world. His popular books, articles, and photographs of his climbs helped broaden the readership of mountaineering literature from the cognoscenti to nonmountaineers. Instead of concentrating on exceptional feats by accomplished climbers, Smythe described the simple joy and delight of being among the hills of the British Isles, the mountains of the European Alps, the Himalayas, and the Canadian Rockies. His accounts were accompanied by excellent photographs; he was considered by many of his contemporaries to be a pioneering and top-class mountain photographer.

Francis Sydney Smythe was born on 6 July 1900 at Ivythorne, Maidstone, to Algernon Sydney Smythe, a timber merchant and property owner, and his second wife, Florence. Smythe was two years old when his father died, leaving him in the charge of an overprotective mother who thought that, because Frank suffered from a persistent heart murmur, he had a dangerously weak constitution. But young Frank Smythe refused to allow his physical condition to limit his life. In fact he first felt the attraction of the mountains during visits to the British hills and to Switzerland when he was seven or eight years old. During his Swiss trip he was given a copy of the famous mountaineer Edward Whymper's *Scrambles amongst the Alps* (1871), which Smythe claimed had a seminal influence in developing his interest in mountaineering.

At the age of thirteen he was sent as a day scholar to Berkenhamsted School, where he developed a love for geography, English literature, and electrical engineering. According to his biographer Harry Calvert in *Smythe's Mountains* (1985), Smythe was a misfit and loner at school who longed to escape the confining atmosphere of the English public school system. As a result he came to be regarded by many of his acquaintances as arrogant, standoffish, and irritatingly self-sufficient, a perception of his character that followed him throughout the rest of his life.

In 1919 Smythe enrolled at Faraday House to become an electrical engineer. He went to Switzerland in 1921 to do an internship in hydroelectric power generation but was disappointed by the Swiss engineering firm's lack of concern for him. Smythe moved to Austria, where he found a position with a company that owned hydroelectric generation plants in Landeck. During his one-year stint as a trainee, he was able to get away to the mountains every weekend and during holidays to climb and walk in the Alps, and within eighteen months he had become a competent skier and taught himself to be an accomplished climber on snow and ice. Smythe sailed to Buenos Aires in 1925 to work as an electrical engineer, but he returned shortly without even having visited the Andes, which is surprising since his hero Edward Whymper wrote eloquently about the South American peaks.

In 1926 he joined the Royal Air Force and was stationed in Egypt. After only a year in the R.A.F., Smythe was discharged in 1927 due to his heart murmur and cautioned not to do any climbing. This warning irritated Smythe, and he felt even more alienated than he had in school. Determined to

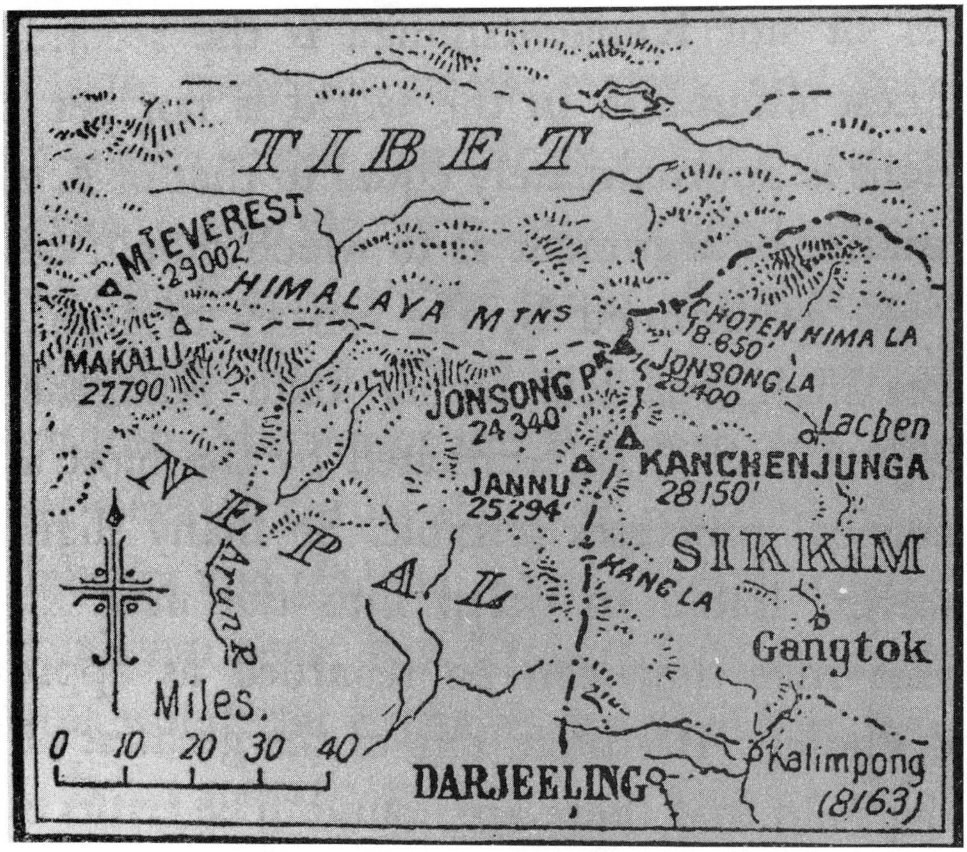

Map of the route Smythe followed while climbing in the Himalayas in 1930 (from The Kanchenjunga Adventure, *1930)*

prove his detractors wrong, he chose climbing as a career, going on to climb some of the highest mountains in the world.

After leaving the R.A.F., Smythe worked for Kodak for a year, where he gained the valuable training and experience in photography that enabled him to become one of the leading mountain photographers of all time. In 1928 he began a full-time career of mountaineering.

Smythe spent the first years of his chosen career, 1928 to 1930, traveling and climbing extensively in the Alps and Corsica. He also contributed five articles in *Blackwood's Magazine* and *Cornhill Magazine.* During this period climbers were competing with each other in establishing new routes on every major summit in the Alps. Although he took part in some of these pioneering efforts, Smythe made few first ascents, as he preferred to travel to the lesser-known areas that he describes in *Climbs and Ski-Runs: Mountaineering and Ski-ing in the Alps, Great Britain and Corsica* (1929), the first of his books.

Climbs and Ski-Runs opens with a description of Smythe's first visit to the hills of the British Lake District as a sick child of three. This was the beginning of a lifelong fascination with mountains; in the first chapter Smythe says, "I began to feel the magic of the hills, the freedom of distance, the joy of being able to look down on a humdrum world and see what seemed so big and important when one was there was very small when seen from the hill." At the age of eight he made his first visit to the Swiss Alps. Smythe describes his first climbs in the British hills, where he taught himself the basics of climbing. He never used a guide, but he did come in contact with other climbers, especially the members of the Yorkshire Ramblers climbing club and Geoffrey Winthrop Young.

From the British hills he moved to the European Alps and climbed in the Dolomites, made a trip to the hills of Corsica, and then was back making his mark on the bigger peaks, especially Mont Blanc. On Europe's highest peak he forsook the normal snow routes to the summit and tried the more-difficult routes to the mountain. With a companion he did a traverse of the Pétéret Ridge, one of the longest climbs in the Alps. Descending, they were caught in a storm, and Smythe led the first successful descent of the Col de Pétéret. In the final chapters of *Climbs and Ski-Runs* Smythe describes his best climbs in the Alps with Professor Graham Brown as they forced two new routes up the Brenva Face of Mont Blanc, but this partnership also brought controversy into Smythe's career. Brown resented Smythe's publishing accounts of their climbs despite having promised that Brown could write the first accounts, and Brown became a lifelong and harsh critic of Smythe at every stage of his career.

Climbs and Ski-Runs has an important place in Smythe's career as a mountaineer and a writer. Smythe gives an overview of his early years in the sport, and in the final chapter he explains his philosophy as a mountaineer. He believed that a full appreciation of mountains was not to be experienced by merely looking at them but by climbing them, declaring, "Civilized life is too complex, too full of superficialities and false doctrines. The philosophy of the hills is a simple one. On them we approach a little nearer to the ends of the Earth and the beginnings of Heaven. Over the hills the spirit of man passes towards his Maker."

Many of Smythe's contemporaries, such as Adrian Lunn and Graham Thomas, found his attempts to philosophize about his mountain experiences a serious weakness in a writer who was at his best in conveying to his reader the adventure of climbing. But Smythe never stopped making these attempts, and in all his books he found ways to somehow inject and elaborate on his philosophy.

In the winter of 1929–1930, while climbing in the Alps, Smythe met Professor G. O. Dyhrenfurth, who was organizing a German expedition to Kangchenjunga, the third highest mountain in the world. Impressed by the young Briton's exploits in the Alps, Dyhrenfurth invited Smythe to join his team. From 1930 until 1938 Smythe spent most of his time in India and the Himalayas, where he attempted to climb Kangchenjunga (1930), made the first ascent of Kamet (1931), discovered the "Valley of Flowers" (1932), and tried three times to climb Mount Everest (1933, 1936, 1938). Between June and August 1930 Smythe wrote five dispatches for *The Times* (London) from Kangchenjunga describing various stages of the expedition. On his return he produced his first book on his Himalayan travels, *The Kangchenjunga Adventure* (1930).

Smythe starts out by revealing his childhood dreams of climbing in the Himalayas from geography lessons in school and listening during his association with the Yorkshire Ramblers to the exploits of Albert F. Mummery and Howard Somervell. Next, in great detail Smythe describes the history of Kangchenjunga, gives the customary profiles of the leader and members of the climbing team, describes the selection and organization of equipment and food and the journey out to India in March. There were problems: obtaining permission to enter Nepal and Tibet, finding porters to transport the expedition to base camp, and hiring Sherpas. However, once the walk to base camp started on 7 April, things went smoothly until they reached it. Then the cliffs and hanging glaciers that barred their chosen route up the western face of the mountain, bad weather, and poor judgment brought the expedition to a halt at Camp Two, where an avalanche killed a Sherpa as they tried to open a route to Camp Three. Smythe had a premonition of such a disaster when he wrote two days before the accident in his 6 May dispatch to *The Times,* "As I write, avalanche after avalanche is roaring off Kangchenjunga, each one seeming to proclaim defiance and warning."

Though they failed to attain their main objective, they climbed some lower peaks in the area, and Smythe had the satisfaction of climbing Jongsong Peak (24,344 feet) and Ramthenga (23,000 feet) in the next few weeks. *The Kangchenjunga Adventure* is different from Smythe's other books in that he writes very little about his mystical vision of the mountains; it is instead a straightforward narrative of a Himalayan expedition, full of details about climbers, equipment, camp life, difficulties of altitude and weather, legends of the Abominable Snowman, remarks on the quaintness of foreign cultures, and the hands-on experience he has gained in organizing Himalayan expeditions. This knowledge was tested the next year when he organized and led the first successful expedition to Kamet.

From April to June 1931 Smythe contributed five more articles to *The Times* on the progress of his expedition; these articles later formed the basis of *Kamet Conquered* (1932). The book starts out with a history of the Himalayas, describes Kamet, and gives the formula for a successful Himalayan venture. Smythe strongly believed that "Assimilation of the experience and lessons from previous expeditions is the first duty of an organizer of a Himalayan expedition. To make the same mistakes as one's predecessors is inexcusable." Taking a cue from his experiences on Kangchenjunga, he selected a cohesive and well-qualified six-man team, which included a young Eric Shipton (later to become one of the best-known mountaineers of the 1930s) on his first Himalayan trip. Smythe hired six Sherpas from Darjeeling, arranged for porters beforehand, and paid special attention to the food. Food is essential for the harmonious working of an expedition, Smythe observes, and the likes and dislikes of each member must be given due consideration. He suggests that if an expedition doubles or trebles its estimates of sugar rations, it will face no problems with morale or energy levels of the members. After as-

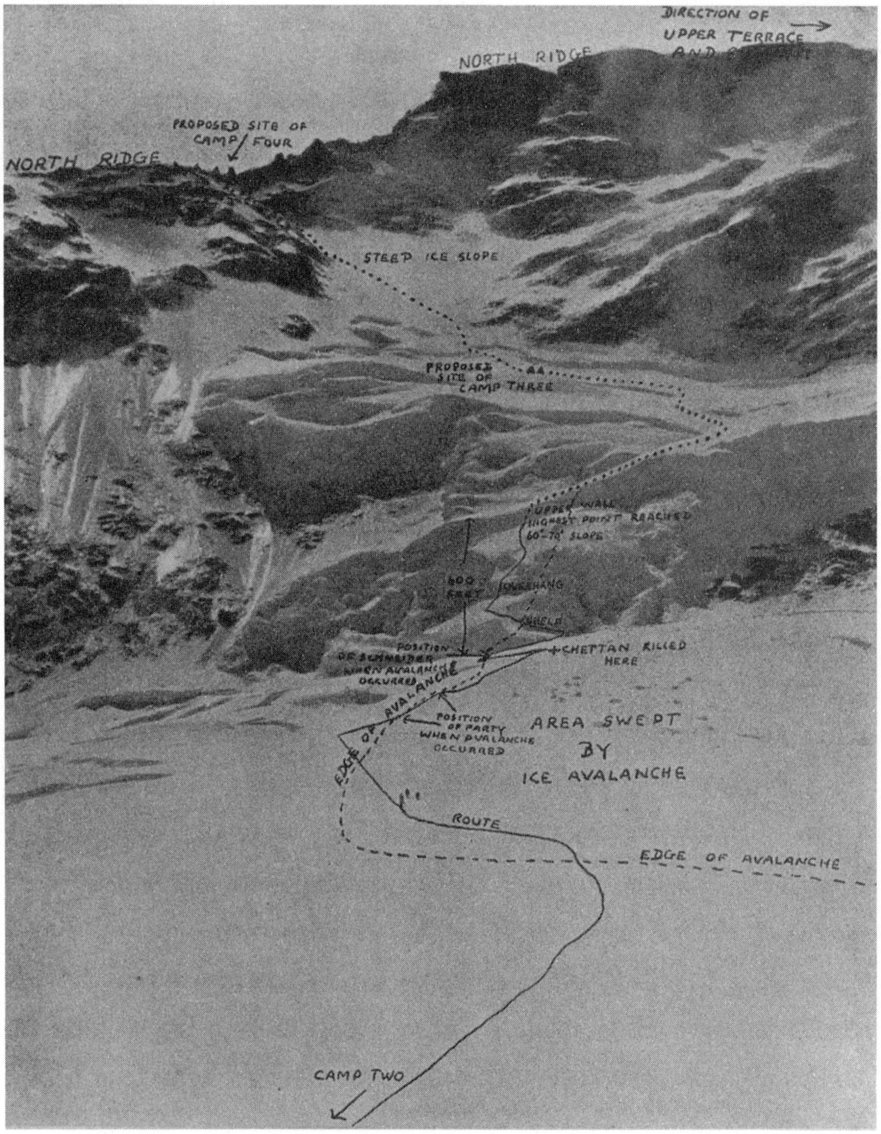

Mount Kangchenjunga's ice wall, on which Smythe has drawn the expedition's route (photograph by Smythe, from The Kangchenjunga Adventure*)*

sembling at Ranikhet in the first week of May, the party left on 18 May, rapidly marched through the foothills, and established their base camp at 15,500 feet on 5 June. From there progress was so rapid and uneventful that in two weeks they set up five high altitude camps and reached the summit on 21 June.

The last ten chapters of *Kamet Conquered* are devoted to the climbs that Smythe and Shipton made on various peaks at the headwaters of the Ganges River. After their success on Kamet, the party exited the Dhaoli Valley by way of the Bhyundar Valley, more famous by the nickname Smythe gave it, "The Valley of Flowers." Smythe was so impressed by the beauty of the valley and the variety of alpine flowers it held that he became an avid gardener and collector of mountain flora for the alpine garden in his country home in Sussex. Smythe's style matches the speed of the climb. He does not dally on reflection but graphically describes each day's activities and exertions with a tautness in the narrative that made his books popular with readers. *Kamet Conquered* is one of the best books on travel and adventure in the Himalayas. Smythe takes the time to describe almost every aspect of climbing in the Himalayas from men to ponies, from food to medicine, from the composition of the rocks to the variety of the flora in the region, and from the physiological aspects of altitude to the mental concerns of those who climb.

In June 1931 he climbed Kamet, which at 25,447 feet was at that time the highest peak ever reached by man, and on his return he married his first wife, Kathleen Mary Johnson, with whom he eventually had three sons. He also completed a film on Kamet, which was shown to King George V and Queen Mary at Buckingham Palace in March 1932. Smythe was involved in a car accident in November of the same year but escaped with minor injuries, from which he recovered in time to join the 1933 Everest expedition.

Every climber dreams of climbing Mount Everest, and Smythe was no exception. Ever since he decided to pursue mountaineering as a career, he had had an eye on the world's highest peak. In 1924 he was not selected for the expedition in which the experienced climber George Leigh Mallory and the young Oxford student Andrew Irvine disappeared near the summit. At the time some influential members of the British climbing establishment thought Smythe was a first-rate climber but a difficult person to get along with. But over the next nine years, with his climbs on Kangchenjunga and Kamet, he enhanced his reputation as a climber so much that when the next Everest expedition was underway in 1933 he was chosen as one of the lead climbers.

Smythe begins his narrative of *Camp Six: An Account of the 1933 Mount Everest Expedition* (1937) in February 1933 in the hill station of Darjeeling in northeast India, which was the jumping off point for all pre–World War II expeditions to Mount Everest. From there he moves on without much delay to the forty-day approach march through Sikkim and Tibet to the base camp on the Rongbuk Glacier. In the opening chapters Smythe vividly describes the long, arduous, uncomfortable, and sometimes dangerous caravan of climbers, Sherpas, porters, and pack animals, the inhospitable surroundings, dry air of the Tibetan plateau, and the constant dust that covered everything: their clothes, sleeping bags, and food. Finally, on 18 April base camp was established on the East Rongbuk Glacier at 16,800 feet. In addition to describing their activities, Smythe sprinkles his narrative with discussions of his ideas and concepts about a mountaineer's life. Lying in his sleeping bag at Camp One he wondered:

> Why are we lying here, when we might be eating and drinking in comfort at sea-level? Yet for some curious reason, I would not exchange the discomfort of Everest for the comfort of sea level. We curse our luck, we curse the discomfort, but we go on with it. Why? I wish I knew. My hands are ingrained with dirt, my face sunscorched and sore, my cracked lips painful. "Why do you do it?" How can we explain when we don't know? And we don't care whether or not we understand–not a bit. We only know that in discomfort, in storm, in the beauty and grandeur of the mountains we have discovered something very much worth while.

Between Camps Five and Six the expedition came upon the remains of the high camps of the 1924 expedition. In addition to some rags of green canvas and collapsed tent poles, the Sherpas found an electric torch that was driven by a dynamo. Even after nine years of lying out in the cold, the torch worked, and there was no rust on it. But the most dramatic find was made by the first summit pair of Wyn Harris and L. R. Wagers, who reached the crest of the northeast ridge. Finding that it was not possible to continue on the ridge, they attempted a traverse by climbing down fifty feet, and there on a slab of rock Harris found an ice ax that could only have belonged to Mallory or Irvine. The ice ax fueled further speculation about the fate of Mallory and Irvine that continues even today. Why was the ice ax lying there? Was it left behind, or did the two have an accident? And the final question, was it left there on the way up or down: did they reach the summit? Smythe believed that they had an accident on the way up.

On 1 June, Shipton and Smythe made their attempt to reach the summit of Everest. They set out at 7 A.M. and planned to climb and descend the last sixteen hundred feet in eleven hours. But about two hours out of camp, Shipton turned back, and Smythe had to continue alone. Avoiding the ridge line, he followed the line that Somervell and E. F. Norton had taken in 1924. Continuing, he traversed the great couloir until he reached the rock band below the summit pyramid of Everest. By 11 A.M. his progress was slow due to the unstable snow and steep slope. Also, being alone, he felt less confident even on simple moves and decided to turn back at twenty-eight thousand feet. The descent was uneventful, but Smythe underwent some interesting experiences. Ever since leaving Shipton he could not overcome a feeling that some strong and friendly presence was accompanying him, and he believed "that in its presence I could come to no harm." When he decided to eat some mint cake, he instinctively divided it into two halves and turned round to offer half to this presence. A little lower down he happened to look toward the northeast shoulder of Everest and thought he saw two dark objects that looked like kite balloons with underdeveloped wings. The objects were visible for quite some time, and they seemed to pulsate with life. After convincing himself that he was not imagining

Sherpa porters of the Kangchenjunga expedition (photograph by Smythe, from The Kangchenjunga Adventure*)*

things, he continued down and reached camp at 12:30 P.M.

Camp Six is a fine example of Smythe's abilities to keep his readers enthralled with a detailed account of the rigors of mountaineering. For instance, in the chapter "The Assault" Smythe describes how a climber had to dress to survive on Everest's summit ridge in the pre-Goretex era. He wore every stitch of clothing he possessed: a Shetland vest, a thick flannel shirt, a heavy camel-hair sweater, six light Shetland pullovers, two pairs of long Shetland pants, a pair of flannel trousers, and over all a silk-lined Grenfell windproof suit, a Shetland balaclava, and another helmet of cloth to protect his head. Overall, *Camp Six* provides an excellent explanation of why and how people risk their lives on the high mountains all around the world. Smythe was able to describe the hardships and both the monotony and the excitement of life as a part of an expedition. The only disappointing part of the book is the quality of the photographs. Smythe was a trained and experienced cameraman, but it seems that the best pictures of the 1933 Everest expedition were put in the official account, *Everest, 1933,* published in 1934 by Hugh Ruttledge, and for *Camp Six* Smythe was left with the second-best photographs.

He was to return to the highest mountain in the world twice more, in 1936 and 1938. In between he continued Alpine rambles, both solo and with others, and published three books. Smythe's love for mountaineering was obvious; after having reached 28,000 feet on Everest in 1933, he was not obsessed with going higher. Instead, in the spring of 1934 he spent six weeks in the northeastern section of the Alps skiing and climbing over terrain that ranged from 1,900 feet to 10,400 feet.

His solo travels in the Alps are described in *An Alpine Journey* (1934). Smythe had visited some of these areas during his early climbing days, but he wanted to do a traverse of the Alps from Bludenz in the Tyrol to Andermatt in Switzerland. This section of the Alps is less frequented by the ordinary tourist or Alpine enthusiast because it does not have glamorous resorts such as Chamonix or Zermatt or the more-well-known peaks such as the Matterhorn or Mont Blanc. In the preface Smythe says that his intention was to see and recapture some of the charms of mountain travel as described by Edward Whymper and other pioneers of mountaineering. He also mentions that mountaineering was no longer confined to the leisured and professional classes; it had become one of the world's greatest sports. But due to the lack of time and resources, most climbers had to choose a particular area and climb in what he calls a "centrist manner." On his decision to travel alone, Smythe says he did not advocate solo climbing but wanted to have the freedom to travel at his own pace, without a fixed plan, and choose any route that took his fancy.

In *An Alpine Journey* Smythe describes his adventures as he skied, walked, and scrambled his way from Bludenz in a southwesterly direction to Andermatt. For the most part the trip was uneventful, and the narration is matter-of-fact. But toward the end of the trip there was some excitement. On the day he reached Andermatt, Smythe was crossing the Fellilucke Pass when a snowslide started just below him, and as Smythe puts it, he had "the privilege to view an avalanche at close quarters." Calvert in *Smythe's Mountains* is more blunt when he says, "a start twenty minutes later would have put a stop to this and any future touring." Later, as Smythe was climbing up to the Clarinden Pass, another avalanche started two hundred feet above him but somehow missed him as it swept by. Despite these incidents, *An Alpine Journey* describes a generally unremarkable excursion. The most noteworthy aspect of the book is the description of obscure areas of the Alps and some of the fifty-three photographs. Smythe's penchant for breathtaking panoramic views from high up are evident in the shots of Piz Linard, Spitzmeilen, the Wetterhorn, Eiger, Mönch, and Jungfrau from the summit of the Weisse Frau.

Though he never wrote a formal account of his life, in *The Spirit of the Hills* (1935) Smythe provides an overview of his career and philosophy of mountaineering, and the book can be considered the first volume of his autobiography. In the first seven chapters of *The Spirit of the Hills* Smythe summarizes his childhood, his early climbs in the British hills, the excursions in the Alps, his expeditions in the Himalayas, and his attempts on Everest. In the last fifteen chapters, which have titles such as "Dawn," "Music," and "The Spiritual," he fulfills the objective outlined in the preface–to "express through the medium of the written word, the meaning of the hills and the reasons that inspire men to climb."

Readers of *The Spirit of the Hills* may agree with Adrian Lunn's view that Smythe was good at describing his mountain adventures but weak at philosophizing. But for readers who are not familiar with Smythe's works, this book is a good place to start. *The Spirit of the Hills* summarizes practically all of Smythe's mountaineering experience before World War II. (Left out of the book are his climbs in North America.) Smythe tells his readers why he chose to devote his life to climbing and how satisfied he is with his achievements. In the last chapter Smythe says, "Mountaineering is a happy pursuit, because it provides through climbing and contemplation a union of the physical and mental qualities." Smythe is prophetic when he says that the indoor and mechanized lifestyle of modern humans will lead to our being ensnared and enslaved by our mode of living and the power and prodigality of our inventions. Our only escape will be in turning to appreciate nature because "the hills have a power for drawing out the best that is within us; on them we are given a full measure of perfect happiness."

Smythe realized that mountaineering was misunderstood and misinterpreted partly because of the competitive spirit associated with the sport. Another reason was the "national" atmosphere surrounding it. Everest was considered a British mountain; Kangchenjunga and Nanga Parbat were viewed as German mountains; and K2 was seen as belonging to the Italians. This tradition tended to promote national prejudices, doubts, and jealousies among climbers. Smythe criticizes the conquering spirit with which individuals approached mountains; he admits that he himself was guilty of such an attitude at various times in his career but says that ultimately he believes man cannot conquer nature.

Smythe returned to the Alps in the summer of 1935, chronicling his experiences in *Over Tyrolese Hills* (1936). Climbing with a companion, Campbell Secord, he traversed the Tyrolese Alps from north to south instead of the usual east to west trek, in an uneventful trip. Although poorly written, the book demonstrates Smythe's ability to write for different audiences. His narratives of exploits on Kangchenjunga and Kamet were meant to bring the thrill of high altitude adventure to the armchair traveler. *Over Tyrolese Hills,* by contrast, was meant to show that ordinary travelers wishing to spend a quiet time away from the crowds might reasonably accomplish their desires by following in the author's footsteps.

The three Everest expeditions, interspersed with visits to the Alps and the Valley of Flowers, kept him away from home for extended periods and led to the dissolution of his marriage to Kathleen in 1937. In the same year, *The Mountain Scene,* Smythe's first collection of mountain photographs, was published. The seventy-eight photos in the book are arranged in eight sections: "The British Hills," "The Eastern Alps," "The Bernese Oberland," "The Pennine Alps," "The Range of Mont Blanc," "Kangchenjunga," "Kamet," and "Mount Everest." Most of the photographs are shots of peaks, ridges, and other mountain views without people. In the introduction Smythe explains he took photographs because he wanted to take home some record of his wanderings to share with friends and family. He goes on to say that almost all the pictures in this collection were snapshots without any setting up. After discussing how painters can manipulate their me-

One of Smythe's companions crosses a bridge over the Lhonak River on the descent to Darjeeling from the Jongsong Peak (photograph by Smythe, from The Kangchenjunga Adventure*)*

dium to express their interpretation of a scene and photographers cannot, Smythe insists that photographers can still create a memorable image by learning the rudiments of the medium such as composition, balance, light and shade, filters, exposure, enlargements, and equipment. Anyone interested in photography would find Smythe's advice helpful.

The Mountain Scene includes some spectacular and unusual views of the Matterhorn, Mont Blanc, Kangchenjunga, Kamet, and the Valley of Flowers. Each section is prefaced with a few paragraphs giving the reader an overview of the area and a history of climbing activities on the various peaks. But even more interesting are the paragraphs that describe each picture. Apart from explaining the scene, Smythe reveals information about exposure, time of day the photograph was taken, and details about the different elements he used in composing a shot, such as the gnarled and weather-beaten solitary pine tree that forms the centerpiece of the photograph "An Outpost Pine: Kuari Pass." *The Mountain Scene* has an important place in Smythe's development as a writer of adventure narratives because it shows that when the format demanded it, he could control his prose and describe his travels in a few well-chosen paragraphs and photographs instead of a whole book. After all, his purpose was "to interest those who enjoy the hills, and to explain the art of moun-

Camping on Mana Peak at twenty thousand feet during the 1937 expedition Smythe describes in The Valley of the Flowers, *1938 (photograph by Smythe, from* British Mountaineers, 1942*)*

tain photography I hope may help readers who like to bring back some pictorial record of their wanderings in the hills."

Smythe had looked forward to returning to the Bhyundar Valley since he and his party had passed through it after his successful 1931 ascent of Kamet. He finally returned in June 1937, staying for three months, and described the trip in *The Valley of Flowers* (1938). Smythe set out from England alone, met up with four of his favorite Sherpas in Ranikhet, hired eleven porters, purchased a goat for fresh meat, marched this caravan for nine days, and set up base camp at the lower end of the valley on 15 June. After traveling with the big Everest expeditions, Smythe found the experience of a small group refreshing, but once he reached the mountains he could not resist the urge to lace up his climbing boots and do some exciting climbs on the peaks surrounding the valley. He spent the time needed to acclimatize by examining and collecting plant specimens until the middle of July, then climbed Nilgiri Parbat (19,346 feet), declaring that it was the most beautiful peak he had ever seen and climbed. On 21 July, Smythe moved the expedition to an adjacent valley at the headwaters of the Ganges River, where they were joined by Capt. P. R. Oliver of the Indian Army. The two Britons attempted a few more peaks, namely Mana (23,866 feet), Nilkanta (21,645 feet), and Dunagiri (23,190 feet). Smythe climbed the first peak solo, but their efforts on the other two failed due to blizzards and difficulties with the routes. He then returned to the Valley of Flowers to collect more specimens, eventually bringing over 250 Himalayan plants back to Britain with him.

For the most part *The Valley of Flowers* is a factual, fast-paced, and exciting account. Smythe seems to be savoring every step and wants to share it with his readers, so he refrains from being unduly reflective of his surroundings. He does slip in a few passages that convey why he considered this trip the happiest holiday of his life and the fulfillment of a six-year dream. He says that he found beauty, health, comradeship, and peace in the Valley of Flowers. As he spent his last evening by the dying flames of the campfire, he wrote, "Everest, Kangchenjunga and Nanga Parbat are duties, but mountaineering in Garhwal is a pleasure, thank God." On his return to England from the Valley of Flowers in September 1937, Smythe devoted the next year to his writing and paid a short visit to the Alps in the spring of 1939, before World War II put an end to any more trips.

From 1938 to 1946 Smythe published twelve books, four of which were volumes of photographs. The first to appear was his second collection of mountain photographs, *Peaks and Valleys* (1938). It has seventy-six photographs arranged in two sections. The first section, called "The European Alps," has thirteen rather dull black-and-white photographs. The second part of the book features sixty-three plates of Smythe's three early expeditions to the Indian Himalayas: to Kamet, the Valley of Flowers, and Dunagiri. As might be expected, Smythe included thirty-three pictures of his beloved Valley of Flowers. These pictures range from panoramic shots of the valley and its surrounding peaks to closeups of flowers, trees, villages, and camp scenes, but the most striking pictures in this section are the shots of Kamet and Dunagiri. In photographs such as "Kamet," "The South-west Ridge of Dunagiri," and "Nanda Devi from the 20,00 Feet Camp," Smythe gives his reader a very clear perspective of the difficult terrain a mountaineer has to overcome at high altitudes.

In the preface Smythe argues that photography is a far superior medium for capturing the beauty of the hills than painting. He says that "simplicity is the soul of beauty in any picture, and specially in mountain photographs." Whereas the artist can be selective about details in a painting, the photographer does not have that option and must cultivate simplicity in composing shots, or a potentially magnificent mountain view will result in a depressing picture. Smythe mentions his inability to use color in showing the true scale and depth of a scene, but he predicts that improvements in color photography would make black-and-white pictures a thing of the past. Smythe believed that if his pictures helped readers share happy days in the hills or experience the keen air of high mountain ridges and icy slopes and the companionship of the campfire, he would be well rewarded. The breathtaking photographs in *Peaks and Valleys* are accompanied by captions that describe Smythe's philosophy of the mountains. In the caption to the photograph "Vista in the Bhyundar Valley," he says, "Peacefulness was the supreme motif and it may be that the photograph, besides revealing a little of the beauty of 'The Valley of Flowers,' also conveys something of this most desirable of natural human qualities."

In *A Camera in the Hills* (1939), his next collection of mountain photographs, Smythe attempts to explain the principles of mountain photography. The book contains sixty-five photographs from his various trips in the European Alps. In a five-page introductory chapter, Smythe discusses a whole range of topics: cameras, lenses, film packs, filters, exposure, lens aperture, lighting, composition, printing, trimming, and enlarging. He also describes for the first time his miniature camera, a 14½-ounce Etui with a Zeiss-Tessar lens that used 2¼-by-3¼-inch film packs.

In the captions, as well as identifying the scene Smythe discusses some of the technical aspects he kept in mind before clicking the shutter. He also provides a log of the month, time of day, length of exposure, lens opening and filter he used, and a few general remarks on the quality of his effort. Some of the pictures, such as "Trees by a Frozen Stream," "Tree Study," "The Matterhorn from the Riffelalp," show that Smythe was a master in using light, shade, and composition to create a picture. Smythe's advice on mountain photography is valid even today in spite of the advances in camera and film technology.

After the two collections of photographs, Smythe's next book was *Edward Whymper* (1940), published after the outbreak of World War II. Smythe had been fascinated by Whymper, the man who conquered the Matterhorn in 1865, since childhood and consciously or not, he had been emulating Whymper ever since; thus it was not surprising that Smythe wrote a biography of his hero. In the preface Smythe acknowledges how Whymper had inspired him and declares his intention to reveal Whymper "not only as a mountaineer, explorer, artist and scientist, but as a man."

Describing Whymper's travels in the Alps and the Andes, Smythe says of Whymper that he was a lonely egotist whose attitudes and ideas changed little during his life: "He gained in experience and knowledge, yet his creative abilities remained on a

Camp 6 of the 1938 British Everest Expedition, with the Northeast Ridge in the background (photograph by Smythe, from British Mountaineers*)*

single plane. He needed a positive philosophy and someone to share it with; he had neither." Smythe alienated many in the British climbing establishment with his biography of Whymper. Ultimately, Smythe duplicated almost all of Whymper's excursions in the mountains, from the Alps to the Canadian Rockies. Even their attitudes toward climbing with guides, aloofness with fellow climbers, and a tendency to push themselves to the limit without consideration for their companions are remarkably similar. The only difference is that Smythe seems to have forced himself to develop a sustaining philosophy that gave him some comfort.

The Adventures of a Mountaineer (1940) is a volume in the series Traveller's Tales, published by J. M. Dent and Sons. Smythe explains in the first chapter that his purpose was to describe how and why he became a mountaineer. He believes that men sometimes want to escape from the cities and the cares of daily life to the beauty and solitude of simple living in the fresh air of the mountains. Mountaineering provides a good opportunity for exercising the body and the mind because it calls for physical effort, nerve and judgment, planning, anticipating danger, and responsibility to fellow climbers. Smythe uses the eleven chapters of *The Adventures of a Mountaineer* to describe every stage of his life as a climber, from the British hills to the Himalayas. Each chapter also includes a lesson in the basics of mountaineering, such as using a rope; developing a sense of judgment and ability to read the weather; understanding the need for perseverance and teamwork; coping with the realities of rivalries on big expeditions; and appreciating the advantages of small, alpine-style expeditions. He concludes with remarks on his experience of challenging the highest mountain in the world.

Apart from the climbing tips, Smythe makes some important observations on his sport. He discusses solo climbing and advises the novice climber to start with easy climbs under expert guidance before venturing out alone. He also emphasizes that young climbers should not tackle great peaks unless they have accumulated enough experience and confidence. Smythe believed that the art of climbing lay not only in reaching the summit but also in returning alive: "He who is destitute of experience may climb safely until confronted by an emergency; then lack of experience may result in a disaster." In the appendix Smythe provides his readers with a bibliography of books and films on mountaineering. *The Adventures of a Mountaineer* will fascinate any reader of travel literature. Though Smythe has been criticized by Adrian Lunn and other critics for overwriting in most of his books, that charge cannot be leveled against this book. Surprisingly, in chapter after chapter Smythe compresses his exploits, previously recounted in three-hundred-page books, into a few pages with great precision and detail.

Next came *Mountaineering Holiday* (1940), a description of Smythe's climbs in the French Alps in 1939. In the last week of July, Smythe left London with his partner, Jim Gavin, for France. Traveling by boat, train, *téléférique* (cable car), and motor coach, they made their way through Paris, Grenoble, and the Dauphiné Alps to La Bérarde, the starting point of their mountaineering holiday. On the way Smythe comments on the French customs officials and peculiarities of French customs regulations, contrasts the French and British railway systems, and applauds French cuisine but sneers at French restaurant decor. On the whole he considers "the French the least sentimental of all races and the greatest realists." Smythe describes his reaction to the mountains, attempting to explain his passion by relating it to the Buddhist philosophy that states that we go from life to life retaining not memory but instinctive knowledge.

My Alpine Album (1940) is a collection of photos that he says were published at the request of readers looking for relief from the war. As it was not possible to visit the high mountains due to the war in Europe, Smythe wanted to invoke happier days spent in the hills for his readers. Smythe believed that to appreciate the beauty of the mountains properly, a person must live in them throughout the four seasons. As he had had the opportunity to do just that, Smythe describes the change in the seasons, snow climbing, climbing techniques, and skiing. Forty-seven photographs are arranged in five sections: "The Eastern Alps," "The Central Alps," "The Bernese Oberland," "The Pennine Alps," and "The Range of Mont Blanc." Each section is introduced with an overview of his climbing in the various areas of the Alps during all four seasons. In a way, *My Alpine Album* can be considered a collection of the best excerpts from Smythe's earlier books describing his exploits in the Alps. Some of the plates may also be familiar to readers because they appeared in other books. Smythe injects some new interest by talking about climbing routes and the technical aspects of photography. A haunting photograph is number thirty-two, "The Matterhorn and the Riffelhorn." From the angle that Smythe took the photo, the Riffelhorn looks strikingly similar to the Matterhorn, which appears to be rising behind it from the mists.

In 1941 Smythe married Nona Miller, a New Zealander. By all accounts this second marriage was happy, and Nona frequently traveled with him, acting as base camp manager and also doing a little climbing. During the war Smythe's experience as a mountaineer resulted in his being sent to Canada in 1943 to select sites for training mountain troops. Though he did not do any climbing, he traveled extensively by car, train, and airplane across a vast area of the Canadian Rockies and Alaska. He used the knowledge gained from this trip to plan his postwar trips to the mountains of Canada.

In 1941 Smythe published *The Mountain Vision* with the cryptic dedication "To 'N,'" a public acknowledgment of his new wife, Nona. In the twenty-three short chapters of the book, he explains what mountains mean to him as a climber. He considers himself fortunate to have climbed in the Himalayas, the Alps, and the British hills because by doing that he had ventured to the very heights of heaven. Each chapter illustrates an aspect of the hills or the mountains. For instance, chapter 2, "The Enjoyment of Mountain Scenery," explains how mountain travelers can become a part of the beauty around them. Chapter 7, "Mountain Peoples," gives thumbnail sketches of the locals in the Swiss Alps, the Himalayan foothills, and the Tibetan Plateau. Some of the chapters, with titles such as "Mount Everest," "Fear," "The Beauty of Flowers," "Clouds," and "Starry Nights," are self-explanatory. On the whole *The Mountain Vision* abounds with information about peaks, climbers, first ascents, accidents, loyal Sherpas, and various incidents from the author's own climbs, but Smythe's evocation of the scenes and his reactions to them are subjective and may have led to the charge that he was trying to create a romantic philosophy of the mountains.

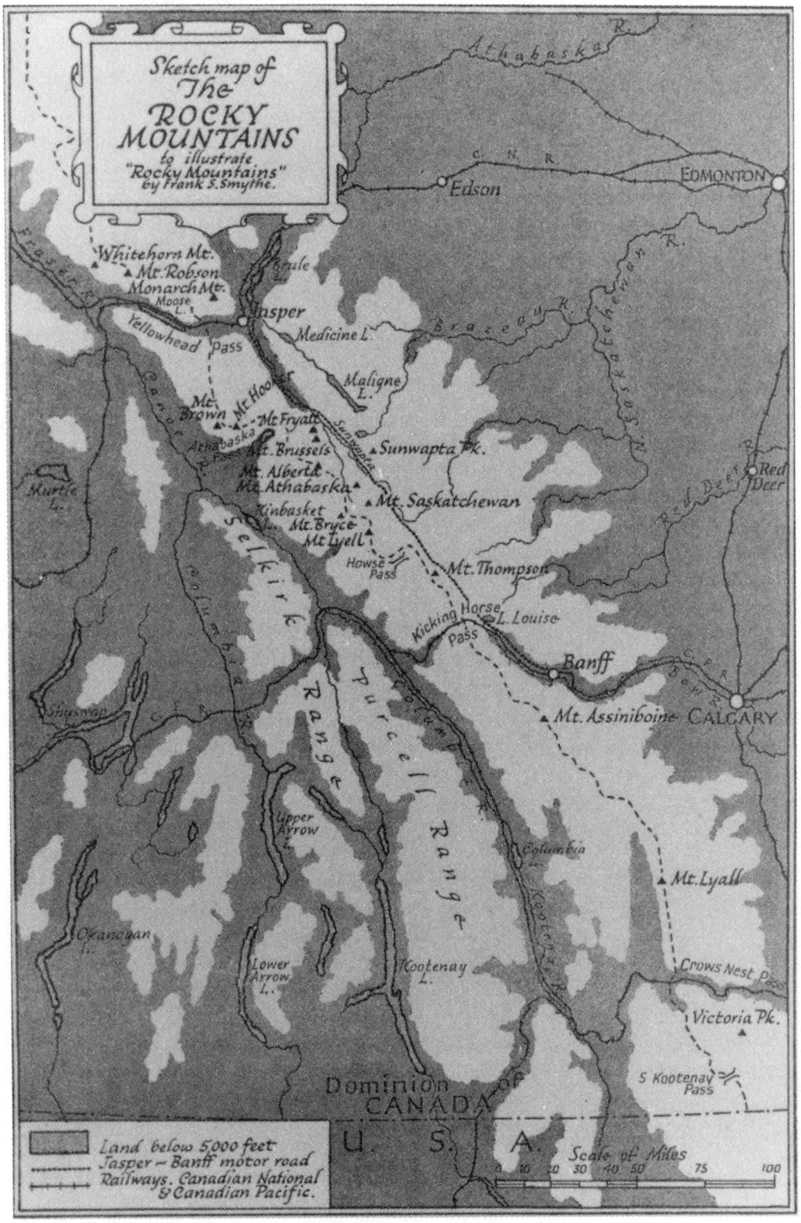

Map of routes Smythe followed in 1946 and 1947 travels in the Canadian Rockies (from Rocky Mountains, *1948)*

Over Welsh Hills (1941) is another wartime book, and it reflects Smythe's irritation at not being able to climb in the Alps or the Himalayas. Instead he is forced to stomp through the hills of Britain and chooses the hills around Snowdon in northern Wales. Curiously enough, in the introduction he discusses his dislike and disdain for the Welsh people for being "welshers," who had charged him five shillings for a sandwich and a synthetic lemonade when he first went there as a fourteen-year-old. Despite his contempt for the Welsh people, he tries to build up the Welsh hills as a respectable area for climbing, remarking that even hills look impressive when they are covered with snow. Smythe also contends that the winds on Welsh hills can be as vicious as those that keep the plume streaming from the summit of Mount Everest.

The book includes fifty-one photographs of Snowdon and surrounding hills. The narrative lacks the excitement of Smythe's descriptions of climbing high mountains but shows Smythe's flair for travel writing. The descriptions of the actual tramps are mundane, but the details about the small villages, the comfort of the inns, hearty breakfasts and other meals draw a picture of a leisurely trip that gave him some satisfaction. Smythe says, "In the British hills a man can rise at a Christian hour, leisurely bathe and dress himself, and tuck away, in peacetime at all events, a substantial breakfast of bacon and eggs, toast, butter, and marmalade before setting forth on his climb." At the end of the book, Smythe the photographer has some tips on how to take better pictures in the moisture-laden atmosphere of the British Isles. As a travel writer Smythe could make even an uneventful excursion engaging to his readers, and the book shows that his commitment to climbing was such that when he could not climb the high mountains, he found pleasure even in the low hills.

British Mountaineers (1942) is the twenty-second volume of a series called Britain in Pictures that attempted to provide an overview of the various facets of British life, literature, and pastimes. Smythe's book was meant to give readers who were not themselves mountaineers a vivid firsthand account of a climber's actual experience. In fact *British Mountaineers* is an incisive history of the development of mountaineering as a sport from the beginning of the eighteenth century to 1941. Smythe genuinely believed that Englishmen were responsible both for the great sport of mountaineering and for opening up the difficult climbing areas in the Alps, Rockies, New Zealand, and Himalayas. The narrative focuses on the exploits of British climbers in three distinct periods. The first period deals with the beginning of the sport in Europe and the exploits of such pioneers as J. D. Forbes, John Ball, Albert Smith, Leslie Stephen, and Whymper and ends with the conquest of the Matterhorn in 1865.

The second period deals with the decline in mountaineering due to the bad publicity from the Matterhorn disaster, when four of the seven climbers who had reached the summit died during the descent, and describes a rejuvenation of the sport in the Himalayas, Andes, Canada, and New Zealand due to the exploits of men such as American William A. B. Coolidge, the first man to make a winter ascent of the Jungfrau in 1874, and the British "prince of rock climbing," Albert F. Mummery, who perished in the first attempt to climb Nanga Parbat in 1895. Smythe calls this second period, which lasted until the end of the nineteenth century, the "Golden Age" of mountaineering. The third and last stage deals mainly with contemporary developments in mountaineering in the Himalayas on such peaks as Everest, Kangchenjunga, K2, Nanga Parbat, Kamet, and Nanda Devi. Smythe discusses the difficulties caused by altitude, logistics, and weather in the high Himalayas. He also reviews the various unsuccessful attempts made on these peaks by such well-known climbers of the 1920s and 1930s as T. G. Longstaff, C. F. Meade, Somervell, Norton, Shipton, George Leigh-Mallory, Noel E. Odell, and himself.

In the concluding chapter Smythe analyzes the progress of mountaineering after World War I. He mentions the national rivalries and jealousies that had begun to plague the sport of climbing and is particularly harsh on the Germans, whose nationalistic insecurities led them to make desperate assaults on the Himalayan giants and brought about the worst mountaineering disaster ever in 1937, when seven German climbers and nine porters were buried by an avalanche on Nanga Parbat. Smythe ends with a word of caution on technical developments in climbing. He feels that climbing with oxygen or using pitons is cheating and hopes that future generations will remember that the charm of mountaineering lies in the use of skill and energy with the minimum of artificial aid. He also hopes that future international rivalries "will help to promote the best and not bring out the worst in men."

Alpine Ways (1942) is another collection of photographs to take readers who like to walk, ski, and climb on a visual tour of the European Alps during World War II, when these areas were off limits due to what Smythe calls "the foul plague of Naziism." In the introduction he disagrees with John Ruskin's comment that mountains are best viewed from below. He also criticizes those individuals who rush from one summit to another, notching up conquests on their ice axes. According to Smythe the best way to enjoy the mountains is by walking, climbing, and stopping to enjoy the views.

The forty-seven photos with titles such as "Reflections: In the Reichen Range," "Misty Window," "Wind Crust," and "Mountain Marigolds" show the depth of Smythe's portfolio. Though a few of the half-dozen views of the Matterhorn had been published in earlier books, the photographs show Smythe's skill in using various features of mountain scenery to compose his shots. Captions furnish additional information on the climbing history of the mountain depicted and technical photographic details. Above all, the pictures demonstrate Smythe's almost mystical view of the Alps: "that there is no nobler contrast between the pastoral and the sublime in all Europe than this, nowhere a closer intimacy between the savage and the gentle, between sterility and fertility."

Snow on the Hills (1946) is a coffee-table book, a collection of forty-seven of Smythe's best pictures with descriptive comments and hints on photographic techniques. In the opening chapter Smythe candidly berates the British for their historical apa-

Nona Smythe and guide, Bruno Engler, in the Rocky Mountains, 1946 (photograph by Smythe from Rocky Mountains*)*

thy to the mountains and snow. He remarks that "snow finds little mention in English Literature and only a fortuitous place in the art up to the end of the eighteenth century." Only toward the middle of the nineteenth century did a change take place as writers and poets began to look toward the mountains and hills for inspiration.

However, Smythe found comfort in the fact that the mountains had a greater influence on people in India, and he says in a caption to one of the photographs that "All mountaineers before they die should travel and climb in Garhwal and Kumaon. True, the valleys are hot and fly ridden, but to stroll over the foothill ridges is sheer joy." He mentions how he felt as he watched the sun rise over the Himalayas from his bed on the veranda of the rest house in Ranikhet and remembered the Hindu saying, "As the dew is dried by the morning sun so are the sins of man by the sight of Himachal. In a thousand ages the gods could not tell thee of the glories of Himachal."

The plates are arranged in four sections titled "The British Hills," "The Alps," "The Canadian Rockies," and "The Himalayas." Some of these pictures had appeared in earlier books, but there are a few, such as those of Mount Robson, Mount McKinley, and views from high on Everest, that are new and exciting, especially the aerial views of Mount Robson and Mount McKinley. They show that Smythe was as good with a camera when he was flying over a mountain as he was when standing on it. The plates of Mount Robson reveal the three faces of the mountain, and together with Smythe's comments they give prospective climbers a clear choice of possible routes to the summit.

In *Again Switzerland* (1947) Smythe describes his return to the mountains in February 1946, after World War II. He considers himself lucky to have escaped the dreary English winter by traveling to the sunshine and snow of Switzerland. Smythe's plan was to traverse the Oberland glaciers from west to east in one trek but bad weather, and poor health forced him to complete this trip in three attempts. Realizing the dangers of crossing glaciers alone, Smythe hired a guide for only the second occasion in his career, having always preferred to travel alone. The first attempt began at Adelboden and lasted only a few days in the nearby ridges. Bad weather and poor health hampered the party's progress, and limited funds due to postwar exchange controls forced Smythe to let his guide go. He then traveled by rail and motor coach to Münster and proceeded in a southeasterly direction toward Goppenstein. On the way he crossed the Galmi, Fiescher, Hugisattel, Fruhstuckplatz, Grunhornlucke, Aletschfirn, Lötschenlucke, Langgletscher, and Lötschental glaciers. Next he moved on to Verbier and teamed up with two others to complete the Haute Route, the classic ski traverse of the Alps. Trips of the type described in *Again Switzerland* are, according to Calvert in *Smythe's Mountains,* "The bread and butter of the average alpinist but they were not for that reason, any the less delectable to Smythe," who found them more fulfilling than his efforts on the "great route."

Again Switzerland reveals that the war had not dulled Smythe's abilities to add color and character to his narratives. In the opening chapter he gives us a graphic preview of modern-day travel as he describes customs and passport checks, aluminum-sheathed airplanes, dark-suited business travelers, stewardesses with blonde untidy hair, the ice crystals building up along the leading edges of the plane's wings, and the deicer sliding out to dislodge them. In the next chapter Smythe makes some unflattering comparisons between English and Swiss hotels. According to him most British provincial hotels are chilly, unfriendly, and barracklike, the food ordinary, and the innkeepers callous. On the other hand even the remotest Swiss hotels are cozy and comfortably furnished; the food is excellent; and the hoteliers are concerned about the immediate material welfare of their guests. The hoteliers are also men of culture, sound taste, and good education. The book contains the usual collection of photographs but with a slight difference: Smythe seems to have incorporated more people in his pictures and even includes a rare photo of himself with a friend having lunch outside the Cabane du Val des Dix.

The Mountain Top was also published in 1947. The book is, according to its subtitle, "an illustrated anthology of the prose and pictures of Frank S. Smythe." It is a forty-five-page, pocket-size selection of passages from *The Mountain Vision* and *The Spirit of the Hills* and photographs from Smythe's previous books. *The Mountain Top* is a good primer for anyone who wishes to get an overview of the author's philosophy of the hills.

Swiss Winter (1948) is another postwar collection of Smythe's pictures. Because of the advances in photography and due to his links with Kodak, Smythe was able to experiment with color film. The book does not deal with any specific climbs but with climbing and skiing in general. In the introduction Smythe explains why people travel to Switzerland. He firmly believes that the Swiss were too relaxed to exploit the bounty that nature had bestowed upon them. It was left to other Europeans, led by the British, who travel to broaden their horizons and are fascinated by the mountains, climbing, and other winter sports, to exploit and popularize travel in Switzerland.

The introduction also has an account of the history and development of skiing as a sport. Smythe mentions that early historians wrote about "Skridfinnar," or "gliding Finns," who hunted on pieces of wood curved like a bow. The early skiers glided and twisted around the bases of rocks, continually swerving from side to side. Some even covered their wooden boards with reindeer skin, but most of these early skiers took to their boards solely for the utilitarian purpose of traveling across difficult terrain, and skiing developed as a cross-country activity. The thrill and glamour of downhill runs were first brought to the Swiss Alps by Britons, who then helped develop it into a sport.

The fifty-six plates reveal Smythe's mastery of mountain photography and growing admiration for color film though he is not sure of its artistic merits. His advice is that to use color effectively the photographer must look primarily for colorful subjects and then compose the picture. Readers would find a good example in plate 42, a telephoto shot of the Matterhorn with the clock tower of the church at Zermatt in the lower right foreground. The picture also shows Whymper's route and the place where the disaster occurred in 1865. Smythe could not help commenting that too many people attempt the Matterhorn, and therefore the mountain has a long and melancholy list of victims who were inexperienced and incompetent climbers.

The postwar return to the Alps was followed by two successful and elaborate trips to the Rocky Mountains of Canada described in *Rocky Mountains* (1948) and *Climbs in the Canadian Rockies* (1950). *Rocky Mountains* combines a description of Smythe's wartime assignment in Canada in 1943 to select training sites for British commandos and a narrative of his subsequent return to Canada, accompanied by his wife Nona, on climbing tours in 1946 and 1947. Smythe was impressed by the vastness of the Canadian Rockies, where people thought nothing of traveling two hundred miles by car. He believed that the mountaineer in the Rockies would have to be first and last a traveler. He advised the climber to not concentrate on one particular district or follow the standard routes described in guidebooks but to travel around as much as possible, as there was still scope for pioneering. In view of the large and unexplored areas of the country, Smythe promptly adapted his travel plans to use amphibious aircraft that were cheaper than pack animals, and he was able to see more places and take more pictures, some of them from the air.

David Wessel, Smythe's climbing partner on the summit of Mount Hungabee, 1946 (photograph by Smythe, from Rocky Mountains*)*

The sixty-four plates show the best that Canada has to offer in Banff, Jasper, Mount Assiniboine, and Mount Robson. Smythe discusses the benefits of traveling by train and car, the comfort level of hotels and lodges, the discomfort from mosquitoes and flies, and the vagaries of the weather. But the pictures are meant only to whet the reader's appetites, which were satisfied subsequently in *Climbs in the Canadian Rockies,* Smythe's last book, published just after his death. It provides the narrative for the pictures that were earlier published in *Rocky Mountains.* In the first chapter of *Climbs in the Canadian Rockies,* Smythe gives a long overview of the geology, climate, flora, and fauna of the Rockies. In the next chapter he describes his wartime experience training soldiers for mountain warfare. Though he did not do any climbing, he flew over Mount Alberta, Mount Robson, and Mount McKinley. From chapter 3 the narrative moves on to his subsequent return visits to Canada. The first one came in 1946, when he was accompanied by his wife, Nona. With their guide, Bruno Engler, and a pack train, the Smythes started out from Jasper and explored the Victoria Cross Range, crossing passes and climbing minor peaks until they reached Lake O'Hara. There Smythe teamed up with a Mr. and Mrs. Gardiner to climb Mount Victoria. Later, Rex Gibson and David Wessel, a young American, joined the group, and they attempted to climb Mount Assiniboine, Mount Brussels, Mount Christie, and finally Mount Robson, which they failed to climb due to poor snow conditions and bad weather. That ended the 1946 trip.

In June 1947 the Smythes returned with the idea of mounting a small expedition to an unknown part of the Rockies north of Jasper. The group consisted of Smythe, Nona, Gibson, Wessel, Henry Hall, and Noel Odell, and it completed a long exploration of the Lloyd George Mountains. Apart from the wealth of information and pioneering effort on the lesser-known section of the Canadian Rockies, *Climbs in the Canadian Rockies* provides a glimpse of Smythe's ambivalence toward climbing gear. Though he had no compunction about using crampons, ropes, and boots with gripping soles, he strongly disapproved of using pitons and other similar climbing aids. He refused to accept credit for the party's ascent of Mount Colin because he had used a piton to protect himself and his rope mates on the crux section of the climb.

Mountains in Colour (1949) is Smythe's only collection of color photographs, and the accompanying text provides a complete overview of all his climbs in mountains on three continents. The book is divided into four sections–"The Himalayas," "The British Hills," "Switzerland," and "The Mountains and Hills of North America"–and has fifty-seven color photographs. This book is also dedicated to Nona, who had accompanied him and helped with the photography of many scenes in this book. The importance of *Mountains in Colour* is that here, almost at the end of his life, Smythe succinctly provides his readers with a summary of his various exploits. Granted that he leaves out much of the detail, but he traces his experiences with mountains, hills, and people in a manner that would entice the reader to sample his other books. The section on the Himalayas concentrates on his first Everest expedition in 1933, but it also gives a fascinating account of the history and progress of climbing in the mountains of India and Nepal, with glimpses into the lives and legends of the Sherpas and Tibetans.

The second section describes the British hills, with the focus on Ben Nevis, Snowdonia, and the Lake District. Smythe has fond memories of the hills and dales where he first reached high places. The third chapter deals with his visits to the European Alps. He describes his early rambles as a sick child and his initiation into photography by his stepsister, who gave him his first camera, a Kodak Brownie, which became one of his most cherished possessions. This section is dominated by a discussion of climbing the Matterhorn and the career of his hero Edward Whymper. The last section deals with Smythe's postwar climbs in the Canadian Rockies and ends with his visit to the hills of New England. Smythe concludes with an appeal to his American friends to lead the world into the same kind of peace and prosperity that they have themselves enjoyed for so long.

At last in 1949 Smythe once again got away to India with plans of revisiting the Valley of Flowers and climbing in other parts of the subcontinent. In May he reached Darjeeling and was reunited with some of his old Sherpas, including Tenzing Norgkay (later one of the first men to conquer Everest), whom he had befriended on his last Everest expedition. While they were making preparations, Tenzing noticed that Smythe was having difficulties with his memory. He kept forgetting his name, where he was, or what month it was. While walking in the streets, he asked for his ice ax although there was no snow. He became delirious and was rushed to a hospital in Calcutta. From there he was flown to England and hospitalized in Uxbridge, where he kept rambling about the mountains and his climbs. He died suddenly on 27 July 1949.

In spite of his many books and articles, Smythe never attempted a thorough assessment of his career as a mountaineer, but there is no doubt that he followed in the footsteps of Whymper, Mummery, and Mallory, a tradition he in turn passed on to others. He was a self-taught climber who was not among the best as a rock climber but who excelled on ice and snow, seeming to flourish as he gained altitude. Smythe was an excellent photographer and is considered by many to be one of the all-time best British mountain photographers.

Though the critics generally agree on how they rate Smythe as a mountaineer and photographer, there are conflicting judgments on the quality of his writing. Some, such as Adrian Lunn, criticize Smythe for churning out so many books in such a short time. Others, such as Raymond Greene, feel he should be commended for bringing a love of the mountains to people who would not have otherwise known it. His attempts to explain his own love of mountains led to what some critics have called a romantic philosophy or religion of the mountains, a philosophy that many readers have found somewhat silly. It is worth remembering that even today the leading climbers cannot explain what it is that drives them repeatedly into the mountain. Throughout his career Smythe was motivated to write about his love for high places, not only to support his climbing but also to share his passion with others; his remark in the opening of *The Adventures of a Mountaineer* can apply to any of his works: "if this book is instrumental in bringing you to the mountains I shall feel well rewarded for having written it."

Biography:

Harry Calvert, *Smythe's Mountains: The Climbs of F. S. Smythe* (London: Victor Gollancz, 1985).

References:

J. H. B. Bell, *A Progress in Mountaineering* (London: Oliver & Boyd, 1950), pp. 150–154, 159, 179–184;

Eric Shipton, *Upon That Mountain* (London: Hodder & Stoughton, 1943), pp. 184–188.

Freya Stark

(31 January 1893 - 9 May 1993)

John C. Hawley
Santa Clara University

BOOKS: *Baghdad Sketches* (Baghdad: Times Press, 1932; enlarged edition, London: Murray, 1937; New York: Dutton, 1938);

The Valleys of the Assassins and Other Persian Travels (London: Murray, 1934; New York: Dutton, 1934);

The Southern Gates of Arabia: A Journey in the Hadhramaut (London: Murray, 1936; New York: Dutton, 1936);

Seen in the Hadhramaut (London: Murray, 1938; New York: Dutton, 1939);

A Winter in Arabia (London: Murray, 1940; New York: Dutton, 1940);

Letters from Syria (London: Murray, 1942);

East Is West (London: Murray, 1945); republished as *The Arab Island: The Middle East, 1939-1943* (New York: Knopf, 1945);

Perseus in the Wind (London: Murray, 1948; Boston: Beacon, 1956);

Traveller's Prelude (London: Murray, 1950);

Beyond Euphrates: Autobiography, 1928-1933 (London: Murray, 1951);

The Coast of Incense: Autobiography, 1933-1939 (London: Murray, 1953);

The Freya Stark Story (New York: Coward-McCann, 1953)–abridgement of *Traveller's Prelude, Beyond Euphrates,* and *The Coast of Incense*;

Ionia: A Quest (London: Murray, 1954; New York: Harcourt, Brace, 1954);

The Lycian Shore (London: Murray, 1956; New York: Harcourt, Brace, 1956);

Alexander's Path: From Caria to Cilicia (London: Murray, 1958; New York: Harcourt, Brace, 1958);

Riding to the Tigris (London: Murray, 1959; New York: Harcourt, Brace, 1960);

Dust in the Lion's Paw: Autobiography, 1939-1946 (London: Murray, 1961; New York: Harcourt, Brace & World, 1962);

The Journey's Echo: Selections (London: Murray, 1963; New York: Harcourt, Brace & World, 1964);

Freya Stark

Rome on the Euphrates: The Story of a Frontier (London: Murray, 1966; New York: Harcourt, Brace & World, 1967);

The Zodiac Arch (London: Murray, 1968; New York: Harcourt, Brace & World, 1969);

Space, Time & Movement in Landscape (London: Her Godson, 1969);

The Minaret of Djam: An Excursion to Afghanistan (London: Murray, 1970);

Turkey: A Sketch of Turkish History, text by Stark and photographs by Fulvio Roiter (London:

Thames & Hudson, 1971); republished as *Gateways and Caravans: A Portrait of Turkey* (New York: Macmillan, 1971);

A Peak in Darien (London: Murray, 1976);

Rivers of Time (Edinburgh: Blackwood, 1982);

Freya Stark in Asolo (Asolo: Magnifica Comunità Pedemontana dal Piave al Brenta, 1984).

Freya Madeline Stark lived for a century, and into that one hundred years she packed a life of extraordinary daring and ingenuity. "Personally I would rather feel wrong with everybody else than right all by myself," she wrote in *Baghdad Sketches* (enlarged edition, 1937); "I like people different, and agree with the man who said that the worst of the human race is the number of duplicates." Such a motto defines not only her approach to the world but also the character of the woman herself. She had no duplicate. The writings that resulted from her constant travels began as wonder-filled accounts of ancient storybook kingdoms of the Middle East and moved impressively toward a reflective consideration of the differences between a nomadic way of life and the stable urbanity that might have been her lot if she had decided to fit the mold of those around her. In these accounts of her own transformation she brought a growing body of readers not only into exotic locales but also to the brink of metaphysical questions about the meaning of life.

Eventually fluent in French, Latin, German, Italian, Arabic, Persian, and Turkish, Stark had written more than two dozen travel books by the time of her death. She had been awarded a Royal Geographical Society Back Grant in 1933 for her travels in Lorestan (the second woman to be so honored), the Burton Memorial Medal of the Royal Asiatic Society in 1934 (the first woman to receive this award), the Royal Geographical Society Founder's Medal in 1942, the Mazzoti Prize for books of exploration, and an honorary doctorate from Glasgow University. She was named Dame of the British Empire in 1972 and was presented the keys to her adopted hometown of Asolo, Italy, in 1984.

As a rule Stark traveled only with a guide or a small party of people, and she was frequently the first Western European woman to venture into many of the locales she described in her books. She has often been compared to Gertrude Bell, another Arabist, but there are differences between the two women. Bell had far greater wealth to support her travels, and she eventually became one of the most powerful women in the British Empire. Stark told friends that Bell was comparatively soft, bringing along servants and lots of baggage and, in Stark's view, never staying in any one place long enough to soak up the local color. Stark relished the sense of having overcome personal obstacles and cultural differences and of having been accepted, after much hard work, by a wide variety of ethnic groups.

A comparison of Stark and Bell would prompt many to favor Stark's assessment of the two women. Whereas Bell seemed hardy, Stark (despite her amazing longevity) was prone to illness. While sharing tents with Bedouin sheiks, traveling through deserts on camel, or living in harems (and taking some of the first photographs of the women with whom she resided), Stark had a constitution that did not seem suited to a traveler. In the first place, she was born two months prematurely. At the age of twenty-two she developed typhoid, pleurisy, and pneumonia. She soon discovered that she had a gastric ulcer. In the course of her journeys she suffered from dysentery, malaria, measles, a weakened heart, dengue fever, and appendicitis. A less determined traveler would surely have retired to her quiet hearth–but not Stark.

As she moved from one country and civilization to the next, from one language to the next, Stark seemed willing and eager to redefine herself and slip into the new world she would be encountering. The consequence of this chameleon character shows itself in the difficulty of categorizing her vocation: she was a travel writer first and foremost but also an historian, an archaeologist, a fine photographer, and, some would say, finally a philosopher, a pioneer in cultural studies and anthropology.

Freya Stark was born in Paris on 31 January 1893, the first surviving child of Robert and Flora Stark, who had been married for thirteen years. The marriage of Stark's parents, who were first cousins, was not a happy one. During Stark's early childhood the family lived in Devon, but in 1901 Flora Stark took Freya and her younger sister, Vera, to live in Asolo, Italy, in the foothills of the Dolomites. Two years later they moved to Dronero, a town in Piedmont. Robert Stark stayed behind in Devon. Flora Stark's connection to Italy had been through her mother, who had lived in Genoa and had entertained such British luminaries as the Trollopes, the Thackerays, and the Brownings. Having been raised in Italy, Flora Stark, who was an artist, had been uncomfortable with the Victorian British ways to which her husband introduced her in England. Like his wife, Robert Stark was a painter, but his principal training was as a sculptor. Freya Stark later said that she inherited from her father a sense of honesty and from her mother a sense of vitality. Her relationship with her mother remained possibly the closest of her life, and she continued writing to her regularly, once a week, until her mother died in

1942. The first letter in Stark's collected letters, written in 1914 when she was just twenty-one, is to her mother and asks, "have we not been growing nearer and nearer? When we go to the next world I hope St. Peter will not know which is which."

When the family moved from Asolo to Dronero, it was because Flora Stark had become involved with Count Mario di Roascio, who was starting a carpet business, which she had helped to finance. One day while walking in the factory Freya Stark caught her hair in one of the looms and was dragged around the wheel. Half her scalp was torn out, and she was in the hospital for four months while skin grafting took place. After the accident she viewed herself as physically unattractive, and for the rest of her life she always wore hats to disguise the side of her face that had been affected.

In 1908 Stark moved to London and began attending W. P. Ker's lectures in English literature at London University. Ker, who was later named professor of poetry at Oxford University, became her first mentor and a lifelong friend. Her major subject was history rather than literature, however, because she had decided that she wanted to spend her life delving into the real world. During World War I she did so by serving as a nurse in Bologna. There she met Guido Ruata, with whom she fell in love and became engaged. Several months later he broke off the engagement because his earlier lover had returned from America. Then, in 1926, Vera Stark died. Freya Stark later saw these two events as the greatest losses of her life. About this time she again took up her studies of Arabic and the Koran, which she had begun in Italy in 1921. She studied first with an Egyptian teacher in London and then at the School of Oriental Studies in 1927. On 18 November 1927, just one year after her sister's death, Stark set off for Beirut. She was thirty-four, and her creative life had finally begun.

From the beginning Stark was fascinated by what she saw, and she slipped into a pattern that was to mark all her travels. She often proceeded on foot, leisurely absorbing the sights and smells and listening carefully. In her stumbling conversations in Arabic she presented herself as a student rather than as one of the typical British women who were generally married to administrators and remained aloof in the colonial compound. Because Stark did not want to be insulated from the roughness of the life around her, she became something of a concern to British authorities, who saw her as having remarkable–possibly reckless–pluck. Though she approved of the goals of the British Empire, she did not see the need to be bound by patriarchal concerns that would have preferred her to spend her days having tea parties, nor did she intend to limit her investigations to those areas that had been visited already by western women. In April she moved to Damascus. After seven months she returned to Europe, having written letters that were eventually published as *Letters from Syria* (1942). In retrospect this account of Stark's first journey east of Italy and her first contact with the Near East has a simple touristic quality in its observations, lacking most of the philosophical reflections that characterize her more polished works. Her first impression of Antioch, for example, was of "a population all suffering from toothache and nothing like the dignified turban of the *Arabian Nights;* but it is the *Arabian Nights* all the same."

Stark in 1928

On this first journey Stark studied Arabic for three months at Brummana, a Syrian village on a slope of the Lebanon Mountains high above Beirut. For a month she lived in a native household in the Muslim quarter of Damascus, where she became sick because of insanitary conditions. She wrote to her mother on 4 April 1928:

> These well-bred Moslems are very agreeable, and just as easy to get on with as well-bred people the world over. Of course, one cannot become intimate unless one

> knows enough of their civilisation to be able to see from their angle. . . . I have long thought of Mohammedanism as one form of Protestantism and far nearer to the spirit of Protestantism than the forms of Christianity here. He [Stark's Muslim host] is convinced that the Koran is superior to the Bible, just as he is convinced that Arabic poetry is superior to the literatures of Europe. This is all interesting in someone who has been in the hands of the missionaries for the *whole* of his education.

Stark was joined in Damascus by her friend Venetia Buddicom, and the two proceeded by car to Baalbek. Their next expedition, in May 1928, was unconventional and adventurous. After the Druse revolt, which had begun in August 1925 and continued until March 1927, the French rulers of Syria were not welcoming intruders, but the two women mounted donkeys, and with a Druse guide called Najm they made a leisurely progress toward Palestine. At the end of eleven days they were at Bosra, where they dismissed their guide and took a car for Jericho and Jerusalem. "I have been received with great friendliness," Stark wrote, "and the village is doing its best to teach me–only too pleased to find someone who has come neither to improve nor to rob, but with a genuine liking for their language." The narrative also includes the sorts of judgments that appear frequently in her mature writing: "Religion is a delicate point," she recorded.

> Now that she [Stark's hostess] realizes I don't want to turn people into Presbyterians, or anything else for that matter, it is all coming out: all the bottled-up feelings since the time when her brother turned Quaker and she came into contact with all the People who Think They Know Better: and never said anything, but just (I believe) hated them more and more. These people never contradict: they listen politely while the convinced missionary goes blundering on–annoyed afterwards that they 'turn around.' But I believe the fact is that they don't 'turn around.' They have simply *never turned at all:* only their politeness is never to say *No* when an Englishman would say so: in fact to say *Yes.*

Nevertheless she warmed to the people and her experiences.

Finally reaching the end of this first journey–and without a sense of all the travel that still lies ahead in her life–the novice gives voice to the simple exhaustion of it all and even the pride of accomplishment. Coming upon the relative comforts of Jerusalem, she remarked,

> How good it has all been: the discomforts vanish, at least from *active* memory; and the loveliness of it all remains and grows. And the joy is that I have been able to do it after all, and the silly old body has really played up rather well considering.

She was thirty-five when she wrote these words.

It was not just the people that fascinated Stark. The landscape itself seems to have had a kind of primal effect on her. On 7 April 1928 she wrote to Robert Browning's son, Pen:

> Yesterday was a wonderful day: for I discovered the Desert! . . . I can't tell you what a wonderful sight it was: as if one were suddenly in the very morning of the world among the people of Abraham or Jacob. . . . I stood in a kind of ecstasy among them. It seemed as if they were not so much moving as flowing along, with something indescribably fresh and peaceful and free about it all, as if the struggle of all these thousands of years had never been, since first they started wandering. I never imagined that my first sight of the desert would come with such a shock of beauty and enslave me right away.

In the fall of 1929 Stark went to Baghdad. Rather than living in the British compound, she stayed with a shoemaker's family in a section of the city that turned out to be in the middle of the prostitutes' quarter. It is not surprising that she wrote to her mother in 1930 that "what one misses here is that the beautiful things are so rarely in beautiful settings: it is almost impossible to feel satisfied, as one does in Italy: always there is a jarring or sordid or cruel touch somewhere. And yet it is indescribably fascinating."

From Baghdad she set out on her first exploratory journey into the area between Iraq and Persia (now Iran) known as Luristan (Lorestan). On this trip, which lasted from April 1930 until October 1931, she intended to visit the castles left behind by the Assassins, a Persian sect of Shia Muslims that flourished in the late eleventh century. The results of her trip were not entirely successful, but she found the experience exhilarating. The British who stayed behind in Baghdad and scoffed at this eccentric lady learned that Stark was a woman with whom they would have to reckon.

Stark's greatest gifts as a travel writer were her capacity to empathize with the people she visited and view her own culture from "within" that of another and to offer the harsh criticism that her hosts might have felt but might not have found the words to express. She addressed this point in her 6 May 1930 letter to her mother:

> Once again I was right and the experts who have been years out here, wrong: they told me the Koran was *no* use now for getting into touch with people. If I had not known the Koran and been able to talk to the old man

> from his own standpoint, he would never have started all these tales. The Koran has been their one source of inspiration for centuries: it is their background–and however Europeanized they may be, one is sure to get nearer to them *really* if one comes at them from behind as it were, through the things they knew as children, or that their parents and nurses knew, than if one comes through the medium of a new civilisation which means something quite different to them than it means to us. When I take the old Mullah's standpoint, I know where I am and what to expect; when I take a European standpoint with a 'civilised' Oriental, I can never know where I am, for I have no means of judging what 'European' means to him: it is certainly not what it means to us.

The trick, of course, was to learn enough to be able to "take the old Mullah's standpoint," and Stark seems to have been unusually capable in this regard.

Stark's writing career began when Duncan Cameron, an editor of the *Baghdad Times,* asked her to continue her explorations and to write about them. She worked at the job for a year and subsequently collected her newspaper reports in *Baghdad Sketches,* published in Baghdad in 1932 and enlarged for publication in England in 1937. At this point in her writing her narrative voice seems to be that of an ambivalent Western traveler who wishes to be the last one inside the gate before the native culture locked out all contaminating foreign influence:

> Whether these Western floods, to which all her sluices are open, come to the East for baptism or drowning, is hard to say. Total immersion in any case she is bound to submit to and we–who love the creature–wait with some misgiving to see in what condition her regenerated head will reappear above the waters; we stand upon the shore and collect such oddments as we find floating in chaos–her customs, religions, her clothes and trinkets and some, alas! of her virtues. We snatch them as they drift for ever out of sight, and encase them in an armour of words–and by so doing, not unhopeful of the future, yet wage our little losing battle against the fragilities of Time.

Stark knew that change would come, and in later writings she actually welcomed it in many respects. Yet her writings reveal her delight in the charms of a culture that was on the brink of transformation beyond recognition. This cementing of the past served as a principal function of her early writing, a function that she later criticized in others.

Cornhill Magazine also published some of Stark's reports on the Druses, which brought her to the attention of John Murray, who was her publisher for most of the rest of her lifetime. Her first contract with him was for *The Valleys of the Assassins and Other Persian Travels* (1934). She dedicated this first endeavor to Ker, who had died in 1923 while on a mountain-climbing expedition with her. The book has little of the reflective poetic language that characterizes Stark's late writing, but it does give some insight into the romantic quality that lay at the heart of her wanderlust. Her preface begins, "An imaginative aunt who, for my ninth birthday, sent me a copy of the *Arabian Nights,* was, I suppose, the original cause of trouble. . . . I must admit that for my own part I travelled single-mindedly for fun." As in her earlier letters from Syria, this reference to the *Arabian Nights* bespeaks her childlike expectations for the Arabic world, her hopes for a genie in a bottle, and her implicit quest for the magic flying carpet.

Stark's guide, Hujjat Allah, with her mule and saddle bags during the journey Stark described in The Valleys of the Assassins and Other Persian Travels *(1934)*

Yet her life in Asolo as a child of a mother with a somewhat dubious reputation and with constant concerns regarding finances also gave Stark what might be described as a Victorian sense of responsibility and purpose that, even in the midst of "fun," forced her to ask: "*Why* are you here alone? and *What* do you intend to *do?*" One thing became quite clear to her in this early outing: she was not simply a

A wedding in the Hadramawt region, photograph taken by Stark in 1935

tourist. She thought, perhaps, that she had a mission. As she wrote to a young fan in 1980, "One should have a quest of one's own–history, literature, photography, anything like a pursuit to give an added reason and interest for travel."

Stark returned to London in 1933, spoke on BBC radio, and became friends with Lord David Cecil and Sir Sydney Cockerell. Becoming something of a celebrity, she set her sights on southern Arabia. In January 1935 she set out for Yemen, seeking Shabwa in the Hadhramaut (Hadramawt), which had been the center of the incense trade. The journey, which required seven days on camel, was one that Europeans had not yet made, and Stark's attempt was also unsuccessful. Along the way she stayed in Shibam, an impressive town of tall structures, but she became so incapacitated by illness that she had to be rescued by the Royal Air Force (RAF). In gratitude and with some chagrin she dedicated her next book, *The Southern Gates of Arabia* (1936), to the fliers. The book received favorable reviews and was followed by *Seen in the Hadhramaut* (1938). As difficult and frustrating as this journey had been for Stark the romantic traveler, Stark the responsible young woman had found her calling as a travel writer.

The subject of *The Southern Gates of Arabia,* Stark wrote, is

> the great frankincense road whose faint remembrance still gives to South Arabia the name of Happy: whose existence prepared and made possible the later exploits of Islam. On its stream of padding feet the riches of Asia travelled: along its slow continuous thread the Arabian empires rose and fell–Mimean, Sabaean, Katabanian, Hadhramaut and Himyar. One after another they grew rich on their strip of the great highway; their policy was urged by the desire to control more of it, to control especially the incense regions of the south and the outlets to the sea: they became imperial and aristocratic, builders of tall cities; they colonized Somaliland and Ethiopia and made themselves masters of the African as well as the Arabian forests. We can scarcely realize what riches their monopoly gave them in days when every altar and every funeral was sweetened with frankincense.

This sense of capturing a bygone era in words that would somehow populate the barren accompanying photographs runs even more insistently through *Seen in the Hadhramaut,* which is principally a series of Stark's photographs of an expedition to such cities as Shibam, Mukalla, Seiyun, and Terim. Stark's intention was "to keep the remembrance of something

Stark and Harold Ingrams in Aden, 1940

very complete, very ancient, very remote, and very beautiful, which may pass for ever from our world." Yet she was never blind in her assessment or imagination of past civilizations. Looking on a world that she knew to be passing from the scene, she had inescapably to view it through the eyes of a proud Englishwoman:

> The civilisation they show was never, I believe, a great civilisation. Its literature, if it had any, has perished; its art, such as we know of it, was bad; the potteries, the small household objects found among its ruins ancient or medieval or still in use to-day, are unimaginative and clumsy. The actual hardships of living in Arabia must ever, perhaps, be too severe for the more fragile flowering luxuries and graces. And yet one thing has come down to us in strange perfection out of the darkness of the Arabian past–an architecture as lovely, austere, and delicate as ever found expression in the dwelling-houses of men.

In her reading of the accounts of nineteenth-century travelers, Stark noticed how little difference there really was between the people of the Hadramawt then and in the 1930s. The implication seems to be that modernization was not arising within the culture but was being brought to it from outside. In this book, which has little text, she managed to take strong positions on imperial overtures that were echoed in progressive forces already growing in the young of the Arab countries. She reprimanded civil servants who shirked their responsibilities "partly out of a natural regard for other people's customs, partly out of a liking–which I share–for old and different ways, and chiefly, perhaps, because of the parsimony of the Treasury." The result, she feared, had been the alienation of the Arab elements that would otherwise have looked on Great Britain as a model. In her view the three most immediate objectives of government in the Hadramawt had to be the elimination of tribal wars, the creation of a local police force able to deal with daily troubles independently of the RAF, and the reestablishment of the ancient irrigation systems that brought fertility to the land. She also condemned the corruption of local peoples by capitalist interests that cared little for the greed they instilled in their wake:

> It is not the Government officials who are responsible for the catastrophe of moral values: knowing and usually loving their people, they do what they can to protect them from themselves and to temper as far as possible the inevitable change. It is the Western expert.

> Whether it be oil or gold, science or excavation, his loyalty is naturally bound, not to the country he visits, but to whatever it is that has sent him from outside. . . . He is like one who, using prussic acid himself for innocuous purposes, leaves the bottle lying promiscuously about among the ignorant.

Without using the word *neocolonialism,* she clearly condemned the exploitation of local talent and, more pointedly, the willingness of Western businessmen to leave the scene before the local population had been sufficiently trained to assume responsible positions. Stark remained a loyal citizen of the British Empire, however, and while she regretted the passing of an earlier, simpler way of life, she did not suggest that the Empire had no business bringing about changes.

Along with Gertrude Caton Thompson and Elinor Gardner, Stark decided to return to the Hadramawt to do some archaeological investigations into the meeting points between African and Arabic cultures during the Roman period. The threesome was not especially compatible, and their 1937–1938 expedition seems to have confirmed Stark's preference for working on her own. The excavations were nonetheless successful and resulted in one of her major works, *A Winter in Arabia* (1940), which was praised for its careful descriptions and its sense of imagination in dealing with other races. *The Spectator* praised her ease and flexibility of idiom and expression; *The New Yorker* called her one of the finest travel writers of the century. *The New York Times Book Review* was also complimentary, as was *The Times Literary Supplement,* which called Stark one of the most unconventional and courageous explorers of her time–a twentieth-century heroine.

Part of the charm of *A Winter in Arabia* depends on its form. Stark chose to write the book in a diary format and set modest goals for it, explaining that "the scientific and more serious records of this venture are to be found elsewhere: this is but a record of actions and reactions that might occur in any small Arabian town unused to Europeans and of a journey from Hureidha to the sea." Reviewers celebrated the fact that readers got to know as much about Freya Stark and her personal reactions to a foreign culture as they learned about the culture itself. Readers were offered rare glimpses of life behind the veil–the subtleties of business and social conduct, the elaborate beauty rituals of the women, and the bitter animosities among rival tribes. Vividly sketching the rich spectacle of a wedding, the eager affection of the children, and the allure of the stark and rocky countryside, she demonstrated the stringent benefit of the people's directness.

In his foreword to *A Winter in Arabia* Sir Kinahan Cornwallis, who had been in the Ministry of the Interior in Iraq, was diplomatic but nonetheless skeptical about Stark's travels:

> The movements of ladies in some of the wilder parts of the country without permission was quite rightly restricted, and unauthorized visits to Persia were strictly forbidden. Miss Stark made light of such bureaucratic red tape; she saved our hair from premature greyness by just going and telling us all about it on her return. She exercised, in fact, on us the same qualities as she showed to the Arabs, and soon built up for herself a privileged position.

Cornwallis's good-natured and backhanded compliment was unusual among civil servants, who often responded to Stark's travel plans in outraged tones, and she wrote that "I am not of those who blame officials for looking upon me with misgiving. Far from it. If they are right in nine cases how should they know, by the mere look of us, that we are that exceptional coincidence, the tenth?" Earlier, however, in a 17 December 1929 letter to her mother, she had written, "What a blessing that Paradise isn't run by our Civil Service, or so few of us would get in."

While Stark was strong willed, she held ambivalent views on women's emancipation. On the one hand she offered the following tongue-in-cheek account of the future for education of women in Arabia:

> "I am not averse to women's education," a liberal sayyid told me . . . in Tarim: "so long as it is not *excessive.* If it is carried on to the age of nine and then stops, I do not think it can do any harm." He looked at me anxiously, afraid that perhaps his modern tendencies were carrying him too far.

At the same time she offered a philosophical caution that seems rooted in conservative essentialist distinctions between the sexes and in a traditionalist feminizing of "the Orient":

> The Orient does not get much done: it looks upon work as a part only–and not too important a part at that–of its varied existence, but enjoys with a free mind whatever happens besides. The Occident, busily building, has its eyes rigidly fixed on the future: Being and Doing, and civilization, a compromise, between them. There is too little of the compromise now. Too much machinery in the West, too little in the East, have made a gap between the active and contemplative; they drift ever more apart. Woman hitherto has inclined to the eastern idea–the stress being laid on what she *is* rather than on what she does; and if we are going to change this, taking for our sole pattern the active

Stark delivering a pro-British speech to a group of Arabs in Cairo, 1940

> energies of men, we are in danger of destroying a principle which contains one-half the ingredients of civilization. Before ceasing to *be,* it is to be hoped that our sex will at least make sure that what it *does* is worth the sacrifice.

Nor did Stark hesitate to alienate her "natural" support community abroad. In an article originally published in the *Baghdad Times* and collected in *Baghdad Sketches,* she wrote:

> it seems a pity that women who slave away at home, at committee meetings, district visiting, local government, and all sorts of meritorious but not amusing things, should grudge time and effort and, let us say it, a good many hours of boredom, to the understanding of what lies around them abroad. A dreadful conclusion is forced on one as one travels. The British appear to be popular wherever they go until they come to settle with their wives.

While preferring the company of men to that of women, Stark also had a "feminine" side. She became well known for her elaborate and fanciful wardrobe, showing up at cocktail parties in Arabic clothing, and at one point demanding that Murray give her a mink coat instead of a monetary advance on her next book. (He refused.)

In *A Winter in Arabia* Stark wrote, "Few pleasures give as much constant satisfaction as the inactive one of sitting quietly while the shows of life go by; it adds to the delight of contemplation the subtle satisfaction that others are fussing about things that leave us personally calm–the feeling that one has after poking an anthill with a stick." While some readers might have characterized this trait as feminine, Stark might have called them Arabic. As she warned her British readers,

> To the Arab, manners are everything; he will forgive any amount of extortion so long as "your speech is good." To us, since the end of the eighteenth century, they have become dangerously unimportant . . . . It is in this heart of our philosophy that we amateurs disagree with your unmitigated expert, whose object is so supremely important that he cannot count, or at any rate notice, the jostling and hurting of others. . . . However important the appointment, one does not run over human bodies to catch one's trains. If this were merely individual it would not matter, but it appears as the very core of difficulty in present dealings with the East, now flooded with experts, of commerce, of science, of oil.

After returning briefly to Europe, which was on the brink of World War II, Stark made a quick trip in 1939 to see Crusader castles. When she returned to London later that year, she began to work with the Ministry of Information as an expert on southern Arabia and was appointed assistant information officer in Aden. The head of this bureau was Stewart Perowne, whom she was later to marry. Her job was to summarize the day's news, which was translated into Arabic and then broadcast. As events became discour-

The house in Baghdad where Stark lived in 1941–1942, (photograph by Stark)

aging, her task was to cast them in the best light, and she became a propagandist. Soon her role became more aggressive. She went into Yemen seeking to rectify rumors that were working against British interests. She showed pro-British movies and spoke to people, mostly women in harems, and came away not only with a sense of success in her public-relations mission but also with a rare Western perspective on the lives of Arabic women. She next worked in Cairo, hoping to counteract Italian attempts to turn Egyptians against the English. In Cairo and later in Baghdad she set up a series of cells called the Brothers and Sisters of Freedom, whose membership eventually swelled to thirty thousand. She was invited to speak at the Muslim university of Azhar, and after Perowne was sent to Iraq, Stark was named temporary attaché at the embassy. Her reflections on these years appeared in *East Is West* (1945), published the same year in the United States as *The Arab Island.*

The principal thesis of the book is that the young effendis, products and propagators of modern education and technologies, were gradually taking over control of the Arab world, which they were likely to bring into some sort of federated unity. Stark dedicated the book to them and to their efforts on behalf of their countries. Her discussion moves progressively through the countries of the Red Sea (Aden, Yemen, and Arabia) to Egypt, Palestine, Syria, Transjordan, and Iraq. She noted that she had not written the book merely for pleasure. In fact there is a sense of urgency in her message. Many things had changed in the Arab world, yet the United States, she believed, was still thinking of an older Middle East. In *A Winter in Arabia* she had complained that "no one in their senses would say, 'I have spent ten years in Holland and therefore I know all about Bulgaria'; but it is a fact that seven people out of ten will assume that a visit to Morocco opens out the secrets of Samarkand. The East is just East in their minds, a homogeneous lump." In book after book she argued that each culture is distinct. Yet in *East Is West* her warning is of a different sort, a suggestion that the West seemed disastrously unable to see the one similarity that was spreading across these many cultures: the rise of modernism.

"The old Arab society," she wrote, "is picturesque, and the modern is becoming less so every hour; artists in words or colours find the sheikh in his draperies easier to deal with than the effendi in his cosmopolitan sameness." Thus in the first instance the problem for the Western powers is one of imagination, of romanticizing and exoticizing whole peoples. Yet, she added,

> even in its conception of the *past,* popular imagination gives to the desert and its nomads far too great a part. What the Arabs represent in history is *the greatest commercial empire of the West between the fall of Rome and the rise of Britain.* In their rich and varied sheaf they gathered, at one time or another, southern Spain and northern India and all that lay between, and penetrated into Europe, so that Malta still remembers them in her language, and Italy in the weaving of her brocades, and the whole of Europe in the traditions of chivalry and the forms of literature that were first imported by the courts of Sicily or Provence. . . . the wall of the Arabian world, against which the crusades threw themselves, was not the wall of the desert. It was the line of trading cities that stretched, and still stretches, from Mosul, Baghdad, and Basra in the east, through Antioch, Alexandretta (now Turkish) Aleppo, Homs, Hama, Damascus, Jerusalem, and Cairo.

Stark did not want to minimize the seventh- and eighth-century eruption that altered the history of the world by spreading the Muslim faith and Arab language. Yet "in speaking of the Arab world it is important to remember that its unity is one of language, largely of religion, and of the civilization they have produced; it is *not* a unity of race." That so small a group of people could impress their language and religion on so many different races suggested to Stark that "the future unifying of the Arab nations seems child's play in comparison." For her, much of the interest of Arab history in the future would chart the progress of two strands: toward individual nationalism and toward commonwealth amalgamation. Her sophisticated understanding of her subject had clearly advanced a great deal beyond her early preoccupation with *Arabian Nights,* and she seemed, in fact, to be accusing the Western powers of sharing her early naïveté.

Stark wrote that Arab liberation had been in their hearts since the middle of the nineteenth century and had actually been accomplished by World War I. It was basically an accomplishment of "the most important factor in the modern Arab world. This is the ascension of the middle class." This group had awakened in response to three factors: "the internal-combustion engine, the (mostly) American educator, and the British Government." Keeping in mind the highly developed sense of dignity in these people, Stark concluded that "what the young effendi needs is the help not so much of a governess as of a brother." The unification of the Arabian peoples would come, she predicted, through the material support and assistance of Britain and through the spiritual unity of Islam.

Her apparent talent at winning over potential enemies brought Stark to the attention of the British government, which in 1943 asked her to help persuade American Jews that the terms of the White Paper of 1939 were reasonable. Malcolm Macdonald's response to demands of Zionists in Palestine, this document suggested that Jewish immigration to Palestine be limited to seventy-five thousand over the next five years and that after that time more would be admitted if the Arabs were willing. Stark strongly supported these terms and thought that the Arabs living in Palestine should not have immigration of Jews forced on them by the Western world. Her views on the matter, however, were perhaps a bit too public and settled to allow her to serve the cause with the necessary equanimity. In *East Is West,* for example, she wrote, "As I sat in the sun, listening to Professor Mayer on Islamic art of the Middle Ages, I wondered what gave the feeling of peace so absent from the Zionist atmosphere of the cities and farms of the plain. . . . It is perhaps toleration, the opposite of the feeling of *exclusion.* This feeling of exclusion haunts one through all the Zionist endeavour in Palestine." Thus in her travel across the United States she contacted anti-Zionist Jews and sought their support in restraining the more militant advocates of immigration. She was not particularly successful in her mission of persuasion and left the United States with some bitterness. She considered the country to be materialistic and shallow and decided that the Jews were the only citizens truly interested in ideas. Later, in editing the angry letters she had written during this period, she apologized and noted, "I should like to say that these letters from America show one aspect only of a people in general: circumstances of less strain, with no artificial direction for contradiction or support, have made later visits particularly delightful and confirmed me in the conviction that my favourite view of a people is not from a platform." With some notable exceptions, such as a congressman who asked that she be deported, Stark remained welcome in the United States.

In 1945 the wife of Archibald Percival, Earl Wavell, the viceroy of India, asked Stark to come to Delhi and help involve Indian women in the war effort. Stark stayed for half a year. While she considered her work there unproductive, she made the most of opportunities to see a last outpost of the British Empire. She was present at Simla when Mohandas Gandhi met with Jawaharlal Nehru, and she was generally well received. She returned to Asolo at the age of fifty-two, a well-known public figure

Stark and Stewart Perowne, whom she married in 1947

who had somehow carved out an almost legendary role for herself as the best kind of English eccentric: individual, free-thinking, imaginative, and consulted by diplomats around the world.

After six months as a "persuasion" officer in northern Italy helping restore good Anglo-Italian relations, she focused her attention on a collection of reflective essays, *Perseus in the Wind* (1948), a light work that served as a breather before her next round of major travel books. The book disappointed critics who found it less weighty than the works they had come to expect from Stark. The book does show the beginning of the sort of observations that filled her later books: "Though it may be unessential to the imagination, travel is necessary to an understanding of men. Only with long experience and the opening of his wares on many a beach where his language is not spoken, will the merchant come to know the worth of what he carries, and what is parochial and what is universal in his choice."

This pause in her travel writing also offered Stark the occasion to reassess her position in the world in such a way that she was able to accept Stewart Perowne's offer of marriage when it arrived by telegram. They were married in London in October 1947. Her reasons for marrying Perowne, a rather dull civil servant who was eight years her junior and apparently a homosexual, seem to have involved some desire for domesticity. By summer 1951 they had decided to divorce. Later that year she dropped his name and from then on called herself "Mrs. Stark."

During these stormy years Stark began writing her autobiography, which eventually appeared in three volumes: *Traveller's Prelude* (1950), *Beyond Euphrates* (1951), and *The Coast of Incense* (1953). Much of this autobiography was written in Libya, where Perowne had been posted. Throughout the three books she alternated letters written in the past with present-day impressions. The result is a composite of memory and reflection, present and past, "plaited in together, as they are in actual life: for it is usually a chord and not a note that we remember." How far her writing had developed is obvious in the cadence of her prose in reflective passages such as the following:

> Looking back through this autobiography and its vicissitudes of nearly half a century, filled as full with sensations and passions as a glass that you ring is filled with sound–the strangest thing about it all perhaps is this–that the person who emerges is still familiar to me, the same optimistic little creature who at two and a half years old set out for Plymouth with three halfpence in her pocket to see the world, whose feelings I can still perfectly well understand and remember, whose equipment will be just as meagre, and whose general attitude of curiosity will be very little different when the gate that clicks behind her is no longer that of the home field alone.

Her divorce from Perowne freed Stark to begin a new phase of her career, which focused on Asia Minor. In 1952 she set out for Smyrna (Izmir) on the west coast of Turkey, hoping to retrace the journey described by Herodotus. Typically, she prepared for this new adventure by learning Turkish. She dedicated the resulting book, *Ionia: A Quest*

(1954), to Harold Nicolson and Vita Sackville-West. In autumn 1952 Stark traveled about the western coast of Asia Minor, visiting fifty-five ruined sites. In only one of them did she meet another tourist. Her letters from this period reveal the sense of loneliness that resulted from her failed marriage, but *Ionia* shows her customary energy and fascination for cultures that were new to her and perhaps to all, or most, of her readers. Some of her observations along the way–such as "the art of government is in the management of people's *feelings*"–may have arisen from her internal struggle, but she was usually more grandiose in her musing, more inspirational in her imagining:

> Some of these vanished cities were buried in the earth, or had sunk away in swamp, so that only a few places of wall, a cornice or shaft of column, remained, neglected or forgotten: in many, the steps of their theatres were split by the roots of trees or hidden, hardly accessible, in thorns. Here, like a manuscript of which most of the words are rubbed away, lay the record of our story, of what–trickling down slopes of time towards us by devious runnels–has made us what we are today. A great longing came to me to know more, and to bring a living image out of these dots and dashes of the past. More particularly, to discover what elements in that breeding ground of civilization can still be planted to grow among us now.

The picture she painted of Asia Minor as she moved away from Ionia and followed the Maeander (Menderes) upstream is of a formless, vast, human-dwarfing geography that was historically humanized by the Greeks and conquered by Rome. Having suffered in her personal life and having seen the vast devastation of World War II, she was prompted by the remains of past civilizations to consider the purpose of so much creation and destruction, so much similarity in the midst of diversity.

Stark was so interested in what she saw in Turkey that she spent more time learning Turkish in Crete in 1954 and then undertook a lighter travel book, *The Lycian Shore* (1956), which includes such observations as the following:

> The life of insecurity is the nomad's achievement. He does not try, like our building world, to believe in a stability which is non-existent; and in his constant movement with the seasons, in the lightness of his hold, puts something right, about which we are constantly wrong. His is in fact the reality, to which the most solid of our structures are illusion.

Stark's next book was the heavily researched and well-received *Alexander's Path* (1958), which focuses on the western and southern coasts of Turkey. Stark had intended to follow the route of Alexander the Great as it had been described by Arrian, but she began to suspect that Arrian had left out some details, including the "whole route between Xanthus and Phaselis, and the campaign against the hill-men." She decided to live along that route for several months, coming in closer contact with country people than she had on her previous visit. She also decided to include more information than former writers had on the geography of Anatolia, the site of the first and most formative year or so of Alexander's adventure, and on the area of Caria and its queen, Ada, who had made Alexander her adopted son when he was only a nineteen-year-old Macedonian prince who had decided to marry her niece. Stark tried to learn what Alexander did between Xanthus and Sagalassus, but she went in the opposite direction from that taken by Alexander. Although critics at the time appreciated her account, it seems speculative and a bit narrowly focused.

Stark's *Riding to the Tigris* (1959), an account of her travels in the interior of Turkey, includes some of her finest reflection on the enterprise of travel to which she had devoted her life. Asking the same fundamental questions that she had raised early in her career, she now had more-pointed responses.

> I began to wonder again why I, and so many others like me, should find ourselves in these recondite places. We like our life intensified, perhaps. Travel does what good novelists also do to the life of every day, placing it like a picture in a frame or a gem in its setting, so that the intrinsic qualities are made more clear. Travel does this with the very stuff that everyday life is made of, giving to it the sharp contour and meaning of art: and unless it succeeds in doing this, its effect on the human being is not, I believe, very great. . . . Most people anyway try to avoid having their feelings intensified: for indeed one must be strong to place oneself alone against the impact of the unknown world.

The statement is emblematic of Stark's life. *Riding to the Tigris* is also one of the best demonstrations of her complex relationship with her native country and with the lands to which she came as a visitor. At one moment she could yearn almost palpably to be an Arab: "It was many years since I had spent a night among the tents; the sight of them, seventy or so in the hollow of the mountain, filled me as it always does with delight and pity; for they seem to me to show what our houses forget or disguise–a security based not on strength but on fragility, at rest on the surface of the world like a seagull on a wave." Yet she could also sound as patriotic as

Photograph of a Lycian tomb taken by Stark during the travels she described in The Lycian Shore *(1956)*

anyone in the Home Office might have hoped, as in this incredible paean to her native country:

> With a nostalgia that hurt like a pain I thought of England; perhaps it was the singing of the waters in the night that brought her so poignantly before me. But it was of her people that I thought: a modest people, where this terrible nationalism is rare and one is not always being told about virtues that one likes to discover for oneself: where, almost alone in the world today, the variety of tastes and opinions, the entrancing *variety* of the world is still encouraged and respected. People, I thought longingly, who when they go about are able here and there to care for other and different people as much as for their own. Perhaps it is only the best of any nation that can do this, and when we owned much of the world we often sent our best: but I was not thinking of being fair in the darkness of the night. The flint, I thought, is fire and the pebble mere stone: and people are civilized when *ideas,* however foreign, will strike a spark inside them: and England is now perhaps among those rare and happy nations where the fierce intellectual qualities of Greece have been toned down to a native goodness like the Turkish–a mixture that could produce civilisation. If that is so, it is the treasure of treasures–and better to be conquered having it than to lack it among the threatening barbarians of our day.

At this point in her life Stark, who was in her early seventies, began to slow her pace. After writing a fourth volume of autobiography, *Dust in the Lion's Paw* (1961), she produced *Rome on the Euphrates* (1966), an account of the Romans' activities along one of the frontiers of their empire over a period of eight hundred years–from 200 B.C. to the Age of Justinian. Her last major travel account, the book is overly derivative and a cumbersome read, but it was an interesting topic for a woman who had lived so long as a bold adventurer on an amazing series of frontiers. Stark admitted that she was only an amateur historian and that she could read little Greek. Why, she wondered, did the Romans fight along this rich Euphrates frontier? Every impartial reading of the evidence suggested that it was a great blunder for two trading communities to fight over this lengthy period rather than seek mutual gain through commerce and traffic. The perennially recurring pattern in the history of northwest Asia, she wrote, is an east-west horizontal of trade cut at recurring intervals by a north-south vertical of war.

Though interested in the vast movements of history, Stark seems to have been most interested in the common people. In *Riding to the Tigris* she had written that "the sheep, plodding through the ages, nose the ground and bury their eyes each in the coat of the one before it, kicking up their own troubles from their own soil, patient, unquestioning, and like mankind resolute to hide their faces from the goal of their marching, trusting to a shepherd that only their leader can see." *Rome on the Euphrates* was inspired by a visit to a group of old women in chadors: "nothing but the hands and the eyes were left to see, but in those outstretched hands and longing eyes such love and sorrow, such timid uncomplaining hope, that I have never forgotten, and think of them, and see them as Euripides saw the Trojan Women, a background or chorus for the quarrelsome nature of man." Feted by diplomats and the powerful in many countries of the West and the East, Stark seems increasingly to have identified with the anonymous individuals who appear outside the flow of political history and completely at home in the larger flow of time.

In 1971 Stark began preparing her many letters for publication. The result was eight volumes of letters (1974–1982) and a one-volume selection, *Over the Rim of the World* (1988). She also spent her remaining years in a series of less-demanding enterprises. *The Zodiac Arch* (1968) is a collection of previously published essays, and *The Minaret of Djam* (1970) is a short travel book about Afghanistan. *Space, Time & Movement in Landscape* (1969) is a beautifully crafted coffee-table book published in a limited edition of five hundred copies. In it she described space, time, and movement as the three enhancers of mood in humankind's relationship with landscape. The text is accompanied by photographs of the Arab and Turkish world. The following story from the book illustrates the interesting metaphysical turn that her aging mind was taking:

> Some years ago I dreamed a disturbing dream. I was dead and found myself, on the far side of the living world, stepping into a lift, behind a neat, plump, and official woman in uniform. I noticed with some misgiving that the lift when it started began to go down, and continued to do so for a long way, past floor after floor of an out-door shaft among dingy houses. Their brick was decayed and their walls were undecorated except by streaks of gutters or of rain. When we reached the bottom, which was a narrow space with a few anaemic grasses imprisoned in its walls, the conductress took up my suitcase, led the way into a mean corridor, opened the door of a small room with bed and cupboard unmitigated by anything except one of these coco-fibre mats that have always been my aversion, and saying: "Well, here you are," left me to myself. I looked to the window–uncurtained–and saw that there was no view: only a blank wall (I must have been reading Sartre). Realising that this was my prospect for eternity, it reflects something of my natural optimism that I murmured (in my dream): "One must make the best of it I suppose," and mercifully woke up. The delight and importance of Space, my first enhancement of landscape, has remained vivid in my mind ever since.

How disturbing she must have found this dream is suggested by an early entry in *A Winter in Arabia,* in which the young traveler observed that "the charm of the horizon is the charm of pilgrimage, the eternal invitation to the spirit of man . . . at the end of days to see before you land that is yet unknown–what enchantment in this world, I should like to know, is comparable to this?"

While these reflections on space are arresting, those on time are even more so. "It must not be thought," she wrote, "that the discovery of Time in a landscape is a mere matter of ruin and decay. It is not the end, but the transitions that enthrall us. . . . The works of men share in the universal discipline and are harmonious as they are subject to the general law of ruin: they are displeasing when they seem to claim a permanence which is not theirs by nature." Then, reminding the reader once again of the vastness of the universe in which all people inevitably find themselves, she added that "a ploughman upon his tractor will appear richer if he is looked at against the incrustation of all the imprisoned movements of his earth." This image could be a metaphor for Stark herself, seen most vividly against the backdrop of her work.

Stark in Nepal at age seventy-seven (photograph by Mark Lennox-Boyd)

Turkey: A Sketch of Turkish History (1971), published in the United States as *Gateways and Caravans* (1971), offers a portrait of Turkey, with text by Stark and photographs by Fulvio Roiter. *Rivers of Time* (1982) is a selection from the more than six thousand mounted prints and perhaps five times as many negatives from Stark's collection of the photographs she took from the 1920s through the 1970s. The book is an excellent reminder that taking photographs usually occupied a quarter of her time given to her expeditions. Praising the historical value of Stark's photographs, Alexander Maitland, in his introduction to the volume, singled out "Freya's studies of women and girls. A number of these, taken in the harim before the last war, show the women unveiled, something no man could have achieved." *Freya Stark in Asolo* (1984) is an essay on that place and her photographs of it. The book was published as part of the Homage to Freya Stark that the Magnifica Comunità Pedemontana held to honor her on the occasion of her ninety-first birthday.

Perhaps the best introduction to Stark's writing is *The Journey's Echo* (1963), a collection of selections from all her major works. In his introduction to the volume Lawrence Durrell described Stark as "one of the most remarkable women of our age–a poet of travel whose Muse has been wholly Arabian in plumage and whose books span nearly half a century of historical time." "A great traveller," he added, "is a kind of introspective; as she covers the ground outwardly, so she advances towards fresh interpretations of herself inwardly. And this is the quality which lends Freya Stark's books the memorable poetic density which is their special *cachet*." This comment is an especially apt assessment of Stark's writing. The reader watches with admiration as the young woman of the early books turns into the wise adult and peaceful older woman who finds in the world around her nothing that is totally foreign.

It was this older woman, clearly reconciled to the final journey that she still faced, who published the extraordinary collection of essays titled *A Peak in Darien* (1976), written not only in the voice of the aged woman but also in that of the little girl who was uprooted from England and from her father, the young woman who was always afraid of being seen as disfigured, the woman abandoned by her lover, the steely explorer of worlds that even men had avoided:

> Solitude has now survived to be perhaps my earliest friend. His thoughtful and kindly presence stands at the edge of every landscape I can remember. . . . And gradually in his company and through his silence I came to realize that solitude is not loneliness, but rather the mingled voice of all things attending to their separate affairs. As the years went by, I came to recognize how fortunate was my early introduction to one who is to be the last of our companions, whose later face can be both cruel and severe.

Stark warned that these essays were not written for believers but "for such among us as are willing to advance as far as honest but purely mundane evidence can take them, and the route is geography rather than religion (though the terminus is probably the same)." In short they are a well-traveled woman's reflections on the heroism possible in accepting one's approaching death.

Stark began as an amateur traveler and archaeologist, a role for which she thought the British were somehow constitutionally fitted:

> There are, I sometimes think, only two sorts of people in this world–the settled and the nomad–and there is a natural antipathy between them, whatever the land to which they may belong. Perhaps it is because we are comparatively recently barbarians, because the stone age lingered longer among us than on the Mediterranean coasts that the English have remained so frequently nomadic at heart. It is the more imaginative attitude in a transitory world.

She ended as an amateur historian and philosopher who concluded that "the actual stature of man is no greater now than it was near his beginning: he is made tall only by standing on the heap of his ages, and using his past." In 1977 she returned to the Euphrates with a BBC film crew, and in 1979, at the age of eighty-six, she was climbing mountains in Annapurna.

Stark recognized that each man or woman is at heart a traveler bound with others by a sense of common enterprise. As she noted with great poignancy in a letter written near the end of her life, her travels gave her "a deepening of the sense of companionship independent of circumstances, national or social or even human, a recognition I had come upon in ignorance among the Druid stones of my childhood on the moors–a sense of safety in the unity of earth: a feeling which must have comforted and strengthened many travellers before me and is, perhaps, the happiest of all reasons for travel."

Letters:

Letters (Salisbury: Russell, 1974–1982)–volume 1: *The Furnace and the Cup 1914–30,* edited by Lucy Moorehead (1974); volume 2: *The Open Door 1930–35,* edited by Lucy Moorehead (1975); volume 3: *The Growth of Danger 1935–39,* edited by Lucy Moorehead (1976); volume 4: *Bridge of the Levant 1940–43,* edited by Lucy Moorehead (1977); volume 5: *New Worlds for Old 1943–46,* edited by Lucy Moorehead (1978); volume 6: *The Broken Road 1947–52,* edited by Lucy Moorehead (1981); volume 7: *Some Talk of Alexander 1952–59,* edited by Caroline Moorehead (1982); volume 8: *Traveller's Epilogue 1960–80,* edited by Caroline Moorehead (1982);

Over the Rim of the World: Selected Letters, edited by Caroline Moorehead (London: Murray, 1988).

Biographies:

Caroline Moorehead, *Freya Stark* (London: Viking, 1985);

Malise Ruthven, *Traveller through Time: A Photographic Journey with Freya Stark* (London: Viking Penguin, 1986);

Molly Izzard, *Freya Stark: A Biography* (London: Hodder & Stoughton, 1993);

Ruthven, *Freya Stark in Iraq and Kuwait* (New York: Garnet, 1994).

Walter Starkie

(9 August 1894 - 2 November 1976)

David C. Judkins
University of Houston

BOOKS: *Jacinto Benavente* (London & New York: Humphrey Milford, Oxford University Press, 1924);

Luigi Pirandello (London & Toronto: Dent/New York: Dutton, 1926); revised and enlarged as *Luigi Pirandello, 1867–1936* (London: John Murray, 1937; New York: Dutton, 1937; revised and enlarged edition, Berkeley: University of California Press, 1965);

Raggle-Taggle: Adventures with a Fiddle in Hungary and Roumania (London: John Murray, 1933; New York: Dutton, 1933);

Spanish Raggle-Taggle: Adventures with a Fiddle in North Spain (London: John Murray, 1934; New York: Dutton, 1935);

Don Gypsy: Adventures with a Fiddle in Barbary, Andalusia, and La Mancha (London: John Murray, 1936); republished as *Don Gypsy: Adventures with a Fiddle in Southern Spain and Barbary* (New York: Dutton, 1937);

The Waveless Plain: An Italian Autobiography (London: John Murray, 1938; New York: Dutton, 1938);

Grand Inquisitor: Being an Account of Cardinal Ximenez de Cisneros and His Times (London: Hodder & Stoughton, 1940);

In Sara's Tents (London: John Murray, 1953; New York: Dutton, 1953);

The Road to Santiago: Pilgrims of St. James (London: John Murray, 1957; New York: Dutton, 1957);

Spain: A Musician's Journey through Space and Time, 3 volumes (Geneva: EDISLI, 1958)–volume 3 comprises a booklet and six phonograph records;

Scholars and Gypsies: An Autobiography (London: John Murray, 1963; Berkeley: University of California Press, 1963);

Homage to Yeats, 1865–1965: Papers Read at a Clark Library Seminar, October 16, 1965, by Starkie and A. Norman Jeffares (Los Angeles: William Andrews Clark Memorial Library, University of California, 1966).

OTHER: "St. James the Apostle," in *Saints and Ourselves: Third Series,* edited by Philip Caraman, S.J. (London: Catholic Book Club, 1958).

TRANSLATIONS: Ramon Pérez de Ayala, *Tiger Juan* (London: Cape, 1933; New York: Macmillan, 1933);

Ramon Ménendez Pidal, *The Spaniards in Their History* (New York: Norton, 1950);

Rodolfo L. Fonseca, *Tower of Ivory* (London: Cape, 1954);

Ignacio Olagüe, *This Is Spain* (London: Cohen & West, 1954);

Miguel de Cervantes Saavedra, *Don Quixote: An Abridged Version Designed to Relate without Digressions the Principal Adventures of the Knight and His Squire,* edited and translated by Starkie (London: Macmillan/New York: St. Martin's Press, 1954);

Lope Félix de Vega Carpio, *Peribañez and the Commendador of Ocaña* (Boulder: University of Colorado Libraries, 1962);

Cervantes, *Don Quixote of La Mancha* [complete version] (New York: New American Library, 1964);

Eight Spanish Plays of the Golden Age, translated, edited, and with an introduction by Starkie (New York: Random House, 1964).

SELECTED PERIODICAL PUBLICATIONS–UNCOLLECTED: "Gypsies of Europe," *Saturday Review of Literature,* 6 (14 September 1929): 128;

"Modern Spain and Its Literature," *Rice Institute Pamphlet,* 16, no. 2 (1929): 47–110;

"Troubadours and Gypsies in Provence," *Nineteenth Century and After,* 106 (October 1929): 556–566;

"With the Gypsies in Transylvania," *Travel,* 61 (September 1933): 18–22, 35, 38;

"Spanish Kaleidoscope: A Background," *Fortnightly,* 147, new series 141 (December 1936): 682–688;

"Ireland To-day," *Quarterly Review,* 271 (October 1938): 343–360;

"U.S. Culture: No Apologies," *Saturday Review,* 41 (26 July 1958): 13–15.

Walter Starkie, a genial, garrulous, and musically talented professor of Spanish and Italian literature, is better known for his unusual means of travel and his inclination toward the nomadic life than for any exotic places he visited. Starkie was raised by a prudish mother and a Victorian father who was determined to train him as a classicist, and much of his life seems to reflect a struggle between the somber occupation of a university don and the romantic lure of a wandering Gypsy life. Frequently the latter tendency won, and it is for his accounts of those periods of rambling that Starkie is mainly remembered. Although he taught and lectured at dozens of universities around the world, his books on the Gypsy life he pursued during summer vacations have delighted readers who did not know and would not have cared that he was also a world-recognized expert on Spanish and Italian literature.

Walter Fitzwilliam Starkie was born in Killiney, County Dublin, Ireland, on 9 August 1894 to William Joseph Miles Starkie, a classical scholar and fellow of Trinity College, Dublin, and May C. Walsh Starkie. The first twenty-five years of Starkie's life are documented in his autobiography, *Scholars and Gypsies* (1963). There he describes the people who were most important to him in his formative years, including Shamus the tinker, who introduced him to the fiddle and the rough life of the itinerant tinker, and the poet, novelist, and short-story writer James Stephens, who reminded Starkie of the mythical Angus Oge, "whom men call the young: he is the sunlight in the heart, the moonlight in the mind: he is the light at the end of every dream, the voice forever calling you to come away." In 1898 William Starkie became president of Queen's College, Galway; two years later he was appointed resident commissioner of national education in Ireland, and the family moved back to Dublin.

Starkie's interest in music was encouraged by a French governess, Mlle Léonie Cora, who was hired to assist in the education of Starkie's three sisters and who played the parlor piano with an intensity Starkie had never before experienced. At her urging he attended a violin concert: "Ever since early childhood I had been fascinated by the sour-sweet tone of the fiddle . . . but the playing of this boy prodigy opened up a nuance of sound; at one moment fierce and strident; at another soft and caressing, it seemed to be part of the body and personality of the virtuoso who played it as he breathed. I returned home in a daze."

Believing that Starkie's classical education was not coming along rapidly enough at St. Stephen's Green School in Dublin, his father sent him to Shrewsbury School in England; he was to enter Oxford after completing the sixth form. The family fortunes suffered during his absence, however, and he was forced to withdraw early for lack of money for tuition; Oxford, of course, was out of the question. Although the headmaster at Shrewsbury, C. A. Alington, urged Starkie's father to allow him to audition for Sir Henry Wood, the conductor of the London Symphony, William Starkie dismissed the suggestion and in 1913 entered him in Trinity College, Dublin. There Starkie would receive a lower tuition rate as the son of a former fellow of the college, and further savings could be realized by having him live at home.

Starkie made the best of his situation: he excelled in his studies, and he regularly attended plays at the Abbey Theatre. He had returned to Dublin shortly after John Millington Synge's death in 1909, and he writes admiringly in *Scholars and Gypsies* of Synge's courage and of William Butler Yeats's defense of Synge's work against detractors at the Abbey. Starkie was in the opening-night audience on 13 January 1910 for Synge's posthumously produced tragedy, *Deirdre of the Sorrows.* "Looking back I can remember no play that produced so deep an impression upon me," he says in *Scholars and Gypsies.*

During this period the political situation in Ireland was becoming increasingly grave, and Starkie was discouraged on visits to England to find little awareness of or interest in the gathering crisis. The outbreak of World War I in 1914 did not ease the tension, and after a short period of cooperation against Germany the Irish began to believe that their efforts were unappreciated by the English. The climax came with the Easter Rebellion of 1916. Starkie, living at home with his parents, heard of the rebellion from the milkman on Monday morning, 24 April. Describing the events of the next few days in *Scholars and Gypsies,* he notes that many people viewed the uprising almost as a sporting event and stood in the streets for a better look while bullets whizzed overhead.

In 1917 Starkie graduated from Trinity College with the second-best record in his class, taking first-class honors in classics, history, and political science. His opinion of the aged senior fellows, to whom he refers as "the Struldbrugs" in an allusion to the elders of Laputa in the third book of Jonathan Swift's *Gulliver's Travels* (1726), however, was not as high as theirs of him: "all that kept them alive was their profound hostility to their colleagues whom they had seen day by day declining towards the tomb. Hatred gave them zest to rise from their beds on Saturday mornings and get themselves transported in cabs into College to vote against any project of reform." These feelings did not extend to the provost, the legendary Dr. John Mahaffy, who was Starkie's godfather and for whom he had great respect and affection.

On graduating, Starkie was offered a teaching position at a boy's school in northern Ireland, but he was unwilling to be sheltered in such a setting while the war continued. Owing to his general poor health and in particular his asthma, combat duty was out of the question. Through his father's connections, however, he was offered a position at the Dominions and Colonial Office in London. The post did not thrust him into the heart of the fray, but he felt more useful there than he would have as a schoolmaster. The job lasted less than a year, mainly because asthma attacks caused Starkie to absent himself frequently from the office on Downing Street. Seeking a position in a warmer climate, he joined a Young Men's Christian Association unit that provided entertainment and comfort for British troops abroad. Starkie was sent to Genoa, Italy, and the experience was a turning point in his life. The city, the people, and the excitement were enormously energizing, especially when contrasted to the divisions and pessimism in Dublin. It was in Genoa that he met the woman who was to become his wife. When he first saw Italia Porchietta, she was singing to patients in a hospital ward. "Her singing was youthful in its freshness," he says in *Scholars and Gypsies,* "but its deep appeal sprang rather from an inherited tradition of centuries. I also remembered how [Baldassare] Castiglione had said that beauty was the result of emotional struggle in past lives."

After the Armistice in November 1918 Starkie and other Y.M.C.A. workers formed a troupe to entertain the soldiers who were awaiting demobilization; they played at Allied camps and bases throughout northern Italy. In the town of Montebello Vicentino, Starkie befriended five Hungarian Gypsy prisoners of war and aided them in acquiring wood to construct makeshift fiddles. To one of them, Farkas, he became a blood brother, and he swore that he would someday visit Farkas in Hungary and mix with the Gypsy's tribe. Starkie may have made the pledge lightheartedly, but the oath would haunt him and would affect the course of his life.

His tour through northern Italy introduced Starkie to the mesmerizing courtesan, Mary Paulon; the early stirrings of Fascism; and the poet and Italian patriot Gabriele D'Annunzio. Starkie was in the crowd in St. Mark's Square in Venice when D'Annunzio publicly called for the annexation of Fiume (Rijeka), Croatia, across the Adriatic from the city.

Six months after the Armistice, Starkie and many of the soldiers he had been entertaining were sent to southern Italy by train. In Taranto, Starkie was given a pair of gray flannel trousers and a shirt in exchange for his uniform and released from further obligations to the Y.M.C.A. His father had written, advising that he return to Dublin to read law, but Starkie found a band of Gypsies and decided to give their way of life a brief trial. "I cannot say that, at the time, I enjoyed the following weeks. . . . living, as I was doing, among vagrants, whose activities would have awakened the suspicions of the police, if there had been an efficient force at the time, I was able to plumb the depths of human poverty." He wandered from Taranto to Reggio with a hunchback; they were joined on the way by a suspicious-looking impresario and a prostitute. In Reggio he slipped away from his companions and took a steamer to Sicily, where he walked from town to town as a wandering minstrel.

Prodded by letters that finally caught up with him, Starkie decided to return to Ireland. First, however, he went back to Genoa, where he and Italia became engaged. Returning to Ireland in 1919, he took an M.A. at Trinity College in 1920; his father died the same year. In August 1921 he married Italia, and after a honeymoon in Spain they settled in Dublin. Italia knew no English and was terrified by the civil war that was raging in Ireland. Starkie maintained an uneasy neutrality in the conflict: he was angered by the clumsy British policy toward Ireland but horrified by the terrorism of the nationalists. He later joked that he was accused of being the "greatest Englishman that ever came out of Ireland."

Starkie received a Ph.D. in Spanish and Italian literature from Trinity College in 1924. In 1926 he was appointed professor of Spanish and lecturer in Italian at Trinity. He and Italia had two children, Landi William and Alma Delfina. The family spent the summers with Italia's parents in Italy, with occasional trips to Spain, and Starkie

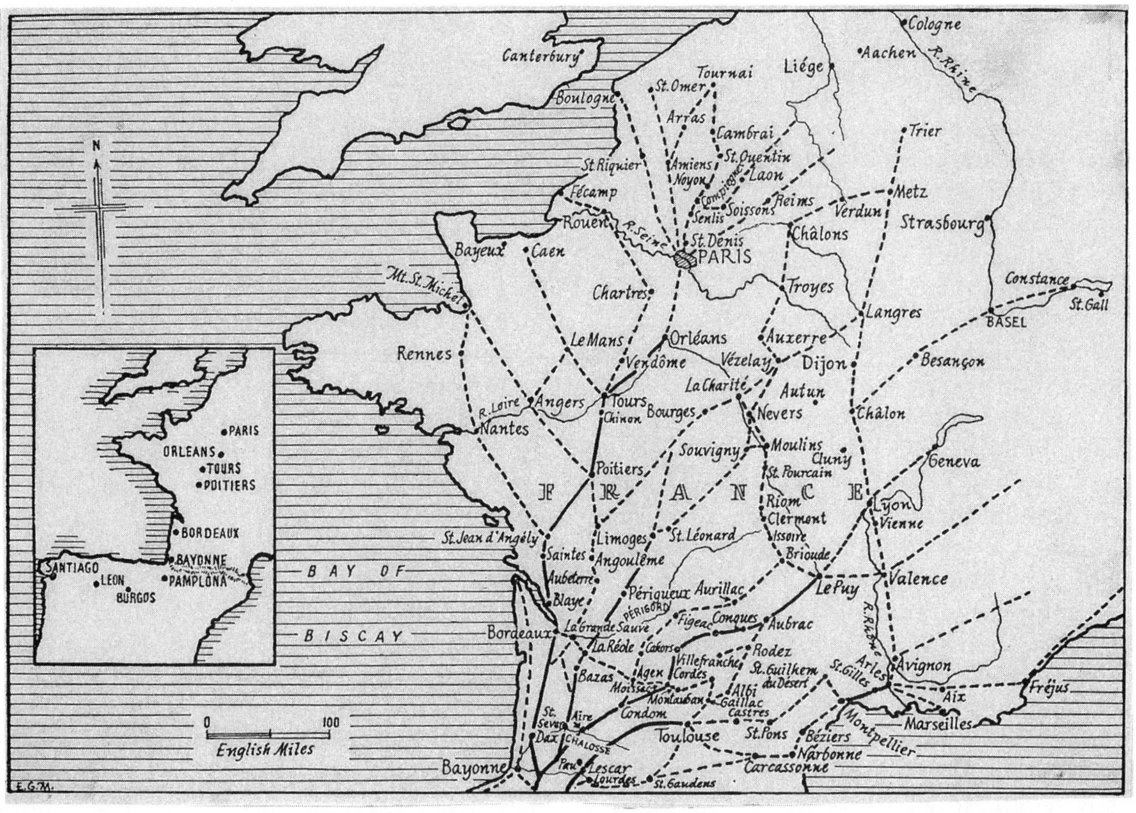

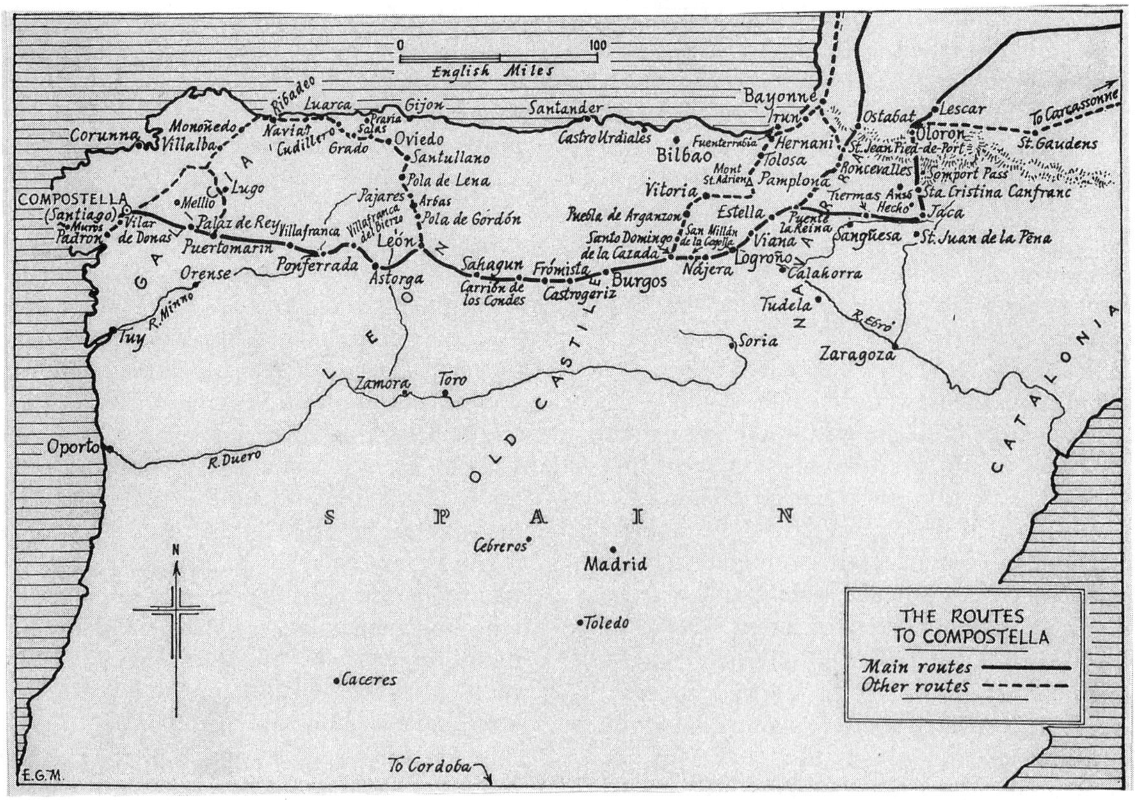

Maps of pilgrim routes, from Walter Starkie's The Road to Santiago *(1957)*

produced critical biographies of dramatists from these countries: *Jacinto Benavente* was published in 1924, two years after the Spanish playwright won the Nobel Prize for literature; *Luigi Pirandello* followed in 1926. Starkie had been captivated by Pirandello when he saw the opening performance of *Six Characters in Search of an Author* in Milan in 1921. The response to the play had been chaotic, and as Starkie looked around the audience he had seen Pirandello himself, "a melancholy, drooping figure with sad eyes." He had been equally impressed when, during his wanderings in Sicily after the war, he had visited Pirandello's hometown, Porto Empedocle, whose main industry was sulfur mining, refining, and exporting: "And there is the great band of workers creeping out of the dark holes in the earth, bearing their loads towards the furnaces," he recalls in *Scholars and Gypsies.* "Never had I seen a more wretched hang-dog crew. The old miners, gnarled and twisted like stunted olive trees, were not as pathetic as the young porters shuffling along like ghosts of the damned. Their pinched, yellow faces, already doomed by the sulphur fumes, malaria and malnutrition, haunted me for many a day, and I recognized for the first time the bedrock of Pirandello's tragic genius."

In 1927 Starkie was invited to join the directorial board of the Abbey Theatre. Recent productions had been fraught with controversy, and Starkie's role was to act as an arbiter among the factions. His position brought him into closer contact with Yeats, Sean O'Casey, and the intellectual life of Dublin.

Starkie, however, was restless. As he writes in *Scholars and Gypsies:*

> In the middle of a serious lecture to a university class, the diabolical Gypsy tunes of Farkas would steal into my brain and make my body tingle for longing to be away on the parched plain near the brown tents listening to the sound of fiddles played at night beneath trees. . . . One night during the spring of 1929 . . . I had a curious telepathic dream in which I saw Farkas through an arch beckoning to me despairingly. I tried and tried to rush to his assistance, but could not pass through the arch. I awoke gasping for breath and bathed in cold sweat, thinking I was dying. I had no doubt in my mind that Farkas had called out to me for help, and I remembered with remorse that I had never fulfilled the oath I had taken exactly ten years before in the Venetian countryside. I looked at my watch and marked the exact time the reminder had come, and I determined to fulfill my promise.

That summer Starkie set out with a rucksack, a violin, and a small amount of money to follow the Gypsy life. His account of his adventures that summer would appear as *Raggle-Taggle: Adventures with a Fiddle in Hungary and Roumania* (1933). Starkie traveled extensively during the academic year, as well: he lectured in Florence, Stockholm, and Uppsala in 1926 and in the United States and Canada in 1929. In 1930 he was visiting professor of Romance languages at the University of Chicago, and in 1931 and 1932 he taught in France. But in 1933, with the publication of *Raggle-Taggle,* he came to be recognized as a folklorist and travel writer as well as a modern-language scholar.

Raggle-Taggle opens with Starkie meeting a Gypsy woman, Anna, who after several glasses of brandy invites him to her room so that she may dance in private to his fiddle. She assures him that her elderly husband is out of town, and they will not be disturbed. "Being of a weak nature and thinking it un-cavalier to refuse a lady, I went to her lodgings." After more glasses of brandy, she prepares to dance for him: "She started to undress with rapidity. Her blue and yellow muslin frock, her petticoat and underclothes slipped off as though someone had pulled aside a curtain." Starkie plays, and Anna dances, until there is a knock at the door and the maid announces that Anna's husband is returning. Starkie quickly makes his exit through a window:

> Grasping my fiddle-case I climbed on to the ledge and found that luckily there was not much of a drop to the ground. As I stood there I had a last fleeting vision of Anna amid a cloud of frills and flounces and then I jumped down into the street.
>
> As I hurried back to my lodgings by devious routes I mentally thanked Anna's husband for his consideration in knocking at the door of his own house. If he had followed the English husband's plan and carried a latch key, the law of husbands would have claimed another victim.

This story sets the tone for Starkie's five books about his travels with Gypsies, vagabonds, and pilgrims: they are not scholarly discussions but lively, anecdotal accounts in the spirit of the people they describe.

Starkie camps one night in a graveyard, and in the early hours of the morning he meets an old man with whom he passes the remainder of the night listening to stories of vampires and werewolves. In Budapest he spends an evening with Magyari Imre, the Gypsy violin king, from whom he learns the magic that Gypsies associate with music. In Transylvania he meets the formidable Hungarian Gypsy fiddler Rostas: "When he looked at you, his queer opal-coloured eyes shone with a malevolent glint and a deep gash across his forehead gave him an expression of fierceness." Through Rostas, Starkie learns that Farkas had died of a fever in Kolozsvár on 19 March 1929, the same night on which he had appeared in Starkie's dream. Starkie accompanies Rostas on a daylong ramble that ends at Rostas's village. He and Rostas play their fiddles in the local bars and cafés that night before returning to the hovel that houses Rostas's wife, three children, mother, brother, and sister-in-law. Between the fleas that attack him in droves and the sister-in-law, who in the depths of the night tries to relieve Starkie of his wallet and, when that fails, turns to amorous embraces and "words of invitation," it would seem that the cross-cultural effort was a disaster. Nevertheless, the reader gets the impression that Starkie has achieved his goal: "The whole scene seemed unreal to me: I could not realize that I was sleeping amid Gypsies in Transylvania." And, after several other frightening adventures, he reflects as he is sailing up the Danube from Bucharest to Belgrade, where he will take the train to Italy and rejoin his wife and children: "Why should humanity sell themselves as slaves to the machine to become soulless robots, having lost all desire for the life of freedom? I wish to rove again among the Gypsies where there are still coppersmiths who make pans by hand, wood-makers who carve by hand, and women who wear hand-embroidered smocks."

The year after *Raggle-Taggle* appeared to wide acclaim, Starkie published *Spanish Raggle-Taggle: Adventures with a Fiddle in North Spain.* Again he meets a collection of prostitutes, beggars, confidence artists, and misfits, but such characters are balanced by beautiful Gypsy dancing girls and, perhaps most of all, by sunny mornings spent tramping alone on country roads. In Ezquioga he joins thousands of pilgrims who hope to see a vision of the Virgin Mary, as some peasant children had a few weeks earlier. In the presence of one of those children, on the hillside where the visions appeared, Starkie seems to see the Virgin for a second as the clouds part.

There are many other adventures as he walks from northern to southern Spain, bisecting the country. In Madrid he dons more acceptable clothing and meets leaders of the Spanish literary community. As he resumes his vagabond life he falls ill, collapsing in El Escorial with double pneumonia. It takes the best part of a month for him to recover sufficiently to return to Dublin.

Don Gypsy: Adventures with a Fiddle in Barbary, Andalusia, and La Mancha (1936) is Starkie's third and longest book of Gypsy travel. He begins his wanderings in Morocco, looking for traces of Gypsy tunes in Arabic music. Back in Spain, in one of his favorite areas, Andalusia, he plays his violin in a circus and at night revelries and meets an old friend named Mariano. He visits the Gypsy camps and some of the most desperate slums in Europe. As in his other books, Starkie reveals a facility not only for meeting and befriending some of the most peculiar, and often frankly evil, characters imaginable but also for knowing just how far to go with them before quietly slipping away.

Starkie enters completely into the way of life he follows. As a linguist, he can understand his subjects and can be understood by them. As a violinist, he has a skill that makes him welcome nearly everywhere. As a scholar, he has an endless curiosity about cultures other than his own. Finally, as a writer, he is able to relate a lively, entertaining, and highly informative account of people and places most readers will never be able–or, in some cases, want–to visit. Whether he is watching a desultory bullfight in a small town, participating in an impromptu music contest in a café, or spending a sleepless night with the "shivers" in a mountain cave, Starkie conveys an enjoyment of life as it is unfolding. He seldom reveals any long-range plans or goals; rather, he ambles along, open to suggestion, allowing life to wash over him. He spends little money, because he thinks that money separates one from the adventures that await the poor; also, he does not carry much money for fear that he will be robbed by his disreputable companions.

On the visit to Spain recounted in *Spanish Raggle-Taggle* Starkie spent some time at a monastery, where he gave a lecture on Gypsy life to the community:

> The Gypsy does what all of us dream; he is beloved of poets, artists, musicians and all those who seek for romance and mystery in this humdrum world. The world has no power over him because he lives by traditions that are a closed book to its rulers. Do not look upon him as an outcast of society because he busies himself in the present without care for the future, and prefers his tents, which he calls moving houses, to the stateliest palaces in cities. Do not look upon him as a lawless scoundrel because his tribal laws are not our own. Remember that he has his observance and penalties, which he enforces without fear or favor. The word given to a Gypsy chief must not be broken, and many a giorgio who transgressed the law of the sons of Egypt found to his cost that Gypsy vengeance reached to the ends of the earth.

It is obvious that Starkie does not take the Gypsies lightly. He does not suggest that they are quaint, misunderstood, or essentially noble. They are a people apart, not because the local population rejects them but because they do not want to join the locals. They have their own code and their own values, and they do not seek assimilation or even friendship. Those who associate with them do so at considerable risk. Nevertheless, they are worth studying.

After Starkie was elected a fellow at Trinity, he and his family spent most summers at the home of Italia's parents, Don Alberto and Donna Delfina, near Genoa. *The Waveless Plain: An Italian Autobiography* (1938) is a memoir of those visits, or, as Starkie calls it in the introduction, "observations and rhythms which had accumulated over the space of twenty years in the mind of a humble wanderer." It is, perhaps, Starkie's least distinguished book: whereas his discussions of Italian culture are interesting if not always penetrating, when he moves into the political arena he is on slippery ground. Granted an interview with Benito Mussolini, he gives a warm ten-page portrait of *Il Duce,* who has brought peace, order, and a sense of destiny to the people of Italy. Starkie also gives a generally sympathetic account of the evolution of Fascism in Italy during the late 1920s and early 1930s. Near the end of the book he describes a visit to Italian troops in Ethiopia. Although he recognizes that the Italian invasion is unpopular in world opinion, he attempts to justify Italy's action by noting that Ethiopia is a possible outlet for Italy's burgeoning population, and he speaks highly of the Italian soldiers' courage and conviction.

After World War II broke out in 1939 Starkie was appointed to the British Council, which charged him with establishing a British Institute in Madrid. In an interview with George Ambrose Lloyd, first Baron Lloyd, president of the British Council, Starkie promised to "put the Raggle-Taggle Gypsies to sleep for the duration." The purpose of the institute was to promote cultural exchanges and understanding between the two countries. It was also hoped that English friendship would help maintain Spain's neutrality. No one could have been better suited for the task than Starkie. During his tenure as director, which lasted from 1940 to 1954, branches of the institute were established in Barcelona, Bilbao, Valencia, and Seville. Starkie resigned his Trinity professorship and fellowship in 1947. The following year he became special lecturer in English literature at the University of Madrid, a post he would hold until 1956.

Starkie's first postwar book, *In Sara's Tents* (1953), takes him back on the trail of the Gypsies. Starkie was nearly sixty years old by this time, but much of the fieldwork for the book had been done fifteen years earlier. The uncompleted manuscript had lain dormant, he says in the book, until 1950, when the ghost of James Stephens, author, minstrel, and Starkie's confidant in his undergraduate years, appeared to him: "He sat there cross-legged upon the table thumbing a guitar softly to himself and gazing at me with a wistful expression." *In Sara's Tents* deals with Gypsy history, music, and culture in a much more general way than Starkie's earlier books before turning to the focus of the narrative, the annual Gypsy pilgrimage to Les Saintes Maries in Provence, France, to pay homage to their patron saint, St. Sara, who the Gypsies believe was Egyptian. Gypsies are not generally Christians, and Starkie seeks in vain for a reason for this pilgrimage. Like so much of Gypsy culture, the practice remains a mystery.

Like *In Sara's Tents, The Road to Santiago: Pilgrims of St. James* (1957) is also more historically oriented than Starkie's earlier books; the travel narrative does not begin until nearly halfway through the text. Also like *In Sara's Tents,* it is an account of a pilgrimage–in this case, a non-Gypsy pilgrimage to the shrine of St. James in Santiago de Compostela, Spain. Now in his early sixties, Starkie takes a modern coach with a friendly conductor instead of walking the dusty pilgrim route. For short jaunts, however, he resumes his tramping and sometimes finds a ride in a peasant's cart. Nevertheless, his journey is sufficiently arduous to lead him to praise the "lonely pilgrims who forsake the rapid-moving supervised pilgrimages and make the long journey guided solely by the myriads of wandering souls in the star-dust of the Milky Way–that galaxy which, as Dante tells us, the common people call 'the Way of St. James.'" Starkie's interest in pilgrimages is as idiosyncratic as his fascination with Gypsies.

Some critics complained that *The Road to Santiago* was "over-long and discursive," and, indeed, one wonders whether the histories of so many statues in so many villages had to be recounted in so much detail. Likewise, the accounts of ancient battles between Moors and Spaniards in which the latter sought St. James's intervention, while well written, might have been left out. But the book does evoke the spirit of the pilgrimage and gives the modern reader a sense of how the medieval practice fits into the culture of modern Spain.

In 1956 Starkie began a series of visiting professorships at American universities, including the University of Texas, New York University, the University of Kansas, the University of Colorado, and the University of California at Los Angeles. In addition, he gave lectures at colleges and smaller universities throughout the country. In an article in *The Saturday Review* (26 July 1958) Starkie called American institutions of higher learning "little paradises of the humanities where the surroundings of the humanistic spirit of professor and student recall the best residential colleges in Europe."

In 1963 Starkie's autobiography, *Scholars and Gypsies,* was published to somewhat muted acclaim. The reviewer for *The Economist* looked forward to a sequel, while others found the reconstructed dialogues of Starkie's childhood somewhat stilted. The greatest fault of the book, one not noted by any of its contemporary critics, is that it covers less than a third of the author's life, and many of the incidents had already been described, often word for word, in *The Waveless Plain.* He dwells at great length on the 1920s and early 1930s and does not discuss his years in Spain or his experiences in the United States.

Starkie died in Madrid, where he had lived for several years, on 2 November 1976. His observations of Gypsy life, while more anecdotal than scholarly, provide rich insights into these shadowy, nomadic people. Just as important, Starkie's life serves as an example. As Julian Moynahan said in reviewing *Scholars and Gypsies* for *The New York Times Book Review* (24 November 1963): "Many lives have been more interesting and enviable in the telling than the living, but not so here. Emerging from the shadow of a somewhat blighted inheritance, Walter Starkie chose and enjoyed a lifelong freedom which most of us throw away with both hands on the day we leave school and take our first jobs."

H. M. Tomlinson
(21 June 1873 - 5 February 1958)

Fred D. Crawford
Central Michigan University

See also the Tomlinson entries in *DLB 36: British Novelists, 1891-1929: Modernists* and in *DLB 100: Modern British Essayists, Second Series.*

BOOKS: *The Sea and the Jungle* (London: Duckworth, 1912; New York: Dutton, 1913); republished, with an introduction by Christopher Morley (New York: Modern Library, 1928); republished, with an introduction by V. S. Pritchett (New York: Time Incorporated, 1964);

The Tramp in a Gale (London: F. Chalmers Dixon, 1912);

Old Junk (London: Andrew Melrose, 1918); republished, with a preface by S. K. Ratcliffe (New York: Knopf, 1920; revised edition, London: Cape, 1933);

London River (London & New York: Cassell, 1921; New York: Knopf, 1921; revised and enlarged, London: Cassell, 1951);

Waiting for Daylight (London & New York: Cassell, 1922);

Katherine Mansfield: An Appreciation (Montreal: Foster Brown, 1923);

Tidemarks: Some Records of a Journey to the Beaches of the Moluccas and the Forest of Malaya in 1923 (London & New York: Cassell, 1924); republished as *Tide Marks: Being Some Records of a Journey to the Beaches of the Moluccas and the Forest of Malaya in 1923* (New York & London: Harper, 1924);

Under the Red Ensign (London: Williams & Norgate, 1926; revised and enlarged, London: Faber & Faber, 1932); republished as *The Foreshore of England: Or, Under the Red Ensign* (New York & London: Harper, 1927);

Gifts of Fortune and Hints for Those About to Travel (New York & London: Harper, 1926); republished as *Gifts of Fortune, with Some Hints for Those About to Travel* (London: Heinemann, 1926);

Gallions Reach: A Romance (London: Heinemann, 1927; New York & London: Harper, 1927);

H. M. Tomlinson in 1949 (photograph by H. Charles Tomlinson)

A Brown Owl (Garden City, N.Y.: Henry & Longwell, 1928);

Illusion, 1915 (New York: Harper, 1928; London: Heinemann, 1929);

Thomas Hardy (New York: Crosby Gaige, 1929);

Côte d'Or (London: Faber & Faber, 1929);

All Our Yesterdays (London: Heinemann, 1930; New York & London: Harper, 1930);

Between the Lines (Cambridge, Mass.: Harvard University Press, 1930);

War Books: A Lecture Given at Manchester University February 15, 1929 (Cleveland, Ohio: Rowfant Club, 1930);

Norman Douglas (London: Chatto & Windus, 1931; New York & London: Harper, 1931; revised and enlarged edition, London: Hutchinson, 1952);

Out of Soundings (London: Heinemann, 1931; New York & London: Harper, 1931);

Easter MCMXXXII (London: Fanfare Press, 1932);

The Snows of Helicon (London: Heinemann, 1933; New York & London: Harper, 1933);

Below London Bridge (London: Cassell, 1934; New York & London: Harper, 1935);

South to Cadiz (London: Heinemann, 1934; New York & London: Harper, 1934);

Mars His Idiot (London: Heinemann, 1935; New York & London: Harper, 1935);

The Master (New York: New School for Social Research, 1935);

All Hands! (London & Toronto: Heinemann, 1937); republished as *Pipe All Hands!* (New York & London: Harper, 1937);

The Day Before: A Romantic Chronicle (New York: Putnam, 1939; London: Heinemann, 1940);

The Wind Is Rising (London: Hodder & Stoughton, 1941; Boston: Little, Brown, 1942);

Ports of Call (London: Corvinus, 1942);

The Turn of the Tide (London: Hodder & Stoughton, 1945; New York: Macmillan, 1947);

Morning Light: The Islanders in the Days of Oak and Hemp (London: Hodder & Stoughton, 1946; New York: Macmillan, 1947);

The Face of the Earth, with Some Hints for Those About to Travel (London: Duckworth, 1950; Indianapolis & New York: Bobbs-Merrill, 1951);

Malay Waters: The Story of Little Ships Coasting Out of Singapore and Penang in Peace and War (London: Hodder & Stoughton, 1950);

The Haunted Forest (London: Hodder & Stoughton, 1951);

Trinity Congregational Church (Poplar [London]: Privately Printed for Rev. Alan Balding, 1952);

H. M. Tomlinson: A Selection from His Writings, edited by Kenneth Hopkins (London: Hutchinson, 1953);

A Mingled Yarn: Autobiographical Sketches (London: Duckworth, 1953; Indianapolis: Bobbs-Merrill, 1953);

The Trumpet Shall Sound (London: Hodder & Stoughton, 1957; New York: Random House, 1957).

OTHER: Edmund Blunden, *The Bonaventure: A Random Journal of an Atlantic Holiday,* introduction by Tomlinson (New York: Putnam, 1923);

"Adelphi Terrace," in *H.W.M.: A Selection from the Writings of H. W. Massingham,* edited by H. J. Massingham (New York: Harcourt, Brace, 1925);

Christopher Morley, *Safety Pins and Other Essays,* introduction by Tomlinson (London: Jonathan Cape, 1925);

"Robert Louis Stevenson," in *Great Names, Being an Anthology of English & American Literature from Chaucer to Francis Thompson,* edited by Walter J. Turner (New York: Dial Press, 1926);

H. Liddell Mack, *Holidays at Sea in Homeland Waters and Beyond,* edited by Prescott Row, prefatory letter by Tomlinson (London: Homeland Association, 1926);

David W. Bone, *Merchantmen at Arms: The British Merchants' Service in the War,* introduction by Tomlinson (London: Chatto & Windus, 1929);

"Almayer's Folly: A Prelude," in *A Conrad Memorial Library: The Collection of George T. Keating* (Garden City, N.Y.: Doubleday, Doran, 1929), pp. 3–7;

Norah Hoult, *Poor Women!,* prefatory letter by Tomlinson (New York: Harper, 1929);

Herman Melville, *Pierre: Or, The Ambiguities,* preface by Tomlinson (New York: Dutton, 1929);

The War: 1914–1917, compiled by Tomlinson, Edmund Blunden, Cyril Falls, and R. Wright (London: The Reader, 1929);

Great Sea Stories of All Nations, edited, with a foreword, by Tomlinson (Garden City, N.Y.: Doubleday, Doran, 1930; London: Harrap, 1930);

C. E. Montague, *A Writer's Notes on His Trade,* introduction by Tomlinson (London: Chatto & Windus, 1930);

Best Short Stories of the War: An Anthology, introduction by Tomlinson (New York & London: Harper, 1931);

Samuel Butler, *Erewhon, or, Over the Range,* introduction by Tomlinson (New York: Cheshire House, 1931);

"Men of Action," in *The American Spectator Year Book,* edited by George Jean Nathan and others, (New York: Frederick A. Stokes, 1934);

"The Upper Amazon," in *An Anthology of Modern Travel Writing,* edited, with an introduction by Tomlinson (New York & London: Nelson, 1936);

"We Correspondents Saw War but Were Forbidden to Tell the Truth," in *The Great War . . . "I Was There!": Undying Memories of 1914–1918, 3 volumes, edited by Sir John Ham-*

merton (London: Amalgamated Press, 1938–1939), III: 1987–1989;

Thomas Cubbin, *The Wreck of the Serica*, edited by Tomlinson (1950).

SELECTED PERIODICAL PUBLICATIONS–UNCOLLECTED: "Fog," *Living Age*, 262 (24 July 1909): 227–230;

"British Merchant Seamen," *Living Age*, 270 (2 September 1911): 600–605;

"Pictures of War," *English Review*, 18 (November 1914): 513–522;

"A War Note for Democrats," *English Review*, 19 (December 1914): 70–77;

"Labour and the War," *English Review*, 20 (June 1915): 348–355;

"Shaw at Armageddon," *Literary Digest*, 305 (10 March 1917): 623–624;

"Wharves of London," *Living Age*, 305 (8 May 1920): 355–361;

"England of Hardy," *New Republic*, 25 (12 January 1921): 190–192;

"England through English Eyes," *Harper's*, 145 (July 1922): 259–264;

"The Day's Run," *Outlook*, 136 (9 January 1924): 60–61;

"Barbarism," *Living Age*, 320 (23 February 1924): 75–78;

"Books at Sea," *Living Age*, 320 (23 February 1924): 377–379;

"From a Log Book," *Living Age*, 322 (20 September 1924): 601–604;

"Concerning the Highbrows," *Saturday Review of Literature*, 2 (22 August 1925): 57–58;

"Letter from London," *Saturday Review of Literature*, 2 (5 December 1925): 394;

"Judges of Books," *Century*, 3 (February 1926): 425–434;

"Two Americans and a Whale," *Harper's*, 152 (April 1926): 618–621;

"Joseph Conrad," *Saturday Review of Literature*, 4 (15 October 1927): 191–192;

"If War Should Come . . . ," *Harper's*, 156 (December 1927): 71–77.

"H. M. Tomlinson, *By Himself*," *Wilson Bulletin*, 5 (September 1930): 20;

"A Journalist's Memoirs," *Fortnightly Review*, new series 128 (1 December 1930): 845–846;

"That Next War," *Forum*, 86 (December 1931): 322–327;

"Nemesis," *Forum*, 88 (September 1932): 130–134;

"Of Ships and Shoes and Sealing Wax," *Scholastic*, 24 (17 March 1934): 5;

"Problems of a Novelist," *Saturday Review of Literature*, 10 (12 May 1934): 685–686;

"A Great Journalist," *Fortnightly*, new series 136 (August 1934): 243–244;

"Ports of Call," *Yale Review*, new series 26 (June 1937): 704–717;

"Propaganda," *Yale Review*, new series 30 (September 1940): 63–74;

"Fish for Britain," *Rotarian*, 64 (February 1944): 28–29;

"Frankenstein in England," *Atlantic Monthly*, 174 (October 1944): 57–59;

"Presiding Spirit," *Atlantic Monthly*, 176 (July 1945): 76–77;

"The Power of Books," *Atlantic Monthly*, 180 (December 1947): 115–119;

"The Master of the 'Rockingham,'" *Atlantic Monthly*, 182 (December 1948): 62–64;

"Adventure in a Shop Window," *Holiday*, 6 (August 1949): 85–86, 88–89;

"Architect with Charm," *John O'London's Weekly* (16 September 1949): 558;

"London as Melville Saw It," *John O'London's Weekly* (11 November 1949): 669;

"The Alien Sea," *Holiday*, 8 (October 1950): 52–59, 77–78, 80–81;

"Thomas Hardy Country," *Holiday*, 14 (November 1953): 54–55, 124, 126–129;

"Call of the Tropics," *Holiday*, 16 (December 1954): 75, 78, 80, 145, 147–150, 152;

"The Ship Herself," *Holiday*, 20 (July 1956): 54–55;

"Historic Ghosts of London," *Holiday*, 23 (January 1958): 14, 16, 19, 21, 130, 132.

During his long and varied literary career, H. M. Tomlinson wrote thirty book-length works that, in terms of sheer volume and variety, place him among the most prolific writers of the modern age. His books include collections of essays, literary criticism, novels, pacifist tracts, history, patriotic essays during World War II, and travel books. His faithful presentations of his view of the world, in terms that communicate his subjective impressions without alienating objective readers, are invaluable guides to the events and spirit of his times. Tomlinson drew almost entirely from his varied and extensive experience. The influence of his style and personality on a younger generation of authors, his role as antiwar spokesman during the between-the-wars period, and his unflagging involvement in the literary milieu of his age make him a noteworthy figure of literary history. Although his eclectic approach to genre defies categorization, his contemporaries regarded him chiefly as a travel writer, and it is as a travel writer that most readers remember him today.

Passing the village of Manicoré aboard the steamer Capella *and dynamite fishing on the Madeira river (woodcuts by Clare Leighton, from the 1930 edition of* The Sea and the Jungle*)*

Henry Major Tomlinson rose to a position of eminence in letters without the assistance of formal education, powerful relatives, or independent means. He was born in Wanstead, Essex, on 21 June 1873. His father, Henry Tomlinson, had sailed a bark during the days of oak and hemp. As a child, his mother, Emily Tomlinson, had sailed with her father, a master gunner who had married the daughter of an officer of the East India Company. Tomlinson was raised in Poplar, a London shipping parish, and even his earliest memories linked him to what he later called the "alien sea." In 1886, when Tomlinson was thirteen, his father lost the family's savings in speculation and died shortly thereafter, so an uncle arranged to remove Tomlinson from school and to place him in a Scottish shipping firm as a clerk.

Tomlinson found his clerkship barely tolerable, but he made only one notable attempt to free himself from the office when, in 1895, he secured the recommendation of Sir Chalmers Mitchell and others as a geologist for the Jackson-Harmsworth expedition to the Arctic. However, he was rejected on the grounds that he would be too frail to endure the hardships of the journey. In 1898 Tomlinson married Florence Hammond, and it seemed that he had reconciled himself to his lot, but in 1904 a heated argument occurred during which his employer lost his temper. Tomlinson answered in kind and found himself out of a job. He was understandably reluctant to tell his wife that he was unemployed as she was pregnant with their first child, Henry Charles (later there would also be two daughters, Florence Margery and Dorothy Mary Major). He wandered to Fleet Street, and by the time he reached home he had arranged with Ernest Parke, editor of the radical half-penny paper *The Morning Leader,* to join the staff. Tomlinson marveled ever after at how easy it had been to obtain his freedom from the clerkship that he detested.

His new career not only freed him from the shipping office but also finally placed him on a ship; within six months he was assigned to cover first the 1904 Naval Maneuvers; then he was sent "by steam trawler, the *Windhover*, to the cod fleet on the Dogger Bank in the days of the Russo-Japanese War," a voyage he described in "Off Shore," an essay included in *London River* (1921).

Although Tomlinson's reputation as a man of letters is largely that of a writer of travel books, surprisingly few of his full-length works are sustained narratives of travel. For all practical purposes Tomlinson's full-length travel books are three in number: *The Sea and the Jungle* (1912), *Tidemarks: Some Records of a Journey to the Beaches of the Moluccas and the Forest of Malaya in 1923* (1924), and *South to Cadiz* (1934). He also wrote lengthy essays of travel, notably "Log of a Voyage, 1935" (*The Turn of the Tide,* 1945) and "After Fifty Years" (about the Tomlinsons' golden honeymoon cruise; *A Mingled Yarn,* 1953), but most of his travel essays were comparatively short. This was not entirely his decision since he wrote most of his travel pieces on commission for such periodicals as *Century, Harper's,* and *Holiday. Tidemarks,* based on a voyage undertaken for *Harper's,* is a series of chapters that had appeared separately as articles.

In his introduction to *An Anthology of Modern Travel Writing* (1936), Tomlinson wrote that "I have never made a voyage for pleasure." This was true in at least one sense: his early excursions, including his voyage up the Amazon that resulted in *The Sea and the Jungle,* were journalistic assignments for *The Morning Leader.* His subsequent journey to Malaya resulted from a commission by *Harper's* after Tomlinson severed his connection with *The Nation.*

Virtually every travel essay he wrote was on assignment. Tomlinson often assumed the pose of a reluctant traveler who could not evade the demands of his editors and who only left his wife and family under protest. The reluctance of Tomlinson to voyage became part of the persona that he was to develop in the course of writing travel narratives. The reluctant traveler, subject to the caprices of unreasonable editors, was a suitable persona for Tomlinson's purpose. It enabled him to assume the stance of a traveler who does not like his assignment and therefore, whether the reader likes it or not, will report only reluctantly. This strategy enhances the reader's credence since the traveler is not trying to impress an audience with his spirit of adventure or his marvelous observations but is merely trying to finish an unsought task. As Tomlinson's account of a journey progresses, this attitude changes as Tomlinson, in spite of himself, becomes enthusiastic, but by then he has established his trustworthiness and can convey his sense of wonder to his audience. The persona has become an important part of the flavor of Tomlinson's travel essays.

Another device that Tomlinson employed frequently was authorial intrusion. He often reminded the reader that he was subject to the limitations of travel narrative, that several conventions of travel books governed his writing, and that he was trying to maintain a scrupulous honesty. In *London River* Tomlinson points out other limits placed on his otherwise unrestricted candor: "I got to the ship's side in time to see a liner's bulk glide by. She would have been invisible but for her strata of lights. She was just beyond our touch. A figure on her, high over us, came to her rail, distinct in the blur of the light of a cabin behind him, and shouted at us. I remember very well what he said, but it is forbidden to put down such words here."

Another distinguishing trait of his travel writing is his use of anecdotal material. He can use the device not only to comment on the marvelous or unusual but also to maintain his stance of objective reporting by ascribing the fabulous to hearsay. Tomlinson frequently includes odd, even outlandish, tales as others have recounted them, but he carefully excludes them from his own direct observation and thus leaves it to the reader to believe or disbelieve the teller of the anecdote.

A fourth trait of Tomlinson's travel narratives is his vivid description of his observations, including a realistic presentation of the hardships of voyaging, often presented with sardonic wit, as in the following passage from *Gifts of Fortune and Hints for Those About to Travel* (1926):

> If the Garden of Eden had been anything like the Amazon jungle, then our first parents would never have been evicted; they would have moved fairly soon on their own account, without giving notice. . . . Tigers, snakes, lovely but malignant nymphs, and head-hunters are not the dangers. What kills men in the wilderness is anxiety, under-nourishment, and mosquitoes.

On occasion Tomlinson presents paragraphs of pure sensory description without philosophical embellishment, as in this passage from *The Sea and the Jungle:*

> Your glance caught a wave passing amidships as a heaped mass of polished obsidian, having minor hollows and ridges on its slopes, conchoidal fractures in its glass. It rose directly and acutely from your feet to a summit that was awesome because the eye traveled to it over a long and broken up-slope; this hill had intervened suddenly to obscure thirty degrees of light; and the imagination shrank from contemplating water which overshadowed your foothold with such high dark bulk toppling in collapse. The steamer leaning that side, your face was quite close to the beginning of the bare mobile down, where it swirled past in a vitreous

> flux, tortured lines of green foam buried far but plain in its translucent deeps. It passed; and the light released from the sky steamed over the "Capella" [the ship] again as your side of her lifted in the roll, the sea falling down her iron wall as far as the bilge. The steamer spouted violently from her choked valve, as it cleared the sea, like a swimmer who battles, and then gets his mouth free from a smother.

He devotes the same care for descriptive language to his rendering of people, jungle scenes, unusual smells, and even the taste of new foods.

Another trait of Tomlinson's travel style is his sense of irony, frequently heavy-handed. In another essay collected in *Gifts of Fortune* he mentions reading

> a recent narrative by an American writer, who had been collecting in Africa for a museum. He confessed that if he had not been a scientist he would have felt some remorse when he saw the infant still clinging to the breast of its mother, a gorilla, whom he had just murdered; so he shot the infant without remorse, because he was acting scientifically. As a corpse, the child added to the value of its dead mother; a nice group. That tableau, at that moment when the job was neatly finished, must have looked rather like good luck when collecting types in a foreign slum. He must have felt happy when skinning the child!

Of the devices enumerated–persona, authorial intrusion, reported anecdote, sensory description, and irony–the last reveals a source of weakness in Tomlinson's sustained travel narratives. In the process of reporting his travels Tomlinson increasingly yields to a desire to polemicize on the state of the world, the folly of progress, the destructive impulses of man, and the pessimistic outlook for the future of modernity. In the case of his later travel narratives, such a focus occasionally detracts from the appeal of his style.

In 1907 Tomlinson completed "The African Coast," a piece of approximately eight thousand words describing his voyage to Algeria, Tripoli, and Sicily. His resistance to his editor unavailing, Tomlinson dutifully takes his journey but hardly mentions Algiers. After noting pessimistically that "the barometer, wherever I am, seems to know when I embark," he devotes a few words to Algiers, boards the French ship *Celestine,* and bids Algiers farewell. Unlike most writers of travelogue, Tomlinson volunteers a few remarks about the dreariness of tourism: "I had travelled from Morocco to Algiers, and was tired of tourist trains, historic ruins, hotels, Arabs selling picture-postcards and worse, and girls dancing the dance of the Ouled-Nails to the privileged who had paid a few francs to see them do it."

Tomlinson turns his attention to the characters aboard the ship, including the solicitous skipper whose efforts to improve Tomlinson's enjoyment of the menu do not assuage his petulance:

> He has an idea I cannot read the menu, so when an omelette is served he informs me, in case I should suppose it is a salad. He makes helpful farmyard noises. There is no mistaking eggs. There is no mistaking pork. But I think he has the wrong pantomime for the ship's beef, unless French horses have the same music as English cows.

Tomlinson describes the "black Mediterranean," which can be "as ugly as the Dogger Bank" in December, and he turns his attention to the suffering deck passengers: "What those Arabs suffered on deck I cannot tell you. I never went up to find out. At Bougie they seemed to have left it all to Allah, with the usual result." The irony of the persona who travels to Algiers but who has virtually nothing to say about the place and who reports sufferings that he has refused to observe is an agreeable change from many travel essays.

His first view of Africa is also unusual:

> Now you understand why it was called the Dark Continent. It looked the home of slavery, murder, rhinoceroses, the Congo, war, human sacrifices, and gorillas. It had the forefront of the world of skulls and horrors, ultimatums, mining concessions, chains, and development. Its rulers would be throned on bone-heaps. You will say (of course you will say) that I saw Africa like that because I was weary of the place. Not at all. I was merely looking at it. The feeling had been growing on me since first I saw Africa at Oran, where I landed. The longer I stay, the more depressed I get.

However, Tomlinson brings himself to disembark at Sfax, where his narrative becomes more lively as his mood improves. He sees a "venerable fellow with an important beard, with a look of wisdom and experience," and even as he regrets his lack of Arabic, the fellow addresses Tomlinson in English. Tomlinson sits down to engage in a conversation that rapidly exhausts the Arab's vocabulary, but others gather to watch the Muslim "draw his finger across his throat in serious and energetic pantomime, and saw me nod in grave appreciation, when he was trying to make me understand what was his sympathy for the Christian conquerors of Sfax." After extricating himself from this embarrassing situation, Tomlinson quickly finds himself in a worse one with an Arab huckster. Joining his "outrageous tourist tweeds with the graceful folds of the robes" in the crowd around the huckster, he has a sudden revelation:

The huckster kept glancing at me, and from grave side-long glances that crowd of men went to the extraordinary length of grim smiles. Suddenly I recognised the trick of that Arab cheapjack. . . . As soon as dignity permitted I passed on, and my dignity did not keep me waiting for any length of time.

Tomlinson, jarred into involvement, begins observing what is going on around him, and the reader, like Tomlinson, finds himself intrigued by the sights and sounds of a strange marketplace. Some of his descriptions are vivid enough to be directions for putting oil on canvas:

Next door . . . was a regular tenant who bred goats, and fed them out of British biscuit-tins. Beyond them the stable was occupied by a party of swarthy ruffians who had arrived with a cargo of esparto grass. In the far corner, a family, crowded out, had been living for weeks under a structure of horrible rags. Smoke, issuing from a dozen seams, gave their home the look of a smouldering haycock.

He begins the final section of his essay with a personal description of the appeal of foreign places that is all the more convincing because he has described his earlier temporary funk:

You probably know there are place-names which, when whispered privately, have the unreasonable power of translating the spirit east of the sun and west of the moon. They cannot be seen in print without a thrill. The names in the atlas which do that for me are a motley lot, and you, who see no magic in them, but have your own lunacy in another phase, would laugh at mine. Celebes, Acapulco, Para, Port Royal, Cartagena, the Marquesas, Panama, the Mackenzie River, Tripoli of Barbary. They are some of mine. Rome should be there, I know, and Athens, and Byzantium. But they are not, and that is all I can say about it.

This passage, characteristic of Tomlinson, invites immediate identification with the reader by free use of the second-person pronoun. Tomlinson even draws the reader into his descriptive passages in this manner. When Tomlinson reaches Tripoli, one of the names that has aroused his imagination, his description becomes richer:

Tripoli, like other towns on these shores, looks as though it were sloughing away. Where stones fall, there they lie. In the centre of the town is a marble triumphant arch in honour of Marcus Aurelius. Age would account for much of its ruin, but not all; yet it still stands cold, haughty, austere, though decrepit, in Tripolitan mud, with mean stucco and plaster buildings about it. The arch itself is filled in, and is used as a dwelling. Its tenant is a greengrocer, and the monument to Marcus Aurelius has an odour of garlic; but it need not be supposed that that was specially repugnant to me. How could the white marble of Marcus, to say nothing of a warmer philosophy no less austere, be acceptable to our senses unless translated, with a familiar odour of garlic, by modern greengrocers?

"The African Coast," as short as it is, gives some indication of the direction his longer travel narratives would take: a highly personalized view of the world, an almost intimate accord between writer and reader, and an apparent disregard for reporting places or events except as they engage Tomlinson's interest or alter his mood.

In 1909, as Tomlinson recalled in 1934, "One day, there dropped in, home from the blue, a relative, a sailor, back once more. He casually discussed his next voyage to a place not yet on the map two thousand miles up the Amazon and its main tributary! I pointed out to him that his ship would, in that case, rise to the altitude of about five hundred feet above sea level." The relative, Tomlinson's brother-in-law, maintained that his trip was real and invited Tomlinson to use a spare cabin and accompany him. Tomlinson, never one to waste an idea, "wrote a light-hearted account of this, and the next day, on the editorial stairs, Ernest Parke murmured, 'That was an amusing lie of yours today.' I assured him that the voyage was to be demonstrated and that I was even invited to go and see it done. 'All right,' he said, 'then go.'" That was the genesis of Tomlinson's best-known travel book, *The Sea and the Jungle*, Tomlinson's account of his voyage to Brazil, his return via Tampa and New York, and his observations and adventures in between. This book, published in 1912, established its author as an interesting new voice in English letters.

Tomlinson begins *The Sea and the Jungle* with a comment warning the reader implicitly that this book is not going to conform in all particulars to the usual travel narrative:

Though it is easier, and perhaps far better, not to begin at all, yet if a beginning is made it is there that most care is needed. Everything is inherent in the genesis. So I have to record the simple genesis of this affair as a winter morning after rain. There was more rain to come. The sky was waterlogged and the grey ceiling, overstrained, had sagged and dropped to the level of the chimneys. If one of them had pierced it! The danger was imminent.

He proceeds to describe his unexpected meeting with the skipper of the *Capella* (without specifically identifying him as his brother-in-law) and the skipper's subsequent success in persuading Tomlinson to serve aboard the steamer as ship's purser. Tomlinson, in the role of the city's prisoner, asks

> "What . . . shall I do about all this?" I waved my arm round Fleet Street, source of all the light I know, giver of my gift of income tax, limit of my perspective. How should I live when withdrawn from the smell of its ink, the urge of its machinery?"
>
> *"That,"* he [the skipper] said. "Oh, damn that!"

After the skipper extends his invitation, Tomlinson finds himself committed to the voyage, but he spends a few pages talking about his feelings, warning the reader that his travelogue will not leave land until he himself does, and preparing to embark. On the *Capella* Tomlinson acquaints himself with the ship's officers and men, discovers in his conversations with sailors that he has not left politics at home, weathers a storm, and begins to understand the mystic identification of the sailors with their ship. He also meets the ship's doctor, who "tried me with such things as fevers, Shaw, Brazilian entomology, the evolution of sex, the medical profession under socialism, the sea and the poets. But my thoughts were in retreat, with the black dog in full cry. It was too cold and damp to talk even of sex."

Tomlinson's duties as purser were comparatively light, judging from how seldom he speaks of them, but he found several subjects to occupy the reader while he waited for the ship to arrive in Para. In addition to discussing the superstitions and loyalties of sailors, their involvement in battening down hatches and resisting an angry sea, and their conversations, Tomlinson describes their foibles. One sailor, named Chips, becomes upset when he cannot find his prized Victoria Cross (a medal awarded only for acts of remarkable heroism), and Tomlinson helps in the search. The object turns up in Chip's sea chest, but as Chips tries to secure it, "a low foreign sailor snatched it from him. The Cross fell to the deck. I recovered it from the feet instantly in a white passion, and chanced to look at it. It confirmed that one, named Chips here, was something in the Royal and Ancient Order of Buffaloes."

After one sailor has related the tale of Handsome Jack (a yarn that recalls the story of Rip Van Winkle) and Tomlinson has heard the English shipping clerk's tale of Captain Davis's shrunken head, the *Capella* prepares to sail from Para to the interior. The ship takes aboard sixty head of cattle, including an extremely rebellious heifer, and proceeds upriver, combining river travel with the irritants of the jungle. Tomlinson discusses the efforts of American engineers and other invaders of the jungle to bring civilization to the interior, and only when he is halfway through his narrative does he confide that "our steamer, the 'Capella,' is taking up supplies for the establishment at Porto Velho, from which the new railway begins, three miles this side of San Antonio." Since the ship was literally in the jungle, Tomlinson had ample opportunity to describe flora and fauna, usually in connection with anecdote:

> Then there are the other things which, so far as most of us know, have no names, though a sailor, wringing his hands in anguish, is usually ready with a name. Today we had such a visitor. . . . He was a bee the size of a walnut, and habited in dark blue velvet. In this land it is wise to assume that everything bites or stings, and that when a creature looks dead it is only carefully watching you. I clapped the net over that fellow and instantly he appeared most dead. Knowing he was but shamming, and that he would give me no assistance, I stood wondering what I could do next; and the cook came along. The cook saw the situation, laughed at my timidity with tropical forms, went down on his knees, and caught my prisoner. The cook raised a piercing cry.

Tomlinson saw enough of insect life to conclude, "I do not wonder [H. W.] Bates remained in this land so long; it is Elysium for the entomologist." Tomlinson speculates for a time on the absurdity of regarding the richness of Brazil merely as a source of rubber, and eventually the *Capella* arrives at Porto Velho. The contrast between the efforts of the ship to arrive and the "bland indifference of Porto Velho to the 'Capella,' which had done so much to get there," bemuses Tomlinson. He meets several interesting people, including Neil O'Brien, whose rumored "dangerously inflammable nature" prevents Tomlinson from finding "common footing with him for some time." He also meets others who have tales to tell, including an Englishman who tells the story of the steam shovel, an anecdote that is reminiscent of the earlier parts of Joseph Conrad's *Heart of Darkness* (1902) in its description of a company's distance from and lack of understanding of the daily realities of its far-flung operations in the jungle.

Tomlinson, becoming restless, fails to convince others to accompany him into the jungle beyond Porto Velho, but providentially an American, "Marion Hill of Texas," invites Tomlinson to take a holiday in the jungle, and although the captain of the *Capella* warns Tomlinson that "if I returned too late I should have to walk home," he accepts the offer. After some exploration, fearing that he will be too late to sail home with the *Capella,* Tomlinson participates in a madcap dash back to Porto Velho by way of railroad handcar. At one point Hill and Tomlinson fear that they will collide with a locomotive, only to discover that what they have mistaken for a headlamp is only a firefly. They return the night before the *Capella* sails homeward, and Tomlinson plans to accompany her until he learns that the return of the *Capella* will be leisurely. When the ship docks at Tampa, Tomlinson takes a train to New York and then returns to England on a Cunard liner.

The Sea and the Jungle provides fascinating reading, but it raises some questions of plausibility that Tomlinson did not resolve. For example, his taking a chance of missing his return trip home, thereby risking at the least a lengthy sojourn at Porto Velho, requires more explanation. Years later, John Gunther's interview with Tomlinson, for the February 1926 *Bookman* (London), indicated other areas where he might have been more thorough in his narrative:

> And what happened to O'Brien, the adventurer in "The Sea and the Jungle"?
>
> "O'Brien," commented his discoverer, "was hanged."
>
> Did Mr. Tomlinson see again the Doctor in "The Sea and the Jungle," whom he left behind precipitously in Para? He did. Doctor James is one of his best friends.

Gunther's questions reflect Tomlinson's omission of names, a travel-writing convention popular among the Victorians. Tomlinson's brother-in-law is merely the skipper, one sailor merely Chips, and another memorable figure merely the Chief. Those few who have names, such as O'Brien and Marion Hill of Texas, would be hard to locate should one wish to verify Tomlinson's depiction of them. There is no reason to doubt Tomlinson's veracity, but despite the charm of his anecdotes, the authenticity of his descriptions, the playfulness of his irony, and the force of his personality, a modern reader (perhaps unduly skeptical) sometimes has the impression that some episodes are imperfectly unified with the basic narrative and that some details remain unnecessarily vague. However, the emphasis in Tomlinson's writing is on perspective rather than on detail.

Except for *The Tramp in a Gale*, a limited edition reprint of an article that had appeared in Ford Madox Ford's *English Review* in September 1912, Tomlinson did not publish another book for some six years. He remained primarily a journalist. In August 1914, he was in Belfast on assignment for *The Daily News*, which had merged with *The Morning Leader*. Civil war in Ireland seemed to be imminent, but the outbreak of the Great War postponed the threatened Irish discord. *The Daily News* sent him to Belgium, and in 1915 he became an official correspondent of the British Armies in France for *The Daily News* and *The Times* (London). He was as close to the thick of the fighting as his status allowed, frequently in danger, and he matched the seriousness of the soldiers with his attempts to report the war accurately. He quickly won a reputation for reliable reporting, and many, including Arnold Bennett, came to regard him as the most trustworthy of the war correspondents. In 1917, after meeting Tomlinson at the front, H. W. Massingham invited him to become associate editor of *The Nation* at £10 per week. A few months after this meeting, Tomlinson was free to accept the offer since one consequence of his honest reporting of the war was to receive orders to return to England. He wryly recalled in 1925:

> When I was recalled from France that spring I ceased to be a war-correspondent because Lord Northcliffe's representative on the Newspaper Proprietors' Association, so I was informed by my own newspaper, had objected to me as a "humanitarian." I don't know what crime that word was intended to imply, but obviously it condemned me, for there can be no answer to it in the nature of things; and as a result I went out of daily journalism to the seclusion of Adelphi Terrace, to sit in an office all day with Massingham.

During his years with Massingham, Tomlinson published three collections of essays–*Old Junk* (1918), *London River* (1921), and *Waiting for Daylight* (1922). These collections established him as a popular author and introduced him as a master of the essay as a literary form. The subjects of these essays were to become recurrent themes in his later writing: the lure of travel, the glory of British naval and mercantile history, the horrors of war, the value of literature, the mysterious attraction of the sea, and personal musings. These collections, often generalized as "travel essays," range in their subjects from a visit to a coal mine, to sighting a foundered sailing ship from a liner, to impressions of London from the point of view of a soldier on leave from Flanders, to the terrors of public speaking, to an interruption by his three children as he tries to write. Tomlinson finds everything interesting and conveys his fascination. An essay by Tomlinson is as likely to be an appreciation of Herman Melville, a capricious look at civilization from the point of view of the future anthropologist, or a description of a family pet, as it is likely to concern travel or the sea. Tomlinson's interest in virtually everything is infectious. *Old Junk* demonstrates the range of Tomlinson's interests. He describes his first impressions of an ocean liner. Having gained his nautical experience aboard ships that he could measure at a glance, Tomlinson now

The Beach of Ternate, with Tidore in the distance, photograph by Tomlinson in Tidemarks *(1924)*

feels that he is not really on a ship, but in a city: "A steward appeared at my door, a stranger out of nowhere, and asked whether I had seen a bag not mine in the cabin. He might have been created merely to put that question, for I never saw him again on the voyage. This liner was a large province having irregular and shifting bounds, permitting incontinent entrance and disappearance."

"Initiation," which focuses on the first voyage of Tomlinson's young son, describes the boy's perplexity during his first encounter with a heavy sea: "As we were about to emerge into the open, the wet, deserted deck fell away, and a grey wave which looked as aged as death, its white hair streaming in the wind, suddenly reared over the ship's side, as though looking for us, and then fled phantom-like, with dire cries. The Boy shrank back for a moment, horrified, but then moved on. I think I heard him sigh."

Tomlinson's descriptive powers lose nothing when his travels take him no farther than a local shop owned by Mr. Monk:

> In one corner of his shop a young lady was caged, for it was also the post office. The interior of the store was confused with boxes, barrels, bags, and barricades of smaller tins and jars, with alleys for sidelong progress between them. I do not think any order ever embarrassed Mr. Monk. Without hesitation he would turn, sure of his intricate world, from babies' dummies to kerosene. There were cards hanging from the rafters bearing briar pipes, bottles of lotion for the hair of school-children, samples of sauce, and stationery.

In this passage Tomlinson has combined the affected irony of the caged woman, an example of his alliteration in lists, and his personal assessment of Mr. Monk's inventory.

He seemed at this time perfectly content to remain in England without further thought of traveling abroad. However, after a series of conflicts with the Rowntree Trust that controlled *The Nation*, Massingham submitted his resignation on 10 December 1922. He continued to edit *The Nation* through June 1923, but for Tomlinson, Massingham was *The Nation*. Accordingly, he left when Massingham did.

Tomlinson was not long in finding employment. *Harper's* magazine commissioned him to tour Malaysia and the Far East, one result of which was *Tidemarks*. The book presented different problems than had *The Sea and the Jungle*. In his earlier full-length travelogue Tomlinson could draw not only from his own inexperience with a long ocean voyage and the nature of the Amazon jungle but also from the drama inherent in an ocean-going vessel's journey more than two thousand miles inland. *Tidemarks* begins with less drama. However, in at least one sense Tomlinson more than compensates for the lack of ready-made adventure. Frederick P. Mayer comments,

> To read "Tide Marks" and see how surprising it is to Tomlinson to set sail on a ship; to see how splendid all the sailors are and how glorious every prospect (nor is man vile), is to be convinced that Tomlinson never rode

a ship before. You believe he is young, inexperienced. You become startled to learn that although he may be easy to surprise, he is not young in years or in experience. You wonder at his fifty or more years.

Mayer qualifies his description of Tomlinson's enthusiasm by noting that "Tomlinson plays with his delight in a thoroughly knowing and sophisticated way"; he realizes "his own extravagance and sometimes plays on it. That takes some of the sting away." In *Tidemarks* this exaggerated extravagance compensates for the absence of a narrative structure such as the circumstantial plot which helped *The Sea and the Jungle* to grip its reader.

Tidemarks has several traits in common with *The Sea and the Jungle*, however. Tomlinson embellishes his account with anecdotes, descriptions of interesting characters, tongue-in-cheek comments on other travelogues, and powerful descriptions of natural and man-made phenomena. However, he frequently comments negatively on the nature of man's progress and also, every time he meets a fellow European, introduces the subject of the Great War. Like his other books of travel, *Tidemarks* begins with a view of Tomlinson's life in London. His editor, Massingham, "was on a journey to interview the proprietor [of *The Nation*], to learn whether he should continue to hold up a lamp in a dark and naughty world, or blow it out. Oil costs money." Tomlinson, at this point, has been visited by a one-armed man selling Christmas cards, and he asks how the man lost his arm. The veteran replies that "if you were a nice lady, I'd say it was cut off by a German on the Somme," but reveals that he had actually lost his arm to infection after being bitten by a British Army mule.

Then Tomlinson begins his voyage. While crossing the Red Sea he converses with the skipper about the hazards of sailing, and the captain tells him a story of a ship striking an uncharted rock in the Red Sea. This anecdote would eventually become an important part of the plot of Tomlinson's novel *All Hands!* (1937) some fourteen years later. When Tomlinson enters new realms, his approach to description differs considerably from the method of his earlier travel writings. Instead of trying to describe what he sees in wholly sensory language, he comments on the significance of what he sees in the context of the England that he has left behind.

> I regretted I could not seek his opinion about Java, a land that was a serious disappointment to me some time before I reached it. The gorgeous East obviously could not be, and ought not to be, so gorgeous as Java's holiday posters, which are in the style of the loudest Swiss art. "Come to Java!" Well, perhaps not. Not while the East Indies are so spacious and have so many other islands; not if Java is like its posters. Why should the East call itself mysterious when it advertises itself with the particularity of a Special Motor Supplement?

When Tomlinson reaches his first Javanese port, Tanjong Priok (Tanjungpriok), he suffers the onslaught of a vicious swarm of mosquitoes and decides to abandon the ship, changing his plans so that he can ride the railway from Tanjong Priok to Batavia (now called Djakarta). According to the guidebook, black monkeys remain on one side of the track while gray monkeys remain on the other. Tomlinson is weary of hearing fellow voyagers repeat this fact, remarking, "By the time you have persuaded the customs officer that you have no explosives in your luggage, that your face and its photograph in the passport really do approximate, and have got the man from the hotel at Weltevreden to understand that you intend to go by train and not in an automobile already wrecked, the monkeys are forgotten."

Soon after the train begins to move, however, a friendly Dutch traveler points out the over-reiterated fact to Tomlinson. "I was going to ask him whether they would forfeit the government subsidy if they broke the contract and spoiled the story," but Tomlinson's peevishness passes, and he "nodded, and looked first at the black tribe, and then at the gray, to show him that his good nature was not wasted on me."

Overall, Tomlinson's observations of Java confirm a pessimism that had begun to grow even before World War I:

> The Javanese agriculturists, ever since they had a civilised government–and that was early in the Christian era–have had to make their fields meet the extortions of so many conquerors before they dared to call any rice their own that now they deserve the glowing testimonial of all directors of empire and great business affairs. Their training has been long and thorough. Hindu, Mohammedan, and European each has taught them the full penalty for Adam's fall; and so the habit of very early rising, and of a long day in the sun, with but a meager expectation of any reward, give them the right aspect of sound and reliable workers.

As the journey proceeds, however, Tomlinson's depression recedes, as it had in "The African Coast." He finds it amusing that a diminutive Javanese woman offers him a selection of Ethel M. Dell's popular English romantic novels, and he moves to a characteristic source of comedy in his travels–his refusal to follow guidebooks or to view such wonders as the "ancient Buddhist tope at Borobudor [Borobudur]." An eminent archaeologist informs Tomlinson that "It is probably the only chance in your life to see one of the most remarkable temples in the world." First Tomlinson resists the notion: "Why, if Buddha were to come to Java, Borobudor is probably the one place he would be careful to avoid!" Then he concludes that there is no escape from the Borobudurs of this world. Wandering about the marketplace and musing on its sights and sounds and smells, he believes he has successfully avoided Borobudur until he is on a train, departing for Sourabaya (Surabaja), "when an official from my hotel, whose anxious face was peering into every coach, presently found me. There had been a mistake. I had not paid for my motor-car to Borobudor. It had waited for me all day. Borobudor?"

This more amiable Tomlinson surfaces in various comments. He notes at one point that Celebes (Sulawesi) "has received less critical attention than Laputa" and rectifies that lamentable oversight, meets an adventurer named Maguire with whom he explores part of the jungle, suffers himself to taste durian (which he finds horrible) at the behest of a missionary who finds the fruit as tempting as the mythical lotus, scales the walls of the volcano Ternate, and generally becomes a more active participant in his travels. However, despite the growing enthusiasm that Tomlinson feels as the result of splash baths and his scaling of Ternate, he cannot forget bitter memories of the war which the smell of the durian evokes: "But for the durian, the spell of Ternate might not have been broken"–

> What was that? I forgot the crimson lor[r]ies. My memory had gone straight back to an old German dugout with its decaying horrors. I thought I must have been mistaken, but advanced cautiously. Nothing could be there, I told myself, that was like the [German] trenches of the Flers line [overrun by the British during the Battle of the Somme]. Confidence returned; the suggestion had gone. Then the ghost passed me again, invisible, dreadful, and I clutched the table, looking round.

He continues his narrative in better spirits, but he restricts himself to recounting a series of episodes (often using the form of diary entries) to describe his progress. This book becomes a pleasing mixture of history, misadventure, suspense, and humor. At one point he remarks, "In 1906 the Dutch were at war with a rajah of the island, who came out with all his court in a sortie, not with the intention of fighting, but of dying to escape dishonor. Brahma does not seem to encourage Falstaffs."

On ship, Tomlinson observes the perplexity of the mate after the latter has discovered women in the crew's quarters, ostensibly selling matches. When the mate appeals to Tomlinson for advice, duty-bound to expel the women but fearing to lose his crew, "I assured him that certainly this was a matter which only our captain could decide. The captain would know what ought to be done, for not only is he an experienced navigator, but a member of the Dutch Reformed Church. I am neither."

Tomlinson and another Englishman, Smith, decide to take a trek through part of the jungle. Shortly after Tomlinson defies the laws of probability by successfully negotiating the slippery log that serves as a bridge over a river, his companion Smith lies down on the trail, too fatigued to move.

> Poor Smith was indeed on his back. . . . He could not go another step. While kneeling beside him, pointing out that he was yet too young to give himself as food for ants, I noticed that my breeches were bloody and had to touch the leeches off my legs with my pipe. . . . I glanced at Smith, and then saw a group of them attached to his belly. He had not noticed them. How soon he was up! How well he stepped out! Even leeches can have their good points.

The prevailing tone of *Tidemarks*, despite such diversions, remains somewhat pessimistic. Even on Tomlinson's return home, when he inquires of a sailor about a rumored SOS call, he learns that the ship has put about because a young hand had gone overboard. "The passengers complain of a draught," the sailor reports before returning to his business. However, on his return, sighting at night the formless shadow that was England, Tomlinson muses that perhaps the presence of England "may have been retired within the night, dominant on its seas, making no sign, knowing the supreme test of all its labors was at hand, vigilant but composed, waiting for another morning to dawn in the hearts of men, when there should be light to build the City of God."

The ending of the travel book holds some promise of hope, but as a whole, *Tidemarks* suffers from Tomlinson's increased pessimism following World War I. Rarely does his narrative proceed more than a page without a reflection or a grim reminder of the nature of the civilization that a traveler hopes to escape. Tomlinson, carrying his taboos with him, has no escape, nor does his reader. John Gunther, in his interview with Tomlinson, raises questions about omissions in *Tidemarks:*

> And what happened to McGuire [*sic*], the Irish adventurer who was turned by war to the East, and who had a better time among tigers in Borneo than with corpses

in France? Mr. Tomlinson, after an expedition with him to the jungle, leaves McGuire in a very precarious position indeed. What happened to him?

"Oh," said Mr. Tomlinson, "he got out, of course. Only fever could kill him."

Gunther also notes that Tomlinson abandoned his boat to scale Ternate and wonders why he did that, as well as how he managed to return. "'I was tired of knocking about,' Mr. Tomlinson told me, 'and I wanted to see something of the life of those islands. I just got off the boat. I knew another one would come along–some day. One did.'"

Although these answers may seem somewhat flippant, they reveal something about Tomlinson's attitude toward the purpose of his travel writing. For Tomlinson such details were trivial compared with his feelings at the time, the immediacy of his experience, and the significance of his observations. His attempt to render his travels vividly, partly aided by the exaggerated enthusiasm Mayer has noted, also accounts for the lack of attention he has paid to transitions between episodes. For Tomlinson his journey was not a unified whole so much as a series of unpredicted adventures.

During the next ten years Tomlinson's collections of essays, widely touted as travel books by dust jackets and reviewers, consisted of essays on other subjects. The grouping of essays closest to being a travel book is *Gifts of Fortune*. The book begins with a lengthy essay discussing travel in general and other essays contain anecdotal material derived from Tomlinson's voyages. "Out of Touch," for example, tells of Tomlinson's meeting a youth during his Amazon voyage. The young man had crossed the Andes to meet a ship, marveled at finding books in Tomlinson's cabin, and admitted that his father was indeed an eminent English judge of Tomlinson's acquaintance. The youth comments, "Fancy your knowing my dad. I thought I was quite out of touch here." Another essay derives from Tomlinson's travels to Malaya. "Elysium" describes his meeting with a missionary who dresses for dinner despite his distance from London. Tomlinson also included "The Rajah," a description of a native in outmoded uniform displaying spangled decorations. Tomlinson's fellow countryman tells him that the rajah is "Quite mad, you know. Used to be a rajah till we turned him out, and thinks he's one still. Just as well to humour the poor old thing."

In a mixed review that appeared in the 1 January 1927 issue of *T. P.'s and Cassell's Weekly*, D. H. Lawrence argued that "*Gifts of Fortune* is not a travel-book. It is not even, as the jacket describes it, a book of travel memories. Travel in this case is a stream of reflections, where images intertwine with dark thoughts and obscure emotion, and the whole flows on turbulent and deep and transitory. It is a reflection, throwing back snatches of image." The chief hint Tomlinson gives to those about to travel, according to Lawrence, is the "sinister suggestion that they had better stay at home," and he summarized his objections to the label in no uncertain terms: "There are travellers and travellers, as Mr. Tomlinson himself makes plain. There are scientific ones, game-shooting ones, Thomas Cook ones, thrilled ones, and bored ones. And none of these, as such, will find a single 'hint' in all the sixty-six hinting pages, which will be of any use to them."

Apparently satisfied to have exposed Tomlinson's "fraud," Lawrence ended his review with a tribute to the book: "Mr. Tomlinson gives us glimpses of a new vision, what we might call the planetary instead of the mundane vision. The glimpses are of extreme beauty, so sensitive to the other life in things. And how grateful we ought to be to a man who sets new visions, new feelings sensitively quivering in us."

During this period Tomlinson was moving in new directions. He wrote three novels, all of which incorporated extensive travel into their plots. *Gallions Reach* appeared in 1927 and won the Femina-Vie Heureuse Prize in 1928. *All Our Yesterdays,* which appeared in 1930, struck most as an antiwar book although little of it focuses on the trenches, and *The Snows of Helicon*, which appeared in 1933, takes its major characters all over the world, frequently implausibly. During this period, Tomlinson also embarked on a lecture tour of the United States, published pamphlets on Thomas Hardy in 1929 and on Norman Douglas in 1931, and toured the United States a second time in 1932, this time to lecture against war. *Côte d'Or* (1929), which many must have bought in the expectation of its being a travel book, focused chiefly on Tomlinson's postwar impressions of the place.

In *South to Cadiz,* Tomlinson's final sustained travel narrative, he demonstrated that the alternative to his earlier approach was to present a unified work at the expense of much of the appeal of his style. It is the least satisfying of his travel books although it employs the same devices that had worked in earlier travel narratives. It is less a travelogue than a commentary on such aspects of modern life as the role of culture, the revolution that resulted in the short-lived Spanish Republic, the role of machinery in modern life, and the prospects of another European war. Included are digressions concerning the successes and failures of democracy and the sad

Tomlinson in 1931

state of world economics during the Great Depression.

The book begins, characteristically, with Tomlinson's attempt to evade his editor's demand that he cover the Economic Conference in Spain. However, he eventually makes the journey with three other journalists–James Bone, Robert Lynd, and Horace Horsnell, to whom he extends apologies in his dedication of the book–and Tomlinson spends almost all his time in their company. Tomlinson describes passing scenery and the oddities inherent in such encounters as that in which he and a railway porter refer to each other as *caballeros,* but the focus of the beginning chapters is on the four travelers discussing such matters as Ernest Hemingway's presenting in *Death in the Afternoon* (1932) a better picture of Spanish countryside than their view can offer; D. H. Lawrence as a novelist; the detrimental impact of nationalism; and other topics. The discussion is entertaining, but not what a reader of travel books might ordinarily expect.

When the four arrive in Madrid, Tomlinson begins to suggest why this book is different: "We found ourselves in the Plaza de las Cortes. That this was Madrid was fairly certain, but we saw at once that if there is an old Madrid it is only a fable to furnish songs for guitars and gramophones. The city looked what it is, the outcome of a political need for a central place where the government could reach out more easily all round."

In Toledo, Tomlinson devotes some time to overt description, mixed with history:

> Nor does it matter which way you turn, for you are sure to get lost. . . . This was a capital of the Goths, portentous early with the row over Arius, for Protestantism began reasonably soon after the Apostles left it to us to do our best. Then the emirs and caliphs came, and protestants of all kinds, for four centuries, had to be tactful. The Christians returned to Toledo a few years after William the Norman landed at Hastings, and the Cid became its alcaide. Its archbishops began their empire of souls and bodies with an authority few emperors have

> possessed, or even desired, and ruled for ages with a magnificence which lingers. You enter the remaining glow and shadow of it. The glory of confident power subdues doubt, but its very brightness is the cause of the dread which lives dumbly within the cold gloom it casts.

The emphasis has shifted from a description of sensory impressions to one overshadowed by historical and political significance. The pattern continues throughout. Tomlinson asks, "Is the generous spirit gone which shaped the cathedrals?" and sees the mean spirit of civilization lurking in barrens and ruins.

In Cadiz, Tomlinson returns to the spirit of anecdote that pervaded his earlier works, but the nature of Spanish anecdotes is political. He reports the conversation of Mr. Pablo, who

> gossiped quietly of the revolution. You could see it gave him pleasure to have a journalist listening to him. That revolution was nothing. It was not bloody. It was only like an orange, which falls when it is very ripe. No trouble, no trouble at all. The people of Cadiz, sir, are always reformers. They had been waiting for it how long? and then the day came. Then they went into the streets. People must go into the streets when there is a revolution, a fiesta. Certainly there was a little burning, but the people were polite. He himself saw that. There was no cruelty. He himself watched, and the reformers went into a church, and came out holding pictures, and other things which are in churches, in their arms, to burn them. But they were not angry. There were many people in the square, and a man who was carrying a picture of the Holy Family to burn pushed it into Mr. Pablo, but he was not rude. He said, "Excuse me. I am truly sorry to crush you."

Shortly thereafter the four journalists encounter a Briton, and Tomlinson has an opportunity to report an anecdote more to his style. This man and his friend Bill had been on HMS *Serpent* during the war, and Bill had taken a photograph as the German warship *Potsdam* sank. Bill had not realized how important an "exclusive" photograph would be to Fleet Street journalists, but he soon discovered its value when he was besieged with offers for the photograph. Befuddled by so many willing to pay unheard-of sums for the photograph, Bill sells it to a man who promised to have the balance of the payment for him on Monday. As the result of waiting for the rest of his money, Bill returned to his ship a day late, and since this occurred in time of war, he was sentenced to five years' imprisonment.

Málaga also provides an opportunity for an anecdote, this time concerning the confusion of the Spanish workmen when they learned that their king had fled the revolution. They wanted to burn a church, but they were advised not to burn something that was their own. Instead they were advised, since they insisted on burning something, to kindle the house of the priest after warning that unfortunate cleric. Tomlinson ponders the meaning of this and related adventures in the hope of discovering something of value. During his reflections he realizes that "I had found Granada, but felt I had lost it as soon as I had found it. Its savour had gone." However, he ends the book on a hopeful note by noticing that, after sundown,"the spread of Granada was the inversion of the lighted heavens. It was a lower density of stars, unwinking and glacial. The universe was a hollow sphere, and the constellations continued below me uninterrupted. Granada was part of the Galaxy."

Tomlinson seems to find meaning in his final view of Granada, but *South to Cadiz,* more reflective and less optimistic than his previous travel books, brightens and fades like a spirit fighting depression. The remembered pleasures of the earlier style occasionally surface, but they submerge under the weight of various philosophical and political reflections. It becomes lighter at the end, but for how long will this last?

Tomlinson's travels over the years took him to Europe, Africa, South America, the Mediterranean, and the Far East, as well as to the United States, where he lectured at Princeton, Yale, Cornell, Columbia, and Harvard, among others. However, travel was only one of his interests. Closely related to his fascination with travel was his love for the shipping tradition, and he combined his experiences, memories, and research to write such historical tributes as *Under the Red Ensign* (1926), *Below London Bridge* (1934), and *Malay Waters: The Story of Little Ships Coasting Out of Singapore and Penang in Peace and War* (1950). He devoted a good deal of his effort to support the pacifist cause between the wars, but he became an energetic propagandist for the war against Hitler from 1939 on.

Tomlinson's three major travel books–*The Sea and the Jungle, Tidemarks,* and *South to Cadiz*–demonstrate the impact that World War I and the postwar years had on Tomlinson's ability to put a cheerful face on the world. The techniques of the travel books do not change, but their proportions do. The three works reveal a marked decline in the entertainment of Tomlinson's enthusiasm and irony, accompanied by a corresponding increase in the philosophical seriousness with which he viewed even the commonplace. His later writing does not uniformly reveal a growing pessimism, but it does become more difficult for him to maintain the light touch in longer narratives as he becomes more assured in his perceptions of impending disaster. Perhaps that is why, after 1935, he changed his approach to the literary marketplace. Except for *Mars His Idiot* (1935), Tomlinson's publications consisted primarily of essays. His only attempts at longer sustained narratives were his novels and *Malay Waters*.

Although Tomlinson's style naturally varied slightly when he wrote in different genres, so that his travel books are distinct from his novels, literary criticism, or chronicles, his essay style changed surprisingly little during his long literary career. His presentation of an amiable and self-deprecating voice, his preference for an anecdotal style, his sensory descriptions, his gentle irony, and his fascination with virtually any topic make his travel books and essays particularly appealing to his readers, who respond to Tomlinson's ability to convey a sense of intimacy, immediacy, veracity, and engaging personality in all his travel narratives. He was an outspoken critic of progress for its own sake, and since he had begun life during the days of oak and hemp and lived into the space age, he had ample evidence at his disposal to argue that the malicious greed or heedless ignorance of financiers, military men, and industrialists had blighted the modern age. His description of modern life in the light of the values of the past that he remembered, vividly conveyed his sense of horror, disillusionment, and disgust with many aspects of modernity. The easy grace of Tomlinson's style was as much the product of his personality and of his wide range of interests as it was of his desire to describe the places that he visited. He combined a full and adventurous life with a prolific and variegated literary career in a way that entitles him to recognition as a minor classic.

Interview:

"Visit with the Author," *Newsweek,* 49 (8 April 1957): 116, 118.

References:

Helen Altick and Richard Altick, "Square-Rigger on a Modern Mission," *College English,* 5 (November 1943): 75–80;

Edmund Blunden, "H. M. Tomlinson," in *Edmund Blunden: A Selection of His Poetry and Prose,* edited by Kenneth Hopkins (New York: Horizon, 1961), pp. 303–308;

Fred D. Crawford, *H. M. Tomlinson* (Boston: Twayne, 1981);

John Freeman, "Mr. H. M. Tomlinson," *London Mercury,* 16 (August 1927): 400–408;

Alva A. Gay, "H. M. Tomlinson, Essayist and Traveller," in *Studies in Honor of John Wilcox by Members of the English Department, Wayne State University,* edited by A. Dayle Wallace and Woodburn O. Ross (Detroit: Wayne State University Press, 1948), pp. 209–217;

J. Ashley Gibson, "H. M. Tomlinson," *Bookman* (London), 62 (April 1922): 6–7;

John Gunther, "The Tomlinson Legend," *Bookman* (London), 62 (February 1926): 686–689;

Alfred F. Havighurst, *Radical Journalist: H. W. Massingham (1860–1924)* (Cambridge: Cambridge University Press, 1974), pp. 155, 275–277, 294–299, 318–319, 322–323;

Stuart Hodgson, *Portraits and Reflections* (New York: Dutton, 1929), pp. 185–191;

Kenneth Hopkins, Introduction to *H. M. Tomlinson: A Selection from His Writings,* edited by Hopkins (London: Hutchinson, 1953), pp. 11–19;

D. H. Lawrence, "*Gifts of Fortune,* by H. M. Tomlinson," in *Phoenix: The Posthumous Papers of D. H. Lawrence,* edited by Edward D. McDonald (New York: Viking, 1936), pp. 342–345;

Robert Lynd, "Mr. H. M. Tomlinson," in *Books and Authors* (London: Cobden-Sanderson, 1922), pp. 226–232;

Frederick P. Mayer, "H. M. Tomlinson: The Eternal Youth," *Virginia Quarterly Review,* 4 (January 1928): 72–82;

T. Michael Pope, ed., *The Book of Fleet Street* (London: Cassell, 1930), pp. 149–150;

J. B. Priestley, "H. M. Tomlinson," *Saturday Review of Literature,* 3 (1 January 1927): 477–478;

Derek Severn, "A Minor Master: H. M. Tomlinson," *London Magazine,* new series 18 (February 1979): 47–58;

Frank Swinnerton, *Background with Chorus: A Footnote to Changes in English Literary Fashion between 1901 and 1917* (London: Hutchinson, 1956), pp. 13, 126–127, 204–208;

Mary A. Taylor, "More Evidence of H. M. Tomlinson's Role in the Melville Revival," *Studies in American Fiction,* 20 (Spring 1992): 111–113;

Edward Weeks, "Authors and Aviators," *Atlantic Monthly,* 172 (November 1943): 58–59;

Stanley Weintraub, *Journey to Heartbreak: The Crucible Years of Bernard Shaw 1914–1918* (New York: Weybright & Talley, 1971), pp. 216–220;

Rebecca West, "A London Letter," *Bookman,* 69 (July 1929): 519–520;

Patrick Edward White, "Varieties of Primitivism in the Travel Books of D. H. Lawrence, Norman Douglas and H. M. Tomlinson," Ph.D. dissertation, University of Iowa, 1980.

Evelyn Waugh

(28 October 1903 – 10 April 1966)

Linda Strahan
University of California, Riverside

See also the Waugh entries in *DLB 15: British Novelists, 1930–1959* and *DLB 162: British Short-Fiction Writers, 1915–1945.*

Evelyn Waugh in 1930 (photograph by Madame Yevonde)

BOOKS: *The World to Come: A Poem in Three Cantos* (N.p.: Privately printed, 1916);

P.R.B.: An Essay on the Pre-Raphaelite Brotherhood, 1847–1854 (Westerham, Kent: Dalrymple Press, 1928);

Rossetti: His Life and Works (London: Duckworth, 1928; New York: Dodd, Mead, 1928);

Decline and Fall: An Illustrated Novelette (London: Chapman & Hall, 1928; Garden City, N.Y.: Doubleday, Doran, 1929);

Vile Bodies (London: Chapman & Hall, 1930; New York: Cape & Smith, 1930);

Labels: A Mediterranean Journal (London: Duckworth, 1930); republished as *A Bachelor Abroad: A Mediterranean Journal* (New York: Cape & Smith, 1930);

Remote People (London: Duckworth, 1931); republished as *They Were Still Dancing* (New York: Farrar & Rinehart, 1932);

Black Mischief (London: Chapman & Hall, 1932; New York: Farrar & Rinehart, 1932);

An Open Letter to His Eminence the Cardinal Archbishop of Westminster (London & Tonbridge: Whitefriars, 1933);

Ninety-Two Days (London: Duckworth, 1934); republished as *Ninety-Two Days: The Account of a Tropical Journey through British Guiana and Part of Brazil* (New York: Farrar & Rinehart, 1934);

A Handful of Dust (London: Chapman & Hall, 1934; New York: Farrar & Rinehart, 1934);

Edward Campion (London: Longmans, Green, 1935; New York: Sheed & Ward, 1935);

Mr. Loveday's Little Outing and Other Sad Stories (London: Chapman & Hall, 1936; Boston: Little, Brown, 1936); enlarged as *Charles Ryder's Schooldays and Other Stories* (Boston: Little, Brown, 1982);

Waugh in Abyssinia (London & New York: Longmans, Green, 1936);

Scoop: A Novel about Journalists (London: Chapman & Hall, 1938; Boston: Little, Brown, 1938);

Robbery under Law: The Mexican Object Lesson (London: Chapman & Hall, 1939); republished as *Mexico: An Object Lesson* (Boston: Little, Brown, 1939);

Put Out More Flags (London: Chapman & Hall, 1942; Boston: Little, Brown, 1942);

Work Suspended: Two Chapters of an Unfinished Novel (London: Chapman & Hall, 1942);

Brideshead Revisited: The Sacred and Profane Memories of Captain Charles Ryder (London: Chapman & Hall, 1945; Boston: Little, Brown, 1945);

When the Going Was Good: Selections Made by the Author from "Labels," "Remote People," "Ninety-Two Days," and "Waugh in Abyssinia" (London: Duckworth, 1946; Boston: Little, Brown, 1947);

Wine in Peace and War (London: Saccone & Speed, 1947);

Tactical Exercise: A New Story (London: Newnes, 1947);

Scott-King's Modern Europe (London: Chapman & Hall, 1947; Boston: Little, Brown, 1949);

The Loved One: An Anglo-American Tragedy (Boston: Little, Brown, 1948; London: Chapman & Hall, 1948);

Work Suspended and Other Stories Written before the Second World War (London: Chapman & Hall, 1948);

Helena (London: Chapman & Hall, 1950; Boston: Little, Brown, 1950);

Men at Arms (London: Chapman & Hall, 1952; Boston: Little, Brown, 1952);

The Holy Places (London: Queen Anne Press, 1952; London: Queen Anne Press / New York: British Book Centre, 1953);

Love among the Ruins: A Romance of the Near Future (London: Chapman & Hall, 1952); republished in *Modern Satire,* edited by Alvin B. Kernan (New York: Harcourt, Brace, 1962), pp. 43–58;

Tactical Exercise (Boston: Little, Brown, 1954);

Officers and Gentlemen (London: Chapman & Hall, 1955; Boston: Little, Brown, 1955);

The Ordeal of Gilbert Pinfold: A Conversation Piece (London: Chapman & Hall, 1957; Boston: Little, Brown, 1957);

The World of Evelyn Waugh (Boston & Toronto: Little, Brown, 1958);

The Life of the Right Reverend Ronald Knox, Fellow of Trinity College, Oxford and Protonotary Apostolic to His Holiness Pope Pius XII (London: Chapman & Hall, 1959); republished as *Monsignor Ronald Knox: Fellow of Trinity College, Oxford and Protonotary Apostolic to His Holiness Pope Pius XII* (Boston: Little, Brown, 1959);

A Tourist in Africa (London: Chapman & Hall, 1960); republished as *Tourist in Africa* (Boston: Little, Brown, 1960);

Unconditional Surrender (London: Chapman & Hall, 1961); republished as *The End of the Battle* (Boston: Little, Brown, 1961);

Basil Seal Rides Again or The Rake's Progress (London: Chapman & Hall, 1963; Boston: Little, Brown, 1963);

A Little Learning: The First Volume of an Autobiography (London: Chapman & Hall, 1964); republished as *A Little Learning: An Autobiography. The Early Years* (Boston: Little, Brown, 1964);

Sword of Honour: The Final Version of the Novels "Men at Arms" (1952), "Officers and Gentlemen" (1955) and "Unconditional Surrender" (1961) (London: Chapman & Hall, 1965); republished as *Sword of Honour: The Final Version of the Novels "Men at Arms" (1952), "Officers and Gentlemen" (1955) and "The End of the Battle" (1961)* (Boston: Little, Brown, 1966);

The Diaries of Evelyn Waugh, edited by Michael Davie (London: Weidenfeld & Nicolson, 1976; Boston: Little, Brown, n.d.);

A Little Order: A Selection from His Journalism, edited by Donat Gallagher (London: Eyre Methuen, 1977; Boston: Little, Brown, 1980);

The Essays, Articles and Reviews of Evelyn Waugh, edited by Gallagher (London: Methuen, 1983);

Evelyn Waugh, Apprentice, edited by Robert Murray Davis (Norman, Okla.: Pilgrim, 1985).

A major figure in twentieth-century British literature, Evelyn Waugh captured in his novels the attitudes, foibles, and virtues of the British upper classes. From the nostalgic romanticism of *Brideshead Revisited* (1945) to the black comedy of *The Loved One* (1948), his fiction presents a world that is exaggerated and distorted but, nevertheless, familiar to his readers. His travel writing, in contrast, describes people, places, and ways of life that are unfamiliar to his audience.

Arthur Evelyn St. John Waugh was born on 28 October 1903 in West Hampstead, a London suburb, to Arthur Waugh, managing director of the publishing firm Chapman and Hall, and Catherine Raban Waugh. Evelyn Waugh remained at home beyond the age that was typical for English boys of his class because of an appendicitis attack he suffered when he was eight. When he did begin boarding school, at age twelve, he had to enroll at Lancing rather than at Sherborne, where he had expected to follow his father and his elder brother, Alec. The scandal surrounding *The Loom of Youth* (1917), Alec Waugh's novel about boarding-school life, had made Evelyn unwelcome at Sherborne. From Lancing, Waugh went on to Hertford College, Oxford, on a scholarship in 1922. He left without a degree in 1924, briefly attended art school in London, and then took low-paying teaching jobs at schools in North Wales and Buckinghamshire. The success of his biography of the painter Dante Gabriel Rossetti, published in 1928, made it possible for him to marry Evelyn Gardner on 27 June of that year; their friends called her "She-Evelyn." That fall she became seriously ill with German measles. With the proceeds from Waugh's *Decline and Fall: An Illustrated Novelette* (1928) and some published articles, they went on a Mediterranean cruise from February to May 1929 to help her recuperate. Instead, her health worsened during the early part of the trip. That summer she left Waugh for another man.

Waugh, circa 1904, with his mother, Catherine Raban Waugh; his father, Arthur; and his older brother, Alec

For his first travel book, *Labels: A Mediterranean Journal* (1930), Waugh revised material from the diaries he had kept while traveling with his wife in 1929. On completing the work he destroyed the diaries. In the book Waugh presents himself as a bachelor–it was published in the United States as *A Bachelor Abroad* (1930)–and invents a young honeymooning couple, Geoffrey and Juliet, to represent himself and his wife. The work begins with Waugh leaving London on an airplane and ends with him debarking from a steamer at Harwich harbor and catching a train that will bring him to London in time for lunch. In between he visits the various cities and ports that then constituted a typical Englishman's tour of the Mediterranean. He titles his travelogue *Labels* because each locale he visits has already been detailed and described to such an extent that the descriptive tag has become more real to most people than the place itself. His purpose is to explore both the geographical site and the cliché and to decide whether the label is appropriate. The romance of travel, symbolized by the honeymooning couple, and the restorative powers of new locations, symbolized by the attractive female invalid Juliet, are the most persistent clichés that Waugh deflates.

Waugh's airplane journey from London to Paris sets the tone for the entire undertaking. Waugh has selected this then-unusual mode of transportation in the spirit of adventure, but he soon laments his choice:

> The chief discomforts of air travelling were, I discovered, those which had drawn me from London, only intensified very severely–cold and noise. The roar of the propellers was shattering. I followed the advice of the company and put cotton wool in my ears, but even so had a headache for some hours afterwards. The cold is worst about one's feet, which are provided with fur-lined footbags.

Waugh's decision literally to descend on Paris was prompted by a desire to infuse the mundane crossing with excitement, but after the first few minutes the flight is "very dull indeed." Waugh's seatmate is not the devil-may-care comrade he expected but a middle-aged woman with an attaché case who makes the trip on business every week. In the end, he concludes, all that can be said for this means of transportation is that it saves time.

In a Paris nightspot a well-dressed Englishwoman–who, Waugh implies, is someone of great importance–deflates the author's ego by terminating their conversation as soon as she realizes that he is not Alec Waugh, whose books she reads and collects. Still, Waugh hopes that this trip and his reporting of it will generate interest in himself and his work: "my hope was that, when someone saw in the gossip page that I was going to Russia, she would say, 'what a very interesting young man, and I must get his life of Dante Gabriel Rossetti out of the circulating library.'" This hope is dashed when he discovers the impossibility of his plan to travel to Russia.

Waugh first encounters the fictitious Geoffrey and Juliet on the train from Paris to Monte Carlo. It is obvious from their "marked concern for one another's comfort" that they are newly married; it is also apparent that Juliet suffers from poor health. They become a literary device that allows Waugh to recount experiences that he and his wife actually had but that would be inaccessible to the single and healthy narrative persona he has created. The narrator observes the experiences as a concerned outsider, not as a participant in the events. Waugh eventually detaches himself from the couple when they head in a different–and supposedly less dangerous–direction at Port Said, Egypt.

The journey from Paris to Monte Carlo by train fares little better in Waugh's estimation than his flight from London to Paris. He admits that he eschewed a "luxurious" train in an effort to recoup the losses he had suffered because of the "minor dishonesties" of the French, who relieved him of an inordinate amount of his change. When he reaches his ship, the *Stella Polaris,* he is not disappointed: "By any standard the comfort of the *Stella* was quite remarkable." Comfort is a crucial concern to the English traveler, and Waugh devotes considerable space to it. Camel riding, generally thought to be uncomfortable, precarious, and frightening, turns out to be "a delightful way of getting about, combining, as it does, complete security with an exhilarating feeling of eminence." On the other hand, some of the highly touted hotels are quite uncomfortable. In one "the bed was, I think, stuffed with skulls," and in another "there were far too many servants in the hall and not enough in the bedrooms." In restaurants the food is frequently expensive and disappointing. Waugh's particular area of expertise is alcoholic beverages (he would later be treated for alcoholism), and he samples and critiques the local spirits. For readers who imbibe he prescribes a hangover cure consisting of beet sugar, Angostura bitters, and cayenne pepper.

Waugh's knowledge and enjoyment of liquor comes second only to his appreciation of art. He presumes his readers' familiarity with Western artists both ancient and modern and mentions only in passing that a splendid work by artist "X" can be seen at place "Y." Although he denigrates certain contemporary Western artists, such as Jean Cocteau, whose work he views in Paris, it is for the "foreign," or non-European, artists that he reserves his most condescending and derogatory comments:

> In Cairo I have noted the pride and superiority which a Western mind must feel when confronted with Arabic art; this feeling is intensified and broadened a hundred times in relation to everything Turkish. They seem to have been unable to touch any existing work or to imitate any existing movement without degrading it.

Waugh finds aesthetic offense in nature, as well as in art. He will often begin an account of a famous landmark with the expected response ("I do not think I shall ever forget the sight of Etna at sunset") but end it with a remark that reverses its meaning ("Nothing I have ever seen in Art or Nature was quite so revolting"). He ridicules his fellow Britons who, influenced by William Makepeace Thackeray's description, see the Rock of Gibraltar as resembling a lion: "due to some deficiency in my powers of observation . . . it appeared like a great slab of cheese." Tourists, who generally remain nameless representatives of their occupations, classes, or nationalities, are typically depicted as naive; they are manipulated by their own preconceived notions and bilked by unscrupulous natives. Americans are the most pitiable because they have traveled across a great ocean in search of historical roots and culture that will continue to elude them. Waugh enjoys the companionship of his fellow Britons; even on the overcrowded ship he can rejoice in "a hundred Englishmen all around me, whistling as they shaved." Natives, on the other hand, are tolerated if they provide local color, like the "gully-gully" men of Port Said, or dismissed as nuisances if their attempts to beg, barter, or entertain are unsolicited.

While modern readers may be appalled by the bigotry of *Labels*, the work fulfills its function as a travel book in an entertaining and informative manner. It became a best-seller, and the critical response was positive. As Christopher Sykes points out in *Evelyn Waugh: A Biography* (1975), "It may be described as a pot-boiler, but strictures on such publications often ignore the qualities and contents of the pot, and the skill of the boiling." Books written for prospective travelers must "boil" the same ingredients: transportation, lodging, sights to see, and the people, both natives and fellow tourists, that one is likely to encounter. Waugh spices these essentials with memorable anecdotes and pithy remarks.

In *Remote People* (1931; republished in the United States as *They Were Still Dancing,* 1932), the second of Waugh's travel books, the narrative voice is that of a more mature and experienced traveler than the one who embarked on the Mediterranean tour. In actuality, the time span separating the two journeys was nominal: the *Labels* journey had commenced in February 1929, while the African trip began in the fall of 1930. Waugh's life, however, had altered in two major ways; one changed his perception of himself, and the other changed his perspective on the world. First, no longer was he a relatively unknown author and journalist. *Labels* did not appear until September 1930, but his novel *Vile Bodies,* which had come out in January of that year, brought him fame and modest fortune–enough to finance part of the African adventure about which he would write in *Remote Places.* The novel's success also gave impetus to his journalistic career, and editors were soliciting pieces from him. This affirmation of his abilities gave Waugh the confidence to approach several newspapers and suggest a commissioned assignment to Ethiopia (also known as Abyssinia) and, having received one from *The Times,* to write with a new sense of authority. The other change was his conversion to Catholicism on 29 September 1930. His conversion would profoundly influence his work for the remainder of his life, and his intimate knowledge of ecclesiastical matters and interest in religious history color *Remote People.*

Waugh's account in *Remote People* of the inception of his journey appears to be essentially truthful. During a dull afternoon in the library at the country home of Sacheverell, Osbert, and Edith Sitwell in Derbyshire, the topic of Ethiopia came up in conversation because of the impending coronation of its ruler, Ras Tafari, as the emperor Haile Selassie. Ethiopia captured Waugh's imagination, and he decided at that moment that he would travel there and witness the historical event. Waugh's motives may have been more complex than the account in *Remote People* suggests, however: he had entered a novelistic dry spell and needed new material and inspiration. The journey succeeded in this endeavor. *Black Mischief* (1932), his third novel, takes place in a fictional African nation and borrows heavily from his experiences on the trip recorded in *Remote People.*

The title of the book is somewhat misleading. The work is not primarily an account of customs of and encounters with indigenous populations in far-off locations. Waugh does record at length his interactions with a variety of people, but most of them are fellow travelers, expatriates, or other individuals for whom Africa is not an ancestral home. The natives are observed with interest, but Waugh seldom interacts with them except by necessity. The reader comes away from *Remote People* knowing little more about the local people than the names of the tribes in the various locations and their relative attractiveness in Waugh's eyes. The work, then, is a travel book that focuses on its author in the act of traveling rather than on the people or places he encounters along the way.

Waugh and his first wife, Evelyn Gardner, about the time of their marriage in 1928 (photograph by Olivia Wyndham, The Sketch*)*

Remote People is divided into four parts. In part 1, "Ethiopian Empire," he discusses his travels in Ethiopia and the event he went there to witness. His eyewitness report of the coronation of Haile Selassie stands on its own as a valuable primary historical document. Waugh claims that most other newspaper accounts of the event were inaccurate, even fictitious. To break the story in their earliest possible editions and thereby preempt their competition, reporters wrote and transmitted their stories before the coronation took place. This practice accounts for the discrepancies in the details reported in the various papers. Waugh is less offended by the yellow journalism than by the journalists' lack of imagination. They can only envision the European cliché of marbled halls–in actuality, the coronation took place in a tent–while Addis Ababa offers a wealth of colorful details that could have enlivened their reports. Waugh's account includes many such details. He describes the spectators, the music, and the ceremony from the point of view of one who is unclear about what he is seeing and unable to discriminate between the significant and the incidental. In spite of his newfound interest in the Catholic mass, he is unable to recognize any aspect of the Coptic ceremony. His companion, "Professor W." (the famous American Byzantinist, Thomas Whittemore), is equally confounded by the events. The disappearance of the emperor- and empress-to-be, along with the clergy, behind a curtain for an hour and a half adds to the confusion. The royal couple eventually emerge, crowned, and the celebrating begins. Waugh concludes his discussion: "If in the foregoing pages I have seemed to give undue emphasis to the irregularity of the proceedings, to their unpunctuality, and their occasional failure, it is because this was an essential part of their character and charm."

While in Ethiopia, Waugh decides to undertake a journey to Debra Lebanos suggested by Professor W. The two, escorted by an American driver and an uninvited native boy, travel to the monastery to discuss theology with the monks and view the holy relics. Their car is filled with supplies, including a hamper of delicacies from the Fortnum and Mason department store and empty Vichy bottles that the professor plans to fill with holy water from the sacred place. The trip is characterized by discomfort and near disaster. The vehicle barely survives the rugged terrain; the tent is unbearable; and the monastery fails to meet their expectations–the relics are of dubious authenticity, and the monks wish only to hear of the coronation. Waugh and the professor spend a miserable night in a bug-infested hut and are served food they find disgusting, including honey in its natural state, with dead bees and bird dung intact. After mass and a quick look around, they cut their visit short, preferring to risk a night on the plain rather than stay at the monastery.

Waugh's Ethiopian adventure concludes with a mule trip to the medieval city of Harar. He describes the countryside, the people, the animals, and the vegetation he sees along the trail. On arrival he finds a gated community with narrow lanes, houses, and rubble. Waugh condemns the two supposedly European inns for their lack of amenities but applauds their boldness in taking advantage of guests who would be unlikely ever to travel that way again, even if offered the best accommodations. He visits the famous bishop, Monsignor Jerome, and Government House and attends a prenuptial party that lasts for a week. His unofficial guide, Mr. Bergebedgian, earns Waugh's respect for his ability to feel at home anywhere and with anyone. In a rare moment of self-awareness, Waugh recognizes that "I shall always be ill at ease with nine out of every ten people I meet."

Waugh then leaves Ethiopia and his newspaper assignment behind and sets out on his own in the Aden protectorate and Zanzibar. He titles this part of his travelogue "The First Nightmare." Here he exclaims: "How wrong I was, as things turned out, in all my preconceived notions about this journey." In Zanzibar he finds the heat intolerable and resents the preemption of the indigenous culture by the immigrant Arabs and Indians. Kenya, on the other hand, resembles Ireland. He enjoys the races, luncheons, and evening picnics, social scenes taken directly from Anthony Trollope's fictional Barchestershire. He might even be deceived into thinking that he was in the south of France except for occasional reminders, such as stinging ants and natives.

The final leg of Waugh's journey takes him through British Africa and the Belgian Congo and finally–and gratefully–onto a ship headed for Southampton. "The Second Nightmare," part 3 of *Remote People,* begins with his difficulties in getting to Kigoma. At this point the book becomes, in Waugh's words, "literally a 'travel book'; that is to say, it deals less with the observation of places than with the difficulties of getting from one place to another." His progress is impeded by erratic schedules, the need to acquire medical certificates, and unreasonable people, such as the captain who ejects Waugh from his ship for failure to provide a ticket for a mythical motor bicycle. Waugh finds himself traveling on a boat and train with a Seventh-Day Adventist missionary who contracts malaria. The nightmare is broken during a short stay in Elizabethville, where the hotel offers "good wine, good cigars and very good food." Waugh then endures a boring six-day train ride to Cape Town, which he deems a "hideous city." With the forty pounds he has left in his pocket he purchases a third-class ticket on a ship leaving the same afternoon and arrives on 10 March 1931 in Southampton. Part 4, "The Third Nightmare," which consists of less than a thousand words, records his first evening back home in London, having dinner in a restaurant.

The reading public responded to Waugh's African travel book with an attitude of detached interest that matched his own attitude to the places he visited: *Remote People* claimed only enough audience to remain on the best-seller list for a week. Reviews were mixed, The negative pieces focused on Waugh's politics, while the positive ones praised his narrative skill.

Waugh endured the "nightmare" of his homeland for almost two years before setting out on another adventure, this time to South America. He recorded the events of this journey in his third travel book, *Ninety-Two Days* (1934). The trip also inspired a short story and a novella.

Waugh's ship, the S. S. *Ingoma,* departs from Tilbury on 2 December 1932. The crossing is remarkable only for its unusually high and rough seas. Waugh finds the other passengers dull, but as seasickness keeps them in their cabins for a large part of the voyage, he is not forced to endure much of their company. He spends a great deal of his time reading books on British Guiana (now known as Guyana). After stops at various islands the ship arrives in Georgetown, British Guiana, on 23 December 1932.

All of his shipboard reading has failed to prepare Waugh for the places he is about to experience. Life in Georgetown seems unamusing and hardly exotic. When two reporters interview him on his arrival, he discovers that he is of interest not on the merit of his literary career but simply because he has come: all arriving first-class passengers rate an interview and a write-up in the local papers. His Christmas dinner at the governor's house is dismal. The governor treats Waugh kindly and puts him in contact with "Mr. Bain" (actually Haynes), the district commissioner, who oversees the first part of Waugh's journey. Waugh soon comes to resent Bain as a spoiler of his fun.

After much moving back and forth of supplies and the planning and abandoning of various forms of transportation, Bain finally secures passage out of Georgetown on a train to New Amsterdam. The mosquito-infested train ride is made even more unendurable by Bain's ceaseless conversation. At one time New Amsterdam enjoyed prosperity and a modicum of civilized society, but the city is now greatly diminished. Waugh encounters the Jordanites, a strange sect named for a deceased Jamaican. On his way out of the city at dawn the next morning, he passes the Lutheran church that attests to the age of Dutch occupation.

At this point Waugh begins his real adventure across plain, savannah, and jungle. His journey on horseback to Kurupukari takes six miserable days. Waugh shows only slight interest in the flora and fauna; he does not describe the native animals unless, like the python in the process of swallowing a huge toad, they frighten him or, like the "cow bird" and the "bell bird," they disturb his rest. When the supply boat fails to arrive in Kurupukari, Waugh and Baines, who have between them a can of milk and a box and a half of biscuits, must survive on native food. The diet in this part of the world comprises, according to Waugh, only two items: *farine,* obtained from the root of the cassava, and *tasso,* which is some sort of dried meat. Eventually the boat arrives and allows Waugh to leave Baines behind and travel farther into the wilderness.

After one abortive attempt Waugh finally succeeds in passing through the forest and stops at the ranch of a Mr. Christie, who suffers from hallucinations, including visions of his dead mistress, and religious mania. This encounter had a profound effect on Waugh. Its significance for his fiction comes from the appearance of the Mr. Christie-like character in the short story "The Man Who Liked Dickens," which first appeared in *Hearst's International and Cosmopolitan* (September 1933) and is considered a classic. The

Frontispiece by Waugh for his first travel book, Labels: A Mediterranean Journal *(1930)*

story formed the basis for the novel *A Handful of Dust* (1934), one of Waugh's masterpieces. The novel ends with Mr. Todd, the renamed Mr. Christie character, holding Tony Last, the hero, captive in the jungle and forcing him to read aloud the works of Charles Dickens.

Waugh's next stop, at St. Ignatius Mission, seems to have been the most pleasant and meaningful experience of the journey. It is a period of rest, learning, and spiritual growth. In contrast, the Benedictine priory in Boa Vista, Brazil, proves disappointing. The name, Boa Vista, has assumed a mythical status for Waugh that is quickly shattered by the reality. None of the monks seems to work hard, yet Waugh finds them to be anything but carefree. Waugh feels uncomfortable and unwelcome at the priory. This sense of not belonging is a surprise to Waugh, who considers himself a member of the worldwide Catholic community, and it is intensified by the language barrier. Conversation is carried on in a strange mixture of German and formal French, and Waugh speaks none of the former and little of the latter. His feelings of disconnection and isolation would become an essential element of Tony Last's experience in *A Handful of Dust.*

From Boa Vista, Waugh plans to continue to Manãos, but circumstances and his disillusionment with Boa Vista lead him to abandon that intention and return by a different route to British Guiana. The trip back is difficult but marked, in Waugh's estimation, by a miraculous event. At one point Waugh foolishly strikes out on his own ahead of his guides and becomes hopelessly lost. A chance meeting with an old Indian saves his life. Calculating the odds against such a coincidence to be 54,750,000 to 1, Waugh decides that the event is explainable only as resulting from the intervention of St. Christopher, to whom he prayed for help.

On his return journey to the coast Waugh endures a final outing that is, perhaps, the most dangerous and debilitating part of his entire undertaking. Accompanying a Father Keary on his ministerial rounds, Waugh experiences nights of numbing cold and the crippling effects of djiggers, insects that bore into the skin and lay their eggs. Waugh's feet become infected and he suffers greatly. His agony is abated somewhat by a forced ten-day respite at Mr. Winter's diamond mine. From there he returns as directly as possible to the coast, where he finds a Canadian ship preparing to leave for Trinidad. Rather than wait for direct passage to England, he boards the vessel and docks in Trinidad in time to celebrate Holy Week. He arrives in England in early May 1933.

Although *Ninety-Two Days* lacks the humor and suspense of *Labels* or the historical significance of *Remote People,* it received generally positive reviews. Sykes says that it "contains some of Evelyn's best travel writing and description of scenery."

Political concerns in Europe during the mid 1930s directed Waugh's attention once again to Africa. The Italian dictator Benito Mussolini's intentions in Ethiopia were causing apprehension, and interest in the country intensified. On the basis of his previous experience there Waugh secured employment as a war correspondent for *The Daily Mail.* Although the success of his venture from a journalistic standpoint is dubious, it resulted in the fourth of his travel books, *Waugh in Abyssinia* (1936).

Waugh prefaces his account of his second journey in Africa with a summary of the history of Ethiopia, which he patronizingly titles "The Intelligent Woman's Guide to The Ethiopian Question." He supports European imperialism in Africa, from which, he thinks, "there has been more gain than loss to the African native." According to Waugh,

> Most people are disposed to settle high political questions in terms of the treatment they have received in casual encounters during their travels; a dishonest taxi-driver or an overbearing policeman. . . . The English, on the whole, are intensely xenophobic, and for this reason their sympathies are most easily aroused on behalf of nations with whom they have least acquaintance.

The rest of *Waugh in Abyssinia* attempts to remedy that situation by acquainting Waugh's readers with those dishonest drivers and overbearing policemen who will reduce their sympathies for the natives of Ethiopia. To emphasize the untrustworthy nature of Ethiopians, and the present regime in particular, Waugh recounts an incident that occurred shortly after Haile Selassie's ascension to the throne: in an exchange of money between the British and the Ethiopians the latter acted in bad faith, but the clever British consul outmaneuvered them by immediately stopping payment on his check. Such incidents, according to Waugh, are common and are indicative of the character of the government and its people.

In chapter 2, "Addis-Ababa during the Last Days of the Ethiopian Empire," Waugh returns to the personal narrative familiar from his earlier travel writings. He arrives at the Ethiopian frontier on 20 August 1935. He is accompanied on the train to Addis Ababa by other foreigners, including a reporter from a Radical newspaper, a Spanish correspondent whose brand of professionalism offers Waugh much amusement, an American doctor, a photographer, and a Mr. F. W. Rickett, whose business in Ethiopia remains unclear at this point. Waugh finds Rickett an amiable companion, though he suspects him of being an arms dealer. Waugh was correct in doubting Rickett's vague story about his "mission" to bring funds to the Coptic Church in Ethiopia, but rather than investigating him Waugh merely wrote to a friend soliciting casual information. Rickett would become the central figure in one of the biggest stories to come out of Ethiopia during this period when he successfully negotiated on behalf of an American firm for the oil rights in the country. Waugh, who was absent from Addis Ababa when the deal was completed, not only failed to break the story, he did not even report it. This omission earned him a severe reprimand from *The Daily Mail.* The deal, which threatened to draw the United States into the conflict in Ethiopia, was soon repudiated by the State Department. In *Waugh in Abyssinia* Waugh, taking advantage of hindsight, dismisses the event as a "brief delusion . . . [by Rickett of] success."

Waugh finds Addis Ababa little changed from his first visit five years before. He provides detailed descriptions of the accommodations, the hospitals, and the two competing establishments that offer the only evening entertainment in the city. The press bureau prevents the reporters from traveling anywhere there might be any fighting, leaving them bored and frustrated. This situation would become the humorous lot of William Boot in Waugh's next novel, *Scoop* (1938).

In search of a story and of relief from the monotony of the capital, Waugh visits the towns of Harar and Jijiga. His memories of Harar have, through the passage of time, been sentimentally embellished, and the present reality bears little resemblance to the

Muslim city he recalls. Waugh's descriptions of the changes are examples of the cruelty that is sometimes found in his writing. He calls the palace under construction "hideous" and reduces the people to caricatures–the chief of police, for example, is "greatly given to the bottle" and stuffs "his nostrils with leaves." Dismissing Harar as a place of little military or personal value, Waugh departs for Jijiga. He arrives in time to observe the arrest of a French count and countess accused of passing military secrets to the Italians. Waugh believes that he has finally achieved a "scoop," but his victory is short-lived. His story goes unnoticed in light of the simultaneous breaking of the oil-rights report by the other major newspapers.

Waugh has no alternative but to return to Addis Ababa and endure the tedium of nonevents. There he receives from his paper an order to investigate an attack on a fictitious hospital in which a nurse was supposedly blown up. Abiding by his employer's instruction to be economical in his reports, Waugh squelches the story in his return cable: "Nurse unupblown." The nurse anecdote is often related by scholars to typify Waugh's brand of humor. In October the emperor orders the expulsion of Count Vinci, the minister of the Italian Legation. His refusal to leave and the dignified manner in which he conducts himself earn Waugh's admiration. Although the press bureau does all it can to discredit Vinci, most of the correspondents refuse to participate in the character assassination.

No other story materializes. Waugh continues to pursue military information throughout Ethiopia, going as far as Dessye, a military outpost in Mohammedan Wolls country. He tells sadly of old men's complaints and joyfully of journalistic camaraderie, but he soon accepts that the world has grown as tired of Ethiopia as he has. On Christmas morning he is in Bethlehem, where "like the rest of the world I began to forget about Abyssinia."

Waugh soon receives orders to return to Ethiopia, and he is the first Englishman to enter the country after its occupation by Italy. He finds superficial changes: the country is more crowded; the shops and cafes have been renamed in Italian; and formerly simple procedures such as currency exchange have taken on sinister aspects and become complicated. In spite of the inconveniences, Waugh judges the changes positively. Everywhere he goes he sees men working and is treated with the utmost courtesy. He concludes that the Italians are bringing peace and progress to a backward nation. Waugh's support of the "eagle of Rome," which characterizes only the final chapters of *Waugh in Abyssinia,* received some adverse criticism, but less than modern readers might expect.

Waugh wearing a lion-skin coat in 1935, during his second trip to Ethiopia

In July 1936 Waugh's marriage to Evelyn Gardner was annulled by the Catholic Church. On 17 April 1937 he married Laura Herbert. They had six children, one of whom, Auberon, grew up to become a novelist.

Those who consider *Waugh in Abyssinia* a travel book flawed by intrusive political digressions might reject the classification of *Robbery under Law: The Mexican Object Lesson* (1939; republished in the United States as *Mexico: An Object Lesson,* 1939) as travel literature altogether. Indeed, the book was politically motivated. The idea of traveling to Mexico and writing a book about it did not originate with Waugh. He was approached by a representative of commercial interests in Latin America and asked to undertake the assignment. The Mexican government of Gen. Lazara Cardenas had nationalized foreign enterprises in the country, chief among them the oil industry. Public sentiment in Britain, sympathetic to the plight of the exploited Mexican workers, tended to favor the confiscations, and the industrialists wanted the other side told by an Englishman who had credibility as a traveler, observer, and writer.

To his credit, Waugh makes no attempt to disguise the purpose of the book. In an introductory chapter and a postscript he states his position and conclusions explicitly, and the work opens with the words, "This is a political book." He also forestalls possible criticism by pointing out in advance that it is, indeed, presumptuous for a writer such as himself, who has spent minimal time in the library in preparation and less than two months in the country, to hold opinions about Mexican affairs at all. Nevertheless, he suggests that since he has traveled much and seen a great deal, his impressions have some validity.

The traveler to Mexico via New York had two options at that time: a steamship that departed weekly for Veracruz or a daily train. Waugh, unaware that American trains were air-conditioned, chooses to journey by ship, which allows him time to observe the attitudes of his fellow tourists and the reactions of the Mexicans to their mainly American visitors. Waugh is struck by the way Americans seem to consider Mexico their playground. He groups these tourists who "play" in Mexico into three categories: holidaymakers, who go to have a good time; sentimentalists, who see Mexico as a spiritual home (the writer D. H. Lawrence is included in this group); and ideologues, who are Marxist pilgrims. The Mexicans, who benefit from the tourist trade, both welcome and resent the visitors. Waugh tells of the ship's purser's advice to the travelers: do not complain, and hold your criticism until you are back home. Waugh agrees that displays of superiority are in bad taste, but to become "unbiased" is impossible. He confesses that he "was a Conservative when I went to Mexico and that everything I saw there strengthened my opinions." Now that he is back home, he need not hold back his complaints. He concludes the first chapter: "The succeeding pages are notes on anarchy."

In the second chapter, "Tourist Mexico," Waugh provides the descriptions of sights, architecture, and entertainment that readers expect from travel literature. In all of these areas he finds Mexico handicapped by shabbiness, noise, and inefficiency. Everything there, including the art, is in need of restoration. In his words–which contrast sharply with those of another English Catholic writer, Graham Greene–Mexico has "more thorns than roses." In this chapter, however, he wants to call attention to the roses. He includes anecdotes about the honest chambermaid and the industrious janitor to demonstrate the character of the people. He journeys to Taxco and Pueblo and finds the former picturesque, the latter dignified. Aficionados of Waugh's style will find two outstanding examples of his wry personal narrative: he tells of his aborted attempt to smuggle a painting out of Mexico, and he claims responsibility for the change in the price of fish in a particular area–the sellers seem to have concluded that if a foreigner enjoys the fish, it must be worth more. These tales are vintage Waugh; but once he discards the role of tourist and assumes that of lecturer, the tone of the book changes.

In spite of his disclaimers regarding his ignorance, Waugh gives a complete overview of the history of Mexico and raises and answers important questions regarding the present and the future of the country. He focuses on the unique nature of Mexican politics, which has created conditions suitable for fascism to flourish. He devotes a chapter to the topic of oil, trying to explain to his fellow Britons the difference between the "Petroland" fantasy of leftist propaganda and the reality of the situation. He fears that ultimately the Mexican idea of enterprise will lead to the Nazification of industry in Mexico.

Another chapter, bearing the ironic title "The Good Neighbour," concerns itself with relations between the United States and Mexico. Waugh draws a parallel for his English readers between American treatment of Mexico and British actions in Ireland. He examines the policies of various American presidents and ambassadors, their ramifications in Mexican history, and their influence on the present-day Mexico. The interference of Presidents Woodrow Wilson and Franklin D. Roosevelt in Mexican affairs warrant much discussion. Though he holds Wilson blameless for conditions in Mexico during his term as president, he considers Roosevelt a Marxist and, therefore, suspect.

In the end, Waugh believes, the failure of the Mexican government to function adequately on every level from agriculture to education will result in the disappearance of Mexico as a sovereign nation. Waugh demonstrates these inadequacies through a critique of the *Plan Sexenal,* or Six-Year Plan Exhibition, held in Mexico City. He finds the exhibition, like the Mexican government itself, to be a sham: many of the articles displayed as examples of Mexican achievement are obviously imports. Waugh pretends to regret drawing attention to such blatant forgeries, as "it is poor sport to bait official guides." He feels no compunction, however, about acquainting his readers with the true condition of agriculture, education, and public works in Mexico under the present regime. His sympathies clearly lie with those whose holdings have been "liberated" by the government "plan." The latter term itself Waugh recognizes as a misnomer, as a plan implies a coordinated approach that is lacking in Mexico. Poor planning has resulted in ignorance and famine.

In Waugh's mind, the most serious error committed by the Mexican government comes from its persecution of the Catholic Church. Chapter 7, "The Straight Fight," explores the need for a strong church in Mexico. Catholicism defines the character of the nation, Waugh says; it united the many cultures and races into one people and made intermarriage a possibility. It provided education and a common heritage through a shared religious history. Without the church the country would become fragmented.

Waugh also counters many of the allegations made against the church. He gives touching examples of poor villagers decorating their local church with cheap gold paint to explain the pleasure that can be provided by a beautiful cathedral in the midst of poverty. The stories of profligate priests and lascivious nuns he rejects as exaggerations. Human nature remains constant, and isolated examples of fallen clergy can always be found, but they are the exception rather than the rule. Most important, the people want their church. Throughout Mexico, small groups are revolting to reclaim their right to the mass. The church must once again be granted property and the right to teach before the Mexican people can be happy and Mexico can have any hope for the future.

Waugh notes that Mexicans celebrate their Independence Day on 16 September, but to him, Mexican independence is less a political fact than a state of mind. Mexicans possess an identity that is recognizable and unique, but their country and their culture may become casualties of a global political battle centered around oil. Waugh mourns such a loss and finds in Mexico's situation a frightening reminder of the vulnerability of other sovereign nations, especially the United Kingdom. He concludes the book on a cautionary note, warning that measures must be taken to prevent leftist governments from creating such disasters at home as well as abroad. Years later, when Waugh chose selections from his travel books for reprinting in a volume titled *When the Going Was Good* (1946), he did not include an excerpt from *Mexico: An Object Lesson.* He recognized the book's overriding concern with politics rather than travel. Many critics in 1939, however, were convinced by Waugh's polemics and responded favorably to the book. But in financial terms the work was less than successful.

Approximately twenty years elapsed between the publication of *Mexico: An Object Lesson* and Waugh's departure on the journey that was to provide material for his final travel book, *Tourist in Africa* (1960). The Waugh who travels to Africa in the last decade of his life has little in common with the innocent abroad who first set foot in Africa, or with the

Waugh and his second wife, Laura Herbert, on their wedding day in 1937

brash reporter of the war in Ethiopia. Waugh is returning to Africa this time neither to gain experience nor to enhance his reputation but for rest and relaxation. At fifty-five, he finds the English winters unpleasant and longs for sunnier climes. He books a cabin on the *Rhodesia Castle,* a one-class sailing ship embarking from Genoa at the end of January 1959, because it is available.

To reach the ship, Waugh must travel through Paris and by train to Italy. He encounters the now-familiar difficulties with tickets and agents, but reports them with the resigned air of a man for whom the world no longer offers any surprises. He observes rather than participates in the adventure. His comment, "as happier men watch birds, I watch men," reveals his newly adopted role of observer. The anecdotes he tells about the men he watches are idle musings rather than the caustic critiques of old. Waugh rallies briefly as he tours Genoa in the company of an old friend, Lady Diana Cooper, identified here only as "Mrs. Stitch." He finds the postwar attempts at restoration in this city impressive and attributes the relative obscurity of the sights to their proximity to Rome and Venice. He concludes that treasures that would create excitement elsewhere appear prosaic in Italy. After a hectic two days transecting Genoa with

Evelyn and Laura Waugh in 1959 at their home, Combe Florey, in Somerset, with their children: Margaret, Harriet, Auberon, Teresa, James, and Septimus (photograph by Mark Gerson)

his vivacious companion, Waugh boards the *Rhodesia Castle* to begin the voyage he terms a "cure."

Life aboard ship is comfortable and uneventful. Waugh finds excitement in the ship's library, which is unusually well stocked, and he indulges in the consumption of two books a day. The eagerly anticipated arrival in Port Said brings disappointment. Gone are the gully-gully men of his earlier visit, and their replacements are attired in Western costume. Aden, too, is characterized by absence. The "mermaids," probably stuffed manatees, that used to be exhibited for a price on the verandas of the hotels, are long forgotten. Their disappearance particularly affects Waugh. These mermaids symbolize for him the passage of time and the erosion of culture. Waugh finds another absence appalling: the absence of sufficient clothing on his fellow tourists. As the ship continues into the Red Sea and the temperature rises, his shipmates wear less and less while the Africans wear more. He contrasts the dignity of long white robes to the outrage of middle-aged flesh baking in the sun. Barbarism encroaches from all directions.

Waugh does not leave the *Rhodesia Castle* until it arrives at Tanganyika. His account of forays from the ship into Kenya include the expected references to Mount Kilimanjaro, Tanga, and Pangani, but they are perfunctory. Book reviews, including one of Eric Rosenthal's *Stars and Stripes in Africa* (1938), and anecdotes, such as his account of the self-coronation of Bishop Homer A. Tomlinson of New York as "king" of Tanganyika, add color and texture to an otherwise prosaic account.

The chapters on Tanganyika and Rhodesia are punctuated with the kind of comments and observations that dismayed or delighted readers of Waugh's earlier travel books. In Tanganyika a safari–which, as Waugh notes, is "a term now used to designate a luxurious motor tour"–provides him with the opportunity to ridicule socialist ideas through a lengthy discussion of the failed "Groundnut Scheme," a British Labour government plan to increase the production of nuts in the country. He relishes a story based on communication problems between Europeans and natives: in one case some Masai, sent to relieve an enemy of their "arms," brought back their severed limbs. Waugh himself is involved in such a confusion. After searching for hours for a place called Tinka-Tinka, he learns that the word is an onomatopoeic term for any mechanical device, such as a pump.

Tourist in Africa did not sell well. It received generally negative reviews, with which Waugh himself agreed. He was not proud of the book. In *The Sunday Times* (25 September 1960) Cyril Connolly called it "quite the thinnest piece of book-making which Mr. Waugh has undertaken" and noted that "the particular pose he affects–of an elderly, infirm and irritable old buffer, quite out of touch with the times–is hardly suited to enthusiasm, a prerequisite of travel writing."

Basil Davidson, writing in the *New Statesman* (24 September 1960), found the work to be full of factual errors.

Tourist in Africa was Waugh's only postwar travel book aside from the collection of excerpts from his previous such writings, *When the Going Was Good.* A work that is often erroneously considered a part of Waugh's travel writings, *The Holy Places* (1952), comprises the script of a radio talk Waugh gave on St. Helena; a reprint of an article he wrote for *Life* (24 December 1951) advocating the preservation and restoration of the Church of the Holy Sepulcher in Jerusalem. Only the preface is new. While some of the material stems from a trip Waugh took to Israel and Jordan in early 1951, it is not an account of the journey.

Waugh died at his home, Combe Florey House in Somerset, on 10 April 1966, apparently of a coronary thrombosis. While a modern reader might be tempted to dismiss Waugh's travel writings as idiosyncratic accounts by a chauvinistic and somewhat pretentious individual, they provide eyewitness reports of people and places seen as only an Englishman of a certain class and time could see them. From them Waugh's contemporary readers learned about unfamiliar lives and locales, and as they vicariously enjoyed his experiences they reaffirmed their commitment to their own customs and way of life. Today readers can still find amusement in Waugh's predicaments and reactions, as well as new insights into foreign cultures. The travel writings also reveal the origins of characters and incidents in some of the works of fiction, including *A Handful of Dust* and *Scoop,* that have assumed a place in the canon of English literature.

Letters:

The Letters of Evelyn Waugh, edited by Mark Amory (London: Weidenfeld & Nicolson, 1980; New Haven & New York: Ticknor & Fields, 1980).

Interview:

Julian Jebb, "The Art of Fiction, XXX: Evelyn Waugh. An Interview," *Paris Review,* 8, no. 30 (1963): 72–85.

Bibliographies:

Robert Murray Davis, Paul A. Doyle, Heinz Kosok, and Charles E. Linck, *Evelyn Waugh: A Checklist of Primary and Secondary Material* (Troy, N.Y.: Whitston, 1972);

Davis, *A Catalogue of the Evelyn Waugh Collection at the Humanities Research Center, The University of Texas at Austin* (Troy, N.Y.: Whitston, 1981);

Davis, Doyle, Linck, Donat Gallagher, and Winnifred M. Bogaards, *A Bibliography of Evelyn Waugh* (Troy, N.Y.: Whitston, 1986).

Biographies:

Christopher Sykes, *Evelyn Waugh: A Biography* (London: Collins, 1975; Boston: Little, Brown, 1977);

Martin Stannard, *Evelyn Waugh: The Early Years 1903–1939* (New York & London: Norton, 1987);

Stannard, *Evelyn Waugh: The Later Years 1939–1966* (New York & London: Norton, 1992);

Selena Hastings, *Evelyn Waugh: A Biography* (Boston: Houghton Mifflin, 1995).

References:

William Deedes, "The Abyssinian Waugh," *Spectator,* 5 May 1959, p. 32;

Paul A. Doyle, *Evelyn Waugh: A Critical Essay* (Grand Rapids, Mich.: Eerdmans, 1969);

D. Paul Farr, "Waugh's Conservative Stance: Defending 'The Standards of Civilization,'" *Philological Quarterly,* 51 (April 1972): 471–484;

Christopher Hollis, *Evelyn Waugh* (London: Longmans, Green, 1954; revised, 1958);

Alvin B. Kernan, "The Wall and the Jungle: The Early Novels of Evelyn Waugh," *Yale Review,* 53 (Winter 1963): 199–220;

David Lodge, *Evelyn Waugh,* Columbia Essays on Modern Writers, no. 58 (New York & London: Columbia University Press, 1971);

David Pryce-Jones, ed., *Evelyn Waugh and His World* (London: Weidenfeld & Nicolson, 1973; Boston: Little, Brown, 1973);

Martin Stannard, ed., *Evelyn Waugh: The Critical Heritage* (London & Boston: Routledge & Kegan Paul, 1984);

Frederick J. Stopp, *Evelyn Waugh: Portrait of an Artist* (London: Chapman & Hall, 1958; Boston: Little, Brown, 1958).

Papers:

The Harry Ransom Humanities Research Center at the University of Texas, Austin, has a major collection of Evelyn Waugh's manuscripts, letters, and personal effects. The Berg Collection at the New York Public Library also has important items.

Travel Writing, 1910–1939

Ackerley, J. R. *Hindoo Holiday: An Indian Journal.* London: Chatto & Windus, 1932.

Atkinson, Sophie. *An Artist in Corfu.* London: Herbert & Daniel, 1911.

Auden, W. H. and Louis MacNeice. *Letters from Iceland.* London: Faber & Faber, 1937.

Bagnold, Ralph A. *Libyan Sands: Travel in a Dead World.* London: Hodder & Stoughton, 1935.

Baillie, Mrs. W. W. *Days and Night of Shikar.* London & New York: John Lane, 1921.

Balfour, John Patrick. *Grand Tour. Diary of an Eastward Journey.* New York: Harcourt, Brace, 1935.

Bates, Daisy Mary. *The Passing of the Aborigines: A Lifetime Spent among the Natives of Australia.* London: Murray, 1938.

Becher, Augusta Emily. *Personal Reminiscences in India and Europe, 1830–1888, of Augusta Becher,* edited by H. G. Rawlinson. London: Constable, 1930.

Belgrave, Charles Dalrymple. *Siwa, The Oasis of Jupeter Ammon.* London: John Lane, 1923.

Bell, Gertrude Lowthian. *Amurath to Amurath: Travels in Asia Minor and Persia.* London: Heinemann, 1911.

Belloc, Hilaire. *The Cruise of the Nona.* London: Constable, 1925.

Belloc. *Many Cities.* London: Constable, 1928.

Benson, Stella. *The Little World.* London: Macmillan, 1925.

Betham-Edwards, Matilda. *In French-Africa: Scenes and Memories.* London: Chapman & Hall, 1912.

Betham-Edwards. *In the Heart of the Vosges and Other Sketches by a "Devious Traveller."* London: Chapman & Hall, 1911.

Brodhurst-Hill, Evelyn. *The Youngest Lion: Early Farming Days in Kenya.* London: Hutchinson, 1934.

Brooke, Rupert. *Letters from America.* London: Sidgwick & Jackson, 1916.

Brooke, Lady Margaret. *Good Morning and Good Night.* London: Constable, 1934.

Brooke, Lady Margaret. *My Life in Sarawak.* London: Methuen, 1913.

Brooke, Sylvia. *Sylvia of Sarawak: An Autobiography.* London: Hutchinson, 1936.

Brown, Lady Richmond (Lilian Mabel Alice). *Unknown Tribes; Uncharted Seas.* London: Duckworth, 1924.

Bruce, Gen. Charles G. *The Assault on Mount Everest, 1922.* London: Arnold, 1923.

Bruce, Mildred. *The Bluebird's Flight.* London: Chapman & Hall, 1931.

Bruce, Mildred. *Nine Thousand Miles in Eight Weeks: Being an Account of an Epic Journey by Motor-car through Eleven Countries and Two Continents.* London: Heath, Cranton, 1927.

Bruce, William Spiers. *Polar Exploration.* London: Williams & Norgate, 1911.

Bryce, James. *South America: Observations and Impressions.* New York: Macmillan, 1912.

Bulstrode, Beatrix (Mrs. Beatrix Gull). *A Tour in Mongolia.* London: Methuen, 1920.

Bunbury, Col. Henry William St. Pierre. *Early Days in Western Australia: Being the Letters and Journals of Lieut. H. W. Bunbury, 21st Fusliers,* edited by Lt. Col. W. Pierre St. Bunbury and W. P. Morrell. London: Oxford University Press, 1930.

Bury, G. W. *Arabia Infelix: or, The Turks in Yamen.* London: Macmillan, 1915.

Bury. *The Land of Uz.* London: Macmillan, 1911.

Butcher, Edith Louisa (Edith Floyer). *Things Seen in Egypt.* London: Seeley, 1910.

Buxton, Noel. *Travels and Politics in Armenia.* London: Smith, Elder, 1914.

Buxton. *Travels and Reflections.* London: Allen & Unwin, 1929.

Cameron, Charlotte. *A Cheechako in Alaska and Yukon.* London: Stokes, 1920.

Cameron. *Mexico in Revolution.* London: Seeley, Service, 1925.

Cameron. *Two Years in Southern Seas.* London: Unwin, 1923.

Cameron. *Wanderings in South-eastern Seas, Etc.* London: Unwin, 1924.

Cameron. *A Woman's Winter in Africa; A 26,000-Mile Journey.* London: Stanley Paul, 1913.

Cameron. *A Woman's Winter in South America.* London: Stanley Paul, 1911.

Carruthers, Douglas. *Arabian Adventure; to the Great Nafud in Quest of the Oryx.* London: Witherby, 1935.

Carruthers. *Unknown Mongolia: A Record of Travel and Exploration in North-west Mongolia and Dzungaria,* 2 volumes. London: Hutchinson, 1913.

Carruthers, ed. *The Desert Route to India: Being the Journals of Four Travellers by the Great Desert Caravan Route between Aleppo and Basca, 1745–1751.* London: Witherby, 1935.

Chapman, Frederick Spencer. *Lhasa, the Holy City: Memoirs of a Mountaineer.* London: Chatto & Windus, 1938.

Chardin, Sir John. *Travels in Persia, 1673–1677.* London: Argonaut, 1927.

Cheesman, Robert Ernest. *In Unknown Arabia.* London: Macmillan, 1926.

Cherry-Garrard, Apsley. *The Worst Journey in the World, Antarctic, 1910–1913.* London: Constable, 1922.

Chesterton, G. K. *What I Saw in America.* London: Hodder & Stoughton, 1922.

Cheston, Mrs. Cecil (Ada Elizabeth). *Young China and New Japan.* London: Harrap, 1933.

Christie, Ella R. *Through Khiva to Golden Samarkand: The Remarkable Story of a Woman's Adventurous Journey Alone through the Deserts of Central Asia to the Heart of Turkestan.* London: Seeley, Service, 1925.

Clementi, Mrs. Cecil (Marie Penelope Rose Eyres). *Through British Guiana to the Summit of Roraima.* London: Unwin, 1920.

Clifton, Violet Mary (Beauclerk). *The Book of the Talbot.* London: Faber & Faber, 1933.

Clifton. *Islands of Queen Wilhelmina.* London: Constable, 1927.

Clifton. *Pilgrims to the Isles of Penance: Orchid Gathering in the East.* London: Long, 1911.

Close, Etta. *Excursions and Some Adventures.* London: Hodder & Stoughton, 1926.

Close. *A Woman Alone in Kenya, Uganda and the Belgian Congo.* London: Constable, 1924.

Cobbold, Evelyn, Lady Murray. *Wayfarers in the Libyan Desert.* London: Humphreys, 1912.

Cobbold. *Kenya: The Land of Illusion.* London: Murray, 1935.

Cobbold. *Pilgrimage to Mecca.* London: Murray, 1934.

Colville, Mrs. Arthur (Olivia). *A Thousand Miles in a Machilla: Travel and Sport in Nyasaland, Argoniland, and Rhodesia, with Some Account of the Resources of Those Countries.* London: Scott, 1911.

Cook, Frederick A. *Life in the Arctic Zone.* Yonkers: Arlington, 1911.

Cook and Robert E. Peary. *My Attainment of the Pole: Being the Record of the Expedition that First Reached the Boreal Center, 1907–1909, with the Final Summary of the Polar Controversy.* New York: Polar, 1911.

Court Treatt, Stella. *Cape to Cairo: The Record of a Historic Motor Journey.* London: Harrap, 1927.

Court Treatt. *Sudan Sand: Filming the Baggara Arabs.* London: Harrap, 1930.

Craig-McKerrow, Margaret. *The Iron Road to Samarcand.* London: De la More Press, 1932.

Craig-McKerrow. *Sudan Sand: Filming the Baggara Arabs.* London: Harrap, 1930.

Crawford, Emily May. *By the Equator's Snowy Peak: A Record of Medical Missionary Work and Travel in British East Africa.* London: Church Missionary Society, 1913.

Cressy-Marcks, Violet Olivia. *Up the Amazon and Over the Andes.* London: Hodder & Stoughton, 1932.

Cunliffe-Owen, Betty. *Silhouettes of Republican Greece (Romances and Refugees).* London: Hutchinson, 1927.

Cunliffe-Owen. *"Thro' the Gates of Memory" (from the Bosphorus to Baghdad).* London: Hutchinson, 1924.

Currie, Jessie Monteath. *The Hill of Good-bye: The Story of a Solitary White Woman's Life in Central Africa.* London: Routledge, 1920.

Currie. *With Pole and Paddle Down the Shiré and Zambesi.* London: Routledge, 1918.

Curzon, George Nathan, Marquess Curzon of Kedleston. *Tales of Travel.* London: Hodder & Stoughton, 1923.

Davies, W. H. *The True Traveller.* London: Duckworth, 1912.

De Watteville, Vivienne. *Out in the Blue*. London: Methuen, 1927.

De Watteville. *Speak to the Earth: Wanderings and Reflections among Elephants and Mountains*. London: Methuen, 1935.

Delafield, E. M. *Straw without Bricks: I Visit the Soviet Union*. London: Macmillan, 1937.

Digby, George. *Red Horizons*. London: Collins, 1939.

Dolman, Alfred. *In the Footsteps of Livingstone: Being the Diaries and Travel Notes Made by Alfred Dolman,* edited by John Irving. London: John Lane, 1924.

Dufferin, Lady Harriot (Blackwood). *My Russian and Turkish Journals*. London: Murray, 1916.

Durham, Edith. *Twenty Years of Balkan Tangle*. London: Allen & Unwin, 1920.

Ellison, Grace. *An Englishwoman in Angora*. London: Hutchinson, 1923.

Ellison. *An Englishwoman in a Turkish Harem*. London: Methuen, 1915.

Eyton-Jones, Theodora. *Under Eastern Roofs*. London: Wright & Brown, 1931.

Farson, James Scott Negley. *Sailing across Europe*. London: Cape, 1926.

Farson. *Seeing Red: Today in Russia*. London: Eyre & Spottiswoode, 1930.

Farson. *Transgressor in the Tropics*. London: Gollancz, 1937.

Fisher, Ruth B. *Twilight Tales of the Black Baganda*. London: Marshall, 1911.

Fitzroy, Yvonne. *A Canadian Panorama*. London: Methuen, 1929.

Flecker, James Elroy. *Some Letters from Abroad*. London: Heinemann, 1930.

Floyer, Edith Louisa. *Egypt as We Knew It*. London: Mills & Boon, 1911.

Ford, Ford Madox. *Great Trade Route*. London: Allen & Unwin, 1937.

Ford. *New York Is Not America: Being a Mirror to the States*. London: Duckworth, 1927.

Ford. *Provence: From Minstrels to the Machine*. Philadelphia & London: Lippincott, 1935.

Forman, Henry James. *Grecian Italy*. London: Cape, 1927.

Forman. *The Ideal Italian Tour*. Boston & New York: Houghton Mifflin, 1911.

Forman. *In the Footsteps of Heine*. Boston & New York: Houghton Mifflin, 1910.

Fox, Ralph. *People of the Steppes*. London: Constable, 1925.

Freshfield, Douglas William. *Below the Snow Line*. London: Constable, 1922.

Fullerton, Amy. *A Lady's Ride through Palestine and Syria; with Notices of Egypt and the Canal of Suez*. London, 1911.

Gardner, Mona. *Menacing Sun*. London: Murray, 1939.

Gaunt, Mary. *Alone in West Africa.* London: Laurie, 1912.

Gaunt. *Reflection–In Jamaica.* London: Benn, 1932.

Gaunt. *Where the Twain Meet.* London: Murray, 1922.

Gaunt. *A Woman in China.* London: Laurie, 1914.

Gerard, Adelaide M. *Et Nos in Arctis.* London: Ballantyne, 1913.

Gibbons, John. *Afoot in Italy.* London: Newnes, 1930.

Gibbons. *Surburban Columbus.* London: Newnes, 1934.

Gibbons. *Tramping through Ireland.* London: Methuen, 1930.

Goodrich-Freer, Ada M. *Things Seen in Constantinople: A Description of This Outpost of the Orient, Its History, Mosques and the Life and Ways of Its People.* London: Seeley, Service, 1926.

Goodrich-Freer. *Things Seen in Palestine.* London: Seeley, Service, 1913.

Gordon, Jan, and Cora J. Gordon. *On Wandering Wheels: Through Roadside Camps from Maine to Georgia in an Old Sedan Car.* New York: Dodd, Mead, 1928.

Gordon and Gordon. *Three Lands on Three Wheels.* London: Harrap, 1932.

Gordon and Gordon. *Two Vagabonds in Albania.* London: John Lane, 1927.

Gordon and Gordon. *Two Vagabonds in Servia and Montenegro–1915.* Harmondsworth: Penguin, 1939.

Gorer, Geoffrey. *Africa Dances: A Book about West African Negroes.* London: Faber & Faber, 1935.

Graham, Robert Bontine Cunninghame. *Cartagena and the Banks of the Sinu.* London: Heinemann, 1920.

Grant, Colquhoun, Mrs. *Through Dante's Land: Impressions in Tuscany.* London: Long, 1912.

Grimshaw, Beatrice Ethel. *Isles of Adventure: Experiences in Papua and Neighboring Islands.* London: Jenkins, 1930.

Gunn, Neil. *Off in a Boat.* London: Faber & Faber, 1938.

Hahn, Emily. *Congo Solo: Misadventures Two Degrees North.* Indianapolis: Bobbs-Merrill, 1933.

Hall, Mary. *A Woman in the Antipodes and in the Far East.* London: Methuen, 1914.

Hamilton, Cicely. *Modern Germanies; as Seen by an Englishwoman.* London: Dent, 1931.

Hamilton. *Modern Italy; as Seen by an Englishwoman.* London: Dent, 1932.

Hamilton, Helen. *Mountain Madness.* London: Collins, 1922.

Hanbury-Tracy, John. *Black River of Tibet.* London: Muller, 1938.

Harris, Audrey. *Eastern Visas.* London: Collins, 1939.

Hasell, (Frances Hatton) Eva. *Across the Prairie: A 3,000 Mile Tour by Two Englishwomen on Behalf of Religious Education.* London: SPCK, 1922.

Hasell. *Canyons, Cans and Caravans.* London: SPCK, 1930.

Hasell. *Through Western Canada in a Caravan.* London: Society for the Propagation of the Gospel in Foreign Parts, 1925.

Herbert, Agnes. *Casuals in the Caucasus: The Diary of a Sporting Holiday.* London & New York: John Lane, 1911.

Herbert. *Korea.* London: Black, 1924.

Hogarth, David George. *Accidents of an Antiquary's Life.* London: Macmillan, 1910.

Howard, Ethel. *Japanese Memories.* London: Hutchinson, 1918.

Howard. *Potsdam Princes.* London: Methuen, 1916.

Howard-Bury, Lt. Col. Charles K., and others. *Mount Everest: The Reconnaisance, 1921.* London: Arnold, 1922.

Hudson, W. H. *A Shepherd's Life: Impressions of the South Wiltshire Downs.* London: Methuen, 1910.

Hull, Edith Maud. *Camping in the Sahara.* London: Nash & Grayson, 1926.

Hutchison, Isobel Wylie. *North to the Rime-ringed Sun: Being the Record of an Alaska-Canadian Journey Made in 1933-34.* London: Blackie, 1934.

Hutchison. *On Greenland's Closed Shore: The Fairyland of the Arctic.* Preface by Dr. Knud Rasmussen. Edinburgh: Blackwood, 1930.

Hutchison. *Stepping Stones from Alaska to Asia.* London: Blackie, 1937.

Hutton, Edward. *The Cities of Lombardy.* London: Methuen, 1912.

Hutton. *The Cities of Romagna and the Marches.* London: Methuen, 1913.

Hutton. *The Cities of Sicily.* London: Methuen, 1926.

Hutton. *A Glimpse of Greece.* London: Medici Society, 1928.

Jenkinson, Anthony. *Where Seldom a Gun Is Heard.* London: Barker, 1937.

Johnstone, Nancy. *Hotel in Flight.* London: Faber & Faber, 1939.

Johnstone. *Hotel in Spain.* London: Faber & Faber, 1937.

Jones, Henry Festing. *Mt. Eryx and Other Diversions of Travel.* London: Cape, 1921.

Kaulback, Ronald. *Tibetan Trek.* London: Hodder & Stoughton, 1934.

King, Agnes Gardner. *Islands Far Away.* London: Sifton, Praed, 1920.

Landor, Arnold Henry Savage. *Everywhere: The Memoirs of an Explorer.* New York: Stokes, 1924.

Landor. *An Explorer's Adventures in Tibet.* New York & London: Harper, 1910.

LeBlond, Elizabeth. *The Old Gardens of Italy; How to Visit Them.* London: John Lane, 1912.

Lewis, Wyndham. *Filibusters in Barbary.* London: Grayson & Grayson, 1932.

Lithgow, William. *Rare Adventures and Painful Peregrinations.* London: Cape, 1928.

Lockhart, Robert H. *Return to Malaya.* London: Putnam, 1936.

Login, E. Dalhousie. *Lady Login's Recollections: Court Life and Camp Life 1820–1904.* London: Murray, 1917.

Lubbock, Percy. *Roman Pictures.* London: Cape, 1923.

Lunn, Sir Arnold Henry. *The Mountains of Youth.* Oxford: Oxford University Press, 1925.

Macartney, Lady Catherine Theodora. *An English Lady in Chinese Turkestan.* London: Benn, 1931.

Macleod, Olive. *Chiefs and Cities of Central Africa. Across Lake Chad by the Way of the British, French, and German Territories.* Edinburgh & London: Blackwood, 1912.

MacNeice, Louis. *I Crossed the Minch.* London: Longmans, Green, 1938.

Mansfield, Charlotte. *Via Rhodesia: A Journey through Southern Africa.* London: Stanley Paul, 1911.

Marsden, Kate. *My Mission to Siberia.* London: Edward Stanford, 1921.

Mills, Lady Dorothy R. M. *Beyond the Bosphorus.* London: Duckworth, 1926.

Mills. *The County of Orinoco, Etc.* London: Hutchinson, 1931.

Mills. *The Golden Land. A Record of Travel in West Africa.* London: Duckworth, 1929.

Mills. *The Road to Timbuktu.* London: Duckworth, 1924.

Mills. *Through Liberia.* London: Duckworth, 1926.

Montague, C. E. *The Right Place: A Book of Pleasures.* London: Chatto & Windus, 1924.

Mordaunt, Elinor. *The Further Venture Book.* London: John Lane, 1926.

Mordaunt. *On the Wallaby through Victoria.* London: Heinemann, 1911.

Mordaunt. *Purely for Pleasure.* London: Secker, 1932.

Mordaunt. *The Venture Book.* London: John Lane, 1926.

Morris, Elizabeth Keith. *An Englishwoman in the Canadian West.* London: Simpkin Marshall, 1913.

Mott-Smith, May. *Africa from Port to Port.* London: Hutchinson, 1930.

Muir, Edwin. *Scottish Journey.* London: Heinemann, 1935.

Muter, Elizabeth (Mrs. D. D.). *My Recollections of the Sepoy Revolt (1857–58) India, China, & New Zealand by Mrs. Muter.* London: Long, 1911.

Newton, Wilfrid Douglas. *Westward with the Prince of Wales.* London: Hurst & Blackett, 1920.

Nichols, Beverley. *No Place Like Home.* London: Cape, 1936.

Norton, Lt. Col. Edward F. *The Fight for Everest, 1924.* London: Arnold, 1925.

Nossiter, Harold. *Northward Ho! Being the Log of a 35-Ton Schooner from Sydney to Plymouth.* London: Witherby, 1937.

O'Brien, Conor. *Across Three Oceans: A Colonial Voyage in the Yacht "Saoirse."* London: Arnold, 1926.

O'Brien, Kate. *Farewell Spain.* London: Heinemann, 1937.

Pickthall, Marmaduke William. *Oriental Encounters: Palestine and Syria (1894–5–6).* London: Collins, 1918.

Pilley, Dorothy. *Climbing Days.* London: Bell, 1935.

Powell, Sydney Walter. *Adventure of a Wanderer.* London: Cape, 1928.

Priestley, J. B. *English Journey: Being a Rambling but Truthful Account of What One Man Saw and Heard and Felt and Thought During a Journey through England During the Autumn of the Year 1933.* London: Heinemann, 1934.

Pritchett, V. S. *Marching Spain.* London: Benn, 1928.

Pryce-Jones, Alan. *People in the South.* London: Cobden-Sanderson, 1932.

Pryce-Jones. *The Spring Journey.* London: Cobden-Sanderson, 1931.

Ratcliffe, Dorothy Una. *Equatorial Dawn: Travel Letters from North, East and Central Africa.* London: Eyre & Spottiswoode, 1936.

Ratcliffe. *News of Persephone: Impressions in Northern and Southern Greece with a Car, a Kettle and Cameras.* London: Eyre & Spottiswoode, 1939.

Ratcliffe. *South African Summer: 5,000 Miles with a Car and a Caravan-trailer.* London: Country Life, 1933.

Ratcliffe. *Swallow of the Sea: Pages from a Yacht's Log.* London: Country Life, 1937.

Ratcliffe. *To the Blue Canadian Hills; a Week's Log in a Northern Quebec Camp.* Leeds: North Country Press, 1928.

Raven-Hart, Rowland. *Canoe Errant on the Mississippi.* London: Methuen, 1938.

Richardson, Gwen. *On the Diamond Trail in British Guiana.* London: Methuen, 1925.

Roome, William J. W. *Tramping through Africa: A Dozen Crossings of the Continent.* London: Black, 1930.

Routledge, Katherine M. *The Mystery of Easter Island: The Story of an Expedition.* London: Hazel, Watson & Viney, 1919.

Routledge and William Scoresby Routledge. *With a Prehistoric People: The Akikúyu of British East Africa, Being Some Account of the Method of Life and Mode of Thought Found Existent amongst a Nation on Its First Contact with European Civilisation.* London: Arnold, 1910.

Ruttledge, Hugh. *Everest, 1933.* London: Hodder & Stoughton, 1934.

Ruttledge. *Everest: The Unfinished Adventure.* London: Hodder & Stoughton, 1937.

Rymill, John. *Southern Lights: The Official Account of the British Graham Land Expedition, 1934-1937.* London: Chatto & Windus, 1938.

Sandes, Flora. *The Autobiography of a Woman Soldier: A Brief Record of Adventure with the Serbian Army, 1916-1919.* London: Witherby, 1927.

Sandes. *An English Woman-Sergeant in the Serbian Army.* London: Hodder & Stoughton, 1916.

Sassoon, Philip. *The Third Route.* London: Heinemann, 1929.

Savory, Isabel. *The Romantic Rousillon: In the French Pyrenees.* London: Unwin, 1919.

Shackleton, Sir Ernest. *South: The Story of Shackleton's 1914-1917 Expedition.* London: Heinemann, 1922.

Sheridan, Clare Consuelo. *Across Europe with Satanella.* London: Duckworth, 1925.

Sheridan. *Arab Interlude.* London: Nicholson & Watson, 1936.

Sheridan. *My American Diary by Clare Sheridan.* New York: Boni & Liveright, 1922.

Sheridan. *Redskin Interlude.* London: Nicholson & Watson, 1938.

Sheridan. *Russian Portraits.* London: Cape, 1921.

Sheridan. *A Turkish Kaleidoscope.* London: Duckworth, 1926.

Sheridan. *West and East.* New York: Boni & Liveright, 1923.

Shipton, Eric. *Blank on the Map.* London: Hodder & Stoughton, 1938.

Shipton. *Nanda Devi.* London: Hodder & Stoughton, 1936.

Sitwell, Constance. *Flowers and Elephants.* London: Cape, 1927.

Smith, Anthony. *Smith and Son: An Expedition into Africa.* London: Longmans, Green, 1933.

Speed, Maud. *Cruises in Small Yachts by H. Fiennes Speed: And a Continuation, Entitled More Cruises by Maud Speed.* London: Imray, Laine, Norie & Wilson, 1926.

Speed. *A Scamper Tour to Rhodesia and South Africa.* London: Longmans, Green, 1933.

Speed. *Through Central France to the Pyrenees.* London: Longmans, Green, 1924.

Speed. *A Yachtswoman's Cruises and Steamer Voyages.* London & New York: Longmans, Green, 1911.

Stack, Reverend James West. *Early Maoriland Adventures,* edited by A. H. Reed. Dunedin, N.Z.: Reed, 1935.

Stack. *Further Maoriland Adventures,* edited by Reed. London: Reed & Foulis, 1938.

Stack. *More Maoriland Adventures,* edited by Reed. Dunedin, N.Z.: Reed, 1936.

Steel, Flora Annie. *The Garden of Fidelity: Being the Autobiography of Flora Annie Steel, 1847-1929.* London: Macmillan, 1929.

Stoneham, Charles. *Africa All Over: Trading, Hunting and Transport.* London: Hutchinson, 1934.

Stopes, Marie C. *A Journal from Japan: A Daily Record of Life as Seen by a Scientist.* London: Blackie, 1910.

Strickland, Diana. *Through the Belgian Congo.* London: Hurst & Blackett, 1925.

Stuck, Hudson. *The Ascent of Denali (Mount McKinley): A Narrative of the First Complete Ascent of the Highest Peak in North America.* New York: Scribners, 1914.

Stuck. *Ten Thousand Miles with a Dog Sled: A Narrative of Winter Travel in the Interior Alaska.* London: Laurie, 1914.

Stuck. *Voyages on the Yukon and Its Tributaries: A Narrative of Summer Travel in the Interior of Alaska.* London: Laurie, 1917.

Sully, James. *Italian Travel Sketches.* London: Constable, 1912.

Sykes, Ella Constance. *Persia and Its People.* London: Methuen, 1910.

Sykes. *Through Deserts and Oases of Central Asia.* London: Macmillan, 1920.

Symons, Arthur. *Cities and Sea-coasts and Islands.* London: Collins, 1918.

Tatchell, Frank. *The Happy Traveller: A Book for Poor Men.* London: Methuen, 1923.

Thomas, Bertram S. *Alarms and Excursion in Arabia.* London: Allen & Unwin, 1931.

Thomas. *Arabia Felix: Across the Empty Quarter of Arabia.* London: Cape, 1932.

Tilman, H. W. *The Ascent of Nanda Devi.* Cambridge: Cambridge University Press, 1937.

Tilman. *Snow on the Equator.* London: Bell, 1937.

Torday, Emil. *Camp and Tramp in African Wilds: A Record of Adventure, Impressions, and Experiences during Many Years Spent among the Savage Tribes round Lake Tanganyika and in Central Africa, with a Description of Native Life, Character, and Customs.* London: Seeley, Service, 1913.

Townley, Lady Susan. *"Indiscretions" of Lady Susan.* London: Butterworth, 1922.

Trevor, Roy. *En Route: A Descriptive Automobile Tour through Nine Countries and over Nineteen Great Passes of Europe.* London: Arnold, 1924.

Trevor. *Montenegro: A Land of Warriors.* London: Black, 1913.

Trevor. *My Balkan Tour.* London & New York: John Lane, 1911.

Tschiffely, A. F. *Southern Cross to Pole Star: Tschiffely's Ride. Being the Account of Ten Thousand Miles in the Saddle through the Americas from Argentina to Washington.* London: Heinemann, 1933.

Tweedie, Ethel Brilliana. *An Adventurous Journey (Russia–Siberia–China).* London: Hutchinson, 1926.

Tweedie. *America as I Saw It; or, America Revisited.* London: Hutchinson, 1913.

Tweedie. *Mainly East (in Prose–Perhaps Posey).* London: Hutchinson, 1922.

Tweedie. *Mexico: From Diaz to the Kaiser.* London: Hutchinson, 1917.

Tweedie. *My Legacy Cruise (The Peak Year of My Life).* London: Hutchinson, 1936.

Vassal, Gabrielle M. *In and Around Yunnan Fou.* London: Heinemann, 1922.

Vassal. *Life in French Congo.* London: Unwin, 1925.

Vassal. *On and Off Duty in Annam.* London: Heinemann, 1910.

Ward, Francis Kingdon. *From China to Hkamti Long.* London: Arnold, 1924.

Ward. *In Farthest Burma: The Record of an Arduous Journey of Exploration and Research through the Unknown Frontier Territory of Burma & Tibet.* London: Seeley, Service, 1920.

Ward. *The Land of the Blue Poppy: Travels of a Naturalist in Eastern Tibet.* Cambridge: Cambridge University Press, 1913.

Ward. *The Mystery Rivers of Tibet: A Description of the Little-known Land Where Asia's Mightiest Rivers Gallop in Harness through the Narrow Gateway of Tibet, Its People, Fauna, & Flora.* London: Seeley, Service, 1923.

Ward. *Plant Hunter's Paradise.* London: Cape, 1937.

Ward. *The Riddle of the Tsangpo Gorges.* London: Arnold, 1926.

Warren, Lady. *Through Algeria and Tunisia on a Motor-bicycle.* N.p.: Houghton, 1923.

Waugh, Alec. *Coloured Countries.* London: Chapman & Hall, 1930. Republished as *Hot Countries.* New York: Farrar & Rinehart, 1930.

Waugh. *Doing What One Likes.* Kensington: Cayme, 1926.

Wazan, Emily Keene, Sharrefa of. *My Life Story,* edited by S. L. Bensusan. London: Arnold, 1911.

Wild, Comdr. Frank. *Shackleton's Last Voyage: The Story of the Quest.* London: Cassell, 1923.

Wilson, Anne Campbell Macleod. *Letters from India.* Edinburgh: Blackwood, 1911.

Woolsey, Gamel. *Death's Other Kingdom.* London & New York: Longmans, Green, 1939.

Young, Geoffrey Winthrop. *On High Hills: Memories of the Alps.* London: Methuen, 1927.

Youngshusband, Sir Francis. *Everest: The Challenge.* London: Nelson, 1936.

Youngshusband. *India and Tibet.* London: John Murray, 1910.

Books for Further Reading

Adams, Percy G. *Travel Literature and the Evolution of the Novel.* Lexington: University of Kentucky Press, 1983.

Adams, ed. *Travel Literature Through the Ages: An Anthology*. New York & London: Garland, 1988.

Aitken, Maria. *A Girdle Round the Earth.* London: Constable, 1987.

Bathe, Basil W. *Seven Centuries of Sea Travel.* London: Barrie & Jenkins, 1972.

Bishop, Peter. *The Myth of Shangri-La: Tibet, Travel Writing and the Western Creation of Sacred Landscape.* Berkeley: University of California Press, 1989.

Brent, Peter. *Far Arabia: Explorers of the Myth.* London: Weidenfeld & Nicolson, 1977.

Brinnin, John Malcolm. *The Sway of the Grand Saloon.* London: Macmillan, 1972.

Burkhardt, A. J., and S. A. Medlik. *Tourism Past, Present, and Future.* London: Heinemann, 1974.

Buzard, James. *The Beaten Track: European Tourism, Literature, and the Ways to 'Culture' 1800–1918.* Oxford: Clarendon Press, 1993.

Callaway, Helen. *Gender, Culture and Empire: European Women in Colonial Nigeria.* Urbana: University of Illinois Press, 1987.

Carrington, Dorothy, ed. *The Traveller's Eye.* London: Pilot Press, 1947.

Clark, Ronald W. *Men, Myths and Mountains.* London: Weidenfeld & Nicolson, 1975.

Clark, William R. (Ronald W. Clark). *Explorers of the World.* London: Aldus Books, 1964.

Cocker, Mark. *Loneliness and Time: The Story of British Travel Writing.* New York: Pantheon, 1992.

Cole, Garold. *Travels in America from the Voyages of Discovery to the Present.* Norman: University of Oklahoma Press, 1984.

Crossley-Holland, Kevin, ed. *The Oxford Book of Travel Verse.* New York: Oxford University Press, 1987.

De Beer, Gavin Rylands. *Travellers in Switzerland.* London & New York: Oxford University Press, 1949.

Dodd, Philip, ed. *The Art of Travel: Essays on Travel Writing.* London: Frank Cass, 1982.

Eisner, Robert. *Travelers to an Antique Land: The History and Literature of Travel to Greece.* Ann Arbor: University of Michigan Press, 1991.

Feifer, Maxine. *Tourism in History: From Imperial Rome to the Present.* New York: Stein & Day, 1986.

Fowler, Marian. *Below the Peacock Fan: First Ladies of the Raj.* New York: Viking, 1987.

Fraser, Keath, ed. *Bad Trips.* New York: Vintage, 1991.

Fussell, Paul. *Abroad: British Literary Traveling Between the Wars.* New York: Oxford University Press, 1980.

Fussell, ed. *The Norton Book of Travel.* New York: Norton, 1987.

Graham-Brown, Sarah. *Images of Women: The Portrayal of Women in Photography of the Middle East, 1860–1950.* New York: Columbia University Press, 1988.

Graves, Robert. *The Long Week End: A Social History of Britain 1918–1939.* London: Faber & Faber, 1940.

Greenhill, Basil, and A. Gifford. *Women Under Sail.* London: David & Charles, 1970.

Gregory, Alexis. *The Golden Age of Travel, 1880–1939.* New York: Rizzoli, 1990.

Holmes, Winifred. *Seven Adventurous Women.* London: Bell, 1953.

Hopkirk, Peter. *Foreign Devils on the Silk Road: The Search for the Lost Cities and Treasures of Chinese Central Asia.* London: Murray, 1980.

Hopkirk. *Trespassers on the Roof of the World: The Race for Lhasa.* London: Murray, 1982.

Hobsbawn, Eric J. *The Age of Empire 1875–1914.* London: Weidenfeld & Nicolson, 1987.

Howarth, Patrick. *When the Riviera Was Ours.* London & Henley: Routledge & Kegan Paul, 1977.

Hudson, Kenneth. *Air Travel, a Social History.* Somerset, U.K.: Adams & Dart, 1972.

Hutchins, Francis. *The Illusion of Permanence: British Imperialism in India.* Princeton: Princeton University Press, 1967.

Jakle, John A. *The Tourist: Travel in Twentieth-Century North America.* Lincoln: University of Nebraska Press, 1985.

Jameson, Fredric. *The Political Unconscious: Narrative as a Socially Symbolic Act.* Ithaca, N. Y. : Cornell University Press, 1981.

Kabbani, Rana. *Imperial Fictions: Europe's Myths of Orient.* London: Pandora, 1994.

Keay, John, ed. *The Royal Geographical Society History of World Exploration.* London: Hamlyn, 1991.

Kowalewski, Michael, ed. *Temperamental Journeys: Essays on the Modern Literature of Travel.* Athens & London: University of Georgia Press, 1992.

Lawrence, Karen R. *Penelope Voyages: Women and Travel in British Literary Tradition.* Ithaca, N. Y.: Cornell University Press, 1994.

Leed, Eric J. *The Mind of the Traveler: From Gilgamesh to Global Tourism.* New York: Basic Books, 1991.

Lochsberg, Winifred. *History of Travel.* Leipzig: Edition Leipzig, 1979.

Lomax, Judy. *Women of the Air.* London: Murray, 1986.

MacCannell, Earle Dean. *The Tourist, A New Theory of the Leisure Class.* London: Macmillan, 1976.

MacGregor, John. *Tibet: A Chronicle of Exploration.* London: Routledge & Kegan Paul, 1970.

MacKenzie, John. *Imperialism and Popular Culture.* Manchester, U.K.: Manchester University Press, 1986.

Macmillan, Margaret. *Women of the Raj.* London: Thames & Hudson, 1988.

Mahood, Molly. *The Colonial Encounter: A Reading of Six Novels.* London: Rex Collings, 1977.

Marsden-Smedley, Philip, and Jeffrey Klinke, eds. *Views from Abroad: The "Spectator" Book of Travel Writing.* London: Grafton, 1988.

Massingham, Hugh and Pauline, eds. *The Englishman Abroad.* London: Phoenix House, 1962.

Melman, Billie. *Women's Orients: English Women and the Middle East, 1718–1918.* Ann Arbor: University of Michigan Press, 1992.

Michael, Maurice Albert, ed. *Traveller's Quest: Original Contributions Towards a Philosophy of Travel.* London: William Hodge, 1950.

Morgan, Susan. *Place Matters: Gendered Geography in Victorian Women's Travel Books about Southeast Asia.* New Brunswick, N.J.: Rutgers University Press, 1996.

Morris, Mary, ed. *Maiden Voyages: Writing of Women Travellers.* New York: Vintage, 1993.

Nevins, Allan. *America Through British Eyes.* New York: Oxford University Press 1948.

Newby, Eric, ed. *A Book of Travellers' Tales.* London: Collins, 1985.

Oliver, Caroline. *Western Women in Colonial Africa.* Westport, Conn.: Greenwood Press, 1982.

Ousby, Ian. *The Englishman's England: Taste, Travel, and the Rise of Tourism.* New York: Cambridge University Press, 1991.

Owen, Charles. *The Grand Days of Travel.* Exeter: Webb & Bower, 1979.

Pakenham, Valerie. *The Noonday Sun: Edwardians in the Tropics.* London: Methuen, 1985.

Pimlott, J. A. R. *The Englishman's Holiday: A Social History.* London: Faber & Faber, 1947.

Pomeroy, Earl. *In Search of the Golden West: The Tourist in Western America.* New York: Knopf, 1957.

Porter, Dennis. *Haunted Journeys: Desire and Transgression in European Travel Writing.* Princeton: Princeton University Press, 1991.

Pratt, Mary Louise. *Imperial Eyes: Studies in Travel Writing and Transculturation.* New York: Routledge, 1992.

Raskin, Jonah. *The Mythology of Imperialism.* New York: Random House, 1971.

Rice, Warner G., ed. *Literature as a Mode of Travel.* New York: New York Public Library, 1963.

Ridley, Hugh. *Images of Imperial Rule.* London: Croom Helm, 1983.

Robinson, Jane. *Wayward Women: A Guide to Women Travellers.* Oxford: Oxford University Press, 1990.

Robinson, ed. *Unsuitable for Ladies: An Anthology of Women Travellers.* Oxford: Oxford University Press, 1994.

Russell, Mary. *The Blessings of a Good Thick Skirt: Women Travellers and Their World.* London: Collins, 1986.

Said, Edward. *Culture and Imperialism.* New York: Knopf, 1993.

Said. *Orientalism.* New York: Pantheon, 1978.

Severin, Timothy. *The Oriental Adventure: Explorers of the East.* London: Angus & Robertson, 1976.

Sigaux, Gilbert. *History of Tourism,* translated by Joan White. London: Leisure Arts, 1966.

Smith, Valene, ed. *Hosts and Guests: The Anthropology of Travel.* Philadelphia: University of Pennsylvania Press, 1977.

Spurr, David. *The Rhetoric of Empire: Colonial Discourse in Journalism, Travel Writing, and Imperial Administration.* Durham, N.C.: Duke University Press, 1993.

Stefoff, Rebecca. *Women of the World: Women Travelers and Explorers.* New York: Oxford University Press, 1991.

Stobel, Margaret. *European Women and the Second British Empire.* Bloomington: Indiana University Press, 1991.

Swinglehurst, Edmund. *Cook's Tours: The Story of Popular Travel.* Poole, U.K.: Blandford, 1982.

Sykes, Christopher. *Four Studies in Loyalty.* London: Collins, 1946.

Tidrick, Kathryn. *Empire and the English Character.* London: Tauris, 1981.

Tidrick. *Heart-Beguiling Araby.* Cambridge: Cambridge University Press, 1981.

Tiltman, Majorie Hessell. *Women in Modern Adventure.* London: Harrap, 1935.

Tinling, Marion. *Women Into the Unknown: A Sourcebook on Women Explorers and Travelers.* New York: Greenwood Press, 1989.

Trease, Robert G. *The Grand Tour.* London: Heinemann, 1967.

Trollope, Joanna. *Britannia's Daughters.* London: Hutchinson, 1983.

Turner, Louise, and John Ashe. *The Golden Hordes.* London: Constable, 1975.

Von Martels, Zwerder. *Travel Fact and Travel Fiction: Studies on Fiction, Literary Tradition, Scholarly Discovery and Observation in Travel Writing.* New York: Brill, 1951.

Ward, Francis Kingdon. *Modern Exploration.* London: Cape, 1946.

West, Herbert Faulkner. *The Mind on the Wing: A Book for Readers and Collectors.* New York: Coward-McCann, 1947.

Williams, Cicely. *Women on the Rope: The Feminine Share in Mountain Adventure.* London: Allen & Unwin, 1973.

Woodcock, George. *Into Tibet: The Early British Explorers.* London: Faber & Faber, 1971.

Contributors

M. D. Allen .... *University Of Wisconsin Fox Valley*
Stanley Archer .... *Texas A&M University*
Dana E. Aspinall .... *University of Montevallo*
Khani Begum .... *Bowling Green State University*
Laura Brady .... *West Virginia University*
Scott R. Christianson .... *Radford University*
Lisa Colletta .... *Claremont Graduate University*
Holly Dworken Cooley .... *Buckeye, Arizona*
Michael Coyle .... *Colgate University*
Fred D. Crawford .... *Central Michigan University*
Marcia B. Dinneen .... *Bridgewater State College*
Thomas Dukes .... *University of Akron*
Elizabeth A. Ford .... *Westminster College*
Jeffrey Gray .... *Seton Hall University*
John C. Hawley .... *Santa Clara University*
Marguerite Helmers .... *University of Wisconsin, Oshkosh*
Chris Hopkins .... *Sheffield Hallam University*
Cecile M. Jagodzinski .... *Illinois State University*
David C. Judkins .... *University of Houston*
Doris H. Meriwether .... *University of Southwestern Louisiana*
Bill V. Mullen .... *Youngstown State University*
Maria Noelle Ng .... *University of British Columbia*
Keith C. Odom .... *Texas Christian University*
Pratul Pathak .... *California University of Pennsylvania*
Dennis M. Read .... *Denison University*
Brian D. Reed .... *Case Western Reserve University*
Carol Huebscher Rhoades .... *Austin, Texas*
Samuel J. Rogal .... *Illinois Valley Community College*
Robert H. Sirabian .... *Mississippi Valley State University*
Linda Strahan .... *University of California, Riverside*
Linda J. Strom .... *Youngstown State University*
D. R. Swanson .... *Wright State University*

Cumulative Index

Dictionary of Literary Biography, Volumes 1-195
Dictionary of Literary Biography Yearbook, 1980-1997
Dictionary of Literary Biography Documentary Series, Volumes 1-16

Cumulative Index

DLB before number: *Dictionary of Literary Biography,* Volumes 1-195
Y before number: *Dictionary of Literary Biography Yearbook,* 1980-1997
DS before number: *Dictionary of Literary Biography Documentary Series,* Volumes 1-16

A

B

C

D

E

F

G

H

K

M

N

O

P

Q

R

S

T

U

V

W

ISBN 0-7876-1850-0
90000
9 780787 618506